THE FIGHT AGAINST IMPUNITY IN EU LAW

The fight against impunity is an increasingly central concept in EU law-making and adjudication. What is the meaning and the scope of impunity as a legal concept in the EU legal order? How does the fight against impunity influence policy and adjudication?

This timely first piece of comprehensive research aims to address these largely unexplored questions, which involve structural institutional and substantive dilemmas underpinning the most recent developments of the European integration process. In recent years, the fight against impunity has become a pressing concern for the European institutions. It has shaped several EU policies and has led to a recurring argument in the case law of the Court of Justice.

The book sheds light on this elusive notion, providing a much-needed conceptual appraisal. The first section examines the scope of the concept of impunity, and its role in the EU decision-making process and in the development of EU competences. Subsequent sections discuss the implications of impunity – and of the fight against it – in a variety of complementary domains, namely the allocation of criminal jurisdiction, mutual recognition instruments, the rise of new surveillance technologies and the external dimension of the Area of Freedom, Security and Justice.

This book is an original and timely contribution to scholarship, which will be of interest to academics, researchers and policymakers alike.

Volume 11 in the series Hart Studies in European Criminal Law

Hart Studies in European Criminal Law

Since the Lisbon Treaty, European criminal law has become an increasingly important field of research and debate. Working with the European Criminal Law Academic Network (ECLAN), the series will publish works of the highest intellectual rigour and cutting edge scholarship which will be required reading for all European criminal lawyers.

The series is happy to consider both edited and single authored titles. The series defines 'European' and 'criminal law' in the broadest sense, so books on European criminal law, justice and policy will be considered. The series also welcomes books which offer different methodological approaches.

Volume 1: *EU Criminal Law after Lisbon: Rights, Trust and the Transformation of Justice in Europe*
by Valsamis Mitsilegas

Volume 2: *Challenges in the Field of Economic and Financial Crime in Europe and the US*
Edited by Vanessa Franssen and Katalin Ligeti

Volume 3: *Chasing Criminal Money: Challenges and Perspectives On Asset Recovery in the EU*
Edited by Katalin Ligeti and Michele Simonato

Volume 4: *Limits to EU Powers: A Case Study of EU Regulatory Criminal Law*
by Jacob Öberg

Volume 5: *The Needed Balances in EU Criminal Law: Past, Present and Future*
Edited by Chloé Brière and Anne Weyembergh

Volume 6: *Redefining Organised Crime: A Challenge for the European Union?*
Edited by Stefania Carnevale, Serena Forlati and Orsetta Giolo

Volume 7: *White Collar Crime: A Comparative Perspective*
Edited by Katalin Ligeti and Stanislaw Tosza

Volume 8: *Criminal Liability of Managers in Europe: Punishing Excessive Risk*
Stanisław Tosza

Volume 9: *The European Union and Deprivation of Liberty: A Legislative and Judicial Analysis from the Perspective of the Individual*
Leandro Mancano

Volume 10: *The Legitimacy of EU Criminal Law*
Irene Wieczorek

The Fight Against Impunity in EU Law

Edited by
Luisa Marin
and
Stefano Montaldo

•HART•
OXFORD • LONDON • NEW YORK • NEW DELHI • SYDNEY

HART PUBLISHING

Bloomsbury Publishing Plc

Kemp House, Chawley Park, Cumnor Hill, Oxford, OX2 9PH, UK

1385 Broadway, New York, NY 10018, USA

HART PUBLISHING, the Hart/Stag logo, BLOOMSBURY and the Diana logo are trademarks of Bloomsbury Publishing Plc

First published in Great Britain 2020

A catalogue record for this book is available from the British Library.

Library of Congress Cataloging-in-Publication data

Names: Marin, Luisa, editor. | Montaldo, Stefano, editor.

Title: The fight against impunity in EU law / edited by Luisa Marin and Stefano Montaldo.

Other titles: Fight against impunity in European Union law

Description: Oxford, UK ; New York, NY : Hart Publishing, an imprint of Bloomsbury Publishing, 2020. | Series: Hart studies in European Criminal Law ; volume 11 | Includes bibliographical references and index.

Identifiers: LCCN 2020026788 (print) | LCCN 2020026789 (ebook) | ISBN 9781509926879 (hardback) | ISBN 9781509926893 (ePDF) | ISBN 9781509926886 (Epub)

Subjects: LCSH: Criminal justice, Administration of—European Union countries. | Criminal law—European Union countries. | Criminal jurisdiction—European Union countries. | Terrorism—Prevention—Law and legislation—European Union countries. | Criminal justice, Administration of.

Classification: LCC KJE9430 .F54 2020 (print) | LCC KJE9430 (ebook) | DDC 345.24—dc23

LC record available at https://lccn.loc.gov/2020026788

LC ebook record available at https://lccn.loc.gov/2020026789

ISBN: HB: 978-1-50992-687-9
ePDF: 978-1-50992-689-3
ePub: 978-1-50992-688-6

Typeset by Compuscript Ltd, Shannon

ACKNOWLEDGEMENTS

This book is an outcome of the research project of the University of Turin 'Offenders' Rehabilitation in the European Union', coordinated by Professor Stefano Montaldo and funded by Fondazione Compagnia di San Paolo.

Compagnia di San Paolo

TABLE OF CONTENTS

Acknowledgements .... *v*
List of Contributors .... *xi*

1. *Introduction: Is There a Fight against Impunity in the EU Legal System?* *1*
Luisa Marin and Stefano Montaldo

PART A
IMPUNITY IN EU LAW: A CONCEPTUAL APPRAISAL

2. *Conceptualising Impunity in the Law of the European Union* *13*
Valsamis Mitsilegas

3. *Fundamental Rights-Oriented Repression in the EU? Exploring the Potential and Limits of an Impunity Rationale to Justify Criminalisation in the EU Legal Order* *47*
Jannemieke Ouwerkerk

4. *The Role of the Fight against Impunity in EU Criminal Policy Preparation and Evaluation* *63*
Wouter van Ballegooij

PART B
THE FIGHT AGAINST IMPUNITY AND THE ALLOCATION OF CRIMINAL JURISDICTION IN THE EU

5. *EU Substantive Criminal Law and Jurisdiction Clauses: Claiming Jurisdiction to Fight Impunity?* *79*
Martin Böse

6. *Between Impunity and the Protection of Fundamental Rights: The Case Law of the CJEU and the ECtHR on the* ne bis in idem *Principle* *99*
Bas van Bockel

7. *Impunity and Conflicts of Jurisdiction within the EU: The Role of Eurojust and Challenges for Fundamental Rights* *117*
Athina Giannakoula

8. *The Fight against Impunity between EU and National Legal Orders: What Role for the EPPO?* 137
Costanza Di Francesco Maesa

PART C
THE FIGHT AGAINST IMPUNITY AND THE EU INSTRUMENTS IMPLEMENTING THE PRINCIPLE OF MUTUAL RECOGNITION IN CRIMINAL MATTERS

9. *The European Supervision Order: The Need for a New Culture of Combating Impunity*....................157
Serena Quattrocolo

10. *Information Sharing as a Tool in the Fight against Impunity in the European Union*....................171
Francesca Galli

11. *Clash of the Titans: The Fight against Impunity versus Social Rehabilitation and the Protection of Fundamental Rights within the Framework of Prisoner Transfers in the EU* 191
Alessandro Rosanò

PART D
IMPUNITY AND NEW SURVEILLANCE TECHNOLOGIES UNDER EU LAW

12. *Stepping Up the Fight against Impunity in EU Law: Access to Immigration Databases by National Law Enforcement Authorities and Europol*....................209
Niovi Vavoula

13. *Enhancing Policing through Algorithmic Surveillance*....................239
Mariavittoria Catanzariti

14. *Fighting Impunity with New Tools: How Big Data, Algorithms, Machine Learning and AI Shape the New Era of Criminal Justice*....................257
Mojca M Plesničar, Aleš Završnik and Pika Šarf

PART E
THE FIGHT AGAINST IMPUNITY AND THE EXTERNAL DIMENSION OF THE AFSJ

15. *International Fight against Impunity and EU Counter-Terrorism Law: The Case of Foreign Terrorist Fighters* 279
Ermioni Xanthopoulou and Theodore Konstadinides

16. *Impunity and EU or Member States' Extradition Agreements with Third Countries*.......299
Stefano Saluzzo

17. *Commercial Data Transfers and Liaison Officers: What Data Protection Rules Apply in the Fight against Impunity When Third Countries Are Involved?*.......317
Christina Eckes and Dominique Barnhoorn

18. *The Court of Justice of the European Union and the International Criminal Court: The Fight against Impunity between Complementarity and Mandatory Requirements*.......339
Aurora Rasi

Index.......355

LIST OF CONTRIBUTORS

Wouter van Ballegooij is a policy analyst at the European Parliament Research Service

Dominique Barnhoorn is a PhD researcher at the Amsterdam Centre for European Law and Governance, University of Amsterdam

Bas van Bockel is Senior Specialist Coordinating Advisor EU Law, Netherlands Council of State, Honorary Judge, District Court Amsterdam, and Senior Lecturer EU Law, Utrecht University

Martin Böse is Professor of Criminal Law, Criminal Procedure and European and International Criminal Law at the University of Bonn

Mariavittoria Catanzariti is a research associate at the Centre for Judicial Cooperation, Robert Schuman Centre for Advanced Studies, European University Institute

Costanza Di Francesco Maesa is Research Fellow in EU Law at the University of Siena

Christina Eckes is Professor of EU Law at the University of Amsterdam

Francesca Galli is a research associate at the Centre for Judicial Cooperation, Robert Schuman Centre for Advanced Studies, European University Institute

Athina Giannakoula is a scientific associate at the Aristotle University and a lecturer at the National School for Judges and Prosecutors of Greece

Theodore Konstadinides is Professor of Law at the University of Essex

Luisa Marin was formerly a Research Fellow in EU Law at the University of Padua and is currently a Marie Curie Fellow at the European University Institute

Valsamis Mitsilegas is Professor of European Criminal Law and Global Security at the Queen Mary University of London

Stefano Montaldo is Associate Professor of EU Law at the University of Turin

Jannemieke Ouwerkerk is Professor of European Criminal Law at Leiden University

Mojca M. Plesničar is an assistant professor at the Institute of Criminology of the University of Ljubljana

Serena Quattrocolo is Professor of Criminal Procedural Law at the University of Eastern Piedmont

Aurora Rasi is Assistant Professor of EU Law at Sapienza, University of Rome

Alessandro Rosanò is Post-doctoral Research Fellow in EU Law at the University of Turin

Pika Šarf is a junior researcher at the Institute of Criminology of the University of Ljubljana

Stefano Saluzzo is an assistant professor in International Law at the University of Eastern Piedmont

Niovi Vavoula is Lecturer in Migration and Security at the Queen Mary University of London

Ermioni Xanthopoulou is Lecturer in Law at the Brunel University London

Aleš Završnik is an associate professor at the Institute of Criminology of the University of Ljubljana

1

Introduction: Is There a Fight against Impunity in the EU Legal System?

LUISA MARIN AND STEFANO MONTALDO

Impunity is a deep-rooted and recurring concern for criminal law, which questions the actual capacity of a penal system to avoid a crime going unpunished and to more generally secure sound and effective administration of justice. This concept embodies a legitimate objective in the public interest and usually triggers institutional and normative reactions aimed at making sure that justice is done. At the same time, leaning on the fine thread between exercise of public coercive powers and protection of fundamental rights, impunity also involves the sphere of victims and (alleged) perpetrators of crimes, because it is closely connected to the search for justice in individual cases and to the inherent limits of substantive and procedural criminal law stemming from constitutional principles.

Even though the concept at issue recalls the basic idea of escaping punishment, its ultimate meaning is elusive and encompasses an expanding scale of implications. At first sight, impunity entails fleeing formal justice, namely the actual delivery of a judicial decision imposing a punishment. Yet, the issuing of a sentence does not preclude de facto impunity, in those cases where, on various grounds, enforcement is blocked because of procedural hurdles or the sentenced person having absconded. From a wider perspective, the concept under consideration also involves a twofold procedural dimension, where an alleged perpetrator escapes trial or in case – at an earlier stage – the investigation phase does not lead to the actual identification of a suspect of a crime. Impunity brings about even more pressing concerns in a cross-border scenario. As early as 1906, Henry Donnedieu de Vabres pointed out that 'la rapidité des voies de communication, la multiplicité des relations entre les peuples, offrent aux delinquents des chances d'impunité qu'ils ne possédaient pas autrefois'.[1]

[1] H Donnedieu de Vabres, *Crimes et délits commis à l'etranger d'après quelques codes récents* (Paris, Rousseau, 1906).

The process of European integration is not immune from impunity concerns, from at least a threefold perspective. In a first decentralised dimension, the enforcement of EU law could be hampered by the diversity of the enforcement systems of the Member States. To limit the dangers of this feature of the EU legal system, the Union can rely on the principle of sincere cooperation to impose on the Member States the duty to sanction – also by means of criminal law – violations of EU law hampering the full effectiveness of its common policies. Following the *Amsterdam Bulb* and *Greek Maize* line of case law,[2] the national authorities are then expected to assimilate situations stemming from EU law to purely domestic ones and to take all necessary measures to protect related interests in light of the principles of equivalence, effectiveness and proportionality, under the scrutiny of the Commission and of the Court of Justice. Secondly, a risk of impunity also lies in the cross-border dimension: that is why a vast array of instruments of horizontal judicial cooperation in criminal matters have been enacted by the EU legislature to facilitate law enforcement in a transnational scenario. Lastly, impunity also constitutes an intrinsic and autonomous supranational concern of the EU itself, which has led the Union to take action to protect its own interests, such as in the case of the establishment of the European Public Prosecutor's Office and of the related legislation aimed at protecting the EU's financial interests.

These dimensions reflect the nature of the EU, but also its complexity, first and foremost represented to a large extent by its reliance on Member States' enforcement systems. Actually, at the EU level, the challenge of impunity reveals the dark side of the domestic authorities' (in)ability to effectively react to crimes having cross-border implications and to behaviours affecting the Union as such or more broadly EU-driven interests underpinning common policies.

Crucially, ignoring technological development and the ensuing availability of refined means to commit crimes and escape law enforcement, across the decades, the European integration process has further amplified EU-wide impunity concerns on two main grounds.

First of all, the establishment of the internal market, with the abolition of controls at the 'internal borders', has provided increased opportunities both for committing crimes with cross-border implications and for fleeing justice.[3] The recurring idea of a boost to the 'free movement of crimes and offenders' as an inevitable side effect of the internal market actually lies at the core of the Member States' decision to start to cooperate in the area of Justice and Home Affairs, back in the 1970s and 1980s, and to develop an increasingly structured EU criminal policy.

[2] Case 50/76 *Amsterdam Bulb* ECLI:EU:C:1977:13; Case 68/88 *Commission v Greece* ECLI:EU:C:1989:339.

[3] A Weyembergh, *L'harmonisation des législations: condition de l'espace pénal européen et révélateur de ses tensions* (Brussels, Editions de l'ULB, 2004).

This can be labelled the 'internal market driver'. Later on, after 9/11, integration was boosted by counterterrorism; more recently, the intertwinement of migration control with security has represented a powerful incentive for coercive surveillance measures which aim to realise a pre-emptive control on migration, stretching the boundaries of impunity and prevention beyond their outer limits.

Overall, the efforts of the EU in confronting impunity must be ascribed to its evolution from a multi-level regulatory polity into a core state powers entity. Though (still) majoritarian narratives frame the EU as a multi-level regulatory polity,[4] or even as a regulatory state,[5] that is firmly focused on regulating markets, emerging interpretations capture the increasing role of the EU in exercising 'core state powers' in several domains,[6] alongside Member States; it is argued here that European integration in the context of the administration of criminal justice can be ascribed to this broader phenomenon, which deserves further research and examination.[7] Next to cooperation in the domain of criminal justice, the emergence of a fully fledged criminal law policy, albeit one with limitations,[8] is an expression of integration in the maintenance of internal security (understood as crime control and administration of justice); to conclude, criminal policy and cooperation in the administration of criminal justice can be framed as the co-exercising of core state powers by the EU and its Member States.

Well before the process of European integration became concerned with the exercise of core state powers, such as internal security and the administration of justice, and when the main focus of integration was economic, the Court of Justice used its powers and discretion to shape and create a new legal order. The dynamic and evolutionary process of becoming a multi-level regulatory polity has been made possible thanks to European principles such as unity, effectiveness and coherence of EU law. In several of the phases of European integration, the fight against impunity has begun to emerge.

In the context of the European integration process, the fight against impunity has acquired new and specific relevance, which reflects the context in which it has developed. The significance of impunity also differs from its conception in the national and international legal orders. In the EU, the fight against impunity is heavily dependent on the concepts of area (of freedom, security and justice), of European legal space and of Member States' territories. Indeed, the contrast to

[4] G Majone, 'The European Community as a Regulatory State' (1996) 5 *Collected Courses of the Academy of European Law* 321.

[5] RD Kelemen, 'Building the New European State? Federalism, Core State Powers, and European Integration' in P Genschel and M Jachtenfuchs (eds), *Beyond the Regulatory Polity? The European Integration of Core State Powers* (Oxford, Oxford University Press, 2013) 211.

[6] Genschel and Jachtenfuchs (ibid) 3ff.

[7] eg Kelemen (n 4) 213 includes only defence, policing, taxation and public administration in the definition of core state powers for the purpose of his analysis.

[8] S Coutts, 'Supranational Public Wrongs: The Limitation and Possibilities of European Criminal Law and a European Community' (2017) 55 *CML Rev* 771.

impunity 'the European way' has been taking shape for decades in the context of European economic integration, which is a dynamic and evolutive process of integration between states, and therefore does not start from nor will lead to a single and uniform legal order.

This process towards the creation of an 'ever closer union' involves the establishment of a single area of freedom, security and justice, in addition to a single market.[9] The fight against impunity in the European legal order is therefore strongly linked with the very nature of the 'area', and also an expression of the core features of the EU.[10]

First of all, the EU has a territory which is an expression of the territories of the Member States. However, the EU does not have the power to determine its territory, but can only control its extension, through new membership, and its contraction, according to Article 50 TEU.

Most importantly, the EU is not a single space, where territory and legal space overlap: the Schengen area, which does not coincide with the area of freedom, security and justice, is a case in point. Moreover, the whole area of freedom, security and justice rests on a pluralistic and fragmented mosaic of national legal orders, which also postulates national enforcement systems, institutions and powers.[11]

If the EU as a legal space coexists with a multitude of territories where different rules apply, what is the function of the fight against impunity within the scope of EU law? What can bind the whole legal system together?

The Court of Justice has been a leading actor in providing answers to these questions; in doing so, it has relied on legal principles such as *effet utile*, effectiveness and unity of EU law. It has also, recently, referred to the constitutional principles common to the Member States, which have been used as sources of reference for the definition of the general principles of EU law, which also include fundamental rights, so crucial in the development of a European constitutional identity. Throughout the process, it has stressed the importance of the uniform interpretation of autonomous concepts of EU law,[12] so that 'united in diversity' does not end up undermining a process of integration through law.

It is precisely within this framework that we have to locate the fight against impunity in EU law, which can be framed as a public interest and European concern for the area of freedom, security and justice, but also more generally for the EU.

However, the nature of the fight against impunity in EU law is not clearly defined. Notwithstanding its role in fostering the development of key Union

[9] Art 3 TEU.

[10] H Lindahl, 'Finding a Place for Freedom, Security and Justice: the European Union's claim to Territorial Unity' (2004) 29 *EL Rev* 461.

[11] N Nic Shuibhne, 'The Territory of the Union in EU Citizenship Law: Charting a Route from Parallel to Integrated Narratives' [2019] *Yearbook of European Law* 1.

[12] V Mitsilegas, 'Autonomous Concepts, Diversity Management and Mutual Trust in Europe's Area of Freedom, Security and Justice' (2020) 57 *CML Rev* 45.

policies, this concept has been notably under-explored so far, especially from an EU law perspective. Hence, the necessity for this book, which has been compiled with a view to paving the way for a more fine-grained appraisal of the notion at issue and of its implications for the EU legal order.

The framework questions this book contributes to the discussion are:

> Which is the morphology of the fight against impunity in the context of the EU legal order? How does the fight against impunity manifest itself?

The book is structured in four parts.

The first part provides a conceptual appraisal of the concept of impunity in the European legal order. **Valsamis Mitsilegas**'s opening chapter addresses impunity as a driver of the European integration process and provides a taxonomy of the concept under consideration, linked to the achievement of internal and external objectives of the Union. As to the internal dimension, the analysis focuses on the protection of the interests – especially the financial ones – of the European Union, and on the establishment of an area of freedom, security and justice without internal frontiers where national legal orders can interact through judicial cooperation mechanisms. The external perspective considers international judicial cooperation of the EU and its Member States with third countries, through the lens of the recent case law on extradition and EU citizenship. The analysis then shifts from the international to the global, by discussing the use of data in the digital world.

Jannemieke Ouwerkerk discusses whether the impunity rationale often placed at the basis for EU choices of criminalisation actually fits the purpose of justifying criminalisation in the EU context. The author starts her analysis by asking if the paradoxical relation between fundamental rights and criminal law can be applied to EU criminal law. Criminal law is at the same time both a protection (shield) for and a threat (sword) to fundamental rights. Can impunity constitute a relevant factor in the exercise of criminalisation powers and, if so, how? The chapter further explores the impunity rationale as a driver for criminalisation, especially discussing the context where it applies, which is about legislating on matters of criminal law. It furthermore advances a number of proposals for a fundamental rights-based impunity rationale in EU criminal law, which are especially interesting because they could contribute to the development of a body of European criminal law, which could respect subsidiarity as well.

Ouwerkerk's chapter is complemented by the one by **Wouter van Ballegooij**, which addresses the role played by concerns about the fight against impunity in the preparation and evaluation of EU criminal policy, from a better regulation perspective. The author contends that the Commission has developed a sophisticated set of better regulation guidelines, which provide guidance on whether a given problem should be tackled at the EU level dependent upon a sequence of preliminary logical steps. Yet the main driver for EU action in criminal law is the seriousness of the offence, and a tighter focus on whose impunity should be prioritised could better reflect the actual need for the adoption of a set of common rules.

The second part of the book is devoted to a traditional component of the impunity discourse, namely the allocation of criminal jurisdiction in a geographic area characterised by advanced political and legal cooperation. In this respect, **Martin Böse** provides an in-depth analysis of the formal clauses on jurisdiction incorporated into EU secondary legislation on substantive criminal law. The chapter classifies relevant provisions depending on the criteria for claiming jurisdiction that they incorporate, namely vicarious and universal jurisdiction, extraterritorial jurisdiction based on the existence of a genuine link and autonomous jurisdictional clauses. The author critically discusses the extraterritorial implications of the outlined clauses, with respect to offences committed within and outside the Union.

This chapter is complemented by **Athina Giannakoula**'s analysis of the soft mechanisms governing (potential) clashes of jurisdiction between the Member States. Specific attention is paid to Framework Decision 2009/948/JHA on prevention and settlement of conflicts of jurisdiction, although this act is described as contributing far from effectively to solving the problem it addresses. The author then turns to the role of Eurojust and to the potential displayed by its guidelines, which she analyses critically in view of the relevant practice and of the possible future normative improvements.

Another distinctive – albeit indirect – element of the coordination of criminal jurisdictions across the EU is the principle of *ne bis in idem* enshrined in Article 50 of the Charter of Fundamental Rights of the Union. Building on the assumption that the present level of protection of the principle at issue by European courts is sufficiently strong, **Bas van Bockel** addresses the delicate relationship between the right not to be tried or punished twice and the interest of the enforcement of material justice. The author contends that the scope of this principle could be nuanced to avoid impunity, in relation to the enforcement requirement included in Article 54 of the Convention Implementing the Schengen Agreement, in some cases of parallel application of criminal and administrative law, and in the event of new and previously undiscovered evidence.

The subsequent chapter deals with the establishment of the European Public Prosecutor's Office (EPPO). The EPPO Regulation represents one of the most illustrative examples of the EU's striving to protect its financial interest, as the rationale underpinning it is precisely to tackle the perpetrators of crimes affecting these interests more effectively, especially where the national authorities are unable to ensure an appropriate level of deterrence. **Costanza Di Francesco Maesa** presents the distinctive features of EPPO's institutional setting and tasks, in particular in relation to the internal organisation of the Office, the identification of the applicable law and the (possible) conflict of competences with national judicial authorities of the non-participating Member States. The critical analysis of these aspects leads the author to consider that the establishment of EPPO marks an important step towards a more effective prosecution system, but also that the current normative framework leaves some problems unresolved and might result in institutional conflicts and procedural blocks.

The third part of the collection focuses on a central element of the impunity narrative in the Union, namely operation of the principle of mutual recognition as a cornerstone of judicial cooperation mechanisms in criminal matters. The numerous and diversified instruments implementing this principle in relation to a varied set of judicial decisions touch upon different aspects of (the risk of) impunity, ranging from the conduct of effective investigations through the European Investigation Order to the possibility to ask for the surrender of a person for purposes of prosecution or execution of a custodial sentence within the framework of the system of the European Arrest Warrant (EAW). Actually, this part alone could have justified the publication of a distinct book, due to the variety and complexity of the issues at stake. As editors, we decided to delimit the analysis to three components of the mutual recognition scenario, namely the European Supervision Order, the cross-border transfer of prisoners under Framework Decision 2008/909/JHA and the ongoing legislative proposal on e-evidence. Any gap left is remedied by Valsamis Mitsilegas's overarching chapter opening the book, which dwells upon the impunity concerns fostering EU legislation on mutual recognition and specifically considers how this driver has shaped Framework Decision 2002/584/JHA on the EAW and its interpretation by the Court of Justice.

Therefore, the mutual recognition part of the book starts with a much-needed appraisal of the widely under-examined Framework Decision 2009/829/JHA on the European Supervision Order. **Serena Quattrocolo** outlines the main features of this Act and points out its unexplored potential in terms of a less discriminatory approach to the choice to impose a non-custodial pretrial measure to an accused person. The author discusses the reasons for the unsatisfactory application of the European Supervision Order by pointing at the difficulty of coping with the strict deadlines that the pretrial phase imposes. Moreover, she contends that the need to interpret the rules governing pretrial measures strictly could hinder mutual recognition, for instance by limiting the room for adaptations of national measures to foreign ones.

Francesca Galli's chapter focuses on the case of information sharing, which represents a recent and controversial development and will give mutual legal assistance a new dimension. The chapter explores the e-evidence proposal, which establishes mechanisms of cooperation where private actors are involved in the information-sharing process and bypasses important instances of judicial scrutiny. In this perspective, the chapter examines the proposal's impact on guarantees for the protection of rights, such as fundamental rights, next to issues of jurisdiction and unclear legal basis. It furthermore examines the contribution of the proposal to the redefinition of integration dynamics, at the vertical and horizontal levels, including in relations with private actors.

The chapter by **Alessandro Rosanò** addresses another crucial instrument of judicial cooperation in criminal matters, namely Framework Decision 2008/909/JHA on the mutual recognition of judicial decisions imposing custodial measures. The transfer of prisoners is an emerging element of the Union's judicial space, as it allows for cross-border enforcement of sentences issued at the domestic level.

As such, it ensures that the European integration process does not frustrate the repressive priorities of the Member States, while it also prioritises the protection of the prisoners' rights. In particular, the chapter analyses the thin line between the effectiveness of judicial cooperation and compliance with appropriate human rights standards in the domain of detention. Moreover, it discusses the status of social rehabilitation as a legal concept and its implications for the mechanism governed by Framework Decision 2008/909/JHA.

The fourth part of the book develops the role of new surveillance technologies in reshaping the contrast to impunity in the EU system and beyond; it especially discusses the consolidation of reliance on databases, and also the emergence of technologies related to the use of Artificial Intelligence (AI) and big data; this is an expression of a broader tendency of 'faith' for new technologies as objective and efficient tools which can contribute to delivering public goods, but what happens in the interplay between humans and technology? Is this shift really neutral or not?

The first chapter discusses the intertwinement between security and migration control that materialises at the EU level in the proliferation of databases which collect personal data. Their attractiveness in regard to the fight against impunity takes shape in the growing tendency by law enforcement authorities and Europol to access these databases. The Schengen Information System, Eurodac and the Visa Information System, together with the proposed Entry/Exit System, the European Travel Information and Authorisation System and the European Criminal Record Information System for third-country nationals, constitute, in a fortunate expression by **Niovi Vavoula**, a 'mille-feuille' of information-processing schemes that found its origin in the fight against terrorism and has subsequently been used in immigration control. The analysis by Vavoula shows us how law enforcement authorities have access to these databases, especially against the background of data protection and privacy perspective, questioning in particular its compliance with European case law. With the simplification of access to these databases by law enforcement authorities, interoperability has added another level of complexity to the whole picture.

In the second chapter, **Mariavittoria Catanzariti** tackles the emergence of algorithmic surveillance in policing, projecting us into predictive policing, which represents a paradigm shift from post-crime policing to proactive measures based on algorithmic predictions. As the chapter warns us, the focus on risk categories threatens to undermine core principles such as presumption of innocence, and the chapter explores in a very timely way the challenges and tensions between predictive policing and civil liberties. Furthermore, it discusses the legal status of inferences and the right to control automated decisions, which are two of the most controversial aspects of the transfer of AI in policing functions. By underpinning predictive policing in the broader context of administration and, more broadly, within the framework of the principle of good administration, the chapter calls for the necessity to reflect upon the role of law and regulation in this domain, and also in relation to the interaction between technology and human beings; the scope of the chapter goes well beyond the relation between AI and policing, and also offers food for thought in relation to other legal and ethical questions emerging from these issues.

This part is completed by a last chapter by **Mojca M Plesničar, Aleš Završnik and Pika Šarf**, which takes the perspective of a broader analysis on how big data, algorithms, machine learning and AI can affect criminal justice. It is complementary to the chapter by M Catanzariti, and it illustrates a number of examples of current deployment of new technologies in the domain of criminal justice, also referring to examples from US experience. The chapter examines a number of cases, from predictive policing to instances of automated decision-making in courts and post-conviction systems, of how new technologies are used in the context of criminal justice, and warns against some of the challenges they imply, for example for fundamental rights and general principles of criminal justice systems. It furthermore addresses some critical aspects of the legal framework surrounding their use which have emerged with reference to the US system, and it discusses the challenges created for fundamental rights by non-transparent decision-making based on algorithms, also discussing the principles of the European Ethical Charter on the Use of Artificial Intelligence in Judicial Systems and their Environment.

The fifth part of the book focuses on the external and international dimension of the fight against impunity, as anticipated in Mitsilegas's conceptual framework.

The first chapter of the part investigates the fight against impunity from the perspective of EU counterterrorism law, focusing on the case of foreign terrorist fighters; this field has seen an expansion since 2014, the date of creation of a 'caliphate' in Syria, with the criminalisation of travelling with a criminal intention, among other changes. **Ermioni Xanthopoulou and Theodore Konstadinides** analyse Directive 2017/541, which updates the EU legal framework by extending the list of preparatory acts and behaviours to be criminalised, also against the background of the relevant international developments. This represents an extension of the boundaries of the fight against impunity in the specific domain of counterterrorism, and, in the thesis of the authors, constitutes a preventive response to impunity, in the form of pre-crime or precautionary criminalisation. The chapter has the merit of stressing the convergences and divergences between European answers and external initiatives, especially from the perspective of the principles of EU criminal and constitutional law.

The second chapter of the part focuses on impunity and EU or Member States extradition agreements with third countries, focusing on the *Petruhhin*, *Pisciotti* and *Raugevicius* cases.[13] **Stefano Saluzzo** analyses them from the perspective of the fight against impunity as a tool used by the Court of Justice to balance competing

[13] Case 182/15 *Aleksei Petruhhin* ECLI:EU:C:2016:630' Case 191/16 *Romano Pisciotti v Bundesrepublik Deutschland* ECLI:EU:C:2018:222; Case 247/17 *Denis Raugevicius* ECLI:EU:C:2018:898.

interests and allow Member States room for manoeuvre, which has nevertheless been limited by the Court of Justice.

The third chapter, by **Christina Eckes and Dominique Barnhoorn**, addresses the question of whether and under what circumstances data protection should prevail over the fight against impunity. It focuses on data cooperation between the European Union and the USA in the context of crime prevention and law enforcement. It examines the limited control mechanisms that are in place to ensure data protection after data has been transferred or otherwise shared in the highly relevant and controversial context of commercial transfers of personal data and in the academically rather neglected context of liaison officers seconded from US to EU agencies within the Area of Freedom Security and Justice. The objective is to identify limits imposed by data protection requirements on data sharing as a means of fighting impunity, responsibilities of EU actors for data that is collected and processed within the EU's jurisdiction, be it public or private actors, and limits of the EU's control over data flows in the twenty-first century.

The last chapter compares two courts, the Court of Justice of the European Union and the International Criminal Court, from the perspective of what the author indicates are interpretative techniques used to fight impunity. **Aurora Rasi** argues that the Court of Justice allegedly expands the scope of EU law when the application of a domestic procedural provision may prevent a national trial. From a reverse perspective, it narrows down the scope of EU law when the application of an EU provision granting individual rights may prevent a national criminal proceeding from taking place. The author finds similarities with analogous interpretation techniques used by the International Criminal Court within the scope of the Rome Statute, and concludes by arguing that the Court of Justice uses the fight against impunity to justify the protection of an overriding public interest of the European Union, similarly to what has happened in the context of the internal market.

PART A

Impunity in EU Law: A Conceptual Appraisal

2

Conceptualising Impunity in the Law of the European Union

VALSAMIS MITSILEGAS

I. Introduction

The fight against impunity has underpinned the development of European integration from as early as the 1980s. In the recent past, anti-impunity concerns have played a key part in the development of the EU into an area of freedom, security and justice. Yet, for all its impact on the content and direction of EU law, the concept of impunity (and, subsequently, of the fight against it) has been notably under-theorised. Recognising that the concept of impunity has been developed in many different contexts and may remain elusive, emotive and vague,[1] this chapter aims to provide a first comprehensive conceptualisation of impunity in EU law, understanding impunity in the sense of evasion of criminal responsibility and punishment in domestic legal systems and under EU law. The chapter will analyse the evolution of anti-impunity legislative and judicial discourses by offering a multi-dimensional taxonomy of the perceived necessity to fight impunity linked with the achievement of a number of broader EU law objectives. In this context, the chapter will highlight four distinct – but interrelated – dimensions of the concept of impunity in EU law, two linked to internal and two to external objectives of EU law. In terms of achieving internal EU law objectives, the concept of impunity will be viewed from the perspective of the need to protect the interests of the European Union (in the case of protecting the financial interests of the EU and the EU budget) and from the perspective of building an area of freedom, security and justice without internal frontiers and where national legal orders interact. The external dimension of anti-impunity will focus on the articulation of the concept in setting the parameters of international judicial cooperation (of the EU and its Member States with third countries), in particular regarding the example of such

[1] On a discussion of the vagueness in the concept of impunity, see JE Vinuales, 'Impunity: Elements for an Empirical Concept' (2007) 25 *Law and Inequality* 115.

cooperation par excellence, extradition. The analysis of the external dimension of (anti-)impunity will then shift from the international to the global: focusing on the use of data in the digital world, the chapter will assess critically the EU's anti-impunity agenda in a transatlantic and global context. Throughout the chapter, the role of the anti-impunity agenda as a driver for European integration will be highlighted. By examining critically the various dimensions of anti-impunity, the analysis will cast light on the key elements of the concept of impunity and evaluate critically the limited extent to which a European concept of impunity, distinct from the interests of Member States and reflecting European values and a European sense of justice, has developed in EU law. The chapter will end with a call to reconceptualise impunity as a rights- and rule-of-law-based common European concept.

II. The Fight against Impunity and the Protection of the Interests of the Union: The Case of the Union's Financial Interests

The fight against impunity has been in constant connection with the need to protect European interests in the field of criminal justice, which are deemed to be distinct from national ones.[2] A key example is the protection of the budget of the European Union. Safeguarding the EU budget has been perceived as a primary European Union interest, and the fight against impunity has acted as a major driver for European integration in the field. Calls for EU intervention to fight against impunity regarding attacks on a European interest (the EU budget) have emerged clearly in the academic study on the *Corpus Juris* funded by the European Commission in the 1990s: the drafters of the *Corpus Juris* put forward a highly centralised model of European criminal law related to the fight against fraud, a model which emanated from the belief that the budget is a uniquely European interest. According to its Explanatory Memorandum, 'the Budget, defined as "the visible sign of a true patrimony common to citizens of the Union …, is the supreme instrument of European policy. To say this emphasises the extreme seriousness of any crime which undermines this patrimony.'[3] At a time of limited EU competence in the field of criminal law, the *Corpus Juris* and institutions such as the European Commission were arguing for further Europeanisation in order to effectively protect the budget as a European interest. Underlying calls for EU intervention has been a perception of mistrust: national authorities are considered

[2] V Mitsilegas, 'The Normative Foundations of European Criminal Law' in R Schütze (ed), *Globalisation and Governance: International Problems, European Solutions* (Cambridge, Cambridge University Press, 2018) 418–52.

[3] M Delmas-Marty (ed), *Corpus Juris* (Paris, Economica, 1997) 12.

unwilling or unable to fight impunity effectively and to protect European interests in the same way or as effectively as they would protect national interests by the use of criminal law.

Over time, the perceived need to fight against impunity in order to protect a distinct European interest has had a significant impact on national law in two ways: in ensuring that national law provides effective protection of the EU interests at stake; and in putting forward legislation at the European Union level aimed at establishing a substantive and institutional framework which would provide an effective response to fraud against the EU budget. These two strands of action have been developing in a complementary manner for more than two decades, with EU institutions playing a key part in leading initiatives in these fields and with the entry into force of the Lisbon Treaty providing considerable acceleration.

The first strand of EU action involved efforts to ensure that Member States provide an equivalent level of protection of EU interests to that provided to national interests in their domestic criminal justice systems. A leading actor in this context has been the Court of Justice, which developed the principle of assimilation in the late 1980s. In its ruling on the *Greek Maize* case,[4] and based on the principles of effectiveness and equivalence, the Court introduced the principle of assimilation: while the choice of penalties is a matter of Member States' discretion, infringements of Community law must be sanctioned under conditions, procedural or substantive, which make the penalty effective, proportionate and dissuasive. Hence, the principle of assimilation plays a paramount role. In this manner, criminalisation may occur at the national level even in cases where it is not expressly required by EU law. The Court stated subsequently that effective national measures in this context 'may include criminal penalties even where the Community legislation only provides for civil sanctions'.[5] The principle of assimilation has since been introduced in the EU Treaties and appears post-Lisbon, along with the principles of effectiveness and deterrence,[6] in Article 325 TFEU.[7] The Court has since used Article 325 TFEU to highlight the obligations incumbent upon national authorities to provide effective protection to the EU budget and thus avoid impunity. The potential of Article 325 TFEU as a Treaty basis to address impunity has been highlighted prominently by the CJEU. In its two rulings in the *Taricco* saga, the CJEU set out the rule that Article 325(1) and (2) TFEU has direct effect and places national authorities, including courts, under the obligation to disapply national law if effectiveness of EU law (and the fight against impunity) is jeopardised. In *Taricco I*,[8] the Court of Justice ruled that Article 325 TFEU itself

[4] Case C-68/88 *Commission v Greece* ECR [1989] 2965, paras 23–25.

[5] Case C-186/98 *Nunes de Matos*, ECR [1999] 4883 para 14.

[6] Art 325(1) TFEU.

[7] According to Art 325(2) TFEU, Member States must take the same measures to counter fraud affecting the financial interests of the Union as they take to tackle fraud affecting their own interests.

[8] Case C-105/14 *Taricco and Others* (*Tarrico I*) ECLI:EU:C:2015:555.

obliges the Member States to counter illegal activities affecting the financial interests of the European Union through effective deterrent measures; in particular, the principle of assimilation obliges them to take the same measures to counter fraud affecting the financial interests of the European Union as they take to counter fraud affecting their own interests.[9] If national provisions are not effective and dissuasive, the Court continued, the national court would have to ensure that EU law is given full effect, if need be by disapplying those provisions, without having to request or await the prior repeal of those articles by way of legislation or any other constitutional procedure.[10] The Court stressed that the Member States' obligations in this context are imposed, inter alia, by EU primary law, namely Article 325(1) and (2) TFEU.[11] These provisions impose on Member States a precise obligation as to the result to be achieved that is not subject to any condition regarding application of the rule, which they lay down.[12] The provisions of Article 325(1) and (2) TFEU therefore have the effect, in accordance with the principle of the precedence of EU law, of rendering automatically inapplicable, merely by their entering into force, any conflicting provision of national law.[13]

The judgment of the CJEU in *Taricco I* set important benchmarks regarding the reach of EU law in order to ensure the avoidance of impunity for breach of European interests. The CJEU responded to what can be seen as a 'cry for help' by a lower national court, with the national judge using the preliminary reference procedure to argue that abuse of national provisions on statute of limitations ensured the impunity of those committing serious fraud against the budget of the Union. The CJEU heeded this call in its response, and attempted to stretch the duration of national criminal proceedings by asking the national judge to disapply any national provisions which lead to impunity. At the same time, the CJEU has used the ruling to push for further EU harmonisation of criminal law against fraud, and led, via its assertion that VAT fraud did indeed form part of fraud against the EU budget, to the eventual inclusion of elements of VAT fraud within the scope of the PIF Directive, which was under negotiation at the time of the ruling. This intervention was of particular significance in view of the fact that the definition of fraud in the PIF Directive forms the basis of the mandate of the European Public Prosecutor's Office (EPPO), which, as will be seen below, forms another strand of fighting impunity against the Union's budget.[14] *Taricco I* has thus introduced

[9] ibid para 37.
[10] ibid para 49 (emphasis added).
[11] ibid para 50.
[12] ibid para 51.
[13] ibid para 52.
[14] On the debate on the inclusion of VAT fraud in the PIF Directive, see F Giuffrida, 'The Protection of the Union's Financial Interests After Lisbon' in R Sicurella, V Mitsilegas, R Parizot and A Lucifora (eds), *General Principles for a Common Criminal Law Framework in the EU* (Milan, Giuffre, 2017) 245–74; R Sicurella, 'A Blunt Weapon for the EPPO? The Long Story of the Directive on the Protection of the Union's Financial Interests, the *Taricco* Case, and the Many Tricks of the Member States to Progressively Stifle It' in W Geelhoed, AWH Meij and L Erkelens (eds), *Shifting Perspectives on the European Public Prosecutor's Office* (The Hague, TMC Asser Press/Berlin, Springer, 2018).

a European concept of the fight against impunity in order to defend European interests: it consists, on the one hand, of detailed obligations by national authorities to disapply national law if the latter serves to boost impunity, and, on the other hand, of setting out the importance of legislation to fight impunity at the national level, in order to address national shortcomings, and at the EU level, to ensure a broad scope of application of EU law.

The *Taricco I* ruling faced vivid reactions in Italy. The Italian Constitutional Court seemed to be at pains to confirm the CJEU emphasis on upholding the effectiveness of Article 325 TFEU. It stated that

> it is certainly not for this Court to attribute to Article 325 TFEU a meaning different from that which it was found to have by the Court of Justice; it is in fact its duty to take note of that meaning and to decide whether it could have been appreciated by the individual who carried out the acts of relevance under criminal law.[15]

However, it found it difficult to accept the CJEU approach as being compatible with the principle of legality, and framed subsequent questions to Luxembourg with a focus on the compatibility of *Taricco I*, with the principle of legality as a supreme principle of the constitutional order or an inalienable human right recognised by the national constitution. Underlying the Italian Constitutional Court's approach may have been a concern for internal constitutional order, with the Court at pains to keep the final say and ultimate control over such questions raised by lower courts itself – a decentralised preliminary reference system empowering lower courts to ask questions related to impunity and constitutional matters directly to Luxembourg and in contrast with the centralised scrutiny of constitutional legality in Italy. Another factor stated in the Italian debate has been the impact of *Taricco I* on the principle of separation of powers, with the CJEU obligation of disapplication in *Taricco I* deemed to place the judiciary into a quasi-legislative role, being called to extensively interpret the law in order to disapply it on a case-by-case basis and under limited guidance by the legislator. The Italian Constitutional Court, however, and importantly, did not refer to Luxembourg questions related to the interpretation of Article 325 TFEU per se, thereby confirming the CJEU's remarkable ruling that Article 325 TFEU entails direct effect.

The CJEU found a compromise in its follow-up ruling in *Taricco II*,[16] upholding its seminal findings on the role of Article 325 TFEU in ensuring an effective fight against impunity on the one hand, while addressing some of the concerns raised by the Italian Constitutional Court on the other. The CJEU reiterated the direct effect of Article 325(1) and (2) TFEU;[17] the duty of disapplication of national provisions incumbent upon national courts;[18] and the finding that the extension of

[15] *Tarrico I* (n 8) para 5.
[16] Case C-42/17 *M.A.S. and M.B.* (*Tarrico II*) ECLI:EU:C:2017:936.
[17] ibid para 38.
[18] ibid para 39.

limitation period does not infringe the principle of legality.[19] However, the CJEU then visibly tried to find a space to accommodate the concerns raised by the Italian Constitutional Court.[20]

The CJEU has attempted to uphold its key findings regarding the applicability of EU law principles and obligations of national authorities to ensure the fight against impunity for violations of EU interests; at the same time, it addressed domestic concerns creating a somewhat artificial temporal dividing line before and after harmonization, with Member States retaining a leeway to act in cases where the EU has not acted. The immediate response by the Italian Constitutional Court was not encouraging, but rather entrenched,[21] with the question being dealt with from an internal balance of power rather than from an anti-impunity perspective. However, this is not a zero-sum game, as Italian domestic rules on limitation periods have been amended to accommodate anti-impunity concerns,[22] and subsequent case law of the Italian Constitutional Court appears to be more open towards applying fully the cooperative mechanisms with the CJEU.[23]

The approach of the CJEU, especially in *Taricco II*, stresses the role of legislation more broadly in addressing both impunity and legal certainty concerns. In this manner, the fight against impunity acts once more as a driver for European integration, by requiring further EU harmonising legislation. However, the fact remains that EU law obligations to ensure the effectiveness of the fight against fraud on the EU budget and to avoid impunity in this context remain even in cases where limited EU harmonisation has occurred – this is particularly the case in the field of criminal procedure, where the impact of EU law on national rules remains unclear and contested. A key question here is the extent to which national authorities must respect fundamental rights when applying their obligations to ensure the effectiveness of EU law in the context of the fight against impunity.

A recent example of the CJEU's approach has been its ruling in *Kolev*,[24] where it focused on the conformity of national procedural measures with fundamental rights in proceedings aimed at safeguarding the EU's financial interests. In *Kolev*, the CJEU extended the obligation stemming from Article 325 TFEU to ensure the effectiveness of EU law expressly in the field of criminal procedure.[25]

[19] ibid para 42.

[20] V Mitsilegas, 'Judicial Dialogue in Three Silences. Unpacking *Taricco*' (2018) 9 *New Journal of European Criminal Law* 38.

[21] V Manes, 'Taricco, *Endgame*' in V Mitsilegas, A di Martino and L Mancano (eds), *The Court of Justice and European Criminal Law. Leading Cases in a Contextual Analysis* (Oxford, Hart Publishing, 2019)188–95.

[22] Law 23 June 2017, no 103, known as 'Orlando reform'. In Gazzetta Ufficiale della Repubblica Italiana, 4 Luglio 2017.

[23] See Constitutional Court, ruling of 23 January 2019, no 20; Constitutional Court, ruling of 20 February 2019, no 63; Constitutional Court, ruling of 10 May 2019, no 112. Furthermore, with the Order of 10 May 2019, no 117, the Constitutional Court has referred to the CJEU a request for a preliminary reference. I am grateful to Michele Caianiello, Giulia Lasagni and Luisa Marin for drawing my attention to these cases.

[24] Case C-612/15 *Kolev and Others* ECLI:EU:C:2018:392.

[25] ibid para 55.

The CJEU proceeded with a delicate balancing act: on the one hand, it called upon the national legislator to amend rules when there is a systemic risk that acts that may be categorised as offences against the Union's financial interests may go unpunished, while also ensuring that the fundamental rights of accused persons are protected;[26] that the national court disapplies, if necessary, national law;[27] and that the referring court ensures that, at the various stages of proceedings, any deliberate and abusive obstruction on the part of the defence to the proper conduct and progress of those proceedings can be overridden.[28] On the other hand, the CJEU stated that fundamental rights cannot be defeated by the obligation to ensure the effective collection of the Union's resources.[29] The CJEU then focused on the requirement to protect the right of accused persons to have their case heard within a reasonable time,[30] which was treated by the Court as a general principle of EU law, enshrined in Article 6(1) of the European Convention on Human Rights (ECHR) and in Article 47 of the Charter of Fundamental Rights of the Union (the Charter).[31] The Court referred to European Court of Human Rights (Strasbourg) case law to determine the temporal applicability of that right in the field of criminal law.[32] However, and while the interpretation of the parameters of a specific rights have again been based on Strasbourg case law, it is noteworthy that the CJEU reverted to its internal 'constitutional' approach, focusing on the general principles of EU law in order to address the broader question of balancing the protection of fundamental rights with the requirement to achieve effective enforcement of EU law in the protection of an EU interest.

This attempt to temper the national courts' duty to fight impunity and ensure the effectiveness of Article 325 TFEU by their duty to respect fundamental rights is also evident in the case of *Dzivev*.[33] In *Dzivev*, the CJEU extended rights protection by stating expressly that the obligation to ensure the effective collection of the European Union's resources does not excuse national courts from the necessary observance of the fundamental rights guaranteed by the Charter and of the general principles of EU law. More precisely, it argued that the criminal proceedings instigated for VAT offences amount to an implementation of EU law, and that those rights and those principles must be respected not only during the criminal proceedings, but also during the stage of the preliminary investigation, from the moment when the person concerned becomes an accused.[34] In a case involving unlawful interception of communications, the CJEU, reminding of the importance

[26] ibid para 65.
[27] ibid para 66.
[28] ibid para 67.
[29] ibid para 68.
[30] ibid para 70.
[31] ibid para 71.
[32] ibid para 71.
[33] Case C-310/16 *Petar Dzivev* ECLI:EU:C:2019:30.
[34] ibid para 33.

of protecting legality and the rule of law,[35] found that EU law cannot require a national court to disapply such a procedural rule, even if the use of that evidence gathered unlawfully could increase the effectiveness of criminal prosecutions, enabling national authorities, in some cases, to penalise non-compliance with EU law.[36]

The trajectory of the Court's approach from *Taricco* to *Dzivev* thus reveals an interesting trend regarding the fight against impunity in terms of the protection of the Union budget. The CJEU has taken full advantage of 'Lisbonisation' in *Taricco I* to set out a clear benchmark of effectiveness and anti-impunity by empowering Article 325 TFEU with direct effect and spelling out far-reaching obligations of disapplication for national authorities, including courts. The CJEU hinted at the importance of further European integration in the form of legislative harmonization, but insisted on the application of these duties in national legal orders even in the face of limited harmonisation – with duties stemming from Article 325 applying also in the fields of criminal procedure and criminal investigations. However, the quest for effectiveness in the fight against impunity is limited by the constitutional requirement for national authorities to respect legality and the rule of law. In a field of law where there is still limited, minimum and piecemeal harmonisation, this European approach of balancing the fight against impunity with the protection of fundamental rights and the rule of law leaves a number of questions of certainty and consistency unanswered, as responses may vary considerably in accordance with national legal systems and policy priorities.[37]

Questions regarding the interaction between EU law obligations and national law in the quest to fight against impunity do not disappear in the event of the existence of harmonisation or unification efforts at the EU level. A key example in point has been the adoption of Regulation (EU) 2017/1939 setting up the EPPO and the questions it raises on the impact of the operations of the EPPO on national legal systems.[38] The establishment of the EPPO has been a breakthrough enabled by the entry into force of the Lisbon Treaty and the express legal basis on the establishment of the EPPO (Article 86 TEU) contained therein. The establishment of a European body competent to safeguard European interests has been a constant demand from the days of the *Corpus Juris*, and its establishment has been based on a logic of mistrust of European institutions – and in particular of the

[35] ibid para 34.

[36] ibid para 39.

[37] See the criticism of AG Bobek in his Opinion in *Dvizev*, noting the challenges to foreseeability (any national court can and should draw appropriate procedural consequences from a finding of incompatibility, which it is entitled to make for itself, without a reference to the CJEU. When extended to the setting aside of national rules of criminal procedure by individual courts in the Member States based on their self-assessment, criminal justice appears to run the risk of becoming an EU-sponsored lottery (para 106) and that, even after the ruling in *Kolev*, the catalysing point set by the Court for any such selective disapplication of offending national rules remains unclear (para 107).

[38] *cf* C Di Francesco Maesa, 'The Fight against Impunity between EU and National Legal Orders: What Role for the EPPO?', ch 8 in this book.

Commission – regarding the ability and willingness of Member States to uphold the effectiveness of EU law and protect the EU budget, and to fight impunity effectively in this context. According to the Commission's Explanatory Memorandum to its proposal for a Regulation establishing a European Public Prosecutor's Office, 'as Member States' criminal investigation and prosecution authorities are currently unable to achieve an equivalent level of protection and enforcement, the Union not only has the competence but also the obligation to act'.[39]

Following lengthy negotiations, the Regulation establishing the EPPO has now been adopted, with the participation of the vast majority of Member States, despite this being framed as an enhanced cooperation measure. The establishment of the EPPO can be seen as a political breakthrough in terms of creating a European mechanism to fight impunity against fraud on the EU budget. Yet the jury is out on whether the EPPO will provide a truly European approach to the prosecution of fraud, along with a related European approach to the protection of rights and the rule of law in this context. These questions will be tested in three main fields when the EPPO becomes operational: the structure of the EPPO (with the Commission's top-down approach being replaced in negotiations by a hybrid, multilayered and very complex scheme of operation of the EPPO); provisions on applicable law (with much – perhaps too much – of the applicable law on the operations of the EPPO left to Member States and not to EU law); and rule of law shortcomings in the scrutiny and accountability of the EPPO (with provisions on the judicial scrutiny of the EPPO by the CJEU being extremely limited). The current structure and design of the EPPO is based on the interaction between this EU body and national legal systems. For those viewing the glass as 'half full', the establishment of a European body to safeguard anti-impunity on the protection of the Union's budget is an overdue and important breakthrough which will lead, in a spillover effect, to further Europeanisation. For the more sceptical commentator, the establishment of the EPPO is a missed opportunity to address not only impunity, but also the legal uncertainty and the rule of law gaps arising from the diffuse applicability of EU law requirements at the national level. It remains to be seen whether operational action on the ground will inevitably lead to greater judicial scrutiny and eventually to further legislative harmonisation in the field.

III. The Fight against Impunity in Europe's Area of Freedom, Security and Justice: Mutual Recognition

Another key instance where the fight against impunity has emerged as an objective of EU law has been in the process of constructing the Union as an area of freedom, security and justice (AFSJ) without internal frontiers. From the very outset,

[39] COM (2013) 534 final, 2.

the Treaties envisaged a borderless area in which the free movement of persons is ensured in conjunction with appropriate measures with respect to, inter alia, the prevention and combating of crime.[40] The fight against impunity plays a key role in the construction of an area without internal frontiers: as with the Schengen logic of strong enforcement action to compensate for the criminogenic risks associated with the abolition of internal border controls, the rationale of the necessity of the fight against impunity is based on the premise that free movement must not lead to perpetrators of crimes evading criminal responsibility and prosecution. In the absence of a high level of harmonisation in the sensitive field of criminal law, the Union has attempted to maximise enforcement in the AFSJ by applying the principle of mutual recognition in criminal matters. Mutual recognition is attractive to Member States resisting further harmonisation or unification in European criminal law, as mutual recognition is thought to enhance interstate cooperation in criminal matters without Member States having to change their national laws to comply with EU harmonisation requirements.[41]

The Union legislator has adopted a series of mutual recognition instruments, ranging from the pretrial to the post-trial stage, with the Framework Decision on the European Arrest Warrant (EAW FD) being emblematic in this context.[42] Mutual recognition is aimed at achieving the extraterritorial reach of national judgments via a system of automaticity in interstate cooperation. Automaticity in interstate cooperation means that a national decision will be enforced beyond the territory of the issuing Member State by authorities in other EU Member States across the AFSJ without many questions being asked and with the requested authority having at its disposal extremely limited (if any) grounds to refuse the request for cooperation.[43] In addition, a key feature of the mutual recognition system is one of speed – with recognition and execution operating under tight deadlines. Effectiveness in the fight against impunity here thus also has a clear temporal dimension, with speed being perceived as essential in achieving justice in the AFSJ.

In nearly two decades of operation of this system of mutual recognition, its main feature has been that the quest for the fight against impunity is linked with the largely uncritical emphasis on the achievement of the enforcement objectives of the issuing Member State, even in the face of considerable differences in national approaches in the field of criminal justice. Although EU law provides a regulatory framework under the principle of mutual recognition, attempts to develop a

[40] Art 3(2) TEU. See also the further articulation of the components of the AFSJ in Title V TFEU (Art 67 TFEU).

[41] V Mitsilegas, 'The Constitutional Implications of Mutual Recognition in Criminal Matters in the EU' (2006) 43 *CML Rev* 1277.

[42] Framework Decision 2002/584/JHA of 13 June 2002 on the European Arrest Warrant [2002] OJ L190/1.

[43] V Mitsilegas, 'The Limits of Mutual Trust in Europe's Area of Freedom, Security and Justice. From Automatic Inter-state Cooperation to the Slow Emergence of the Individual' (2012) 31 *Yearbook of European Law* 319.

European concept of the fight against impunity in the operation of mutual recognition in criminal matters, taking into account the divergent interests of both the cooperating states and the affected individuals, have been limited. The fight against impunity is exhausted in serving the enforcement objectives of the issuing Member State. Thus, the abolition of the requirement to verify dual criminality has been found by the CJEU to be compatible with the principle of legality,[44] and the verification of dual criminality as such has been narrowly construed;[45] execution must happen in principle, with limited grounds for refusal (including on fundamental rights grounds) arising (at least initially)[46] and executing Member States not allowed to expect the application of their own, higher constitutional standards of protection if the lower standards of the issuing state are deemed to be compliant with EU law.[47]

Furthermore, the executing state can introduce a series of criminal procedural safeguards in the execution of the EAW, but only if these do not undermine the execution deadlines set out by the EAW FD;[48] the concept of detention will not include periods of curfew if this is not permitted by the law of the issuing state, even if this is allowed by the law of the executing state.[49] In other case law, the CJEU stated that periods of deduction of the sentence possible under the law of the executing state will not apply if not provided by the law of the issuing state;[50] the executing state is not permitted to enforce a sentence via the imposition of a fine, even though this is the only option permissible under its national law for this kind of case, if enforcement in the issuing state take place under a custodial sentence;[51] and the executing authority is not allowed to substitute its own assessment of the criminal responsibility of the minor in cases of differences between the issuing and the executing states on the delimitation of the age of criminal responsibility.[52]

[44] Case C-303/05 *Advocaten voor de Wereld* [2007] ECR I-3633.

[45] Case 289/15 *Grundza* ECLI:EU:C:2017:4.

[46] Case C-396/11 *Radu* ECLI:EU:C:2013:39.

[47] Case C-399/11 *Melloni* ECLI:EU:C:2013:107. For a commentary, see LFM Besselink, 'The Parameters of Constitutional Conflict after Melloni' (2014) 39 *EL Rev* 531; A Torres Pérez, 'Melloni in Three Acts: From Dialogue to Monologue' (2014) 10 *European Constitutional Law Review* 308; V Mitsilegas, 'Mutual Recognition, Mutual Trust and Fundamental Rights after Lisbon' in V Mitsilegas, M Bergström and T Konstadinides (eds), *Research Handbook on EU Criminal Law* (Cheltenham, Edward Elgar, 2016) 148–68.

[48] Case C-168/13 PPU *Jeremy F* ECLI:EU:C:2013:358.

[49] Case C-294/16 PPU *JZ v Prokuratura Rejonowa Łódź –Śródmieście* ECLI:EU:C:2016:610.

[50] Case C-554/14 *Ognyanov* ECLI:EU:C:2016:835. For a discussion, see S Montaldo, 'Offenders' Rehabilitation and the Cross-Border Transfer of Prisoners and Persons Subject to Probation Measures and Alternative Sanctions: A Stress Test for EU Judicial Cooperation in Criminal Matters' (2019) 5 *Revista Brasilera de Direito Processual Penal* 925, 953–54.

[51] Case C-514/17 *Sut* ECLI:EU:C:2018:1016. Para 47 requires the sentence to 'actually be enforced, in order to ensure that the custodial sentence imposed is enforced and thereby to avoid any risk of that person going unpunished'.

[52] Case C-367/16 *Piotrowski* ECLI:EU:C:2018:27.

Additionally, the executing state must ensure that a custodial sentence is actually enforced on its territory if it applies the grounds for refusal under Article 4(6) EAW FD, even if its national law provides otherwise – linking again the fight against impunity with the requirement of the actual enforcement of a custodial sentence.[53] All these rulings demonstrate a failure of imagination in developing a European concept of enforcement to tackle the fight against impunity under mutual recognition which takes into account the legal systems of the Member States involved and, importantly, the fundamental rights and interests of the individuals subject to these enforcement measures and their integration and rehabilitation. Rather than viewing the territory of the Union as a single area of freedom, security and justice with a common sense of justice, the CJEU has developed a paradigm of mutual recognition which, with few exceptions, privileges uncritically the enforcement objectives of the issuing state and the idea of justice as expressed in the national law of the issuing state.

This model of mutual recognition prioritising the achievement of the enforcement objectives of the issuing state has not been unqualified, however. Recent years have witnessed a series of attacks on this model, mainly reflecting the post-Lisbon requirement for the Union and its Member States when implementing Union law to comply fully with fundamental rights and the rule of law. Taking fundamental rights and the rule of law seriously has become essential in ensuring and maintaining the very credibility of the system of mutual recognition, with an uncritical emphasis on enforcement jeopardising the 'buy-in' to the system of national authorities, including national courts. A European concept of the fight against impunity has thus emerged in this context, with fundamental rights and the rule of law underpinning the system of mutual recognition in criminal matters in three main respects.

First, we have moved from a system of mutual recognition based on perceived or blind trust to a system of mutual recognition based on earned trust as regards the possibilities of the executing authorities to check meaningfully whether execution of a judgment complies with fundamental rights and the rule of law.[54] A turning point in this context has been the ruling of the CJEU in *Aranyosi and Căldăraru*, which launched a model of dialogical cooperation between the national authorities if the executing one has concerns of non-compliance of the execution of an EAW with fundamental rights.[55] The CJEU has since extended this model of scrutiny to include rule-of-law concerns.[56] While the precise parameters of cooperation and

[53] Case C-579/15 *Poplawski I* ECLI:EU:C:2017:503; Case C-573/17 *Poplawski II* ECLI:EU:C:2019:530. See the remarks on the creation of a risk of impunity in para 86 of *Poplawski II*.

[54] V Mitsilegas, 'Resetting the Parameters of Mutual Trust: From *Aranyosi* to *LM*' in Mitsilegas et al (n 21) 421–36; on the concept of blind trust, see K Lenaerts, 'La Vie après l'Avis: Exploring the Principle of Mutual (Yet Not Blind) Trust' (2017) 54 *CML Rev* 805.

[55] Joined Cases C-404/15 and C-659/15 PPU *Pál Aranyosi and Robert Căldăraru* ECLI:EU:C:2016:198.

[56] Case C-216/18 PPU *Minister for Justice and Equality (Défaillances du système judiciaire)* ECLI:EU:C:2018:586.

scrutiny of mutual trust post-*Aranyosi* are currently being fleshed out by national courts and the CJEU,[57] this development is of great significance as it departs from a rationale privileging the uncritical fight against impunity on the basis of the interests of the issuing state to a model of enforcement underpinned by a European duty of scrutiny of fundamental rights and rule of law compliance on the ground.

Linked to this development is the second step towards a European benchmark of safeguards to underpin mutual recognition enforcement efforts: the development by the CJEU of an autonomous European concept of judicial independence and judicial authority to underpin the operation of mutual recognition.[58] Linked to broader efforts by the CJEU to safeguard and further define the parameters of the rule of law in the Union legal order, the development of autonomous concepts containing European rule-of-law benchmarks in this context serves to set limits to executive power and to ensure that enforcement under mutual recognition is underpinned by full judicial protection and remedies.

The question of remedies appears prominently in the third way in which the paradigm of mutual recognition is being transformed: via legislative harmonisation rather than judicial intervention. Making use of the express legal basis provided by the Lisbon Treaty under Article 82(2) TFEU, the Union legislator has adopted a series of measures on the rights of the defendant in order to facilitate mutual recognition. Notwithstanding this functional legal basis and the granting of Lisbon competence to adopt minimum standards only, the result has been the adoption of a series of Directives covering a range of rights in criminal procedure, including the right to interpretation and translation,[59] the right to information,[60] the right of access to a lawyer,[61] the right to legal aid,[62] the right to procedural safeguards for children[63] and the presumption of innocence, and the right to be

[57] See, eg Case C-128/18 *Dorobantu* ECLI:EU:C:2019:857, which can be seen as signifying a return to *Melloni*.

[58] See recently Joined Cases C-508/18 *OG (Public Prosecutor's Office of Lübeck)* and C-82/19 PPU PI *(Public Prosecutor's Office of Zwickau)* ECLI:EU:C:2019:456; Case C-509/18 *PF (Prosecutor General of Lithuania)* ECLI:EU:C:2019:457. For an analysis, see V Mitsilegas, 'Autonomous Concepts, Diversity Management and Mutual Trust in Europe's Area of Criminal Justice' (2020) 57 *CML Rev* 45.

[59] EU Parliament and Council Directive 2010/64/EU on the right to interpretation and translation in criminal proceedings [2010] OJ L280/1.

[60] EU Parliament and Council Directive 2012/13/EU on the right to information in criminal proceedings [2012] OJ L142/1.

[61] EU Parliament and Council Directive 2013/48/EU on the right of access to a lawyer in criminal proceedings and in European arrest warrant proceedings, and on the right to have a third party informed upon deprivation of liberty and to communicate with third persons and with consular authorities while deprived of liberty [2013] OJ L294/1.

[62] EU Parliament and Council Directive 2016/1919/EU on legal aid for suspects and accused persons in criminal proceedings and for requested persons in European arrest warrant proceedings [2016] OJ L297/1.

[63] EU Parliament and Council Directive (EU) 2016/800 on procedural safeguards for children who are suspects or accused persons in criminal proceedings [2016] OJ L132/1.

present at the trial in criminal proceedings.[64] The scope of these Directives to insert a meaningful European rights approach to the anti-impunity framework of mutual recognition is considerable: they apply across the board in national systems (not only to cross-border cases, but also purely domestic ones), must have full effectiveness, bring forward the full implementation scrutiny by the European Commission and the CJEU, entail (in many of their key provisions) direct effect and constitute benchmarks for other areas of EU criminal justice, including the operation of the EPPO. An uncritical fight against impunity via mutual recognition has thus been tempered by a series of fundamental rights standards adopted via secondary EU law, and which may have a transformative effect in the protection of fundamental rights and in the reshaping of the paradigm of mutual recognition in the AFSJ.[65] What is noteworthy here is that concerns arising from an enforcement-based paradigm of mutual recognition have acted as a driver of European integration in criminal matters not in terms of adopting further enforcement measures, but in terms of adopting measures on fundamental rights which will serve as benchmarks for the European system of mutual recognition in Europe's SFSJ.

IV. The Fight against Impunity in Europe's Area of Freedom, Security and Justice: Transnational *ne bis in idem*

Another instance where the fight against impunity has been tempered by the protection of fundamental rights in Europe's AFSJ specifically concerns the evolution of the principle of transnational *ne bis in idem* in European criminal law.[66] There is a certain symmetry between the extraterritoriality in the application of the principle of mutual recognition in criminal matters and the extraterritoriality in the transnational *ne bis in idem*, but while the former aims at extraterritorial enforcement within the AFSJ, the latter aims at extraterritorial protection of individuals and their legal certainty, in order to ensure meaningful free movement within a borderless area. It is worth reminding here that the principle of transnational *ne bis in idem* has a concrete and distinct Schengen heritage, appearing in a number of provisions of the Schengen Implementing Convention, which the

[64] EU Parliament and Council Directive 2016/343/EU on the strengthening of certain aspects of the presumption of innocence and of the right to be present at the trial in criminal proceedings [2016] OJ L65/1.

[65] V Mitsilgegas, 'Legislating for Human Rights after Lisbon: The Transformative Effect of EU Measures on Procedural Rights in Criminal Proceedings' in M Fletcher, E Herlin-Karnell and C Matera (eds), *The European Union as an Area of Freedom, Security and Justice* (London, Routledge, 2017) 201–15.

[66] See Bas van Bockel, 'Between Impunity and the Protection of Fundamental Rights: The Case Law of the CJEU and the ECtHR on the *ne bis in idem* Principle', ch 6 in this book.

CJEU was called to interpret following the incorporation of the Schengen *acquis* in EU law by the Amsterdam Treaty. Initially, the Court interpreted the principle of transnational *ne bis in idem* broadly. This broad interpretation was underpinned by the existence of mutual trust in an area where national criminal procedural laws, including rules on *ne bis in idem* as such, have not been harmonised. The need to achieve the effective enjoyment of free movement takes precedence over national priorities with regard to the fight against impunity.

This teleological approach is evident in the Court's interpretation of both elements of *bis* and *idem*. On the concept of *bis*, the Court has included, in the concept of 'finally disposed of', cases whose outcome was settled without involving a substantive examination of their merits. These include cases of a settlement ('transaction') between the defendant and the prosecution terminating the prosecution,[67] as well as cases of time-barred prosecutions.[68] The Court's reasoning was put forward with great clarity in the landmark case of *Gözütok and Brügge*, where the Court placed emphasis on the purpose of the integration of the Schengen *acquis* into the Union legal order. The Court noted that such integration 'is aimed at enhancing European integration and, in particular, at enabling the Union to become more rapidly the area of freedom, security and justice which is its objective to maintain and develop'.[69] Examining specifically Article 54 of the Convention Implementing the Schengen Agreement (CISA, Schengen Convention), the Court emphasised its objective to ensure that no one is prosecuted on the same facts in several Member States on account of having exercised his right to freedom of movement.[70] The Court stated that nowhere in the EU Treaty or the Schengen Convention 'is the application of Article 54 of the Convention made conditional upon harmonisation, or at least approximation, of the criminal laws of the Member States relating to procedures whereby further prosecution is barred',[71] and added that, in those circumstances,

> there is a necessary implication that the Member States have *mutual trust* in their criminal justice systems and that each of them recognises the criminal law in force in the other Member States even when the outcome would be different if its own national law were applied.[72]

[67] Joined Cases C-187/01 and C-385/01 *Gözütok and Brügge* [2003] ECR I-1345.

[68] Case C-467/04 *Gasparini* ECR [2006] I-9199.

[69] *Gözütok and Brügge* (n 67) para 37.

[70] ibid paras 35–38. See also the Opinion of AG Ruiz-Jarabo Colomer, paras 42–43.

[71] *Gözütok and Brügge* (n 67) para 32.

[72] ibid para 33 (emphasis added). See also the Opinion of Advocate General Ruiz-Jarabo Colomer, delivered on 19 September 2002, paras 119–24, and para 55, where the AG states that 'the construction of a Europe without borders, with its corollary of the approximation of the various national legal systems, including the criminal systems, presupposes that the States involved will be guided by the same values'.

The Court's teleological approach thus presumes mutual trust in the absence of harmonisation of criminal justice systems.[73] Unlike its use in the EAW system, this presumption of trust serves here to enhance, not challenge, the protection of fundamental rights in Europe's AFSJ.

The same approach has also based the Court's interpretation of *idem*. The Court has proceeded towards defining *idem* autonomously.[74] In the leading case of *Van Esbroek*,[75] it rejected the idea of defining *idem* on the basis of the legal classification of the act in national law. Given that there is no harmonisation of national laws, the legal classification or the legal interest protected at the national level 'might create as many barriers to freedom of movement within Schengen as there are legal systems'.[76] On similar grounds, the Court has rejected the use of the concept of the legal interest (*Rechtsgut*) in national law as a determining factor for *idem*.[77]

The Court has taken into account to a greater extent national considerations in relation to the *bis*.[78] The Court has required for the application of Article 54 CISA that a decision is given after a determination has been made as to the merits of the case[79] and that a national decision definitely bars further prosecution at the national level.[80] However, the decisive factor in the applicability of the *ne bis in idem* principle continues to be the law of the first Member State which has dealt with the case. In the case of *M*, the Court confirmed that the assessment of the 'final' nature of the criminal ruling at issue must be carried out in light of the law of the Member State in which that ruling was made.[81] Thus, it reaffirms the priority of the requirement of legal certainty for the affected individual in Europe's area of criminal justice.

However, recent years have witnessed a shift in the Court's approach, from a legal certainty/free movement emphasis to the prioritisation of the enforcement views of the 'second' Member State wishing to prosecute. In *Spasic*,[82] the Court of Justice had to assess whether the enforcement condition to the principle of *ne bis*

[73] See also the Court's similar reasoning in *Gasparini*, where the Court included time-barred prosecutions within the scope of Art 54 CISA notwithstanding the concerns by Advocate General Sharpston that this approach would disregard the fact that substantive justice has not been delivered in the present case.

[74] For further analysis, see V Mitsilegas, 'Managing Legal Diversity in Europe's Area of Criminal Justice: The Role of Autonomous Concepts' in R Colson and S Field (eds), *EU Criminal Justice and the Challenges of Legal Diversity. Towards A Socio-Legal Approach to EU Criminal Policy* (Cambridge, Cambridge University Press, 2016) 125–60.

[75] Case C-436/04 *Van Esbroek* ECR [2006] I-2333.

[76] ibid para 35.

[77] Case C-288/05 *Jürgen Kretzinger* ECR [2007] I-6641, in particular para 33.

[78] On the latter point, see A Weyembergh and I Armada, 'The Principle of *ne bis in idem* in Europe's Area of Freedom, Security and Justice' in Mitsilegas et al (n 47) 189–209.

[79] Case C-469/03 *Miraglia* EU:C:2005:156, para 30.

[80] Case C-491/07 *Turanský* EU:C:2008:768, para 36.

[81] Case C 398/12 *M* judgment of 5 June 2014, Para 36.

[82] Case C-129/14 PPU *Spasic* judgment of 27 May 2014.

in idem under Article 54 CISA is compatible with Article 50 of the Charter. The Court found that the additional condition laid down in Article 54 CISA constitutes a limitation of the *ne bis in idem* principle that is compatible with Article 50 of the Charter.[83] The Court accepted the argument put forward by the German and French governments that the condition laid down in Article 54 CISA does not call into question the *ne bis in idem* principle as such, but is intended, inter alia, to avoid a situation in which a person definitively convicted and sentenced in one contracting state can no longer be prosecuted for the same acts in another contracting state and therefore ultimately remains unpunished if the first state did not execute the sentence imposed.[84] Moreover, the Court went on to find that the limitation of *ne bis in idem* is proportionate as it is intended to prevent the impunity of persons definitively convicted and sentenced in an EU Member State. According to the Court, where the sentence has not yet been executed, allowing the authorities of another contracting state to prosecute the same person for the same acts amounts to avoiding the risk that the person concerned would enjoy impunity by virtue of his leaving the territory of the state in which he was sentenced.[85] The Court was not convinced by the Commission's argument that EU secondary law instruments providing for consultations between national authorities (including the Framework Decision on Conflicts of Jurisdiction) addressed this objective. The Court noted that these instruments are not capable of fully achieving the objective pursued.[86] According to the Court, these Acts cannot ensure that persons definitively convicted and sentenced in the European Union will not enjoy impunity if the state which imposed the first sentence does not execute the penalties imposed.[87]

The CJEU's approach in *Spasic* is striking.[88] It is a marked departure from the view of Advocate General Jääskinen, who found that the generalised application of the execution condition in Article 54 CISA does not satisfy the proportionality criterion and cannot be regarded as a justified interference with the right not to be tried or punished twice in criminal proceedings.[89] The ruling is also at odds with the Court's case law on *bis* and *idem*, with the earlier emphasis on the presumption of mutual trust being transformed in *Spasic* to an institutionalisation of mutual distrust. The Court seems to have little time for the deliberative and consultative mechanisms introduced by EU law and aimed at facilitate interstate cooperation in cases of conflicts of jurisdiction. The Court finds these mechanisms to be weak, but this weakness is explained by Member States' reluctance to harmonise standards

[83] ibid para 54.
[84] ibid para 58 and reference to *Kretzinger* (n 77) para 51.
[85] *Spasic* (n 82) paras 63 and 64, respectively.
[86] ibid para 68.
[87] ibid para 69.
[88] V Mitsilegas, 'The Symbiotic Relationship between Mutual Trust and Fundamental Rights in Europe's Area of Criminal Justice' (2015) 6 *New Journal of European Criminal Law* 460.
[89] View delivered on 2 May 2014, paras 91–103.

further in the field. This lack of harmonisation is allowed here to foment distrust and allow multiple interventions by national enforcement authorities for the same acts.[90] This approach has profound consequences for the protective function of *ne bis in idem*. In *Spasic*, the Court effectively introduces a security rationale within a fundamental right. However, not only does this rationale (and the emphasis on the need to avoid impunity) not fall within the scope of *ne bis in idem*, but the Court's interpretation also opens the door towards divergent interpretations and levels of protection between domestic *ne bis in idem* cases involving the implementation of EU law (interpreted in conformity with Article 50 of the Charter) and transnational *ne bis in idem* cases under Article 54 CISA.[91] The Court's approach in *Spasic* also does very little for the achievement of legal certainty in Europe's area of criminal justice and raises the spectre of serious impediments to the enjoyment of free movement.

A similar shift in approach can be seen in the case of *Kossowski*,[92] where the Court accepted the argument of the second Member State that the investigation of the case in the first Member State was not sufficiently detailed and that therefore the *ne bis in idem* protection did not arise.[93] The CJEU thus seems to accept the mistrust of the first state by the second state and accept one of the two state's (and arguably the more draconian) approach on the conduct of criminal investigations, by requiring an unclear – and for some arbitrary – extra benchmark of 'detailed investigation'.[94] Here a European approach limiting the fight against impunity on the grounds of truly European considerations of legal certainty and free movement within Europe's borderless AFSJ give way to the precedence of unilateral perceptions of effective enforcement by individual Member States which have the potential to render important protective principles toothless and devoid of a common meaning reflecting a common sense of justice within the EU.

V. The Fight against Impunity and International Cooperation in Criminal Matters

Another dimension of the fight against impunity in EU law involves its external dimension. Anti-impunity considerations have arisen before the CJEU in

[90] On these instruments, see A Giannakoula, 'Impunity and Conflicts of Jurisdiction within the EU: the Role of Eurojust and Challenges for Fundamental Rights', ch 7 in this book.

[91] See further M Wasmeier, '*Ne bis in idem* and the Enforcement Condition: Balancing Freedom, Security and Justice?' (2014) 4 *New Journal of European Criminal Law* 534.

[92] Case C-486/14 *Kossowski* ECLI:EU:C:2016:483.

[93] ibid paras 53–54.

[94] In this context, see the remarks of Nowak, noting the arbitrary nature of the concept of 'sufficiently detailed examination': C Nowak, 'Impact of the Case C-486/14- *Kossowski* at the National Level' in Mitsilegas et al (n 21) 239. Noting the case and context-dependent nature of this test, and the obvious limits to external control this can entail, see also K Ambos, 'Judgment (Grand Chamber) C-486/14 *Piotr Kossowski*, 29 June 2016' in Mitsilegas et al (n 21) 235.

a series of cases concerning extradition requests from third countries to EU Member States.[95] These requests covered a wide range of legal situations: extradition requests for the purpose of prosecution in cases where the third country in question had not concluded an extradition agreement with the EU (this was the case of Russia in *Petruhhin*[96]); extradition requests for prosecution by countries which had concluded an extradition agreement with the EU (namely the US case *Pisciotti*[97]); and extradition requests for the purposes of execution of the sentence by countries with no extradition agreement with the EU (again a case involving Russia – *Raugevicius*[98]). In all three cases, the CJEU was essentially asked to position the fight against impunity within the constitutional question of the extent to which cooperation is possible while upholding EU law. In response, and notwithstanding the nuances in these rulings, the CJEU has elevated the fight against impunity in the context of international cooperation and its effectiveness as a key objective of EU law subject to two conditions: that cooperation complies with EU values and that it respects, to some extent, EU citizenship rights.

In terms of the need to respect EU values, the CJEU has explicitly used its internal *Aranyosi* test developed in the context of the EAW as the external benchmark of Member State action in the field of extradition. This is an important reminder that international cooperation cannot happen at the expense of the protection of fundamental rights and cannot undermine the Union's own standards and values.[99] The CJEU added a second layer of scrutiny and examined the extent to which EU citizenship could act as a further protection against extradition requests from third countries. It noted that the Union is to contribute to the protection of its citizens in its relations with the wider world,[100] questioning the extent to which such protection extends to extradition requests against EU citizens located in Member States other than the state of nationality. The development of bilateral international cooperation arrangements between Member States and third countries aimed at fighting impunity must be seen here within the broader obligations and values of the European Union as a whole, both in terms of the relationship between national law and EU law and in terms of the requirement of the EU to uphold its fundamental principles on the global stage.

The evolution of the CJEU case law thus far has presented a nuanced protection against extradition on citizenship grounds. The Court set a promising initial benchmark in *Petruhhin*, where it focused on the need to protect free movement and invoked the need to give priority to internal EU cooperation mechanisms over international ones. The Court accepted that preventing the risk of impunity is a

[95] On this topic, see S Saluzzo, 'Impunity and EU or Member States' Extradition Agreements with Third Countries', ch 17 in this book.
[96] Case C-182/15 *Petruhhin* ECLI:EU:C:2016:630.
[97] C-191/16 *Pisciotti* ECLI:EU:C:2018:222.
[98] Case C-247/17 *Raugevicius* ECLI:EU:C:2018:898.
[99] *Petruhhin* (n 96) para 44 – see reference to Art 3(5) TFEU.
[100] ibid.

legitimate objective of EU law.[101] However, measures which restrict a fundamental freedom such as the one set out in Article 21 TFEU can be justified by objective considerations only if the interests which they are intended to secure cannot be attained by less restrictive means.[102] If the state of nationality has jurisdiction pursuant to its national law to prosecute that person for offences committed outside its territory,[103] it will be granted the opportunity to issue an EAW, which takes precedence over the international extradition request.[104] In other words, as Costa has noted, the EU citizenship exception gives rise to protection against extradition, but only if the offence can be prosecuted in the EU.[105] In this way, the CJEU has attempted to ensure that impunity does not occur while trying to uphold citizenship rights by establishing not a duty, but merely an opportunity for the country of nationality to issue an EAW via the evocation of the principle of sincere cooperation.[106] The protection offered by the Court to EU citizens is thus derivative, depending on action by the state of nationality.[107] With this caveat, *Petruhhin* has been an important ruling in setting potential limits to the uncritical fight against impunity in the context of international cooperation in criminal matters – with EU fundamental rights benchmarks and citizenship rights setting limits to such cooperation.

The extent of these limits has been tested in the follow-up case of *Pisciotti*.[108] *Pisciotti* differed from *Petruhhin* in two main respects: it involved an EU national who was in transit from an EU Member State (an Italian national in transit at Frankfurt airport); and it involved a situation where the EU had in fact signed an extradition agreement with the third country concerned (the USA). The CJEU found that this agreement, as well as national law, including constitutional law governing bilateral extradition relations with third countries (which may prohibit the extradition of own nationals to third countries), must be applied in accordance with EU law, including primary EU law.[109] The CJEU then referred back to *Petrunhin* regarding the requirement of approaching the need to prevent impunity in the international sphere without disproportionately restricting the free movement of EU citizens.[110] However, the CJEU's conceptualisation of the protective function of EU citizenship in the context of international cooperation was rather limited. The CJEU did not place Member States under the duty to treat

[101] ibid para 37 and reference to *Spasic*.
[102] ibid para 38.
[103] ibid para 50.
[104] ibid para 48.
[105] MJ Costa, 'The Emerging EU Extradition Law. *Petruhhin* and Beyond' (2017) 8 *New Journal of European Criminal Law* 192.
[106] *Petruhhin* (n 96) para 42.
[107] Costa (n 105) 198.
[108] *Pisciotti* (n 97).
[109] ibid paras 39–43.
[110] ibid paras 44–48.

EU citizens in the same way as their own citizens in cases of extradition requests by third countries (which could mean a prohibition of extradition if this is the case of own nationals and an obligation to assume prosecution at the national level). This approach would both give meaning to EU citizenship rights and ensure the avoidance of impunity. Rather, the Court chose to develop further its approach to *Petruhhin*, whereby essentially citizenship rights are taken into account by giving precedence to the enforcement will of the country of nationality of the requested person.

In *Pisciotti*, this derivative protection found its expression in the CJEU giving precedence to an EAW in relation to an extradition request from the USA, notwithstanding the nuanced wording of the EU–USA extradition agreement in this regard.[111] The only question for Germany in this context was whether to adopt an action which was less prejudicial to free movement and surrender the EU citizen to his EU state of nationality (Italy) rather than to the USA.[112] Thus, the only way forward in this case would be for Germany to inform Italy and, should the latter decide to issue an EAW, to execute the warrant provided that the Member State has jurisdiction, pursuant to its national law, to prosecute the person for offences committed outside its territory.[113] In this case, the Italian authorities chose not to issue an EAW in respect of Mr Pisciotti.[114] The *Pisciotti* ruling was rightly criticised for failing to uphold a protection based on EU citizenship. As Coutts has eloquently noted, in *Pisciotti* the relationship shifts from one of a Union citizen, deriving protection from the Union legal order, to a one of a national citizen, over whom the state claims a privileged relationship of authority, before and above the claims of other third states.[115] Indeed, such protection may essentially be offered on grounds of nationality, and not of a broader European understanding of EU citizenship within Europe's AFSJ – a European approach which has been weakened further in *Pisciotti* by the failure of the CJEU to refer expressly to the requirement for EU fundamental rights standards to form the benchmark for external action on extradition for the EU and its Member States.

The CJEU's restrictive approach in *Pisciotti* may be explained by the facts of the case, namely that it involved an EU citizen in transit via another EU Member State. The CJEU's response was slightly different in the subsequent case of *Raugevicius*, which involved a permanent resident EU citizen.[116] Mr Raugevicius was a dual Russian–Lithuanian national, resident in Finland and subject to a Russian extradition request to enforce a sentence. The CJEU reiterated its statements on the limits to the fight against impunity posed by free movement[117] and applied this

[111] ibid para 53.
[112] ibid para 50.
[113] ibid para 51.
[114] ibid para 55.
[115] S Coutts, 'From Union Citizens to National Subjects: *Pisciotti*' (2019) 56 *CML Rev* 536.
[116] *Raugevicius* (n 98) 533.
[117] ibid paras 28–32.

reasoning to extradition requests for the enforcement of sentences.[118] Unlike in *Pisciotti*, however, here the Court projected its internal case law on citizenship protection in intra-EU EAW cases into the external field. By reference to the internal case of *Wolzenburg*,[119] the CJEU found that, in view of the aim of preventing the risk of impunity, Finnish nationals and nationals of other Member States who reside permanently in Finland and demonstrate a certain degree of integration into that state are in a comparable situation.[120] The CJEU found that Articles 18 and 21 TFEU require that nationals of other Member States who reside permanently in Finland and whose extradition is requested by a third country for the purpose of enforcing a custodial sentence should benefit from the provision preventing extradition from being applied to Finnish nationals and may, under the same conditions as Finnish nationals, serve their sentence on Finnish territory.[121] In contrast, if a citizen may not be regarded as residing permanently in the Member State which has received the extradition request, the issue of his extradition is to be settled on the basis of the applicable national or international law.[122] The Court constructed citizenship protection here in light of permanent residence under national law. However, this protection is further underpinned by the requirement to comply with EU benchmarks: the Court reiterated that, in the absence of EU law on extradition with Russia, Member States are still required to exercise the power to adopt domestic provisions in accordance with EU law.[123] Citing *Petruhhin*, the Court confirmed the obligation of a Member State intending to extradite a national from another Member State to a third country not to infringe Charter rights, and in particular Article 19 of the Charter.[124]

In terms of their impact on the conceptualisation of the fight against impunity in EU law, this sequence of cases paints a complex and nuanced picture. First of all, the Court confirms that the fight against impunity in the context of international cooperation in criminal matters, and in particular in the context of extradition arrangements between EU Member States and third countries, is a legitimate objective of EU law. Here, it can thus be seen that the effectiveness of international cooperation is elevated as a distinct objective in EU law.[125] Secondly, it can be seen that the fight against impunity on the international stage is far from unqualified. EU law sets important parameters and limits to international cooperation. The first set of limits involves full compliance with internal EU fundamental rights standards – as also reiterated by the CJEU in two out of its three rulings in the

[118] ibid para 34.
[119] Case C-123/08 *Wolzenburg* ECLI:EU:C:2009:616.
[120] *Raugevicius* (n 98) para 46.
[121] ibid para 47.
[122] ibid para 48.
[123] ibid para 45.
[124] ibid para 49; *Petruhhin* (n 96) para 60.
[125] Coutts (n 115) 536 notes that impunity reflects a more abstract principle here, that justice be done more generally.

field. The challenge for the European Union when emerging as a global actor is to uphold and promote its values worldwide, and these values can be seriously challenged in the context of international cooperation in criminal matters with third states whose benchmarks and standards vary significantly from EU norms.

The significance of rulings such as *Petruhhin* and *Raugevicius* is not only the express reminder by the Court that internal EU benchmarks apply externally, but also that these standards govern action by EU Member States in their bilateral relations with third states even in the absence of EU rules on extradition with the third countries concerned. This can certainly be said on the back of these judgments for cases involving extradition requests by third countries involving citizens of other EU Member States – but it is submitted that this also applies in cases involving extradition requests by third countries involving own nationals of EU Member States. This is an area where, in view of EU action in the field, Member States are bound by EU law in their external action.[126] While fundamental rights provide here a truly European benchmark for conceptualising the fight against impunity and setting its parameters in international cooperation, the same cannot be said in terms of the development of protection against extradition on the grounds of citizenship of the Union.

The CJEU's choice of dealing with these cases from a citizenship perspective has been of great significance in bringing these cases within the scope of EU law, to ensure that EU law protection is achieved. As Nic Shuibhne has eloquently noted, the Court's primary concern is to keep the business of Union citizens within the territory of the Union as much as possible, with the purpose of protecting the Union citizen from the uncertain consequences of exposure to 'outside'.[127] However, in the evolution of the case law of the Court, protection against an uncritical fight against impunity privileging the interests of the non-EU requesting state has been based not so much on a European concept of citizenship and rights, but rather on a derivative model, which has degenerated in cases like *Pisciotti* from a model of protection based on citizenship to a model of protection based on nationality. This approach leaves EU citizens at the mercy of the choices of their country of nationality, which may or may not see a strong need to protect that individual concerned on the basis of the various links arising in the specific case. It potentially creates a great disparity in the treatment of EU citizens within the AFSJ. The case for a reconsideration on the basis of a European model of protection based more firmly on equality and non-discrimination appears to be due.

[126] I have developed this point in V Mitsilegas, 'Transatlantic Counter-Terrorism Cooperation after Lisbon' (2010) 3 *Eucrim* 111.

[127] N Nic Shuibhne, '"The Territory of the Union" in EU Citizenship Law: Charting a Route from Parallel to Integrated Narratives' (2019) 38 *Yearbook of European Law* 267.

VI. The Fight against Impunity and the Globalisation of Law Enforcement: The Case of Digital Evidence

Another dimension of the fight against impunity in EU law is inextricably linked with processes of globalisation. The growing importance of the generation and use of personal data in the digital world is key in this context. The proliferation of the generation, use and processing of personal data as part of the everyday life in the digital world and the central role that private companies such as telecommunications or internet companies play in the handling and exploitation of such data[128] have the potential to change law enforcement paradigms in the quest for the fight against impunity. In this process, the state is increasingly required to co-opt the private sector in the fight against impunity. This privatisation of law enforcement was noted by criminologists some time ago,[129] and appeared prominently in EU and international law in the context of the fight against money laundering.[130] However, the privatisation of law enforcement and surveillance in the digital world raises a number of further challenges both as regards the protection of fundamental rights and the rule of law, and as regards defining the parameters of applicable law in a world of data where jurisdictional fault lines may prove to be increasingly difficult to demarcate. The fight against impunity by going after personal data generated from everyday life in the global context thus blurs boundaries in two respects: in terms of actors of enforcement, where the boundaries between the public and the private are being blurred; and in terms of the applicable law, where the boundaries between EU law on the one hand and national laws and the law of third countries on the other hand are being blurred – in a field where global law enforcement efforts to have maximum access to everyday personal data are not necessarily accompanied by a protective global level playing field of fundamental rights and the rule of law.

A key example of the challenges posed by the fight against impunity in the global digital world involves recent attempts to develop legal regimes enabling maximum access by law enforcement authorities to digital data which may be used as evidence – with the European Commission tabling a proposal for a Regulation on European Production and Preservation Orders for electronic evidence in criminal matters.[131] The draft Regulation establishes a system compelling private service providers offering services in the EU to produce or preserve electronic

[128] S Zuboff, *The Age of Surveillance Capitalism* (London, Profile Books, 2019).

[129] On the responsibilisation strategy, see D Garland, 'The Limits of the Sovereign State: Strategies of Crime Control in Contemporary Society' (1996) 36 *British Journal of Criminology* 445.

[130] I have expanded on the privatisation on crime control in the context of anti-money laundering law in V Mitsilegas, *Money Laundering Counter-Measures in the European Union: A New Paradigm of Security Governance versus Fundamental Legal Principles* (The Hague, Kluwer Law International, 2003).

[131] COM (2018) 225 final.

evidence, regardless of the location of the data, upon receipt of orders issued by public authorities in EU Member States. According to the proposal, such orders (the European Production Order and the European Preservation Order) can be served on providers of electronic communication services, social networks, online marketplaces, other hosting service providers and providers of internet infrastructure, such as IP address and domain name registries, or on their legal representatives where they exist. The draft Regulation thus establishes a direct channel of communication between the issuing (public) authority and private service providers, with European Production Orders and European Preservation Orders addressed directly to a legal representative designated by the service provider (to facilitate this, the Commission has also tabled in parallel a draft Regulation laying down harmonised rules on the appointment of legal representatives.[132] The addressees must in principle comply with the orders and react swiftly: upon receipt of a European Production Order, the addressee must ensure that the requested data is transmitted directly to the issuing authority or the law enforcement authorities as indicated in the Order at the latest within 10 days upon receipt. The Commission has justified the system proposed in the draft Regulation on the basis of the special features of the internet and of the operations of electronic service providers, linked with the perceived need for greater speed in the gathering and transmission of electronic evidence. The second paragraph of the Explanatory Memorandum to the draft Regulation states that:

> Given the borderless nature of the internet, such services can be provided from anywhere in the world and do not necessarily require physical infrastructure, a corporate presence or staff in Member States where the services are offered or in the internal market as a whole. They also do not require a specific location for the storage of data, which is often chosen by the service provider on the basis of legitimate considerations such as data security, economies of scale and swiftness of access. As a result, in a growing number of criminal cases involving all types of crime, Member State authorities require access to data that might serve as evidence and that is stored outside their country and/or by service providers in other Member States or third countries.

Based on the premise that e-evidence is a 'special case' along these lines, the draft Regulation introduces a paradigm change.[133] It establishes a system whereby cooperation takes place directly between a public authority in the issuing Member State and the private sector – departing from existing models of judicial cooperation and mutual recognition in EU law, which are based on cooperation and communication between public authorities in Member States. This change is not without controversy and raises three main concerns in terms of the protection of fundamental rights at the EU and at the global level. First, the system introduced

[132] COM (2018) 226 final.

[133] See V Mitsilegas, 'The Privatisation of Mutual Trust in Europe's Area of Criminal Justice' (2018) 25 *Maastricht Journal of European and Comparative Law* 263.

by the draft Regulation on e-evidence dispenses with the layer of judicial control and scrutiny of a request for evidence in the executing Member State. This layer of control is of paramount importance in the EU architecture of judicial cooperation in criminal matters on the basis of mutual recognition. The most mature measure of mutual recognition adopted thus far, which actually concerns the exchange of evidence – the Directive on the European Investigation Order[134] – promotes speed and efficiency in judicial cooperation while providing for a number of safeguards to be taken into account by the judicial authorities of the executing Member State, including fundamental rights considerations. The proposal on e-evidence dispenses with this system, delegating fundamental rights scrutiny to the private sector.

This approach leads effectively to the privatisation of mutual trust in Europe's area of criminal justice, which raises the second concern regarding the protection of fundamental rights. The Commission's proposal on e-evidence marks a fundamental shift in the scheme of cooperation in criminal matters in the EU, from a system of cooperation and communication between public (and mainly judicial) authorities to one of cooperation and communication between public authorities in the issuing state and private companies. The proposed system places undue responsibility on private providers to safeguard fundamental rights. Private providers do not enjoy equality with public authorities in terms of cooperation – this is evident by the very fact that they are subject to sanctions for infringements of their obligations under the Regulation. This lack of equality cannot underpin any meaningful relationship of mutual trust between public authorities and the private sector, which is placed largely in a subordinate position in terms of compliance with e-evidence requests from a public authority.[135] The draft Regulation does include provisions on fundamental rights safeguards, but asking private companies to fully scrutinise these whilst at the same time facing the prospect of sanctions for non-compliance may prove to be a tall order.

This asymmetry between the public and the private sector in terms of cooperation in criminal matters raises a third fundamental rights concern when the Commission's proposal is viewed in a global context. As mentioned above, the proposal lowers the threshold of fundamental rights protection within the EU by dispensing with a layer of judicial control in the executing Member State. The emergence of this privatised model of mutual trust as an EU benchmark may, in effect, lead to a race to the bottom in terms of fundamental rights protection at a global level. The general approach in the Commission's draft Regulation seems to be in line with the provisions in the recently adopted US Clarifying Lawful Overseas Use of Data (CLOUD) Act, which compels service providers to disclose all data

[134] Directive 2014/41/EU of the European Parliament and of the Council of 3 April 2014 regarding the European Investigation Order in criminal matters [2014] OJ L130/1.

[135] Lenaerts (n 54), referring to the link between equality and mutual trust.

in their possession regardless of the location of this data.[136] The CLOUD Act was adopted partly in response to the *Microsoft* litigation, where the requirement for the authorities of an EU Member State to approve a request for evidence by the US authorities via the mutual legal assistance route was tested.[137] The CLOUD Act has three elements in common with the Commission's Regulation on e-evidence: it attempts to bypass mutual legal assistance safeguards and the layers of fundamental rights scrutiny they entail; it establishes a direct link between public authorities and the private sector; and it bypasses the concept of territoriality in terms of the location of personal data. In this manner, transatlantic convergence leads to the development of a global level playing field privileging prosecutorial and law enforcement efficiency over fundamental rights concerns. These efforts have not been accompanied by parallel efforts to create a global level playing field in the area of privacy and data protection, and it is only a matter of time before the limits to this new paradigm are exposed by courts, at least on this side of the Atlantic.

Attempts by the European Commission to change the internal EU paradigm of judicial cooperation in the field of digital evidence are inextricably linked with efforts to extend this paradigm at the transatlantic and global levels. In addition to the EU approach mirroring the US approach in the CLOUD Act, the Justice and Home Affairs Council has authorised the European Commission to negotiate agreements on digital evidence with the USA.[138] In its Recommendation for a Council Decision, the Commission justified the opening of negotiations on the grounds that the current EU–US mutual legal assistance arrangements are too slow and that there is fragmentation in the applicable legal framework, with the transatlantic agreement aimed at complementing the internal EU e-evidence proposal by addressing conflicts of law.[139] The EU–US Agreement on digital evidence under negotiation would aim to complement the protective standards set out in the EU–USA Umbrella Agreement.[140] The same Justice and Home Affairs Council authorised EU negotiations on the second additional protocol of the Council of Europe Cybercrime Convention, which will develop provisions on digital evidence. The aim of this move would be to address conflicts of law,[141] as

> while cybercrime and other offences entailing electronic evidence on computer systems are thriving and while evidence relating to these offences is increasingly stored on

[136] For the background, see J Daskal, 'Unpacking the CLOUD Act' (2018) 11 *Eucrim* 220.

[137] For a background to the Microsoft saga, see CEPS, *Access to Electronic Data by Third-Country Law Enforcement Authorities. Challenges to EU Rule of Law and Fundamental Rights* (Brussels, July 2015).

[138] Justice and Home Affairs Council adopted conclusions on 6/7 June 2019.

[139] Recommendation of a Council Decision authorising opening of negotiations between the EU and the US on cross-border access to electronic evidence for judicial cooperation in criminal matters, COM (2019) 70 final, 1–4.

[140] ibid 10.

[141] COM (2019) 71 final, 5.

> servers in foreign, multiple, shifting or unknown jurisdictions, that is, in the cloud, the powers of law enforcement remain limited by territorial boundaries.[142]

However, as far as the EU is concerned, its bilateral agreement with the USA should take precedence over the Council of Europe Protocol.[143]

The role of the European Union in developing a transatlantic and global level playing field regarding digital evidence is noteworthy. Unlike the development of the passenger name record (PNR) system (where the EU responded to the unilateral imposition of US domestic law requirements via the conclusion of transatlantic agreements, and then internalised this paradigm in EU law),[144] here the EU develops internal legislation first (mirroring US legislation in the field), and negotiates a transatlantic level playing field in parallel, while using its power within the Council of Europe to establish a global level playing field on digital evidence.[145] This strategy is problematic from both a human rights and a rule-of-law perspective. From a human rights perspective, it advocates a new paradigm of privatisation which results in the transfer to the state of everyday personal data, disregarding the key EU law benchmarks of judicial authorisation and judicial independence. From a rule-of-law perspective, the EU is part of efforts to globalise this system, which would undermine its internal human rights benchmarks and values, which the Union is bound to apply in external actions. The EU has opted to establish a transatlantic level playing field via the conclusion of a sectoral agreement, notwithstanding the established concerns on the adequacy of the US privacy and data protection system and its limited compatibility with EU law.

At the same time, the EU has chosen to negotiate standards on digital evidence – which would have profound fundamental rights consequences – within the framework of a Council of Europe instrument whose principal aim is not to protect human rights and which is not exclusively focused on mutual legal assistance. Regional standards with a global reach will be developed by an instrument framed as a 'cybercrime' proposal; however, the exclusive framing of digital evidence as a cybercrime issue is misleading and may lead to limited scrutiny of the fundamental rights implications of the relaxation of safeguards in mutual legal assistance and to the introduction of lower standards through the back door. Calls for an effective fight against impunity in the global, digital context may undermine the very values upon which the Union claims to be based, values which, as seen above, the Union must uphold and promote in its external actions.

[142] ibid 1.

[143] ibid 7.

[144] On the development of PNR standards, see V Mitsilegas, 'Immigration Control in an Era of Globalisation: Deflecting Foreigners, Weakening Citizens Strengthening the State' (2012) 19 *Indiana Journal of Global Legal Studies* 3.

[145] The Council of Europe Convention on Cybercrime is open to states beyond Council of Europe members.

VII. Conclusion: Reimagining Impunity in Europe's Area of Justice

This chapter has attempted to demonstrate that, while the quest for the fight against impunity has acted as a driver for advancing European integration, this drive has not necessarily led to a truly European concept of impunity or a coherent approach to the fight against it. The fight against impunity has fostered European integration primarily to ensure the protection of internal Union interests and objectives – the protection of the budget and the financial interests of the Union, and the construction of Europe's borderless area of freedom, security and justice. As regards the fight against impunity of perpetrators of fraud against the EU budget, Europeanisation has evolved in a twofold manner: in strengthening the impact of EU enforcement objectives and constitutional principles on the domestic legal systems and obligations of Member States, with the Court granting direct effect directly to Treaty provisions (Article 325 TFEU) and calling for the disapplication of national law which does not meet the Union objectives of effectiveness; and in establishing European institutions aimed at ensuring anti-impunity, in the form of the European Public Prosecutor's Office, where for the first time a Union agency has been entrusted with criminal law coercive powers in domestic legal systems of the Member States. While in both these instances the impact of Union enforcement to ensure anti-impunity may be significant, Europeanisation leaves a number of questions unclear as regards the relationship between Union law and national law – with questions of legal certainty remaining acute in this context. Moreover, the question of the place of the protection of fundamental rights and the rule of law in action to fight against impunity becomes more and more relevant the more European integration advances, with the Court of Justice increasingly grappling with questions of delimiting the constitutional parameters of rights and the rule of law to the fight against impunity and the effectiveness of enforcement objectives of EU law.

Similar issues arise with regard to the conceptualisation of impunity in the construction of Europe's AFSJ. A key feature in this context has been attempts to advance European integration to fight impunity without aspiring necessarily to a high level of legislative harmonisation in the sensitive field of criminal law. Two parallel trends can be discerned in this context. On the one hand, the application of the principle of mutual recognition in criminal matters has organised interstate cooperation in Europe's AFSJ under a concept of impunity which in many respects fails to reflect a European sense of justice. Cooperation takes place largely with the aim of privileging the enforcement objectives and the justice system of the issuing Member State, with justice considerations of the executing Member State or of the affected individuals largely disregarded. Three recent trends temper this one-sided approach and serve to put forward a more European, rights-based concept of impunity: the move from blind to earned trust via the on-the-ground scrutiny of compliance with fundamental rights and the rule of law in the execution of mutual recognition instruments; the development of autonomous EU law concepts giving flesh to judicial independence and providing rule-of-law underpinnings to the operation of the system of mutual recognition; and, more ambitiously, legislative harmonisation in the field of defence rights, with standards underpinning the operation of mutual recognition in criminal matters. While, in the enforcement field of mutual recognition, we thus see a slow trend from uncritical anti-impunity based on the interest of the state of enforcement to the development of European benchmarks of fundamental rights and the rule of law underpinning interstate cooperation and mutual trust, we have witnessed the opposite trend in the extra-territorial application of rights in Europe's AFSJ. The analysis presented here focused in detail on the development of this trend in the context of the application of the transnational *ne bis in idem* principle. In this context, the impressive beginnings of the case law of the Court of Justice, which placed *ne bis in idem* within a truly European, Schengen context of honouring rights and certainty in a borderless AFSJ, has been gradually replaced by a vision of rights limited by an uncritical focus on the fight against impunity based on the view of justice and the perception of effective enforcement which is not pan-European, but is purely domestic and pertains to the law of the Member State which has felt that it did not have the opportunity to prosecute. In this manner, the CJEU fuels distrust between Member States and increasingly disregards legal certainty and the position of the individual within the AFSJ.

Further challenges in conceptualising impunity arise from the external dimension of the fight against impunity. The analysis has demonstrated that the Court of Justice has in principle accepted effective international cooperation in criminal matters as a legitimate objective justifying the aim of EU law to fight impunity, in the context of extradition relationships between EU Member States and third states. The cases arising before the Court of Justice all involved an EU citizenship dimension, namely requests by third countries to extradite EU citizens residing in a Member State other than the one of their nationality. The significance of this line of case law for the protection of EU citizens against an uncritical fight against impunity lies in two facts: in the fact that the Court of Justice used the citizenship dimension in order to ascertain a link with EU law of bilateral extradition arrangements of Member States with third countries, even if there is no extradition agreement between the Union and the third state in question – thus placing Member State action firmly within the scope of EU law; and in exporting, or extending, the internal EU fundamental rights benchmark developed in *Aranyosi* to the Union and Member States' external relations on extradition – with the fight against impunity in the context of extradition requests by third countries being placed within European parameters of fundamental rights and rule of law protection.

What has been less obvious in terms of providing a European conceptualisation of the fight against impunity in these cases has been the Court's reluctance to utilise an EU-wide protection of EU citizenship, instead reverting to protection based on the nationality of the requested person. The Court has thus failed to develop a meaningful protection on the basis of the principles of equality and non-discrimination, and has shied away from projecting the AFSJ as a unified space and territory for the purposes of the protection of Union citizens subject to extradition requests by third countries.

In contrast to the reluctance of the Court to develop a meaningful concept of Union territory for the purposes of the protection of EU citizens in the context of international cooperation in criminal matters, the European Commission has been attempting to project a unified vision of Europe's territory in the context of extending the possibilities of law enforcement in the field of digital evidence. The design here is to shift responsibility to the private sector and to establish responsibility of private providers on a pan-European basis, on the basis of EU-wide legal representation. The Commission's approach is justified on maximum anti-impunity grounds and on the grounds that technology has changed the rules of the game of enforcement. It blurs the boundaries of public–private cooperation and, in doing away with a key layer of judicial scrutiny in the field of transfer of personal data as evidence, it undermines essential safeguards of fundamental rights and rule-of-law protection as developed in the Union's internal *acquis* on judicial cooperation and mutual recognition, most notably the *acquis* on independence of the authorities' operating cooperation and on mutual trust. The challenges of the Commission's shifting paradigm of law enforcement cooperation to the internal EU *acquis* and the strengthened fundamental rights safeguards it entails are further compounded by the framing of its proposals within a global and transatlantic perspective – with EU law seen as a response to similar developments in the United States under the CLOUD Act and with the attempt to establish a regional, if not global, level playing field on digital evidence via Council of Europe initiatives. Globalising an uncritical fight against impunity in this regard will challenge the Union's internal *acquis* and undermine the constitutional duty for the Union to uphold and promote its values in its external action.

In view of this mixed and evolving picture, this contribution argues in favour of reimagining the fight against impunity in EU law, by striving to develop a European concept of impunity underpinned by full respect of EU values, and in particular the protection of fundamental rights and the rule of law. In this process, three key elements of the concept of impunity need to be rethought: time, space and the actors of anti-impunity. This process of reconceptualising impunity will begin in the courts, but may in some instances involve further legislative intervention and harmonisation at the EU level.

The anti-impunity objectives have been served by both the extension and shortening of time. Extension of time has been sought in the context of the protection of the Union's financial interests by the duty of national courts to disapply national provisions on limitation periods and to extend these periods in order to allow effective prosecution of serious fraud cases. As demonstrated in the *Taricco* litigation, EU disapplication requirements may lead to considerable (at least perceived) legal uncertainty at the national level, and a discussion of EU-wide harmonisation of limitation periods (as has already happened to some extent in the adoption of the post-Lisbon PIF Directive) may be a way forward to achieving a European understanding of time in this context. Harmonisation in this context, underpinned by legal certainty safeguards for the individuals subject to prosecution, may also serve to address enforcement concerns by the second state in *ne bis in idem* cases, while at the same time achieving true legal certainty for affected individuals in Europe's AFSJ – with further prosecution not allowed on the grounds of the second state's reluctance to act speedily under lengthy national limitation periods. A similar rethinking of time to ensure a European concept of impunity based on a European concept of justice is required with regard to the calculation of imprisonment and detention periods in the context of cooperation under mutual recognition – with the CJEU currently uncritically privileging the justice approaches of one of the two states in the system. On the other hand, fighting impunity has involved the shortening of time, by the requests of law enforcement authorities for speed in interstate, international and public–private cooperation. This has been the case in the operation of the principle of mutual recognition in criminal matters, under tight deadlines, and in the Commission's proposals on digital evidence, where speed in preservation and production of evidence is a key priority. In the field of mutual recognition, the Court of Justice (and national authorities executing EAWs) have shown the way by de facto tempering requirements of speedy cooperation with the need to take time to ensure meaningful scrutiny of the fundamental rights and rule-of-law implications of the execution of a decision. An uncritical requirement of speed as justification for digital evidence proposals and the paradigmatic shift they entail is in urgent need of reconsideration: while the perceived need for speedy action in the digital world may be addressed by measures entailing the preservation of data, the issue of their speedy production by the private sector is a separate matter and should not occur at the expense of meaningful safeguards of judicial scrutiny, as in the general system of judicial cooperation and mutual recognition in EU law.

Reimagining the element of space is key in reconceptualising impunity in EU law. An ongoing tension in designing EU responses to the fight against impunity has been meeting the constitutional aim of constructing an AFSJ without internal frontiers, without such an area being accompanied by a legal concept of a single area or a single Union jurisdiction – hence an AFSJ continues to consist of national legal territories and jurisdictions. This construction of physical and legal space renders the question of the relationship between national and EU law of ongoing importance, raising questions of applicable law, legal certainty and, ultimately, rule of law. Tensions between developing a European concept of anti-impunity within a borderless AFSJ on the one hand and national priorities and considerations on the other have been present almost throughout this analysis. In the fight against fraud on the EU budget, the concept of the Union as a 'single legal area' underpinning the establishment of the EPPO proposed by the Commission has been abandoned in negotiations, with their outcome being a system relying substantially upon the different national applicable laws – with their relationship with EU law being a matter which will be 'under construction' and subject to potential legal uncertainty.

Similar issues of legal uncertainty have arisen in light of the lack of EU harmonisation regarding enforcement and periods of limitation in the *Taricco* and post-*Taricco* litigation. In the field of mutual recognition, the established system of interaction between national systems with limited harmonisation has led to the development of an EU system based on a limited European sense of justice, prioritising national enforcement and anti-impunity objectives and national legal choices at the expense of a European approach. In the external field, protection of EU citizens in extradition proceedings ultimately reverts back to their state of nationality, with a common Union area as a protective space not being fully projected externally – while, on the other hand, the Commission attempts to internalise global data collection concerns and to use the Union as a single space in order to undermine judicial scrutiny guarantees developed within the very context of interstate cooperation in mutual recognition. In all these cases, a key element in developing a European concept of (anti-)impunity is to reflect upon the development of a European concept of rights, rule of law and justice to underpin the fight against impunity. The significant strides forward in the field of mutual recognition – in the form of fundamental rights scrutiny and autonomous concepts developed by the Court of Justice, but also by legislative harmonisation in the field of defence rights – are emblematic examples in this context.

Further reflection on rights and justice in a common European space is inextricably linked with the need to reflect further on the actors of anti-impunity. Recent developments have demonstrated a shift away from traditional state-to-state cooperation mechanisms in fighting impunity. On the one hand, cooperation and enforcement mechanisms have been extended to include EU bodies and agencies with coercive powers (the EPPO) and, in another direction, private companies in the field of digital evidence. On the other hand, the scope of state-to-state cooperation has been narrowed by the Court of Justice in the operation of the EAW system by limiting the concept of competent authority to one of independent judicial authority. This step has been key to safeguarding the effective protection of fundamental rights and the rule of law in the fight against impunity in EU law, and the principle behind this approach should be applicable across the board in delimiting the scope and powers of the authorities competent in the fight against impunity in EU law. These are some of the steps which may lead to the development of a true European concept of impunity underpinned by a common sense of justice based on the effective and real protection of fundamental rights and the rule of law in EU law across and beyond the Union.

3

Fundamental Rights-Oriented Repression in the EU? Exploring the Potential and Limits of an Impunity Rationale to Justify Criminalisation in the EU Legal Order

JANNEMIEKE OUWERKERK

I. Introduction

The quest for the potential and limits of an impunity rationale to justify EU-level criminalisation of conduct brings up the close relationship between human rights and criminal law – a relationship with a rather paradoxical character, though. Whereas human rights traditionally serve to afford *protection from* the criminal law, the repressive and coercive powers of the criminal law have also been called on, precisely *to protect* human rights. This has become particularly noticeable in the case law of the dominant human rights actor in Europe: the European Court of Human Rights (ECtHR).

Under the development of the concept of positive obligations,[1] ECtHR case law has inferred obligations for states to use the criminal law to prevent impunity and, hence, to effectively safeguard the rights of victims of fundamental rights infringements. Probably the most well-known is the Court's judgment in *X and Y v the Netherlands*. In this case, the father of a mentally ill young girl complained of his inability to institute criminal proceedings against the individual

[1] The 1968 *Belgian Linguistic* case was the first case in which the ECtHR accepted a duty to take action, after which the concept developed further and was gradually interpreted as not only applying in the relationships between states and individuals, but also in the horizontal relationships between individuals, provided that the state can be held responsible for violations of ECHR rights between them. See JF Akandji-Kombe, *Positive Obligations under the European Convention on Human Rights. A Guide to the Implementation of the European Convention on Human Rights* (Strasbourg, Council of Europe, 2007) 14–15.

who allegedly raped her; under the Dutch law at that time, criminal proceedings could only be instituted upon a complaint lodged by the victim herself. In its judgment, the Court held that this constituted a violation of the right to respect for private life under Article 8 of the European Convention on Human Rights (ECHR):

> the protection afforded by the civil law in the case of wrongdoing of the kind inflicted on Miss Y is insufficient. This is a case where fundamental values and essential aspects of private life are at stake. Effective deterrence is indispensable in this area and it can be achieved only by criminal-law provisions; indeed, it is by such provisions that the matter is normally regulated.[2]

In subsequent judgments, the requirement to take recourse to the criminal law has appeared much more often in ECtHR case law, both in the context of Article 8[3] and under other articles, such as Article 2 (right to life)[4] and Article 3 (prohibition of torture).[5] In most of these cases, the actual complaints concerned procedural obstacles in states' law enforcement machineries, such as in the *X and Y* case. But there have also been cases dealing directly with offence definitions and their interpretations in criminal courts. For instance, in the case of *MC v Bulgaria*, the applicant complained about the legal interpretation of the definition of rape, according to which physical resistance by the victim had to be proven.[6] The Court held that such an interpretation violates both Article 3 and Article 8 ECHR as it fell short of the requirements under states' positive obligations 'to *establish* and apply effectively a criminal-law system punishing *all forms* of rape and sexual abuse'.[7]

As mentioned, in most of the other cases, complaints were primarily dealing with procedural obstacles during criminal investigations and prosecutions. Nevertheless, in many such cases, positive obligations to criminalise conduct have been adopted too. The Court's reasoning in such cases usually relies on the very acceptance of positive obligations to enact criminal prohibitions in the area of crime concerned – which, in turn, requires that such prohibitions can be

[2] *X and Y v the Netherlands* App no 8978/80 (ECtHR, 26 March 1985) para 27.

[3] See, eg *MC v Bulgaria* App no 39272/98 (ECtHR, 4 December 2003); See also *KU v Finland* App no 2872/02 (ECtHR, 2 December 2008).

[4] See, eg *Osman v United Kingdom* App no 23452/94 (ECtHR, 28 October 1998), confirmed several times, eg in *Mastrometto v Italy* App no 37703/97 (ECtHR, 24 October 2002); *Nikolova & Velichkova v Bulgaria* App no 7888/03 (ECtHR, 20 December 2007); *Cesnulevicius v Lithuania* App no 13462/06 (ECtHR, 10 January 2012).

[5] Most well known is *MC v Bulgaria* (n 3), which gave rise to an issue under both Art 8 ECHR and Art 3 ECHR. The Court's ruling in this case has been confirmed a number of times, eg in *DJ v Croatia* App no 42418/10 (ECtHR, 24 July 2012).

[6] Under Bulgarian criminal law, rape was defined by reference to the means used by the perpetrator, ie 'force' or 'threats', and there were indications in Bulgarian case law that for those means to be proven, evidence of physical resistance was mostly required: see *MC v Bulgaria* (n 3) paras 169ff.

[7] *MC v Bulgaria* (n 3) para 185 (emphasis added).

effectively applied in practice, meaning that procedural rules resulting in leaving crime unpunished can be held to violate ECHR rights.[8]

In doing so, the ECtHR has acknowledged that the criminal law is not only a potential 'threat', but can also be a 'protection' for fundamental rights.[9] In other words, in the application of criminal law, human rights can function both as a 'shield' and as a 'sword'.[10]

The shield function of fundamental rights in the application of the criminal law reflects very well its primary and traditional role of affording protection from the indiscriminate and excessive use of the criminal law. Therefore, it has never really been called into question. However, it is quite another story where fundamental rights function as a sword, triggering the application of criminal law. From a historical perspective, this is hardly surprising. Besides, in response to the ECtHR's use of the criminal law option, it has been pointed out that this has constituted a potentially problematic paradigm shift. This is because it remains unclear whether and how the ECtHR takes sufficient account, in its judgments, of relevant interests other than fundamental rights interests alone, such as the desirability and effectiveness of the criminal law option, or the existence of adequate alternatives to criminal law responses.[11]

Can similar or otherwise critical observations also be made with regard to the functioning of fundamental rights in the application of EU criminal law? Initially primarily an organisation for trade and economic cooperation, the present-day European Union is, moreover, considered a fundamental rights actor too. Lately, the EU has been quite active in the criminal law domain. This raises the question how fundamental rights actually function in the context of EU criminal law, and

[8] See again *X and Y v the Netherlands* (n 2) and accompanying text. See also *KU v Finland* (n 3), regarding the inability of Finnish law enforcement officials to oblige a service provider to reveal the identity of a person who on its website had placed a defamatory dating advertisement in the name of a 12-year-old boy. According to the Court, this procedural obstacle constituted a violation of the applicant's rights under Art 8 ECHR since the inability to identify the offender compromises effective criminal investigations and prosecutions in cases such as the underlying case, paras 46, 49–50.

[9] The terms 'threat' and 'protection' are borrowed from M. Delmas-Marty's chapter on 'Le paradoxe pénal' in: M. Delmas-Marty & C. Lucas de Leyssac (eds), *Libertés et droits fondamentaux*, Paris: Seuil 1996, p. 368, where she states: 'le droit pénal semble tout à la fois protection et menace pour les libertés et droits fondamentaux'.

[10] A 2007 edited volume has been dedicated to this paradox: Y Cartuyvels et al (eds), *Les droits de l'homme, bouclier ou épée du droit penal?* (Brussels, Presses de l'Université Saint-Louis, 2007). See also F Tulkens, 'The Paradoxical Relationship between Criminal Law and Human Rights' (2011) 9 *Journal of International Criminal Justice* 578, fn 5 and accompanying text.

[11] PHPHMC van Kempen, *Repressie door mensenrechten. Over positieve verplichtingen tot aanwending van strafrecht ter bescherming van mensenrechten* (Utrecht, Wolf Legal Publishers, 2008) 66, 80; JW Ouwerkerk, 'Criminalisation as a Last Resort: A National Principle under the Pressure of Europeanisation?' (2012) 3 *New Journal of European Criminal Law* 239–240. See also para 2 of Tulkens's concurring opinion to the ECtHR judgment in *MC v Bulgaria* (n 3), in which she underlines that 'it is also important to emphasise *on a more general level*, as, indeed, the Court did in *X and Y v the Netherlands* itself, that "[r]ecourse to the criminal law is not necessarily the only answer"'.

in particular whether and how impunity may constitute a relevant factor in the exercise of criminalisation powers.

This chapter provides an attempt to answer these questions and offers food for further reflection on the matter. To that end, it starts with a brief account of how the close relationship between fundamental rights and criminal law has come into play in the EU legal order, and to what extent this relationship has become affected by the 'shield and sword' paradox (section II). Subsequently, it explores the limits and potential of applying a fundamental rights-oriented impunity rationale to the adoption of criminalisation duties in the EU legal order. To that end, it discusses, first, the incompleteness of such an approach (section III); and, secondly, how such an impunity rationale could and should function in the exercise of EU criminalisation powers (section IV), both from an institutional lawmaking perspective (section IV.A) and from a substantive perspective (section IV.B). This chapter closes with some final remarks.

II. EU Criminal Law and the Emergence of Fundamental Rights in the EU Legal Order

Since the entry into force of the Treaty of Lisbon, the protection and further advancement of fundamental rights have obtained a prominent place in the institutional legal framework of the EU. The EU Charter of Fundamental Rights (the Charter) is now a legally binding instrument (Article 6(1) TEU) and the EU is legally obliged to accede to the ECHR (Article 6(2) TEU). Moreover, respect for human rights has been recognised as a foundational value of the EU (Article 2 TEU).[12] This development has been welcomed by many, not least by criminal law experts.[13] Especially since the introduction and implementation of the mutual recognition principle, there has been a widely shared concern that EU action in the criminal law domain has been too one-sided, focusing on cross-border law enforcement and repression without proper attention for due process rights.[14] The increased attention for fundamental rights protection under the Lisbon

[12] For further on this development, see G de Búrca, 'The Road Not Taken: The EU as a Global Human Rights Actor' (2011) 105 *The American Journal of International Law* 649.

[13] See, eg both inside and outside the criminal law domain: E Herlin-Karnell, *The Constitutional Dimension of European Criminal Law* (Oxford, Hart Publishing, 2012) 231–32; F van den Berghe, 'The EU and Issues of Human Rights Protection: Some Solutions to More Acute Problems' (2010) 16 *European Law Journal* 112; S Douglas-Scott, 'A Tale of Two Courts: Luxembourg, Strasbourg and the Growing European Human Rights Acquis' (2006) 46 *CML Rev* 629.

[14] In the specific context of the European Arrest Warrant mechanisms, concerns and reliefs have been described well by L Mancano, 'A New Hope? The Court of Justice Restores the Balance between Fundamental Rights Protection and Enforcement Demands in the European Arrest Warrant System' in C Brière and A Weyembergh (eds), *The Needed Balances in EU Criminal Law. Past, Present and Future* (Oxford, Hart Publishing, 2017).

regime has therefore been argued to have constituted a paradigm shift in the EU criminal justice area:

> the construction of Europe's area of criminal justice has moved from a paradigm privileging the interests of the state and of law enforcement under a system of quasi-automatic mutual recognition to a paradigm where the rights of individuals affected by such system are brought to the fore, protected and enforced in EU law.[15]

The many complaints that no sufficient attention was paid to due process rights in criminal proceedings prior to Lisbon suggests that a stronger engagement of the EU with fundamental rights was generally expected to particularly boost and strengthen the shield function of fundamental rights in the application of EU-governed criminal law measures – expectations that at least partly may have been fulfilled through the gradual adoption of Directives on procedural rights for suspects in criminal proceedings. Between 2010 and 2016, a respectable number of common minimum norms has been adopted, covering the rights to interpretation and translation, the right to information, the right of access to a lawyer, the right to communicate with third persons and consular authorities, the presumption of innocence, the right to be present at trial, the right to state-paid legal aid, and rights specific to children who are suspected of crime.[16]

In addition to this obvious protective approach, it must at the same time be observed that the EU Court of Justice (CJEU) has recognised the prevention of impunity as a relevant interest in assessing the scope of fundamental rights protection in the context of criminal proceedings. In the *Spasic* case, dealing with the scope of the *ne bis in idem* principle, the CJEU was asked whether the so-called enforcement condition laid down in Article 54 of the Convention Implementing the Schengen Agreement (CISA)[17] is compatible with Article 50 of the Charter, in which Union-wide protection against double prosecutions and

[15] V Mitsilegas, *EU Criminal Law after Lisbon. Rights, Trust and the Transformation of Justice in Europe* (Oxford, Hart Publishing, 2016) 183.

[16] Directive 2010/64 on the right to interpretation and translation in criminal proceedings [2010] OJ L280/01; Directive 2012/13 on the right to information in criminal proceedings [2012] OJ L142/1; Directive 2013/48 on the right of access to a lawyer in criminal proceedings and in European arrest warrant proceedings, and on the right to have a third party informed upon deprivation of liberty and to communicate with third persons and with consular authorities while deprived of liberty [2013] OJ L294/1; Directive 2016/343 on the strengthening of certain aspects of the presumption of innocence and of the right to be present at the trial in criminal proceedings [2016] OJ L65/1; Directive 2016/800 on procedural safeguards for children who are suspects or accused persons in criminal proceedings [2016] OJ L132/1; Directive 2016/1919 on legal aid for suspects and accused persons in criminal proceedings and for requested persons in European arrest warrant proceedings [2016] OJ L297/1.

[17] Art 54 CISA reads as follows: 'A person whose trial has been finally disposed of in one Contracting Party may not be prosecuted in another Contracting Party for the same acts provided that, if a penalty has been imposed, it has been enforced, is actually in the process of being enforced or can no longer be enforced under the laws of the sentencing Contracting Party.' The CISA has been integrated into EU law; the currently applicable protocol is Protocol 19 to the Treaty of Lisbon [2012] OJ C326/1.

double punishments would apply irrespective of whether the sanction has been imposed.[18] The CJEU ruled in the affirmative,[19] arguing that the *ne bis in idem* principle, enshrined in Article 54 CISA, has a twofold aim, ie to prevent impunity and to ensure legal certainty:

> The *ne bis in idem* principle set out in Article 54 CISA is intended not only to prevent, in the area of freedom, security and justice, the impunity of persons definitively convicted and sentenced in the European Union but also to ensure legal certainty through respect for decisions of public bodies which have become final, in the absence of harmonisation or approximation of the criminal laws of the Member States.[20]

Under the principle's aim to avoid impunity, it was also held that the application of the enforcement condition does constitute a limitation of the *ne bis in idem* principle, albeit a proportionate limitation in view of the very aim to avoid impunity: 'It follows that the execution condition laid down in Article 54 CISA does not go beyond what is necessary to prevent, in a cross-border context, the impunity of persons definitively convicted and sentenced in the European Union.'[21]

The arguments that have been put forward by the CJEU in the *Spasic* case demonstrate that the scope of protection of fundamental rights in the EU legal order is not necessarily defined by protective rationales; in *Spasic*, the CJEU explicitly relied on an impunity rationale.[22] The *Spasic* judgment therefore illustrates how an impunity rationale can trigger the limitation of fundamental rights protection in EU law and, hence, can give rise to the application of law enforcement activities which could not have been applied under a protective rationale-based interpretation of Article 50 of the Charter. Therefore, although the *Spasic* case concerns a case of cross-border judicial cooperation, the judgment demonstrates well how the relationship in EU law between fundamental rights and criminal law has become affected by the 'shield and sword' paradox.

The increased engagement of the EU with fundamental rights makes it plausible to expect more occasions to come in which fundamental rights may be invoked to justify the use of criminal law measures. One of these occasions regards the further development of an EU criminalisation policy. Fundamental rights interests, in more general terms, have indeed been invoked in this context, in particular in the exercise of criminalisation competences under Article 83(1) TFEU (regarding the so-called Euro-crimes). For instance, preambles to the latest Directives in the areas of child sexual abuse and terrorism state that these Directives concern offences that constitute serious violations of fundamental rights.[23]

[18] Art 50 of the Charter states: 'No one shall be liable to be tried or punished again in criminal proceedings for an offence for which he or she has already been finally acquitted or convicted within the Union in accordance with the law.'

[19] Case C-129/14 *Spasic* ECLI:EU:C:2014:586, para 74.

[20] ibid para 77.

[21] ibid para 72.

[22] Indicated as a 'security rationale' in Mitsilegas (n 15) 90.

[23] Recital 1 of the Preamble to Directive 2011/93 on combating the sexual abuse and sexual exploitation of children and child pornography [2011] OJ L335/1 reads as follows: 'Sexual abuse and

Impunity arguments have been invoked too in the context of criminalisation legislation, though always rather implicitly. On several occasions, the European Commission has accompanied its criminalisation proposals with the argument that differences in scopes of national criminal prohibitions hinder the optimal application of judicial cross-border cooperation mechanisms. For instance, in the context of child sexual abuse, it was held that shared definitions of offences in this field would prevent criminals from choosing national jurisdictions with more lenient criminal laws to commit their crimes, but also that shared norms would facilitate cross-border cooperation, hence the fight against such crimes.[24] Such reasoning amounts to a security or impunity argument, for it suggests that a reduction of disparities in substantive criminal law may lower the chances that perpetrators go unpunished.

Now the question arises how convincing such an impunity argument is, and can be – and, hence, whether impunity concerns justify the development of a fundamental rights-oriented criminalisation policy in the EU legal order. The following sections will share some exploratory reflections on these questions, in an attempt to contribute to the scholarly debate on the matter.

III. The Reductionist Nature of a Fundamental Rights-Oriented Approach

In discussing whether criminalisation processes should be governed by fundamental rights-based arguments, a first significant question that arises is to what extent such fundamental rights-based arguments can be decisive in justifying

sexual exploitation of children, including child pornography, constitute serious violations of fundamental rights, in particular of the rights of children to the protection and care necessary for their well-being, as provided for by the 1989 United Nations Convention on the Rights of the Child and by the Charter of Fundamental Rights of the European Union'; and in Recital 2 of the Preamble to Directive 2017/541 on combating terrorism [2017] OJ L88/6 it is stated that 'Acts of terrorism constitute one of the most serious violations of the universal values of human dignity, freedom, equality and solidarity, and enjoyment of human rights and fundamental freedoms on which the Union is founded'.

[24] European Commission, Proposal for a Directive of the European Parliament and of the Council on combating the sexual abuse and sexual exploitation of children and child pornography, and replacing Council Framework Decision 2004/68/JHA, COM (2010) 94 final (the proposal was originally submitted as a draft Framework Decision, COM (2009) 135 final, but following the entry into force of the Lisbon Treaty, the proposal was amended into a draft Directive), Explanatory Memorandum, 2, para 1; Commission Staff Working Document, Impact Assessment, Accompanying document to the Proposal for a Directive of the European Parliament and of the Council on combating the sexual abuse and sexual exploitation of children and child pornography, and replacing Council Framework Decision 2004/68/JHA, SEC (2009) 355 final, paras 2.2, 2.4, 3.1 and 4.3. For more examples of such reasoning in Commission's proposals, see J Ouwerkerk, 'The Potential of Mutual Recognition as a Limit to the Exercise of EU Criminalisation Powers' (2017) 7 *European Criminal Law Review* 9, followed by a critical appraisal from the perspective of mutual recognition.

criminalisation of conduct. In addressing this question, I would like to point out the inherently reductionist[25] nature of a rights-oriented approach.

As convincingly demonstrated by legal scholarship in the field of criminal procedure theory, it is problematic to frame doctrines in this area predominantly in terms of individual rights. That is not only because the contours of such a rationale are unclear (what exactly does the term 'rights' encompass?), but also – and perhaps more importantly – because such a framing would wrongfully suggest that in responding to procedural violations committed in the course of criminal proceedings there is only one relevant question, ie the question whether a procedural violation constitutes a violation of an individual fundamental right.[26] Put differently, approaching matters of procedural violations solely from the perspective of rights ignores the (potential) relevance of other perspectives. Consequently, it also ignores the complexity of criminal procedural standards and their underlying values, which requires the consideration of other perspectives too when determining how to address violations of such procedural standards. Pitcher has shown what the consequences would be when a mere rights rationale (which she refers to as 'the protective rationale') would be applied to the problem of unlawfully obtained evidence in the pretrial stage of criminal proceedings:

> the rationale for excluding unlawfully obtained evidence lies in the need to protect … rights of the suspect and accused (ie the rights underlying *declared* standards for the conduct of criminal investigations) … Under the protective rationale, then, once it has been established that the evidence in question was obtained by a rights violation (specifically, by violation of the accused's rights), that evidence should, *in principle*, be excluded. Accordingly, under the protective rationale exclusion is the primary response to pretrial impropriety, and the sole predicate event to the exclusion of evidence is the fact that the evidence in question was obtained in violation of accused's rights (by the public authorities charged with investigating and prosecuting crime).[27]

Consequently, as Pitcher subsequently points out, other factors are not taken into account, not even those factors that are considered highly relevant under the rationales that have been shaping rules on pretrial investigations:

> For example, while a relevant consideration under the deterrence rationale, whether the law enforcement officer acted deliberately in obtaining the evidence by improper means is not a relevant consideration under the protective rationale … Different rationales for responding to pretrial impropriety require (or allow) different factors to be taken into account, so that when certain factors are excluded from consideration … this may lead to certain rationales and the values underpinning them being overlooked.[28]

[25] The term 'reductionist' is borrowed from KM Pitcher, 'Rights-Analysis in Addressing Pre-trial Impropriety: An Obstacle to Fairness?' in J Jackson and S Summers (eds), *Obstacles to Fairness in Criminal Proceedings. Individual Rights and Institutional Forms* (Oxford, Hart Publishing, 2018) 273.

[26] See, eg P Roberts, 'Excluding Evidence as Protecting Constitutional or Human Rights?' in L Zedner and JV Roberts (eds), *Principles and Values in Criminal Law and Criminal Justice: Essays in Honour of Andrew Ashworth* (Oxford, Oxford University Press, 2012) 183; Pitcher (n 25).

[27] Pitcher (n 25) 277 (original emphasis).

[28] ibid 278. See also Roberts (n 26) 183.

The individual rights-oriented rationale thus has a reductionist character in the context of criminal procedural law, for it is not well suited to capturing all relevant rationales and underlying values that are at stake, and bears the risk of wrongfully overlooking them. For instance, imagine that, in an individual case, law enforcement authorities commit a number of procedural violations in the course of gathering evidence. But imagine also that the suspect in this case may – overall – not have been prevented from receiving a fair trial (eg in the sense of Article 6 ECHR); from a fundamental rights point of view, no response is required. However, the procedural violations might still be considered to constitute severe violations of the integrity of the criminal proceedings. Such a serious conclusion may well trigger a response, though perhaps a different one than warranted under a fundamental rights-oriented approach (ie exclusion of evidence).[29]

The reductionist nature inherent in the individual fundamental rights-oriented approach to procedural violations also has implications for the position of such an approach in the context of legislating on matters of substantive criminal law. To commence, I would like to recollect the 'shield and sword' paradox this chapter started with: fundamental rights protection may offer a reason to extend the scope of certain criminal prohibitions, but fundamental rights protection may also demand that they be limited, or even abolished. This underscores that even where fundamental rights protection would be the single perspective from which criminalisation issues would be approached, the impunity argument can never be decisive. That would one-sidedly reflect the sword function of the criminal law, whereas fundamental rights instruments traditionally also include rights that particularly express the shield function that fundamental rights also aim to fulfil in the context of criminal law (eg the principles of legality and proportionality).

Besides, in determining the reach of substantive criminal law, there are a number of other factors that are traditionally taken into account for very justifiable reasons. These include factors that cannot be classified as rights of individuals, but nonetheless must be considered likewise significant, for they play an indispensable part in the development of a reasonable and balanced body of substantive criminal law – a multipurpose body of law after all, pursuing, indeed, the protection of fundamental rights, but also the protection of many other values, norms and societal customs. It does this by means of regulating what conduct is acceptable and what is not, and under what conditions individuals can be held liable or, rather, excused. Considering the aim of this chapter, I confine myself to mentioning only a few of these other non-fundamental rights-related factors. Most obvious are factors of principle, such as the existence of other possible answers to address the unwanted behaviour (expressing the *ultima*

[29] Pitcher (n 25) 292ff. For more elaboration on this (though available in Dutch only), see KM Pitcher and M Samadi, 'Integriteit als perspectief bij de rechterlijke reactie op vormverzuimen (2018) 59 *Delikt en Delinkwent* 731.

ratio principle[30]) or the magnitude of the problem. Other relevant factors are of a more pragmatic nature, such as the actual prosecutability of conduct (including predictable evidentiary problems) and the capacity of the available law enforcement machinery. Their relevance has long since been recognised in the context of national criminal law, and they are increasingly copied at the level of EU criminal law.[31] They concern factors that acknowledge both the complexity and the multipurpose nature of substantive criminal law, and the variety of rationales that underpin it.

To conclude, due to their reductionist character, the criminalisation policy of the EU cannot be solely based on fundamental rights, nor can impunity arguments be decisive. Such would carry the unforgiveable risk of overlooking other relevant factors and their underlying values. The fundamental rights perspective must be taken into account, all the more since the EU has increasingly been engaging with fundamental rights,[32] though without losing sight of, first, the shield function that fundamental rights must fulfil in shaping the criminal law, and, secondly, the complexity and multipurpose nature of the criminal law. In the following section, I reflect on how such a task fits into the applicable lawmaking process of the EU, and how the legislator could further advance its efforts in this regard.

IV. The Functioning of Fundamental Rights-Based Impunity Rationales in EU Legislative Practice Concerning Matters of Substantive Criminal Law

The following will show that the EU lawmaking process applicable to criminalisation acts is, in principle, well suited to using the various relevant rationales to determine the scopes of EU-level criminal prohibitions (section IV.A). Subsequently, however, it will be argued that the pursuit of developing a reasonable and balanced EU-level body of substantive criminal law would benefit from more explicit attention in the legislative procedure to particular offence definitions, instead of maintaining the perspective of the crime areas these definitions fall into (section IV.B).

[30] Compare n 11 and accompanying text.

[31] See, eg European Parliament Resolution of 22 May 2012 on an EU approach to criminal law, P7_TA(2012)0208, under point I; European Commission Communication, 'Towards an EU Criminal Policy: Ensuring the effective implementation of EU policies through criminal law', COM (2011) 573 final, para 2.2.1. See also P Asp et al, 'A Manifesto on European Criminal Policy (European Criminal Policy Initiative)' (2009) 4 *Zeitschrift für Internationale Strafrechtsdogmatik* 707.

[32] As demonstrated in section II.

A. Institutional Perspective

This section comprises two intertwining parts. First, it demonstrates that the institutional positioning of criminal law competences in the EU legal order facilitates the taking into account of a variety of relevant rationales when EU action is being considered. Based on that, the second claim is that the EU lawmaking process further encourages the legislature to incorporate such different, sometimes competing, rationales and balance them against each other.

As demonstrated in the introduction of this chapter, the use of fundamental rights-based arguments to extend the scope of national criminal prohibitions has been developed in the context of human rights law, predominantly under the Strasbourg doctrine of positive obligations. It has also been mentioned that this development in ECtHR case law has been criticised, in particular out of concern that the Strasbourg Court would fail to take sufficient account of other factors that are considered relevant in determining the scope of substantive criminal law. In its case law on positive duties to criminalise conduct, the Court does occasionally refer to other factors, though this does not seem to be a consistent practice.[33] Clearly, the question is whether, and to what extent, the Court actually ought to consider these other perspectives, for its duty is to 'ensure the observance of the engagements undertaken by the High Contracting Parties in the Convention and the Protocols thereto' (Article 19 ECHR). Would a similar concern be justified in the context of EU criminal law? Not necessarily.

Within the EU legal order, the conferred powers to enact legislation regarding matters of substantive criminal law are part of a bigger whole – a whole of competences that covers both procedural and substantive criminal law, as well as police and judicial cooperation and the setting up of law enforcement agencies (laid down in Chapters IV and V of Title V TFEU). Yet, from a wider perspective, criminal law competences fall under the broader policy field called the 'area of freedom, security and justice' (AFSJ), which also covers civil law, asylum law and migration law (Title V TFEU). And even beyond the AFSJ, criminal law powers cohere with other powers and principles, such as the power to maintain a borderless area and to safeguard the free movement of persons therein.[34] In exercising its competences in the field of criminal law, the EU must adhere to the EU Charter on Fundamental Rights (Article 6 TEU), as well as to the governing principles of subsidiarity and proportionality (Article 5 TEU). Consequently, longer term AFSJ and criminal law policies usually concern the areas as a whole, rather than being

[33] See, eg *KU v Finland* (n 3) para 48, where it states that 'in view of the difficulties in policing modern societies, a positive obligation must be interpreted in a way which does not impose an impossible or disproportionate burden on the authorities, or, as in this case, the legislator. Another relevant consideration is the need to ensure that powers to control, prevent and investigate crime are exercised in a manner which fully respects the due process and other guarantees which legitimately place restraints on criminal investigations and bringing offenders to justice'.

[34] *cf* Mitsilegas (n 15) 125; J Ouwerkerk, *Herijking van Uniestrafrecht. Over grondslagen voor strafrechtelijke regelgeving in de Europese Unie* (The Hague, Boom juridisch, 2017).

focused on one specific competence in a certain area.[35] Consequently, lawmaking on specific matters, such as criminalisation, is unlikely to be taken in isolation or by applying a single perspective, such as the perspective of impunity. The institutional positioning of criminal law within the EU legal order stipulates rather that several other factors are taking into account when designing new laws.

Such is being further facilitated through the existence of a well-prescribed and rather detailed legislative process, applicable to criminal law affairs. Usually, upon a Commission's proposal, generally accompanied by an impact assessment, the close involvement of national governments' perspectives (via the European Council) and the European Parliament in such legislative processes secures the possibility of careful weighing up all (perhaps competing) interests involved in the assessment of whether specific behaviours justify the adoption of criminal prohibitions at the EU level. Although there is still much room to critique the way in which this is being done in practice, research shows that usually a variety of factors are invoked and debated.[36] It justifies the intermediate conclusion that the EU is, in principle, well suited to involving fundamental rights considerations in its criminalisation policy without losing sight of other factors and their underlying rationales. Be that as it may, the following subsection will explain why the existing practice of lawmaking in the field of criminal law nevertheless deserves to be criticised for how it employs the rights argument and the underlying impunity rationale.

B. The Precise Subject of an Impunity Rationale: Areas of Crime versus Particular Definitions of Offences

To invoke fundamental rights in order to justify the adoption of criminalisation duties can be rather appealing for the Member States, and are perhaps easily convincing – in particular, when one considers the areas of crime in which the EU is competent to act: terrorism, human trafficking, sexual exploitation of women and children, etc (Article 83(1) TFEU). It goes without saying that these acts constitute gross violations of fundamental rights. Who would not want to prevent impunity for those committing them? But here it is important to observe that recent EU legislative measures regarding criminalisation in these areas of crime

[35] See, eg the so-called 'Stockholm programme', adopted in 2009, establishing a five-year policy programme for Justice and Home Affairs, entitled 'An Open and Secure Europe Serving and Protecting the Citizens', Council doc 17024/09 (Brussels, 2 December 2009).

[36] See some overviews (for different purposes) in J Ouwerkerk, 'Evidence-Based Criminalisation in EU Law: Evidence of What Exactly?' in J Ouwerkerk J Atltena, J Öberg and S Miettinen (eds), *The Future of EU Criminal Justice Policy and Practice. Legal and Criminological Perspectives* (Leiden, Brill/Nijhoff, 2019) 50–56; Ouwerkerk (n 24) 9–15. See also analyses on specific types of crime, eg V Mitsilegas, 'The Normative Foundations of the Criminalization of Human Smuggling: Exploring the Fault Lines between European and International Law' (2019) 10 *New Journal of European Criminal Law* 77; J Öberg, 'Is It 'Essential' to Imprison Insider Dealers to Enforce Insider Dealing Laws?' (2014) 14 *Journal of Corporate Law Studies* 111.

do not concern the core crimes. After all, the latest Directives regarding these areas of crime did not define for the first time what according to EU law is to count as terrorism, human trafficking or sexual exploitation; these were already defined in previous legislation which has now been replaced by new, more extensive provisions (adopted under the umbrella of the Lisbon Treaty).[37] These latest Directives rather deal with so-called 'related offences'. The question really is how convincing fundamental rights-based justifications and impunity arguments are in relation to those related offences.

Before turning to this question, it is instructive to illustrate how the rights argument has been used in the latest EU Directive on Terrorism. Directive 2017/541 aims to replace its 2002 predecessor, merely by extending the scopes of prohibited conduct related to terrorism.[38] To that end, Directive 2017/514 covers an impressive number of newly incriminated types of conduct, called 'offences related to terrorist activities'. It concerns: public provocation to commit a terrorist offence, recruitment for terrorism, providing training for terrorism, receiving training for terrorism, travelling for the purpose of terrorism, organising or otherwise facilitating travelling for the purpose of terrorism, and terrorist financing.[39] In the explanatory notes to its proposal for this Directive, the Commission explicitly mentioned the serious violations of fundamental rights that 'acts of terrorism' constitute, for which reason it considers EU action in the field justified.[40] In an account of evaluations of then existing legislation as well as impact assessments, the Commission further elaborated on the relationship between fundamental rights protection and the need for stronger terrorism legislation. It explicitly mentions that the proposed measures 'have as final objective the protection of fundamental rights of victims and potential victims, in particular the right to life and the right to physical and mental integrity'.[41] But whether and to what extent the protection of fundamental rights also requires the incrimination of all aforementioned terrorism-related offences, or whether that specific argument only applies to the core terrorist offences, has not been explained. Only in rather general terms has it been stated that criminal prohibitions must in any case 'comply with the principles of necessity, proportionality, and legality, with appropriate safeguards to ensure accountability and judicial redress'.[42]

These general wordings and references related to fundamental rights protection strongly suggest that the fundamental rights argument has merely been

[37] Directive 2017/541 on combating terrorism [2017] OJ L88/6; Directive 2011/36 on preventing and combating trafficking in human beings and protecting its victims, replacing Council Framework Decision 2002/629/JHA [2011] OJ 2011 L101/1; Directive 2011/93 on combating sexual abuse (n 23).

[38] Council Framework Decision 2002/475/JHA on combating terrorism [2002] OJ L164/3.

[39] Directive 2017/541 (n 37) Art. 5–11.

[40] European Commission, Proposal for a Directive of the European Parliament and of the Council on combating terrorism and replacing Council Framework Decision 2002/475/JHA on combating terrorism, COM (2015) 625 final, 1, para 1.

[41] ibid 13, para 3.

[42] ibid 13–14, para 3.

used to justify legislative action at the level of the crime area concerned (here, terrorism), instead of justifying legislative action at the level of particular offence definitions within this specific crime area. This corresponds to what has happened regarding other areas of crime, such as human trafficking and sexual exploitation. Whereas the latest (and in the meantime adopted) Commission's proposals for new Directives in these areas also aim to define criminal prohibitions concerning 'related offences' only, accompanying justifications have predominantly been put forward relating to the respective areas of crime, without mentioning consistently specific proposals regarding 'related offences'.[43]

The practice described above may be problematic, because it wrongfully suggests that justifications at the level of a crime area automatically equate with justifications at the level of specific incriminations. After all, one argument may well justify incrimination of the core offence (terrorist attack), but will not necessarily justify either incrimination of a related act (eg terrorist financing)[44] or incrimination of acts in a pre-emptive or anticipative stage (eg attempts and preparatory acts). Therefore, in order to further advance a legitimate criminalisation policy, and a fair position of rights-oriented impunity arguments therein, it is necessary to use such arguments in a much more specific manner than has been done so far. Instead of linking them to the applicable crime area as a whole, they should be made in relation to particular criminal prohibitions.

V. Final Remarks

It has been demonstrated in this chapter that the EU's increased engagement with fundamental rights has triggered both their shield and their sword function in the context of criminal law. Fundamental rights have, on the one hand, been invoked to protect citizens from the application of the criminal law, but, on the other hand, have also been invoked to trigger the very application of the criminal law, for instance by compelling Member States to enact certain criminal prohibitions in their national legal orders. The latter use of fundamental rights-based arguments shows an increased attention for the impunity rationale in EU substantive criminal law.

[43] Regarding human trafficking, see Recitals 1 and 11 to Directive 2011/36 on preventing and combating trafficking in human beings and protecting its victims [2011] OJ L101/1; Commission Staff Working Document, Impact Assessment, Accompanying document to the Proposal for a Council Framework Decision on preventing and combating trafficking in human beings, and protecting victims, SEC (2009) 359, in particular paras 2.7 and 5.3.3. Regarding sexual offences, see the Explanatory Memorandum to the European Commission's Proposal for a Directive (n 24) 2, para 1 and 8, para 3; see also the accompanying Impact Assessment (n 24), in particular paras 2.2 and 2.8.

[44] Especially if one considers the very broad scope of the applicable provision: Art 11 of Directive 2017/541 (no 37) requires the prohibition of 'providing or collecting funds, by any means, directly or indirectly, with the intention that they be used, or in the knowledge that they are to be used, in full or in part, to commit, or to contribute to the commission of, any of the offences referred to in Articles 3 to 10'.

In a subsequent exploration of the potential and limits of such an impunity rationale in the context of EU criminalisation policy, it has been argued that the utmost limit of a right to impunity follows from the inherent reductionist nature of rights-based arguments. Would such arguments be made decisive, there is a real risk that other factors of relevance to the criminalisation process would wrongfully be overlooked. Against that background, it has been shown that decision-making processes in the context of EU criminal law and policy are quite well suited to focusing on all interests at stake in determining the scope of substantive criminal law at the EU level. However, to further advance legitimate law, and policy-making in EU criminal law, it has been recommended that justifications for EU-level incrimination must be given, to an increasing extent, at the level of specific offence definitions, rather than at the level of crime areas only. Here also lies a task for legal scholarship on EU criminal law which, contrary to national-oriented scholarship on substantive criminal law, predominantly discusses competences and the exercise thereof in relation to areas of crime, but should feel encouraged to increasingly engage with discussing specific definitions of offences, including those that qualify as related offences or pre-emptive or anticipative acts of crime.

4

The Role of the Fight against Impunity in EU Criminal Policy Preparation and Evaluation

WOUTER VAN BALLEGOOIJ

I. Introduction

The triangulation of the fight against impunity, the concept of better regulation and the rule of law raises the questions of the fight against *whose* impunity should be prioritised at the EU level and what tools are available within and beyond the EU criminal law toolkit to win it. With these questions in mind, this chapter discusses how the fight against impunity has been reinforced through EU policy preparation and evaluation. In this context, the chapter describes the origins of the concept of better regulation at the EU level and how the European Commission and Parliament have applied it across the EU policy and legislative cycle covering the process of preparation and adoption of EU measures, and continuing during the process of their transposition and implementation (section II). It then elaborates on the application of better regulation criteria in the area of EU criminal law. In this area, the fight against impunity is often cited (explicitly or implicitly) to demonstrate the added value of a particular action or cooperation at the EU level either in an impact assessment accompanying a legislative proposal or, more generally, in strategic policy documents. The extent to which action and cooperation at the EU level has added value in the fight against impunity has also been assessed ex post (although it has not been properly and comprehensively evaluated at this stage) (section III). Subsequently, the example of the European Public Prosecutor's Office is discussed, also taking into account that the fight against impunity includes tackling violations of the rule of law (section IV), before the chapter concludes with a number of recommendations on how the fight against impunity may be further embedded in the EU (criminal) policy cycle (section V).

II. EU Policy Preparation and Evaluation: Origins and Application of the Concept of Better Lawmaking

EU policy preparation and evaluation is guided by the concept of better regulation.[1] The exact aims of this concept, however, remain somewhat nebulous. This is already clear from the definition provided by the European Commission, which contains a number of negations that have been italicised below to illustrate this point:

> Better regulation is *not* about 'more' or 'less' EU legislation; *nor* is it about deregulating *or* deprioritizing certain policy areas or compromising the values that we hold dear: social and environmental protection, and fundamental rights including health – to name just a few examples. Better regulation is about making sure we actually deliver on the ambitious policy goals we have set ourselves.[2]

Despite these denials, the concept of better regulation can be traced back to debates that have taken place since the 1980s on the need for deregulation, meaning reducing government regulation of the economy. At the EC/EU level, discussions about de- and re-regulation came together with debates regarding the governance of the internal market. The deregulatory effect of the prohibition of national measures restricting the free movement of goods, persons and services from other Member States raised the question of the extent to which consumer and environmental protection, for example, need to be harmonised at the EU level. As European integration progressed, this discussion was extended to other EU policy areas, including the area of freedom, security and justice. For example, Article 82(2) TFEU provides a legal basis for establishing minimum rules concerning the rights of individuals in criminal procedure 'to the extent necessary to facilitate mutual recognition of judgments and judicial decisions and police and judicial cooperation in criminal matters having a cross-border dimension'. At the same time, for supranational regulation to be legitimate, citizens have to hold trust in EU institutions. In a White Paper on European governance adopted in 2001,[3] this dilemma was aptly described:

> Today, political leaders throughout Europe are facing a real paradox. On the one hand, Europeans want them to find solutions to the major problems confronting our societies. On the other hand, people increasingly distrust institutions and politics or are simply not interested in them.

Part of the solution was found in the introduction of the concept of better regulation.

[1] European Commission, 'European Governance – A White Paper', COM (2001) 0428, [2001] OJ C287/1–29.

[2] European Commission, 'Better Regulation for Better Results – An EU Agenda' (Communication) COM (2015) 215, para 1.

[3] Above n 2, 1.

The natural development towards 'more' EU legislation faced increasing scrutiny after the lack of trust expressed by part of the European citizenry in several referenda concerning the draft Treaty establishing a Constitution for Europe, the Lisbon Treaty and Brexit. Against this background, it is not a coincidence that the Juncker Commission (2014–2019) sought to regain that trust by being 'serious about being big on big things and small on small things'.[4] The same trend was visible in the first work programme presented by the Von der Leyen Commission (2019–2014), with a strong emphasis on a 'European Green Deal' and 'a Europe fit for the digital age'.[5] These priorities had to be reconsidered in view of the need to coordinate a common European response to the outbreak of COVID-19. Better regulation therefore certainly has to do with prioritising certain policy areas, in which EU action is perceived to be legitimate. The Commission's own Eurobarometer surveys show that trust in the EU has decreased over the handling of the relatively high number of migrants seeking access to the EU through irregular means in 2015–2016 and the continued lack of ability of Member States to come to an agreement on how to reform the EU's Common European Asylum System.[6] At the same time, immigration is an area in which citizens expect the Union to deliver on its aims.[7]

Various interinstitutional agreements on better lawmaking have been adopted between the European Commission, the European Parliament and the Council of the European Union.[8] From these agreements, it has become clear that the better lawmaking criteria have to be applied throughout the whole policy and legislative cycle covering the process of preparation and adoption of EU measures and continuing during the process of their implementation and application. Better lawmaking implies that EU intervention should be prepared in an open and transparent manner, informed by the best available evidence and backed by the comprehensive involvement of stakeholders.[9] Compliance with these better regulation criteria has become ever more important to show that EU intervention

[4] The Juncker Commission, 'The Right Team to Deliver Change', speech, Brussels, 10 September 2014 http://europa.eu/rapid/press-release_SPEECH-14-585_en.htm; For a critical reflection, see A Alemanno, 'How Much Better Is Better Regulation, Assessing the Impact of the Better Regulation Package on the European Union- A Research Agenda' (2015) 6 *European Journal of Risk Regulation* 344.

[5] European Commission, 'Commission Work Programme 2020, A Union that Strives for More' (Communication) COM (2020) 37.

[6] W van Ballegooij, 'Cost of Non-Schengen: Civil Liberties, Justice and Home Affairs Aspects' (EPRS, 2016): W van Ballegooij and C Navarra, 'The Cost of Non-Europe in Asylum Policy' (Brussels, EPRS, 2018).

[7] European Commission, 'Standard Eurobarometer 90' (November 2018) 28 http://ec.europa.eu/commfrontoffice/publicopinionmobile/index.cfm/Survey/getSurveyDetail/surveyKy/2215.

[8] Interinstitutional agreement on better law-making [2013] OJ C321/1; Interinstitutional agreement on better law-making [2016] OJ L123/1.

[9] European Commission, 'Better Regulation for Better Results' (n 2) paras 2, 3.

respects the principle of subsidiarity[10] in areas of shared competence between the Union and the Member States. The principle has two aspects:

- 'the Union shall act only if and in so far as the objectives of the proposed action cannot be sufficiently achieved by the Member States' (the 'necessity/relevance test'[11]);
- but can rather 'by reason of the scale or effects of the proposed action, be better achieved at Union level' (the 'EU added value' test).[12]

Furthermore, in accordance with the proportionality principle, EU action must be limited to what is necessary to achieve the objectives of the European Union Treaties.[13]

In line with its right of initiative,[14] the Commission has developed the most sophisticated procedure for better regulation.[15] When preparing an EU intervention,[16] Commission officials have to follow better regulation guidelines, which are complemented by 'toolboxes' providing more specific and operational guidance.[17] In particular, these toolboxes describe when there is a need for the preparation of an impact assessment collecting evidence to assess whether the envisaged initiative is justified.[18] In particular, inception impact assessments should identify and describe the problem to be tackled,[19] establish objectives,[20] formulate policy options (and indicate their appropriate legal basis)[21] and finally assess the key social, economic, environmental, fundamental and human rights impacts of these options.[22] In the context of this chapter, the specific toolbox on how to assess and address the potential impact of the various policy

[10] Art 5(3) TEU,[2012] OJ C326/1; Protocol (No 2) on the application of the principles of subsidiarity and proportionality [2008] OJ 115/206.

[11] European Commission, 'Better Regulation Toolbox #5. Legal Basis, Subsidiarity and Proportionality' https://ec.europa.eu/info/sites/info/files/file_import/better-regulation-toolbox-5_en_0.pdf, 28–30.

[12] ibid.

[13] Art 5(4) TEU; Protocol (No 2).

[14] Art 17(2) TEU.

[15] Commission Staff Working Document, 'Better Regulation Guidelines' SWD (2017) 350.

[16] Legislative or non-legislative, spending programmes or other measures.

[17] European Commission, 'Better Regulation Toolbox', https://ec.europa.eu/info/better-regulation-toolbox_en.

[18] European Commission, 'Better Regulation Toolbox #9. When Is an Impact Assessment Necessary?' https://ec.europa.eu/info/sites/info/files/file_import/better-regulation-toolbox-9_en_0.pdf.

[19] European Commission, 'Better Regulation Toolbox #14. How to Analyse Problems?' https://ec.europa.eu/info/sites/info/files/file_import/better-regulation-toolbox-14_en_0.pdf.

[20] European Commission, 'Better Regulation Toolbox #16 How to Set Objectives?' https://ec.europa.eu/info/sites/info/files/file_import/better-regulation-toolbox-16_en_0.pdf.

[21] European Commission, 'Better Regulation Toolbox #17 How to Identify Policy Options?' https://ec.europa.eu/info/sites/info/files/file_import/better-regulation-toolbox-17_en_0.pdf.

[22] European Commission, 'Better Regulation Toolbox #19 Identification/Screening of Impacts' https://ec.europa.eu/info/sites/info/files/file_import/better-regulation-toolbox-19_en_0.pdf; tool #28 fundamental & human rights,https://ec.europa.eu/info/sites/info/files/file_import/better-regulation-toolbox-28_en_0.pdf.

options on the fight against fraud should also be pointed out.[23] Following stakeholder consultation and a positive opinion on the draft impact assessment report by the Commission's Regulatory Scrutiny Board,[24] the proposal and its accompanying impact assessment may proceed for adoption by the College of Commissioners. Furthermore, evaluations of the implementation of EU legislation have gained increasing importance.[25] These evaluations are aimed at gauging whether the objectives of EU intervention have been met and, if so, whether this has happened in the most efficient manner. It should also be seen whether the intervention has led to a coherent tackling of the problem and whether it is still relevant given the current context. An overall estimation of the 'EU added value' of the intervention builds on the results of the first four evaluation criteria.[26]

Besides the European Commission's commitment towards conducting impact assessments of its initiatives, in the 2003 Interinstitutional agreement on better law-making between the EU institutions,[27] for the first time reference was made to the possibility of the European Parliament and Council conducting impact assessments prior to the adoption of any substantive amendments.[28] So far, the Council has not made use of that possibility. However, the Parliament, and notably its Research Service (EPRS), inter alia produces 'appraisals' of the strengths and weaknesses of the Commission's impact assessments and complementary or substitute impact assessments in cases where a Parliamentary Committee deems that certain aspects have been dealt with inadequately or not at all in the original Commission proposal,[29] and assessments of the impact of its own amendments upon the request of a Committee.[30] Furthermore, the EPRS produces European Implementation Assessments to support Parliament in drawing up Reports on the Implementation of EU legislation,[31] 'Cost of Non-Europe' reports and European Added Value Assessments accompanying requests for proposals for Union Acts

[23] European Commission, 'Better Regulation Toolbox #25. Prevention of Fraud' https://ec.europa.eu/info/sites/info/files/file_import/better-regulation-toolbox-25_en_0.pdf.

[24] European Commission, 'Better Regulation Toolbox #3. Role of the Regulatory Scrutiny Board' https://ec.europa.eu/info/sites/info/files/file_import/better-regulation-toolbox-3_en_0.pdf.

[25] European Commission, 'Better Regulation Toolbox #43. What is an Evaluation and When Is It Required?' https://ec.europa.eu/info/sites/info/files/file_import/better-regulation-toolbox-43_en_0.pdf.

[26] European Commission, 'Better Regulation Toolbox #46. Designing the Evaluation' https://ec.europa.eu/info/sites/info/files/file_import/better-regulation-toolbox-46_en_0.pdf.

[27] [2003] OJ C321/1.

[28] Interinstitutional agreement on better law-making [2003] OJ C321/1, para 30: 'Where the codecision procedure applies, the European Parliament and Council may, on the basis of jointly defined criteria and procedures, have impact assessments carried out prior to the adoption of any substantive amendment, either at first reading or at the conciliation stage.'

[29] European Parliament, Conference of Committee Chairs, 'Impact Assessment Handbook, Guidelines for Committees' www.europarl.europa.eu/EPRS/impact_assesement_handbook_en.pdf, para 15.

[30] ibid para 16; C Collova, 'How Does ex ante Impact Assessment Work in the EU?' (Brussels, EPRS, 2015).

[31] I Anglmayer, 'Evaluation and ex post Impact Assessment at the EU Level' (Brussels, EPRS, 2016).

put forward by the European Parliament in accordance with Article 225 TFEU.[32] The Commission has to reply to such proposals within three months.[33]

Before concluding this section on EU policy preparation and evaluation, it should be mentioned that better regulation also entails striving for high-quality EU legislation. A 'Joint Practical Guide' provides a number of principles to be followed, including that 'legal acts of the Union shall be drafted clearly simply and precisely' to ensure the equality of citizens before the law and legal certainty.[34] These aspects, which are of the utmost importance in the area of criminal law, will be examined further in the following section.

III. The Implementation of Better Lawmaking Criteria in the Area of EU Criminal Law

As discussed, the concept of better regulation is a response to the deregulatory effect of European economic integration and a safeguard for the legitimacy of EU intervention and the EU as an actor therein. However, as the development of EU criminal law is equally guided by the principle of mutual recognition[35] and legitimacy of EU action is a fortiori important in an area so closely related to national sovereignty, as further underlined in the relevant legal bases for action provided for by the TFEU,[36] and fundamental rights, notably compliance with the Charter of Fundamental Rights of the European Union (the Charter),[37] the application of better lawmaking to this area also deserves careful scrutiny.[38] In this context, one may also assess the extent to which the area of freedom, security and justice, and notably a 'high level of security',[39] has been 'delivered'

[32] Art 225 TFEU: 'The European Parliament may, acting by a majority of its component Members, request the Commission to submit any appropriate proposal on matters on which it considers that a Union act is required for the purpose of implementing the Treaties. If the Commission does not submit a proposal, it shall inform the European Parliament of the reasons.'

[33] Interinstitutional Agreement between the European Parliament, the Council of the European Union and the European Commission on Better Law-Making [2016] OJ L123/1.

[34] European Commission Legal Service, *Joint Practical Guide of the European Parliament, the Council and the Commission for persons involved in the drafting of European Union Legislation* (Brussels, 2016) https://publications.europa.eu/en/publication-detail/-/publication/3879747d-7a3c-411b-a3a0-55c14e2ba732/language-en/format-PDF/source-86102285, ss 1.1 and 1.2.

[35] Art 67(3) TFEU; W van Ballegooij, *The Nature of Mutual Recognition in European Law, Re-examining the Notion from an Individual Rights Perspective with a View to Its Further Development in the Criminal Justice Area* (Antwerp, Intersentia, 2015).

[36] For a more general reflection on the application of the principles of subsidiarity and proportionality in the area of EU criminal law, see E Herlin Karnell, *The Constitutional Dimension of European Criminal Law* (Oxford, Hart Publishing, 2012), ch 4, s IV; W de Bondt and S Miettinen, 'Minimum Criminal Penalties in the European Union: In Search of a Credible Justification' (2015) 21 *European Law Journal* 722.

[37] [2012] OJ C326/391.

[38] W van Ballegooij, 'Measuring the Added Value of EU Criminal Law' [2016] *Eucrim* 90.

[39] Art 3(2) TEU; Art 67(3) TFEU.

through the application of better lawmaking criteria to EU initiatives in the area of criminal law.[40]

In general, it may be pointed out that the concept of better regulation has not yet been fully embraced in the area of EU criminal law. Many measures have been adopted without an impact assessment, including as regards their effects on fundamental rights and human rights.[41] For the ones adopted before the entry into force of the Lisbon Treaty on 1 December 2009, this could partially be explained by the many Member State initiatives, notably under the guise of the fight against terrorism.[42] However, also since then, whilst Commission legislative proposals tend to include general statements on the effectiveness of the proposals and their compliance with fundamental rights, they often forgo detailed impact assessments, citing urgency and other reasons for the omissions.[43] Furthermore, a comprehensive evaluation of the EU's security policies as regards their relevance, coherence, effectiveness, efficiency and compliance with fundamental and human rights is lacking.[44] The Commission did, however, conduct a comprehensive assessment in 2017, which may be viewed as a positive first step.[45] As regards effectiveness, it should be noted that some instruments, like the Framework Decision on Organised Crime,[46] have been purposefully drafted in ambiguous language to avoid a clash with the various national legal traditions ('constructive ambiguity'[47]). This makes it very difficult to establish the extent to which this measure contributes to a more effective fight against organised crime by the Union and its Member States.[48] As regards fundamental rights, national and European judges have partially filled gaps in EU legislation, notably providing safeguards for the

[40] W van Ballegooij, 'Area of Freedom, Security and Justice: Cost of non-Europe (Brussels, EPRS, 2019).

[41] European Commission, 'Better Regulation Toolbox #28. Fundamental Rights and Human Rights' https://ec.europa.eu/info/sites/info/files/file_import/better-regulation-toolbox-28_en_0.pdf.

[42] F de Londras, 'Reviewing the Effectiveness of EU Counterterrorism Policies' in S Carrera and V Mitsilegas (eds), *Constitutionalising the Security Union, Effectiveness, Rule of Law and Rights in in Countering Terrorism and Crime* (Brussels, CEPS, 2017) 45–53; W van Ballegooij and P Bakowski, *The Cost of Non-Europe in the Fight against Terrorism* (Brussels, EPRS, 2018) ch 1.3.1.

[43] European Commission, 'Better Regulation Toolbox #9' (n 18). As regards the proposal for a Directive on combating terrorism, the justification for the absence of an impact assessment was 'the urgent need to improve the EU framework to increase security in the light of recent terrorist attack including by incorporating international obligations and standards': 'Proposal for a Directive on combating terrorism and replacing Council Framework Decision 2002/475/JHA on combating terrorism' COM (2015) 625 final.

[44] van Ballegooij and Bakowski (n 42) 19.

[45] European Commission, 'Ninth Progress Report towards an Effective and Genuine Security Union' COM (2017) 407 final; European Commission Staff Working Document, 'Comprehensive Assessment of EU Security Policy' SWD (2017) 278 final.

[46] Council Framework Decision 2008/841/JHA of 24 October 2008 on the fight against organised crime [2008] OJ L300/42.

[47] For a definition, see euABC.com, http://en.euabc.com/word/222.

[48] 'Report from the Commission to the European Parliament and the Council based on Article 10 of Council Framework Decision 2008/841/JHA of 24 October 2008 on the fight against organised crime' COM (2016) 448 final.

protection of personal data, procedural rights and humane detention conditions.[49] However, such ex post intervention often comes too late or is unable to properly remedy the suffering of victims of fundamental rights violations.

This is not to underestimate the difficulties that applying better regulation criteria, and more specifically establishing the added value of EU criminal law, pose. The European Commission measures the added value of EU criminal law based on the extent to which it strengthens the confidence of citizens in exercising their free movement rights, enhances mutual trust among judiciaries and law enforcement, ensures the effective enforcement of EU law in areas such as the protection of the environment or illegal employment, and ensures a consistent and coherent system of legislation.[50] An example is the impact assessment accompanying the Commission proposals regarding interoperability between EU information systems for security, border and migration management,[51] in which it was stated that 'The new facilities are also expected to generate increased public trust by ensuring that their design and use increases the security of European citizens'.[52] However, one may criticise the justification provided by the Commission in questioning whether one should not rather focus on 'better' instead of 'more' information sharing in seeking to ensure a high level of security.[53]

The Council[54] and the Parliament[55] have not developed general guidelines on the added value of EU criminal law, but have so far limited themselves to guidelines for the adoption of substantive criminal law, stressing the need for factual evidence for the adoption of criminal sanctions. This is based on the principle that criminal law should only be used as a last resort (*ultima ratio*).[56] While these are lofty objectives and initiatives, they do not amount to a firm substantive foundation for an EU criminal justice system based on the rule of law, in which all interests,

[49] G Gonzales Fuster, 'A Security Union in Full Respect of Fundamental Rights: But How Effectively Respectful?' in Carrera and Mitsilegas (n 42) 87–92; W van Ballegooij and P Bárd, 'Mutual Recognition and Individual Rights; Did the Court Get It Right' (2016) 7 *New Journal of European Criminal Law* 439.

[50] European Commission, 'Towards an EU Criminal Policy: Ensuring the Effective Implementation of EU Policies through Criminal Law' (Communication) COM (2011) 573, 5.

[51] Impact Assessment (SWD (2017) 473, SWD (2017) 474 (summary)) of a Commission proposal for a regulation of the European Parliament and of the Council on establishing a framework for interoperability between EU information systems (borders and visa) and amending Council Decision 2004/512/EC, Regulation (EC) No 767/2008, Council Decision 2008/633/JHA, Regulation (EU) 2016/399 and Regulation (EU) 2017/2226 (COM (2017) 793) and of a Commission proposal for a regulation of the European Parliament and of the Council on establishing a framework for interoperability between EU information systems (police and judicial cooperation, asylum and migration) (COM (2017) 794).

[52] Impact Assessment (SWD (2017) 473) (ibid) 19; K Eisele, 'Initial Appraisal of a European Commission Impact Assessment, Interoperability between EU Information Systems for Security, Border and Migration Management' (Brussels, EPRS, 2018).

[53] van Ballegooij and Bakowski (n 42) ch 1.3.4.

[54] 'Council Conclusions on Model Provisions Guiding Council's Criminal Law Deliberations' (30 November 2009) www.consilium.europa.eu/uedocs/cms_Data/docs/pressdata/en/jha/111543.pdf.

[55] European Parliament resolution of 22 May 2012 on an EU approach to criminal law (2010/2310 (INI)), P7_TA (2012)0208.

[56] *cf* A Klip, *European Criminal Law, An Integrative Approach*, 3rd edn (Cambridge, Intersentia, 2016) 241–43.

including that of the defence,[57] are properly represented. Instead, the following argument featuring on the Commission's Directorate General for Justice under the heading 'EU strategy on criminal justice' still prevails: 'Serious organised crime is often committed across borders. To prevent "safe havens" for criminals, EU countries' laws should be more aligned.'[58] This sometimes rather artificial reasoning aimed at bringing matters within the scope of EU competence seems to deflect from the real objective of enhancing security by reducing the prevalence of serious criminality.[59]

The factual evidence for cross-border criminality, obstacles to law enforcement cooperation and effective enforcement referred to, including (threat) assessments produced by EU agencies, criminal justice statistics, data resulting from academic research and stakeholder consultations and surveys, is, however, often not complete, nor easily comparable across the EU's jurisdictions due to differences in criminal law and procedure. In any event, such evidence may be interpreted in different ways, depending on the perspective taken (law enforcement, victim, suspect, society).[60] In this context, the monitoring and evaluation of EU measures has proven to be particularly challenging. Even on the core criterion of effectiveness, one should not only check how the legislation has been transposed by the Member State concerned; it is also important to see how prosecutors and ultimately courts apply the new provisions. To get a proper view of that, one probably needs to wait longer than three to five years after a measure is adopted.[61] Beyond coherence of the measure internally and within EU law more generally, one can also not escape wider reflections on the impact of the measure on the legal systems concerned and the way in which they choose to address certain criminal phenomena. Finally, in recognition of the fact that lawyers do not have an absolute monopoly on wisdom, an interdisciplinary approach is needed involving criminologists, social scientists and other disciplines, depending on the offence concerned.

As demonstrated, the implementation of better lawmaking criteria in the area of EU criminal law has faced challenges, which are grounded in EU institutional developments and the specificities of criminal law, but also the methodological predispositions of better regulation, relying heavily on the extensive collection of (economic) data. As will be demonstrated in the next section, which discusses

[57] For elements to assess effective criminal defence in a particular jurisdiction, see E Cape, Z Namoradze, R Smits and T Spronken, *Effective Criminal Defence in Europe* (Antwerp, Intersentia, 2010) 5, 6.

[58] European Commission, 'EU Strategy on Criminal Justice' https://ec.europa.eu/info/policies/justice-and-fundamental-rights/criminal-justice/eu-strategy-criminal-justice_en.

[59] Art 67 (3) speaks, rather unhelpfully, in terms of the Union endeavouring to ensure a 'high level of security'.

[60] S Carrera et al, 'The Cost of Non-Europe in the Area of Organised Crime', Annex I to W van Ballegooij and T Zandstra, 'The Cost of Non-Europe in the Area of Organised Crime and Corruption', European Parliament Research Service, 2016, s 2.4; P Bárd, 'The Benefits of the EU from a Criminal Law Perspective' (*Social Security Network/CEPS blogspot*, 2016) www.societalsecurity.net/blog/ceps-blog-post-benefits-eu-criminal-law-perspective-0.

[61] For an example, see A Scherrer, W van Ballegooij, European Implementation Assessment: Directive 2011/93/EU Combating sexual abuse of children (Brussels, EPRS, 2017).

the example of the establishment of the European Public Prosecutor's Office, these predispositions may also shroud the actual added value of an EU initiative, particularly one that seeks to enhance the fight against impunity.

IV. European Public Prosecutor's Office

As discussed in the previous section, the added value of EU criminal law is mostly expressed in qualitative terms, though quantitative considerations also play a role, certainly when it concerns measures that might be very costly or when large financial gains may be expected.[62] A prime example is the establishment of the European Public Prosecutor's Office (EPPO).[63] As discussed in more detail elsewhere,[64] the impact assessment accompanying the Commission proposal on the EPPO[65] had an economic dimension. It estimated that the total value of offences against the EU's financial interest amounted to €3 billion.[66] However, on this point, the impact assessment admitted that an exact estimate could not be given due to weaknesses in the available data and the inherent difficulties in measuring the scale of undetected criminal activities.[67] The impact assessment was based on four policy options for the establishment of the EPPO ranging from a centralised EPPO to a decentralised EPPO (the preferred option of the Commission) and to a college-type EPPO (closer to the ultimate model agreed by the Member States), and the creation of an EPPO unit within Eurojust. Having in mind other research,[68] the €300 million expected annual benefits to the EU budget of the preferred policy option due to a reduction in fraud were probably overestimated.

Moreover, the impact assessment overlooked the gains that the EPPO might bring by strengthening the hand of 'national' prosecutors. This is perhaps due to the sensitivities that surround making such an argument. The 'elephant in the room' is that public prosecutors in certain Member States do not prioritise EU fraud cases due to their complexity and the risk of having to go up against suspects who are either politically active or are 'protected' by those in power. The independence and expertise of the EPPO can offer an outcome there.

[62] van Ballegooij (n 38) 90–94.

[63] Council Regulation (EU) 2017/1939 of 12 October 2017 implementing enhanced cooperation on the establishment of the European Public Prosecutor's Office ('the EPPO') [2017] OJ L283/1; *cf* C Di Francesco Maesa, 'The Fight against Impunity between EU and National Legal Orders: What Role for the EPPO?', ch 8 in this book.

[64] W van Ballegooij, 'European Public Prosecutor's Office – A View on the State of Play and Perspectives from the European Parliament' in W Geelhoed, L Erkelens and A Meij (eds), *Shifting Perspectives on the European Public Prosecutor's Office* (The Hague, Springer, 2018) 27–38.

[65] European Commission, 'Impact Assessment accompanying the Proposal for a Council Regulation on the establishment of the European Public Prosecutor's Office' SWD (2013) 274, August 2013.

[66] ibid 56.

[67] ibid 57.

[68] W van Ballegooij and T Zandstra, 'The Cost of Non-Europe in the Area of Organised Crime and Corruption' (Brussels, EPRS, 2016) 9.

However, besides the establishment of the EPPO, one may also need to enhance the effectiveness of the judicial systems in a number of Member States more generally. As Di Francesco Maesa points out in her chapter in this book,

> the EPPO has no competence to ensure that criminal convictions adopted by national judicial authorities are effectively enforced at the national level; the execution phase is still exclusively entrusted to the domestic authorities. The EPPO is merely responsible for investigating, prosecuting and bringing to trial the perpetrators of offences falling within its competence, while the national courts are responsible for settling the cases brought before them by the EPPO.[69]

Monitoring the effectiveness, efficiency and independence of judicial systems could be tackled through the development of an annual European Union monitoring report on democracy, the rule of law and fundamental rights with country-specific recommendations, as demanded by the European Parliament,[70] and the further enhancement of judicial cooperation by means of training and coordination through EU agencies.

Currently two EU Member States (Poland[71] and Hungary[72]) are subject to the Article 7(1) EU procedure aimed at establishing 'a clear risk of a serious breach' of EU values based, inter alia, on accusations of their governments seeking to undermine judicial independence. Several other Member States[73] are also under scrutiny by EU institutions. Following the CJEU judgment in the *LM* case,[74] judicial authorities have to follow a two-pronged test to decide whether to execute European Arrest Warrants issued by judicial authorities from Member States where judicial independence – and thereby the right to a fair trial as per Article 47 of the Charter – is in doubt. First, on the basis of objectivity, the executing court must assess reliable, specific and properly updated material concerning the operation of

[69] Di Francesco Maesa (n 63) 3.

[70] European Parliament resolution of 25 October 2016 with recommendations to the Commission on the establishment of an EU mechanism on democracy, the rule of law and fundamental rights (2015/2254(INL)), P8_TA-PROV(2016)0409; W van Ballegooij and T Evas, 'An EU Mechanism on Democracy, the Rule of Law and Fundamental Rights', European Added Value Assessment accompanying the Legislative initiative report (Rapporteur Sophie in' t Veld) PE.579.328 (Brussels, EPRS, October 2016); Annex I, L Pech, E Wennerström, V Leigh, A Markowska, L De Keyser, A Gómez Rojo and H Spanikova, '-An EU Mechanism on Democracy, the Rule of Law and Fundamental Rights'; Annex II, P Bárd, S Carrera, E Guild and D Kochenov, with a thematic contribution by W Marneffe, 'Assessing the Need and Possibilities for the Establishment of an EU Scoreboard on Democracy, the Rule of Law and Fundamental Rights'.

[71] European Commission, 'Proposal for a Council Decision on the Determination of a Clear Risk of a Serious Breach by the Republic of Poland of the Rule of Law' COM (2017) 835 final.

[72] European Parliament resolution of 12 September 2018 on a proposal calling on the Council to determine, pursuant to Article 7(1) of the Treaty on European Union, the existence of a clear risk of a serious breach by Hungary of the values on which the Union is founded, P8_TA-PROV(2018)0340.

[73] European Parliament resolution of 15 November 2017 on the rule of law in Malta, P8_TA(2017)0438; European Parliament resolution of 13 November 2018 on the rule of law in Romania, P8_TA-PROV(2018)0446.

[74] CJEU, Case C-216/18 PPU *Minister for Justice and Equality v LM* ECLI:EU:C:2018:586; P Bárd and W van Ballegooij, 'Judicial Independence as a Precondition for Mutual Trust? The CJEU in *Minister for Justice and Equality v LM*' (2018) 9 *New Journal of European Criminal Law* 353.

the justice system in the issuing Member State and determine whether there is a real risk of a breach of the fair trial rights of the person concerned, also with regard to a potential lack of independence of the courts.[75] Secondly, if the first element of the test is satisfied, the executing judiciary must specifically and precisely assess whether, in the case at hand, there are substantial grounds for believing that the requested suspect will run the real risk of being subject to a breach of the essence of the right to a fair trial.[76]

In the national follow-up to *LM*, the Supreme Court of Ireland, after underlining the difficulty of applying the second prong of the test laid down by the CJEU,[77] held that the threshold of evidence pointing to such a real risk had not been reached.[78] Hence the appeal against his surrender was dismissed.[79] However, as reported by Wahl,[80] more recently, the Higher Regional Court of Karlsruhe set aside an EAW against a Polish national who was to be surrendered to Poland for the purpose of criminal prosecution. The court argued that a fair trial for the requested person was not guaranteed in Poland following recent reforms that had an impact on the disciplinary regime of the judiciary in Poland.[81]

This case underlines the Achilles heel of EU criminal law. Without a clear foundation in the rule of law, the fight against impunity of criminals and 'rule of law' backsliding regimes will persist. It should not be overlooked that neither Hungary nor Poland is part of the EPPO.[82] In accordance with the interpretation of the CJEU,[83] mutual trust may only be suspended by the Council, but what does that mean for cooperation between the EPPO and Member States subject to Article 7(1) TEU procedures?[84]

V. Recommendations on how the Fight against Impunity May be Further Embedded in the EU Criminal Policy Cycle

EU policy preparation and evaluation is guided by the concept of better regulation. Its origins can be traced back to debates on deregulation, including the

[75] Case C-216/18 PPU (ibid) para 61.
[76] ibid para 68.
[77] Supreme Court of Ireland of 12 November 2019, *Minister for Justice & Equality* v *Celmer* [2019] IESC 80, paras 81-83.
[78] ibid paras 84–87.
[79] ibid; *Minister for Justice & Equality* v *Celmer* [2019] IESC 80, para 88.
[80] T Wahl, 'Fair Trial Concerns: German Court Suspends Execution of Polish EAW' (*Eucrim*, 2 April 2020) https://eucrim.eu/news/fair-trial-concerns-german-court-suspends-execution-polish-eaw/.
[81] Higher Regional Court of Karlsruhe, decision of 17 February 2020, https://oberlandesgericht-karlsruhe.justiz-bw.de/pb/,Lde/6096769/.
[82] Council Regulation (EU) 2017/1939 (n 63).
[83] Case C-216/18 PPU (n 74) paras 71, 72.
[84] Council Regulation (EU) 2017/1939 (n 63) Art 105.

deregulatory effect of European economic integration and the extent to which re-regulation was needed at the EC and later the EU level. Better lawmaking furthermore serves as a response to objections to EU integration as such and as a means to enhance trust in the EU. Moreover, better regulation is meant to ensure that the EU achieves its objectives in the most effective, efficient and coherent manner through relevant measures. In this way, the EU can show its added value, which is one of the main elements of the subsidiarity principle.

The Commission has developed a very sophisticated set of better regulation guidelines and toolboxes, which force its officials to go through a sequence of logical steps before arriving at the conclusion that a certain problem needs to be tackled at the EU level and ensuring that relevant impacts of the various policy options are fully taken into account. Better regulation guidelines also detail a number of evaluation criteria that allow officials to check whether an EU intervention has added value. This exercise should also provide useful background information for any future initiatives in line with the notion of a policy and legislative cycle. Since the entry into force of the Lisbon Treaty, the European Parliament has developed its own capacity in the area of impact assessment and evaluation, mirroring that of the Commission but applied to its own rights to request the Commission to propose EU legislation and to propose amendments to Commission proposals.

Better regulation is certainly relevant for the area of EU criminal law, as it is equally guided by the principle of mutual recognition. The proper application of better regulation criteria should also enhance trust and legitimacy of EU action in an area closely related to national sovereignty and fundamental rights. In particular, it could refocus the Union on the core project of 'delivering' an area of freedom, security and justice, currently under threat by various crises, ranging from compliance with EU values to managing migration and providing public security. In reality, as discussed in section III, proper impact assessments have been few and far between in this domain, and there have not been any evaluations that have met the better regulation criteria. Before the entry into force of the Lisbon Treaty, this could be blamed on the dominance of the Member States in this policy area. However, even since then, the Commission has taken the escape routes that are still available (urgency, etc) in order for it not to conduct an impact assessment, including on major and sensitive pieces of legislation concerning the fight against terrorism.[85] This urgency/emergency/crisis argument is quite compelling in this volatile area, which has been completely redirected, since the 'refugee crisis', which was actually a governance crisis, towards migration related crimes (smuggling, travelling for terrorist purposes, etc). The situation is not helped by the artificial way in which the case for EU action is still constructed, notably that a crime is serious and perpetrators might cross borders, thereby escaping justice, and that EU citizens will feel safer crossing borders if criminality is addressed in a similar matter among Member States. Rather than basing itself on such artificial

[85] eg COM (2015) 625 final (n 43) 12.

arguments, an effective EU criminal policy should rather develop a comprehensive approach towards reducing the prevalence of serious criminality in society. In other words: the fight against *whose* impunity should be prioritised at the EU level and which tools are available within and beyond the EU criminal law toolkit to win it. In this context, one might critically assess the priority setting in the EU policy cycle for organised and serious international crime, based on threat assessments developed by Europol.[86] It is submitted that further involving the European Parliament and national parliaments in establishing priorities in the context of an EU criminal policy cycle[87] might result in strengthening the fight against impunity of those seeking to undermine the rule of law and the related organised crime and corruption.

Taking this perspective also sheds a different light on the establishment of the EPPO. Of course, one might hope its establishment will lead to a decrease in EU fraud and an increase in the recovery of assets. But one can also not escape the 'elephant in the room', which is that it is also there to enhance the rule of law, including effective law enforcement action against those who might otherwise escape justice because they are too powerful for national prosecutors to tackle on their own. This example underlines the relationship between the development of EU criminal law, including the EPPO, and the mantra of mutual recognition based on mutual trust, with the need to monitor and enforce democracy, the rule of law and fundamental rights in the Member States. The EPPO can enhance prosecutions, but it cannot ensure judicial independence. The fight against impunity cannot be won without addressing the impunity of those undermining the rule of law.

[86] Explained on the Europol website, www.europol.europa.eu/empact.
[87] van Ballegooij (n 40) 10.

PART B

The Fight against Impunity and the Allocation of Criminal Jurisdiction in the EU

5

EU Substantive Criminal Law and Jurisdiction Clauses: Claiming Jurisdiction to Fight Impunity?

MARTIN BÖSE

I. Introduction

In a globalised world, cross-border crimes confront national criminal justice systems with a number of challenges. Increasing mobility and the almost limitless possibilities of modern communication technology stand in sharp contrast to the territorial boundaries of state sovereignty and the limited capacity of the states to effectively enforce their criminal law. In order to prevent criminals from seeking refuge in countries with lower criminal law standards and thereby escaping from justice, building a network of jurisdictions has been an appealing idea: by extending their jurisdiction to crimes committed abroad, states may be able to produce a dense web of overlapping national jurisdictions that do not allow any criminal to slip through.[1] This reasoning is the underlying rationale of the principle of universal jurisdiction.[2] But there are also doubts whether networking jurisdiction would be able to sustain the fight against impunity of cross-border crime as it may give rise to conflicts of jurisdiction and subject individuals to parallel or subsequent prosecution and legal uncertainty about the criminal law to be applied.[3]

[1] M Böse and F Meyer, 'Introduction' in M Böse, F Meyer and A Schneider (eds), *Conflicts of Jurisdiction in Criminal Matters in the European Union – Volume I: National Reports and Comparative Analysis* (Baden-Baden, Nomos, 2013) 7, 9.

[2] C Ryngaert, *Jurisdiction in International Law* (Oxford, Oxford University Press, 2008) 107.

[3] P Caeiro, 'Jurisdiction in Criminal Matters in the EU: Negative and Positive Conflicts, and Beyond' [2010] *Kritische Vierteljahresschrift für Gesetzgebung und Rechtswissenschaft* 366, 374; O Lagodny, 'Empfiehlt es sich, eine europäische Gerichtskompetenz für Strafgewaltskonflikte vorzusehen?', expert opinion prepared for the German Federal Ministry of Justice (March 2001) www.uni-salzburg.at/fileadmin/oracle_file_imports/460066.PDF (15 June 2020) 101ff; J Vogel, 'Internationales und europäisches ne bis in idem' in A Hoyer, HE Müller, M Pawlik and J Wolter (eds), *Festschrift für Friedrich-Christian Schroeder zum 70. Geburtstag* (Heidelberg, CF Müller, 2006) 877, 891–92.

In the European Union, these concerns have been fostered by legislative measures on the harmonisation of criminal law providing for extraterritorial jurisdiction and new cooperation instruments (such as the European Arrest Warrant) facilitating transnational criminal law enforcement. On the other hand, the European Union is based upon a normative framework that allows – and calls for – measures to avoid and resolve conflicts of jurisdiction (Article 82(1)b) TFEU) and to protect the fundamental rights of EU citizens as the transnational dimension of the *ne bis in idem* principle illustrates (Article 54 the Convention Implementing the Schengen Agreement, Article 50 of the Charter of Fundamental Rights of the European Union (EU-CFR)).

This chapter analyses and evaluates the jurisdiction clauses in EU legislation on substantive criminal law. First, some preliminary clarifications are made about the term 'jurisdiction' (section II).[4] Then, an overview of the jurisdictional rules that have originated from international treaties or have emerged from autonomous EU legislation is presented (section III). This is followed by a discussion on the legitimacy of the clauses providing for extraterritorial jurisdiction and the presentation of alternative solutions to avoid impunity of perpetrators (section IV). Section V concludes.

II. Concepts of Jurisdiction

In international law, the term 'jurisdiction' encompasses three types of jurisdiction that widely correspond to the division of states' sovereign powers between the legislature, judiciary and executive: jurisdiction to prescribe, to adjudicate and to enforce. A definition of these terms that can be considered as a common basis is given in the American Law Institute's *Third Restatement of Foreign Relations Law of the United States.*[5] According to this definition, jurisdiction to prescribe means that a state makes its criminal law applicable to the activity of a person, ie it makes a certain conduct a criminal offence under its national law.[6] A state's jurisdiction to adjudicate is defined as the power to subject persons or things to the process of its courts[7] – in the current context, to establish a domestic forum for a criminal trial. In criminal proceedings, this is closely linked to jurisdiction to enforce, which explicitly covers the state's power to punish noncompliance with its law or regulations.[8]

[4] See M Böse, 'Choice of Forum and Jurisdiction' in M Luchtman (ed), *Choice of Forum in Cooperation Against EU Financial Crime* (The Hague, Eleven, 2013) 73ff; M Böse, F Meyer and A Schneider, *Conflicts of Jurisdiction in Criminal Matters in the European Union – Volume II: Rights, Principles and Model Rules* (Baden-Baden, Nomos, 2014) 21ff.

[5] American Law Institute (ed), *Restatement (Third) of the Law – The Foreign Relations of the United States*, vol 1 (§§ 1–488) (St Paul, MN, American Law Institute Publishers, 1987), § 401; see also European Committee on Crime Problems, *Extraterritorial Criminal Jurisdiction* (Strasbourg, European Committee on Crime Problems, 1990) 18.

[6] ibid § 401(a).

[7] ibid § 401(b).

[8] ibid § 401(c).

Another distinction is drawn between primary and derivative jurisdiction. Primary jurisdiction has its origin in the state's interest in maintaining its legal order and ensuring adequate protection of its own legal interests. This is the case when a state claims jurisdiction to prescribe by making a conduct a criminal offence under its national law.[9] As a consequence, the state has to provide for a domestic forum and establish jurisdiction of its law enforcement authorities and courts to enforce its criminal law. There is thus a functional link between the jurisdiction to prescribe and the jurisdiction to enforce: if a state has a vital interest in extending the scope of its national law, this implies an interest in its enforcement as well.[10]

By contrast, a state exercising derivative jurisdiction refers not to its own interest in maintaining its legal order, but to the correspondent interest of a foreign state which claims primary jurisdiction but is unable to exercise its jurisdiction to enforce.[11] In this situation, derivative jurisdiction helps to ensure that the offender will not escape from justice.[12] The state that exercises the jurisdiction of another state represents this state and derives its *ius puniendi* from that state. Thus, the jurisdictional basis is the so-called principle of representation, or vicarious jurisdiction.

III. Jurisdiction Clauses Originating from International Crime Control Treaties

To a large extent, Framework Decisions and Directives harmonising criminal law have emerged from international crime control treaties. As a consequence, the jurisdictional rules in these harmonising measures originate from international treaty law. This applies all the more as the Union has acceded to several of these treaties and thus entered into an obligation to implement them into EU law.[13]

[9] F Jeßberger, *Der transnationale Geltungsbereich des deutschen Strafrechts* (Tübingen, Mohr Siebeck, 2011) 11; T Vander Beken, G Vermeulen, S Steverlynck and S Thomaes, *Finding the Best Place for Prosecution* (Antwerp, Maklu, 2002) 59.

[10] M Böse, 'Vor §§ 3 ff' in U Kindhäuser, U Neumann and HU Paeffgen (eds), *Nomos-Kommentar zum Strafgesetzbuch*, 5th edn (Baden-Baden, Nomos, 2017) no 8; see also A Eser, 'Kritische Würdigung der Modellentwürfe' in A Sinn (ed), *Jurisdiktionskonflikte bei grenzüberschreitender Kriminalität – Conflicts of Jurisdiction in Cross-Border Crime Situations* (Osnabrück, V&R unipress, 2012) 557, 562. In the draft model B proposed by Sinn, the choice of the forum determines the applicable law: ibid 611–12; in this regard, see the critical remarks of Eser (ibid) 562.

[11] F Jeßberger (n 9) 11–12; R Linke, 'Zwischenstaatliche Kompetenzkonflikte auf dem Gebiet des Strafrechts' in D Oehler and PG Pötz (eds), *Aktuelle Probleme des Internationalen Strafrechts – Heinrich Grützner zum 65. Geburtstag* (Hamburg, R v Decker's, 1970) 85, 90; Vander Beken et al (n 9) 15, who distinguish two variants of derivative jurisdiction (substitution and adoption of proceedings).

[12] To that extent, the forum state will have an (indirect) interest in exercising derivative jurisdiction. Like with international cooperation in criminal matters, solidarity with the state having primary jurisdiction is also based on the principle *do ut des*, ie, the benefits expected from future cooperation with the state that has been assisted in criminal law enforcement.

[13] UN Convention against Illicit Traffic in Narcotic Drugs and Psychotropic Substances (20 December 1988) 1582 UNTS 95; UN Convention against Transnational Organized Crime of (15 November 2000) 2225 UNTS 209 (UNTOC); Council of Europe, Convention on the Prevention

Not surprisingly, international treaties and EU harmonising measures provide for territorial jurisdiction and rules further elaborating on the territorial link or establishing jurisdiction over domestic ships and aeroplanes (flag principle). Admittedly, these rules determine the scope of criminal jurisdiction; the concept of building a network of jurisdiction to fight impunity mainly relies on extraterritorial jurisdiction. Therefore, the following overview will be confined to the various forms of extraterritorial jurisdiction.

The idea of extending jurisdiction to crimes committed abroad has been built upon the common interest of states in effectively combating serious transnational and/or international crimes. This common interest is reflected in various international treaties and customary international law defining the elements of crime and conferring an obligation upon states to penalise the corresponding conduct under national law.[14] In EU law, the legislative measures are based upon the competence to adopt minimum rules on the definition of criminal offences and sanctions in the areas of particularly serious crime with a cross-border dimension (Article 83(1) TFEU).

A. The Principle *aut dedere aut iudicare* (Vicarious Jurisdiction)

For an effective prosecution of international crimes, the harmonisation of national criminal law is not sufficient, as the perpetrator might still escape from justice by seeking refuge in another country that has no jurisdiction over the crime and refuses to surrender the suspect. There are two options to bring the perpetrator to justice: establishing extraterritorial jurisdiction or granting extradition. The functional link between these alternative options was first elaborated in the late Middle Ages, and was then further developed to the principle *aut dedere aut iudicare*.[15] This principle was not only implemented in early extradition treaties of the nineteenth century, but also in several treaties on international crimes.[16]

of Terrorism (16 May 2005) CETS 196; Council of Europe, Convention on Laundering, Search, Seizure and Confiscation of the Proceeds from Crime and on the Financing of Terrorism (16 May 2005) CETS 198. For the impact of international crime control treaties on EU legislation on the approximation of criminal law, see E Fahey, 'Joining the Dots: External Norms, AFSJ Directives and the EU's Role in the Global Legal Order' (2016) 41 *EL Rev* 105, 112–13, 116–18; V Mitsilegas, 'The European Union and the Implementation of International Norms in Criminal Matters' in M Cremona, J Monar and S Poli (eds), *The External Dimension of the European Union's Area of Freedom, Security and Justice* (Frankfurt am Main, Peter Lang, 2011) 239, 251–56.

[14] For universal jurisdiction, see Ryngaert (n 2); for the European Union and extraterritorial jurisdiction, see AS Massa, 'Jurisdiction in England and Wales and in the Netherlands: A Comparative Appraisal with a European Touch' in A Klip (ed), *Substantive Criminal Law of the European Union* (Antwerpen, Apeldoorn, Maklu, 2011) 103, 118–19.

[15] See the detailed analysis of C Maierhöfer, *Aut dedere – aut iudicare* (Berlin, Duncker & Humblot, 2006) 54ff, with further references.

[16] ibid 98ff, 131ff.

The idea that the common interest in fighting international crimes requires supplementary provisions on cooperation and jurisdiction in order to prevent the perpetrator from escaping justice was taken up for the first time in the International Convention on the Suppression of Counterfeiting Currency of 1929.[17] Because extradition and prosecution were understood to be equivalent alternatives, the obligation to adjudicate was subject to the same conditions as extradition (extradition request, lack of obstacles to extradition).[18] The link to extradition requirements reveals that this concept of *aut dedere aut iudicare* is closely connected to the general regime of international cooperation in criminal matters. Accordingly, the option *iudicare* is limited to jurisdiction to adjudicate; it does not cover jurisdiction to prescribe: the adjudicating state is acting on behalf of the state requesting extradition and, thus, exercises derivative jurisdiction.[19] This understanding of the principle of *aut dedere aut iudicare* is still prevalent in international treaties such as (with regard to the refusal to extradite own nationals) the Convention on Cybercrime of 2001[20] and the UN Conventions against Illicit Traffic in Narcotic Drugs and Psychotropic Substances of 1988 and against Transnational Organized Crime of 2000.[21]

In EU criminal law, the Framework Decision against Counterfeiting of the euro directly referred to the jurisdiction clauses of the international convention of 1929.[22] However, this Framework Decision has now been replaced by a Directive providing for extraterritorial jurisdiction on the basis of the active personality principle and a revised model of *aut dedere aut iudicare* that is no longer linked to an extradition request (see section III.B below).[23] Unlike the Cybercrime Convention, the Directive on Attacks against Information Systems does not refer at all to the principle *aut dedere aut iudicare*.[24] In contrast, the Framework Decisions on Illicit

[17] International Convention on the Suppression of Counterfeiting Currency (20 April 1929) 112 LNTS 371.

[18] Art 8, para 2 and Art 9, para 2 of the Convention (ibid).

[19] Böse (n 4) 73, 77.

[20] Art 22, para 3 of the Convention on Cybercrime (23 November 2001) ETS 185; see also the treaties listed by Maierhöfer (n 15) 337–38.

[21] Art 4, para 2, lit a, no ii and Art 6, para 9, lit a of the UN Convention against Illicit Traffic in Narcotic Drugs and Psychotropic Substances (n 13); Art 15, para 3 and Art 16, para 10 UNTOC (n 13); UN Commentary on the UN Convention against Illicit Traffic in Narcotic Drugs and Psychotropic Substances (1988) 4.32 (pp 112–13), 6.40 (p 169): vicarious administration of justice. With regard to the UNTOC, see N Boister, *Transnational Criminal Law* (Oxford, Oxford University Press, 2012) 147.

[22] Art 7, para 1 of Council Framework Decision 2000/383/JHA of 29 May 2000 on increasing protection by criminal penalties and other sanctions against counterfeiting in connection with the introduction of the euro [2000] OJ L140/1.

[23] Art 8, para 2, lit a of Directive 2014/62/EU of the European Parliament and of the Council of 15 May 2014 on the protection of the euro and other currencies against counterfeiting by criminal law, and replacing Council Framework Decision 2000/383/JHA [2014] OJ L151/1.

[24] Art 12 of Directive 2013/40/EU of the European Parliament and of the Council of 12 August 2013 on attacks against information systems and replacing Council Framework Decision 2005/222/JHA [2013] OJ L218/8.

Drug Trafficking and on the Fight against Organised Crime correspond to the international treaty provisions.[25]

B. The Principle *aut dedere aut iudicare* (Universal Jurisdiction)

The next generation of international treaties followed a more ambitious approach and did not subject the principle *aut dedere aut iudicare* to the extradition regime. In the aftermath of the Second World War, the Geneva Conventions[26] prepared the ground for this new understanding in order to fight the impunity of war crimes,[27] and the Convention for the Suppression of Unlawful Seizure of Aircraft of 1970[28] established this new concept as a blueprint for a number of international crime control treaties.[29] According to the latter Convention, each contracting state shall establish its jurisdiction over the offence if the offender is present on its territory and is not extradited to another state. So, the obligation to adjudicate does not depend upon a request for extradition and even applies when no state that has primary jurisdiction is willing to prosecute.[30] Similar provisions have been incorporated into the UN Conventions for the Suppression of Terrorist Bombings and of the Financing of Terrorism.[31]

In EU legislation, this model has been implemented in the Directive on Counterfeiting Currencies,[32] whereas the Directive on Combating Terrorism requires the refusal of an extradition request and thereby adheres to the former model of *aut dedere aut iudicare* (vicarious jurisdiction, section III.A above).[33]

[25] Art 8, para 3 of Council Framework Decision 2004/757/JHA of 25 October 2004 laying down minimum provisions on the constituent elements of criminal acts and penalties in the field of illicit drug trafficking [2004] OJ L335/8; for the requirement of an extradition request, see the corresponding proposal by the Commission, 'Proposal for a Council Framework Decision laying down minimum provisions on the constituent elements of criminal acts and penalties in the field of illicit drug trafficking' COM (2001) 259 final, 11; Art 8, para 3 of Council Framework Decision 2008/841/JHA of 24 October 2008 on the fight against organised crime [2008] OJ L300/42.

[26] Geneva Conventions of 12 August 1949 for the Amelioration of the Condition of the Wounded and Sick in Armed Forces in the Field (I), for the Amelioration of the Condition of the Wounded and Sick and Shipwrecked Members of Armed Forces at Sea (II), relative to the Treatment of Prisoners of War (III) and relative to the Protection of Civilian Persons in Time of War (IV).

[27] Art 49(2) of Geneva Convention I; Art 50(2) of Geneva Convention II; Art 129(2) of Geneva Convention III; Art 146(2) of Geneva Convention IV; in this regard, see Maierhöfer (n 15) 161–62.

[28] Art 4, para 2 of the Convention for the Suppression of Unlawful Seizure of Aircraft (16 December 1970) 860 UNTS 105.

[29] Maierhöfer (n 15) 137–38, 338ff.

[30] For a detailed analysis, see Maierhöfer (n 15) 338ff.

[31] Art 6, para 4 and Art 8, para 1 of the UN Convention for the Suppression of Terrorist Bombings (15 December 1997) 2149 UNTS 256; Art 7, para 2 and Art 10, para 1 of the International Convention for the Suppression of the Financing of Terrorism (9 December 1999) 2178 UNTS 197.

[32] Art 8, para 2, lit a Directive 2014/62 (n 23).

[33] Art 17, para 4 of Directive 2017/541/EU of the European Parliament and of the Council of 15 March 2017 on combating terrorism and replacing Council Framework Decision 2002/475/JHA and amending Council Decision 2005/671/JHA [2017] OJ L88/6.

According to the new understanding of the principle *aut dedere aut iudicare*, the adjudicating state does not act on behalf of the state where the crime has been committed, but in the common interest of the international community that there shall be no safe haven for criminals.[34] As a consequence, the obligation to adjudicate does not even require that the crime is a punishable act at the place where it was committed. The criminal sentence is instead based upon international law and its implementation in the adjudicating state.[35]

This concept changes the character and scope of the obligation to establish jurisdiction over the relevant international crime: a state defining the criminal offence and the punishment to be applied does not only exercise jurisdiction to adjudicate, but jurisdiction to prescribe. According to the principle *nullum crimen, nulla poena sine lege* (Article 7 of the European Convention on Human Rights, Article 49 EU-CFR), the offender must be able to foresee that his conduct will be punishable under the law of the adjudicating state.[36] Since the obligation to adjudicate is only subject to conditions to be met after the crime has been committed (presence of the suspect, no extradition), each contracting state must establish its jurisdiction over the relevant international crime beforehand, irrespective of the place where the crime is committed.[37] In short, the second generation of treaties implementing the principle *aut dedere aut iudicare* implies an obligation to establish universal jurisdiction to prescribe.

C. Extraterritorial Jurisdiction Based upon a Genuine Link

The statement that international crimes are subject to universal jurisdiction is, however, subject to the requirement that there is a corresponding international consensus, ie an international obligation that a certain conduct shall be subject to criminal punishment.[38] The scope of extraterritorial jurisdiction must not extend to states that are not bound by this obligation because they have not ratified the treaty and a corresponding obligation under customary law does not exist yet. Ergo, recourse to universal jurisdiction will violate the territorial sovereignty of that state.[39]

In that case, however, extraterritorial jurisdiction may be established on the basis of a genuine link established under international law (eg active personality).

[34] Maierhöfer (n 15) 345, 347.
[35] Böse (n 1) 41, 119.
[36] Böse (n 1) 41, 119–20.
[37] With regard to the similar problem of naturalised citizens and the problem of retroactive application of the active personality principle, see Böse (n 4) 73, 83–84.
[38] Thereby, the requirement of the principle *nullum crimen sine lege* is met as the relevant conduct constitutes 'a criminal offence under … international law' (Art 7 ECHR); see *Kononov v Latvia* App no 36376/04 (ECtHR, 17 May 2010) paras 205ff.
[39] KF Gärditz, *Weltrechtspflege* (Berlin, Duncker & Humblot, 2006) 153–54; F Jeßberger (n 9) 187–88, 279–80.

This approach is reflected in the most recent generation of international crime control treaties. These treaties still refer to the principle *aut dedere aut iudicare*, but tighten the net of jurisdictions by calling upon the contracting states to extend extraterritorial jurisdiction over the corresponding crime even further. For instance, the UN Conventions against Illicit Traffic in Narcotic Drugs and Psychotropic Substances (1988) and against Transnational Organized Crime (2000) provide a basis for the optional establishment of extraterritorial jurisdiction over crimes committed by nationals and habitual residents (active personality and active domicile principle).[40] In the UN Convention for the Suppression of Terrorist Bombings of 1997, extraterritorial jurisdiction on the basis of the active personality principle is mandatory, whereas recourse to the passive personality principle, to the protective principle and to the active domicile principle is optional.[41] The Council of Europe Convention on the Protection of Children against Sexual Exploitation and Sexual Abuse (Lanzarote Convention) even provides for mandatory jurisdiction on the basis of the active personality and the active domicile principle, which must not be made subject to the double criminality requirement (unrestricted active personality principle).[42] The drafters of the Lanzarote Convention wanted to ensure that serious forms of sexual exploitation (the phenomenon of sex tourism in particular) are prosecuted regardless of whether or not the relevant conduct is a criminal offence under the law of the state in which the crime is committed.[43]

In this regard, EU legislation widely corresponds to international treaty law. According to the Framework Decisions on Illicit Drug Trafficking and on the Fight against Organised Crime, extraterritorial jurisdiction over own nationals is merely an option,[44] whereas the Directive on Combating Terrorism obliges the Member States to establish extraterritorial jurisdiction on the basis of the active personality and domicile principle and the protective principle.[45] Mandatory extraterritorial jurisdiction on the basis of (unrestricted) active personality has been incorporated into the EU Directive on Sexual Exploitation of Children on the basis of the very same reasoning as the Lanzarote Convention.[46]

[40] Art 4, para 1, lit b, no i of the UN Convention against Illicit Traffic in Narcotic Drugs and Psychotropic Substances (n 13); Art 15, para 2, lit b UNTOC (n 13).

[41] Art 6, para 1, lit c and para 2, lit c of the UN Convention for the Suppression of Terrorist Bombings (n 31); see also Art 15, para 2, lit a UNTOC (n 13).

[42] Art 25, para 1, lit d and para 4 of the Council of Europe Convention on the Protection of Children against Sexual Exploitation and Sexual Abuse (26 October 2007) ETS 201.

[43] Explanatory report to the Convention (n 42) para 171 https://rm.coe.int/CoERMPublicCommonSearchServices/DisplayDCTMContent?documentId=09000016800d3832 (15 June 2020).

[44] Art 8, para 1, lit b and para 2 Framework Decision 2004/757/JHA; Art 7, para 1, lit b Framework Decision 2008/841/JHA.

[45] Art 19, para 1, litt c and e Directive 2017/541/EU (n 33).

[46] Art 17, para 1, lit b and para 4 of Directive 2011/93/EU of the European Parliament and of the Council of 13 December 2011 on combating the sexual abuse and sexual exploitation of children and child pornography, and replacing Council Framework Decision 2004/68/JHA [2011] OJ L335/1.

Although the EU legislator has not consistently transposed the jurisdictional rules under international treaty law into EU criminal law, it is quite obvious that EU legislation on jurisdiction in criminal matters is to a considerable extent shaped by international crime control treaties.[47] This influence notwithstanding, the scope of traditional jurisdictional rules has been extended and further developed significantly by EU criminal law.

This holds particularly true for the prominent role of the active personality principle in more recent legislation, providing for mandatory extraterritorial jurisdiction even if there is no corresponding obligation under international law.[48] In addition, several harmonising measures have extended the scope of the active personality principle to residents (active domicile principle), either on a mandatory[49] or an optional[50] basis.

Furthermore, EU criminal law has refined the active personality principle with regard to legal persons. Several autonomous jurisdictional clauses extend the Member States' jurisdiction to crimes committed for the benefit of a legal person established in their territory.[51] Since the benefit for the legal person is one of the key elements to establishing corporate criminal liability,[52] the reasoning of these provisions is to establish extraterritorial jurisdiction over crimes committed by domestic corporations by recourse to the active personality principle.[53]

D. Autonomous Jurisdictional Clauses in EU Criminal Law

The overview of jurisdiction clauses in EU criminal law is completed by a final look at jurisdictional clauses in harmonising measures on criminal law enforcement of the Union's policies (Article 83(2) TFEU). This applies in particular to the Directive on the Protection of the Environment through Criminal Law,[54]

[47] For the impact of international crime control treaties on EU legislation, see generally Fahey (n 13) and Mitsilegas (n 13).

[48] Art 8, para 1, lit b Directive 2014/62/EU (n 23); with regard to unrestricted active personality, see also Art 10, para 1, lit b and para 3, lit a of Directive 2011/36/EU of the European Parliament and of the Council of 5 April 2011 on preventing and combating trafficking in human beings and protecting its victims, and replacing Council Framework Decision 2002/629/JHA [2011] OJ L101/1.

[49] Art 19, para 1, lit c Directive 2017/541/EU (n 33).

[50] Art 12, para 3, lit a Directive 2013/40/EU (n 24); Art 10, para 2, lit a of Directive 2018/1673/EU of the European Parliament and of the Council of 23 October 2018 on combating money laundering by criminal law [2018] OJ L284/22.

[51] Art 7, para 1, lit c Framework Decision 2008/841/JHA (n 25); Art 19, para 1, lit d Directive 2017/541/EU (n 33).

[52] See Art 5, para 1 Framework Decision 2008/841/JHA (n 25); Art 17, para 1 Directive 2017/541/EU (n 33).

[53] C Kreß and N Gazeas, '§ 19 Terrorismus' in U Sieber, H Satzger and B von Heintschel-Heinegg (eds), *Europäisches Strafrecht*, 2nd edn (Baden-Baden, Nomos, 2014) para 53.

[54] Directive 2008/99/EC of the European Parliament and of the Council of 19 November 2008 on the protection of the environment through criminal law [2008] OJ L328/28.

the Directive on Ship-Source Pollution,[55] the Directive against Employment of Illegally Staying Third-Country Nationals,[56] the Directive on Market Abuse[57] and the Directive on the Fight against Fraud to the Union's Financial Interests.[58] As these measures are not based on an international treaty, the rules on jurisdiction may be called autonomous jurisdictional clauses in EU criminal law.

In part, these autonomous clauses still rely on traditional jurisdictional links that have been incorporated into other EU legislative measures and corresponding international treaties. This holds particularly true for the active personality principle, which serves as a mandatory basis for extraterritorial jurisdiction even if there is no corresponding international crime control treaty at all.[59] Another jurisdictional basis linked to active personality refers to the personal status of the offender as an official of the Union or one of its Member States; this optional basis of extraterritorial jurisdiction can be found in the Directive on the Fight against Fraud to the Union's Financial Interests.[60]

On the other hand, the Directive on the Protection of the Environment through Criminal Law, the Directive on Ship-Source Pollution and the Directive against Employment of Illegally Staying Third-Country Nationals do not entail any jurisdictional clause at all and thereby clearly do not require Member States to establish extraterritorial jurisdiction.[61] This restrictive approach may be based upon the reasoning that criminal jurisdiction is accessory to the territorial scope of the EU legislation to be enforced through criminal law; if the latter does not apply outside the Union, the corresponding criminal law does not, either.

IV. Critical Assessment

Even though the majority of jurisdictional clauses in EU criminal law originate from international crime control treaties, a coherent approach of the EU legislator on the implementation of international treaties into EU law and on the scope and content of autonomous clauses on jurisdiction is still lacking. Notwithstanding

[55] Directive 2009/123/EG of the European Parliament and of the Council of 21 October 2009 amending Directive 2005/35/EC on ship-source pollution and on the introduction of penalties for infringements [2009] OJ L280/52.

[56] Directive 2009/52/EC of the European Parliament and of the Council of 18 June 2009 providing for minimum standards on sanctions and measures against employers of illegally staying third-country nationals [2009] OJ L168/24.

[57] Directive 2014/57/EU of the European Parliament and of the Council of 16 April 2014 on criminal sanctions for market abuse [2014] OJ L173/17 (Market Abuse Directive).

[58] Directive 2017/1371/EU of the European Parliament and of the Council of 5 July 2017 on the fight against fraud to the Union's financial interests by means of criminal law [2017] OJ L198/29.

[59] Art 8, para 1, lit b Directive 2014/62/EU (n 23); Art 11, para 1, lit b Directive 2017/1371/EU (n 58).

[60] Art 11, para 2 and para 3, lit c Directive 2017/1371/EU (n 58).

[61] See, however, Art 8 of Council Framework Decision 2003/80/JHA of 27 January 2003 on the protection of the environment through criminal law [2003] OJ L29/55, providing for mandatory jurisdiction on the basis of the territoriality and the flag principle.

the general objective to avoid impunity of the offender, it is still an open question whether and to what extent EU criminal law should confer an obligation upon Member States to establish extraterritorial jurisdiction over harmonised offences. As the need for extraterritorial jurisdiction may depend upon whether the crime has been committed within or outside the Union, the following analysis shall distinguish these two scenarios.

A. Extraterritorial Jurisdiction over Crimes Committed within the Union

Where a crime has been committed on the territory of a Member State (ie within the Union), EU legislation on the harmonisation of criminal law obliges that Member State to establish and exercise territorial jurisdiction and to bring the perpetrator to justice. Since all legislative measures on the harmonisation of substantive criminal law provide for territorial jurisdiction, there will be at least one Member State that is in charge of prosecution and adjudication, and, due to the obligations under EU law, there will be no safe havens for criminals in the Union. A risk of impunity may only arise where the competent Member State – the Member State where the crime has been committed – is either unable or unwilling to prosecute the offender.

Both situations are supposed to be quite exceptional. The competent Member State may be unable to prosecute a criminal who has fled to another Member State where that Member State does not execute a European Arrest Warrant issued for the purpose of prosecution because one of the explicit grounds for refusal applies or because, due to the conditions for his detention in the issuing Member State, the person to be surrendered would be exposed to a real risk of inhuman or degrading treatment (Article 4 EU-CFR).[62] In such a case, the Framework Decision on the European Arrest Warrant does not oblige the executing Member State to prosecute its own nationals and residents.[63] Nevertheless, recourse to the active personality principle is not necessary to avoid impunity, but recourse to vicarious jurisdiction will provide a sufficient basis for extraterritorial jurisdiction. Such a solution corresponds to existing EU legislation on the request-based concept of *aut dedere aut iudicare* (eg the Framework Decision on Organised Crime). There is no need to establish primary jurisdiction in order to enforce harmonised criminal law.

This model will not, however, be sufficient to avoid impunity where the competent state is unwilling to prosecute and, as a consequence, is unwilling to issue a request for extradition (a European Arrest Warrant) or a prosecution request.

[62] Joined Cases C-404/15 and C-659/15 PPU *Aranyosi and Căldăraru* (CJEU, Grand Chamber, 5 April 2016) para 104.

[63] However, for European Arrest Warrants issued for the purpose of the execution of a criminal sentence, see Art 4(6) of Council Framework Decision 2002/584/JHA of 13 June 2002 on the European arrest warrant and the surrender procedures between Member States [2002] OJ L190/1.

In these cases, there may be a need for extraterritorial jurisdiction. Instead of territorial jurisdiction of the Member State, one might even draw upon the concept of European territoriality that does not refer to a single Member State's territory, but to the territory of the Union,[64] ie the common area of freedom, security and justice (Article 3(2) TEU, Article 67 TFEU).[65] In EU criminal law, such a concept has been developed in the *Corpus Juris* on the protection of the Union's financial interests.[66] According to the principle of European territoriality, the territories of the Member States constitute a single legal area for the investigation, prosecution, trial and enforcement of sentences.[67] As a consequence, each Member State will have jurisdiction over any 'European' offence (*Europa-Delikt*) that has been committed within the Union.[68] This approach, however, is inextricably linked to a set of fully harmonised and directly applicable criminal law provisions on fraud, market rigging, misappropriation of funds etc and the corresponding penalties.[69] In contrast, the existing Framework Decisions and Directives do not provide for a uniform criminal law, but establish a minimum standard that leaves a margin of discretion to the Member States on how to define the elements of crime and the applicable sanctions. In particular, it is up to the Member States to decide on whether or not to go beyond this standard, and, to the extent that EU law allows for a margin of discretion (eg in the area of child pornography), the national legislator is still free not to criminalise a certain conduct.[70] The European territoriality principle would, however, undermine the choice for a restrictive criminal policy because it would enable any Member State to prosecute a conduct irrespective of whether it constituted a criminal offence under the law of the Member State where the conduct took place.[71]

[64] See Case C-34/09 *Ruiz Zambrano* (CJEU, Grand Chamber, 8 March 2011) para 44 ('territory of the Union'); Case C-87/12 *Ymeraga* (CJEU, 8 May 2013) para 36 ('territory of the European Union').

[65] For the concept of Union territory, see L Azoulai, 'Transfiguring European Citizenship: From Member State Territory to Union Territory' in D Kochenov (ed), *EU Citizenship and Federalism. The Role of Rights* (Cambridge, Cambridge University Press, 2017) 178ff; for the relationship between EU citizenship and the area of freedom, security and justice (and its territorial scope), see H van Eijken and TP Matguery, 'The Federal Entrenchment of Citizens in the European Union Member States' Criminal Laws: Or How EU Citizenship Is Shaping Criminal Law' in Kochenov (ibid) 561, 566–67, 580–81.

[66] M Delmas-Marty (ed), *Corpus Juris: Introducing Penal Provisions for the Purpose of the Financial Interests of the European Union* (Economica, Paris, 1997); M Delmas-Marty and JAE Vervaele (eds), *The Implementation of the Corpus Juris in the Member States*, vol 1 (Intersentia, Antwerp, 2000) 189ff.

[67] Delmas-Marty and Vervaele (n 66) 188, referring to Art 18, para 1 of the *Corpus Juris* (n 66).

[68] J Vogel, 'Gesetzlichkeitsprinzip, territoriale Geltung und Gerichtsbarkeit' in K Tiedemann (ed), *Wirtschaftsstrafrecht in der Europäischen Union – Freiburg Symposium* (Köln, Heymanns, 2002) 91, 96, 99, 454.

[69] Delmas-Marty and Vervaele (n 66) 189ff; with regard to other European offences, see also Tiedemann (ibid) 453ff.

[70] On offences related to child pornography where the person appearing to be a child was in fact 18 years of age or older at the time of depiction or where it is established that the material is produced and possessed solely for private use, see, eg Art 5, paras 7 and 8 Directive 2011/93/EU (n 46).

[71] For criticism on extraterritorial jurisdiction under EU law, see Caeiro (n 3) 378–79. For similar reasons, the case law on EU citizenship and Union territory (n 64) has not yet replaced the concept of Member State territory. For a detailed analysis, see Azoulai (n 65) 178ff.

Furthermore, even where the conduct is a criminal offence according to the minimum standards of EU criminal law, it should be borne in mind that a decision not to prosecute a criminal offence is not per se illegitimate, but may – even where EU law establishes an obligation to criminalise and punish the corresponding conduct – result from a legitimate exercise of prosecutorial discretion. Establishing primary extraterritorial jurisdiction of other Member States would not only enable them to prosecute and punish the offender where the primarily competent Member State failed to comply with its obligations under EU law, but also to override the legitimate decision of the competent authority of that Member State not to prosecute the suspect. For instance, it is not a matter for German or French law enforcement authorities to investigate and prosecute drug offences committed by the owner of a 'coffeeshop' in the Netherlands if the requirements for non-prosecution under Dutch law were met.[72]

In sum, extraterritorial jurisdiction – and the principle of European territoriality in particular – favours a punitive criminal law approach and tends to eliminate or at least undermine the Member States' leeway not to punish a certain conduct. In other words, the EU rules on jurisdiction should not focus on the risk of 'under-punishment' only, but also consider the risk of 'over-punishment'. Furthermore, it should be taken into account that EU law provides for mechanisms to enforce the implementation of EU criminal law, namely infringement proceedings before the Court of Justice (Article 258 TFEU). Where a Member State does not properly implement EU criminal law in its domestic legislation and court practice, and thereby runs the risk that criminal offences as defined by EU law go unpunished, the Commission may bring the matter before the Court of Justice, arguing that the Member State has failed to comply with its obligation to effectively enforce EU law (Article 4(3) TEU).[73] This option will be particularly relevant for a lack of enforcement resulting from systemic deficiencies in national criminal justice systems and the Member States' obligation to effectively protect the Union's financial interests (Article 325 TFEU).[74] Where such a systemic risk cannot be established, the European Public Prosecutor's Office may initiate criminal investigations into crimes affecting the Union's financial interests (Article 86 TFEU).[75] In the latter case, the EU legislator expressly acknowledged the priority of territorial jurisdiction of the Member State where the crime has been committed (Article 26(4) EPPO-Regulation). Thus, there is apparently no pressing need to establish extraterritorial jurisdiction over crimes committed in another Member State.

[72] With regard to the exercise of universal jurisdiction, see Böse (n 4) 101–02 and references therein.

[73] In this regard, see Case C-68/88 *Commission v Greece* (CJEU, 21 September 1989) paras 23ff; Case C-265/95 *Commission v France* (CJEU, 9 December 1997) paras 32ff.

[74] Case C-105/14 *Taricco* (CJEU, 8 September 2015) para 47; Case C-42/17 *MAS and MB* (CJEU, 5 December 2017) para 35; Case C-612/15 *Kolev* (CJEU, 5 June 2018) paras 63, 76.

[75] Art 26 of Council Regulation 2017/1939/EU of 12 October 2017 implementing enhanced cooperation on the establishment of the European Public Prosecutor's Office ('the EPPO') [2017] OJ L283/1.

The restrictive approach is mirrored in the autonomous jurisdictional clauses that are not based upon international treaties. The Market Abuse Directive obliges Member States to establish extraterritorial jurisdiction over crimes committed by their own nationals, but subject to the condition that the crime is an offence where it was committed (double criminality requirement).[76] Admittedly, jurisdiction is not linked to an extradition request, but the reference to the *lex loci delicti commissi* takes up a key element of vicarious jurisdiction. The focus on territorial jurisdiction finds further support in the Directives that do not even provide for a jurisdictional clause, so do not require a Member State to establish extraterritorial jurisdiction over crimes committed in another Member State (section III.D above).

B. Extraterritorial Jurisdiction over Crimes Committed outside the Union

Where a crime has not been committed on the territory of a Member State, any rule establishing extraterritorial jurisdiction must not violate the territorial sovereignty of the third state where the crime has been committed. In this regard, EU legislation on the harmonisation of criminal law is subject to the same requirements (genuine link) as international crime control treaties or national criminal law. Such a genuine link can be based upon the bond of loyalty between a state and its citizens (active and passive personality) or the sovereign state's right to defend its national interests against attacks from abroad (protective principle).[77] The question is whether and to what extent the EU legislator can or should rely upon these traditional jurisdictional rules that refer to the bond between the state and its nationals on the one hand and the state's sovereign right to protect its security, financial and economic interests on the other. As far as Member States have transferred their sovereign powers to the Union, the Union may have a legitimate interest in the protection of its own interests and its citizens, too.

As a consequence, the EU legislator may rely on the protective principle in order to protect its own interests against crimes committed in third countries. This applies to the protection of the common currency of the Economic and Monetary Union (Art 3 TEU) (the euro) and the Union's financial interests. In this regard, the existing legislation is based upon a rather cautious approach: whereas the Framework Decision of 2000 required the Member States of the eurozone to establish jurisdiction over counterfeiting offences related to the euro irrespective of the nationality of the offender and the place where the crime was committed,[78] extraterritorial jurisdiction under the Directive on the Protection of the euro against

[76] Art 10, para 1, lit b Directive 2014/57/EU (n 57).

[77] For a detailed analysis, see F Jeßberger (n 9) 191ff, 239ff, 252ff and references therein.

[78] Art 7, para 2 Framework Decision 2000/383/JHA (n 22).

Counterfeiting by Criminal Law adheres to the principle *aut dedere aut iudicare* and/or requires a territorial link (presence of the perpetrator or detection of counterfeit euros).[79] Notwithstanding these restrictions, extraterritorial jurisdiction does not require an extradition request, nor is it subject to the double criminality requirement. Accordingly, it entails an obligation to establish primary jurisdiction. Likewise, the Directive on Combating Terrorism obliges each Member State to establish jurisdiction over offences against EU institutions or agencies based on its territory.[80] In both Directives, the requirement of a territorial link shall avoid conflicts of competences and establish jurisdiction of the Member State that appears to be best placed for prosecution.

As far as the protection of the Union's financial interests is concerned, the corresponding Directive does not provide for mandatory extraterritorial jurisdiction based upon the protective principle.[81] Instead, it relies on the active personality principle and calls upon Member States to establish (optional) extraterritorial jurisdiction over crimes committed by Union officials and by its own officials.[82] Whereas the loyalty of Union officials may qualify as an interest of the Union triggering the protective principle, crimes committed by a Member State's nationals and/or officials are not specifically linked to such interests. Apparently, the EU legislator does not consider the Union's financial interests a sufficient link to justify the exercise of extraterritorial jurisdiction under the protective principle.

Instead of the protective principle, the active personality and domicile principle and, to some extent, the passive personality principle are the main bases for the extraterritorial scope of EU criminal law.[83] The question, however, is still whether the underlying rationale of these principles provides a legitimate basis for extraterritorial jurisdiction.

The principle of active personality is based upon the citizen's duty to respect his home country's law even when abroad.[84] But why should a state insist on obedience with regard to conduct outside its territory? A general duty of citizens to abide by the law of their home country seems to rely on the anachronistic concept of absolute and unconditional obedience to the sovereign,[85] but does not provide a valid argument for such a general obligation.[86] On the contrary, if a

[79] Art 8, para 2 Directive 2014/62/EU (n 23).

[80] Art 19, para 1, lit e Directive 2017/541/EU (n 33).

[81] However, with regard to the active personality principle, see Art 11, para 1, lit b Directive 2017/1371/EU (n 58).

[82] Art 11, para 2 and para 3, lit c Directive 2017/1371/EU (n 58).

[83] From the perspective of the Union, the principle of active and passive personality should not rely on nationality (principle of non-discrimination, Art 18 TFEU), but upon the perpetrator's (or the victim's) status as an EU citizen or permanent resident.

[84] C Blakesley, 'Extraterritorial Jurisdiction' in C Bassiouni (ed), *International Criminal Law – Vol. II: Procedural and Enforcement Mechanisms*, 2nd edn (New York, Transnational Publishers, 1999) 33, 61–62; for the origins of the active personality principle, see D Oehler, *Internationales Strafrecht*, 2nd edn (Köln, Heymanns, 1983) 49ff.

[85] See the criticism raised by Oehler (n 84) 142–43 and 445.

[86] For a more detailed analysis, see Böse (n 1) 41, 91ff.

certain conduct is not prohibited in another country, it is up to the EU legislator to provide reasons why a conduct that is perfectly legal at the place where it occurred should be punishable according to EU law, respectively the law of the Member States. In a case on the mutual recognition of driving licences, the Court of Justice explicitly stated that an EU citizen may exercise his right to free movement for the purpose of benefiting from legislation less stringent than the law of his home country.[87]

The passive personality principle raises even more serious concerns: the state's responsibility for protecting its own nationals is undoubtedly a legitimate objective. The question, however, is whether extraterritorial jurisdiction on the basis of the passive personality principle is an appropriate means to that end.[88] As the perpetrator often does not care about the victim's nationality, a dissuasive effect will be a pure fiction. This argument is mirrored in the concern that the offender is confronted with a criminal law that is not at all foreseeable to him because he is not aware of the facts that determine the applicable criminal law. Finally, there is no need for additional protection by the criminal law of the victim's home country because the criminal law of the state where the crime is committed usually provides for adequate protection of potential victims.

Nevertheless, there may be cases where offences committed abroad could seriously undermine the criminal law provision at stake: if potential offenders can easily escape from criminal punishment by moving abroad, this impunity could lead to an erosion of trust in the validity of criminal law because its enforcement would depend upon the offender's wealth and cleverness.[89] This rationale, however, only applies to permanent residents, not to nationals living abroad. Furthermore, a circumvention of criminal law protecting individuals usually requires a victim to be protected by domestic law. In such cases, extraterritorial jurisdiction should be based upon a combination of the active domicile and the passive domicile principle. The Directives on Human Trafficking and Sexual Abuse and Exploitation of Children seem to follow such a reasoning because they entail an obligation to establish extraterritorial jurisdiction irrespective of whether the conduct is a criminal offence at the place where it was committed.[90] Nevertheless, they rely on the sole ground of active personality and thereby go beyond what is necessary to provide effective protection of EU citizens and other EU residents.

This critical assessment stands in sharp contrast not only to existing EU legislation, but also to international crime control treaties that provide for mandatory extraterritorial jurisdiction on the basis of the active personality principle. The aim of these jurisdictional clauses is to stretch the ambit of criminalisation and to prepare the ground for universal jurisdiction. EU legislation, however, should

[87] Case C-467/10 *Criminal proceedings against Akyüz* (CJEU, 1 March 2012) para 76.

[88] For a more detailed analysis, see Böse (n 1) 41, 87ff.

[89] Böse (n 1) 41, 94ff.

[90] Art 10, para 1, lit b and para 3, lit a Directive 2011/36/EU (n 48); Art 17, para 1, lit b and para 4 Directive 2011/93/EU (n 46).

not rely on this auxiliary function of active personality (and similar jurisdictional rules) because it aims at harmonisation of substantive criminal law of its Member States. Unlike the United Nations or other international organisations, the Union does not provide for an institutional framework for establishing universal crimes on a treaty basis, and thus should not rely on jurisdictional bases to that end. As far as the Union has acceded to international crime control treaties, the treaty provisions on jurisdiction must be incorporated into EU law, but the Union should not go beyond the scope of these provisions. Accordingly, autonomous jurisdictional clauses should rely on EU law and/or EU interests only.

The concerns about the active and passive personality principle may provoke the question whether these criteria are wholly irrelevant for establishing jurisdiction. The answer is yes – and no. The objections to extraterritorial jurisdiction based upon active and passive personality are related to primary jurisdiction: extraterritorial jurisdiction to prescribe should be established by the nationality of the offender (or the victim) in exceptional cases only (circumvention of domestic criminal law). By contrast, reference to the active and passive personality principles does not meet similar objections as far as these principles serve as a basis for the establishment of a domestic forum (jurisdiction to adjudicate).[91] Obviously, there is a legitimate interest of the victim to actively participate in the criminal proceedings and, thus, to have the trial be held in his home country. Correspondingly, a legitimate interest of the suspect to be tried in his home country cannot be denied, either.[92] This understanding corresponds to the fact that the principle of active personality is closely linked to the ban on extradition of nationals: a state that does not extradite its own national must establish extraterritorial jurisdiction in order to ensure that the offender will not escape from justice. In this case, however, prosecution can be based upon vicarious jurisdiction; recourse to the active or passive personality principle is not necessary.[93] As far as a domestic forum shall enable the offender and/or the victim to exercise his or her procedural rights effectively, one might even say that the determination of the forum should be based upon residence rather than nationality as pure reliance on the latter would be in breach of the principle of non-discrimination (Article 18 TFEU).[94]

As the treaty provisions on the principle *aut dedere aut iudicare* (section III.A above) have illustrated, vicarious jurisdiction is an alternative to extradition and forms part of international cooperation in criminal matters. However, its potential scope is not limited to transnational crimes; rather, vicarious jurisdiction may provide a general and autonomous basis for extraterritorial jurisdiction that can be exercised in the interests of the defendant, the victim or the good administration

[91] Böse (n 4) 73, 82, 83.

[92] In this regard, see Art (1)b of the European Convention on the Transfer of Criminal Proceedings; see also Art 8 of the Model Rules proposed by Böse et al (n 4) 381, 411ff.

[93] Böse (n 4) 73, 83–84.

[94] For a detailed discussion, see Böse (n 4) 45ff, 69ff; see also Case C-182/15 *Proceedings relating to the extradition of Petruhhin* (CJEU, 6 September 2016) paras 30ff; M Böse, 'Mutual Recognition, Extradition to Third Countries and Union Citizenship: *Petruhhin*' (2017) *CML Rev* 1781, 1788ff.

of justice. A corresponding treaty instrument is the European Convention on the Transfer of Proceedings in Criminal Matters of 15 May 1972.[95] The scope of the Convention is not limited to serious cross-border crime, but applies to any offence. In EU law, a corresponding instrument could be established under the treaty basis on cross-border cooperation in criminal matters (Article 82 TFEU).[96] The adoption of such a cooperation instrument would supplement jurisdiction clauses in harmonising measures and render extraterritorial jurisdiction over crimes committed within the Union superfluous.

V. Conclusion

Jurisdictional clauses in EU criminal law mainly originate from international crime control treaties, but these treaties have not been incorporated into EU legislation on the harmonisation of serious cross-border crime (Article 83(1) TFEU) in a consistent and coherent manner. In combination with the jurisdictional rules in harmonising measures aiming at the enforcement of the Union's policy (Article 83(2) TFEU), a patchwork of traditional bases for establishing and exercising extraterritorial jurisdiction has emerged.

It cannot be denied that the EU legislator must comply with its obligations under international law and implement binding treaty provisions on jurisdiction in criminal matters. As far as international treaties leave a margin of discretion or do not cover the relevant offence, it is upon the EU legislator to decide on whether and to what extent extraterritorial jurisdiction is necessary and appropriate to ensure that the perpetrator will not escape from justice. In its assessment, the legislator must balance the interest in effective transnational law enforcement with the fundamental rights of the defendant because extraterritorial jurisdiction may give rise to conflicts of jurisdiction that expose the potential offender to the risk of multiple prosecution and to legal uncertainty about the applicable law.

These divergent interests can be reconciled by addressing them on different levels, namely jurisdiction to prescribe and jurisdiction to adjudicate and to enforce: as a rule, jurisdiction to prescribe should be limited to territorial jurisdiction. As a matter of principle, there is no need for extraterritorial jurisdiction over crimes committed within the Union (section IV.A above). If an international treaty provides for subsidiary universal jurisdiction (*aut dedere aut iudicare*, section III.B above), the provision shall be incorporated into EU law. As far as the crime is committed against the Union (eg the euro as the common currency of the Economic and Monetary Union), extraterritorial jurisdiction should be based on the protective principle rather than universal jurisdiction (sections III.A and

[95] European Convention on the transfer of proceedings in criminal matters (15 May 1972) ETS 73.

[96] See the Draft Council Framework Decision on the transfer of proceedings in criminal matters (30 June 2009), Council Document 11119/09 and Council Document 16437/1/09 (26 November 2009).

IV.B above). In contrast, extraterritorial jurisdiction on the basis of the active and passive domicile principle should be established in exceptional cases only (sections III.C and IV.B above).

On the other hand, extraterritorial jurisdiction to adjudicate and to enforce is less problematic insofar as it is based upon the principle of vicarious jurisdiction and forms part of the general framework of mutual legal assistance in criminal matters. In this context, recourse to the principles of active and passive domicile principle appears legitimate and may provide guidance for the choice of the forum. Article 82(1) lit b TFEU provides for a treaty basis to adopt a legal framework for the transfer of criminal proceedings within the Union; such a cooperation instrument could replace most provisions on extraterritorial jurisdiction in EU criminal law.[97]

It follows from the foregoing that the scope of extraterritorial jurisdiction to prescribe under EU criminal law should be reconsidered. Wherever a crime committed abroad is subject to domestic criminal law, this will not only expose the offender to legal uncertainty about the applicable law, but may also affect the preventive function of criminal law (*positive Generalprävention*, section IV.B above). The EU legislator should bear in mind that the establishment of extraterritorial jurisdiction has only symbolic value if it cannot be exercised in practice because the state where the crime has been committed is not willing to cooperate.

[97] See the Model Rules proposed by Böse et al (n 4) 439ff.

6

Between Impunity and the Protection of Fundamental Rights: The Case Law of the CJEU and the ECtHR on the *ne bis in idem* Principle

BAS VAN BOCKEL

I. Introduction

A. Impunity and Fundamental Rights Protection: False Positives and False Negatives

The principle of *ne bis in idem*[1] is a fundamental right which guarantees that a defendant will not be prosecuted more than once on the basis of the same offence, act or facts. The principle is a 'rational principle of civic order'[2] that minimises the arbitrary element in legal norms and decisions. The principle touches on the 'very essence of the right to a fair trial'.[3] The burdens of double prosecution for the individual 'include the duplicated costs of legal representation, coercive measures to the person and property, and psychological burdens associated with the extended procedures and the absence of finality'.[4] The principle forms a fundamental

[1] For more background on the *ne bis in idem* principle, see, amongst (many) others: A Weyembergh, 'La jurisprudence de la CJ relative au principe *ne bis in idem*: une contribution essentielle à la reconnaissance mutuelle en matière pénale' in A Rosas, E Levits and y Bot (eds), *The Court of Justice and the Construction of Europe: Analyses and Perspectives on Sixty Years of Case-law – La Cour de Justice et la Construction de l'Europe: Analyses et Perspectives de Soixante Ans de Jurisprudence* (Berlin, Springer, 2013) 539; A Rosanò, '*Ne Bis Interpretatio In Idem*? The Two Faces of the *Ne Bis In Idem* Principle in the Case Law of the European Court of Justice' (2017) 18 *German Law Journal* 39; F Alicino, 'Il ne bis in idem comunitario e la cooperazione giudiziaria tra gli Stati membri dell'Unione europea: due facce di una stessa medaglia' (2005) 6 *Diritto pubblico comparato ed europeo* 1509.

[2] The term was coined by P Selznick, P Nonette, and H Vollmer (eds) *Law, Society and Industrial Justice* (Piscataway, Transaction Publishers, 1980) 11.

[3] *Nikitin v Russia* App no 50178/99 (ECtHR, 20 July 2004) para 57.

[4] M Fletcher, 'The Problem of Multiple Criminal Prosecutions: Building an Effective EU Response' (2007) 26 *Yearbook of European Law* 10 http://eprints.gla.ac.uk/3811/1/Jurisdicition2_and_ne_bis_in_idem.pdf.

requirement under the rule of law, an important guarantee for the proper and fair administration of criminal justice, and a corollary of the finality of judicial decisions.

For the purpose of discussing the relation between a fundamental right like *ne bis in idem* and impunity in this chapter, it is necessary to consider the relationship between impunity and fundamental rights somewhat more generally. Impunity is a particularly broad and multifaceted concept. It has been described, inter alia, as 'the exemption from accountability, penalty, punishment, or legal sanction for perpetrators of illegal acts'.[5] Impunity is not absolute, but exists by degrees in social (and legal) reality. A certain degree of impunity is in fact acceptable and even necessary for some of the reasons discussed below, whereas a higher degree of impunity (eg for more severe categories of crimes) sooner or later becomes unacceptable. A reason why a degree of impunity is acceptable or necessary is that legal systems and societies as a whole could become overburdened if no single illegal act ever went unpunished. Trial and punishment come at a cost, not only to society, but also to the perpetrator, both immediately as well as in the longer run. Statistics, for example, indicate that in the Netherlands many younger perpetrators who escape prosecution for crimes they committed go on to lead societally productive lives.[6] Impunity can also result directly from the legal process itself, with its inbuilt procedural requirements and fundamental guarantees. These procedural requirements and guarantees, however, serve a fundamental and overriding purpose in democratic societies under the rule of law. Such impunity may therefore be justified under certain circumstances in order for constitutional rights and principles to prevail over the interest of the enforcement of ordinary laws. If, for example, the decisive evidence relating to a particular crime was obtained by the authorities in an illegal manner during the investigative phase, the consequence can (and should) be that the evidence in question is rendered inadmissible, even if this means that a defendant who would otherwise have been convicted ultimately escapes further prosecution or punishment. Acquittals on various 'technical', procedural grounds often intuitively offend our sense of justice, but they are – to an extent – the price that must be paid in the wider interests of justice. The question is therefore what degree of impunity is deemed acceptable in the interests of the protection of fundamental rights. The possible answers to this question clearly go beyond mere legal analysis, and involve public opinion and political deliberation.

[5] MM Penrose, 'Impunity, inertia, Inaction, and Invalidity: A Literature Review' (1999) 17 *Boston University International Law Journal* 269. This chapter necessarily departs on a practical, ordinary language meaning of the notion of 'impunity', as any more fundamental approach necessarily entails a socio-legal analysis of the concept that goes well beyond the scope of this study. See also C Di Francesco Maesa, 'The Fight against Impunity between EU and National Legal Orders: What Role for the EPPO?', ch 8 in this book.

[6] This is inferred by experts from, amongst other factors, the 'peak' in crime suspects around age 18: https://www.cbs.nl/nl-nl/achtergrond/2016/47/criminaliteit.

Ne bis in idem is certainly one procedural rule which has often been accused of 'merely working to the advantage of criminals', and it has often been attacked (especially in popular media) for that reason. In particular, the common law equivalent of *ne bis in idem*, the double jeopardy rule in the USA and in common law countries, has in the past attracted a great deal of criticism.[7] This has led to legislative initiatives in various parts of the Anglo-Saxon world seeking changes to the law to allow for a retrial in some cases, in particular where new and previously undiscovered evidence comes to light after an acquittal or mistrial for the same historical facts.

Every fundamental procedural requirement that works to the advantage of defendants likely entails some risk of impunity. 'Getting off on a technicality' is, and should be, a real possibility. Without this possibility, every procedural misstep, no matter how serious from a fundamental rights perspective, would remain free from legal consequence. Under those circumstances, there would be no 'fair trial'. It is safe to assume that more stringent procedural requirements can generally lead to more situations in which a defendant is under-punished, acquitted or not tried at all on procedural grounds entirely connected to the manner in which the investigation or prosecution was conducted. Conversely, less stringent procedural requirements may lead to situations where defendants' rights are inadequately protected, and where errors on the parts of enforcers, prosecutors and judges go uncorrected or fail to benefit defendants. It is also accepted wisdom that laxer procedural standards increase the risk of wrongful convictions and other miscarriages of justice.

For analytical purposes, the problem can simply be framed as one of 'false positives' v 'false negatives' (false positives being situations in which a defendant is 'wrongfully' tried and/or punished due to lax or flexible procedural or evidentiary standards, and false negatives being situations in which a defendant is 'wrongfully' acquitted or not tried at all due to stringent technical-legal requirements). Needless to say, where the line should be drawn is subject to debate, and the possible answers depend on one's perspective, political persuasion and other factors. The age-old adage in English criminal law known as *Blackstone's ratio* is that 'it is better that ten guilty persons escape than that one innocent suffer'.[8] Public opinion pulls in the opposite direction, and often for understandable reasons.

[7] There are countless examples, ranging from the OJ Simpson case in the USA to the high-profile Deidre Kennedy case in Australia from 1973 (which continues to shock that nation, and resulted in 'Deidre's Law' being passed in Queensland in 2014, amending the double jeopardy rule). Other examples include the Stephen Lawrence and 'babes in the woods' cases in the UK.

[8] As stated in William Blackstone's seminal work *Commentaries on the Laws of England* (first published around 1760). Blackstone's 'ratio' or 'rule' became a maxim that was absorbed by the UK's legal system by the early 19th century.

B. Justification of the Approach Taken

Following Blackstone's ratio, the standard approach would be to assess the weaknesses that are in the present doctrinal make-up of the *ne bis in idem* principle as it emerges from the case law of European courts, and to address those weaknesses.[9] However, in keeping with the overall aim of the book, this chapter proposes to do the opposite: to examine the kinds of situations in which the application of the *ne bis in idem* principle should perhaps be nuanced or mitigated in the interests of the enforcement of material justice, and in order to avoid impunity. This approach is based on an important assumption: that the present level of *ne bis in idem* protection from the case law of the European courts is – at least doctrinally – sufficiently strong. This deserves some further explanation, as well as a little additional background on previous jurisprudential developments.

The argument presented here is that both the EU Court of Justice (CJEU) and the European Court of Human Rights (ECtHR) have adopted a broad and protective approach to the interpretation of the element of *idem*, ie what must be understood as 'the same' act or facts, and that this interpretation of the element of *idem* is decisive for protective force afforded by the *ne bis in idem* principle. Because of these jurisprudential developments, the 'European' *ne bis in idem* rule now offers a high level of protection, in keeping with its rationale and its status as a fundamental human right. The case law by the CJEU on Article 54 of the Convention Implementing the Schengen Agreement (CISA) has been seminal in this regard. In *Van Esbroeck*, the CJEU was faced with this question for the first time. In his Opinion, the Advocate General (AG) argued that 'if, instead of the acts alone, account were taken of the offences or of the rights protected by the prohibition of the said acts, the *ne bis in idem* principle would never function at the international level'.[10] Following the Opinion of the AG, the CJEU held that 'the wording of Article 54 of the CISA, "the same acts", shows that that provision refers only to the nature of the acts in dispute and not to their legal classification'.[11] According to the CJEU, it follows from this that 'the possibility of divergent legal classifications of the same acts in two different Contracting States is no obstacle to the application of Article 54 of the CISA'.[12] Furthermore, 'the criterion of the identity of the protected legal interest cannot be applicable since that criterion is likely to vary from one Contracting State to another'. The only relevant criterion for the application of Article 54 CISA is the 'identity of the material acts, understood in the sense of the existence of a set of concrete circumstances which are inextricably linked together in time, in space and by their subject-matter'.[13] The CJEU therefore

[9] This is the approach in B van Bockel, *The* ne bis in idem *Principle in EU Law* (Alphen aan den Rijn, Kluwer Law International, 2010).
[10] Para 47 of the Opinion.
[11] Para 27 of the judgment.
[12] Para 31 of the judgment.
[13] Paras 36–38 of the judgment.

held that, in the context of the specific facts of the case, 'import' and 'export' of illegal substances should in principle be seen as a set of facts which are 'inextricably linked' together in an area without internal borders, such as the EU. Since then, this approach has been confirmed and refined in several decisions.

The approach taken by the CJEU appears to have had a decisive influence on the ECtHR. In its *Zolotukhin* judgment, the Grand Chamber of the ECtHR embraced a similarly broad, objective approach to the interpretation of the element of *idem*, whilst expressly denouncing its own earlier case law on this point.[14] Referencing, amongst other things, the case law of the CJEU on this point, it held that 'Article 4 of Protocol No. 7 ECHR [European Convention on Human Rights] must be understood as prohibiting the prosecution or trial of a second "offence" in so far as it arises from identical *facts or facts* which are substantially the same'.[15] It further held that:

> the use of the word 'offence' in the text of Article 4 of Protocol No. 7 cannot justify adhering to a more restrictive approach. It reiterates that the Convention must be interpreted and applied in a manner which renders its rights practical and effective, not theoretical and illusory … The Court further notes that the approach which emphasises the legal characterisation of the two offences is too restrictive on the rights of the individual, for if the Court limits itself to finding that the person was prosecuted for offences having a different legal classification it risks undermining the guarantee enshrined in Article 4 of Protocol No. 7 rather than rendering it practical and effective as required by the Convention … Accordingly, the Court takes the view that Article 4 of Protocol No. 7 must be understood as prohibiting the prosecution or trial of a second 'offence' in so far as it arises from identical facts or facts which are substantially the same.'[16]

The importance of this approach lies in the fact that the ECtHR has fundamentally rejected any recourse to more formal (and therefore more arbitrary) criteria that tie in with the legal qualification of the act or facts, such as the 'essential elements' of an offence as defined in national criminal law. In adopting this approach, the Grand Chamber also fully brought its case law in line with that of the CJEU on Article 54 CISA. The *Zolotukhin* judgment therefore killed two birds with one stone in terms of strengthening *ne bis in idem* protection in Europe. A more 'objective' approach, based on the historical rather than the legal act or facts, offers stronger protection for the individual and strengthens legal certainty by rendering the *ne bis in idem* principle more predictable in its application. The judgment could therefore be seen as requiring a high degree of objectivity in assessing the underlying facts of the case. The *ne bis in idem* principle has thus been given an adequately protective substance. A valid question could be whether the principle

[14] It considered that 'the existence of a variety of approaches to ascertaining whether the offence for which an applicant has been prosecuted is indeed the same as the one of which he or she was already finally convicted or acquitted engenders legal uncertainty incompatible with a fundamental right': *Sergey Zolotukhin v Russia* App no 1493/03 (ECtHR (GC), 10 February 2009) para 78.

[15] ibid para 82.

[16] *Sergey Zolotukhin v Russia* App no 1493/03 (ECtHR (GC), 10 February 2009) paras 82 and 83.

is not, by now, overly protective under some circumstances, leading to a risk of impunity, and this question is explored in the remainder of this chapter (from three different angles). What is meant by this, coming back to the basic analytical framework presented earlier, is that the risk of false negatives (where a subject is wrongfully exempted from prosecution or punishment) outweighs that of false positives (where the *ne bis in idem* fails to offer adequate protection).

The remainder of this chapter therefore focuses on mitigating the possibility of false negatives. Even though it was justified by arguing here that the *ne bis in idem* principle in EU law now, in principle, offers a sufficiently high level of protection, it is also clear that the principle remains a controversial fundamental right and that its interpretation and application continues to raise some thorny issues. *Ne bis in idem* protection in Europe is by no means undisputed, as evidenced by two recent judgments of the ECtHR, *Rola v Slovenia*[17] and *Mihalache v Romania*, in which the Court showed itself to be very divided on the interpretation of some aspects of the principle.[18] There is no doubt that the question whether *ne bis in idem* protection in the EU is sufficiently strong is, and will likely remain, up for debate. Clearly, good reasons can be presently found to argue that the protection under the *ne bis in idem* principle in Europe should be strengthened further in some respects, and the aim of this chapter is not to refute those reasons (which will be discussed further in section II below).

C. Framing the Question of Impunity and *ne bis in idem*

Three issues readily present themselves when considering whether, at present, the *ne bis in idem* principle can lead to false negatives: the parallel application of criminal and administrative law; the so-called 'enforcement requirement' from Article 54 CISA; and the exception possibility in the case of new and previously undiscovered evidence (*novum*). The issues and arguments involved, however, differ:

1. In the case of the parallel application of criminal and administrative law, the argument that will be made is that the present developments in the case law of the European courts, which have attracted a great deal of criticism, are ultimately necessary and inevitable in order to avoid a degree of impunity that could result randomly from procedural circumstance, such as the order in which administrative and criminal proceedings are conducted.
2. In the case of the enforcement requirement, the argument presented here is that its importance for the prevention of impunity is perhaps underestimated, and that it would be a mistake to abolish it, as has been advocated publicly by the Commission on several occasions.

[17] *Rola v Slovenia* App nos 12096/14 and 39335/16 (EctHR, 4 June 2019).
[18] *Mihalache v Romania* App no 54012/10 (ECtHR (GC), 8 July 2019).

3. In the case of *novum*, the position taken here is that the exception possibility is a vital and integral part of the *ne bis in idem* principle, and therefore reflects the essence of that right.

II. The Parallel Application of Criminal and Administrative Law

A. Background: *A and B v Norway* and the 'Italian Cases' before the CJEU

Recently, there have been several developments in the case law of the European courts on the *ne bis in idem* principle relating to the issue of cumulation of administrative and criminal proceedings. This point has come to the fore in particular because many states allow for simultaneous administrative and penal sanctioning of tax offences. The Strasbourg Court recently handed down a number of judgments in such cases, and at the end of 2016 the Grand Chamber ruled, in its judgment in *A and B v Norway*, that cumulative penalisation under administrative and criminal law will not violate the *ne bis in idem* principle provided the administrative and criminal procedures can be considered as a 'coherent whole'.[19] The Grand Chamber's approach has met with significant criticism, primarily because it is thought that this approach could substantially weaken *ne bis in idem* protection. On 20 March 2018, the CJEU ruled in three Italian cases relating to this same issue,[20] and these are discussed here. The question as to what extent the CJEU indeed models its interpretation on *A and B v Norway* is addressed, and some relevant differences between the protection of *ne bis in idem* under EU law and the ECHR are identified. It has by now become clear that the issues raised by *A and B v Norway* have left the ECtHR itself sharply divided.

The central question in all three of the Italian cases is whether the possibility of punishing certain financial offences (VAT offences, market manipulation and trading with inside information) under Italian law violates the *ne bis in idem* principle. The answer to this question chiefly depends on whether both proceedings

[19] *A and B v Norway* App nos 24130/11 and 29758/11 (ECtHR (GC), 15 November 2016) §§ 121–22. For comments, see G Lo Schiavo, 'The Principle of ne bis in idem and the Application of Criminal Sanctions: Of Scope and Restrictions: CJEU 20 March 2018, Case C-524/15, *Luca Menci*; CJEU 20 March 2018, Case C-537/16, *Garlsson Real Estate SA and Others v Commissione Nazionale per le Società e la Borsa (Consob)* CJEU 20 March 2018, Joined Cases C-596/16 and C-597/16, *Enzo Di Puma v Consob and Consob v Antonio Zecca*' (2018) 14 *European Constitutional Law Review* 644; B van Bockel, 'Annotatie bij ECtHR 15 November 2016, nrs 24130/11 en 29758/11, *A and B t. Noorwegen*' (2017) 1 *European Human Rights Cases*.

[20] Case C-524/15 *Luca Menci* ECLI:EU:C:2018:197; Case C-537/16 *Garlsson Real Estate SA, Stefano Ricucci, Magiste International SA v Commissione Nazionale per le Società e la Borsa (Consob)* ECLI:EU:C:2018:193; Joined Cases C-596/16 and C-597/16, *Enzo di Puma v Antonio Zecca* ECLI:EU:C:2018:192.

and punishments can be classified as 'criminal', and whether they concern the same facts (*idem*). First, as is well known, the classification of what is 'criminal' for the purposes of Article 50 is independent from the classification under domestic law. In the cases at hand, the nature and severity of the administrative penalties imposed led the CJEU to classify them as criminal. Further, none of these cases raised any doubts as to the identity of the facts under consideration. Given that such would result in a limitation of the right not to be tried or punished twice for the same offence under Article 50 of the Charter of Fundamental Rights of the European Union (the Charter), the question is whether such limitation can be justified under Article 52(1) of the Charter. According to the provision, any limitation must have been provided for by law, must respect the essence of the right and must be proportionate in light of objectives of general interest recognised by the Union, or the protection of rights of others. The ECtHR had already ruled that, in order for dual proceedings to comply with *ne bis in idem*, the state would need to show that the two procedures were sufficiently closely connected both in substance and in time, meaning that they must have been complementary and temporally closely connected, and that the overall punishment was proportionate and foreseeable. To assess whether a sufficiently close connection in substance existed, the ECtHR looks at: (i) whether the proceedings pursued complementary purposes, thus addressing, both *in abstracto* and *in concreto*, different aspects of the misconduct; (ii) whether the institution of dual proceedings was foreseeable; (iii) whether duplication in the collection and assessment of evidence was avoided as much as possible, with both proceedings relying on the same establishment of the facts; and, above all (iv) whether the second proceeding in sentencing takes account of the punishment already doled out, thus ensuring the overall proportionality of the penalties imposed.[21]

In the *Garlsson* judgment, the CJEU reiterates that the stipulation from Article 52(3) of the Charter (that the meaning and scope of the Charter rights that are also contained in the ECHR shall be the same) ought to be read as safeguarding the necessary consistency, without, however, affecting the autonomy of EU law and the CJEU.[22] This part of the judgment echoes Opinion 2/13,[23] in which the CJEU rejected the EU's accession to the ECHR. By and large, the approach taken by the CJEU accords with that of the ECtHR, in particular in requiring: (i) that the penal and administrative proceedings and penalties pursue additional objectives; (ii) a legal basis which renders it sufficiently clear and foreseeable that the offences in question may be subject to a duplication of proceedings; (iii) rules on coordination, ensuring that any disadvantages for those affected are limited to what is strictly necessary; and (iv) rules opening up the possibility of ensuring the severity of all penalties imposed is limited to what is strictly necessary in

[21] *A and B v Norway* (n 19), para 132.
[22] *Garlsson et al* (n 20) paras 24–26.
[23] Advisory Opinion 2/13 (CJEU, 18 December 2014) ECLI:EU:C:2014:2454.

relation to the seriousness of the offence – as is also enshrined in Article 49(3) of the Charter. Although this formulation is not identical to that of the ECtHR in *A and B v Norway* (chiefly in that the CJEU does not formulate any requirement of temporal connection between the proceedings), there is substantial overlap. In his Opinion of the case, AG Campos Sanchez-Bordona proposed a different approach. The Opinion argues that Article 50 of the Charter does not:

> permit double punishment by way of a criminal penalty (or proceedings), on the one hand, and by way of a tax penalty (or proceedings), on the other, where it can be said that the latter is genuinely criminal in nature, notwithstanding that it is classified under national law as solely administrative. I repeat that, in those circumstances, 'if the tax penalty is criminal in nature for the purposes of Article 50 of the Charter and has become final … that provision precludes criminal proceedings in respect of the same acts from being brought against the same person'.[24]

The Court, however, chose not to follow the Opinion on this point, which would have allowed for a higher level of protection under the Charter than under the ECHR. It therefore seems that a deliberate choice was made to follow the ECtHR doctrine from *A. and B* instead of maintaining the level of protection from the *Akerberg Fransson* judgment.

B. Analysis

Some comments are in order. The AG is no doubt right in pointing out that the level of protection afforded by the *ne bis in idem* principle is lowered in *A and B* and subsequent judgments. There are also good grounds to argue why such a lowering of the level of protection is neither necessary nor appropriate in the EU context, as the AG convincingly and eloquently does in his Opinion. Finally, the Opinion is also right in pointing out that the road that the ECtHR chose to travel in *A and B* further complicates the interpretation and application of the *ne bis in idem* principle on the European level. In plain terms, it makes for some pretty unsightly and complex case law. At the same time, however, the most basic purpose of the *ne bis in idem* principle is essentially to ensure that a subject is troubled only once by the consequences of his or her actions. It is considered perfectly acceptable as a matter of *ne bis in idem* that multiple charges are brought, or even multiple procedures are initiated simultaneously, in respect of the same historical act or facts. In the event that all of those charges are brought in the context of criminal proceedings, the adequate coordination of those charges or procedures should not pose many problems. The subject in question will be convicted or acquitted in several separate proceedings, ending in a single judgment or set of judgments which would normally be delivered at the same point in time.

[24] Para 109 of the Opinion.

The fact, however, is that many Member States have opted for a system allowing for a combination of criminal law and administrative law measures in respect of a given infringement, each with its own specific purpose. In many legal systems, this combination does *not* allow for the seamless coordination of different procedures, as different sets of procedural rules and different judicial bodies are involved. The doctrine that the ECtHR arrived at in *A and B* essentially accepts that reality as a matter of *ne bis in idem*, whilst laying down rather stringent (and, for some legal systems, perhaps even unrealistically strict) requirements as far as the integration and coordination of criminal and administrative proceedings are concerned, in order to protect the individual and alleviate the burden of multiple criminal and administrative proceedings posed upon that individual as far as possible. At least from the viewpoint of the ECtHR, such a pragmatic solution seems acceptable, and still accords with the spirit and fundamental purpose of the *ne bis in idem* principle. All the while, it must be admitted that it is little more than a '*solution de depannage*', and that it significantly complicates the interpretation and application of the *ne bis in idem* principle. It is, however, not easy to see how the ECtHR could have arrived at any other, more satisfactory or elegant solution to this particular issue. Whether the same could be said from the viewpoint of the CJEU may be up for debate, as the AG points out, but it should also be pointed out that the existence of two separate lines of European case law on this particular point may also have complicated matters. In the present situation, at least a high level of convergence is maintained between the case law of the two European courts. This, in itself, is already quite helpful for the national judiciary, which is faced with the significant task of interpreting and applying all this in everyday judicial practice.

The test the CJEU formulates for duplication of proceedings plays out slightly differently in each of the three cases. In *Garlsson et al*, the companies in question had already been finally criminally convicted and punished, raising the question whether they could subsequently be penalised under administrative law. The CJEU held that this would exceed what is strictly necessary, at least where the criminal conviction was such as to punish the offence in an effective, proportionate and dissuasive manner – which was left for the referring court to determine.[25] *Menci* concerned a criminal prosecution after the imposition of a final administrative fine, and in this case the CJEU did not take issue under Article 50 of the Charter. It would therefore appear that a criminal prosecution is permitted if it follows an administrative one without violating the *ne bis in idem* principle, but not the other way around. That finding would seem to tie in with the rationale for dual punishment in many Member States. In *Di Puma*, what was at issue was again an administrative fine after a criminal prosecution, but this time the accused had been finally acquitted rather than convicted. Here the CJEU is more pronounced, and finds that this sequence of events clearly exceeds what is necessary, and that

[25] *Garlsson et al* (n 20) para 59.

Article 50 of the Charter precludes such.[26] The only reference to the ECHR in this case relates to the ultimate option of reopening a finally decided criminal case in extraordinary circumstances, under Article 4(2) Protocol 7.[27] These different outcomes may go some way to explaining why it is only in *Menci* that the CJEU explicitates that, although it is in no way bound by, and that its interpretation does not conflict with or fall below the threshold of protection under, the ECHR.

In order to clarify, it is useful to consider the judgment and the facts of the case in more detail. In the case of *Menci*, the Italian tax authorities imposed a €85,000 fine on Mr Menci for failure to pay VAT. After the time at which that fining decision became final, Mr Menci was prosecuted before a criminal court. The Italian court referred a question for a preliminary ruling to the CJEU, asking whether Article 50 of the Charter, read in light of Article 4 of Protocol 7 ECHR, stands in the way of bringing criminal proceedings for failure to pay VAT after a time at which an administrative penalty has (finally) been imposed in respect of the same facts.

In its judgment, the CJEU first of all notes that EU law requires that Member States take all legislative and administrative measures appropriate to ensure collection of VAT and to prevent fraud.[28] Furthermore, pursuant to Article 325 TFEU, they must counter any illegal activities which affect the financial interests of the Union through effective deterrent measures. In principle, the Member States are at liberty to choose the exact measures and penalties. Criminal penalties are, however, 'essential' in serious cases of VAT evasion, bringing the case within the scope of EU law. The CJEU holds that, in spite of the referring court's references to the ECHR, the answer to the referred question must be given in the light of the *ne bis in idem* principle as enshrined in Article 50 of the Charter. Under that provision, the Court rules that the administrative fine should be considered to be of a 'criminal' nature in the sense of the Charter, in light of its severity and punitive purpose. At the same time, however, it leaves the final assessment in this regard with the referring court. Moreover, both the fine and the criminal proceedings concern Menci's failure to pay VAT, meaning they pertain to a set of concrete circumstances which were inextricably linked together, thus constituting identical material facts within the purview of Article 50 of the Charter. This means that Italian law allows for a duplication of proceedings constituting a limitation of the *ne bis in idem* principle, leading the CJEU to assess whether this limitation can be justified under Article 52(1) of the Charter.

The CJEU furthermore holds that the legitimate aim of collecting VAT is of sufficient gravity to potentially justify cumulating administrative and criminal law responses. This requires the proceedings and penalties to pursue complementary

[26] Joined Cases C-596/16 and C-597/16, *Enzo Di Puma v Consob and Consob v Antonio Zecca* paras 44–45.

[27] ibid para 35.

[28] Art. 2 and 273 of Council Directive 2006/112/EC of 28 November 2006 on the common system of value added tax [2006] OJ L347/1.

aims relating to different aspects of the same unlawful conduct, a matter which is further left for the referring court to determine. The Court also holds that the Member States may in principle punish any VAT offence by administrative penalties, whilst imposing criminal penalties for serious violations. Such duplication of proceedings: (i) must at all times remain proportionate; (ii) may not exceed what is appropriate and necessary; and (iii) must form the least onerous means to achieve the aim. The legislation in question must be clear and precise, so as to guarantee predictability where there is a duplication of proceedings. For the Italian legislation, this appears to be so. Further, the legislation must ensure that the disadvantages suffered by those affected are limited to what is strictly necessary, meaning that there must be rules for the coordination of proceedings. Rules must also ensure that the severity of cumulative punishments does not become disproportionate. Italian law complies with these requirements, and it is for the national judiciary to apply this in a manner that avoids any disproportionate disadvantages for the accused. Finally, the CJEU considers that it must take account of Article 4 of Protocol 7 ECHR in its interpretation of Article 50. It finds that its interpretation in this case does not conflict with the ECtHR's approach to cumulating administrative and criminal proceedings in tax offence cases, as that court also allows cumulation where the proceedings are sufficiently closely connected in substance and time.[29] It is worth pointing out that it is only in the *Menci* judgment that the CJEU expressly finds that a duplication of proceedings is, in principle, allowed. In finding that its interpretation does not fall below the protection granted under the ECHR, the CJEU does, however, overlook the ECtHR's criterion of a *temporal* connection between the two sets of proceedings – the lack of which can in and of itself give rise to a violation of Article 4 of Protocol 7 ECHR.

There are a number of differences between EU and ECHR law which may influence the approach taken by the courts. Article 4 of Protocol 7 ECHR is clearly limited to duplication of proceedings within one state, whereas Article 50 of the Charter also operates transnationally within the Union.[30] The EU has created an area of freedom, security and justice,[31] removing internal borders, which implies that citizens ought also to be protected against duplication in criminal proceedings. In fact, the rules for taxation in case of transnational trade which are at issue in these cases are precisely where states have often concluded treaties to prevent entrepreneurial activities from attracting double taxation. Taking this into account, it makes perfect sense to also provide protection against double punishment (penalisation) by different Member States, or by the Union and a Member State. But it is also this difference in scope of application which at times makes it less evident to accord identical levels of protection of *ne bis in idem* in both systems. The requirement of foreseeability of double penalisation is, for instance,

[29] *A and B v Norway* (ECtHR, 15 November 2016) CE:ECHR:2016:1115JUD002413011, § 132.

[30] By way of example, see *Krombach v Frankrijk* App no 67521/14 (EHRM, 20 February 2018), ECLI: CE:ECHR:2018:0220DEC006752114.

[31] Art 67 TFEU.

quite different for individuals who are penalised administratively in one state and criminally in another, as compared to individuals who are penalised twice in the same state. Double penalisation may not always prove sufficiently foreseeable in cross-border situations.

It is uncertain whether the criteria as formulated here will even be applied in the same way in cases of duplication of procedures across borders, as it was newly formulated in these Italian cases. Member States will in any case need to be aware of the increased protection the CJEU provides in case of criminal acquittals; for example, it found in *Di Puma* that a subsequent administrative fine was excessive and in breach of *res judicata*. This also means that the various national and European authorities can still hinder each other, because if the prosecutorial authorities of one state are a little bit too cavalier in bringing a prosecution for which they cannot in the end provide the relevant evidence, thus causing the prosecution to end in an acquittal, this will prevent other Member States or the Commission from later imposing an administrative fine. All this may limit the Member States in their action radius, but it also fits neatly within the system of mutual trust as instituted by the Union, and moreover achieves precisely what *ne bis in idem* was meant to: safeguarding individuals from repeated punitive interferences.

Another difference between the protection of *ne bis in idem* in the EU and ECHR systems is found in the system of limitations. Under the Charter, limitations of Article 50 can be justified as long as they meet the requirements set out in Article 52(1). Under the ECHR, there is, in principle, no room for the justification of an interference once a duplication of proceedings falls within the scope of *ne bis in idem*, although Article 4(2) of Protocol 7 provides the possibility for the reopening of a case. This would at first glance indicate a higher level of protection under the ECHR than under the Charter, but, as has been set out in this chapter, the two courts nonetheless come to similar interpretations, allowing for a duplication of proceedings in certain circumstances. This is not to say the protection levels in both systems are now necessarily identical in each possible situation: the ECHR appears to provide a higher level of protection through its requirement of a temporal connection between the two sets of proceedings, whereas the Charter may prove more protective in its attention to the order in which administrative and criminal penalties are imposed.

The ECtHR supervises Member States' conduct in light of the ECHR, which is its main function and purpose. For the CJEU, this is merely one of its functions as an organ of the EU, because the EU has self-standing and extensive legislative and executive competences. In cases such as those at issue here, the Union moreover has a stake in the outcome, as collecting VAT and countering market manipulation safeguards the financial interests of the EU itself. In that respect, EU law even requires states to take effective and deterrent measures to safeguard these interests.[32] In this regard, an international human rights court, although of course

[32] See Case C-42/17 *MAS and MB (Taricco II)* ECLI:EU:C:2017:936.

weighing national interests against individual protection of human rights, has a different perspective, because its primary aim will consistently be the protection of fundamental rights. For the CJEU, this is merely one goal, and it will more readily be required to engage in a balancing exercise because EU law itself imposes duties of effectively penalising certain financial offences. This issue surfaces explicitly in *Di Puma*, as the CJEU was faced with the question whether Member States were under an obligation to impose administrative fines even after a criminal conviction, in order to effectively deter financial offences. Even though this does not necessarily mean the ECtHR and CJEU adopt different interpretations, it is not unlikely that weighing a fundamental right against national interests has a different connotation for a court than weighing a fundamental right against the interests of the EU, of which the court itself forms a part. This might also explain why the CJEU, despite being spurred on to do so by its AG, decides not to provide a higher level of *ne bis in idem* protection than under the ECHR.

III. The Enforcement Requirement from Article 54 CISA: The Case Law of the CJEU on Article 54 CISA

Out of the *ne bis in idem* provisions in force on the European level, only Article 54 CISA requires that if a penalty has been imposed, 'it has been enforced, is actually in the process of being enforced or can no longer be enforced' under the laws of the sentencing contracting party. Article 4 of Protocol 7 ECHR and Article 50 of the Charter do not require that the penalty has been enforced.

The CJEU therefore interprets the enforcement condition very generously, so as to include out-of-court settlements and suspended sentences, in keeping with the principle of mutual recognition between the Member States and Article 54 CISA's aim of promoting free movement. In the seminal *Gözütok & Brügge* judgment,[33] the CJEU held that if the conditions of an out-of-court settlement are met, this will be considered as a 'penalty which has been enforced', for the purposes of Article 54 CISA. In *Kretzinger*,[34] the court was faced (amongst other things) with the question whether a *suspended* custodial sentence must be treated as a penalty which has been enforced or one which is actually in the process of being enforced. The CJEU considered that it would be

> inconsistent, on the one hand, to regard any deprivation of liberty actually suffered as enforcement for the purposes of Article 54 CISA and, on the other hand, to rule out the possibility of suspended sentences, which are normally passed for less serious offences, satisfying the enforcement condition in that Article, thus allowing further prosecutions.

[33] Joined Cases C-187/01 and C-385/01 *Gözütok and Brugge* [2003] ECR I-1345.
[34] Case C-288/05 *Kretzinger* (CJEU, 18 July 2007).

The *Bourquain* judgment by the CJEU provides a clear illustration of why it would be problematic to abolish the enforcement requirement. Mr Bourquain, a German national, served in the French foreign legion in North Africa around 1960. He was stopped by a fellow serviceman (also a German national) during an attempted desertion and shot his comrade dead with a pistol. He subsequently escaped to the German Democratic Republic and was sentenced to death *in absentia* by the French Permanent Military Court 'zone Est Constantinoise' for the murder of a fellow legionnaire. After the German reunification, Mr Bourquain was again prosecuted for the same murder, this time by the German authorities. In the proceedings, Mr Bourquain relied (amongst other things) on his previous French conviction from 1961. The German court contacted the authorities in France, and the public prosecutor of the Tribunal aux armées de Paris confirmed that the criminal conviction had acquired the force of *res iudicata*, and that the sentence could no longer be executed in France for several reasons (including the fact that a general pardon had since been issued by the French Republic for all crimes committed in Algeria). The Landesgericht Regensburg referred several questions to the CJEU for a preliminary ruling. Notwithstanding the fact that the CISA was never in force at all in the Algerian territory where Mr Bourquain was sentenced to death, and was not in force in France at the time that the sentence was passed by a competent authority of that state, the CJEU held that Article 54 CISA applies *ratione temporis* to criminal prceedings such as those at issue in the main proceedings because the CISA had entered into force in both Germany and France by the time the second proceedings were brought against Mr Bourquain. The CJEU held that it was sufficient that the penalty could no longer be enforced – regardless of the fact that it was clear that the penalty probably could never have been executed in the first place as a matter of French law.

Little or nothing is known of the reasons (if any) why Article 4 of Protocol 7 ECHR and Article 50 of the Charter do not require anything on the point of the enforcement of the sentence. It is perhaps surprising, considering that it can be difficult for a state to enforce a penalty against a subject. The last century saw armed conflict and upheaval in many parts of Europe, and there are many examples of circumstances – like in the case of *Bourquain* – under which the surrender or extradition of a subject could not be effectuated, or where foreign states refused to enforce sentences. Under those circumstances, it would be reasonable to allow for a second prosecution if justice was not fully done when the first sentence was handed down but could not be enforced because the subject actively and successfully avoided such. Many instruments, like the European Arrest Warrant, are now in place to make it much less likely that a subject is successful in escaping trial or punishment by crossing a border. The fact remains, however, that impunity is, and always has been, a general problem in criminal law. It is a problem that is certainly mitigated, but probably not removed by EU criminal law instruments so that developments in EU criminal law as such cannot justify the abolition of a fundamental requirement of the *ne bis in idem* rule.

The CJEU has acknowledged this in the judgment in *Zoran Spasic*.[35] The case concerned a Serbian national who, at the time of the preliminary ruling before the CJEU, was being prosecuted in Germany for a fraud committed in Italy against a German national. He had already been convicted for this fraud and sentenced to one year of imprisonment and a fine in Italy. At the time of the German trial, the Italian conviction had become final and executable. However, although the fine had been paid by Mr Spasic, the custodial part of the sentence remained non-executed. Two preliminary questions were submitted by the German judge to the CJEU. First, is the enforcement clause of Article 54 CISA compatible with Article 50 of the Charter? Secondly, is this condition satisfied by the execution of only one part of the sentence, when it is composed of two independent penalties?

In answering the first question, the CJEU qualified the enforcement requirement as a 'limitation' of the right enshrined in Article 50 of the Charter. The Court held that the limitation was indeed proportionate, for several reasons. The first was that the enforcement condition of Article 54 CISA does not call into question the essence of *ne bis in idem* as per Article 50 of the Charter.[36] Secondly, the Court ruled that the condition pursues an objective of general interest within the area of freedom, security and justice, namely the prevention of impunity. Finally, the court held that the enforcement requirement is necessary, given that the instruments of mutual recognition (the European Arrest Warrant and the Framework Decision on the Mutual Recognition of Custodial Sentences for their Cross-Border Enforcement) were not 'equally effective' in preventing impunity.

IV. An Exception to the *ne bis in idem* Rule to Avoid Impunity? The Need for a *novum* Rule

Only Article 4 of Protocol 7 ECHR, in paragraph 2 of that provision, allows for 'the reopening of the case … if there is evidence of new or newly discovered facts, or if there has been a fundamental defect in the previous proceedings'. The *ne bis in idem* rules at the EU level do not provide for any similar exception possibility. Article 55 CISA does allow for certain exceptions to Article 54 CISA, but those exceptions concern situations in which the 'essential interests' of a Member State are at issue, and are therefore of a fundamentally different nature than those contained in Article 4 of Protocol 7 ECHR.

For this reason, there is no CJEU case law to date on the *novum* exception in the context of Article 54 CISA or Article 50 of the Charter: such an exception does not exist. There is by now some case law before the ECtHR on the possibility of the 'reopening of proceedings'. That court has on several occasions examined whether the power to reopen the proceedings 'was exercised by the authorities so

[35] CJEU Case C-129/14 PPU.

[36] Para 58 of the judgment.

as to strike, to the maximum extent possible, a fair balance between the interests of the individual and the need to ensure the effectiveness of the system of criminal justice'. An observation from this could be that although this leaves a considerable margin of discretion for the state, it also confirms the central importance of the *ne bis in idem* principle as a fundamental human right and its function as a guarantee of legal certainty.[37] The ECtHR case law, however, provides little guidance on the fundamental question that is raised when we consider the exception possibility to the *ne bis in idem* rule in the light of the issue of impunity: is the *novum* exception fundamental in this regard, and should it be incorporated into Article 54 CISA and Article 50 of the Charter?

It is squarely proposed here that it should. The argument is not sophisticated or legalistic: it is simply a question of how one weighs the interest of the protection of a fundamental right like *ne bis in idem* against that of the risk of impunity. It is within the application of the *ne bis in idem* principle that the tension between the interests of the individual and the need to ensure the effectiveness of the system of criminal justice often become particularly apparent, as evidenced by some of the cases referred to in the introductory part of this chapter.[38] Although the importance of the *ne bis in idem* rule should obviously never be underestimated, the interest of preventing impunity should also weigh in heavily, especially in situations where a subject was successful in hiding or destroying the evidence, or in misleading the justice system. Under those exceptional circumstances, the possibility of an exception to the *ne bis in idem* principle forms an important and necessary instrument for achieving a fair balance between those two fundamental interests by avoiding unacceptable impunity.

What appears certain is that the possibility of exceptions to the *ne bis in idem* principle at the EU level therefore forms an aspect of the principle which has so far received too little attention, and which merits much more thorough consideration and study.[39] At present, without guidance from the case law of the European courts, we can only point to cases in foreign jurisdictions (like the *OJ Simpson* case) in which the absence of a *novum* exception led to unacceptable impunity, or the *Kennedy* case, in which the same led to hard-fought and far-reaching changes in the law many decades later.

[37] In the recent Grand Chamber judgment in *Mihalache v Romania* App no 54012/10, the ECtHR for the first time shed some more light on its interpretation of para 2 of Art 4, Protocol 7 ECHR. Although the arguments raised there certainly merit further discussion, they are immaterial to the argument presented here.

[38] The OJ Simpson and Deidre Kennedy cases in particular illustrate the profound societal impact that such rare cases can have.

[39] It has been suggested that a mistrial could, for the purposes of the principle of finality, be considered a factor that could mitigate the finality of the judgment (a 'flawed' decision would not be 'final'). The CJEU has, however, repeatedly emphasized that the 'finality' of the previous decision is primarily a question for national law (see CJEU Case C-486/14 *Kossowski*). In addition, this does not touch on the main, and most poignant issue: that of new and previously undiscovered evidence.

V. Findings

In keeping with the overall aim of this book, this chapter has examined the kinds of situations in which the application of the *ne bis in idem* principle should (perhaps) be nuanced or mitigated in order to avoid impunity. Three issues were discussed in that regard: the so-called 'enforcement requirement' from Article 54 CISA; the parallel application of criminal and administrative law; and the exception possibility in the case of new and previously undiscovered evidence (*novum*). Regarding the first two, it was argued that although the issue may in theory result in impunity through the application of the *ne bis in idem* rule, that risk is now adequately avoided through jurisprudential developments. In particular, and although each case raises many new questions and issues, the *Garlsson*, *Menci* and *Di Puma* judgments have ostensibly ruled out any possibility of impunity through the application of the *ne bis in idem* principle between the administrative and criminal law spheres. There is, however, no doubt that critics are right to point out that this has somewhat weakened *ne bis in idem* protection in Europe, and perhaps to a degree that may be unacceptable to some. Nevertheless, it is hard to see a clear alternative solution to the issues raised in those cases.

The *Spasic* judgment is of particular importance in many regards. In that judgment, the CJEU ruled, amongst other things, that the requirement of the enforcement of the sentence from Article 54 CISA is 'necessary to meet the objective of general interest' of preventing impunity. Although the judgment has received widespread criticism, it is argued here that the Court made a sensible and laudable choice in this regard.

As for the exception possibility of *novum*, it was argued that essentially the same reasons as those found in *Spasic* could apply. In the case of new and previously undiscovered evidence, a retrial may be necessary in the interests of preventing impunity. This is, of course, subject to the requirements set forth in the case law of the ECtHR on this point. The *ne bis in idem* provisions found in EU law, however, do not provide for such an exception possibility, and it was argued that such a possibility should in fact be incorporated into both Article 54 CISA and Article 50 of the Charter.

7

Impunity and Conflicts of Jurisdiction within the EU: The Role of Eurojust and Challenges for Fundamental Rights

ATHINA GIANNAKOULA

I. Introduction – Identification of the Problem

From the outset of constructing an EU area of freedom, security and justice, impunity, which could be roughly defined as the inability to hold criminal proceedings for an act whose punishability appears to be justified and necessary, was included in discussions on the justification of the EU's competence to act in the field of criminal law. Most notably, the approximation of the constituent elements of serious criminal offences was connected (among other factors) to the need to deal with relevant weaknesses in the judicial systems of the national legal orders, based on the thought that such weaknesses could attract organised crime groups to specific Member States.[1] Furthermore, the notion of impunity appears to be a factor in the definition of 'effectiveness' with regard to criminal sanctions, as the latter are considered to be effective when national provisions do not make it practically impossible or excessively difficult to impose the penalty provided for in each case;[2] in this respect, the CJEU[3] has linked national criminal law provisions on the

[1] Council doc 9959/99, paras 6–9.

[2] See Joined Cases C-387/02, C-391/02 and C-403/02 *Berlusconi and others* EU:C:2004:624, Judgment of 3 May 2005, Opinion of Advocate General Kokott, paras 88–89; also A Klip, *European Criminal Law*, 3rd edn (Cambridge, Intersentia, 2016) 76ff; E Herlin-Karnell, 'Commission v Council: Some Reflections on Criminal Law in the First Pillar' [2007] *European Public Law* 69, 77; M Faure, 'Effective, Proportional and Dissuasive Penalties in the Implementation of the Environmental Crime and Ship-source Pollution Directives: Questions and Challenges' (2010) 6 *European Energy and Environmental Law Review* 256.

[3] See Case C-105/14 *Taricco and Others* EU:C:2015:555, Judgment of 8 August 2015, para 58. On this case, see F Viganò, 'Supremacy of EU Law v (Constitutional) National Identity: A New Challenge for the Court of Justice from the Italian Constitutional Court' (2017) 7 *European Criminal Law Review* 103. Compare Case C-42/17 *MAS and MB* EU:C:2017:936, Judgment of 5 December 2017, para 62, where the CJEU sets limits; on this case, see M Bassini and O Pollicino, 'Defusing the Taricco

statute of limitations to a similar estimation with reference to the effective protection of the EU's financial interests.[4]

Being a key aspect of EU criminal law, fighting impunity and enhancing the protection of legal interests against crime has also been promoted in the EU by expanding the scope of national criminal laws through clauses calling for the establishment of extraterritorial jurisdiction by the Member States.[5] By adding such clauses in legal instruments adopted to approximate the definitions of criminal offences and their sanctions, the EU has been aiming to reduce the chances of a criminal offence falling under its competence not being prosecuted by any Member State. However, in doing so, it has contributed to increasing the chances for conflicts of jurisdiction to occur, ie for judicial authorities in various Member States to initiate criminal proceedings against a person for the same conduct; in other words, by aiming to avoid 'negative' conflicts of jurisdiction (ie where no Member State can prosecute an act), EU law has resulted into favouring 'positive' ones (ie where more Member States prosecute or punish a person for the same act).[6]

At the same time, (positive) conflicts of jurisdiction are increasingly problematic in the EU area of freedom, security and justice, even in relation to national provisions on extraterritorial jurisdiction which have been adopted irrespective of EU's intervention.[7] For the actual extent of the problem to be identified, one must take into account not only the estimation that cross-border crime has increased,[8] but also the fact that, under EU law, conflicts of jurisdiction should not be tolerated: on the one hand, Member States have conferred upon the EU competence to

Bomb through Fostering Constitutional Tolerance: All Roads Lead to Rome' (*Verfassungsblog*) https://verfassungsblog.de/defusing-the-taricco-bomb-through-fostering-constitutional-tolerance-all-roads-lead-to-rome/; D Burchardt, 'Belittling the Primacy of EU Law in Taricco II' (*Verfassungsblog*) https://verfassungsblog.de/belittling-the-primacy-of-eu-law-in-taricco-ii/; A Giannakoula, 'Commentary on the Decision of the European Court of Justice of 5th December 2017' (2018) 1 *Revue Hellénique de Droit Européen* 84 (in Greek). For both judgments, see M Kaiafa-Gbandi, 'Supranational Determination of Criminal Repression: Ideological Axes of the Development of EU Criminal Law' (2018) 7 *Poinika Chronika* 497 (in Greek).

[4] See the explicit connection between impunity and Art 325 TFEU in F Zimmermann, 'Conflicts of Criminal Jurisdiction in the European Union' in P Asp and M Ulväng (eds), *Essays on European Criminal Law* (Uppsala, Iustus, 2015) 151–52.

[5] On this, see M Böse, 'EU Substantive Criminal Law and Jurisdiction Clauses: Claiming Jurisdiction to Fight Impunity?' ch 5 in this book; P Caeiro, 'Jurisdiction in Criminal Matters in the EU: Negative and Positive Conflicts, and Beyond' (2010) *Kritische Vierteljahresschrift für Gesetzgebung und Rechtswissenschaft*, 366; H Satzger, *International and European Criminal Law* 2nd edn (Munich, Beck, 2018) 10; K Ligeti and Gavin Robinson (eds), *Preventing and Resolving Conflicts of Jurisdiction in EU Criminal Law. A European Law Institute Instrument* (Oxford, Oxford University Press, 2018) 21; Klip (n 2) 218.

[6] See distinction and analysis in Caeiro (n 5) 369ff; see also Zimmermann (n 4) 152; Ligeti and Robinson (n 5) 16.

[7] M Kaiafa-Gbandi, 'Jurisdictional Conflicts in Criminal Matters and their Settlement within EU's Supranational Settings' (2017) 7 *European Criminal Law Review* 30, 31–32.

[8] See Eurojust, Guidelines for Deciding "Which Jurisdiction Should Prosecute?'" [2016] 1 www.eurojust.europa.eu/doclibrary/Eurojust-framework/Casework/Guidelines%20for%20deciding%20which%20jurisdiction%20should%20prosecute%20(2016)/2016_Jurisdiction-Guidelines_EN.pdf; Europol, 'Internet Organised Crime Threat Assessment 2018' www.europol.europa.eu/internet-organised-crime-threat-assessment-2018.

prevent and resolve conflicts of jurisdiction in the context of judicial cooperation in criminal matters (currently in Article 82 TFEU);[9] on the other hand, conflicts of jurisdiction are directly connected to specific breaches of fundamental legal principles guaranteed at the EU level. Most commonly, the *ne bis in idem* principle is evoked;[10] however, it is rightly argued that parallel criminal proceedings for the same conduct also affect the *nullum crimen nulla poena sine lege processu* principle and may hamper the good administration of justice.[11]

In view of the above, the issue of who should prosecute and punish an offence when a number of Member States have the jurisdiction to do so has been widely discussed by the legal scholarship, not just in recent years, but also even before the Lisbon Treaty had entered into force.[12] Nevertheless, there is still no EU legislative Act addressing the issue in a complete and effective manner. This chapter deals with the subject of positive conflicts of jurisdiction (hereafter just 'conflicts of jurisdiction') as side-effects or direct consequences of fighting impunity within the EU. In this respect, it aims to highlight its most important aspects and to appraise recent developments and perspectives, eventually focusing on Eurojust as the main and most decisive actor in the field. Against this background, it examines the suitability of national provisions and the *ne bis in idem* principle to address the problem, the existing EU legislative framework and the respective soft-law rules introduced by Eurojust, and, finally, the most important challenges arising both from the legal framework and from practical implementation, especially with regard to the fundamental principles of EU law and in relation to the notion of impunity in the EU.

II. Critical Evaluation of the Rules Addressing the Problem

A. National Provisions and the *ne bis in idem* Principle

As already mentioned, conflicts of jurisdiction are by no means a phenomenon attributed solely to the EU; consequently, one could look for rules to apply when

[9] M Böse, 'The Legal Basis (Art. 82 TFEU)' in M Böse, F Meyer and A Schneider (eds), *Conflicts of Jurisdiction in Criminal Matters in the European Union – Volume II: Rights, Principles and Model Rules* (Baden-Baden, Nomos, 2014) 131ff; M Wasmeier, 'The Legal Basis for Preventing and Resolving Conflicts of Criminal Jurisdiction in the TFEU' in Ligeti and Robinson (n 5) 100ff; Caeiro (n 5) 369ff.

[10] Framework Decision 2009/948/JHA on prevention and settlement of conflicts of exercise of jurisdiction in criminal proceedings [2009] OJ L328/42 (FD) recital 3; Eurojust (n 8) 1.

[11] See section III.A below.

[12] See, indicatively, the following chapters in B Schünemann (ed), *A Programme for European Criminal Justice* (Munich, Carl Heymanns Verlag, 2006): B Schünemann, 'The Foundations of Trans-national Criminal Proceedings' 344, 357ff, N Bitzilekis, M Kaiafa-Gbandi and E Symeonidou-Kastanidou, 'Alternative Thoughts on the Regulation of Transnational Criminal Proceedings in the EU' 493ff; H Fuchs, 'Regulation of Jurisdiction and Substantive Criminal Law' 365–66. See also Böse et al (n 9)

such conflicts occur in the legislations of the Member States. Taking the (recently redrafted)[13] Greek Criminal Code (GrCC) as an example, Article 9(1) therein dictates that prosecution is excluded for offences committed abroad in three particular sets of cases,[14] which concern the Greek judicial authorities' extraterritorial jurisdiction on the basis of the principles of active personality and of passive personality.[15] However, when these criteria are not fulfilled,[16] the Greek authorities may prosecute a person for an act who is also being prosecuted by a foreign authority or even already tried by a foreign court, bearing just the obligation to deduct during sentencing any period of time served abroad (Article 10 GrCC). In addition, the GrCC has explicitly covered the application of the *ne bis in idem* principle[17] only since the 2019 reform and only in reference to judgments of courts of other Member States.[18] In total, the Greek rules on dealing with conflicts of jurisdiction have been considered to predominantly express national interests,[19] have

381ff; Ligeti and Robinson (n 5) 16ff; European Law Institute, 'Draft Legislative Proposals for the Prevention and Resolution of Conflicts of Jurisdiction in Criminal Matters in the European Union' (2017) www.europeanlawinstitute.eu/fileadmin/user_upload/p_eli/Publications/Conflict_of_Jurisdiction_in_Criminal_Law_FINAL.pdf; T Vander Beken, G Vermeulen, S Steverlynck and S Thomaes, *Finding the Best Place to Prosecute* (Antwerp, Maklu, 2002); Zimmermann (n 4) 170ff; Klip (n 2) 450ff; Kaiafa-Gbandi (n 7) 40ff; Caeiro (n 5) 374ff; M Munivrana Vajda, 'The Trust is Not Blind – Reviewing the Idea of Mutual Trust in the EU in the Context of Conflicts of Jurisdiction and Ne Bis In Idem Principle' (2018) 2 *EU and Comparative Law Issues and Challenges Series* 329; P Ortolani, 'Conflicts of Jurisdiction in Criminal Law: Lessons from European Civil Procedure' (19 January 2017) https://ssrn.com/abstract=2902046, http://dx.doi.org/10.2139/ssrn.2902046.

[13] It was voted on 6 June 2019 and entered into force on 1 July 2019.

[14] That is when: a person has been acquitted abroad, or has been convicted and has served or is serving his or her sentence; or, according to the applicable foreign law, the act/sentence is time-barred, the perpetrator pardoned or a complaint is necessary and one has not been filed; or a court of another Member State has issued a 'final' judgment for the same act.

[15] These principles (Arts 6 and 7 GrCC) are considered to achieve a 'balanced' contribution of the Greek legal system to fighting crime and impunity at an international level: see N Chatzinikolaou, T Papakyriakou, A Zachariadis and M Kaiafa-Gbandi, 'Country Report "Greece"' in M Böse, F Meyer and A Schneider (eds), *Conflicts of Jurisdiction in Criminal Matters in the European Union – Volume I: National Reports and Comparative Analysis* (Baden-Baden, Nomos, 2013) 202ff.

[16] Most importantly, when crimes are committed in the Greek territory (Art 5 GrCC) or fall within the scope of universal jurisdiction or the protective principle (Art 8 GrCC); in general, great concern has been expressed on the expansion of Art 8 GrCC – see Chatzinikolaou et al (n 15) 221 and references therein.

[17] On the principle in relation to impunity, see B van Bockel, 'Between Impunity and the Protection of Fundamental Rights: the Case Law of the CJEU and the ECtHR on the *ne bis in idem* Principle' ch 6 in this book.

[18] Before the 2019 reform, the principle applied owing to Art 54 of the Convention Implementing the Schengen Agreement and Art 50 of the EU Charter of Fundamental Rights (the Charter). For this, see M Kaiafa-Gbandi in M Kaiafa-Gbandi and E Symeonidou-Kastanidou's revision of I Manoledakis, *Criminal Law – General Part Compendium*, 7th edn (Athens, Sakkoulas, 2005) 113ff (in Greek). On the EU provisions on the principle, see indicatively M Böse, 'Fundamental Rights of the EU-Charter' in Böse et al (n 9) 131ff; B van Bockel 'The "European" *Ne Bis in Idem* Principle: Substance, Sources and Scope' in B van Bockel (ed), *Ne Bis in Idem in EU Law* (Cambridge, Cambridge University Press, 2016) 21ff; PP Paulesu, 'Ne bis in idem and Conflicts of Jurisdiction' in RE Kostoris (ed), *Handbook of European Criminal Procedure* (Berlin, Springer International Publishing, 2018) 402ff; Kaiafa-Gbandi (n 7) 34–40.

[19] Kaiafa-Gbandi (n 7) 33.

a limited scope and function unilaterally;[20] thus, such rules would be unsuited to serve the objective of resolving conflicts of jurisdiction at the EU level. This estimation is still valid, in spite of the fact that, in an even more recent development, a new provision was added to the Greek Code of Criminal Procedure (Article 57(4)) according to which a public prosecutor may abstain from prosecuting an offence, when informed, through judicial cooperation procedures, that a prosecution for the same events is pending in another Member State; the provision is certainly novel, but brief and of narrow scope of application (as it only covers the stage before initiating criminal proceedings).

The above-mentioned observations do not concern solely the Greek example; on the contrary, they appear to be rather indicative of the way conflicts of jurisdiction are approached at a national level across the EU. As research in Member States has shown, the respective national provisions do not as a rule entail procedures that could effectively deal with all the aspects of the issue; most importantly, they do not address the needs to avoid the initiation of parallel proceedings and to guarantee the fundamental rights of the persons involved.[21] In the same direction, it is interesting to also refer to a review of the Spanish system as an example of a system that originally lacked rules on the settlement of international conflicts of jurisdiction in criminal matters but was later enriched with such rules. In this respect, it is revealed that, although the system was reformed based on the current EU legislation on resolving conflicts of jurisdiction, it is still insufficient, as it misses key mechanisms in the process of settling the conflicts and it functions unilaterally when judicial decisions have to be made.[22]

On the other hand, the *ne bis in idem* principle is a self-standing concept, with autonomous aims and content.[23] Consequently, while it is of great significance from the perspective of resolving jurisdictional conflicts too, it does not constitute an adequate solution to the relevant problems. More specifically, it may protect an individual from being punished twice for the same act, but, as it applies only after a final decision has been issued in one Member State, it allows for parallel criminal proceedings to exist, meaning that a person may have to defend him- or herself in two (or more) different legal systems in the EU. In addition, it does not entail any rules in relation to the central issue of determining which Member State should prosecute in a certain case. At the same time, since the first Member State to issue a final decision may be one with a very weak link to the criminal offence in question, coincidence can prove to be a critical factor, while the principle even leaves room for manipulation (ie forum shopping) and (partial) impunity.[24]

[20] Chatzinikolaou et al (n 15) 245.

[21] M Böse, F Meyer and A Schneider, 'Comparative Analysis' in Böse et al (n 15) 442–43, 460–63.

[22] M Carmona Ruano, 'Prevention and Settlement of Conflicts of Jurisdiction (Spanish System)' in Ligeti and Robinson (n 5) 119ff.

[23] Caeiro (n 5) 376.

[24] On these, see European Criminal Policy Initiative (ECPI), 'A Manifesto on European Criminal Procedure Law' (2013) 11 *Zeitschrift für Internationale Strafrechtsdogmatik* 430, 435, 441; P Asp, *The Procedural Criminal Law Cooperation of the EU – Towards an Area of Freedom, Security & Justice – Part 2*

Therefore, dealing with conflicts of jurisdiction in the EU has to be pursued with a mechanism that directly addresses the problem and corresponds to the current traits of the area of freedom, security and justice.

B. Framework Decision 2009/948/JHA: A Frail Legislative Effort

In 2009, the EU adopted Framework Decision 2009/948/JHA on the prevention and settlement of conflicts of exercise of jurisdiction in criminal proceedings (the FD).[25] In spite of its ambitious title and although it could have been of noteworthy value, given that it seeks to 'prevent situations where the same person is subject to parallel criminal proceedings' in more Member States with regard to the same facts (thus covering a wider scope than the *ne bis in idem* principle), the procedures it introduced did not match the effectiveness of other measures included in EU instruments in the field of judicial cooperation in criminal matters, especially mutual recognition instruments.

Specifically, the FD establishes a procedure for the competent national authorities to contact each other and confirm the existence of parallel criminal proceedings, and a framework for subsequent direct consultations between such authorities, in order to reach consensus on a solution that would avoid breaching the *ne bis in idem* principle and wasting time and resources;[26] should direct consultations fail, Member States are called on to cooperate with Eurojust,[27] which is considered 'particularly well suited' to providing such assistance.[28] In contrast, the FD does not entail criteria for the consultations to be based on; instead, it refers Member States to Eurojust's respective guidelines for inspiration (hereafter Eurojust Guidelines).[29]

(Stockholm, Jure, 2016) 91–93; V Mitsilegas, *EU Criminal Law after Lisbon* (Oxford, Hart Publishing, 2016) 84ff; Munivrana Vajda (n13) 323, 329; Caeiro (n 5) 367, 376; Kaiafa-Gbandi (n 7) 34ff (38); Klip (n 2) 285; Satzger (n 5) 10, 148ff; Zimmermann (n 4) 164ff. See also indicatively Case C-398/12 *Criminal proceedings against M* EU:C:2014:65, Opinion of Advocate General Sharpston, para 51: 'At present, there are no agreed EU-wide rules on the allocation of criminal jurisdiction. The application of the *ne bis in idem* principle resolves the problem in a limited, sometimes an arbitrary, way. It is not a satisfactory substitute for action to resolve such conflicts according to an agreed set of criteria.'

[25] For previous (Initiative on the *ne bis in idem* principle; Commission's Green Paper on conflicts of jurisdiction) and parallel (Initiative on the transfer of criminal proceedings) to the FD efforts to regulate the matter in the context of EU criminal law, see M Böse, 'Models and Instruments for solving conflicts of jurisdiction' in Böse et al (n 9) 342ff.

[26] FD, Art 2 and recital 3.

[27] FD, Art 12(2).

[28] FD, recital 14.

[29] FD, recital 9.

In reality, the FD is somewhat reserved towards the very processes it introduces: on the one hand, it does not render the result of any consultation binding on the Member States;[30] on the other hand, it asks for Member States not to request information on probable parallel criminal proceedings light-heartedly, but to do so only when reasonable grounds exist, and it specifies these grounds in a rather 'strict' manner (ie a national authority is justified in contacting the competent authority in another Member State if it already has some information on parallel criminal proceedings either implied by a request for mutual legal assistance or provided by the suspect or a police authority).[31] Obviously in the same direction, it is clarified that applying the FD 'should not give rise to a conflict of exercise of jurisdiction which would not occur otherwise'.[32] In reality, these provisions are the only ones functioning in the direction of preventing the occurrence of parallel criminal proceedings and thus of conflicts of jurisdiction. Even so, the EU approach according to this legislative Act could be understood as expressing a lack of trust in the handlings of other Member States and favouring national sovereignty,[33] or at the very least reflecting the procedural challenges that emerge in the effort to settle such conflicts. Indeed, the FD does not contain any measures to support the practical application of the main EU notion it introduces, ie that prosecution in one Member State should satisfy the principle of mandatory prosecution in all the others,[34] although the promotion of such a notion would obviously require an EU intervention. Likewise, it does not regulate any procedural matters that relate to the proceedings or to the rights of the persons affected,[35] thus lacking key conditions concerning its applicability and its essential compatibility to the Charter of Fundamental Rights of the Union (the Charter).

In view of the above, it is quite apparent that the existing general EU legislative tool on jurisdictional conflicts is not effective nor advanced enough to cope with the critical aspects of the problem discussed.[36] Nevertheless, the FD, adopted on

[30] In addition, see FD, recital 11 ('no Member State should be obliged to waive or to exercise jurisdiction unless it wishes to do so').

[31] See FD, recital 5.

[32] FD, recital 12, sentence 1.

[33] Klip (n 2) 452 refers to 'reluctance'.

[34] FD, recital 12, sentence 2.

[35] Although the FD was adopted before the Lisbon Treaty entering into force, and therefore before the introduction of Directives on procedural rights, it only contained a weak relevant reference in recital 17, mentioning that the FD 'does not affect any right of individuals to argue that they should be prosecuted in their own or in another jurisdiction, if such right exists under national law'. See the criticism in K Ambos, *European Criminal Law* (Cambridge, Cambridge University Press, 2018) 160ff; Mitsilegas (n 24) 92; Böse (n 25) 347ff; Kaiafa-Gbandi (n 7) 39; Zimmermann (n 4) 166; ECPI (n 24) 435, 440. Of course, even under the current EU legal framework, it would still be necessary to establish specific formal procedures on resolving conflicts of jurisdiction for rights to be exercised (eg if there is no open procedure on deciding which forum should prosecute, it is not possible for the person involved to ask to be heard) and even specific provisions on the rights (eg a specific legal remedy against a decision on choosing forum, or at least a specific reference to the obligation to provide such remedy).

[36] Klip (n 2) 534.

the very last day before the Lisbon Treaty entered into force, is still maintained by the EU[37] and expressly referred to by new Directives.[38]

C. Special Legislative Provisions: A Step Further

Apart from the general rules on resolving conflicts of jurisdiction introduced by FD 2009/948/JHA, EU legislation has sporadically provided for additional ones that are linked to specific criminal offences and thus function as *lex specialis* compared to the FD. The respective provisions have been included in Framework Decisions and Directives adopted to approximate the definitions of criminal offences and their penalties; interestingly, such Acts do not habitually deal with conflicts of jurisdiction, although they do regularly require national legislators to establish extraterritorial jurisdiction. Today, the ones in force concern organised crime,[39] terrorism,[40] money laundering[41] and corruption.[42] As far as the relevant provisions[43] are concerned, it is worth noting that, whereas the Acts adopted until 2001 only entailed the obligation of the Member States to cooperate 'with a view to centralising the prosecution', the rest of the Acts enumerate factors to be taken into account when deciding which Member State shall prosecute the criminal offence in question.[44]

In total, in spite of entailing criteria for the selection of the appropriate authority,[45] the special EU rules on dealing with conflicts of jurisdiction appear

[37] On the binding effect of Framework Decisions that are still in force, see Arts 9–10 of Protocol 36 of the TEU; V Mitsilegas, S Carrera and K Eisele, 'The End of the Transitional Period for Police and Criminal Justice Measures Adopted before the Lisbon Treaty: Who Monitors Trust in the European Criminal Justice Area?', CEPS Paper No 74 (December 2014); T Blanchet, 'The Genesis of Protocol 36' (2015) 4 *New Journal of European Criminal Law* 434; H Satzger, 'Legal Effects of Directives Amending or Repealing Pre-Lisbon Framework Decisions' (2015) 4 *New Journal of European Criminal Law* 528; A Giannakoula, 'Framework Decisions under the Lisbon Treaty: Current Status and Open Issues' (2017) 7 *European Criminal Law Review*, 275.

[38] See eg Directive (EU) 2019/713 on fraud and counterfeiting of non-cash means of payment [2019] OJ L123/18, recital 21; Directive 2011/36/EU on human trafficking [2011] OJ L101/1, recital 5; Directive 2013/40/EU on attacks against information systems [2013] OJ L218/8, recital 27.

[39] Art 7(2) of Framework Decision 2008/841/JHA on organised crime [2008] OJ L300/42.

[40] Art 19(3) of Directive (EU) 2017/541 on terrorism [2017] OJ L88/6.

[41] Art 10(3) of Directive (EU) 2018/1673 on money laundering [2018] OJ L284/22.

[42] Art 9(2) of the Convention on Corruption involving EU officials [1997] OJ C195/2.

[43] See Art 6(2) of the PIF Convention [1995] OJ C316/49; Art 7(3) of Framework Decision 2000/383/JHA on counterfeiting of currency [2000] OJ L140/1; Art 11(2) of Framework Decision 2001/413/JHA on counterfeiting of non-cash means of payment [2001] OJ L149/1; Art 9(2) of Framework Decision 2002/475/JHA on combating terrorism [2002] OJ L164/3; Art 10(4) of Framework Decision 2005/222/JHA on information systems [2005] OJ L69/67; Art 7(4) and (5) of Framework Decision 2005/667/JHA on ship-source pollution [2005] OJ L255/164. See also the acts currently in force. See further Klip (n 2) 453–54; Böse (n 25) 353ff.

[44] The Framework Decision on ship-source pollution (later annulled by Case C-440/05 *Commission v Council* EU:C:2007:625, Judgment of 23 October 2007) introduced criteria suitable for cases where legal persons are involved in committing criminal offences.

[45] The factors mainly cited are the territory where the offence was committed, the offender's nationality/residency, the victims' country of origin and the territory where the offender was found. There is

to be affected by, and in the end participate in, the fluidity of the relevant framework. Most notably, there is no evident reason why these rules have been linked to the specific offences; indeed, as some of the crucial third pillar Acts have been replaced with Directives, in one case the rules on resolving conflicts of jurisdiction have been repeated in the succeeding Directive,[46] while in the others they have been abandoned, either without any further statement[47] or with a reference to FD 2009/948/JHA added to their context;[48] of course, as the FD does not contain general rules concerning the criteria that should guide the choice of jurisdiction, repeating the special rules in the new Directives would not have been redundant. Also, special rules were introduced not only before but also after the adoption of the FD,[49] with no substantial differences in the content and structure between those formulated before and those formulated after the FD, although the adoption of a general instrument in the field should normally have made a difference. At the same time, the FD does not refer to any of the relevant Acts that pre-existed. The rules themselves do not vary based on the criminal offence they are linked to. Finally, they have no added value as to the procedure to be followed to resolve a conflict of jurisdictions.

Consequently, the special EU rules on dealing with conflicts of jurisdiction currently in force apply in parallel to FD 2009/948/JHA and to the Eurojust Guidelines, and, in principle, they have 'advantages' over them. First of all, they refer both to resolving and preventing conflicts of jurisdiction. Specifically, consultation under FD 2009/948/JHA concerns Member States where parallel proceedings already exist and thus it aims at resolving the respective conflicts; on the contrary, cooperation under the special rules concerns Member States that 'can validly prosecute on the basis of the same facts' and thus also covers even earlier stages, where conflicts have not yet occurred. Secondly, because they introduce criteria, the special EU rules provide a more complete framework in the fields they concern and they serve legal certainty in a clearer manner than the FD;[50] on the other hand, unlike the Eurojust Guidelines, they form part of legislative Acts, and thus are binding by nature. Still, given the inappropriateness of the national legal frameworks and the absence of general EU rules establishing a concrete procedure for them to apply within,[51] they lack in practical enforcement.

no indication that the order of the factors is binding, although always citing them in the same order obviously implies a suggested preference.

[46] Regarding terrorism.

[47] Regarding counterfeiting of currency, ship-source pollution and also fraud, which, however, is covered by Regulation (EU) 2017/1939 on the establishment of the European Public Prosecutor's Office (EPPO) [2017] OJ L283/1.

[48] Regarding information systems and non-cash means of payment.

[49] Regarding terrorism and money laundering.

[50] Böse (n 25) 356.

[51] In this regard, see the procedure introduced by Art 26(4) of the EPPO Regulation. Also, compare the procedure of Art 16(1) of Framework Decision 2002/584/JHA on the European arrest warrant (EAW) [2002] OJ L190/1.

D. The Role of Eurojust and its Guidelines: The Actual EU Framework for Resolving Conflicts of Jurisdiction

Eurojust holds a key position in the process of resolving conflicts of jurisdiction between the EU Member States.[52] It is mainly charged with informing Member States of investigations and prosecutions that may concern them and consulting with the European Judicial Network, asking specific national authorities to undertake an investigation or prosecution when it considers them to be best suited for the task, while, in cases where Member States cannot agree on who should investigate or prosecute a criminal offence, Eurojust issues reasoned written opinions on the subject, which are not binding to the parties involved.[53]

Nonetheless, the most significant relevant contribution by Eurojust is not regulated by its founding legal Acts. As mentioned above, since 2003, Eurojust has been publishing guidelines on the resolution of conflicts of jurisdiction. Although FD 2009/948/JHA acknowledges them and they have long served as the only EU point of reference available on the topic,[54] the Eurojust Guidelines have not yet transformed into official EU criteria for determining the proper national authority to investigate or prosecute a criminal offence, as they are still functioning outside the scope of EU legislation.

According to their most recent version (2016), the Eurojust Guidelines claim to support the idea introduced by the FD that, in the EU area of freedom, security and justice, the principle of mandatory prosecution should be considered fulfilled in all the national legal systems that operate under it, when any Member State prosecutes a criminal offence.[55] As far as the decision on where to prosecute is concerned, the Eurojust Guidelines present a number of factors that are to be taken into account.[56] Regarding these, Eurojust clarifies that, as a general rule, every factor should be given a different priority and weight in each case; therefore, the sequence of the factors is not binding and does not amount to one eliminating any other. Most importantly, though, this also means that it is never possible to know in advance which factor will prevail, even in somewhat similar cases.

[52] See Art 85(1)(c) TFEU as the current primary law provision conferring competence to Eurojust in the field of resolving (not preventing) conflicts of jurisdiction; Arts 6, 7 and 13 of Council Decision 2002/187/JHA [2002] OJ L63/1, which is to remain in force until 12 December 2019; Arts 4 and 21 of Regulation (EU) 2018/1727 [2018] OJ L295/138. See also S Gless and T Wahl, 'A Comparison of the Evolution and Pace of Police and Judicial Cooperation in Criminal Matters: A Race between Europol and Eurojust?' in C Brière and A Weyembergh (eds), *The Needed Balances in EU Criminal Law. Past, Present and Future* (Oxford, Hart Publishing, 2017); Mitsilegas (n 24) 94ff; Kaiafa-Gbandi (n 7) 39.

[53] The special provisions on resolving conflicts of jurisdiction currently in force and the relevant provision on the EAW (section II.C above) also provide for referring to Eurojust.

[54] According to Eurojust, the guidelines are even used by some Member States as a reference point when they develop their own rules or guidelines on settling conflicts of jurisdiction: Eurojust (n 8) Part I, para 5.

[55] Eurojust (n 8) Part II, para 4.

[56] In brief, the factors are territoriality; location of suspect/accused; availability and admissibility of evidence; obtaining evidence from witnesses, experts etc; possibility to offer witness protection; victims' interests; stage of proceedings; length of proceedings; legal requirements; sentencing powers; possibility to recover proceeds of crime; costs and resources; Member States' priorities.

In spite of this general rule, according to Eurojust, a 'preliminary presumption' should be made that, if possible, prosecution should take place based on territoriality; thus, a form of priority is indeed recognised. Even so, the criterion is not definite enough to provide for concrete results, since it includes both the place of the commission of the act and the place where the outcome occurs, which, for cross-border crime, may not lead to any actual solutions regarding the choice of the authority that should prosecute.

Moreover, in addition to guidelines on how to evaluate the proposed factors, Eurojust also determines when certain factors should not be taken into account, apparently in an effort to preclude forum shopping on behalf of the prosecutorial authorities. This means, for example, that, while the potential outcome of the proceedings in one jurisdiction should be considered as a factor, the decision on where to prosecute should not be made solely in order to avoid a legal obligation that exists in a specific Member State. Similarly, while it should be ensured that the potential penalty in a legal system reflects the seriousness of the offence in question, a jurisdiction should not be chosen just because it provides for the highest penalty. And, while the powers available to restrain, recover, seize and confiscate the proceeds of crime should be evaluated, judicial authorities should not 'decide to prosecute in one jurisdiction rather than another just because such prosecution would result in a more effective recovery of the proceeds of crime'.

Obviously, the said approach of Eurojust that some factors should not be taken into account in certain cases is correct; however, these cases may not always be easy to distinguish. For example, it could prove difficult to ignore a high penalty in practice, since the level of a penalty provided for by law is crucial in relation to the statute of limitations, which in turn has been directly connected to the effective protection of the EU's financial interests by the CJEU.[57] Likewise, at a time when the EU promotes freezing and confiscation through advanced substantive[58] and procedural[59] criminal law Acts, Eurojust's above-mentioned requirement may become hard to apply or even be perceived as conflicting with the general trend of EU criminal law regarding recovering proceeds of crime. Consequently, for these restrictions to be effective, the relevant factors should be precluded as criteria to be taken into account not just in some cases but in all cases (ie the penalty level should not be a factor). Otherwise, forum shopping may even be favoured by the respective clauses and, in any case, more uncertainty as to the authority to be selected is generated.

Furthermore, some of Eurojust's criteria are in fact 'weakened' by the Guidelines themselves, when Eurojust correctly notes that EU mutual recognition legal instruments[60] may provide for possibilities that render particular factors

[57] See n 3.

[58] Directive 2014/42/EU on freezing and confiscation [2014] OJ L127/39.

[59] Regulation (EU) 2018/1805 on the mutual recognition of freezing orders and confiscation orders [2018] OJ L303/1.

[60] The European Arrest Warrant (EAW), Framework Decision 2008/909/JHA on mutual recognition of judgments imposing custodial sentences or measures involving deprivation of liberty and Directive 2014/41/EU on the European Investigation Order (EIO).

of secondary importance; in other words, it is apparently suggested that it is not necessary to choose the jurisdiction where the suspect resides or where most of the evidence is available when the penalty can be executed in another Member State, or both the suspect and the evidence can be 'transferred' by means of the proper instrument of judicial cooperation. Indeed, the same argument could be used in relation to other EU instruments (eg the Regulation on the Mutual Recognition of Freezing/Confiscation Orders) or even other EU decision-making procedures (eg the approximation of criminal penalties under Article 83 TFEU as the proper method to deal with the penalty level concerning a certain offence).

From a different perspective, however, mutual recognition instruments may affect cross-border criminal proceedings in the opposite manner and thus complicate situations where conflicts of jurisdiction occur. The EU Acts mentioned just above allow (under varying conditions) for EAWs, EIOs and national judicial decisions not to be executed when they concern criminal offences which have been committed outside the territory of the issuing state and wholly or partially on the territory of the executing state.[61] Therefore, 'concentrating' persons and evidence in one Member State through EU instruments of judicial cooperation is more probable when this is also the territory where the criminal offence was committed. Furthermore, non-execution of EAWs is also possible in clear cases of conflicts of jurisdiction, primarily when the person to be surrendered is being prosecuted in the executing Member State for the same act.[62]

Finally, just like the FD, Eurojust connects the effort to settle conflicts of jurisdiction with respecting the *ne bis in idem* principle, making no reference to any other rights or principles of law being potentially affected. This concludes a legal framework, both binding and soft law, not addressing the core problems related to conflicts of jurisdiction in criminal matters in the EU.

III. Shortcomings and Future Perspectives

A. Assessing the True Dimension of the EU Rules Construed to Deal with Conflicts of Jurisdiction

(i) Challenges Arising from the Legal Framework

In order to better estimate the impact of the EU legal framework on dealing with conflicts of jurisdiction, one should assess it against the problems it is called to

[61] See Art 4(7) of Framework Decision 2002/584/JHA, Art 9(1)(l) of Framework Decision 2008/909/JHA, Art 11(1)(e) of Directive 2014/41/EU and Art 8(1)(d) of Regulation (EU) 2018/1805.

[62] Art 4(2) of Framework Decision 2002/584/JHA. Greece, in order to deal with the obligation to surrender own nationals, has transposed the said condition as grounds for *mandatory* non-execution (Art 11(h) of Law 3251/2004). See Council doc 13416/2/08, especially point 4.8.

address. The first problem obviously concerns the possible infringement of the *ne bis in idem* principle in the future, as pointed out in the relevant EU texts; since it is established in EU primary law that only one judgment declaring a person guilty or innocent with regard to a specific act should exist in the EU, it is fair to argue that only one criminal court should adjudicate the respective case.

Another problem, not tackled by the EU, concerns the burden of parallel criminal proceedings on the defendant. In the field of criminal justice, a person's most fundamental rights (personal freedom, property, honour) are affected not only by a conviction, but, even earlier, by the criminal proceedings themselves; in view of this, as well as for the purpose of serving the good administration of justice and determining the truth, criminal procedure in European countries is composed of guarantees and rights stemming directly from principles encompassed in legal texts of constitutional status and of national and international law origin.[63] As a result, it is not acceptable for a defendant to face criminal proceedings in more than one Member State for the same act, especially within the EU, where mutual trust, mutual recognition and approximation of national criminal laws have long been employed to develop a common area of freedom, security and justice.[64] Indeed, multiple prosecutions arising from a conflict of jurisdictions entail that the accused needs to defend him- or herself in front of the authorities of more Member States, or that he or she has to endure investigating acts to be repeated in more legal systems or for them to take place in different legal regimes. As a result, there is an evident problem with regard to the principle of proportionality and to the essential ability of the accused to exercise his or her rights emerging from the right to a fair trial (eg to be represented by a lawyer in all the Member States involved).[65]

A third issue concerns the objective of fighting impunity and punishing crime effectively. In cases where the criminal activity of a person affects more Member States and, consequently, gives rise to multiple prosecutions against him or her, an unresolved conflict could cause one or more of the prosecuting authorities to step back and not conduct an effective investigation or not share their findings. This could result into leaving aspects of the crime unravelled or unrevealed to their investigating counterparts and letting the perpetrator receive a lesser punishment than the one he or she deserves. Such an outcome obviously contradicts the aims of judicial cooperation in criminal matters. At the same time, however, it is equally clear that, in a legal order governed by the rule of law, such as the one of the EU,[66] pursuing effectiveness should be delineated by the obligation to respect fundamental legal principles and rights.

[63] N Androulakis, *Fundamental Concepts of Criminal Procedure*, 4th edn (Athens, PN Sakkoulas, 2012) 29 (in Greek).

[64] Kaiafa-Gbandi (n 7) 31–32.

[65] See ECPI (n 24) 435; Zimmermann (n 4) 155; Kaiafa-Gbandi (n 7) 39–40.

[66] See Art 2 TEU; European Commission, 'Further Strengthening the Rule of Law within the Union State of Play and Possible Next Steps' (Communication) COM (2019) 163 final.

So, in assessing the EU rules on conflicts of jurisdiction against the need to address the outlined core problems, the following points should be highlighted. First, it is apparent that ensuring that the criminal activity in question will be effectively investigated and punished is a goal that is clearly set by the Eurojust Guidelines. Against this background, the flexibility allowed by the relative legislative provisions, thus permitting the Guidelines' criteria that are most appropriate in each case to be taken into account, is considered an asset of the examined legal framework.

Secondly, in relation to preventing infringements of the *ne bis in idem* principle, it goes without saying that the FD is surely aiming to address the problem. However, since the EU legislator has not provided the negotiating parties with detailed and binding criteria to apply when determining which Member State should prosecute a case, has not adopted a procedure to transfer and concentrate proceedings in the selected Member State and has not introduced rules on terminating the conflicting proceedings in the Member States not selected to prosecute, there is still too much room left for parallel criminal proceedings to take place in the EU and for the *ne bis in idem* principle to function as a much needed barrier.

Thirdly, and most importantly, the factors mentioned just above reveal that the EU is far from ensuring the adequate protection of the defendant's rights when more Member States initiate criminal proceedings against the defendant for the same activity.[67] In reality, what is viewed as flexibility from an effectiveness perspective amounts to problematic legislative lacunas from a fundamental rights standpoint; similarly, the ability to decide which authority should prosecute by prioritising and weighing various factors in a different manner in each particular case has a severe cost to foreseeability. Consequently, the mere fact that the Member State to prosecute is chosen after the act, based on non-fixed criteria, infringes the right to be tried by a tribunal established by law.[68] In addition, the lack of foreseeability means that the procedural criminal law to be applied, eg regarding the admissibility of evidence, remains for a long time unknown to the person under investigation, undermining his or her right to a fair trial in the sense that he or she may with good reason be unable to take full advantage of the possibilities and remedies provided by the national law which will be finally selected to apply in his or her case. Moreover, the lack of foreseeability naturally extends to substantive criminal law as well; when committing the act in question, the perpetrator may very well be unaware of the punishment provided for under the law of

[67] See respective criticism in Böse (n 18) 109ff, 151ff; Caeiro (n 5) 377ff; ECPI (n 24) 441–42; Kaiafa-Gbandi (n 7) 39, 43; Mitsilegas (n 24) 94; Satzger (n 5) 11; Zimmermann (n 4) 153ff.

[68] On this, see also M Panzavolta, 'Choice of Forum and the Lawful Judge Concept' in M Luchtman (ed), *Choice of Forum in Cooperation Against EU Financial Crime* (The Hague, Eleven International Publishing, 2013) 159; A Marletta, 'Forum Choice in the Area of Freedom, Security and Justice' in Ligeti and Robinson (n 5) 119ff.

the Member State where he or she will be eventually tried, contrary to the fundamental requirements of the principle of legality guaranteed under Article 49 of the Charter.[69]

In addition to these serious shortcomings, it is obvious that a choice made based on criteria linked to the effectiveness of criminal procedures may in fact be equivalent to forum shopping on the part of the prosecutorial authorities, in the sense of choosing the forum that is most favourable for a conviction. Yet, there should be a consistent stance towards forum shopping at the EU level. Since it is the aim of the EU to prevent offenders from pursuing impunity by manipulating the criminal justice system, there should also be a commitment to effectively punish crime without allowing criminal law authorities to abuse the justice system.[70] In fact, the latter should be even stronger, because in the field of criminal law the state and the defendant are not equal parties, given that the state is equipped with significant powers, which culminate in the right to employ coercive measures against the defendant.

Therefore, the EU legal framework on settling conflicts of jurisdiction has failed to introduce an effective solution to the issues it should have addressed, but it has also caused additional problems, which clearly contradict the Charter.

(ii) Challenges Concerning Practical Implementation (2018 Eurojust Report)

Further points of concern emerge from the 2018 Report of Eurojust on the cases handled in the period 2009–2017,[71] as certain practices followed in the context of dealing with conflicts of jurisdiction confirm or even enhance problems deriving from the current legal framework. Most importantly, these practices highlight the predominance of the criterion of the effectiveness of the proceedings.

First of all, according to Eurojust, the 'location of the suspect or of the evidence/witnesses' is identified as a factor that may be decisive in determining which Member State shall prosecute even in cases where the criminal offence has taken place within one Member State.[72] This is interesting, because most commonly the

[69] On this, see also Fuchs (n 12) 362, 364; M Luchtman, 'Choice of Forum and the Prosecution of Cross-Border Crime in the European Union – What Role for the Legality Principle?' in Luchtman (n 68) 46. On the principle of legality in the context of mutual recognition, see indicatively S Gless, 'A New Test for Mens Rea? Safeguarding Legal Certainty in a European Area of Freedom, Security and Justice' (2011) 1 *European Criminal Law Review* 116.

[70] See Zimmermann (n 4) 157, 168: 'there is always a reasonable concern that forum shopping might occur when prosecution authorities of different Member States are allowed to determine the state of trial by means of consultations'.

[71] 'Report on Eurojust's casework in the field of prevention and resolution of conflicts of jurisdiction 2018' (Report) www.eurojust.europa.eu/doclibrary/Eurojust-framework/Casework/Report%20on%20Eurojust%20casework%20in%20the%20field%20of%20prevention%20and%20resolution%20of%20conflicts%20of%20jurisdiction%20(2018)/2018_Eurojust-casework-on-conflicts-of-Jurisdiction_EN.pdf.

[72] ibid 9.

models proposed for dealing with conflicts of jurisdiction[73] suggest that, when the territoriality principle does not answer the question 'where to prosecute', only then can other factors be taken into account, ie when the commission or the result of a criminal offence involves the territory of more than one Member State. Although Eurojust's practical approach is not precluded by the legal framework, it should be clear that it favours uncertainty and the lack of foreseeability.

A second point of concern arises from Eurojust's stance towards parallel criminal proceedings. In the Report, such proceedings are expressly described as 'very beneficial' for investigating and combating cross-border crime.[74] To this end, not only is it noted that in certain cases, when a request to execute an instrument of judicial cooperation brings a criminal offence to the attention of the authorities in a Member State, that Member State may open its own investigation (instead of just responding to the request), but Eurojust also admits to triggering parallel criminal proceedings itself.[75]

Thirdly, and related to the previous point, the Report comments on the difficulties concerning the transfer of proceedings (eg it is time-consuming; formalities and differences in national laws complicate it and add to the delay; it is not always easy for a Member State to agree to handle the concentrated proceedings; the principle of mandatory prosecution prohibits certain national authorities from agreeing to step back).[76] At the same time, it is argued that occasionally there is no reason to formally transfer proceedings to one Member State (and formally end them in the rest), because a Member State may have already collected all the evidence gathered in the others through mutual recognition instruments. In such cases, according to the Report, the other Member States involved should cease the proceedings or at least suspend them (and obviously wait for the *ne bis in idem* principle to preclude new trials). However, 'ceasing' and 'suspending' do not insure a person against enduring multiple criminal proceedings in the same manner; and, most importantly, the Report is not concerned with how the proceedings will be suspended or ceased in those Member States that do not provide for such a possibility, since no EU legal instrument has introduced such procedures.

The implementation of the EU legal framework on conflicts of jurisdiction as described in the Report can only be assessed as deeply problematic. The practice of triggering parallel criminal proceedings directly contradicts the letter and the spirit of the FD, which expressly calls on the parties involved not to cause new conflicts of jurisdiction.[77] Consequently, the said practice in essence opposes the very concept of preventing conflicts of jurisdiction in the EU. In addition, it is inconsistent with other aspects of EU law as well, since parallel criminal proceedings appear to be used as alternatives to official judicial cooperation mechanisms.[78]

[73] See n 12.
[74] Report (n 71) 3, 5.
[75] Report (n 71) 3, 6.
[76] Report (n 71) 11–12.
[77] See explicitly FD recital 12, sentence 1.
[78] In this context, they may even disable the legislative provisions permitting the non-execution of mutual recognition instruments (see section II.D above).

Moreover, it expresses a clear disregard for the suspect/defendant's rights, since the existing shortcomings concerning the procedures of resolving conflicts and transferring proceedings are neither dealt with nor (at the very least) functioning as substantive deterrents to causing new conflicts.

Even more worryingly, Eurojust appears to consider parallel proceedings as mere tools for fighting crime more effectively. Since triggering new prosecutions against the same person for the same act, which amounts to causing a conflict of jurisdictions, is employed as a means to get more evidence within a legal framework that does not provide for a procedure to resolve the conflict, then obviously this is not a discussion on resolving conflicts of jurisdiction, but a process for collecting more evidence, regardless of the cost of parallel proceedings.

B. Thoughts on a Future Reform of the Legal Framework

The significance of dealing with the challenges arising from conflicts of jurisdiction in the EU has long been evident in the legal literature. As a result, and unlike the approach of the EU, there have been important proposals on the principles and the rules that should govern the choice of forum when conflicts occur, while some go as far as regulating the allocation of jurisdiction, so as to drastically preclude the very possibility of a conflict.[79] The issues that stand out regarding the problems identified above mainly concern the need to lift the burden of parallel criminal proceedings at the earliest stage possible, to guarantee procedural rights for the persons involved and to provide for a concrete legislative framework that shall enhance legal certainty and ensure foreseeability of the authority that should prosecute in case of a conflict.

There is no doubt that coping with the respective problems is an extremely complicated matter. The decision about where to prosecute affects the entire course of the criminal proceedings, and must entail solving a series of key issues; at the same time, it is directly linked to the concept of national sovereignty and to the ability of any Member State to punish crime and exercise its powers of imposing coercive measures on persons. Because of these issues, it puts the degree of mutual trust and the compatibility between the national judicial systems achieved so far within the area of freedom, security and justice to the test. Moreover, the proposals set forth to date show that the question whether conflicts of jurisdiction should be addressed with far-reaching EU measures, which will enhance

[79] See n 12. The territoriality principle prevails in the proposals, either due to the concept that a person is (rightly expected to be) familiar with the legislation of the place where he or she has chosen to act or because the legal order that suffers the consequences of the criminal offence is considered to be the one that most needs a public response to it. A binding hierarchy of other criteria is often presented, relating mainly to the nationality or residence of the offender; conversely, factors concerning effectiveness, eg the location of the evidence, are debatable, as they are the most unpredictable ones. There is also provision of remedies appropriate for the specific proceedings (eg right of the accused to be informed of the procedure, right to judicial review of the decision on the choice of forum).

the supranational character of EU criminal law, or with modest rules, which will respect more clearly the different legal systems and traditions of the Member States as defined in Article 67 TFEU, is an open one. However, there is one certainty: the EU must intervene without delay to provide adequate protection to fundamental rights, as obliged by the Charter.

To this end, it is worth stressing that, of the different stages at which EU rules can in theory apply with regard to a conflict of jurisdictions (ie to prevent a conflict from occurring at all; or, if one has already occurred, to resolve it; or later, if it has not been resolved, to address its consequences through the *ne bis in idem* principle), it is the EU rules corresponding to the last stage that have been developed the furthest to date, due to CJEU's case law on the *ne bis in idem* principle. However, it is EU rules covering the first stage, ie establishing mechanisms to prevent conflicts of jurisdiction,[80] that would be of obvious added value, since they could preclude parallel criminal proceedings from occurring. In any case, it is of the utmost significance to emphasise the following: any EU intervention should be based on the fundamental choice to focus on the conflicts themselves, as complex situations setting serious challenges to procedural criminal law and to provisions of the Charter, rather than as an appendix to the operation of judicial cooperation in cross-border cases. The 2018 Eurojust Report revealed that this has become another area of EU activity where effectiveness collides with legality. The discussion regarding the impact of the obligation to ensure effectiveness on rights or even law principles may be of central importance in the area of freedom, security and justice, but the 'cost' that legality and abiding by the rule of law have on effectiveness is definitely not an EU issue alone. On the contrary, it is precisely the mission of the rule of law, functioning as the backbone of any democracy, to delimit state powers and, in this manner, protect citizens from abuse and legalise all state activity that does not cross these limits. It is due to this legalising effect that respecting the rule of law serves the effectiveness of state action in the long term. And, in this sense, it remains to be fully acknowledged in the EU that legality and effectiveness are not contradictory concepts.

IV. Conclusions on the Link between Fighting Impunity and Conflicts of Jurisdiction in the EU

Revisiting the initial remarks on the connection between fighting impunity in the EU and conflicts of jurisdiction, one may conclude that the aspect of the notion of impunity that is of relevance here is the goal of punishing crime effectively;

[80] Preventing conflicts can be conceived (i) by reducing clauses calling for the establishment of extra-territorial jurisdiction from EU legal acts; (ii) by allocating jurisdiction in such a manner that only one court in the EU has competence to prosecute each criminal act; or (iii) as an alternative to (ii), by determining rules to apply so as to decide which among the different courts that have competence should initiate the criminal proceedings (in which case, regulating the transfer of proceedings would also be necessary).

in this respect, it is directly linked to the obligations addressed to the Member States to establish extraterritorial jurisdiction in fields of crime falling within the EU's competence, but also to the genesis of specific conflicts of jurisdiction and to the 'mechanisms' in place to deal with the conflicts. However, it has furthermore become clear that conflicts of jurisdiction in criminal matters in the EU are not just a side effect of the effort to diminish legal loopholes that allow for crime to prosper, but are in addition a tool placed at the service of judicial cooperation. In this context, the introductory observation that conflicts of jurisdiction cannot be tolerated in the EU is reinforced for a number of reasons. Most significantly, the respective competence prescribed in Article 82 TFEU, which is integral for the construction of one area of freedom, security and justice in the EU,[81] is yet to be exercised satisfactorily, allowing for soft-law solutions entailing uncertainty and even disregard for legislative provisions. Significant room is left for rights included in the Charter to be violated, not only in relation to the *ne bis in idem* principle, but also in relation to the principle of proportionality, the right to a fair trial and the principle of legality in the aspect of foreseeability. Finally, the general requirement to respect the rule of law in the EU needs to be affirmed further by aligning practice to the legislation.

The fight against impunity in the EU presents significant challenges for preventing and resolving conflicts of jurisdiction in criminal matters. In fact, the field of conflicts of jurisdiction is a most indicative example of how perceiving the fight against impunity as an abstract (and very general, or even absolute) objective may have a serious impact on the quality (see the violations of fundamental EU law principles and rights) and the effectiveness (see the lack of binding force) of EU legislation. Conversely, adopting concrete measures to deal with specific issues of impunity would be much more beneficial in terms of efficiency, and with less cost to legality. This becomes apparent, for example, if one compares the current problematic handlings concerning parallel criminal proceedings to a possible future regime, where triggering criminal prosecutions would, as a rule, be prohibited (so as to respect EU law principles and rights), but (bearing in mind the peculiarities of the area of freedom, security and justice) it could be allowed as an exception, under predetermined and regulated conditions, when real cases of impunity actually occur. Indicatively, it could be permitted when the national authorities in a Member State are reluctant to prosecute due to high-level state corruption, or when no Member State is willing to prosecute or maintain the prosecution of a complex cross-border case.

Consequently, the much-needed drastic legislative regulation of preventing and resolving conflicts of jurisdiction in the EU must abstain from considering impunity as a vaguely perceived danger; instead, it must aim to address realistic situations of impunity in a concise manner and to confirm legality as a precondition for substantive and functional effectiveness of EU law.

[81] In comparison, no Member State would permit a situation where more than one of its national courts would hold parallel criminal proceedings for the same case.

8

The Fight against Impunity between EU and National Legal Orders: What Role for the EPPO?

COSTANZA DI FRANCESCO MAESA

I. Introduction

In a European territory without border checks, cross-border crimes and crimes specifically affecting European interests pose important challenges to national criminal justice systems. Rapidly growing mobility and the rapid expansion of new technologies are not compensated by the capacity of the Member States (MS) to prosecute effectively the perpetrators of these offences and to enforce their criminal law. In this context, the Regulation establishing a European Public Prosecutor's Office (EPPO Regulation)[1] has been adopted at the EU level. The EPPO Regulation aims to tackle more effectively the perpetrators of offences affecting the Union's financial interests and to enhance deterrence by increasing the number and effectiveness of criminal investigations and prosecutions against the perpetrators of such offences throughout the Union's territory.

In this context, this chapter aims to test the normative force of the concept of impunity within the context of the EPPO Regulation. In particular, the analysis seeks to ascertain whether the EPPO Regulation's objective of avoiding impunity, stated in the recitals,[2] is effectively translated into its provisions. To that end, it commences with a brief account of the different meanings of the concept of impunity contained within the EPPO Regulation (section II). Thereafter, it assesses whether the structure of the EPPO allows it to achieve the objective of preventing impunity (section III.A and B), then seeks to ascertain whether the rules on the forum choice and the cases of conflict of competence between the EPPO and the

[1] Council Regulation (EU) 2017/1939 implementing enhanced cooperation on the establishment of the European Public Prosecutor's Office (EPPO Regulation) [2017] OJ L283/1.

[2] Recital 12 EPPO Regulation declares that the EPPO Regulation's objective is to 'enhance the fight against offences affecting the financial interests of the Union by setting up the EPPO', thus to avoid the impunity of the perpetrators of such offences. For an in-depth analysis, see section II.B below.

national authorities are adequate for achieving the objective of ensuring an area of freedom, security and justice (AFSJ) where the impunity of someone who has already been sentenced is avoided (section III.C and D). In the conclusion, it is argued that the EPPO Regulation does not achieve those objectives. In fact, it does not seem that the EPPO is fully equipped to perform its tasks. In this regard, the final remarks outline some possible solutions for addressing these flaws.

II. Terms of the Analysis: A Definition

A. Impunity

Impunity is a multifaceted and pervasive notion, which can be used in a variety of contexts and with different aims. The basic meaning of the notion corresponds to 'exemption from punishment' (in-punity, or in-poena from the Latin).[3] However, this expression can be interpreted in at least three different ways. According to its initial narrow meaning, the concept of 'impunity' is strictly connected to the adoption of a judicial authority's formal decision. A second, broader meaning, on the other hand, also encompasses those cases in which the suspects of crimes not only escape the penalty imposed by a judgment, but escape the trial itself. A final meaning provides an even wider definition, also including those cases of de facto impunity. This section scrutinises which meaning should be used to test the normative force of the concept of impunity in the context of the EPPO Regulation.

As mentioned above, according to a narrow interpretation, the meaning of the term 'impunity' is closely related to the concept of 'punishment' and the judge's formal decision imposing a penalty. The formal 'imposition of a penalty as retribution for an offence'[4] by a judicial authority is deemed to be a constitutive element of impunity. A criminal cannot, in fact, escape the punishment before he or she has been found guilty and sentenced. Thus, in this sense, 'fight against impunity' means avoiding the perpetrators of crime, convicted by a criminal court, going unpunished. However, in assessing the relevance of this first meaning to this chapter, it should be noted that the EPPO has no competence to ensure that criminal convictions adopted by national judicial authorities are effectively enforced at the national level; the execution phase is still exclusively entrusted to the domestic authorities. The EPPO is merely responsible for investigating, prosecuting and bringing to trial the perpetrators of offences falling within its competence, while the national courts are responsible for settling the cases brought before them by the EPPO. Therefore, that formal approach to the notion of 'impunity' is not relevant to this analysis and is not considered any further in this chapter.

[3] *Oxford Dictionary of English*, 3rd edn (Oxford, Oxford University Press, 2010).
[4] ibid.

However, there are at least two other scenarios in which the concept of 'impunity' comes into play at an earlier stage, ie before the perpetrator is sentenced.

First, international criminal law shows that in some cases alleged perpetrators of serious international crimes not only escape the punishment imposed by a judicial decision, but are not even subjected to criminal proceedings.[5] In this context, 'impunity' has been defined as:

> the impossibility, de jure or de facto, of bringing the perpetrators of violations to account … since they are not subject to any inquiry that might lead to their being accused, arrested, tried and, if found guilty, sentenced to appropriate penalties, and to making reparations to their victims.[6]

Therefore, from this point of view, fighting against impunity also means avoiding the suspects of crimes absconding before or during the trial.[7] However, this particular meaning of the term 'impunity' is not analysed further in this chapter either, since other instruments, ie judicial and police cooperation instruments and mechanisms aimed at ensuring the mutual recognition of judgments and judicial decisions,[8] have been adopted at the European level to fight against that absconding risk.[9]

The third meaning of 'impunity' is of particular relevance for these purposes. While, at the European level, a clear definition of this notion does not yet exist, the Court of Justice (the Court) has provided useful interpretative guidance. The Court's case law concerns, in particular, the prosecution of offences affecting the Union's financial interests, which are also the offences falling within the EPPO's competence.[10] In this respect, the Court stated that the provisions adopted at the

[5] See JA Le Clercq Ortega and GR Sánchez Lara (eds), *Global Impunity Dimensions. Global Impunity Index 2017* (Fundación Universidad de las Américas, Puebla, UDLAP, 2017).

[6] Commission on Human Rights, 'Updated Set of principles for the protection and promotion of human rights through action to combat impunity, Impunity – Report of the independent expert to update the Set of principles to combat impunity, Diane Orentlicher (sixty-first session, Item 17 of the provisional agenda Promotion And Protection of Human Rights, 2005)' (Updated Impunity Principles). See also MM Penrose, 'Impunity – Inertia, Inaction, and Invalidity: A Literature Review' (1999) 17 *Boston University International Law Journal* 276.

[7] See, particularly with reference to international terrorism, C Paulussen, 'Impunity for International Terrorists? Key Legal Questions and Practical Considerations' (ICCT Research Paper, 2012) 5–6. See also A Rasi, 'The Court of Justice of the European Union and the International Criminal Court: the Fight against Impunity between Complementarity and Mandatory Requirements', ch 18 in this book.

[8] See, eg Council Framework Decision on the European arrest warrant and surrender procedures between Member States (EAW Framework Decision) [2002] OJ L190/1; Directive 2014/41/EU of the European Parliament and of the Council regarding the European Investigation Order in criminal matters (EIO Directive) [2014] OJ L130/1. See also the European legislation on the European Evidence Warrant, freezing of assets and evidence, confiscation orders, exchange of information on convictions/criminal records, pre- and post-trial measures, mutual recognition of protection measures and mutual recognition of financial penalties.

[9] In general, such a scenario may also unfortunately transpire in respect of particularly serious crimes under international law. For a definition of such crimes, see Commission on Human Rights, 'Promotion and protection of Human Rights, Impunity, Report of the independent expert to update the Set of Principles to combat impunity, Diane Orentlicher (sixty-first session 2005)' point 13.

[10] See Case C-105/14 *Ivo Taricco and Others* [2015] paras 45–47; for an analysis of the relationship between the interpretation given in the *Taricco* judgment and the respect of the fundamental rights enshrined in the Charter, see Case C-310/16 *Dzivev and Others* [2019].

national level to counter fraud and any other illegal activities affecting the financial interests of the Union must ensure that the perpetrators of those offences do not enjoy de facto impunity.[11] MS must ensure that national provisions facilitate the effective investigation and prosecution of offences against the Union's financial interests.[12] 'Even though the penalties and administrative and/or criminal procedures relating to those penalties … fall within the [Member States'] procedural and institutional autonomy', 'that autonomy is nevertheless limited by the principle of effectiveness, which requires that such penalties be effective and dissuasive'.[13] The need to ensure that the domestic measures are effective and dissuasive thus obliges MS to

> ensure that the procedural rules applicable to the prosecutions of offences affecting the financial interests of the European Union are not designed in such a way that there arises, for reasons inherent in those rules, *a systemic risk* that acts that may be categorised as such offences *may go unpunished*, and also to ensure that the fundamental rights of accused persons are protected.[14]

MS are thus obliged to ensure that the perpetrators of offences against the Union's financial interests do not enjoy de facto impunity but that, on the contrary, they are effectively prosecuted. Deficiencies in the national system with regard to the measures adopted to counter any illegal activities affecting the Union's financial interests do not justify flaws in the protection of those interests.[15] National provisions which ensure de facto impunity for the perpetrators of those crimes are thus to be considered incompatible with EU law.[16] The only limit is represented by respect for the general principles of the European legal system and the fundamental rights of the individuals involved in the investigations, as enshrined in the Charter of Fundamental Rights of the Union.[17] This is the background against which the EPPO is expected to add value to the fight against crime and impunity.

After a brief description of the objectives pursued by the EPPO Regulation, the next subsection will consider whether the promises underpinning the establishment of the EPPO have actually been met.

[11] See *Ivo Taricco and Others* (n 10) paras 46–47; Case C-612/15 *Kolev and Others* [2018] paras 50ff; Case C-47/17 *MAS and MB* [2017], Opinion of AG Bot, paras 83, 87, 106.

[12] In this respect, with particular reference to rules of criminal procedure, see *Dzivev and Others* (n 10) para 29; Case C-419/14 *WebMindLicenses* [2015] para 65; *Kolev and Others* (n 11) para 55. That is a corollary of the general obligation of equivalence and effectiveness established by the Court in the 'Amsterdam Bulb' (Case 50/76 *Amsterdam Bulb BV v Produktschap voor Siergewassen* [1977] ECR 137) and 'Greek maize' (Case 68/88 *Commission v Greece* [1989] ECR 2965) cases.

[13] See *Dzivev and Others* (n 10) para 30; Case C-574/15 *Scialdone* [2018] para 29.

[14] See *Dzivev and Others* (n 10) para 31 (emphasis added). See also, in the same vein, *Ivo Taricco and Others* (n 10) paras 45–47.

[15] National provisions that are incompatible with Art 325 TFEU must in fact be disapplied by the competent judicial authority. See *Ivo Taricco and Others* (n 10) paras 48, 49ff.

[16] See Art 325 TFEU.

[17] See *Dzivev and Others* (n 10) para 33ff.

B. The Concept of Impunity in the EPPO Regulation

As far as the objectives of the EPPO Regulation are concerned, the Commission's proposal on the establishment of the EPPO,[18] which, in this regard, was later incorporated into the recitals of the EPPO Regulation,[19] expressly clarifies that the EPPO is set up for the following purposes: to fight more effectively against offences affecting the Union's financial interests, to enhance deterrence due to increased risk of investigation and prosecution throughout the Union's territory, to further strengthen the development of an AFSJ and to consequently increase EU citizens' trust in EU institutions.[20] In other words, the ultimate aim of establishing the EPPO is to develop the AFSJ further by enhancing the fight against the impunity of perpetrators of offences affecting the Union's financial interests. Although the term 'impunity' is not explicitly mentioned in the EPPO Regulation, the fight against this phenomenon is the guiding objective in shaping the structure and powers of the EPPO.

In the Commission's view, an effective fight against the impunity of perpetrators of offences against the Union's financial interests is a necessary condition for strengthening the trust of EU citizens in EU institutions and in the AFSJ. As the former EU Justice Commissioner Viviane Reding stated: 'Criminals who exploit legal loopholes to pocket taxpayers' money should not go free because we do not have the right tools to bring them to justice.'[21] In this context, the concept of impunity is seen to be strictly interconnected with the concepts of effectiveness, deterrence and trust.[22] More precisely, effective investigations and prosecutions are seen as a way of avoiding the impunity of criminals committing offences against the financial interests of the Union. Similarly, it is closely related to deterrence, as effective prosecution contributes to discouraging people from perpetrating crimes. At the same time, by avoiding the risk of impunity and creating an area in which people can freely and safely circulate, the trust of EU citizens and businesses in the EU as a supranational polity is enhanced. This multifaceted dimension of the concept of 'impunity' is also mirrored in the case law of the Court, which highlights the close relationship between the objective of ensuring an AFSJ without internal frontiers, as referred to in Article 3(2) TEU, and the need to avoid a denial of the victims' right to justice. The Court affirmed accordingly that preventing the risk of impunity represents a legitimate objective of the EU.[23] The EPPO is

[18] Commission, 'Proposal for a Council for a Regulation on the establishment of the European Public Prosecutor's Office' (Commission's Proposal) COM (2013) 534 final, point 3.3, 5.

[19] See Recitals 1, 3, 12 EPPO Regulation.

[20] See Commission's Proposal, point 3.3, 5.

[21] European Commission, 'Protecting Taxpayers' Money against Fraud: Commission Proposes European Public Prosecutor's Office and Reinforces OLAF Procedural Guarantees', Press Release (2013) http://europa.eu/rapid/press-release_IP-13-709_en.htm.

[22] See Commission's Proposal, point 3.3, 5.

[23] See Case C-191/16 *Romano Pisciotti v Bundesrepublik Deutschland* [2018] para 47; Case C-182/15 *Aleksei Petruhhin* [2016]; Case C-220/18 PPU *ML* [2018].

certainly a step forward in this direction; nevertheless, the author will argue that it is the result of a compromise solution, which raises some concerns as to its actual capacity of tackling impunity.

III. EPPO Regulation and the Fight against Impunity

This section seeks to discuss whether the current EPPO Regulation achieves the objective of at least reducing the risk of impunity of perpetrators of offences affecting the Union's financial interests. In the author's opinion, the EPPO Regulation leaves many legal loopholes open, which may represent a breeding ground for financial crimes. Although the EPPO Regulation aims to give the EPPO the power to carry out effective investigations and prosecutions,[24] the final version of the Regulation does not, in fact, create the best conditions for achieving that objective for a number of reasons. The following paragraphs will thus focus on the analysis of the legal inconsistencies of the EPPO Regulation, which are likely to allow criminals to escape justice and facilitate the creation of 'safe havens'.[25]

A. The Structure of the EPPO

The EPPO's structure is one of the most problematic features likely to affect the effectiveness of its investigations and prosecutions, and consequently to weaken its capacity to reduce the risk of impunity. In particular, the intergovernmental features characterising the EPPO's structure, coupled with its complex and multilayered dimension, results in the fragmentation of its powers to decide and investigate. The reason for this lies mainly in the difficulty of combining the European dimension of investigation and prosecution with the different legal systems of 22 MS.[26] The shortcomings related to the current EPPO's structure have already been analysed by many scholars who have commented on the Regulation.[27] We therefore refer

[24] It should be noted that 'effective prosecutions' is mainly intended by the Commission as 'more prosecutions'. See Commission's Proposal, point 3.3.

[25] This expression has been used by A Csuri, 'The Proposed European Public Prosecutor's Office – from a Trojan Horse to a White Elephant?' (2016) 18 *Cambridge Yearbook of European Legal Studies* 122, 139.

[26] Reference is made to the 22 MS participating in the enhanced cooperation to set up the EPPO (Austria, Belgium, Bulgaria, Croatia, Cyprus, Czech Republic, Estonia, Finland, France, Germany, Greece, Italy, Latvia, Lithuania, Luxembourg, Portugal, Romania, Slovakia, Slovenia, Spain, the Netherlands and Malta, which recently notified its willingness to participate in the enhanced cooperation). In this regard, see S Allegrezza and A Mosna, 'Cross-Border Criminal Evidence and the Future European Public Prosecutor. One Step Back on Mutual Recognition?' in L Bachmaier Winter (ed), *The European Public Prosecutor's Office – The Challenges Ahead* (Cham, Springer, 2018) 151.

[27] In this regard, see, *ex multis*, K Ligeti, 'The European Public Prosecutor's Office: Which Model?' in A Klip (ed), *Substantive Criminal Law of the European Union* (Antwerp, Maklu, 2011) 51ff; K Ligeti and M Simonato, 'The European Public Prosecutor's Office: Towards a Truly European Prosecution

to those studies for an in-depth analysis of the EPPO's intergovernmental, collegiate model. This analysis, on the other hand, mainly focuses on the aspects of the EPPO's structure which potentially make its investigations and prosecutions ineffective, thereby hampering the capability of avoiding the risk of impunity of the perpetrators of offences falling within its competence.

The Regulation defines the EPPO as an 'indivisible body operating as a single Office',[28] which is nevertheless to be organised at two different levels, centralised and decentralised.[29] The centralised level is composed of a Central Office consisting of the College, the Permanent Chambers, the European Chief Prosecutor, the Deputy European Chief Prosecutors, the European Prosecutors and the Administrative Director.[30] The decentralised level includes 'European Delegated Prosecutors who shall be located in the Member States'.[31] All the different bodies composing the EPPO are to work together in order to ensure the functioning of the Central Office.

The College is responsible for 'the general oversight of the activities of the EPPO' and 'shall take decisions on strategic matters, and on general issues arising from individual cases',[32] but it is not allowed to 'take operational decisions in individual cases'.[33] The responsibility for the EPPO's investigations belongs to the European Delegated Prosecutors (EDPs) handling the case, who are to carry out the investigations and prosecutions.[34] The significant part of the investigative and prosecutorial tasks of the EPPO is therefore performed at the national level by 'active members of the public prosecution service or judiciary of the respective Member States which nominated them', who wear a 'double hat'.[35] In turn, the European Prosecutors 'supervise the investigations and prosecutions for which the European Delegated Prosecutors handling the case in their Member State of origin are responsible',[36] while the Permanent Chambers 'shall monitor and

Service?' [2013] *New Journal of European Criminal Law* 10–12; K Ligeti (ed), *Toward a Prosecutor for the European Union – Volume I: A Comparative Analysis* (Oxford, Hart Publishing, 2013).

[28] Art 8(1) EPPO Regulation.

[29] See Art 8(2) EPPO Regulation. In this regard, for an explanation of the structure of the EPPO, see, *ex multis*, V Mitsilegas and F Giuffrida, 'Raising the Bar? Thoughts on the Establishment of the European Public Prosecutor's Office' (CEPS, 2017) https://www.ceps.eu/system/files/PI%20 2017-39%20Mitsilegas_Giuffrida_0.pdf; Bachmaier Winter (n 26).

[30] In this sense, see Art 8(3) EPPO Regulation.

[31] See Art 8(4) EPPO Regulation.

[32] See Art 9(1)(2) EPPO Regulation.

[33] See Art 9(2) EPPO Regulation.

[34] See Art 13(1) EPPO Regulation.

[35] The expression 'double hat' refers to the double nature of the EDPs, who 'may also exercise functions as national prosecutors, to the extent that this does not prevent them from fulfilling their obligations under th[e] Regulation' (Art 13(3) EPPO Regulation). The European Chief Prosecutor and the European Prosecutors, in contrast, are considered as 'temporary agents' according to the Staff Regulations of the European Union. See Art 96(1) EPPO Regulation.

[36] See Art 12(1) EPPO Regulation. In this respect, Ivan Korčok, President-in-Office of the Council during the European Parliament debate, highlighted that, due to the significant differences existing between the criminal justice systems of the participating MS, 'it is clear that only a prosecutor with his or her background in a given legal system will be able to know exactly what actions are most appropriate and efficient in that given state' (European Parliament, debates on Tuesday 4 October 2016, point 17)

direct the investigations and prosecutions conducted by the European Delegated Prosecutors' and 'ensure the coordination of investigations and prosecutions in cross-border cases'.[37]

Therefore, the decision on whether or not to prosecute an offence over which the EPPO has competence depends on interactions between the Permanent Chambers, the supervising European Prosecutors and the EDPs. Moreover, decisions on whether or not to prosecute an offence are taken at a different level (the centralised one, and specifically by the Permanent Chambers) from the level (the decentralised one) at which investigations and prosecutions are carried out in accordance with the applicable national law, ie ordinarily the law of the Member State whose EDP is handling the case.[38] The multiplication of decision-making centres and layers consequently increases the possibility of incoherent, cumbersome and dysfunctional proceedings within the EPPO. Investigations and prosecutions carried out by the EPPO face the risk of being ineffective because its decision-making and operational powers are split into two different levels: centralised and decentralised. This may lead to both lengthy proceedings and delays in taking important investigative and prosecutorial decisions, as well as to possible contradictory decisions at the two different decision-making levels.[39] This situation may trigger contradictory opinions of the EPPO's members about whether or not to prosecute and may cause delays in making such decisions, which in some cases may involve the crimes becoming time-barred or otherwise not prosecuted due to national procedural rules.

The possibility for perpetrators of offences falling within the EPPO's competence to exploit the shortcomings of the system in order to escape justice may particularly arise when the EDP handling the case disagrees with the supervising European prosecutor (SupEP) and/or the Permanent Chamber (PC), and thus does not follow their instructions. The EPPO Regulation states that the EDPs 'shall follow the direction and instructions of the Permanent Chamber in charge of a case as well as the instructions from the supervising European prosecutor'.[40] If the EDP handling the case does not follow the instructions of the competent PC or of the SupEP, the case may be reallocated to another EDP[41] or, in exceptional cases, to the SupEP him or herself.[42] However, the Regulation does not clarify at which stage of the investigations this could happen. The decision may, therefore, even be taken at an advanced stage of the investigations and the new EDP may have to familiarise him- or herself, in a short period of time, with all the relevant

http://www.europarl.europa.eu/sides/getDoc.do?type=CRE&reference=20161004&secondRef=TOC&language=en. However, for an exception, see Art 12(2) EPPO Regulation.

[37] See Art 10(1)(2) EPPO Regulation.

[38] Art 5(3) EPPO Regulation.

[39] See Mitsilegas and Giuffrida (n 29) 8.

[40] Art 13(1) EPPO Regulation.

[41] Art 28(3) EPPO Regulation.

[42] See Art 28(4) EPPO Regulation.

information and evidence gathered by the EDP previously handling the case.[43] The possible positive outcome of the reallocation thus depends on a variety of factors, such as the workload of the EDP to whom the case is reallocated, the time that he or she can spend in studying the new case, his or her relationship with the former EDP handling the case and the stage at which this reallocation mechanism is activated. It is nevertheless likely that this reallocation mechanism, instead of making the EPPO's investigations smoother and quicker, will complicate the situation and hinder effective investigations. Another scenario to be considered is one in which the EDP handling the case and the SupEP intend to prosecute the criminal offence at issue, while the PC intends to dismiss it. The EPPO Regulation states that the PC 'cannot decide to dismiss the case if a draft decision proposes bringing a case to judgment'.[44] However, the PC, under the conditions established in Article 34 of the EPPO Regulation, may transfer the case to the national authorities, which may decide autonomously on whether to dismiss or prosecute the case.

Conversely, it may be that the EDP handling the case and the SupEP intend to dismiss the case, while the PC disagrees and thinks the case should continue. Can the PC force the EDP and the SupEP to bring the case to judgment? Article 39 of the EPPO Regulation does not envisage such a possibility.[45] Thus, if the EDP and the SupEP decide to dismiss a case, the central level of the EPPO, ie the competent PC, cannot order them to bring the case to judgment. Thus, the perpetrators of the offences against the Union's financial interests may go unpunished without the central level having the power to avoid it.

This demonstrates that any contradictory opinions of different members of the EPPO on the same case may cause problems. Issuing a decision could take time, and the decision could ultimately be to dismiss the case or to transfer it back again to the national authorities with the risk of evidence being lost and the limitation period elapsing. In such a scenario, the added value of the EPPO in avoiding the fragmentation of investigative and prosecutorial powers with a view to circumventing the impunity of perpetrators of offences affecting the Union's financial interests is difficult to see.

B. Applicable Law

Another critical feature of the EPPO Regulation is the frequent reference to national law, both in general terms[46] and in specific provisions concerning the procedures that the EPPO should follow for taking investigative measures.[47] The normative multilayered system established by the Regulation which relies on

[43] However, it should be noted that the Regulation establishes that, in exceptional cases, the investigations may be undertaken personally by the SupEP, who is a temporary agent of the Union. See Art 28(4) EPPO Regulation.

[44] See Art 36(1) EPPO Regulation.

[45] But see Art 39(2) EPPO Regulation.

[46] See Art 5(3) EPPO Regulation.

[47] See Art 30(5) of the EPPO Regulation. See also, eg Arts 26(1) and 30 EPPO Regulation.

the national law of the MS appears to be inconsistent with the objective of creating a European prosecutorial body able to avoid the problems emerging from 'the fragmentation of national prosecutions in the area of offences committed against the Union's financial interests'.[48] The apparent coherence of the body, which is described as an 'indivisible body operating as a single Office',[49] in fact conceals its ongoing fragmentation. The diversity of applicable procedural rules increases the risk of impunity of criminals, who may choose to commit the crime in a place where the threshold for executing the investigative measures and/or the conditions under which they are ordered are more favourable to them, eg in a Member State where it will be declared time-barred before the criminal penalty laid down by law can be imposed by a final judicial decision.[50]

That risk is particularly high in the case of cross-border crimes,[51] where the handling EDP applies procedural rules different from those applied by the assisting EDP. Since the procedural rules in the MS participating in the EPPO differ, it may in fact be the case that a certain measure exists in one Member State but not in another, or that the same investigative measure cannot be used under the conditions requested by the handling EDP in the Member State where it should be executed.

If the measure requested is not available in a similar domestic case in the Member State where the measure is to be executed, the EPPO Regulation provides that the assisting EDP should consult with the handling EDP and solve the matter bilaterally.[52] An analogous system of consultation and notification is established in the EIO Directive.[53] However, the EPPO Regulation on this point is

[48] Recital 12 EPPO Regulation.

[49] Art 8(1) EPPO Regulation.

[50] In this respect, it should be noted that, even though the perpetrators of offences falling within the EPPO's competence are not always rational individuals, those crimes, in most cases, are committed on the basis of a cost–benefit analysis. The reason is twofold. In the first instance, only PIF offences which are serious and cause or are likely to cause significant damage fall within the EPPO's competence (see section III.C below). As a result, particularly when they are of a cross-border nature, such as in the case of carousel fraud, they are committed by companies or shell companies specifically created to commit such offences. Organised crime is also sometimes involved because of the high profit deriving from such crimes. The seriousness of the offences, the high profit deriving from them and the nature of the perpetrators of those crimes provide some empirical support for the assumption that companies committing such crimes, especially carousel fraud, decide, in most cases, whether to abide by the law on the basis of a cost–benefit analysis. That statement is not contradicted by the analysis of De Bondt and Miettinen, who refer to forum shopping as a rationale for harmonising minimum penalties at the EU level: W De Bondt and S Miettinen 'Minimum Criminal Penalties in the European Union: In Search of a Credible Justification' (2015) 21 *European Law Journal* 722. On this point, they state, in particular, that the approximation of minimum penalties 'is insufficient to achieve a satisfactory level of convergence'. 'Unification, the wholesale harmonisation of all elements of penalty systems, could in principle be effective. However, this is politically difficult' (722). In their opinion, therefore, only unification could avoid the risk of forum shopping, while there is no evidence that forum shopping can be avoided through the approximation of minimum penalties. The same opinion is held in the text, where the author argues that minimum harmonisation does not solve the problem of forum shopping.

[51] See Art 31 EPPO Regulation.

[52] If the matter cannot be solved bilaterally, the mechanism foreseen in Art 31(7)(8) EPPO Regulation applies.

[53] Art 10(5) EIO Directive.

'rather confusing'.[54] If the assigned measure does not exist in the executing state, Article 31(6) of the EPPO Regulation applies, but the wording of this provision is rather unclear.[55] At first glance, it appears that the system envisaged by the EPPO Regulation prevails, but if 'the assigned measure does not exist in a purely domestic situation, but would be available in a cross-border situation covered by legal instruments on mutual recognition or cross-border cooperation',[56] the EDPs, in agreement with the supEP, may make recourse to instruments of mutual recognition or cross-border cooperation.

The recourse to the EIO, in the absence of a uniform EPPO procedure, may be beneficial, and could contribute to creating a more coherent scheme.[57] The precondition for establishing a special scheme for EPPO investigations was the 'assumption that the EPPO will be a single legal office, operating in a single legal area'.[58] However, the EPPO Regulation does not establish a single legal area for EPPO investigations, as the EPPO gathers evidence according to different national laws and does not involve a uniform EPPO procedure. As a result, for cross-border crimes, the mechanism is complex and time-consuming, as there are many persons and many different legal frameworks involved.[59] The reasoning based on the fact that the EPPO operates in a single legal area, therefore, is not an adequate rationale for limiting the recourse of the EPPO to the EIO.[60]

The recourse to the EIO and other mutual recognition instruments, on the contrary, could be a way for the EPPO to limit the risk of criminals exploiting the differences between the national legal systems in order to go unpunished. The fragmentation of the procedural rules of the participating MS penalises the effectiveness of the EPPO's investigations; thus, it does not reduce the risk of de facto impunity, which the EPPO Regulation was created to eliminate, especially in cross-border cases, which are supposedly the cases in which the EPPO should provide added value and improve the current situation significantly.

C. Conflict of Competence between the EPPO and the National Authorities of the Participating MS

The way in which conflicts of competence between the EPPO and the national authorities of the participating MS are resolved is another challenge.

[54] L Bachmaier Winter, 'Cross-Border Investigations under the EPPO Proceedings and the Quest for Balance' in Bachmaier Winter (n 26) 127.

[55] As noted by Bachmaier Winter (ibid) 127, in fact, 'according to Article 31(2) the measures that any EDP can "assign" are those listed in Article 30 EPPO Regulation, so I do not see how there can be a problem due to the non-existence of the measure'.

[56] Art 31(6) EPPO Regulation.

[57] See A Csúri, 'Towards an Inconsistent European Regime of Cross-Border Evidence: The EPPO and the European Investigation Order' in W Geelhoed, LH Erkelens and AWH Meij (eds), *Shifting Perspectives on the European Public Prosecutor's Office* (The Hague, TMC Asser Press, 2018) 141, 150–151.

[58] ibid. See also Art 25(1) Commission proposal.

[59] According to Art 31(3) EPPO Regulation, the competent PC shall in fact decide in accordance with the Regulation and the applicable national law.

[60] See Csúri (n 57) 150.

The EPPO Regulation is based on a shared competence between the EPPO and the national authorities of the participating MS.[61] Conflicts of competence between them may arise, and the EPPO Regulation is expected to provide adequate resolution mechanisms of these conflicts to avoid the risk of certain offences not being prosecuted by the EPPO or by the national authorities, such that the perpetrators of those offences enjoy de facto impunity.

As regards the EPPO's competence, the EPPO Regulation establishes that, save for certain exceptions, it is competent 'in respect of the criminal offences affecting the financial interests of the Union that are provided for in Directive (EU) 2017/1371, as implemented by national law'.[62] The EPPO's competence is thus determined by reference to the national law implementing the PIF Directive.[63]

Even from a substantive criminal law perspective, as mentioned above with respect to the procedural rules,[64] the EPPO, despite the declared intention to create a central European prosecution office, lacks a truly vertical scheme. Its overall coherence thus depends on national implementing laws. This delimitation of the EPPO's competence affects the uniformity and coherence of the EPPO's competence itself. It may in fact be the case that a domestic provision 'that is considered to implement the Directive actually – in terms of criminalising certain conduct – goes beyond the specific obligations stemming from the corresponding provision of the PIF Directive'.[65] If that were the case, the same conduct may be considered an offence falling within the EPPO's competence according to the national law of a given Member State, whereas it may not be considered such if committed within the jurisdiction of another Member State. The coherent interpretation of the EPPO's competence is further undermined by the system of exceptions referred to in Article 25(2)(3) of the EPPO Regulation, which lists the cases in which the EPPO should refrain from exercising its competence.[66] Furthermore, Article 25(2) of the EPPO Regulation, which refers to cases where the EPPO may exercise its competence, provides exceptions to these exceptions.[67] As a result, the perpetrators of offences affecting the Union's financial interests could benefit from differences existing between different MS and decide to commit a given offence in a Member State in which it is not considered to fall within the EPPO's competence rather than in a Member State in which it is considered to fall within the EPPO's

[61] See Recital 13 and Arts 22ff EPPO Regulation. Contra, see Art 11(4) Commission's Proposal.

[62] See Art 22(1) EPPO Regulation.

[63] Directive (EU) 2017/1371 on the fight against fraud to the Union's financial interests by means of criminal law (PIF Directive) [2017] OJ L198/29. See C Di Francesco Maesa, 'Directive (EU) 2017/1371 on the Fight against Fraud to the Union's Financial Interests by Means of Criminal Law: A Missed Goal?' (2018) *European Papers, European Forum* www.europeanpapers.eu/en/europeanforum/directive-EU-2017/1371-on-fight-against-fraud-to-union-financial-interests.

[64] See section III.B above.

[65] HH Herrnfeld, 'Choice of Forum and Case Allocation in the EPPO Regulation' in K Ligeti and G Robinson (eds), *Preventing and Resolving Conflicts of Jurisdiction in EU Criminal Law* (Oxford, European Law Institute, 2018) 291, 297.

[66] See, however, the exception to the exception mentioned in Art 25(3) EPPO Regulation.

[67] See, in particular, Art 25(2)(a)(b) EPPO Regulation.

competence. The scenario is even more challenging in the event of 'inextricably linked' offences[68] and of crime with a transnational dimension (eg, as it is committed on the territory of different MS, if a national of one Member State commits the crime on the territory of another Member State, or if the main financial damage has occurred in a different state from that in which the hub of the criminal activity is located).

The allocation of the competence to investigate and prosecute an offence 'inextricably linked' to criminal conduct which falls within the EPPO's competence is a key concern.[69] In principle, these cases must be handled by the EPPO, except where

> the maximum sanction provided for by national law for an offence falling within the scope of the [EPPO's competence] is equal to or less severe than the maximum sanction for an inextricably linked offence … unless the latter offence has been instrumental to commit the offence falling within the scope of [the EPPO's competence].[70]

This wording fails to determine the area of intervention of the EPPO, thereby giving rise to possible conflicts of competence. In the absence of a clear criterion, both the EPPO and the national authorities could claim jurisdiction or decline it. These provisions pose additional challenges in the case of cross-border crimes, as such situations impose a twofold decision: the allocation of competence between the EPPO and the MS, and the identification of the MS enjoying jurisdiction.[71]

Moreover, problems of allocation of competence may also arise after the start of an investigation. The EPPO may exercise its right of evocation or it may refer the case to the competent national authorities at a later stage of the investigation.

In particular, the EPPO may exercise its right of evocation and require the competent national authorities to refrain from 'carrying out further acts of investigation in respect of the same offence'[72] if it becomes aware of the fact that an investigation in respect of a criminal offence for which it could be competent is already being undertaken by the competent national authorities.[73] On the other hand, the EPPO may decide to refer the case to the competent national authorities at any stage of the proceedings if it finds out that the case does not fall within its competence.[74] Accordingly, if the competent national authorities do not agree to

[68] See Art 22(3) EPPO Regulation.

[69] The notion of 'inextricably linked offences' is only described in Recital 54 of the EPPO Regulation with a cryptic formulation, which refers to the *ne bis in idem* case law. Against such interpretation, see, nevertheless, Case C-129/14 PPU *Spasic* [2014] paras 58, 61–64.

[70] In that case, the EPPO is to refrain from exercising its competence and is to refer the case to the competent national authority. See Art 25(3) EPPO Regulation.

[71] The criteria on forum choice are set down in Art 26(4–7) EPPO Regulation. cp Art 27(4) Commission's Proposal.

[72] See Art 27(5) EPPO Regulation.

[73] See Art 27(3) EPPO Regulation. Before deciding whether to exercise its right of evocation, the EPPO shall consult the competent authorities of the MS concerned, but if it decides to exercise it, the competent authorities shall transfer the file to the EPPO (Art 27(4)(5) EPPO Regulation).

[74] See Art 34 EPPO Regulation. Furthermore, Recital 61 of the Regulation establishes that 'When a judicial or law enforcement authority of a Member State initiates an investigation in respect of a

take over the case within a maximum period of 30 days, the EPPO shall remain competent to prosecute or dismiss the case.[75] However, if the competent national authorities do take over the case, they 'should preserve their full prerogatives under national law to open, continue or dismiss the investigation'.[76] It may nevertheless occur that, once the case is referred to the national authorities, it is already close to becoming time-barred or to coming across other procedural obstacles. Effective investigation and prosecution are thus precluded.

At first sight, it seems that the EPPO should be in charge of deciding whether or not to exercise its competence and to decide when it can investigate and prosecute an offence. However, a deeper examination of the EPPO Regulation shows that, in reality, the choice of who is competent to investigate and prosecute is dependent upon national law provisions and is mainly in the national authorities' hands. The latter are those responsible for informing the EPPO that, according to their national law, an offence falling within its competence has been committed.[77] They are also those competent to decide, in the case of disagreement between them and the EPPO, the question of whether the criminal conduct falls within their competence or that of the EPPO.[78] Therefore, the decision on the attribution of competence is taken by the national authorities on the basis of national law and varies from one Member State to another. In this regard, the only improvement envisaged by the EPPO Regulation, in comparison with the Commission's Proposal, is the possibility granted to the national authorities of referring the case to the Court of Justice for a preliminary ruling on 'the interpretation of Articles 22 and 25 of th[e] Regulation in relation to any conflict of competence between the EPPO and the competent national authorities'.[79] However, even in this case, the Court cannot annul the decision taken by the national authorities, as it does not fall within the scope of its competence.

The referral of the case to national authorities could, in the end, be a disguised way of dismissing the case; and the real decision in that regard lies with the national authorities. The risk of impunity is, therefore, not avoided by the current legal framework. On the contrary, the current situation of fragmentation of the applicable rules may be exploited by the perpetrators of offences affecting the Union's financial interests and could lead to their de facto impunity.

criminal offence and considers that the EPPO could not exercise its competence, it should inform the EPPO thereof, in order to allow the latter to assess whether it should exercise competence'.

[75] See Art 34(5) EPPO Regulation.

[76] See Recital 77 EPPO Regulation.

[77] See Art 24(2) EPPO Regulation.

[78] See Art 25(6) EPPO Regulation. As regards the expression 'national authorities', Recital 62 EPPO Regulation clarifies that 'The notion of competent national authorities should be understood as any judicial authorities which have competence to decide on the attribution of competence in accordance with national law'.

[79] Art 42(2)(c) EPPO Regulation.

D. Conflict of Competence between the EPPO and the National Authorities of the Non-participating MS

The case of conflict of competence between the EPPO and the national authorities of the participating MS should be distinguished from the case of conflict of competence between the EPPO and the national authorities of the non-participating MS. The establishment of the EPPO through enhanced cooperation in fact creates even more problems with regard to non-participating MS unable or unwilling to cooperate with the EPPO's requests for judicial cooperation, which could become a 'safe haven' for perpetrators of offences falling within the EPPO's competence.[80]

The EPPO Regulation does not cover the cases of conflict of competence between the EPPO and non-participating MS. In fact, the Regulation does not obligate non-participating MS. However, cases of conflict of competence may arise in various situations, such as offences falling within the EPPO's mandate which are either committed on the territory of non-participating MS or have a cross-border dimension, thus affecting the territory of both participating and non-participating MS.[81] Similarly, problems may arise when ancillary offences 'inextricably linked' to criminal conduct, falling within the EPPO's material scope of competence, are committed on the territory of a non-participating MS.[82]

The forms of cooperation envisaged by the EPPO Regulation are nevertheless scarce and have a limited scope of application.[83] In particular, the relationships that can be established by the EPPO with the non participating MS are the same as those that can be established between the EPPO, third countries and international organisations.[84] Working arrangements on the exchange of information and on the secondment of liaison officers to the EPPO are concluded on a voluntary basis. The content of these agreements, and also whether or not to conclude them, depends on the willingness of the non-participating MS. The designation of contact points in the non-participating MS is described in the Regulation as a possibility but not an obligation.[85] The relationship between the EPPO and the

[80] See C Di Francesco Maesa, 'Repercussions of the Establishment of the EPPO via Enhanced Cooperation EPPO's Added Value and the Possibility to Extend its Competence' (2017) 3 *Eucrim* 156, 157ff.

[81] V Mitsilegas, 'Follow-up Evidence to the House of Lords European Union Committee for Their Inquiry on "The Impact of the European Public Prosecutor's Office on the United Kingdom"' (4th Report HL Paper, session 2014–2015) 53.

[82] See Di Francesco Maesa (n 80) 157ff.

[83] See Art 105 EPPO Regulation.

[84] In this regard, see Art 104 EPPO Regulation.

[85] Art 105(2)(3) EPPO Regulation. In addition, para 3 of Art 105, which was eventually included in the EPPO Regulation after discussions in the Council, provides that the EPPO is able to rely on existing EU instruments of judicial cooperation in its relations with non-participating Member States 'In the absence of a legal instrument relating to cooperation in criminal matters and surrender' between the EPPO and the competent authorities of the non-participating MS. See A Weyembergh and C Briere, 'The Future Cooperation between OLAF and the European Public Prosecutor's Office' (Study for the Policy Department for Budgetary Affairs, 2017) http://www.europarl.europa.eu/RegData/etudes/IDAN/2017/603789/IPOL_ IDA(2017)603789_EN.pdf 25.

non-participating MS will thus be characterised by fragmentation, and 'it will rely on working agreements, of which there may be as many different ones as there are non-participating MS'.[86]

Therefore, these instruments are inadequate for ensuring effective coordination between the EPPO and the non-participating MS, and for avoiding the creation of a 'grey area' in which the perpetrators of offences falling within the EPPO's competence may escape justice. In this regard, a possible solution may be to adopt, as has been proposed,[87] a separate instrument to regulate in detail the relationship between the EPPO and the competent authorities of non-participating MS. It would be particularly useful if this instrument contained detailed rules on support by the non-participating MS of the EPPO's investigations and established rules for solving the conflict of jurisdiction between the EPPO and the national authorities of the non-participating MS and fostering the exchange of information between them. In this sense, a clarification of the relationship of the EPPO with Eurojust and OLAF (the European Anti-Fraud Office), when non-participating MS are involved, would be useful.[88] Admittedly, this is currently just a theoretical option.

IV. Conclusion

The above analysis has demonstrated that the EPPO Regulation does not fully achieve the objective of avoiding the risk of impunity of perpetrators of offences affecting the Union's financial interests. Despite being an important step towards a more efficient prosecution system within the area of freedom, security and justice, the strong and significant intergovernmental features of the EPPO, coupled with the definition of the EPPO's competence and powers by reference to national law, seriously undermines its effectiveness and, consequently, its deterrent effect. The existence of different substantive and procedural national laws gives criminals the opportunity to exploit loopholes created by the EPPO Regulation; rather than being deterred from committing offences against the Union's financial interests, they will, therefore, find ways of escaping justice.

In the author's opinion, the only possible way of removing the risk of impunity to any significant extent would be to create a centralised, truly European, Public Prosecutor's Office, with its competence defined by European common substantive rules and its powers delimited by European common rules of procedure.[89]

[86] See Di Francesco Maesa (n 80) 158.

[87] 'Proposal for a Regulation on the establishment of the European Public Prosecutor's Office – Discussion paper on cooperation between EPPO and non-participating Member States, Brussels', Council doc 12341/16 (19 September 2016).

[88] See Di Francesco Maesa (n 80) 158.

[89] See, eg K Ligeti, 'Model Rules for the Procedure of the EPPO' (2012) http://eppo-project.eu/design/eppodesign/pdf/con-verted/index.html?url=c982b9eef093cee8cebfbfcb2b0556d1.pdf&search=.

This would be the only solution capable of reducing the risk of impunity of perpetrators of offences affecting the Union's financial interests.[90] This is further demonstrated by the Swiss example, which shows that the most effective way of avoiding risks of impunity and effectively investigating and prosecuting crimes having a cross-border dimension or crimes affecting the Confederation's fundamental interests is to create a uniform penal code and a uniform code of criminal procedure.[91] In the absence of uniform provisions in the common territory of the cantons (for Switzerland) and Member States (for Europe), criminals may exploit legal differences between jurisdictions in order to escape justice.

The existence of legal loopholes which can be exploited by criminals to escape justice also significantly weakens the deterrent effect of the EPPO. In this context, the trust of citizens in EU institutions and the need to further enhance an area of freedom, security and justice in which EU citizens can enjoy freedom of movement and can rely upon respect of their fundamental rights is also at stake. Citizens are, in fact, likely to lose their trust in the reliability of EU institutions to punish effectively those criminals who depredate resources from the EU budget, ie their own resources as European taxpayers. All the foregoing issues combined can only result in bringing into discussion the very foundations of the objective of avoiding impunity at the EU level. That objective, it should not be forgotten, is, pursuant to the Court of Justice's case law, closely connected with the need to develop further an area of freedom, security and justice.

It could, therefore, even be questioned whether preventing the risk of impunity can still be considered a legitimate objective of the EPPO Regulation.

[90] For a more in-depth analysis of the reasons justifying this statement, see C Di Francesco Maesa, 'Verso una Procura europea? Tra effettività e diritti fondamentali' (DPhil thesis, Alma Mater Studiorum – University of Bologna, Université de Strasbourg, 2013).

[91] For a description of the Swiss system, see C Siebert, 'L'Evolution du modèle suisse de l'entraide judiciaire et de la coopération intercantonale en matière pénale' in JAE Vervaele (ed), *European Evidence Warrant. Transnational Judicial Inquiries in the EU* (Antwerp, Intersentia, 2005) 187; S Gleß, 'Aus 29 mach 1 – die jüngsten Bemühungen um die Vereinheitlichung des Strafverfahrensrechts in der Schweiz' (2001) 113 *Zeitschrift für die gesamte Strafrechtswissenschaft* 419; J Ouwerkerk *Quid Pro Quo? A Comparative Law Perspective on the Mutual Recognition of Judicial Decisions in Criminal Matters* (Antwerp, Intersentia, 2011).

PART C

The Fight Against Impunity and the EU Instruments Implementing the Principle of Mutual Recognition in Criminal Matters

9

The European Supervision Order: The Need for a New Culture of Combating Impunity

SERENA QUATTROCOLO

I. Introduction

Framework Decision 2009/829/JHA,[1] introducing the European Supervision Order (ESO), provides national judicial authorities with a list of pretrial supervision measures to be applied to suspects who are not nationals of or residents within the Member State of the proceedings. The measure will be supervised by the authority of the executing Member State.

The ESO is one of the latest pieces of legislation set forth under the 'third pillar' system. It belongs to what has been defined as a 'third wave' in the third pillar law,[2] along with a number of other Framework Decisions, covering a wide range of areas, such as the harmonisation of substantive criminal law, mutual recognition, the work of the EU criminal justice bodies such as Europol and Eurojust, and the development of standards to regulate the proliferation of third pillar mechanisms, to collect, analyse and exchange personal data.

Actually, it looks more consistent with the second, rather than the first, 'season' of the EU judicial cooperation in criminal matters. The first season, from the entry into force of the Maastricht Treaty to that of the Lisbon Treaty, is said to have been characterised by a repressive trend, aimed at promoting a more effective reaction to crime, especially to transborder crime.[3] The European Arrest Warrant Framework Decision (EAW) is the clearest example of it, with efficiency and rapidity of the surrendering process overarching the defence's rights and guarantees.[4]

[1] Council Framework Decision 2009/829/JHA, [2009] OJ L294/20.

[2] V Mitsilegas, 'The Third Wave of Third Pillar Law: Which Direction for EU Criminal Justice?' (2009) 34 EL Rev 523.

[3] RE Kostoris (ed), *Handbook of European Criminal Procedure* (Berlin, Springer, 2018) 8.

[4] D Sayers, 'Protecting Fair Trial Rights in Criminal Cases in the European Union: Where Does the Roadmap Take Us' (2014) 14 *Human Rights Law Review* 733, 755.

The main topic of this book is the fight against impunity in the EU, and the current part is based on a review of the effectiveness demonstrated by mutual recognition instruments in contrasting crime. However, if, for many of the tools considered here, it is a matter of assessing their effectiveness after a first period of implementation, for the ESO it is still a matter of considering its potentialities. The reason for this depends on two intertwined aspects. First, the ESO proved to be a fairly multifaceted instrument, both repressive and protective at the same time, impinging on some of the most delicate aspects of the domestic criminal proceedings. Therefore, secondly, its implementation was unsurprisingly slow.[5] In this chapter, I will elaborate on the specificity of the ESO, and try to highlight how ambitious and potentially useful the instrument is.

In section II, I will address the structure of Framework Decision 2009/829/JHA and the regulation of the instrument. In section III, I will analyse the elements making the ESO an extremely innovative tool, to grant more effectiveness to the criminal system. Finally, in section IV, I will conclude upon what application the ESO could hopefully have in the future.

II. The Structure and Functioning of the ESO

A few days before the entry into force of the Lisbon Treaty, Framework Decision 2009/829/JHA (the Framework Decision) established the 'application … of the principle of mutual recognition to decisions on supervision measures as alternatives to provisional detention'.

In particular, the aim of the initiative, based on a Commission proposal, was to enhance

> the protection of the general public through enabling a person resident in one Member State, but subject to criminal proceedings in a second member State, to be supervised by the authorities in the State in which he or she is resident whilst awaiting trial.

The need for such instrument was based on the assessment of the risk of discrimination (recital no 5)[6] of non-resident accused, who are almost automatically remanded in custody,[7] even when residents in the same conditions enjoy alternative measures. Such risk depended on the fact that, before the Framework Decision, the existing regime provided only two alternatives for non-resident

[5] See 'Green Paper on the Application of the EU Criminal Justice Legislation in the Field of Detention' (COM (2011) 327 final) 7, which raises a question about uniformity in the implementation and application of the ESO across the participating Member States.

[6] For a general (but paradigmatic) example of the detrimental situation of foreign prisoners (either sentenced or remanded in custody, illegal immigrants, etc) in Europe, see J Warr, 'The Deprivation of Certitude, Legitimacy and Hope: Foreign National Prisoners and the Pains of Imprisonment' (2016) 16 Criminology and Criminal Justice 307.

[7] I Durnescu, 'Framework Decisions 2008/847 and 2009/829: State of Play and Challenges' (2017) 18 *ERA Forum* 357.

accused – provisional detention or unsupervised movement – as no mutual recognition instrument was available for supervision measures.

The measure, in fact, was part of a coherent and complementary legislative package, along with Framework Decisions 2008/909/JHA and 2008/947/JHA,[8] addressing the issue of EU citizens' detention in another Member State, different from the one of legal residence. According to the recitals of Framework Decision 2009/829/JHA, the instrument is aimed at enhancing 'the right to liberty and the presumption of innocence in the European Union'.[9] In fact, not only can the ESO have a positive impact on preserving the private and social life dimension of the accused,[10] but, by demonstrating that the latter can be properly supervised in the other Member State, it may induce the judicial authority of the criminal proceedings to impose probation or alternative sanctions instead of a prison sentence in case of conviction.[11]

From this angle, the new tool is designed to extend mutual recognition as much as possible,[12] contributing significantly to the creation of an effective area of freedom, security and justice. In fact, as underlined in sections II.A and II.B below, the measure is conceived as a proactive engagement of the national executing authority, constantly monitoring the accused, on the basis of a foreign judicial authority decision: it implies (see, in particular, section III.D below) not only high levels of confidence, but also effective standards in practical cooperation between national judicial and law enforcement authorities of the two Member States. Thus, the ESO embodies the concept of a measure aimed at circulating in a real common area of freedom, security and justice. The following analysis will show if and how this model was successful.

A. Definitions and Competent Authorities

Moving on to definitions, the Framework Decision refers to supervision measures as 'obligations and instructions imposed on a natural person', on the basis of the national law of the issuing Member State, as an alternative to provisional detention. Accordingly, the 'decision on supervision measures' is an enforceable decision by a competent authority of the issuing Member State, within a criminal

[8] See European Commission, 'Report from the Commission to the European Parliament and the Council on the implementation by the Member States of the Framework Decisions 2008/909/JHA, 2008/947/JHA and 2009/829/JHA on the mutual recognition of judicial decisions on custodial sentences or measures involving deprivation of liberty, on probation decisions and alternative sanctions and on supervision measures as an alternative to provisional detention' (COM (2014) 57 final).

[9] Framework Decision 2009/829/JHA, Recital 4.

[10] Alternative supervision measures are indicated as a crucial means in fighting the abuse of pre-trial detention all over the world. See a Penal Reform Organisation study at https://cdn.penalreform.org/wp-content/uploads/2016/04/10-point-plan-Pre-trial-detention-WEB_final.pdf.

[11] COM (2014) 57 final (n 8) 5.

[12] L Klimek, *Mutual Recognition of Judicial Decisions in European Criminal Law* (Berlin, Springer, 2016) 103ff.

proceeding, imposing one or more alternative measures on a natural person. It is the responsibility of the Member States to notify the General Secretariat of the list of national competent authorities.[13] The Member States can decide to identify a central authority in charge of assisting the competent authorities at the territorial level.

The functioning of the instrument is based on a list of supervision measures that can be applied by the judicial authority of the issuing Member State in any criminal case, regardless of the seriousness of the offence.[14] Provided that the domestic conditions for the application of a pretrial coercive measure are met, the national competent authority can apply one of the measures listed in Article 8(1) of the Framework Decision[15] to the accused who is lawfully and ordinarily residing in another Member State if pretrial detention is not needed in the case. The accused must be willing and consenting to return to his or her residing state, or to a third Member State (Article 9(2)) – in which case, the Member State of lawful residence shall consent to such replacement.

In addition to the list of supervision measures, Member States can notify the General Secretariat if they are ready to monitor further, more sophisticated, supervision measures, such as those listed in Article 8(2) of the Framework Decision.[16] The national decision applying the alternative measure is forwarded to the competent judicial authority[17] of the executing Member State, together with the certificate mentioned in Article 10(2):[18] the certificate describes in detail the nature and the length of the applied measure. The receiving authority must reply within 20 days, accepting or refusing to supervise the measures that have been imposed by the authority of the issuing Member State. Meanwhile, the supervision of the applied measures is still under the competence of the issuing authority (Article 11(1)). The transfer of competence will occur only upon recognition by the executing authority, which must be officially communicated to the issuing one.

[13] Exceptionally, it can be also a non-judicial authority (Art 4(2)).

[14] T Rafaraci, 'The Application of the Principle of Mutual Recognition to Decisions on Supervision Measures as an Alternative to Provisional Detention' in S Ruggeri (ed), *Liberty and Security in Europe* (Osnabrück, Universitätverlag Osnabrück, 2013) 70.

[15] The list covers six measures: obligation to inform the executing state authority of any change of residence; obligation not to enter localities, places or defined areas; obligation to remain in a specified place; limitation to the right of leaving the territory of the state; obligation to report to the police, at specified times; and obligation to avoid contact with specific persons.

[16] The list covers: obligation not to engage in specified activities in relation with the offence allegedly committed; prohibition to drive a vehicle; obligation to deposit a sum of money or similar guarantee; obligation to undergo therapeutic treatments or addiction treatments; and obligation to avoid contact with specific objects in relation with the alleged offence.

[17] Art 6 of the Framework Decision provides that the Member States inform the general Secretariat of the judicial authorities designated for the purpose (or even non-judicial if so provided by the national law, except for the decisions under Art 18, para 1, let c), and Art 7 allows for the designation of a central authority to assist with administrative purposes. See Durnescu (n 7) 358.

[18] Under the EAW Framework Decision, there is no need to transmit the national decision at the basis of the EAW: Rafaraci (n 14) 73.

B. The Procedure

The Framework Decision sets forth only non-mandatory grounds for refusing the recognition of the decision applying alternative measures. They are listed in Article 15, covering both formal aspects and material ones: *bis in idem*; double criminality[19] (with the exception of a list of 32 offences, if punishable in the issuing state by a custodial sentence or other deprivation of liberty of at least three years);[20] statute of limitation; immunity; age; and the case where the executing state should refuse to surrender the person on the basis of an EAW, were the latter to breach the supervision measures.

If the measure imposed in the issuing Member State is not compliant with the law of the executing Member State, the latter authority must adapt – with a certain degree of discretion[21] – the foreign measure to those provided by the domestic law, in relation to corresponding domestic offences (Article 13), provided that the new measure is not more severe than the original one. The monitoring of the measure falls entirely under the law of the executing state, although all the subsequent decisions, such as renewal, review, withdrawal or modification, are within the competence of the issuing authority. The latter will be entitled to issue an EAW in case of breach of the supervision measures. The subsequent decisions may be subject to formal recognition by the executing authority, although such recognition cannot lead to a new examination of the grounds for refusing the original decision; in any case, if the measure has been modified, the executing authority can adapt the modified measure to the domestic regulation or refuse to supervise it (Article 18(4)).

Article 11 provides for cases in which the executing authority, having recognised the foreign decision, may withdraw from its duty to supervise the measures, on the basis of several different reasons.

What makes the procedure peculiar (see section III.D below) is the high level of cooperation imposed on the judicial authorities of the two Member States concerned. Consultations and exchange of information are imposed throughout the proceedings, from before the alternative measure decision has been forwarded until the expiration of the effects of that decision (Articles 19, 20 and 22). Moreover, during the supervision, the executing authority must promptly inform the issuing authority about any difficulty impinging on the effective supervision of the measure, in particular the impossibility of finding the person (the cases are listed in Article 20.2), as well as any breach of the duties imposed with the supervision order. Were the issuing authority to issue an EAW against the same person (for this or any other reason), the authority supervising the measure should surrender

[19] ibid.

[20] Member states were free to declare that they would not apply the clause abolishing the double criminality control for some of the 32 offences, on the basis of their domestic constitution.

[21] R Jurka and I Žentelytė, 'European Supervision Order – Is It the Ballast for Law Enforcement or the Way out of the Deadlock' (2017) 31 *Journal of European Criminology* 36.

her, with no exception, based on Article 2(1) of the EAW Framework Decision (punishable with at least 12 months of imprisonment, or punished with at least 4 months' custodial sentence). One of the annexes to the Framework Decision is a form for reporting breaches of the measure, or any other findings that the issuing authority must be informed about, in view of an eventual decision.

Interestingly, the costs of the procedure shall be borne by the executing state, except for those arising exclusively on the territory of the issuing state.

On the basis of this general overview, it is possible to argue that the functioning of this mutual recognition instrument is highly discretionary. Because of the wide range of differences existing between the domestic regulations in the field of pretrial coercive measures and the innate delicacy of any pretrial decision about liberty, the Framework Decision tends to regulate only the general aspects of the process, implying a very high (and ambitious) level of cooperation, case by case, between the judicial authorities involved in the matter.

III. The Specificities of ESO

Framework Decision 2009/829/JHA has now finally reached a good level of implementation, at least from a formal point of view. In fact, after a period of very low rates of transposition,[22] today only Ireland remains outside of the ESO system, although that status is subject to review. The UK opted in, with four different measures incorporating the Framework Decision into the national legislation (also in Scotland and Gibraltar),[23] as did Denmark.

Nevertheless, we must acknowledge that the instrument has not yet reached a good level of application.[24] There are several indications of this.[25] There is a general lack of official rates and figures, which would appear to confirm that the number

[22] A Tinsley, 'Protecting Criminal Defense Rights through EU Law: Opportunities and Challenges' (2013) 4 *New Journal of European Criminal Law* 461, 467. Many Member States implemented the measure only after a long period of time, such as France, Italy, Luxembourg, Germany and Cyprus.

[23] See the official report on the implementation of the Framework Decision at https://eur-lex.europa.eu/legal-content/EN/NIM/?uri=CELEX:32009F0829 and https://www.ejn-crimjust.europa.eu/ejn/EJN_Library_StatusOfImpByCat.aspx?l=EN&CategoryId=39.

[24] For the UK Extradition Review Panel position, see D Mansell, 'The European Arrest Warrant and Defence Rights' (2012) 2 *European Criminal Law Review* 36, 43. For more recent data (October 2018) about the UK situation, see https://www.fairtrials.org/news/european-arrest-warrant-invoking-alternative-measures-remains-uphill-struggle-defendants-uk; for a general, critical overview on the practical application of ESO (September 2015), see B Min, 'The European Supervision Order for Transfer of Defendants: Why Hasn't It Worked?' https://www.penalreform.org/blog/the-european-supervision-order-for-transfer-of-defendants/#_edn3. More recently, see the 2019 Report on Justice in Europe by Fair Trials International, still referring to the abuse of pretrial detention, with indirect reference to ESO at 32: https://www.fairtrials.org/sites/default/files/publication_pdf/LEAP_Annual_Report_2018-2019_0.pdf.

[25] L Bachmaier Winter, 'Mutual Recognition Instruments and the Role of the CJEU: The Grounds for Non-execution' (2015) 6 *New Journal of European Criminal Law* 505, 512.

of ESO cases seems to be almost insignificant. This is certainly true for Italy,[26] where only one decision has been delivered so far by the Italian Supreme Court, concerning the interpretation of d.lgs. 36/2016.[27] Based on a case law review, the Italian legal system has so far handled 12 cases of ESO, the majority of which were passive – that is to say, requests coming from foreign courts.

In the European literature, there have been relatively few studies focusing on the ESO,[28] and this confirms that there have not been any relevant issues about interpretation: scarce application, absence of interpretative issues and few comments in the literature.

Moving on from this awareness, it is important to reflect upon the causes of this non-successful level of application, and to try to understand whether the reasons are 'structural' or 'practical'.

A. Fighting Impunity but Enhancing the Presumption of Innocence

From a formal point of view, the ESO is an instrument of mutual recognition, based on the need to enhance the circulation of judicial decisions. As such, it seems to fit into the 'traditional' pattern of mutual recognition: the issuing authority in a Member State adopts a typical domestic decision or judgment, which is meant to be executed by the judicial authority of another Member State, provided that some basic requirements are met.

As previously said, the Commission proposal was based on the acknowledgement that foreign nationals tend to be submitted to pretrial detention on the sole basis that they do not have strong ties with the Member State in which the criminal proceeding is pending, revealing that the absence of such ties is considered to be a relevant index of flight risk. Official rates and figures demonstrate that, usually, non-resident EU citizens suffer pretrial detention more than nationals or long-term residents,[29] inducing an effect of discrimination between these groups.[30] The discriminatory effect impinges on many aspects of the accused's personal situation: the imposition of pretrial detention in another Member State almost always implies loss of job, detriment for family and private life relationships, and several other negative consequences related to the absence from the home territory. The

[26] R Del Coco, 'Il d.lgs. 15 febbraio 2016 n. 36: "fungibilità europea e misure alternative alla detenzione"' in T Bene and A Marandola (eds), *Cooperazione giudiziaria internazionale* (Milan, Giuffré, 2016) 75ff.

[27] Cassazione penale, sezione II, 26526/2017.

[28] However, see L Mancano, *The European Union and Deprivation of Liberty* (Oxford, Hart Publishing, 2019) para 8 II; I Rusu, 'The Recognition of Legal Supervision Measures as an Alternative to Detention on Remand in European Union' (2012) 34 *Acta Universitatis Danubius Juridica*, 34ff.

[29] Recital no 5 of the Framework Decision.

[30] JB Banach-Gutierrez, 'Globalised Criminal Justice in the European Union Context – How Theory Meets Practice' (2013) *New Journal of European Criminal Law* 154, 165.

aim of the Framework Decision was to prevent such a discriminatory effect, providing the national authorities with an ad hoc instrument. Actually, the inner sense of the supervision order is to eradicate a common trend and habit of national courts and judges to couple the absence of stable ties to the country of the criminal proceeding with the risk of flight. As already said, the goal of preserving family and social ties (also in view of facilitating rehabilitation and reintegration after serving an eventual sentence) is compliant with other EU instruments and, in some way, also with the EAW.[31]

In this sense, the instrument truly reflects the basic aim of the area of freedom, security and justice and, in this sense, has proved more ambitious than similar mutual recognition tools, introducing a certain number of peculiarities. I focus more deeply on each of these below.

B. A Particular Aspect within the General Issue of Pretrial Detention 'Overuse'

It has been repeatedly highlighted that, within the EU, the recourse to pretrial detention is massive.[32] Both European institutions and academia have focused on this issue in the past decades, showing how urgent an intervention that can reverse the current trend is. Although Article 5 of the European Convention on Human Rights (ECHR) provides a normative framework in which pretrial detention is clearly conceived as the *extrema ratio*, or last resort,[33] figures demonstrate that the trend is not going to decrease.[34]

In this context, a significant phenomenon, as said, is that of the application of pretrial detention to foreign nationals, based on their personal condition. Depending on the seriousness of the crime, foreign nationals tend to be submitted to pretrial detention while nationals would not in similar conditions. This means that domestic judges, although able to rely on a list of less coercive pretrial measures,[35] deem that foreigners accused of a crime are likely to flee the country and thus avoid the pending criminal proceedings against him or her, so conclude that they should be remanded in custody. So, while nationals or residents facing

[31] Rafaraci (n 14) 69; S Montaldo, 'Offenders' Rehabilitation: Towards a New Paradigm for EU Criminal Law?' (2018) 8 *European Criminal Law Review* 223ff; A Martufi, 'The Paths of Offender Rehabilitation and the European Dimension of Punishment: New Challenges for an Old Ideal?' (2018) 25 *Maastricht Journal of European and Comparative Law* 672.

[32] See Fair Trial International, 'A Measure of Last Resort? The Practice of Pre-trial Detention Decision-Making in the EU' https://www.fairtrials.org/publication/measure-last-resort.

[33] M Macovei, *The Right to Liberty and Security of the Person. Human Rights Handbook No 5* (Strasbourg, Council of Europe, 2002) 8.

[34] See Fair Trial International (n 34).

[35] Not every domestic system applies the concept of pretrial detention as *extrema ratio* in the same strict way promoted by the interpretation of the ECtHR: P Spagnolo, 'L'assetto codicistico tra gradualità e adeguatezza' in P Bronzo, K La Regina and P Spagnolo (eds), *Il pluralismo delle misure cautelari personali* (Padua, Cedam, 2017) 17.

similar accusations would be submitted to non-custodial measures, foreigners are deprived of their liberty. Significative numbers and figures were reported in the Commission staff working document accompanying the draft of the Framework Decision:[36] according to the prevision in the document, more than 8000 people per year could undergo a supervision order rather than pretrial detention.

As said, before the introduction of the ESO, there was a gap in the mutual recognition panorama, inducing judicial authorities to submit foreigners to pre-trial detention, rather than to more lenient measures. The lack of a system of mutual recognition of non-custodial measures impinged significantly on this attitude of the judicial authorities: the result was a 'all or nothing' situation, in which pretrial detention represented the sole instrument to keep control of foreign nationals accused of a crime, who could otherwise leave the country with no control over the execution of an eventual non-custodial measure. Now that Article 8(1) of the Framework Decision provides for a list of supervision measures granted by all Member States, national courts and judges[37] can rely on the fact that the execution of their non-custodial measures will be undertaken by the judicial authority of the lawful state of residence (or other Member State, under the conditions set forth in Article 9(2) of the Framework Decision).

In light of these remarks, it is possible to argue that the situation existing prior to the implementation of the ESO was subject to a serious limitation. With regard to non-resident accused persons, national judicial authorities could always rely, at least theoretically, on the whole range of domestic pretrial measures, whether custodial or non-custodial. However, in the absence of a system of European supervision of less coercive measures, the only way to nullify a foreigner's risk of flight was to fall back to pretrial detention. In this sense, the grounds for what has proved to be practical discrimination between nationals and foreign nationals are understandable. The potential risk of flight has many implications with regard to the defendant's participation in the trial and, in this sense, for the satisfaction of the state's punitive power, but also for the victim's rights and interests.[38]

Having said this, the Framework Decision is crystal clear in excluding that the foreign national has a right to a non-custodial measure, based on the Framework Decision itself, as highlighted in Article 2(2) of the Framework Decision. It is up to the national authority to evaluate if, according to the national legislation and its interpretation of it, a non-custodial measure, listed in Article 8 of the Framework Decision, suits the need of that specific case. However, the range of alternative

[36] SEC (2006) 1080.

[37] Or non-judicial authorities, as provided by Art 6(2) of the Framework Decision.

[38] Actually, Art 2(1) of the Framework Decision refers to the 'improvement in the protection of victims and of the general public', apparently highlighting a preventive function of the ESO. Although mentioned in the text, this aspect is not particularly convincing, as the alternative – pretrial detention – has an incapacitation effect which is possibly more effective. Nevertheless, the victim has a clear interest in the defendant's presence at trial and, in light of this, the ESO can play an important role.

solutions provided for by the domestic law are now potentially available for foreign supervision, allowing the competent national authority to freely decide which precautionary measure best serves the need of each specific case.

C. The Need for a Cultural Change in Practitioners: Getting Used to a New Tool

This brings us to focus on the first specificity of the ESO. National courts, judges and other competent authorities must change their traditional decision-making process, which should now cover the whole range of possible non-custodial measures, in order to assess whether any of them suits the specific needs of the case.

Today, a comparative study on the ESO in our jurisdictions should assess, first, whether the competent authorities are aware of the possibility of applying a supervision order on a non-custodial measure. According to Article 2(2) of the Framework Decision, if it is true that the non-national or resident accused has no right to a non-custodial measure, the competent authority should give reasons for this, especially in those countries in which pretrial detention is considered to be the 'last resort'. Italy is an example. In Italy, the competent judge must give reasons why a less coercive measure than detention does not suit the specific needs of the case. When the accused person is a non-national EU citizen or a non-resident, the judicial evaluation shall now cover the whole list of available measures: thus, on the basis of both the domestic criminal procedure regulation and the list of measures mentioned in Article 8 of the Framework Decision (and, presumably, reported in any national law implementing the Framework Decision),[39] the national judges can decide to apply a non-custodial measure, relying on the possibility to start a supervision process.[40]

Secondly, a comparative study should assess whether counsel are aware of the possibility to ask for an ESO or to challenge a pretrial detention measure imposed on a non-national, on the basis that the judge did not consider alternative measures

[39] Spagnolo (n 37) 21: the measures listed in Art 8(1) may not coincide with the domestic ones. It happens in Italy, where there are some relevant differences between the effects of the European and the domestic measures.

[40] As to Italy, however, d.lgs. 36/2016 expressly set forth that the competent authority, to start a supervision order, is the public prosecutor. The national implementation regulation is based on a two-tier process: first, a judge applies (on the basis of a request by the prosecutor) the suitable pretrial measure, according to Art 275 of the Italian Criminal Procedure Code; then the prosecutor starts, at his or her own discretion, the procedure for the European supervision, by forwarding the decision to another European authority. This two-tier process implies strong prosecutorial discretion in starting the ESO or not, and that discretion is undisputed, as the sole and unique decision ever delivered by the Italian Supreme Court (n 19) about d.lgs.36/2016 confirmed that the prosecutor is free to consider whether the transfer of the accused (who has to consent) is suitable or not. In this context, the prosecutorial decision overlaps the judicial one: even though the judge deemed an alternative measure suitable for the case, the prosecutor may subsequently decide that he or she is not going to start the supervision process, on the basis of a formal request by the accused.

applicable by the ESO. Practitioners on both sides of the bench need to get used to the instrument in order to take advantage of all its potentialities. And the scarce judicial application of the instrument demonstrates that counsels are not yet used to asking for it, as a viable alternative to remand in custody, for their clients:[41] changes in judicial habits and trends tend to be enhanced by counsel's action, stimulating the courts to reflect upon alternative options and interpretations.

For this reason, there is an urgent need for qualified training, for all practitioners, on the ESO, with the aim of boosting the application of alternative measures and, as a consequence, of reducing both pretrial detention and the number of EAWs, especially for petty offences.[42]

D. Getting Used to Consultation with Foreign Courts

A second specificity is related to the fact that the Framework Decision prescribes (in Article 22) consultations between the competent authorities throughout the supervision procedure and, in particular, during its preparation. This provision is valuable because, based on what will be presented hereinafter as the third specificity, there may be relevant differences between the national legal orders, even though the list of measures in Article 8 of the Framework Decision is binding for all Member States. However, the idea of preliminary consultations before the application of a pretrial coercive measure is certainly not familiar to many of the judicial authorities of the Member States. First of all, these are decisions taken immediately after the perpetration of the acts, which implies rapidity in the application of the measure. In many jurisdictions, the pretrial coercive measure is imposed in a non-adversarial procedure, in which the competent authority decides upon a request by the prosecutor or the police.[43] It is a challenging target, for the competent authorities, to set up effective consultations with foreign colleagues in the context of a speedy procedure, like the pretrial ones.[44] Once again, the limit here is neither theoretical nor practical, but, rather, cultural: it will take some time for the competent authorities to start including consultations with foreign colleagues in the pretrial coercive measures application process. Nevertheless, it should prove extremely fruitful, because of the lack of harmonisation from the point of view of pretrial instruments. The European Judicial Network should play a key role in promoting awareness in the European judiciary about the seriousness

[41] In some countries, eg Italy, the implementing regulation implies that the ESO procedure is started on the basis of a proactive request by the accused (or his or her counsel): Art 5 d.lgs.36/2016.

[42] Rafaraci (n 14) 77.

[43] For a comparative study, see S Ruggeri in S Ruggeri (ed), *Liberty and Security in Europe* (Osnabrück, Universitätverlag Osnabrück, 2013) 185ff.

[44] This justified, in the light of some domestic implementation regulation, the creation of a two-tier process: first the alternative measure is applied according to the national law; then (eventually) the competent authority starts the ESO procedure, by forwarding the certificate to the foreign authority.

of the problem and the existence of a specific solution. At the same time, law schools should engage both in lifelong professional training for the judiciary and in preparing more EU-law-aware graduates.

E. Good Reasons to Overcome Strict Interpretations

There is a third specificity of the instrument, impinging on its difficult start-up. The area of pretrial coercive measures is clearly one of the most sensitive aspects of criminal proceedings. It is regulated not only by Article 5 ECHR, but often by national constitutions and detailed procedural rules. Abidance to statutory law and to strict interpretative patterns is crucial in the field of interim limitations of liberty.[45]

It is not unusual for domestic Supreme Courts to highlight the importance of respecting legal provisions in the application and execution of pretrial measures. Not only must the grounds for application be clearly regulated by law, but also the execution must be strictly compliant with the rule of law. Such a strict interpretation may hamper mutual recognition and, in particular, the ESO. First, the measures listed in Article 8 of the Framework Decision and accepted by all the (implementing) Member States may comply only in part with the domestic provisions. This is the case, for example, in Italy. Some of the provisions covered by the Framework Decision do not match exactly with national interim coercive measures, as there are differences both in the classification of the different measures (for example, measure c in Article 8, the obligation to remain at a specified place, matches with the Italian provision of home arrest; however, in the Italian system, home arrest is considered a form of pretrial detention, and not a non-custodial measure)[46] and in the level of coercion. Thus, on the one hand, the lack of flexibility – often prescribed by the supreme courts in liberty matters – can represent a serious limit to the effectiveness of the ESO. On the other hand, early consultations between competent authorities seem to be the best way to overcome such a potential flaw. Based on this, a more relaxed approach could be allowed, letting the interests of mutual recognition prevail over strict interpretation,[47] when the competent authorities have previously and personally assessed the substantial equivalence of one of the alternative measures provided by the executing state.

[45] P Rackow and C Birr, 'Recent Developments in Legal Assistance in Criminal Matters' (2010) 2 *Goettingen Journal of International Law* 815, 815ff.

[46] The CJEU ruled upon the concept of 'detention' in Case C-294/16 *JZ* (www.curia.europa.eu), which concerned the EAW, and concluded that: 'measures such as a nine-hour night-time curfew, in conjunction with the monitoring of the person concerned by means of an electronic tag, an obligation to report to a police station at fixed times on a daily basis or several times a week, and a ban on applying for foreign travel documents, are not, in principle, having regard to the type, duration, effects and manner of implementation of all those measures, so restrictive as to give rise to a deprivation of liberty comparable to that arising from imprisonment and thus to be classified as "detention" within the meaning of that provision, which it is nevertheless for the referring court to ascertain'.

[47] Spagnolo (n 37) 23.

IV. Conclusions

To conclude, it is important to highlight the enormous potentiality of this instrument, not only in combating impunity, but also in realising the most genuine meaning of the concepts of 'mutual trust' and 'mutual recognition'.

There are at least three crucial reasons not to concede the failure of the instrument. The specificities analysed above make the ESO a highly ambitious instrument, much more so than other mutual recognition tools. The implementation of the Framework Decision has been so slow that the ESO is still a novelty in many of our jurisdictions. Thus, it is not possible to argue that the low level of application is due to structural problems, rather than practical ones. In fact, although challenging in its aims, the instrument is based on a high level of respect for internal procedures. Unlike the EAW, it does not tend to regulate all the steps of the process meticulously. In particular, the key feature of the tool is that it does not aim to impose on the domestic authorities new and harmonised criteria in the choice of pretrial coercive measures. National decision-makers are free to apply their own national criteria and alternative measures, relying on the new opportunity to ask for supervision in another European Member State. Thus, it is possible to argue that the ESO is crucial in allowing a more general and effective application of national regulations and provisions, as it represents a compelling instrument to apply the existing alternative measures also to non-resident European citizens.

However, the success of this instrument relies on a relevant change in legal culture by all the practitioners involved in criminal proceedings. We all have to acknowledge that, within the EU, the fight against impunity ultimately goes hand in hand with the respect of fundamental rights, and the ESO seems to be an excellent example of this trend.

10

Information Sharing as a Tool in the Fight against Impunity in the European Union

FRANCESCA GALLI

I. Introduction

The increasing use of online services as well as information and communication technologies requires law enforcement and judicial authorities to collect electronic information daily, for both prevention and investigation purposes. This information would not be available to public authorities without the cooperation of private actors such as technology companies or service providers, which share, process, transmit and/or store information across borders.

Cross-border law enforcement access to electronic information traditionally takes the form of mutual legal assistance (MLA) instruments. Conventional forms of MLA[1] constitute the lowest degree of informational integration. Created for the exchange of raw material for investigation purposes, which at a later stage could become evidence at trial, MLA is at the opposite side of the scale of interoperable information systems – currently under the spotlight – which confer direct and unmediated information access to competent law enforcement authorities.[2]

This chapter addresses a number of intertwined issues. It first investigates whether and to what extent MLA is undergoing major changes, challenging existing dynamics of law enforcement and judicial cooperation, and redefining the roles of the actors involved. Secondly, it explores whether and how such developments in information sharing allow for a quicker and easier access to

[1] See, eg Council Act of 29 May 2000 establishing in accordance with Article TEU the Convention on Mutual Assistance in Criminal Matters between the Member States of the European Union.

[2] The regulations on the interoperability between EU information systems have been adopted by the Council on 14 May 2019 but not yet published in the EU Official Journal. For a comment, see D Curtin, 'Security of the Interstice and Inter-operable Data Sharing: A First Cut' in S Carrera and V Mitsilegas (eds), *Constitutionalising the Security Union: Effectiveness, Rule of Law and Rights in Countering Terrorism and Crime* (Brussels, CEPS, 2017) 65–72.

information in cross-border crime cases and thus allegedly contribute to the fight against impunity, bypassing, inter alia, issues of jurisdiction. The new proposals for EU legislation on electronic evidence[3] are in fact akin to those instruments which developed around the principle of mutual recognition to compensate the negative implications of free movement of persons on Member States' criminal justice systems, including the risk of impunity. In fact, from a law enforcement perspective, a quicker and unmediated access to information held by internet service providers could, for instance, prevent criminals absconding. Thirdly, it highlights that instruments of judicial cooperation come at a cost and challenge existing criminal procedure guarantees for the protection of individual rights. In fact, cross-border access to data outside established legal channels of mediated assistance poses a number of challenges to fundamental rights, with reference to issues such as 'jurisdiction transfer' (or operations outside its own jurisdiction); unclear legal basis; and/or lack of compliance with (EU) data protection rules.

After a short overview of the main features of new modes of MLA (section II), the chapter addresses whether and how cross-border direct access of law enforcement authorities to electronic information actually or potentially redefines integration dynamics, including the existing distribution of competences between the EU and Member States (section III) and among competent authorities of different kinds,[4] including private actors (section IV). Having identified several common trends in the dynamics of cooperation, the chapter draws some preliminary conclusions, including with reference to the fight against impunity and its costs.

II. Developments in the Judicial and Law Enforcement Access to Data in a Transnational Context

Three main types of access exist globally: mediated, unmediated and hybrid. EU Member States have traditionally used the model of mediated access to authorise law enforcement to have access to data in a transnational context. In this model, an authority in the requesting state wishing to obtain access to data under the jurisdiction of another state sends an MLA request to the designated central authority

[3] 'Proposal for a Regulation of the European Parliament and of the Council on European Production and Preservation Orders for electronic evidence in criminal matters' COM (2018) 225 final – 2018/0108 (COD); 'Proposal for a Directive of the European Parliament and of the Council laying down harmonised rules on the appointment of legal representatives for the purpose of gathering evidence in criminal proceedings' COM (2018) 226 final – 2018/0107 (COD).

[4] In EU law the notion of competent authority has a specific meaning, identifying a judicial or law enforcement authority with a number of characteristics or a public order authority in charge of managing cooperation procedure. See specifically Art 67 TFEU (general provisions), Art 87 TFEU (police cooperation) and passim in Title V. As I shall argue in section IV, the reference to private actors in the EU proposal for legislation on e-evidence interestingly challenges the existing notion.

of that country with recognised competence to order access to data transfers from private companies. Access to data is thus supervised by the designated authority and an independent court/tribunal of the requested country. Each specific method of mediated access is regulated by national legal provisions, and different rules and oversight systems also apply to the issuing of requests, depending on the constitutional and institutional framework established in the country concerned. The 'unmediated access model' lacks the scrutiny of an independent judicial authority in the requested state to validate the lawfulness of accessing and processing data. Under this model, a third country may assert the authority under its own national law to access electronic data stored in the EU territory. The risk is to create multiple conflicts of law when, in spite of the requesting country's power, the transfer of data triggers legal effects in the country where a private company is requested to hand over data. The 'hybrid access model' raises similar challenges due to the lack of a proper oversight system by an independent judicial authority. It is also affected by accountability and transparency deficits with reference to the decision allowing for access to information.[5]

In 2014, the adoption of the European Investigation Order (EIO) was a major step forward in the international cooperation in information sharing among EU Member States.[6] The EIO became the sole legal instrument regulating the exchange of evidence and MLA between EU Member States.[7] The EIO helps to overcome the undesirable fragmentation of legal instruments for the collection and transfer of evidence between EU Member States, in compliance with the defendants' fundamental rights. This major legal development expressly establishes the fundamental rights parameters of the operation of the mutual recognition principle.[8] The provision frames blind mutual trust among Member States and confirms that the presumption that all Member States comply with fundamental rights at all instances is rebuttable.

[5] See, eg S Carrera et al, *Access to Electronic Data by Third-Country Law Enforcement Authorities, Challenges to EU Rule of Law and Fundamental Rights* (CEPS, Brussels, 2015); J Vervaele, 'Mutual Legal Assistance in Criminal Matters to Control (Transnational) Criminality' in G Fornasari and D Sartori (eds), *European Criminal Justice in the Post-Lisbon Area of Freedom Security and Justice* (Trento, EdiTN, 2014) 139.

[6] Directive 2014/41/EU regarding the European Investigation Order in criminal matters [2014] OJ L130/1 (EIO Directive).

[7] The Directive replaced, as of 22 May 2017 (the transposition deadline for Member States), the corresponding provisions applicable between Member States bound by the 1959 Council of Europe Mutual Legal Assistance Convention (ETS 30) and its 1978 and 2001 Protocols (ETS 99 and ETS 182), the 2000 Convention implementing the Schengen Agreement and the EU 2000 Mutual Legal Assistance Convention and its 2001 Protocol, the Framework Decision on the European Evidence Warrant (2008/978/JHA) and the relevant provisions of the Framework Decision on the mutual recognition of freezing orders (2003/577/JHA).

[8] S Ruggeri, 'Introduction to the Proposal of a European Investigation Oder: Due Process Concerns and Open Issues' in S Ruggeri (ed), *Transnational Evidence and Multicultural Inquiries in Europe* (Berlin, Springer, 2014) 1; S Allegrezza, 'Collecting Criminal Evidence Across the European Union: The European Investigation Order Between Flexibility and Proportionality' in Ruggeri (ibid) 51–67; see also Carrera et al, *Access to Electronic Data* (n 5) 48–54.

In fact, over the years, the inclusion of an express ground of refusal to recognise and execute a judicial decision on fundamental rights grounds has been a central issue in the development of the application of the principle of mutual recognition in criminal matters. Before the entry into force of the Lisbon Treaty, EU mutual recognition instruments in the third pillar contained references to the respect of fundamental rights but did not include a specific ground for refusal in this regard.[9]

Particularly, in Opinion 1/2013, the CJEU inferred that, when implementing EU law, Member States are required to presume that fundamental rights have been observed by the other Member States. This presumption imposes two negative obligations on the Member States. First, they may 'not demand a higher level of national protection of fundamental rights from another Member State than that provided by EU law'.[10] Secondly, 'save in exceptional cases', Member States are prevented from 'check[ing] whether that other Member State has actually, in a specific case, observed the fundamental rights guaranteed by the EU'.[11]

The path towards the adoption of the EIO was lengthy and difficult. A major challenge was fostering the swift and efficient cross-border judicial cooperation in criminal investigations in the EU and the admissibility of the evidence obtained abroad, while ensuring a high standard of procedural rights of the defendants.[12]

A. Cross-Border Direct Access of Law Enforcement Authorities to Information

Current trends in cross-border cooperation often fall outside existing legal channels of transnational judicial cooperation. Such 'direct' cooperation is not a new phenomenon; it has been going on for decades. However, it has become increasingly challenging, as the functioning of many new communication technologies is not always covered by existing legislation; plus, a number of global service providers are located outside the territory where investigations take place, with consequent jurisdictional challenges.[13] Moreover, service providers are often

[9] See I Armada, 'The European Investigation Order and the Lack of European Standards for the Gathering of Evidence. Is a Fundamental Rights-Based Refusal the Solution?' (2015) 1 *New Journal of European Criminal Law* 8.

[10] Opinion 2/13, EU:C:2014:2454, para 192.

[11] ibid. For a comment, see M Bossuyt, 'The Principle of "Mutual Trust" in Opinion 2/13' in Š Imamović, M Claes and B De Witte (eds), 'The EU Fundamental Rights Landscape after Opinion 2/13' (2016) Maastricht Faculty of Law Working Paper, 15–25; E Bribosia, 'Fundamental Rights and Mutual Trust in the European Union – The Story of a Clash Foretold?' in Imamović et al (ibid) 26–36.

[12] L Bachmaier, 'Mutual Recognition and Cross-Border Interception of Communications: The Way Ahead of the European Investigation Order' in C Brière and A Weyembergh (eds), *The Needles Balances in EU Criminal Law: Past, Present and Future* (Oxford, Hart Publishing, 2017).

[13] A number of Member States, including Belgium and the UK, have tried to address the challenge adopting new legislation or practices with major extraterritorial implications. On recent Belgian legislation and case law, see V Franssen, 'The Belgian Internet Investigatory Powers Act – A Model to Pursue at European Level?' (2017) 3(4) *European Data Protection Law Review* 534; on the UK Investigatory Power Act 2016, see L Cropper, 'The Investigatory Powers Act 2016 – A 'Snoopers' Charter' or

confronted with conflicting legal obligations arising from national provisions and practices, leading to serious challenges in the effective protection of (suspects' and non-suspects') fundamental rights.

The collision between the territoriality of legal provisions and the 'unterritoriality' of data[14] challenges existing MLA mechanisms in criminal matters. Such mechanisms are considered lengthy and complex, and thus are notoriously slow. Therefore, it is questionable whether MLA in criminal matters is a mechanism that functions when cross-border digital information is concerned. Where easily moved (corrupted or destroyed) electronic information is concerned, time is an essential factor in criminal investigations. Therefore, law enforcement authorities often disregard existing MLA mechanisms and address requests for information directly to foreign service providers via mechanisms of voluntary disclosure,[15] bypassing the judicial authority where service providers are established, or targets are habitually resident. The practice of voluntary disclosure is predominantly applied by US service providers[16] as this possibility is specifically foreseen in the Electronic Communications Privacy Act.[17] When companies are located in a third state, a conflict of laws may emerge if national provisions forbid the handing over of data.[18] As argued in depth in section IV.B below, such mechanisms already constitute a de facto extraterritorial reach of national investigative powers, as well as an extension of the 'sword' function of criminal law via a further 'privatisation of security'.

B. The Commission Proposals on e-Evidence

In this context, the Commission has presented two proposals on e-evidence which would enable law enforcement authorities to request ('production request') or compel ('production order') a third party, ie a service provider, in another Member State to disclose personal data about a user, without the request or order having

a Legitimate Surveillance Tool for Today's Society?' (*Privacy, Security and Information*, 2 April 2017) https://privacylawblog.fieldfisher.com/2017/the-investigatory-powers-act-2016-a-snoopers-charter-or-a-legitimate-surveillance-tool-for-todays-society.

[14] See J Daskal, 'The Un-territoriality of Data' (2015) 125 *Yale Law Journal* 326.

[15] For interesting data on voluntary disclosure practices from 2017, see the transparency reports of Apple (www.apple.com/privacy/transparency-reports/), Facebook (https://govtrequests.facebook.com/about/#), Google (www.google.com/transparencyreport/), Microsoft (www.microsoft.com/about/csr/transparencyhub/), Twitter (https://transparency.twitter.com/) and Yahoo (https://transparency.yahoo.com/government-data-requests).

[16] US service providers can only disclose metadata (traffic data and network data) and not content data; and this distinction was the point of departure of the famous *Microsoft* case in 2018: *United States v Microsoft* No 17-2, 584 US (2018). Cross-border cooperation with US service providers is practised by more or less all parties to the Budapest Convention (Council of Europe (Budapest) Convention on Cybercrime, ETS no 185), although there are considerable differences in the use of this option between parties.

[17] See 18 US Code §2702 www.law.cornell.edu/uscode/text/18/2702.

[18] See, eg the so-called 'blocking statute' under the US Electronic Communication Privacy Act.

to go through a law enforcement or judicial intermediary in the other Member State.[19]

The package proposed encompasses both a Regulation on the European Production and Preservation Orders for electronic evidence in criminal matters (on the basis of Article 82(1) TFEU)[20] and a Directive on the Appointment of Legal Representatives (on the basis of Articles 53 and 62 TFEU).[21] Cooperation will take the form of a European Production Order Certificate (EPOC) or European Preservation Order Certificate (EPOC-PR) directly from an issuing authority in one Member State to the legal representative of service providers in another Member State. Both types of order may only be issued in the context of criminal proceedings during either the pretrial or trial phase. Compliance by service providers must not depend on the location of the data solicited.[22]

It is noteworthy that the scope of the Regulation clearly exceeds the traditional telecommunications providers; it aims to include internet access services, 'internet-based services enabling inter-personal communications such as Voice over IP, instant messaging and e-mail services', as well as 'cloud and other hosting services' and 'digital marketplaces', and the providers of online services and platforms such as Skype, WhatsApp, Telegram, Dropbox and eBay would also be covered. Providers of internet domain names and IP numbering services are relevant because they 'can provide traces allowing for the identification of an individual or entity involved in criminal activity'.[23]

The proposal has been welcomed by part of the digital technology industry in Europe, which considers that it presents a real opportunity to update EU law enforcement authorities' access to electronic data with regard to criminal investigations, whilst maintaining European users' privacy and other fundamental rights.[24] Industries have, however, expressed a number of concerns and advocated for a

[19] Council Conclusions, Luxembourg, 9 June 2016 https://ec.europa.eu/home-affairs/sites/home affairs/files/what-we-do/policies/organized-crime-and-human-trafficking/council_conclusions_on_improving_criminal_justice_in_cyberspace_en.pdf. It should be noted that the e-evidence proposal was not approved before the 2019 European Parliament elections. On November 2019, the LIBE Committee of the European Parliament presented MPE Birgit Sippel's draft report on the E-Evidence draft Regulation which constitutes a huge departure from both the Council General approach and the initial proposal of the Commission. The EP report is far more protective of fundamental rights and could open a new debate with stakeholders and NGOs. For more details, see T Christakis, 'E-Evidence in the EU Parliament: Basic Features of Birgit Sippel's Draft Report' (*European Law Blog*, 21 January 2020) https://europeanlawblog.eu/2020/01/21/e-evidence-in-the-eu-parliament-basic-features-of-birgit-sippels-draft-report/.

[20] COM (2018) 225 final – 2018/0108 (COD) (n 3).

[21] COM (2018) 226 final – 2018/0107 (COD) (n 3).

[22] This specification reflects the long-standing discussions revolving around the US *Microsoft* case (n 16).

[23] See 'Proposal for a Regulation of the European Parliament and of the Council on European Production and Preservation Orders for electronic evidence in criminal matters' COM (2018) 225 final, Explanatory Memorandum, 14.

[24] 'DIGITALEUROPE calls on e-evidence proposal to protect European users' privacy & fundamental rights' (*DIGITALEUROPE*, 10 December 2018) www.digitaleurope.org/resources/digitaleurope-calls-on-e-evidence-proposal-to-protect-european-users-privacy-fundamental-rights/. For a more in-depth analysis, see DIGITALEUROPE's position paper on the proposed e-evidence package, 2 August 2018.

number of additional safeguards, including: clarifying that the default first point of call should be the enterprise customer of all cloud service providers; strengthening of good faith immunity provisions; introducing more realistic time frames for responding to requests; improving transparency measures; and safeguarding legal representatives from personal liability.

Some academics have questioned the added value of the proposal compared to existing MLA treaties and the EIO.[25] In particular, Böse has argued that the added value of the new cooperation regime, which is a quick and effective access to provider data, is mainly based on the abolition of cooperation obstacles and procedures ensuring effective protection of fundamental rights.[26]

With reference to legal remedies, the new threshold of the Commission's proposal certainly does not reach a similar level of protection as the requirements provided by individual Member States to access sensitive data.[27] For instance, comparing the EIO with the EPO, the recent European Parliament study highlights the still further reduced number of grounds for refusal at both the issuing and enforcement stages: 'the EIO Directive has maintained traditional rules of cross-border cooperation such as the double criminality requirement and the analogous application of thresholds for particularly intrusive investigative measures (art 11(1)(g) and (h) EIO)';[28] the new draft Regulation removes all of these. As a result, an EPO could be executed in a Member State even when the requested state has higher national protection standards in place than the issuing state.[29]

By contrast, the proposal seems to be very much in line with data protection requirements.[30] The draft European Production Order Regulation is full of references to the EU data protection package. Article 11 provides that the addressee of an EPOC or EPOC-PR must refrain from informing that person,[31] unless the

[25] CCBE position on the Commission proposal for a Regulation on European Production and Preservation Orders for electronic evidence in criminal matters, 19 October 2018, www.ccbe.eu/fileadmin/speciality_distribution/public/documents/SURVEILLANCE/SVL_Position_papers/EN_SVL_20190228_CCBE-recommendations-on-the-establishment-of-international-rules-for-cross-border-access-to-e-evidence.pdf.

[26] M Böse, 'An Assessment of the Commission's Proposals on Electronic Evidence' PE 604.989 (Directorate General for Internal Policies of the Union, September 2018) 46.

[27] On the potential impact of the e-evidence proposal on defence rights, see, eg Fair Trials' letter to Birgit Sippel on the e-Evidence Proposal www.fairtrials.org/sites/default/files/publication_pdf/Fair-Trials-Letter-Birgit-Sippel-e-evidence.pdf.

[28] Böse, 'An Assessment of the Commission's Proposals on Electronic Evidence' (n 26) 22.

[29] The result would be similar to the situation explored by the CJEU in *Melloni*. It is, of course, a critical dynamic, but it is likely to develop in many cases if the conditions put forward in the judgment are respected. This means, in sum, that Member States can set higher national standards even in a situation set by EU law, but only to the extent that the subject matter has not been completely regulated by the Union. Member States would otherwise undermine the effectiveness of EU law and violate the principle of primacy of EU law. See Case C-399/11 *Stefano Melloni v Ministerio Fiscal* (26 February 2013); for a comment, see A Torres Pérez, 'Melloni in Three Acts: From Dialogue to Monologue' (2014) 10 *European Constitutional Law Review* 308.

[30] On this issue, see in detail G Robinson, 'The European Commission's e-Evidence Proposal' (2018) 3 *European Data Protection Law Review* 347.

[31] In compliance with Art 23 of the General Data Protection Regulation: Regulation (EU) 2016/679 of the European Parliament and of the Council of 27 April 2016 on the protection of natural persons

issuing authority requests that this be done. Where the service provider has not already informed the data subject that their data has been subject to an EPOC or EPOC-PR, the issuing authority shall inform the target thereof once there is no longer a risk of jeopardising the investigation.[32] By virtue of Article 17, once apprised of the situation, the person whose data was obtained via an EPO has the right to effective remedies under the EU data protection *acquis* and under national law before the court in the issuing state. This is the case irrespective of whether the individual is a suspect or accused person or not, and hence whether or not they are involved in criminal or civil proceedings. According to Article 18, immunities and privileges in respect of transactional or content data obtained by virtue of an EPO granted under the law of the Member State of the addressee (the service provider) are to apply in criminal proceedings in the issuing state.

What happens across the Atlantic has influenced EU legislative developments in this field deeply. Particularly relevant has been the *Microsoft* case, concerning the unmediated access of law enforcement authorities to data held by private companies, where the US Supreme Court was expected to decide whether territorial borders matter when it comes to data,[33] but the case has subsequently been mooted by the CLOUD Act (Clarifying Lawful Overseas Use of Data Act). In response to the uncertainty highlighted by the case, the CLOUD Act, passed on 23 March 2018,[34] specifies that all of the 1986 Stored Communications Act's provisions on required disclosure apply regardless of the location of the communications or records.[35]

The CLOUD Act provides, inter alia, an explicit legal basis for the US Government to conclude bilateral executive agreements with other foreign governments on access to data (including content data) held by US service providers and vice versa. US service providers could then respond to valid legal orders of competent foreign authorities, thus bypassing the pre-existent legal prohibition under the US Electronic Communication Privacy Act (the so-called 'Blocking Statute'), which has been a major obstacle for EU–US cooperation in this field.

For the purpose of this chapter, it is useful now to highlight major changes with reference to modes of law enforcement cooperation, which mirror similar

with regard to the processing of personal data and on the free movement of such data, and repealing Directive 95/46/EC) (Text with EEA relevance) [2016] OJ L119/1–88.

[32] In accordance with Art 13 of the Police Data Protection Directive: Directive (EU) 2016/680 of the European Parliament and of the Council of 27 April 2016 on the protection of natural persons with regard to the processing of personal data by competent authorities for the purposes of the prevention, investigation, detection or prosecution of criminal offences or the execution of criminal penalties, and on the free movement of such data, and repealing Council Framework Decision 2008/977/JHA.

[33] *Microsoft* (n 16).

[34] HR 4943 – The Clarifying Lawful Overseas Use of Data Act, 6 February 2018 (the CLOUD Act). For a comment, see ST Mulligan, 'Cross-Border Data Sharing under the CLOUD Act' R45172 (Congressional Research Service, 23 April 2018).

[35] The Stored Communications Act is a law that addresses voluntary and compelled disclosure of 'stored wire and electronic communications and transactional records' held by third-party internet service providers. It was enacted as Title II of the Electronic Communications Privacy Act of 1986 (ECPA). See 18 USC, cha 121, paras 2701–12.

transformations in the interoperability domain.[36] The next three sections explore the impact of new modes of MLA on competence, which in broad terms is understood to encompass the concepts of 'jurisdiction' and 'task'. First, information sharing via direct cooperation challenges the existing dynamics of integration, including both harmonisation and the principle of mutual recognition, thus affecting the sharing of competences between the EU and Member States. Secondly, new modes of MLA lead to a blurring of information-sharing tasks between several law enforcement actors for different purposes, and also an increasing involvement of private actors in information management activities.

III. Cross-Border Access to Data by Law Enforcement Authorities and Integration Dynamics

A. Approximation and Mutual Recognition as the Cornerstone of Judicial Cooperation

The concept of mutual recognition, in combination with the harmonisation/approximation of substantive and procedural law, has been considered a cornerstone of judicial cooperation in both civil and criminal matters for many years.

The approximation of criminal law has various functions in the establishment of the area of freedom, security and justice (AFSJ). Most importantly, it enables smooth judicial cooperation through various mechanisms based on mutual trust, particularly mutual recognition.[37]

In the AFSJ, successful operation of the principle of mutual recognition implies that Member States must trust each other when it comes to complying with fundamental rights.[38] This means that the principle of mutual recognition presupposes mutual trust and comity among national judiciaries.[39]

[36] F Galli, 'Interoperable Law Enforcement. Cooperation Challenges in the EU Area of Freedom Security and Justice' (2019) RSCAS Working Paper 15.

[37] See A Weyembergh, *Le rapprochement des législations, condition de l'espace pénal européen et révélateur de ses tensions* (Brussels, Éditions de l'Université de Bruxelles, 2004); A Weyembergh, 'The Functions of Approximation of Penal Legislation within the EU' (2005) 12 *Maastricht Journal of European and Comparative Law* 149.

[38] For an in-depth analysis of the principle of mutual recognition, see S Peers, 'Mutual Recognition and Criminal Law in the European Union: Has the Council Got It Wrong?' (2004) 41 *CML Rev* 5; V Mitsilegas, 'The Constitutional Implications of Mutual Recognition in Criminal Matters in the EU' (2006) 43 *CML Rev* 1277; A Suominen, *The Principle of Mutual Recognition in Cooperation in Criminal Matters – A Study of the Principle in Four Framework Decisions and in the Implementation Legislation in the Nordic Member States* (Cambridge, Intersentia, 2011) 51–55.

[39] L Bay Larsen, 'Some Reflections on Mutual Recognition in the Area of Freedom, Security and Justice' in P Cardonnel, A Rosas and N Wahl (eds), *Constitutionalising the EU Judicial System: Essays in Honour of Pernilla Lindh* (Oxford, Hart Publishing, 2012) 148.

Policy developments in the AFSJ have been characterised by a firm belief in the added value of approximation and mutual recognition, also in the fight against impunity, ie to prevent criminals from escaping justice. Taking the national legislation of the requesting state as the point of reference has increasingly become accepted in information sharing via mutual assistance mechanisms in criminal matters. In addition, the approximation of national legislation in specific fields has fostered the underlying mutual trust required.

B. Alternative Cooperation Dynamics

The European Union is now practising and proposing in the AFSJ 'alternative' cooperation mechanisms which do not aim at a formal harmonisation or approximation of national provisions. The coordination of Member States' policies and national law enforcement activities, particularly with reference to cross-border challenges, is entrusted to the exchange of information based on commonly agreed general principles and goals. By contrast, more traditional models of European integration insist on the harmonisation/approximation of legal provisions to common standards and the redistribution of competences and rights to the advantage of the supranational level. Mutual recognition has so far applied mainly to judicial cooperation. Introducing the mutual recognition philosophy in the field of law enforcement cooperation would have important implications which will undoubtedly facilitate and expedite information exchanges.[40] Some authors suggest that there should be no question at all of mutual recognition in this context.[41]

As assessed in detail in the following paragraphs, it is questionable whether mutual recognition and harmonisation alone can describe the dynamics of integration in law enforcement cooperation, particularly with reference to information sharing.

(i) The Choice of a Regulation as the Most Suitable Legal Instrument

The e-evidence proposal does not sideline approximation/harmonisation as the most significant asset in the integration process, although it challenges the traditional understanding and functioning of the mutual recognition principle.

With reference to harmonisation, it is noteworthy that the Commission has chosen a Regulation as the most suitable legal instrument, even in the realm of

[40] See G Vermeulen et al, *Availability of Law Enforcement Information in the European Union. Between Mutual Recognition and Equivalent Right of Access* (Antwerp, Maklu, 2005).

[41] G Vermeulen, 'Mutual Recognition, Harmonisation and Fundamental (Procedural) Rights Protection' in M Martin (ed), *Crime, Rights and the EU: The Future of Police and Judicial Cooperation* (London, Justice, 2008) 94.

EU criminal procedure. Hitherto, the Union had only adopted Directives on the basis of Article 82(1) TFEU. The choice is significant because a Regulation would allow the drafting of uniform rules in cross-border procedures, as well as the uniform implementation of such rules at the Member State level.[42] However, a number of issues are challenging. The direct applicability of a Regulation would demand provisions to be sufficiently precise in their wording when drafted. Thus, a well-elaborated legal framework is crucial. The proposed Regulation would in fact establish an innovative and unprecedent legal framework in the field of criminal procedure and foster direct cooperation between the judicial authorities of one Member State and service providers located or active in a different Member State, bypassing the traditional mandatory intervention of another judicial authority in the requested Member State.

Some have argued that the choice of a Regulation instead of a Directive as a legal instrument is not only a paradigm shift in the criminal law area, but it also risks lowering the higher national standards by means of EU legislation.[43] In addition to clearly defined rules for the purpose of legal certainty, the proposed Regulation should also regulate procedural safeguards and legal remedies. In this regard, it is also relevant to note that measures concerning procedural harmonisation to facilitate, inter alia, mutual admissibility of evidence between Member States may, according to Article 82(2), be adopted only by means of Directives.[44]

(ii) A Suitable Legal Basis?

Furthermore, as explored in the fourth section of this contribution, these proposals witness an additional shift away from traditional MLA agreements, involving the 'direct' cooperation between law enforcement authorities seeking to obtain electronic evidence and foreign service providers in (at times, exclusive) control of it. The envisaged framework of direct cooperation between judicial authorities of the issuing Member State and private companies in another Member State goes far beyond the well-established legislative practice and a traditional understanding of mutual recognition of judicial decisions (Article 82(1)2(a) TFEU) as cooperation between the judicial or equivalent authorities of the Member States (Article 82(1)2(d) TFEU).

There are therefore doubts as to whether Article 82(1) TFEU provides a legal basis for a mechanism of direct cooperation between law enforcement authorities and service providers, and the Commission's choice is therefore controversial. Only in cases where the service provider refuses to comply with the order of the issuing Member State will the authorities of the Member State where the service provider is established (or has chosen to appoint its legal representative for the EU)

[42] See the arguments of the Commissions in Explanatory Memorandum to the Proposed Regulation (n 23) 6.
[43] CCBE position on the Commission proposal (n 25) 1–2.
[44] ibid.

be involved. Some authors argue that Article 82(1)(a) is a more convincing choice for a legal basis. The proposed investigative tool would in fact ensure the recognition of a judicial decision (either a Production or Preservation Order) of a Member State throughout the entire Union. An order issued by the issuing Member State would thus have the same legal effect, and thus be enforced in the same manner, as an order issued by the Member State hosting the service provider.[45]

Although the issues at stake differ to some extent and the reasoning of the Luxembourg Court cannot be fully transposed to the other case, one could draw a parallel with the compatibility issues that arose in Opinion 1/15 on the EU–Canada PNR (passenger name record) agreement.[46] In the so-called PNR Opinion, the CJEU ruled that the involvement of non-judicial authorities questioned the use of Article 82(1) TFEU (under a strict interpretation) as the appropriate legal basis – in combination with Article 87(2)(a) TFEU – for concluding such an agreement.[47]

In addition, Article 89 TFEU is very clear in making EU legislation on extraterritorial operations of law enforcement authorities subject to specific requirements. By virtue of this Treaty provision, the Union may lay down conditions and limitations for judicial and police authorities of the Member States (Articles 82 and 87 TFEU) to operate on the territory of another Member State. Given the significant interference with the territorial sovereignty of the enforcing Member State, the TFEU provides for two safeguards: the operation must be carried out in liaison and in agreement with the authorities of the Member State whose territorial sovereignty is affected (Article 89(1) TFEU), and the adoption of the legislative measure requires a unanimous Decision of the Council entailing the veto power of every Member State to protect its territorial sovereignty (Article 89(2) TFEU).[48]

The EU policy-maker has tried to go beyond the traditional integration modalities. However, this has made the choice of a suitable legal basis even more difficult.

IV. The Reshuffling of Responsibilities between Different Actors

It is noteworthy that the proposed Regulation would only apply to ongoing criminal investigations. The new investigative instruments proposed are thus far

[45] V Franssen, 'The European Commission's e-Evidence Proposal: Toward an EU-wide Obligation for Service Providers to Cooperate with Law Enforcement?' (*European Law Blog*, 12 October 2018).

[46] Opinion 1/15 of the Court on the EU–Canada PNR agreement, delivered on 26 July 2017. For a comment, see C Kuner, 'International Agreements, Data Protection, and EU Fundamental Rights on the International Stage: Opinion 1/15 (EU–Canada PNR) of the Court of Justice of the EU' (2018) 55 *CML Rev* 857.

[47] 'that agreement does not provide for the transfer of PNR data by the European authorities to the Canadian authorities, but rather for the transfer of such data by private entities, namely the airline companies, to the Canadian authorities. Accordingly, it is difficult to conclude that those provisions come under judicial and police cooperation as such': Opinion 1/15, para 33.

[48] Böse (n 26).

from mass surveillance or crime prevention tools. Subscriber and access data are considered less sensitive in nature,[49] justifying less stringent legal conditions for their production and a larger scope of application – the European production order could therefore be issued by a prosecutor or a judge (not just any judicial authority) for any type of offence, regardless of its seriousness. By contrast, the production of transactional and content data requires the intervention of a judge and is limited to certain categories of offences: offences punishable by a maximum imprisonment of at least three years and a number of harmonised offences that 'typically' involve electronic information.[50] Finally, the European preservation order would apply to all offences, without distinction, and could be ordered by a prosecutor or a judge.

Some authors consider prosecutors to fall into the categories of law enforcement authorities as, in certain Member States, they are not fully autonomous from the executive power and thus could not be considered independent judicial authorities.[51] For instance, the proposed regulation also involves the cross-border execution of production and preservation orders that have been issued and validated by prosecutors alone and are therefore not judicial decisions. Nevertheless, the proposed cross-border information sharing mechanism indicates very clearly the competent authorities authorised to issue either a production or a preservation order.

On this point, an interesting recent reference is a preliminary ruling from the Irish Supreme Court where the CJEU had to assess, within the framework of a European Arrest Warrant case, how the independence from the public prosecutor is to be decided. The Luxembourg Court ruled that:

> The concept of an 'issuing judicial authority', within the meaning of Article 6(1) of Council Framework Decision 2002/584/JHA of 13 June 2002 on the European arrest warrant and the surrender procedures between Member States, as amended by Council Framework Decision 2009/299/JHA of 26 February 2009, must be interpreted as not including public prosecutors' offices of a Member State which are exposed to the risk of being subject, directly or indirectly, to directions or instructions in a specific case from the executive, such as a Minister for Justice, in connection with the adoption of a decision to issue a European arrest warrant.[52]

This is the first definition of who is an independent issuing authority in the context of mutual recognition proceedings at the EU level and constitutes a major turning point.

[49] Interestingly, the ECtHR, in its recent decision *Big Brother Watch*, held that it was unsustainable to treat the content of communications and metadata/communications data differently in terms of their potential for privacy intrusion – in other words, the interception of metadata can be just as intrusive as the interception of content. See M Milanovic, 'ECtHR Judgment in *Big Brother Watch v UK*' (*EJIL: Talk!*, 17 September 2018); M Milanovic, 'Human Rights Treaties and Foreign Surveillance: Privacy in the Digital Age' (2015) *Harvard International Law Journal* 56, 141.

[50] Art 5(4) e-Evidence Proposal.

[51] As defined in the EIO Directive (n 6).

[52] Joined Cases C-508/18 and C-82/19 PPU *Minister for Justice and Equality v OG and PI* (27 May 2019).

A. Law Enforcement Authorities

The Commission package may be severely criticised on different aspects of the powers of the competent (public) authorities involved in the issuing state, as it clashes with the traditional understanding of the territoriality principle. The European Parliament study raises concerns the approach of the European Commission to allowing the unilateral extension of enforcement jurisdiction within the EU (and not only outside its border). The proposal shifts the competence of assessing the legality of the order from the executing authority to the issuing authority. In particular, law enforcement authorities in the issuing Member State must verify the legality of the data requested under the law of the requested Member State. Fulfilling such an obligation would not, however, serve the issuing Member State's own national interest, so there could be an incentive to bypass this step.

First, the proposed regime of direct cross-border access to service providers' data would reach beyond the territorial boundaries of the issuing Member State and would thereby affect the sovereignty of other states. A unilateral extension of enforcement jurisdiction may thus compromise the functioning of international cooperation in criminal matters and foster conflicting obligations of service providers. In fact, the creation of a transnationally binding order may interfere with the sovereignty of the Member State in whose territory the order is to be executed (the enforcing Member State).

It is noteworthy that the scope of the proposed regulation reaches even beyond the border of the EU, as it encompasses companies that provide services within the EU. In fact, the e-evidence proposal would have a number of important policy consequences, not only for EU-based cloud customers, technology companies and law enforcement authorities, but also for technology companies and cloud customers based outside of the Union. By requiring providers within its jurisdiction to appoint a legal representative that can comply with Member State production and preservation orders, the Regulation would give law enforcement authorities across the EU the ability to compel providers based outside the EU to produce data – potentially even regardless of which entity in the provider's corporate group has possession or custody over the data. This reading could result in a significant expansion of Member State jurisdiction over digital data held by service providers located outside the EU.

Secondly, the proposed cooperation regime is based on the place where the service provider is offering its services, instead of the storage location, as grounds for jurisdiction. Service providers may thus end up in a situation where they must provide user data to law enforcement authorities of any country from whose territory these services can be accessed. Access to service providers' data will thus be governed by multiple jurisdictions without the service provider or its customer being able to foresee the conditions and restrictions under the cooperation regime to be applied. There would in fact be legal uncertainty as to the state competent to exercise enforcement jurisdiction and thus to access user data. The connecting factor should be strictly construed in order to enable the user to foresee which enforcement regime(s) will apply to his or her data. The situation could be exacerbated should this model be copied by third countries, which could put in place extraterritorial enforcement rules to access data stored in the EU, with a risk of clashing with the General Data Protection Regulation.

B. The Role of Private Actors: Beyond the 'Public–Private' Divide

The information society has substantially changed the ways in which law enforcement authorities can obtain information and evidence. Beyond their own specialised databases, competent authorities have access to huge amounts of data on all types of public and private databases.

Nowadays, the legal systems in most Western countries thus face relevant changes in the politics of information control. The rise of advanced technologies has magnified the capability of new players to control both the means of communication and data flows. To an increasing extent, public authorities are sharing their regulatory competences with an indefinite number of actors by imposing preventive duties on the private sector, such as information-gathering and sharing (eg on telecommunication companies for data retention purposes).[53] This trend is leading to a growing privatisation of surveillance practices. In this move, key players in private information society (producers, service providers, key consumers) are given law enforcement obligations.

Information sharing functions across national boundaries and across the traditional public–private divide. Most of the web giants are established overseas, so that private actors often – voluntarily or compulsorily – transfer data to third countries. Companies do not just cooperate with public authorities, but effectively and actively come to play a part in bulk collection and security practices. They identify, select, search and interpret suspicious elements by means of so-called 'data selectors'. Private actors, in this sense, have become 'security professionals' in their own right.[54]

Systematic government access to private sector data is carried out not only directly, via access to private sector databases and networks, but also indirectly, through the cooperation of third parties, such as financial institutions, mobile phone operators, communication providers and the companies that maintain the available databases or networks.

[53] V Mitsilegas, 'The Transformation of Privacy in an Era of Pre-emptive Surveillance' (2015) 20 *Tilburg Law Review* 35; HE De Busser, 'Privatisation of Information and the Data Protection Reform' in R Leenes, S Gutwirth and P De Hert (eds), *Reloading Data Protection: Multidisciplinary Insights and Contemporary Challenges* (Berlin, Springer, 2013) 129–49.

[54] See D Bigo, 'Beyond National Security, the Emergence of a Digital Reason of State(s) Led by Transnational Guilds of Sensitive Information: The Case of the Five Eyes Plus Network' in B Wagner, MC Kettermann and K Vieth (eds), *Research Handbook on Human Rights and Digital Technology* (Cheltenham, Edward Elgar, 2019) 33.

Personal data originally circulated in the EU for commercial purposes may be transferred by private intermediaries to public authorities, often also overseas, for other purposes, including detection, investigation and prosecution. The significant blurring of purposes among the different layers of data gathering – for instance, commercial profiling techniques and security – aims to exploit the 'exchange value' of individuals' fragmented identities, as consumers, suspects of certain crimes, 'good citizens' or 'others'.

Private actors are not just in charge of the operational enforcement of public authority decisions in security matters; they are often the only ones with the necessary expertise, and therefore they profoundly shape decision-making and policy implementation. Their choices are nevertheless guided by reasons such as commercial interest and they are often unaccountable.

By virtue of the proposed Regulation on e-Evidence, the responsibility to ensure that MLA requests do not encroach upon fundamental rights is deferred to a service provider – a private person, ie 'the addressee'[55] – without the intervention of the public competent authority of the service provider's host Member State. As argued by Mitsilegas, the draft e-evidence proposals introduce a paradigm shift, called the 'privatisation of mutual trust', departing from the existing models of judicial cooperation and mutual recognition in EU law. A system of direct cooperation between public authorities and private companies would in fact replace the cooperation between public authorities in different Member States.[56]

Cooperation with the private sector already exists in other policy areas. For instance, judicial decisions in civil matters can be enforced by private actors with no need to involve public authorities in the executing Member State. However, in the field of judicial and police cooperation in criminal matters, the cross-border enforcement of judicial decisions has so far required the involvement of the competent public authority (most often a judicial one) in the executing Member State.[57] The proposed Regulation thus entails a fundamentally different approach.

Considerations of a practical nature raise concerns with reference to due process guarantees of requests and legal foreseeability. Addressees are responsible for determining whether one of the several grounds for refusal to the execution of a production and preservation order applies. The crucial weakening of the degree of judicial control at the executing stage is dictated by practical considerations to foster effectiveness.

[55] Art 14(4) e-Evidence Proposal.

[56] V Mitsilegas, 'The Privatization of Mutual Trust in Europe's Area of Criminal Justice: The Case of e-Evidence' (2018) 25 *Maastricht Journal of International and Comparative Law* 263.

[57] The implementation of the mutual recognition principle which entails the interaction between public authorities on both sides of a border. This holds true in cases of a final judicial decision imposing a custodial sentence or a fine as much as in decisions relating to the investigation of a crime via a European Arrest Warrant or a European Investigation Order. See, eg Art 8 of Council Framework Decision 2008/909/JHA of 27 November 2008 on the application of the principle of mutual recognition to judgments in criminal matters imposing custodial sentences or measures involving deprivation of liberty for the purpose of their enforcement in the European Union [2008] OJ L327/27.

The extent to which possible 'manifest' fundamental rights concerns will be taken into account in the processing of production and preservation orders may vary from one service provider to another; the broad scope of the proposal, covering *any* criminal offence, carries the risk of swamping service providers with requests, despite the fact that many of them do not have legal departments to conduct such assessments. And processing requests from law enforcement authorities will entail significant costs (in terms of both financial and human resources), especially for small and medium enterprises and start-ups; however, provisions on financial help fail to properly address these legitimate concerns.[58] The decision on whether or not to disclose the data may therefore be subject to business considerations.

The proposal would put companies in the role of public judicial authorities and lead to an undesirable privatisation of security. There are considerable doubts as to whether service providers are in a position to provide for effective individual rights protection within the framework of international cooperation in criminal matters, checking the compatibility of production and preservation orders, inter alia, with the EU Charter. The service provider is subject to an obligation to produce the requested data, and, unlike a public authority, runs the risk of being subject to enforcement measures and sanctions in case of non-compliance. Besides, the six-hour deadline envisaged for processing emergency requests from law enforcement authorities sheds further doubts on the ability of service providers to conduct an in-depth assessment that ensures adequate protection of individuals' rights.

Such a major delegation of states' responsibility for the protection of individual rights would require a detailed regulation of the service provider's responsibilities, procedural safeguards (for instance, the requirement of a reasoned decision) and supervision by the competent authority. As the mechanism proposed by the Commission lacks such a regulatory framework, it leaves a loophole in the protection of individual rights and bears the risk that the standard of protection under the law of the enforcing Member State could not be maintained.

These concerns are heightened by the absence of clear-cut criteria on which service providers should rely to perform their assessment. As regards individual rights in particular, a service provider may oppose an order if it 'manifestly violates' the provisions of the Charter or if it is 'manifestly abusive'.[59] It is not clear what a 'manifest' violation of the Charter or a 'manifest' abuse entails. This approach contradicts the obligation of clarity and precision in EU legislation required by the CJEU's jurisprudence,[60] an obligation that is nevertheless essential to allow the individuals concerned to enjoy sufficient guarantees that their data will be

[58] Reimbursement of costs may be claimed before the competent authorities of the issuing state, provided that this possibility is foreseen under national law. See Art 12 e-Evidence Proposal.

[59] Art 14(4)(f) e-Evidence Proposal.

[60] See Joined Cases C-293/12 and C-594/12 *Digital Rights Ireland and Seitlinger and Others* EU:C:2014:238; Joined Cases C-203/15 and C-698/15 *Tele2 Sverige AB v Postoch telestyrelsen* and *Secretary of State for the Home Department v Tom Watson, Peter Brice, Geoffrey Lewis* ECLI:EU:C:2016:970.

effectively protected against risks of abuse and unlawful access and use.[61] Plus, the manifest violation must be apparent solely from the information contained in the order. As the production order certificate does not contain further information on the facts of the case nor a thorough necessity and proportionality analysis, a human rights assessment will hardly be possible, and a request for additional information is not foreseen. Moreover, the service provider is not even allowed to refuse to execute the order and to oppose its enforcement if the requested information is protected by a privilege or immunity under domestic law (Articles 8 and Article 14(4) of the draft Regulation).

In many cases, the defence will have little access to the service provider, for example, if the investigation is carried out without his or her knowledge, or the service provider is located outside the EU. In addition, the current proposal only provides a possibility for the suspect or accused person to challenge the decision to issue a production or preservation order in the issuing state.[62] This means that the recognition and execution of the request by the service provider cannot be challenged by the person whose data is at stake. Thus, although existing data protection provisions are fine, as argued above, the involvement of a private actor could hinder their practical enforcement in certain circumstances.

Service providers and traditional telecommunications providers seem highly reluctant to enter into any legality and fundamental rights assessment of production and preservation orders. Such a task also raises important questions with reference to the liability of these providers towards their own customers.

The delineation of which service providers would be requested to cooperate with public authorities under the proposed legal framework is equally significant. The proposed Regulation targets specific subcategories of service providers: providers of electronic communications services, of information society services 'for which the storage of data is a defining component of the service provided to the user', and of internet domain names and IP numbering services. No exception is made for small service providers, for which the additional administrative and financial burden is likely to be very significant, and possibly even unrealistic. Services for which data storage is only an ancillary component are excluded. It is yet not clear which services would be excluded on this basis.

V. Concluding Remarks

In recent decades, EU Member States have increased their efforts in the fight against terrorism, organised crime and illegal immigration, which have gradually developed a cross-border dimension, accentuated by the dismantling of internal

[61] Case C-362/14 *Schrems* ECLI:EU:C:2015:650, para 91.
[62] Art 17(1) e-Evidence Proposal.

border controls. In the wider context of transnational cooperation, information exchanges are essential in fighting cross-border crime and in ensuring a high level of security in the EU, and thus in the fight against impunity. However, the enhanced efforts to fight against impunity via new means of MLA come at a cost, in terms of the protection of fundamental rights. Clearly there should be no impunity for the most serious crimes. If states have the primary responsibility for investigating and prosecuting the most serious crimes, cooperation is essential in order to accomplish that mission because evidence is often spread across different countries and investigations must therefore take place across national borders. Information exchanges are necessary to effectively investigate and prosecute cross-border crimes, and to avoid impunity. In the context of globalisation and of modern technology and communication, there is certain a need to establish new instruments taking into account new modes of assistance to enhance prosecution efforts.

This chapter has explored how information management – and particularly MLA – is witnessing a paradigm change in the dynamics of law enforcement and judicial cooperation within the EU's AFSJ. This is particularly the case with reference to the growing involvement of private actors in information management activities.

Mutual legal assistance is in fact undergoing major changes, specifically with the envisaged development in the EU of cross-border production and preservation orders. The proposed cross-border direct interaction between competent public authorities and service providers first challenges the traditional understanding of mutual recognition as cooperation between judicial or equivalent authorities of the Member States. The new instruments envisaged would only apply to ongoing judicial investigations and would thus involve only judicial authorities and not a broad range of law enforcement authorities with blurred tasks. Yet, under the new regulatory framework under discussion, private actors, namely service providers, would be requested to take up new roles and responsibilities in MLA procedures. It is doubtful, however, whether they will be in a position to provide for effective individual rights protection. Such unilateral extension of enforcement jurisdiction may compromise the functioning of international cooperation in criminal matters and foster conflicting obligations for service providers. A most interesting change and potential challenge in new modes of MLA is that direct cross-border access to service providers' data would reach beyond the territorial boundaries of the issuing Member State and would thereby affect the sovereignty of other states.

11

Clash of the Titans: The Fight against Impunity versus Social Rehabilitation and the Protection of Fundamental Rights within the Framework of Prisoner Transfers in the EU

ALESSANDRO ROSANÒ

I. Introduction

Framework Decision 2008/909/JHA[1] introduced an advanced tool of judicial cooperation whose purpose is twofold. On the one hand, it aims to speed up transfers of prisoners between EU Member States through a cooperation mechanism between judicial authorities that is not based upon the consent of either the sentenced person or the governments of the states involved in the procedure;[2] on the other hand, it pursues the social rehabilitation of the sentenced persons to allow them to serve part of their sentence in a state with which they have significant family, linguistic, cultural, social, economic or other links.[3]

The purpose of this chapter is to identify the role that the fight against impunity may play in the context of that Framework Decision and whether that purpose

[1] Council Framework Decision 2008/909/JHA of 27 November 2008 on the application of the principle of mutual recognition to judgments in criminal matters imposing custodial sentences or measures involving deprivation of liberty for the purpose of their enforcement in the European Union [2008] OJ L327/27.

[2] See recitals 4 and 5.

[3] See recital 9, Art 3(1) and Art 4(6). On social rehabilitation in EU law, see S Montaldo, 'Offenders' Rehabilitation: Towards a New Paradigm for EU Criminal Law?' (2018) 8 *European Criminal Law Review* 223; A Martufi, 'The Paths of Offender Rehabilitation and the European Dimension of Punishment: New Challenges for an Old Ideal?' (2019) 25 *Maastricht Journal of European and Comparative Law* 1. More generally on social rehabilitation, see E Rotman, *Beyond Punishment. A New View on the Rehabilitation of Criminal Offenders* (Praeger, Greenwood Press, 1990).

can be deemed to be consistent with the objective of social rehabilitation, on the one hand, and the protection of fundamental rights, on the other.

One may wonder what relationship may exist between these three elements. Generally speaking, impunity means the situation of someone not being held accountable for a crime. Thus, it should be regarded as a common feature of lawless societies, being a form of lawlessness in itself.[4] As a consequence, the fight against impunity should be interpreted as a way of establishing, re-establishing and promoting the rule of law.[5] The idea of constraints, meaning limitations to power, is typical of the notion of the rule of law. Therefore, the fight against impunity must take place consistently with the value of the rule of law and with the idea of limitations to power. Social rehabilitation and the protection of fundamental rights should then be considered limitations to the fight against impunity, as their purpose is to oppose both a lawless impunity and a limitless fight against impunity.[6]

Social rehabilitation would work as a limitation as it would make it possible for the offender to be engaged in a pathway towards gaining greater responsibility and attaining a more meaningful life, while society could restrain him or her through available means of social control.[7] Whereas this individual perspective is essential to the nature of punishment itself, successful post-release social reinsertion also pursues the public interest of avoiding future recidivism. However, this collective dimension cannot justify any means of re-education. A similar dynamic applies

[4] See N Roht-Arriaza, 'Punishment, Redress, and Pardon: Theoretical and Psychological Approaches' in N Roht Arriaza (ed), *Impunity and Human Rights in International Law and Practice* (Oxford, Oxford University Press, 1995).

[5] See generally W Schroeder, *Strengthening the Rule of Law in Europe: From a Common Concept to Mechanisms of Implementation* (London, Bloomsbury, 2016); R Bellamy (ed), *The Rule of Law and the Separation of Powers* (London, Routledge, 2017); T Kostadinides, *The Rule of Law in the European Union: The Internal Dimension* (London, Bloomsbury, 2017).

[6] The nature of social rehabilitation in the EU legal framework is unclear. According to some Advocates General, it should be regarded as a general principle of EU law: see, eg Case C-582/15 *Van Vemde* [2016], published in the electronic Reports of Cases, Opinion of AG Bot, para 48; for a general overview, see A Rosanò, '*Beshkov* or the Long Road to the Principle of Social Rehabilitation' (2018) 4 *European Papers* 433. However, the CJEU has never uttered a word on the topic. Furthermore, there are reasons to believe that social rehabilitation might be seen as a fundamental right belonging to the individual: see S Montaldo, 'Offenders' Rehabilitation and the Cross-Border Transfer of Prisoners and Persons Subject to Probation Measures and Alternative Sanctions: A Stress Test for EU Judicial Cooperation in Criminal Matters' (2019) 3 *Revista Brasileira de Direito Processual Penal* 924. However, considering the features of the EU legal system, as fundamental rights are general principles of EU law, the outcome would be the same: whether it is a fundamental right or not, social rehabilitation would be a primary source of EU law. Therefore, for the purpose of this chapter, social rehabilitation should be considered as a general principle of EU law, and not as a fundamental right. In this regard, as recalled in Case C-145/09 *Tsakouridis* [2010] ECR I-11979, Opinion of AG Bot, para 50, pursuant to Art 10(3) of the International Covenant on Civil and Political Rights, the penitentiary system of the signatory states shall comprise treatment of prisoners, the essential aim of which shall be their reformation and social rehabilitation. All Member States of the EU are parties to the Covenant; it can therefore be said that the Covenant expresses some core values that are shared by these states which may be recognised by the Court of Justice as general principles of supranational law.

[7] See Roht-Arriaza (n 4).

to fundamental rights, which place constraints on the exercise of public coercive powers.

For the purposes of this chapter, the question is to what extent the effectiveness of judicial cooperation mechanisms allowing for the cross-border enforcement of a sentence can prioritise certainty of punishment, in the presence of serious fundamental rights concerns.[8]

As far as Framework Decision 2008/909/JHA is concerned, the fight against impunity entails more specifically certainty of punishment or, rather, certainty of enforcement of the (foreign) sentence, provided that it is consistent with the aforementioned general constraints.[9]

To address this issue, an overview on the Framework Decision's main provisions is provided (section II). The chapter then focuses on the importance attached in the case law of the Court of Justice of the European Union (CJEU), which deals with that instrument, on the need to avoid impunity, highlighting that social rehabilitation seems to play the role of a secondary objective (section III). Thereafter, the shift in the legislative and jurisprudential paradigm on the protection of fundamental rights in the context of judicial cooperation mechanisms in criminal matters is highlighted to ascertain if this also applies to Framework Decision 2008/909/JHA (section IV). More specifically, the analysis aims to assess if the *Aranyosi and Căldăraru* test applies to the Framework Decision in question (section V). Finally, some concluding remarks are provided on the role that social rehabilitation may

[8] However, one should distinguish between an international law approach and an EU law approach to fundamental rights. From an international law point of view, fundamental rights are synonymous with the fight against impunity, as they are the key features established or re-established after a period of dictatorship or of systemic violations of basic values: K Engle, 'Anti-impunity and the Turn to Criminal Law in Human Rights' (2015) 100 *Cornell Law Review* 1070, 1077. Thus, impunity refers to an exemption from punishment, a failure to remedy fundamental rights violations, a cause of these violations and an obstacle to peace and stability, while fundamental rights and the fight against impunity refer to accountability: P Akhavan, 'Beyond Impunity: Can International Criminal Justice Prevent Future Atrocities?' (2001) 95 *American Journal of International Law* 7; G Robertson, 'Ending Impunity: How International Criminal Law Can Put Tyrants on Trial' (2005) 38 *Cornell International Law Journal* 649.

[9] Apart from the issues related to social rehabilitation and the protection of fundamental rights, there is another problem regarding the application of Framework Decision 2008/909/JHA: its connection with and encroachment on other instruments of judicial cooperation in criminal matters, such as Framework Decision 2002/584/JHA on the European Arrest Warrant (EAW). This topic is not tackled here because of its procedural nature, while the purpose of this chapter is to address some teleological issues and some aspects related to the protection of fundamental rights as general principles of EU law. However, in some cases, the overlapping of the two instruments of judicial cooperation may lead to de facto impunity. This may concern a situation where the sentenced person has fled the state in which he or she was convicted, finding shelter on the territory of a state where the sanction might be executed following a transfer. The authorities of the sentencing state may resort to an EAW in order to obtain his or her surrender, or they might decide to proceed according to Framework Decision 2008/909/JHA. The lack of expertise on the part of the judicial authorities and of a careful assessment regarding the place of execution of the sentence and the chances of social rehabilitation in that location may delay the decision by the competent authorities or lead to a situation where both procedures are initiated, which is likely to determine a contradictory outcome (the sentenced person must stay and be transferred at the same time).

play in national legal systems in changing the CJEU's case law and the need to rely on scrutiny on the part of the European Court of Human Rights (ECtHR) when it comes to the protection of fundamental rights (section VI).

II. Framework Decision 2008/909/JHA, its Main Provisions and the Report of the European Commission

The 2001 Programme of measures to implement the principle of mutual recognition of decisions in criminal matters highlighted the will to re-evaluate existing judicial cooperation mechanisms related to final decisions on custodial sentences.[10] The intention expressed therein was possibly to replace those procedures with new ones that would lead to the application of the principle of mutual recognition to the transfer of sentenced persons between the Member States.[11]

In view of these aspects of the Programme, Austria, Finland and Sweden proposed the adoption of a Framework Decision.[12] The idea was to introduce a new judicial cooperation instrument, known as the European Enforcement Order. The issuing of an order by the authorities of a Member State would permit the execution of a custodial sentence or another measure limiting personal liberty in another Member State. More specifically, the proposal identified the executing Member State as any Member State of which the sentenced person was a national or in which that person had their permanent legal residence or with which they had other close links. The consent of the sentenced person for the transfer to take place was only mandatory in the latter case, while all other situations involved a mere right to express a personal opinion.

Despite some difficulties, due to the opposition expressed by Poland[13] related to the high number of Polish inmates serving their sentence in the prisons of the other Member States,[14] a compromise text was eventually approved by the Council and Framework Decision 2008/909/JHA came into force on 5 December 2008.

As it was based upon the principles of mutual trust between national judicial authorities and of mutual recognition of foreign judicial decisions,[15] the procedure

[10] Council, Programme of measures to implement the principle of mutual recognition of decisions in criminal matters [2001] OJ C12/10.

[11] ibid measures 14 and 16.

[12] Initiative of the Republic of Austria, the Republic of Finland and the Kingdom of Sweden with a view to adopting a Council Framework Decision on the European enforcement order and the transfer of sentenced persons between Member States of the European Union [2005] OJ C150/1.

[13] Council, Press release, 2768th Council Meeting, Justice and Home Affairs, Brussels, 4–5 December 2006, C/06/341, 15801/06, 11.

[14] Council, Press release, 2781st Council Meeting, Justice and Home Affairs, Brussels, 15 February 2007, C/07/16, 5922/07, 10.

[15] See generally C Janssens, *The Principle of Mutual Recognition in EU Law* (Oxford, Oxford University Press, 2013); L Klimek, *Mutual Recognition of Judicial Decision in European Criminal Law* (Berlin, Springer, 2017).

laid down by this instrument was centred on the duty on the part of the receiving authority to recognise the foreign judgment and to execute the transfer request.

For the purposes of the transfer, the decision to submit a transfer request is transmitted by the competent authorities in the issuing state to those of the Member State of which the sentenced person is a national, the Member State to which he or she will be deported or any other Member State that consents to the forwarding of the judgment.[16] The judgment is forwarded together with a certificate, translated into the official language or one of the official languages of the executing state.[17] The sentenced person's consent is needed unless the judgment is forwarded to the Member State in which he or she is resident or to which he or she will be deported, or the Member State to which he or she fled or returned before the conclusion of the proceedings pending against him or her, or following the conviction in the issuing state. In any case, the sentenced person has the right to express his or her opinion on the transfer. The authority of the issuing state must take this into account when deciding whether or not to transfer the sentenced person. Furthermore, this opinion must be forwarded to the executing state.[18]

As the Framework Decision applies the principle of mutual recognition, this implies the abolition of the double criminality check in relation at least to a list of 32 categories of offences[19] and the exhaustive identification of grounds for denying recognition.[20]

Partial recognition and execution are allowed,[21] and the recognition may be postponed if the certificate is incomplete or does not correspond to the judgment.[22] If there are no grounds for refusal or postponement of recognition of the judgment, the authority of the executing state recognises the decision transmitted, making any necessary adaptations with regard to the duration or nature of the sentence if these are not compatible with national law. However, the adapted sentence may not aggravate the sentence passed in the issuing state.[23]

The decision must be recognised by the executing Member State as soon as possible, and in any case within 90 days from receipt of the judgment and certificate.[24]

[16] Framework Decision 2008/909/JHA, Art 4(1).

[17] ibid Art 22(1).

[18] ibid Art 6.

[19] ibid Art 7. On the abolition of the double criminality check and the instruments of judicial cooperation in criminal matters, see N Keijzer, 'The Fate of the Dual Incrimination Requirement' in E Guild, L Marin (eds), *Still Not Resolved? Constitutional Issues of the European Arrest Warrant* (Nijmegen, Wolf Legal Publishers, 2009) 61; E van Sliedregt, 'The Dual Criminality Requirement' in N Keijzer and E van Sliedregt (eds), *The European Arrest Warrant in Practice* (The Hague, TMC Asser Press, 2009).

[20] Framework Decision 2008/909/JHA, Art 9. On the list of grounds for denying recognition and the instruments of judicial cooperation in criminal matters, see L Klimek, *European Arrest Warrant* (Berlin, Springer, 2015) 145–80.

[21] Framework Decision 2008/909/JHA, Art 10.

[22] ibid Art 11.

[23] ibid Art 8.

[24] ibid Art 12(1) and (2).

The enforcement of the sentence is governed by the law of the executing state, including the grounds for early or conditional release,[25] whereas amnesty and pardon may be granted by both states involved in the procedure and the review of the judgment may only be decided by the issuing Member State.[26]

As such, this mechanism obliterates the role of the sentenced person and of the political branch, as it does not rely on their consent.[27] Furthermore, it speeds up the procedure, by imposing on the executing authority strict deadlines for issuing a decision. From this point of view, Framework Decision 2008/909/JHA replaces the pre-existing rigid and bureaucratic mechanisms in the relationships between the Member States.[28]

However, there are some issues that need to be taken into account. In its report of 2014 on the status of implementation of the Framework Decision, the European Commission highlighted that only five states – namely, Denmark, Finland, Italy, Luxembourg and the UK – had transposed it in time.[29] Another 13 had done so when the deadline had already expired, while 10 had failed to communicate their implementation measures.[30] Furthermore, a number of issues arising from the practice of the national authorities were put under the spotlight. More specifically, the Commission complained that the sentenced person is not always informed of the start of the transfer procedure.[31] As a consequence, he or she is unable to provide a personal opinion. Furthermore, the choice made by some states to expand the conditions for adapting the sentence, to introduce new grounds for refusal or to make some of the existing ones optional was criticised.[32] Finally, the report underlined that some states had not set a deadline for their national courts to decide on

[25] ibid Art 17(1) and (3).

[26] ibid Art 19.

[27] See generally CL Blakesley, 'The Practice of Extradition from Antiquity to Modern France and the United States: A Brief History' (1981) 4 *Boston College International and Comparative Law Review* 39; E Edmonds-Poli and D Shirk, 'Extradition as a Tool for International Cooperation: Lessons from the US–Mexico Relationship' (2018) 33 *Maryland Journal of International Law* 215.

[28] For instance, one may consider the Convention on the Transfer of Sentenced Persons, concluded in Strasbourg on 21 March 1983 within the framework of the Council of Europe and ratified by 66 countries, including 19 outside the Council. On the topic, see E Muller-Rappard, 'The Transfer of Sentenced Persons – Comments on the Relevant Council of Europe Legal Instruments' (1991) 3 *Pace International Law Review* 155; J Ddamulira Mujuzi, 'Legal Pluralism and the Convention on the Transfer of Sentenced Persons in Practice: Highlighting the Jurisprudence of the European Court of Human Rights on the Transfer of Sentenced Persons within and to Europe' (2015) 47 *The Journal of Legal Pluralism and Unofficial Law* 324.

[29] Commission, 'Report from the Commission to the European Parliament and the Council on the implementation by the Member States of the Framework Decisions 2008/909/JHA, 2008/947/JHA and 2009/829/JHA on the mutual recognition of judicial decisions on custodial sentences or measures involving deprivation of liberty, on probation decisions and alternative sanctions and on supervision measures as an alternative to provisional detention' COM (2014) 57 final, 6.

[30] ibid.

[31] ibid 7–8.

[32] ibid 9–10.

appeals against the transfer decision.[33] Therefore, the Commission expressed some dissatisfaction, urging the Member States to transpose the Framework Decision fully and consistently.

On their part, legal scholars have highlighted some flaws in the Framework Decision under discussion. According to some of them, the major problem concerns the failure to define social rehabilitation as a purpose pursued by the Framework Decision,[34] while others have focused on the lack of a right of veto that should be held by sentenced persons regarding their transfer.[35]

Others have highlighted the failure to provide deadlines for the procedures in the issuing Member State, and the failure to provide an obligation for that Member State to inform the sentenced person of the detention conditions in the executing Member State.[36]

Some commentators have added that the real purpose of the Framework Decision is to reduce the costs of foreign inmates, claiming that social rehabilitation is just a secondary consequence or a mere desire.[37] Others have highlighted the difficulties involved in actually implementing mutual trust between Member States. In fact, practitioners have expressed doubts regarding prison conditions, judiciary independence or the level of corruption in other Member States, as they may act as limits to mutual trust and lead to mutual scepticism.[38]

[33] ibid 10.

[34] A Martufi, 'Assessing the Resilience of "Social Rehabilitation" as a Rationale for Transfer: A Commentary on the Aims of Framework Decision 2008/909/JHA' [2018] *New Journal of European Criminal Law* 43. See also E de Wree, T Vander Beken and G Vermeulen, 'The Transfer of Sentenced Persons in Europe. Much Ado about Reintegration' [2009] *Punishment & Society* 111.

[35] See P Faraldo-Cabana, 'Transferring Non-consenting Prisoners' in S Montaldo (ed), *The Transfer of Prisoners in the European Union. Challenges and Prospects on the Implementation of Framework Decision 2008/909/JHA* (The Hague, Eleven, 2020) 61–78. According to Faraldo-Cabana, 'by abolishing the offender's right to veto, the EU expects to maximise the offenders' chances of social rehabilitation while ensuring the cross-border enforcement of custodial sentences and measures involving deprivation of liberty. … However, … the fact that consent is considered to be an obstacle may indicate that offenders do not feel that transfer is of benefit to their reintegration or that it is in any way a favour'.

[36] See, in the context of the 'STEPS 2 Resettlement. JUST/2011/JPEN/AG/4605' project, I Durnescu, 'Obstacles and Solutions in the Implementation of the FD 2008/909/JHA' http://steps2.europris.org/wp-content/uploads/2016/07/Annex-4.6.-Workstream-1-Obstacles-and-Solutions-in-the-implementation-of-the-FD-2008909JHA.pdf.

[37] M Pleić, 'Challenges in Cross-Border Transfer of Prisoners: EU Framework and Croatian Perspective' in D Duić and T Petrašević (eds), *EU Law in Context – Adjustment to Membership and Challenges of the Enlargement* (Osijek, Josip Juraj Strossmayer University of Osijek, 2018) 380.

[38] In the context of the 'Improving the transfer of persons pursuant to mutual recognition of judicial decisions in criminal matters and the citizens' fundamental rights protection. JUST/2014/JCOO/ AG/ CRIM/7755' project, see T Marguery, M Simonato, B Oude Breuil and N Peris Brines, 'Part V. Comparative Analysis and Recommendations' https://euprisoners.eu/wp-content/uploads/sites/153/2017/11/EUPrisoners-Part-V-comparative-report.pdf. Furthermore, the authors of this report highlighted some issues related to the procedural safeguards. For instance, the regulation of the right of access to a lawyer may differ according to whether the Member State acts as the issuing or executing state, while the right to access the documents of the proceedings and the right to obtain translated documents are not granted uniformly.

III. Avoiding Impunity versus Social Rehabilitation: A View from the Court

It has been said that

> by pursuing the aim of a free circulation of final judicial decisions in criminal matters, the EU appears concerned with the risk of impunity that may result as a consequence of the increased mobility of EU citizens across borders. It is then no surprise that other mutual recognition instruments contain explicit reference to the need to protect the general public, as fewer restrictions on the free circulation of citizens across the EU may entail higher threats to individual and public security.[39]

Other scholars have also highlighted the connection between the mobility of European citizens and the risk of impunity.[40] These concerns were addressed – and actually further confirmed – by the Court of Justice in the *Ognyanov* case, which conveys the idea of an ongoing clash between the fight against impunity and social rehabilitation as the purpose pursued through Framework Decision 2008/909/JHA.

In *Ognyanov*,[41] the CJEU dealt with the case of a Bulgarian national sentenced to imprisonment in Denmark, who, while imprisoned in a Danish prison, worked for one year, eight months, and 20 days. Following his transfer to Bulgaria, some doubts were raised as to the determination of the length of the sentence he still had to serve. In fact, under Bulgarian law, two days of work are equivalent to three days of deprivation of liberty, unless the issuing state has already reduced the sentence. This means that Mr Ognyanov would have qualified for a significant reduction in his sentence and, most importantly, for an early release. Therefore, the Sofia City Court referred some questions to the CJEU to ascertain if it was possible to reduce the sentence in light of Bulgarian law.

The CJEU held that under Framework Decision 2008/909/JHA, only the enforcement of the sentence is governed by the law of the executing Member State. That should be interpreted as meaning that only the execution of the sentence following the transfer falls under the competence of the law of the executing

[39] See Martufi (n 34) 48. As far as other mutual recognition instruments are concerned, Martufi refers to Framework Decision 2008/947/JHA on the application of the principle of mutual recognition to judgments and probation decisions with a view to the supervision of probation measures and alternative sanctions.

[40] See, eg P Faraldo-Cabana, 'One Step Forward, Two Steps Back? Social Rehabilitation of Foreign Offenders under Framework Decisions 2008/909/JHA and 2008/947/JHA' [2019] *New Journal of European Criminal Law* 164.

[41] Case C-554/14 *Ognyanov* [2016], published in the electronic Reports of Cases. For a comment, see J Ddamulira Mujuzi, 'The Transfer of Offenders between European Countries and Remission of Sentences: A Comment on the Grand Chamber of the Court of Justice of the European Union's Judgment in Criminal Proceedings against Atanas Ognyanov of 8 November 2016 Dealing with Article 17 of Council Framework Decision 2008/909/JHA' [2017] *European Criminal Law Review* 289; S Montaldo, 'Judicial Cooperation, Transfer of Prisoners and Offenders' Rehabilitation: No Fairy Tale Bliss. Comment on *Ognyanov*' (2017) 3 *European Papers* 709.

Member State. As regards the determination of the sentence, the issuing Member State retains its competence and this cannot be disputed in light of a more favourable provision existing in the executing Member State. To deem otherwise would lead to a retroactive application of the executing Member State's national law to the part of the sentence already served in the issuing Member State, which would amount to a breach of the principle of mutual recognition.[42]

Technically speaking, the CJEU cannot be criticised for its interpretation followed in this judgment, as this is how mutual recognition works. However, legal fragmentation – meaning the different legal regimes existing in the Member State – leads to varied approaches to social rehabilitation from state to state. As can clearly be seen from this case, on the one hand, Bulgarian law attached significant importance to work in prison as a way of reintegrating the inmate into the social context; on the other hand, Danish law focused much more on the punitive aspects of imprisonment.[43] As a consequence, impunity was avoided, as Mr Ognyanov could not benefit from early release or a reduction in sentence, but had to serve his remaining sentence in Bulgaria in its entirety. From a social rehabilitation perspective, this is questionable, as the cross-border transfer had the effect of neutralising the offender's engagement in a rehabilitation programme. The purely punitive component of the sentence is granted de facto priority, while no room is left for a coherent and uninterrupted social rehabilitation pathway.[44]

The CJEU had the opportunity to clarify its approach in this regard. In fact, a Slovak court had referred some questions to assess whether there are grounds for refusing to recognise and enforce the judgment if it is not proven that there are family, social or professional ties from which it could be assumed that the enforcement in the executing Member State would be beneficial from a social rehabilitation perspective. However, the CJEU decided that there was no need to adjudicate on the questions as, in the case in question, the authority of the issuing Member State had withdrawn its request for recognition of the relevant judgment. Therefore, there was no pending case before the Slovak court and the questions referred to the CJEU had become merely hypothetical.[45]

[42] *Ognyanov* (ibid) 40–49.

[43] Therefore, one should not criticise the CJEU for the solution provided, but Denmark for not attaching importance to social rehabilitation.

[44] However, one cannot say that the CJEU has endorsed the fight-against-impunity-no-matter-what kind of approach adopted by some Member States. In *Ognyanov*, the Court simply took note of the Danish provisions regarding an area of law not falling under any of the EU competences. In another case (Case C-579/15 *Popławski* [2017], published in the electronic Reports of Cases, para 23), the Court held that legislation of a Member State which implements Framework Decision 2002/584/JHA on the European Arrest Warrant by providing that 'its judicial authorities are, in any event, obliged to refuse to execute a European Arrest Warrant in the event that the requested person resides in that Member State, without those authorities having any margin of discretion, and without that Member State actually undertaking to execute the custodial sentence pronounced against that requested person, thereby creating a risk of impunity of that requested person, cannot be regarded as compatible with that Framework Decision'.

[45] See Case C-495/18 *YX* [2019], published in the electronic Report of Cases. Nevertheless, the Slovak court underlined that the Court's judgment could have been relevant for the decision in

IV. A Paradigm Shift: The Fight against Impunity versus the Protection of Fundamental Rights

The protection of fundamental rights has always been an issue with regard to EU instruments of judicial cooperation in criminal matters. Considering the model provided by the Framework Decision on the European Arrest Warrant (EAW),[46] one surely recalls that it does not provide for grounds for non-execution of an EAW related to a possible incompatibility between the EAW and those rights. In truth, it is simply stated that it respects fundamental rights[47] and it does not have the effect of modifying the obligation to respect them.[48]

This kind of approach, based on a sort of unquestionable presumption vis-à-vis the consistency between the EAW and the protection of fundamental rights, has been confirmed in other instruments[49] and, in this regard, Framework Decision 2008/909/JHA makes no exception. In fact, the very same provisions regarding the relationship between the Framework Decision and the fundamental rights enshrined in the EU legal order can also be found in this Framework Decision,[50] while the Framework Decision does not envisage a specific ground for refusal related to the protection of those rights.

Many scholars have criticised this approach, as it conveyed the idea that the protection of fundamental rights was not an issue in the EU, as a high level of protection had already been achieved. It took time before things changed.[51]

another case pending before it. Thus, it seems likely that the CJEU will have to rule on this topic, sooner or later.

[46] Council Framework Decision 2002/584/JHA of 13 June 2002 on the European Arrest Warrant and the surrender procedures between Member States [2002] OJ L190/1. On the topic, see NM Schallmoser, 'The European Arrest Warrant and Fundamental Rights. Risks of Violation of Fundamental Rights through the EU Framework Decision in Light of the ECHR' [2014] *European Journal of Crime, Criminal Law and Criminal Justice* 135; M Fichera, 'EU Fundamental Rights and the European Arrest Warrant' in S Douglas-Scott and N Hatzis (eds), *Research Handbook on EU Law and Human Rights* (Cheltenham, Edward Elgar, 2017) 418.

[47] Council Framework Decision 2002/584/JHA, recital 12.

[48] ibid Art 1(3).

[49] See, eg Council Framework Decision 2008/947/JHA of 27 November 2008 on the application of the principle of mutual recognition to judgments and probation decisions with a view to the supervision of probation measures and alternative sanctions [2008] OJ L337/102; Council Framework Decision 2009/829/JHA of 23 October 2009 on the application, between Member States of the European Union, of the principle of mutual recognition to decisions on supervision measures as an alternative to provisional detention [2009] OJ L294/20.

[50] Recital 13 and Art 3(4) of Framework Decision 2008/909/JHA.

[51] See, eg S Peers, 'Mutual Recognition and Criminal Law in the European Union: Has the Council Got It Wrong?' [2004] *CML Rev* 5; V Mitsilegas, 'The Limits of Mutual Trust in Europe's Area of Freedom, Security and Justice: From Automatic Inter-state Cooperation to the Slow Emergence of the Individual' [2012] *Yearbook of European Law* 312. More generally, see V Mitsilegas, 'The Symbiotic Relationship between Mutual Trust and Fundamental Rights in Europe's Area of Criminal Justice' [2015] *New Journal of European Criminal Law* 457; K Lenaerts, '*La vie après l'avis*: Exploring the Principle of Mutual (Yet Not Blind) Trust' [2017] *CML Rev* 805; T Wyschmeyer, 'Generating Trust through Law? Judicial Cooperation in the European Union and the "Principle of Mutual Trust"' [2017] *German*

In 2014, the European Parliament urged the European Commission to amend the Framework Decision on the EAW by adding a specific mandatory refusal ground where there are substantial grounds to believe that the execution of the measure would be incompatible with the executing Member State's obligation in accordance with Article 6 of the Treaty on the European Union and the Charter of Fundamental Rights.[52]

The Commission did not comply with that request. However, that very same year, the Directive on the European Investigation Order (EIO) was passed,[53] whose Article 11(1)(f) provides for the non-recognition or non-execution of an EIO where there are substantial grounds to believe that the execution of the investigative measure indicated in the EIO would be incompatible with the executing state's obligations concerning the protection of fundamental rights in the EU legal framework.

In December 2020, the new Regulation on the Mutual Recognition of Freezing Orders and Confiscation Orders will come into force,[54] whose Articles 8 and 19 provide for the grounds of non-recognition and non-execution of freezing orders and confiscation orders, respectively. In both cases, the authorities of the executing Member State shall not recognise or execute the orders if, in exceptional situations, there are substantial grounds to believe, on the basis of specific and objective evidence, that the execution of the confiscation order would, in the particular circumstances of the case, entail a manifest breach of a relevant fundamental right as set out in the Charter of Fundamental Rights, particularly the right to an effective remedy, the right to a fair trial or the right of defence.

This shift on the normative side has been followed by a change in the case law of the CJEU. It took some time, however, before this happened. As is known, in *Melloni*,[55] the Court stated that, where an EU legal act calls for national implementing measures, national authorities and courts are not allowed to apply national standards of protection of fundamental rights if this compromises the primacy, unity and effectiveness of EU law. Furthermore, in *Radu*,[56] it was held that the

Law Journal 339; C Rizcallah, 'The Challenges to Trust-Based Governance in the European Union: Assessing the Use of Mutual Trust as a Driver of EU Integration' [2019] *European Law Journal* 37.

[52] European Parliament resolution of 27 February 2014 with recommendations to the Commission on the review of the European Arrest Warrant.

[53] Directive 2014/41/EU of the European Parliament and of the Council of 3 April 2014 regarding the European Investigation Order in criminal matters [2014] OJ L130/1. On the topic, see I Armada, 'The European Investigation Order and the Lack of European Standards for Gathering Evidence: Is a Fundamental Rights-Based Refusal the Solution?' [2015] *New Journal of European Criminal Law* 8.

[54] Regulation (EU) 2018/1805 of the European Parliament and of the Council of 14 November 2018 on the mutual recognition of freezing orders and confiscation orders [2018] OJ L303/1. For a comment, see A Rosanò, 'Congelamento e confisca di beni. Le novità del diritto dell'Unione europea nel quadro della cooperazione internazionale' (*Eurojus.it*, 2019) http://rivista.eurojus.it/congelamento-e-confisca-di-beni-le-novita-del-diritto-dellunione-europea-nel-quadro-della-cooperazione-internazionale/.

[55] Case C-399/11 *Melloni* [2013], published in the electronic Reports of Cases. For a comment, see V Skouris, 'Développements récents de la protection des droits fondamentaux dans l'Union européenne: les arrêts *Melloni* et *Åkerberg Fransson*' [2013] *Il diritto dell'Unione Europea* 229; LFM Besselink, 'The Parameters of Constitutional Conflict after *Melloni*' [2014] *EL Rev* 531.

[56] Case C-396/11 *Radu* [2013], published in the electronic Reports of Cases.

authorities of the executing Member State cannot refuse to execute an EAW on the grounds that the requested person was not heard in the issuing Member State before the warrant was issued. Finally, in *Lanigan*,[57] the Court ruled that EU law does not preclude the holding of the requested person in custody even if the total duration for which that person has been held in custody exceeds the time limits set under the Framework Decision on the EAW, provided that the duration is not excessive in light of the characteristics of the procedure followed in the case in the main proceedings, which is a matter to be ascertained by the national court.

It was only in 2016 that the CJEU adopted a different approach. In *Aranyosi and Căldăraru*,[58] the Court held that, where there is objective, reliable, specific and properly updated evidence of systemic deficiencies in the detention conditions in the issuing Member State, the executing judicial authority must determine if there are substantial grounds to believe that the individual affected by an EAW will be exposed to a real risk of inhumane or degrading treatment, in the event of his or her surrender to that Member State. To that end, the executing judicial authority must request supplementary information from the issuing judicial authority and postpone its decision on the surrender of the individual concerned until it obtains that information. If the existence of that risk cannot be discounted within a reasonable time, the executing judicial authority must decide if the surrender procedure should be ended.[59]

This line of reasoning has been confirmed in the Minister for Justice and Equality judgment,[60] where the Court applied the *Aranyosi and Căldăraru* test to a situation where the breach of the rule of law and, more specifically, the independence of the issuing Member State's judiciary may give rise to a violation of the right to a fair trial. Furthermore, the Court confirmed its approach in *Generalstaatsanwaltschaft (Conditions de détention en Hongrie)*,[61] where it was held that the judicial authority of the executing Member State must assess only the

[57] Case C-237/15 PPU *Lanigan* [2015], published in the electronic Reports of Cases. For a more detailed analysis of the CJEU's case law, see S Montaldo, 'On a Collision Course! Mutual Recognition, Mutual Trust and the Protection of Fundamental Rights in the Recent Case-Law of the Court of Justice' (2016) 2 *European Papers* 965; J Ouwerkerk, 'Balancing Mutual Trust and Fundamental Rights Protection in the Context of the European Arrest Warrant. What Role for the Gravity of the Underlying Offence in CJEU Case Law?' [2018] *European Journal of Crime, Criminal Law and Criminal Justice* 103.

[58] Joined Cases C-404/15 and C-659/15 *Aranyosi and Căldăraru* [2016], published in the electronic Reports of Cases.

[59] ibid 88–89, 94–95. For a comment, see G Anagnostaras, 'Mutual Confidence Is Not Blind Trust! Fundamental Rights Protection and the Execution of the European Arrest Warrant: *Aranyosi and Căldăraru*' [2016] *CML Rev* 1675.

[60] Case C-216/18 PPU *Minister for Justice and Equality* [2018], published in the electronic Reports of Cases. For a comment, see P Bárd and W Van Ballegooij, 'Judicial Independence as a Precondition for Mutual Trust? The CJEU in *Minister for Justice and Equality v LM*' [2018] *New Journal of European Criminal Law* 353; D Sarmiento, 'A Comment on the CJEU's Judgment in *LM*' [2018] *Maastricht Journal of European and Comparative Law* 385.

[61] Case C-220/18 PPU *Generalstaatsanwaltschaft (Conditions de détention en Hongrie)* [2018], published in the electronic Reports of Cases. See A Rosanò, '"Du côté de chez Aranyosi", ovvero ancora su come la Corte di giustizia ha chiarito alcuni aspetti applicativi del test "Aranyosi e Căldăraru"' [2019] *Diritti umani e diritto internazionale* 427.

detention conditions in the prisons in which the person is likely to be detained and only the actual and precise detention conditions that are relevant for determining if that person will be exposed to a real risk of inhumane or degrading treatment. Finally, in *Dorobantu*,[62] the CJEU ruled that, in the absence of minimum standards regarding the personal space available to each detainee under EU law, the judicial authority of the executing Member State must take account of the minimum requirements set under Article 3 of the European Convention on Human Rights.

Therefore, it could be said that there has been a shift in the relationship between the protection of fundamental rights and judicial cooperation in criminal matters, as the former is no longer taken for granted when it comes to the latter. This shift in the relevant paradigm calls for a review of existing judicial cooperation instruments applying the principle of mutual recognition to judgments and decisions in criminal matters. In fact, they should all be amended in line with the model provided by the Directive on the EIO and the Regulation on the Mutual Recognition of Freezing Orders and Confiscation Orders, in order to provide for a ground for refusal related to the protection of fundamental rights.[63]

Should this not happen, an extension may be required to the scope of application of the *Aranyosi and Căldăraru* test to those instruments.

V. Would It Be Possible to Apply the *Aranyosi and Căldăraru* Test to Framework Decision 2008/909/JHA?

It follows from the above that, as Framework Decision 2008/909/JHA applies the principle of mutual recognition to the cross-border transfer of sentenced persons, the *Aranyosi and Căldăraru* test may be used to cope with possible fundamental rights issues arising in its application.

Crucially, in line with the EAW system, such violations may be likely to concern the prohibition of inhumane or degrading treatment, should the detention conditions in the issuing Member State not meet certain standards set by the ECtHR.[64]

[62] Case C-128/18 *Dorobantu* [2019], published in the electronic Reports of Cases. See note 62.

[63] As desirable as it may be, this review is far from being achieved. For instance, in its Work Programmes for the years 2018 and 2019, the Commission does not mention this among the objectives regarding the area of freedom, security and justice: see 'Commission Work Programme 2018: An Agenda for a More United, Stronger and More Democratic Europe' COM (2017) 650 final; 'Commission Work Programme 2019: Delivering What We Promised and Preparing for the Future' COM (2018) 800 final. The need to strike a balance between fundamental rights and the effectiveness of judicial cooperation instruments (meaning, the need to find a balance between the protection of fundamental rights and security issues) seems to prevent any amendment of the existing acts. On the search for the right balance in the area of freedom, security and justice, see L Bachmaier Winter, 'Fundamental Rights and Effectiveness in the European AFSJ. The Continuous and Never Easy Challenge of Striking the Right Balance' [2018] *Eucrim* 56; C Rijken, 'Re-balancing Security and Justice: Protection of Fundamental Rights in Police and Judicial Cooperation in Criminal Matters' [2010] *CML Rev* 1455.

[64] *Muršić v Croatia* App no 7334/13 (ECtHR, 20 October 2016).

However, violations related to the right to liberty,[65] the right to a fair trial[66] and the right to private and family life[67] may not be ruled out.

Thus, from a strictly factual point of view, the situation related to possible violations of fundamental rights seems to be the same in the cases of both the EAW and the procedure set out under Framework Decision 2008/909/JHA.

However, after a closer analysis, one may conclude that what is identical on a factual level is not that similar on an operational level. In fact, operatively speaking, there is a significant difference between the application of that test to an EAW or a transfer procedure. In the former case, it is the authority of the executing Member State that is asked to evaluate the situation related to the protection of fundamental rights in the issuing Member State. In the latter case, the same authority would be asked to do so with regard to the executing Member State, meaning the Member State to which it belongs.

Leaving aside the political viability of a judicial authority[68] expressly admitting that some fundamental rights are not respected in the state it represents, such a decision would be quite dangerous, as it would provide a substantial ground for lodging applications with the ECtHR. One can imagine how difficult it would be to represent before the ECtHR a state whose court had admitted that it is in violation of one or more fundamental rights.

Furthermore, one should consider the consistency issues related to the application of the *Aranyosi and Căldăraru* test. In fact, when dealing with the same

[65] Consider someone held in detention when his or her health conditions are not compatible with such a limitation of personal freedom. On the topic, see *LB v Belgium* App no 22831/08 (ECtHR, 2 January 2013); *WD v Belgium* App no 73548/13 (ECtHR, 6 September 2016); L Mancano, 'Storming the Bastille: Detention Conditions, the Right to Liberty and the Case for Approximation in EU Law' [2019] *CML Rev* 61.

[66] Consider the case of a sentenced person transferred to a Member State where the independence of the judiciary is not respected. In this regard, see N Chronowski and M Varju, 'Two Eras of Hungarian Constitutionalism: From the Rule of Law to Rule by Law' [2016] *Hague Journal on the Rule of Law* 271; TT Koncewicz, 'The Capture of the Polish Constitutional Tribunal and Beyond: of Institution(s), Fidelities and the Rule of Law in Flux' [2018] *Review of Central and East European Law* 116.

[67] This may concern access to toilet facilities and the right to privacy of a detainee. In this regard, see *Szafrański v Poland* App no 17294/12 (ECtHR, 15 March 2016).

[68] In some Member States, non-judicial authorities are involved in transfers of sentenced persons. This raises a problem concerning the application of the *Aranyosi and Căldăraru* test as 'in several cases offenders do not have a right to object to a transfer, and they do not enjoy any judicial remedy against it. If no judicial authority is involved at all, this risks creating a gap in judicial protection, especially concerning a possible violation of fundamental rights in the executing state. It may be difficult, perhaps even impossible, for the defence to challenge a decision to transfer even if reliable and updated information exists concerning deficiencies in the detention conditions in the executing state. In addition, even if an administrative authority is competent to decide on the transfer and is aware of the existence of the *Aranyosi and Căldăraru* test, it seems difficult to expect that it will have the same independence and expertise as a court when applying the *Aranyosi and Căldăraru* test': see T Marguery, 'Towards the End of Mutual Trust? Prison Conditions in the Context of the European Arrest Warrant and the Transfer of Prisoners Framework Decisions' [2018] *Maastricht Journal of European and Comparative Law* 713.

situation, some courts may suspend the transfer procedure as they believe fundamental rights are not properly protected, while others may not share the same view and may recognise the foreign decision, thus allowing the transfer.[69]

Therefore, there are reasons to believe that the application of the test to Framework Decision 2008/909/JHA would prove detrimental for the purpose of protecting fundamental rights. This calls for a different approach. A reverse-*Solange* kind of test – meaning a test based on the role played by the CJEU as a centralised controller in the event of systemic violations of fundamental rights by the Member States – would certainly prevent the consistency issues,[70] as the assessment would be conducted only and exclusively by the CJEU. However, it is questionable whether a national court would be willing to activate a preliminary reference procedure before the CJEU just to be told that in its state, the protection of fundamental rights is not working properly. Furthermore, one might wonder whether the Court's assessment would amount to a decision on the merits, which the Court is precluded from making.

Thus, it is quite likely that the solution lies in Strasbourg rather than in Luxembourg. A sentenced person to be transferred to a Member State in whose prisons his or her rights would be likely to be violated would have every right to lodge an application with the ECtHR not only against the executing Member State, but also against the issuing Member State that subjected him or her to that situation.

To conclude, at the time of writing, no specific test has been applied to Framework Decision 2008/909/JHA.[71] Considering the fundamental rights issues related to the transfer of sentenced persons to another Member State, it is likely that the problem will be brought before the CJEU, sooner or later. Whether the Court will develop a specific test or adapt *Aranyosi and Căldăraru* is not easy to tell. However, what can be said is that the lack of a fundamental rights test ends up increasing the above-mentioned prioritisation of the punitive aspects related to the transfers of sentenced persons.

[69] This kind of issue has already arisen following the *Minister for Justice and Equality* judgment. While a Dutch court decided not to execute some EAWs issued by Polish judicial authorities due to the problems related to the independence of the judiciary and the right to a fair trial in Poland, some Irish and English courts recognised the decisions and allowed the surrender of the arrested persons.

[70] For the reverse-*Solange* approach, see A Von Bogdandy, M Kottmann, C Antpöhler, J Dickschen, S Hentrei and M Smrkolj, 'Reverse *Solange* – Protecting the Essence of Fundamental Rights against EU Member States' [2012] *CML Rev* 489.

[71] In the context of a project funded by the Justice Programme 2014–2020 of the European Union (RePers – Mutual Trust and Social Rehabilitation into Practice, GA 766441; see http://www.eurehabilitation.unito.it), it has been highlighted that some Member States (eg Italy and Spain) do not perform any form of control regarding this matter, while others (eg Romania) have introduced a mechanism allowing for a reduction in the length of the sentence for every day spent in prison under inhumane or degrading conditions. In other cases (Germany), the competent authorities prefer not to transfer the sentenced person.

VI. Conclusion

In this chapter, it is argued that Framework Decision 2008/909/JHA is an advanced tool of judicial cooperation whose text and application seem to be excessively focused on security issues, meaning that it avoids the impunity of the transferred person. Social rehabilitation amounts to a mere desire, and the protection of fundamental rights is not properly considered.

In this regard, some reforms are needed. As far as social rehabilitation is concerned, considering what the CJEU ruled in *Ognyanov*, this would require the Member States to reconsider the role that this concept may play in the development and application of their criminal policy. In the absence of this kind of intervention, it seems unlikely that any help may come from the case law of the Luxembourg Court, which would lead to a situation where the fight against impunity is destined to prevail over other purposes.

With regard to the protection of fundamental rights, a paradigm shift is needed for the mechanism to be consistent with these sources of primary law. It might take the form of either an amendment to the Framework Decision in the context of a general review of existing judicial cooperation instruments in criminal matters lacking a specific ground for refusal related to the fundamental rights situation in the issuing Member State or an extension in the scope of the *Aranyosi and Căldăraru* test. However, this test may not be helpful, as it was not developed for situations where the authority of the executing Member State assesses the situation related to the protection of fundamental rights in its own state. A different approach, based on a direct intervention of the CJEU, also might not prove decisive.

Therefore, it is argued that sentenced persons who have been transferred and subjected to a violation of their fundamental rights should bring an action before the ECtHR not only against the executing Member State, but also against the issuing one.

PART D

Impunity and New Surveillance Technologies Under EU Law

12

Stepping Up the Fight against Impunity in EU Law: Access to Immigration Databases by National Law Enforcement Authorities and Europol

NIOVI VAVOULA

I. Introduction

In an era of globalised crime, the evolution of digital technologies has opened up new possibilities for the use of personal data, particularly in the law enforcement context, with reliance on technology championed as a panacea for the fight against impunity. At the EU level, efforts to facilitate the flow of personal data have been translated in two main strands of legislative action: the proliferation of legal channels of information exchange among national and EU bodies, with progressive expansion outside the EU,[1] and the maximisation of access by law enforcement authorities to immigration databases, despite the undoubtedly different objectives of managing migration and combating crime. These initiatives involve a 'mille-feuille' of information-processing schemes that has been set up, currently comprising three operational databases – the Schengen Information System (SIS II, formerly SIS), Eurodac and the Visa Information System (VIS) – and three on paper – the Entry/Exit System (EES), the European Travel Information and Authorisation System (ETIAS) and the European Criminal Record Information System for third-country nationals (ECRIS-TCN).[2] Largely justified by counter-terrorism concerns[3] – both in the aftermath of 9/11[4] and in recent years[5] – these

[1] V Mitsilegas, *EU Criminal Law* (Hart Publishing, 2009) ch 5.

[2] For a detailed analysis on databases for third-country nationals, see N Vavoula, *Immigration and Privacy in the Law of the European Union: The Case of Databases* (Brill Nijhoff, forthcoming).

[3] See V Mitsilegas, 'Contrôle des Étrangers, des Passagers, des Citoyens: Surveillance et Anti-Terrorisme' (2005) 58 *Cultures et Conflits* 155.

[4] See, eg the European Council, Declaration on combating terrorism (25 March 2004) 7.

[5] See, eg the European Agenda on Security (COM (2015) 185 final), as well as the numerous progress reports that unwrap it.

databases establish the conditions of EU surveillance and are accessed by national law enforcement authorities and Europol, either as part of their security mandate (SIS II and ECRIS-TCN) or because their consultation constitutes one of their ancillary objectives (Eurodac, VIS, EES and ETIAS).

This chapter aims at critically evaluating the modalities of law enforcement access to the latter category of information systems, as explained above, from a privacy and personal data protection standpoint. To that end, the next section provides a compact outline of the existing and forthcoming databases, so as to inform the subsequent analysis. Moving to the core, the provisions according to which national law enforcement bodies and Europol may consult immigration data are analysed. In that respect, a comparative table is submitted to form the basis for the critical appraisal that follows. Drawing on primary materials and relevant jurisprudence by both the European Court of Human Rights (ECtHR) and the EU Court of Justice (CJEU) on surveillance, this chapter disputes the necessity and effectiveness of law enforcement access and questions the proportionality of the relevant rules. Finally, the reforms to the procedure stemming from the forthcoming interoperability among the different information systems are also discussed.

II. EU Databases for Third-Country Nationals: A Sketch

Over the past three decades, an elaborate framework of large-scale information systems has emerged, whereby a wide array of personal data, including biometrics, collected by different categories of third-country nationals are stored and further processed for a wide range of purposes, spanning from modernising immigration control to law enforcement. The flexible and dynamic nature of databases that enables adaptability to the evolving digital technologies and perceived threats to the EU has meant that the systems are used for a multiplicity of purposes.

A. The Flexible Intelligence Weapon: SIS II

Perhaps the best-known database is the SIS II, the purpose of which is to maintain a high level of security within the Schengen area.[6] At the heart of the compensatory measures for the abolition of internal border controls,[7] the SIS II registers

[6] The legal bases of the SIS II are: Regulation (EU) 2018/1860 [2018] OJ L312/1; Regulation (EU) 2018/1861 [2018] OJ L312/14; Regulation (EU) 2018/1862 [2018] OJ L312/56.

[7] For a detailed overview of the SIS, see E Brouwer, *Digital Borders and Real Rights: Effective Remedies for Third-Country Nationals in the Schengen Information System* (Martinus Nijhoff, 2008).

'alerts' on various categories of persons and objects such as people wanted for arrest for extradition, missing persons, or persons or objects subject to discreet, inquiry or specific checks.[8] In addition, it stores alerts on third-country nationals to be refused entry into or to stay in the Schengen area,[9] or subject to return proceedings.[10] Hence, by its very hybrid nature, the SIS II serves as both immigration and criminal law instrument. In connection to each alert, the SIS II stores basic alphanumeric information, as well as biometric data (fingerprints, photographs, palm prints) and DNA files in certain cases,[11] and is complemented by SIRENE (Supplementary Information Request at the National Entries), which enables searches for supplementary information in cases of a 'hit'.

B. The Multifunctional Tool: VIS

The VIS was conceptualised in the aftermath of the 9/11 events[12] to modernise the administration, issuance and checks of short-stay visas by enabling the exchange of personal data on short-stay visa applicants.[13] Its overarching aim is to assist in the development of the common visa policy; however, no fewer than seven wide-ranging sub-purposes are set out, among which is the prevention of threats to the internal security of the EU Member States.[14] To that end, a separate instrument has been adopted, Decision 2008633/JHA (VIS Decision),[15] that lays down the modalities by which law enforcement authorities and Europol may consult visa data. Overall, the system stores a broad range of personal data, including fingerprints and photographs of all persons subject to visa requirements, irrespective of the status of their visa application (refused, granted, revoked).[16]

[8] Regulation 2018/1862, Art. 26–41.

[9] Regulation 2018/1861, Art. 20–31.

[10] Regulation 2018/1860, Art 3.

[11] Regulation 2018/1862, Art. 42–43.

[12] A Baldaccini, 'Counter-terrorism and the EU Strategy for Border Security: Framing Suspects with Biometric Documents and Databases' (2008) 10(1) *European Journal of Migration and Law* 31.

[13] Council Decision 2004/512/EC [2004] OJ L213/5; Regulation (EC) 767/2008 [2008] OJ L218/60, as amended by Regulation (EC) 810/2009 [2009] OJ L243/1 (VIS Regulation).

[14] These are: (i) facilitating the visa application procedure; (ii) preventing 'visa shopping'; (iii) facilitating the fight against fraud; (iv) facilitating checks at external border crossing points and within national territory; (v) assisting in the identification of persons that do not meet the requirements for entering, staying or residing in a Member State; (vi) facilitating the implementation of the Dublin mechanism; and (vii) contributing to the prevention of threats to Member States' internal security. On the ranking of these purposes by the CJEU, see below.

[15] Council Decision 2008/633/JHA [2008] OJ L218/129 (VIS Decision). The need for a separate EU instrument is attributed to the then pillar structure. A bridging clause (Art 3) linked the Regulation with the Decision.

[16] VIS Regulation, Art 9. A reform of the VIS legal basis is currently negotiated, so that the personal scope of the database will cover holders of residence permits, residence cards and long-stay visas. See COM (2018) 302 final.

C. The 'Truth Serum': Eurodac

Eurodac was created[17] with the aim of assisting in the administration of the Dublin system on the allocation of the Member State responsible for examining an application for international protection.[18] To that end, the system processes the fingerprints of all asylum seekers over the age of 14,[19] as well as those persons found irregularly crossing the external borders or staying on national territory,[20] to check whether these have already been recorded by another Member State.[21] If a Eurodac check reveals that the fingerprints have already been recorded in another Member State, the individual may be sent to that Member State.[22] A year after the database had begun its operation, the 2004 Hague Programme called for 'an innovative approach to the cross-border exchange of law enforcement information'.[23] Following years of discussions, Regulation 602/3013 was adopted in June 2013,[24] opening up the database to national law enforcement authorities and Europol.[25]

D. The Schengen Hotel: EES

Influenced by similar initiatives in the USA, in 2013 the Commission presented three legislative proposals – the so-called 'Smart Borders Package' – including a proposal to establish an Entry/Exit System (EES) that will record border crossing both at the entry and exit of third-country nationals admitted for a short stay.[26] Due to proportionality concerns,[27] the Commission originally left the registration of biometrics and law enforcement access outside the scope of the proposal.

[17] Council Regulation 2725/2000 [2000] OJ L316/1; Council Regulation 407/2002 [2002] OJ L62/1.

[18] Dublin Convention [1997] OJ C254/1, replaced by Regulation 343/2003 [2003] OJ L50/1 (Dublin II Regulation) and Regulation (EU) 604/2013 [2013] OJ L180/31 (Dublin III Regulation).

[19] Art. 9–13 of the recast Eurodac Regulation.

[20] Art. 14–17 of the recast Eurodac Regulation. However, the fingerprints of migrants found irregularly staying are not centrally stored, but only compared with existing records.

[21] A Eurodac reform is underway that expands the personal and material scope of the database: by requiring the registration of records on irregular stayers, by increasing the categories of personal data collected, by modifying the storage period, by lowering the fingerprinting obligation to encompass children over the age of six and by adding photos. See COM (2016) 272 final.

[22] For an analysis, see E Guild, 'Unreadable Papers? The EU's First Experiences with Biometrics: Examining Eurodac and the EU's Borders' in J Lodge (ed), *Are You Who You Say You Are? The EU and Biometric Borders* (Wolf Legal Publishers, 2007) 32.

[23] The Hague Programme [2004] OJ C53/1, 7.

[24] Regulation 603/2013 [2013] OJ L180/1 (recast Eurodac Regulation).

[25] Denmark, Iceland, Liechtenstein, Norway and Switzerland do not apply any of the law enforcement related provisions and protocols are required.

[26] COM (2013) 95 final. The other proposals involved a 'Registered Travellers Programme' (COM (2013) 97 final) and amendments to the Schengen Borders Code (COM (2013) 96 final).

[27] For criticism, see, among others, EDPS [2014] OJ C32/25 (executive summary); Article 29 Data Protection Working Party, Opinion 05/2013 on Smart Borders (WP206, 2013); Standing Committee of Experts on International Immigration, Refugee and Criminal Law (Meijers Committee), Note on the Smart Borders Proposals (COM (2013) 95 final, COM (2013) 96 final and COM (2013) 97 final) (CM1307, 2013).

Later, the package was withdrawn entirely. In the aftermath of the 2015 terrorist events, the EES was adopted in November 2017.[28] The EES is also a multipurpose tool: it will enhance the efficiency and automation of border checks; assist in the identification of irregular migrants and overstayers; combat identity fraud and misuse of travel documents; and strengthen internal security by allowing law enforcement authorities access to travel history records.[29] To those ends, it will record the identities of third-country nationals, by storing alphanumeric data, four fingerprints and a facial image, along with details of their travel documents, which will be linked to electronic entry and exit records.

E. The Screening Test: ETIAS

The movement of visa-free travellers will also be monitored through the European Travel Information and Authorisation System (ETIAS), enacted in September 2018.[30] The ETIAS Regulation solidifies the link between immigration control and security, as one of its main objectives is to contribute to a high level of security by thoroughly assessing whether travellers pose a 'security risk'.[31] The database serves many other purposes, including the prevention of irregular migration and the contribution to the prevention, detection and investigation of terrorist offences and other serious offences.[32] To achieve these aims, all visa-exempt travellers shall be obliged to obtain authorisation prior to their departure by disclosing a series of personal data.[33] A pre-screening procedure shall take place on the basis of cross-checking against databases, certain screening rules based on risk indicators;[34] and a special ETIAS watch list of individuals suspected of terrorism or other serious crimes.[35]

F. The Missing Chain between Law Enforcement and Immigration Control: ECRIS-TCN

The latest member in the databases' family is the European Criminal Records Information System for Third-Country Nationals (ECRIS-TCN).[36] The latter emerged as a necessity in the law enforcement context as, in order to obtain complete information on previous convictions of third-country nationals, states

[28] Regulation (EU) 2017/2226 [2017] OJ L32720 (EES Regulation).
[29] Regulation 2017/2226, Art 6(1).
[30] Regulation (EU) 2018/1240 [2018] OJ L61/1 (ETIAS Regulation).
[31] Regulation 2018/1240, Art 4(a).
[32] ibid Art 4(b)–(f).
[33] ibid Art 17.
[34] ibid Art 33.
[35] ibid Art 34.
[36] Regulation (EU) 2019/816 [2019] OJ L135/1 (ECRIS-TCN Regulation); Directive 2019/884 [2019] OJ L151/143.

were obliged to send 'blanket requests' to all other Member States. The ECRIS-TCN will be a centralised system for the exchange of criminal records on convicted third-country nationals and stateless persons, including dual nationals, and is meant to complement the ECRIS system through which information on the criminal records of EU nationals is exchanged.

III. Access to Immigration Data by National Law Enforcement Authorities and Europol: An Ancillary Objective

The analysis above demonstrates that every database processing personal data of third-country nationals is at the disposal of national law enforcement authorities, at least to a certain extent, either because of its direct law enforcement (security) rationale, as in the cases of the SIS II and the ECRIS-TCN, or because criminal law is listed as an ancillary objective, as is the cases of Eurodac, VIS, EES and ETIAS. With regard to the former category, access by domestic law enforcement authorities and Europol is restricted only in terms of the purpose for which the processing of records may take place and there are no further limitations as regards the conditions and procedure of access to the systems or the offences for which the data may be consulted. As for the latter category, the databases are conceived and designed as multipurpose tools serving a series of objectives, spanning from modernising immigration control to law enforcement, thereby heavily blurring the boundaries between immigration and criminal law.[37]

That consultation of immigration data for law enforcement purposes is merely an ancillary objective has been clarified by the CJEU in a case that arose in relation to the VIS.[38] The UK, which, pursuant to its opt-out privileges, does not form part of it (since this constitutes a development of the Schengen *acquis* in which it does not participate), sought annulment of the VIS Decision on the grounds that it constitutes a police cooperation measure. In line with the opinion of Advocate General Mengozzi, the Court upheld the VIS Decision, basing its reasoning on the effectiveness and special nature of Schengen cooperation. Although it contended that the aim of the VIS Decision falls within the sector of police cooperation, it opined that the content is related to both the common visa policy and police cooperation.[39] The Court observed that

> [The VIS Decision] provisions nevertheless contain conditions restricting access to the VIS … which make clear that they organise in essence the ancillary use of a database

[37] V Mitsilegas, 'The Border Paradox: The Surveillance of Movement in a Union without Internal Frontiers' in H Lindahl (ed), *A Right to Inclusion and Exclusion? Normative Fault Lines of the EU's Area of Freedom, Security and Justice* (Hart Publishing, 2009).

[38] Case C-482/08 *UK v Council* [2010] OJ I-10413.

[39] ibid paras 50–51.

Table 1 Modalities of Access to Immigration Control Databases by National Law Enforcement Authorities and Europol

A. National Law Enforcement Authorities

	VIS (VIS Decision)	Eurodac (Recast Eurodac Regulation)	EES (EES Regulation)	ETIAS (ETIAS Regulation)
Authorities	Designated authorities (Art 3(1)); (One or more) Central Access Point(s) (Art 3(3)).	Designated authorities, except for agencies or units exclusively responsible for intelligence relating to national security (Art 5(1)); Verifying authority is (one or more) national authority(ies) or a unit of an authority (Art 6(1)); National Access Point(s).	Same as VIS (Art 29).	Same as VIS (Art 50).
Offences	Terrorist offences and serious crimes (Art 2(c) and (d))	Terrorist offences and serious crimes punishable by a custodial sentence or a detention order for a maximum period of at least three years (Art 2(1)(j) and (k))	Same as Eurodac (Art 3(1)(24)–(25))	Same as Eurodac (Art 3(1)(15)–(16))
Conditions of access	Article 5(1) 1. Access must be necessary for the prevention, detection or investigation of terrorist offences and other serious crimes; 2. Specific case;	1. Article 20(1) 2. Prior comparisons with national fingerprint databases and the automated fingerprinting identification systems (AFIS) of all Member States unless there are reasonable grounds to believe that such comparison will not lead to identification; 3. Access must be necessary for the prevention, detection or investigation of terrorist offences and other serious crimes, which means that there is an overriding public security concern, which makes the searching of the database proportionate;	Article 32 1. Same as VIS; 2. Same as VIS; 3. Evidence or reasonable grounds to consider that the consultation will contribute to the prevention, detection or investigation of a criminal offence, in particular when there is substantiated suspicion that the suspect, perpetrator or victim falls under the category covered by the EES Regulation;	Article 51(1) 1. Same as VIS; 2. Same as VIS; 3. Same as EES.

	VIS (VIS Decision)	Eurodac (Recast Eurodac Regulation)	EES (EES Regulation)	ETIAS (ETIAS Regulation)
	3. Reasonable grounds to consider that consultation will substantially contribute to the prevention, detection or investigation of any criminal offence within the scope of access.	4. Specific case (no systematic comparisons) 5. Reasonable grounds to consider that the comparison will substantially contribute to the prevention, detection or investigation of any criminal offence within the scope of access, in particular when there is a substantiated suspicion that the suspect, perpetrator or victim falls under the category covered by the recast Eurodac Regulation.	4. Prior search has been conducted in national databases; 5. For searches with fingerprints a prior search must have launched in the Member States' AFIS. Conditions (4) and (5) do not apply when there are reasonable grounds to believe that a comparison with the systems of the other Member States will not lead to the verification of the identity or in cases of urgency.	
Procedure	Reasoned written or electronic request by a designated authority; Verification that the conditions of access have been fulfilled (Art 4(1)); In exceptional cases of urgency, oral requests are also acceptable and verification will take place ex post (Art 4(2)).	Reasoned electronic request; Verification that the conditions of access have been fulfilled; Transmission of the request by the verifying authority to the National Access Point (Art 19(1)); In exceptional cases of urgency, where there is a need to prevent an imminent danger associated with a terrorist offence or other serious criminal offence, the verification will take place ex post (Art 19(3)).	The standard procedure is the same as the VIS (Art 31(1)); In a case of urgency, where there is a need to prevent an imminent danger to the life of a person associated with a terrorist offence or another serious crime, verification of the conditions of access may take place ex post (Art 31(2)).	Same as the EES (Art 51).

(continued)

Table1 *(Continued)*

	VIS (VIS Decision)	Eurodac (Recast Eurodac Regulation)	EES (EES Regulation)	ETIAS (ETIAS Regulation)
Transfer to third countries or an international organisation	Prohibited, unless in an exceptional case of urgency, subject to the consent of the Member State that entered the data into the VIS (Art 8(4)).	Prohibited. This prohibition shall also apply if those data are further processed at the national level or between Member States (Art 35(1)); Personal data which originated in a Member State and are exchanged between Member States following a 'hit' shall not be transferred if there is a serious risk that, as a result of such transfer, the data subject may be subjected to torture, inhuman and degrading treatment, or punishment or any other violation of their fundamental rights (Art 35(2)).	Prohibited. This prohibition shall also apply if those data are further processed at the national level or between Member States (Art 41(1)); Derogation: in an exceptional case of urgency subject to the following conditions; (i) the transfer must be necessary for the prevention, detection or investigation in the territory of the Member States or in the third country concerned; (ii) the designated authority has access to the data; the transfer is carried out in accordance with the Directive 2016/680; a duly motivated request has been submitted; the reciprocal provisions of any information of entry/exit records held by the requesting third country to the Member States operating the EES is ensured (Art 41(6)).	Same as the EES (Art 65(2) and (5)).

B. Europol

	VIS	Eurodac	EES	ETIAS
Conditions	Within the limits of Europol's mandate and where necessary for the performance of its tasks and for the purposes of a specific analysis or an analysis of a general nature and of a strategic type, provided that VIS data is rendered anonymous (Art 7).	Within the limits of Europol's mandate and where necessary for the performance of its tasks: 1. Prior comparisons against data stored in systems accessible by Europol must have not led to the identification of the data subject; 2. Comparison must be necessary to support and strengthen action by Member States in preventing, detecting or investigating terrorist offences or other serious criminal offences, which means that there is an overriding public security concern which makes the searching of the database proportionate; 3. Specific case; 4. There must be reasonable grounds to consider that the comparison will substantially contribute to the prevention, detection or investigation of any of the criminal offences in question, in particular where there is a substantiated suspicion that the suspect, perpetrator or victim of the criminal offence in question falls in the categories covered by Eurodac (Art 21).	1. Consultation must be necessary to support and strengthen action by Member States in preventing, detecting or investigating terrorist offences or other serious crimes within Europol's mandate; 2. Specific case; 3. There must be evidence or reasonable grounds to consider that consultation will contribute to the prevention, detection or investigation of the offences at stake, in particular where there is a substantiated suspicion that the suspect, perpetrator or victim of an offence falls under the category covered by the EES Regulation (Art 33(1)); 4. Access to the EES to identify an unknown suspect, perpetrator or suspected victim is allowed under the same conditions and if prior consultation of databases accessible by Europol has not made it possible to identity the person in question (Art 33(2)).	Same as the EES, with the added condition that consultation must take place solely on the basis of specific search keys (Art 53)

> concerning visas, the principal purpose of which is linked to the control of borders and of entry to the territory and which is therefore available, merely by way of consultation, for police cooperation purposes on a secondary basis only, solely to the extent that use for those purposes does not call into question its principal use.[40]

The aforementioned proclamations are also relevant to the cases of Eurodac, EES and the ETIAS. These may also be consulted by national law enforcement authorities and Europol under specific conditions, which are tailor-made based on the specificities of each database. Indeed, despite any variations, the significant deviation from their original immigration context is reflected in that law enforcement access is subject to a series of limitations: first, consultation of immigration data is only reserved to cases involving the prevention, detection or investigation of terrorist offences and other serious crimes; and secondly, a specific procedure is foreseen that requires the verification that a series of bespoke conditions of access have been met. For the purposes of this chapter, a comparative table illustrating the modalities of law enforcement access to databases by national bodies and Europol is provided (Table 1), the design of which corresponds to the chronological order in which each legal instrument was adopted.

IV. Law Enforcement Access to Immigration Control Databases: An Appraisal

In *Weber and Saravia*,[41] the ECtHR held that the transmission of data to other authorities and the subsequent use by them that enlarges the group of individuals with knowledge of the personal data intercepted and can therefore lead to investigations being instituted against the persons concerned amounts to a further separate interference with the right to private life.[42] Similarly, in *Digital Rights Ireland*,[43] concerning the retention of telecommunications data for law enforcement purposes, the CJEU contended that access by the competent national authorities to the data constitutes a separate interference with privacy, in line with the case law of the ECtHR.[44] By analogy, consultation of immigration data by national law enforcement bodies and Europol constitutes an interference with the rights to private life and protection of personal data, in addition to the interference to which initial collection and storage of personal data in massive databases amounts.[45] In order to justify this interference, the requirements of Article 52(1)

[40] ibid para 52.
[41] *Weber and Saravia v Germany* (2008) 46 EHRR SE5.
[42] ibid para 79.
[43] Joined Cases C-293/12 and C-594/12 *Digital Rights Ireland Ltd v Ireland* ECLI:EU:C:2014:238.
[44] ibid para 35.
[45] The systematic collection and storage of personal data has been repeatedly found to constitute an interference with the right to private life, irrespective of whether the data will be further used or the collection took place in an intrusive manner. See *Amann v Switzerland* (2000) 30 EHRR 843; *Rotaru v Romania* (2000) 8 BHRC 43.

of the Charter (provided for by law, respect of essence and proportionality) must be fulfilled.

A. The Normalisation of Law Enforcement Access and the Erosion of the Purpose Limitation Principle

Despite some resistance, the necessity of making available immigration data to law enforcement authorities and Europol has never been questioned; if anything, the evolution of the legal framework on databases for third-country nationals testifies that the nexus between migration and security has solidified in an ongoing '(in) security continuum' that supplies the field of migration with security concerns related to crime control.[46] This link was first expressly articulated in the Hague Programme:

> the management of migration flows, including the fight against illegal immigration should be strengthened by establishing *a continuum of security measures* that effectively links visa application procedures and entry and exit procedures at external border crossings. Such measures are also of importance for the prevention and control of crime, in particular terrorism. In order to achieve this, a coherent approach and harmonised solutions in the EU on biometric identifiers and data are necessary.[47]

In the case of the VIS, which laid the foundation stone of multipurpose systems that grant access to law enforcement bodies, the necessity for this additional objective is encapsulated in the Preamble to the VIS Decision, where it is stated that:

> It is essential in the fight terrorism and other serious crimes for the relevant services to have the fullest and most-up-to-date information in their respective fields in order to perform their tasks. The Member States' competent national services need information if they are to perform their tasks. The information in the VIS may be necessary for the purposes of preventing and combating terrorism and serious crimes …

This justification is characterised, at best, as very weak. The fact that information 'may be necessary' in the fight against terrorist and other serious crimes does not automatically mean that it must be available to law enforcement bodies and Europol without further reasoning. Law enforcement access is not inherent in the system and constitutes a significant change, the necessity and effectiveness of which should have been properly assessed on a periodic basis. The latest statistical data reveal that between 2015 and 2017 only eight Member States performed almost 28,000 searches, 83% of which are attributed to three states (France, Germany and Switzerland).[48] Around 800 of these searches were conducted under the urgent procedure.[49] In its 2016 report on the evaluation of the VIS,

[46] D Bigo, *Polices en Réseax. L' Éxperience Européenne* (Presses de Sciences Po, 1996).
[47] See n 23, para 1.7.2. Emphasis added.
[48] eu-LISA, VIS Technical Report 2018, 26.
[49] ibid 26 and 29.

the Commission suggests that eight of 26 Member States had never accessed the VIS for law enforcement purposes, with the use being gradually increased.[50] Regrettably, neither report provides further information as to the number of 'hits' on the basis of VIS searches, possible false matches, follow-up in cases of 'hits' and how many requests for access have been refused.

Justifying consultation for criminal law purposes in the case of Eurodac has been even more problematic due to the inherent vulnerability of asylum seekers as a group of individuals in need of protection. Testament to the complexity of the matter is the fact that the Commission presented no less than four legislative proposals,[51] including one blocked by the European Parliament,[52] before the latter would eventually cave in to the desires of the Member States.[53] Strikingly, the references to the necessity of granting access to law enforcement agencies are minimal. Recital 8 of the recast Regulation merely states that

> It is essential in the fight against terrorist offences and other serious criminal offences for the law enforcement authorities to have the fullest and most up-to-date information if they are to perform their tasks. The information contained in Eurodac is necessary for the purposes of the prevention, detection or investigation of terrorist offences … or other serious criminal offences.

In comparison to VIS, the EU legislature is more assertive, but a connection between asylum seekers and criminality such as that inevitably made by the Regulation implies that asylum seekers as a group of people are targeted for compelling reasons. Such justification is, however, missing;[54] the only information regarding the usefulness of asylum seekers' data for law enforcement purposes comes from a discussion document submitted to the European Council during negotiations by three Member States (Austria, the Netherlands and Germany).[55] These states – along with a few others – seem to have been keeping asylum seekers' fingerprints in their national AFIS as a matter of internal design of databases.[56]

[50] COM (2016) 655 final.

[51] COM (2008) 825 final; COM (2009) 342 final and COM (2009) 344 final; COM (2010) 555 final; COM (2012) 254 final.

[52] The one of 2009.

[53] For details, see N Vavoula, 'The Recast Eurodac Regulation: Are Asylum Seekers Treated as Suspected Criminals?' in C Bauloz et al (eds), *Seeking Asylum in the European Union: Selected Protection Issues Raised by the Second Phase of the Common European Asylum System* (Brill, 2015).

[54] EDPS, 'Opinion of the European Data Protection Supervisor on the amended proposal for a Regulation of the European Parliament and of the Council on the establishment of "EURODAC" for the comparison of fingerprints for the effective application of Regulation (EU) No [… / …] (Recast version)' [2013] OJ C28/3 (executive summary), 13.

[55] Council Document 16990/12 (3 December 2012). The Dutch pointed out that between 2007 and 2011 access to national asylum seekers' fingerprints database was admitted in 356 cases, and in 134 cases (38%) such comparison led to one or more criminal identifications. In Germany, where the national AFIS includes the fingerprints of both asylum seekers cases and criminal cases, around 40% of criminal identifications resulted from a comparison with the fingerprint data of asylum seekers. Moreover, in Austria, which applies the same system as Germany, between 2007 and 2011, criminal identifications were possible in 310 cases.

[56] See SEC (2009) 936 final.

As a result, if another Member State wished to consult information under the Prüm Decision from their databases,[57] it would have access to asylum seekers' data as well. However, the requested Member State did not have that option. It thus appears that the way domestic AFIS were constructed in some Member States, and the consequent lack of reciprocity, had a significant impact in the adoption of the measure. This approach indicates that asylum seekers form a suspect population whose data should be available for processing in the context of law enforcement, a view that is institutionalised and supported at the EU level. As a result, the example of the recast Eurodac Regulation demonstrates how certain Member States exported their internal problem of how their national AFIS were designed to the EU.[58] Besides, their submission does not include any information on the criminal proceedings themselves or final convictions. Finally, the feedback from Germany and Austria does not concern terrorism and serious crimes only, but all types of offences.[59]

As for statistical data, significant discrepancies in domestic practices and fragmentary and inconsistent application are evident here as well. In 2018, law enforcement authorities performed 296 searches, with a match being found in 201 cases.[60] These searches were undertaken by nine Member States, with two-thirds of them credited to Germany. No information is provided as to the aftermath of the relevant matches, and there is no further breakdown as to whether the matches involves victims or suspected perpetrators.

The case of the EES is also interesting: 'Given the high number of personal data contained in the EES', the Commission proposal of 2013 postponed a decision on whether to include law enforcement access to the system at a later stage.[61] Member States were clearly dissatisfied with this approach, with no fewer than 20 of them expressing their wish to grant law enforcement authorities access to the EES data from the outset of its operations.[62] The Commission was concerned with the lack of proportionality between, on the one hand, the data collected and stored in the EES, and, on the other hand, the usefulness of EES data in combating serious crime due to difficulties in ascertaining the rate of success on the basis of using such data.[63] At the same time, opening up the EES to law enforcement authorities influenced two other aspects: the issue of whether to include biometric data and the duration of the retention period.[64] As a result, other sensitive features were

[57] Council Decision 2008/615/JHA [2008] OJ L210/1.

[58] See A Geddes, 'International Migration and State Sovereignty in an Integrating Europe' (2001) 39(6) *International Migration* 21.

[59] V Eechaudt, 'Access to EURODAC by Law Enforcement Authorities – An Assessment' (University of Groningen, 2011) 8 http://rechten.eldoc.ub.rug.nl/FILES/root/Scripties/accetoeub/Vincent_Eechaudt_-Scriptie_-_E_1.pdf.

[60] eu-LISA, Eurodac – 2018 Statistics, 8.

[61] COM (2016) 194 final, recital 23.

[62] Council Document 9863/13 (28 May 2013) 5.

[63] ibid.

[64] SWD (2013) 47 final, 22. See Council Document 10720/13 (7 June 2013) 9. Council Document 13806/13 (19 September 2013) 6.

directly affected and pre-fixed in order to accommodate this functionality, thus giving in to the risk that law enforcement access 'obscures the discussion on the desired form' of the database.[65] Be that as it may, in the revised proposal of 2016, which was adopted under the pressure of realising a 'Security Union'[66] in the aftermath of a series of terrorist events across Europe, the usefulness of EES data was justified by reference to the VIS, highlighting that

> Member States have reported cases of people who died violently and whose identification was only possible through accessing the VIS. Other cases reported are related to human being trafficking, terrorism or drug trafficking for which the access to VIS data allowed the investigators to make substantial progress.[67]

As for the ETIAS, the Commission proposal simply took it for granted that, in an era of globalised crime, the ETIAS data may be useful in order to establish evidence and information related to a person suspected of having committed a crime or be the victim of a crime.[68] The fact that the forthcoming EES, the revised proposal of which was already on the negotiating table, will also store records on visa-free travellers that will be accessed by law enforcement authorities and Europol was not commented upon.[69]

This approach comes as no surprise; once resistance in relation to more heated dossiers, such as Eurodac and the EES, was curbed, it was inevitable that the trend of law enforcement access would be generalised, especially in the case of the ETIAS, which includes security among its objectives. Therefore, opening up databases established primarily for administrative purposes to law enforcement has become the norm, even though the justification is invariably flimsy and the actual effectiveness of such access is still in the embryonic stage, with limited anecdotal information. Therefore, with the generalisation of surveillance of third-country nationals came the normalisation of law enforcement access to the systems under the unspoken application of the principle of availability. Behind the trend of granting access to immigration data by law enforcement authorities is the perception that, once data has been collected and is already stored, there is no reason why these should not be available even for objectives unrelated to their original context. This is all the more so considering the billions of euros invested in the development of new databases. This understanding has a series of consequences: first, the possibility of function creep through the erosion of the purpose limitation principle is evident.[70] This principle suggests that data must be collected for a specified, explicit and legitimate purpose, and must not be further processed in

[65] Standing Committee of Experts on International Immigration, Refugee and Criminal Law (Meijers Committee) (n 27) 5.
[66] COM (2016) 230 final.
[67] COM (2016) 194 final, 6.
[68] COM (2016) 731 final, 11.
[69] EDPS, Opinion 3/2017, 14.
[70] This is particularly visible in the case of Eurodac, which was opened up to law enforcement authorities at a later stage.

a manner that is incompatible with that purpose. Law enforcement access challenges the outer boundaries of the purpose limitation principle, with the threshold for incompatibility being difficult to reach. Furthermore, law enforcement access is a prime example of preventive justice through risk assessment, whereby emphasis is placed on identifying unknown threats by assigning risk to different suspect populations.[71] Third-country nationals collectively are thus viewed as de facto risky individuals suspected of criminality, whose movement constitutes an inherently dangerous activity that must be controlled and monitored. Databases as risk technology tools could thus be redeployed from the immigration control domain to the fight against impunity in an attempt to 'feign control over the uncontrollable'.[72] However, the stigmatising effect of law enforcement access, which has been stressed in *S and Marper*,[73] particularly since the data are stored for a significant period of time,[74] has been largely disregarded.[75]

B. The Use of Stored Immigration Data for Law Enforcement Purposes: The Curious Case of Databases

The use of data for additional purposes other than those for which they were originally collected is not uncommon. In Opinion 1/15 regarding the compliance with the right to private life of the draft EU–Canada Agreement on the transfer and processing of passenger name record (PNR) data,[76] the CJEU did not object to the additional use of PNR data for law enforcement purposes *in abstracto*,[77] but called for increased safeguards. A distinction was made between retention and use of PNR data before the arrival of air passengers, during their stay in Canada and after their departure. Whereas the retention of data prior to their departure for Canada was found proportionate in relation to all air passengers,[78] during the stay of passengers who have been admitted entry, the CJEU opined that the use of PNR data must be based on new circumstances justifying that use.[79] As for the retention after the departure of passengers from Canada, the CJEU took the view that passengers subjected to entry and exit checks should be regarded as 'not presenting, in principle, a risk' for terrorism and serious crime,[80] therefore, there

[71] L Amoore and M de Goede (eds), *Risk and the War on Terror* (Routledge, 2008).
[72] U Beck, 'The Terrorist Threat: World Risk Society Revisited' (2002) 19(4) *Theory, Culture & Society* 39, 41.
[73] *S and Marper v UK* (2009) 48 EHRR 50, para 122.
[74] Depending on the respective legal bases, data may be held between five and 10 years.
[75] As regards Eurodac, see EDPS, 'Opinion on the Proposal of 2012 (n 54) para 39; UNHCR, 'An Efficient and Protective Eurodac' (November 2012) 10–11.
[76] Opinion 1/15 ECLI:EU:C:2017:592.
[77] ibid paras 148–49.
[78] ibid para 197.
[79] ibid para 200.
[80] ibid para 204.

would not appear to be, once they have left, a connection – even a merely indirect connection – between their PNR data and the objective pursued by the envisaged agreement which would justify that data being retained.[81] As such, the continued storage of all air passengers data after departure was deemed disproportionate and only in specific cases, where

> objective evidence is identified from which it may be inferred that certain air passengers may present a risk in terms of the fight against terrorism and serious transnational crime even after their departure from Canada, it seems permissible to store their PNR data beyond their stay in Canada.[82]

These pronouncements sit at odds with the function of databases as multipurpose tools. Consultation of their personal data for law enforcement purposes may still take place, although the person will have undergone pre-vetting and may have been found not to pose any risk for terrorism and serious crime. Ultimately, tying together different objectives signifies that third-country nationals are at a disadvantageous position, destined to retain the stigma of a risky individual without ever being able to lift it. In turn, databases represent a first-class tool against impunity, whereby individuals remain potential persons of interest for as long as their data is stored. A potential way forward in line with Opinion 1/15 would be to 'block' from law enforcement access the records of *bona fide* persons who have undergone pre-vetting and have been found not to pose a security risk and to 'mark' certain data of risky individuals on the basis of objective evidence, so that these may be accessible by law enforcement bodies.[83]

C. Progressive Refinement of the Modalities of Access: Real or Cosmetic Changes?

With the consolidation of the trend to grant law enforcement authorities and Europol access to immigration data, another question arises: are the modalities of access clear and limited enough? In *Digital Rights Ireland*, the CJEU was dissatisfied with the absence of any objective criterion determining the limits of the access and their subsequent use, as well as the lack of substantive and procedural conditions concerning this access.[84] These proclamations were reiterated in *Tele2*.[85] As Table 1 shows, in the present case, access is governed by harmonised rules, whereby numerous provisions are replicated almost verbatim or with some variations in the

[81] ibid para 205.
[82] ibid para 207.
[83] The mere fact that an individual is an irregular migrant should not be considered as objective evidence on which to base suspicion.
[84] *Digital Rights Ireland* (n 43) para 61.
[85] Joined Cases C-203/15 and C-698/15 *Tele2 Sverige AB v Post-och Telestyrelsen, and Secretary of State for the Home Department v Tom Watson, Peter Brice, Geoffrey Lewis* ECLI:EU:C:2016:970, para 117.

legal instruments (such as that routine access by national law enforcement bodies is proscribed or that consultation must contribute in some way to the prevention, detection or investigation of terrorist offences or other serious crimes). The variations in the rules denote significant efforts to refine the respective rules. No eagle's eye is required to notice that the provisions in the recast Eurodac Regulation have been expanded and are clearer than those prescribed in the VIS Decision, and these are largely replicated in the EES and ETIS legal regimes. This shift is attributed to two main reasons: the controversy surrounding the reform of Eurodac, leading to extensive negotiations; and the timing of the EES and ETIAS proposals in the aftermath of the landmark judgments in *Digital Rights Ireland*, *Tele2* and Opinion 1/15, which imposed significant limitations to states' powers to conduct surveillance activities.[86]

Be that as it may, the modalities of access fall short of the pronouncements of the European Courts, with the problematic features involving the conditions of access, the categories of the offences for which consultation is allowed and the designated national authorities.

(i) Exceptional or Disproportionate Access to Immigration Data?

The exceptional character of law enforcement access to immigration data is evident from the fact that domestic law enforcement authorities are not given carte blanche and routine access is forbidden.[87] Designated authorities may consult a specific system in relation to a particular case and no systematic searches or 'fishing expeditions' may take place. However, the threshold for necessity is significantly different among the underlying systems:

1. In the case of the VIS, there must be *reasonable grounds* to consider that consultation will *substantially contribute* to the fight against terrorism or other serious crimes, the definition of which is explained below.
2. As regards Eurodac, in addition to these conditions, necessity means that there must be 'an overriding security concern which makes the searching of the database proportionate'.
3. The specificity of a case arises in particular when the request for comparison is connected to a specific and concrete situation, to a specific and concrete danger associated with a terrorist offence or other serious criminal offence, or to specific persons in respect of whom there are serious grounds for believing that they will commit or have committed any such offence.
4. The EES and the ETIAS legal bases drop the requirement for 'substantial' contribution and introduce the possibility that national authorities base their request on evidence *or* reasonable grounds. In both cases, the

[86] See Council Document 9009/14 (5 May 2014) 8.
[87] How this safeguard will be circumvented with interoperability is covered below.

EU legislature has also clarified that there must be a substantiated suspicion that the suspect, perpetrator or victim falls within the personal scope of the database at stake.

5. Another key difference observed in the Eurodac and EES rules is that other sources – in particular, national fingerprint databases and the automated fingerprinting identification systems of all Member States – must have been exhausted prior to searching these databases. However, a caveat is included: when there are reasonable grounds to believe that such comparison will not lead to the identification of the data subject (or in cases of urgency, in the case of the EES), no such search must have taken place.[88]
6. With regard to the expedited procedure in cases of urgency, it is notable that the VIS Decision does not define when there is an exceptional case of urgency. In the recasting of the Eurodac Regulation, it was clarified that such a case is when there is need to prevent an imminent danger associated with a terrorist offence or other serious criminal offences. The EES and ETIAS legal bases further specify that the danger must involve the life of a person. However, both instruments do not make reference to 'exceptional' cases of urgency, but merely to cases of urgency, thus seemingly recognising that an ex post verification of the conditions of access, despite being urgent, may not qualify as an exceptional state.
7. There are no specific conditions of access by Europol in the VIS Decision, therefore access is not exceptional or sufficiently limited.

Despite the aforementioned reforms, the current wording on modalities of access raises concerns. First, with regard to the VIS and Eurodac in particular, the threshold for allowing access could have been set higher by requiring the existence of factual indications as a basis for reasonable grounds.[89] Such an approach was endorsed by the ECtHR in *Zakharov v Russia*,[90] where it was held that, in order for the authority to authorise surveillance, there must be reasonable suspicion against the person concerned, understood as 'factual indications for suspecting that person of planning, committing or having committed criminal acts or other acts that may give rise to secret surveillance measures'.[91] As for the cases of the EES and ETIAS, it is notable that though a requirement of 'evidence' as a basis for the request was added, this is merely a cosmetic change because the request may be based on reasonable grounds only. Secondly, whereas the legal instruments provide some clarifications to make the modalities of access less vague, in practice the conditions of access are not substantially altered, because the revised rules are fraught with exceptions, with a key example being the consultation of other

[88] Recital 32 of the recast Eurodac Regulation explains that this situation may arise when 'a case does not present any operational or investigative link to a given Member State'.

[89] Mitsilegas, 'The Border Paradox' (n 37) 58.

[90] *Zakharov v Russia* (2015) ECHR 1065.

[91] ibid para 260.

databases as an added condition of access. Thirdly, access to VIS and ETIAS data could have been made dependent on exhaustion of other sources, particularly information stored in other databases, such as the national AFIS and the national AFIS of other Member States, pursuant to the Prüm scheme. This would have mitigated – at least to some extent – concerns that travellers (visa and non-visa holders alike) are under suspicion of wrongdoing simply because they are third-country nationals. Fourthly, with regard to the transfer of data in urgent cases, it is regrettable that the VIS Decision does not provide a definition or guidelines as to what constitutes an urgent case.[92] Finally, access to data by Europol raises concerns for several reasons: with respect to the VIS, the differentiated regime in comparison to national authorities is unjustified and, therefore, disproportionate. The mere reference to Europol's tasks means that consultation of VIS data is not restricted to specific cases and there is no need to substantially contribute to the purpose of the access.[93] It could merely involve 'enhancing the general information position of Europol or improving the quality of Europol data'.[94] This wide access by Europol defies the exceptional character of law enforcement access and may even lead to extensive risk assessments of visa applicants particularly in the context of analyses of general or strategic nature. Furthermore, it must be stressed that since the retention periods may be further extended, the only restriction provided in the legal bases is the existence of ongoing investigations.[95] Access to immigration data may amount to an almost indefinite storage period at Europol database.

(ii) Defining Terrorism and Serious Crimes

The material scope of law enforcement access to immigration data involves the prevention, detection or investigation of terrorist offences and other serious crimes only.[96] This is in line with *Digital Rights Ireland*, where the CJEU stressed the need for an explicit rule asserting that access and use must involve merely the prevention, detection or prosecution of serious offences.[97] Furthermore, the Court highlighted in *Tele2* that in cases where the interference with the rights to private life and personal data protection is particularly serious, only the objective of fighting serious crime is capable of justifying such a measure.[98]

[92] F Boehm, *Information Sharing and Data Protection in the Area of Freedom, Security and Justice – Towards Harmonised Data Protection Principles for Information Exchange at EU-level* (Springer, 2012) 354.
[93] ibid 352.
[94] Council Document 5049/07 (4 January 2007) 4.
[95] Boehm (n 92) 365.
[96] It is noteworthy that consultation of databases does not concern the prosecution of such offences, as is the case of PNR data. Compare with Directive (EU) 2016/681 [2016] OJ L119/132.
[97] *Digital Rights Ireland* (n 43) para 60.
[98] *Tele2* (n 85) para 102.

As mentioned in the respective legal instruments,[99] terrorist crimes correspond or are equivalent to those referred to in Articles 3–12 of Directive (EU) 2017/541 on combating terrorism,[100] whereas serious crimes are considered those specified in Article 2(2) of Framework Decision 2002/584/JHA on the European Arrest Warrant.[101] In the case of the VIS, there is no further specification; however, in the legal instruments of Eurodac, EES and ETIAS, these serious crimes must be punishable under national law by a custodial sentence or a detention order for a maximum period of at least three years.[102] The fact that the offences in question are specified by reference to other EU instruments does not present a legality issue. In *Kennedy v UK*,[103] the applicant claimed that the term 'serious crime' as set out in the British Act in question was not sufficiently clear. In this regard, the ECtHR opined that, as long as the term is further clarified in the interpretative provisions of the contested act and the act itself, the foreseeability requirement would be met.[104] In Opinion 1/15, the CJEU was satisfied that the definitions of 'terrorist offences' and 'serious transnational crime' were provided with clarity and precision by requiring that they be punishable by a maximum deprivation of liberty of at least four years or a more serious penalty as defined by Canadian law.[105] In *Advocaten voor de Wereld*, the Court found that the legality of the list of offences in Article 2(2) was respected, 'since the actual definition of those offences and the penalties applicable are those which follow from the law of "the issuing Member State"'.[106]

However, it must be stressed that the delineation of terrorist acts has been susceptible to consecutive reforms in the Directive on Combating Terrorism as a response to the phenomenon of 'foreign terrorist fighters' and new trends in terrorism. In that respect, the inclusion of additional offences, such terrorist travel, has been rightly criticised as raising legality concerns, due to its vagueness and leading to legal uncertainty.[107] Therefore, immigration data may be consulted in relation to criminal offences that do not stand the legality test due to lack of clarity in their definition.

Furthermore, with regard to the demarcation of serious crimes, it is noteworthy that the VIS Decision does not specify a particular penalty framework of the crimes encompassed, an issue that has been subsequently addressed in the cases of Eurodac, EES and ETIAS. Therefore, in the case of the VIS, the lack of threshold as

[99] See above in the comparative table.
[100] Directive (EU) 2017/541 [2017] OJ L88/ 6.
[101] Framework Decision 2002/584/JHA [2002] OJ L190/1. The list involves categories of offences for which the requirement for double criminality is abolished.
[102] Recast Eurodac Regulation, Art 2(1)(k).
[103] *Kennedy v UK* (2011) 52 EHRR 4.
[104] ibid para 159.
[105] Opinion 1/15, paras 176–77.
[106] Case C-303/05 *Advocaten voor de Wereld VZW v Leden van de Ministerraad* ECLI:EU:C:2007:261.
[107] See E Xanthopoulou and T Konstadinides, 'International Fight against Impunity and EU Counter-Terrorism Law: The Case of Foreign Terrorist Fighters' ch 15 in this book.

regards the penalty framework raises proportionality concerns. The barrier is quite low for the rest of the databases as well; despite the fact that, in comparison to VIS, a further specification for serious crimes is provided, the barrier is also relatively low particularly in those Member States whose criminal law allows potentially long custodial sentences for fairly minor crimes.[108]

(iii) The Authorities Designated at the National Level: A Convoluted Legal Landscape

With the exception of Eurodac, where there is a distinction between the verifying authority and the Central Access Point, there are two authorities that intervene in order to provide law enforcement access: the 'designated' authority submits the request to the Central Access Point, which acts as the verifying authority. Both authorities are identified at the national level. The list is then communicated to eu-LISA and the Commission, without control or check at the EU level, for example by the Commission (which used to be the recipient of the lists) or eu-LISA.[109] One may wonder whether the EU may interfere in the designation process. The recast Eurodac Regulation excluded intelligence services already at the legislative level, therefore there may be leeway for EU intervention ex post. In such a case, designation would be in breach of Article 5 of the recast Eurodac Regulation, enabling intervention through the initiation of infringement proceedings. Furthermore, in cases where Member States have either gone beyond their designating power by granting access to authorities which do not have a clear link to law enforcement or vaguely refer to certain national authorities, without providing sufficient clarifications, formal letters asking for clarifications by the Member States or warnings similar to those employed in the early stages of infringement proceedings may be useful tools. Member States may proceed to changes in their respective lists, which follow the same procedure of communication and publication. Furthermore, at the national level, each Member State must keep a list of the operating units within the designated authorities that are authorised to access the systems. As regards the exact nature of the 'designated' bodies entrusted with the task of consulting the respective systems, the definition merely refers to authorities that are 'responsible for the prevention, detection or investigation of terrorist offences and other serious crimes', without further specification or limitation.[110] As regards the verifying authorities, the legal bases for Eurodac, EES and ETIAS clarify that the designated and verifying authority can be within the same organisation,[111] with the preceding VIS Decision being silent

[108] S Peers et al, *EU Immigration and Asylum Law*, 2nd edn (Brill, 2015) 437.

[109] For the VIS list, see Declaration [2013] OJ C236/1; the Eurodac list is not publicly available but was provided by Prof Guild, who obtained it through a freedom of information request to the Commission.

[110] The recast Eurodac Regulation exempts intelligence services. See below.

[111] Recast Eurodac Regulation, Art 6(1); EES Regulation, Art 29(3)(2); ETIAS Regulation, Art 50(2).

on this issue. Emphasis is placed on the need for independence of the authority, which should not receive instructions from the designated authorities regarding the outcome of the verification process.[112] Similar rules exist in relation to Europol, whereby access is reserved for a specialised unit within the organisation but acting independently.

The aforementioned rules allow Member States a large amount of discretion to designate any authority they consider related to law enforcement, without further scrutiny at the EU level; the mere publication of the lists suffices for ticking the legality box. However, the uncritical acceptance of the lists provided by Member States has led to a series of irregularities and bad practices. A regular shortcoming of the communicated authorities is the vagueness as to which specific bodies or units within the authorities are authorised, since, in many cases, a general reference to a ministry is preferred. It may be the case that national police departments are not even explicitly listed and the relevant ministry to which they organically belong is mentioned, whereas in other cases, Member States have submitted very detailed information encompassing elaborate listings of regional bodies and units across the Member State.[113] From a technical standpoint, Member States are not required to draft the lists in a specific, detailed manner, and flexibility is foreseen so as to reflect the existing divergences in administrative governance. However, from a legality point of view, this is not a satisfactory approach that allows for transparency and clarity; given that the authority must be responsible for the prevention, detection and investigation of a terrorism offence or other serious crime, the list should make clear which particular directory or unit within an authority is specifically designated, preferably followed by a brief explanation of the reason behind the designation. Furthermore, it is not uncommon for authorities that seem unrelated to law enforcement to also be listed,[114] as well as military services.[115]

The flexibility allowed to Member States in allocating 'designated authorities' is further reflected in the inclusion of intelligence services. Intelligence services are traditionally understood as bodies that provide independent analysis of information related to the external and internal security of a state and the

[112] ibid.

[113] This is the case of the Italian and French list of authorities that may access Eurodac and the German designated authorities in the case of the VIS. Furthermore, in the case of Austria, local administrative authorities (*Bezirkshauptmannschaft*) are also enabled to access the VIS. In the Belgian, Finnish, Lithuanian, Luxembourgish and Danish lists of authorities, the designated and verifying authorities enlisted are the same without further information. In Bulgaria's list of designated authorities on top of authorities such as the national police, the list refers to 'other authorities competent for the prevention, detection and investigation of terrorist acts and serious crimes' without any further specification.

[114] With respect to Eurodac, Italy has designated three authorities (Command for Health Protection, Command for Agricultural and Food Policies and Command for the Protection of Labour) which do not fit. Furthermore, the VIS is accessed by the Dutch Food and Consumer Product Safety Authority and the Inspectorate of Human Environment and Transport.

[115] More worryingly, military services have also been designated in Latvia (Military and Intelligence Security Service) and Poland (Military Counter-Intelligence Service and Military Intelligence Service).

protection of vital national interests. Article 4(2) TEU provides that 'national security remains the sole responsibility of each EU Member States, whereas the Law Enforcement Directive is not applicable to activities of agencies and units concerning national security'.[116] However, the scope of the national security exemption particularly as regards the extent to which intelligence services are included within the term of 'competent authorities' is debatable, due to the various and often unclear separations between the areas of law enforcement and national security in individual Member States. This is particularly apparent in the case of counterterrorism, since terrorism is regarded as a threat to both national security and law and order. As a result, the division of competences amongst intelligence and law enforcement authorities varies throughout the EU Member States, as do the modalities of their information exchanges. It may be the case that certain agencies at the national level are vested with tasks related to both law enforcement and intelligence analysis. That intelligence services are not a priori completely excluded from the scope of the term 'designated authorities' is evident from the explicit exclusion of intelligence services in Article 5(1) of the recast Eurodac Regulation. Thus, unless otherwise indicated, the definition of designated authorities may cover intelligence services, particularly in cases whereby the boundaries of their competence as well as their nature are mixed.[117] This limitation, which was added during negotiations,[118] shows that the vulnerable status of asylum seekers was taken into account in developing the modalities of law enforcement access. However, the EU does not have competence to legislate on issues of national security. It is therefore unclear how this provision will be enforced.[119] For example, Bulgaria has decided that its State Agency for National Security, which is an intelligence service, should have access to Eurodac (and VIS) data despite the proscription.

In the light of the above, a way forward, apart from checking the list of authorities, as mentioned earlier, would be to understand the concept of 'authorities responsible for the prevention, detection and investigation of terrorism offences and serious crimes' as an autonomous concept of EU law, guidance on the content and limits of which would be provided by the CJEU should this issue arise.

As for the verification that the conditions of access have been fulfilled, in *Digital Rights Ireland* and *Tele2 and Watson*, the CJEU set the threshold particularly high. The Court required that, prior to access by the competent national agencies, the conditions of access must be reviewed by a court or by an independent administrative body whose decision seeks to limit access to the data and their use to what is strictly necessary for the purpose of attaining the objective pursued and which intervenes following a reasoned request of those authorities submitted within the framework of procedures of prevention, detection or

[116] Directive (EU) 2016/680 [2016] OJ L119/89, recital 14 and Art 2(3)(a).

[117] Intelligence services are listed in the VIS list by Germany, Greece, Malta, Poland and Romania.

[118] Compare with the Commission proposal, COM (2012) 254 final, Art 5(1).

[119] C Jones, 'Analysis – 11 Years of Eurodac' (*Statewatch*, 2014) http://www.statewatch.org/analyses/no-235-eurodac.pdf.

criminal prosecutions.[120] In the case of databases, it is clear that the verifying authority may be a law enforcement authority, which may also form part of the same organisation as the agency seeking access. Though this policy choice may make practical sense, as the verifying authority could perhaps better understand the needs of a criminal investigation, it is likely that the decision regarding the fulfilment of conditions could be biased, particularly if the officials involved are situated within the same organisation and/or the same premises.[121] The multiple references to the independence of the verifying authority in the legal bases (particularly in the cases of Eurodac, EES and ETIAS) in reaching their decisions, which are spread throughout the Regulation, albeit necessary, may prove inadequate.[122] This is because, once the verifying authority has concluded that the conditions of access have been fulfilled, there is no other mechanism prior to the transmission to ensure that this assessment was indeed accurate. It should be recalled that such consultations may take place not only within a formal investigation of a criminal offence, but also at earlier stages in the context of crime prevention. The fact the individuals are not informed about consultations of their data in order to jeopardise the outcome of investigations means that the individual may only find out about the processing if they so request ex post. Remedies at the national level shall also be applicable when challenging the outcome and lawfulness of consultation on trial by the defence. However, if consultation of data stored in a particular database that led to a negative result (and thus may not be part of the file) was unlawful, there would be no judicial remedies for the individual whose data was accessed, who may only file a complaint with the national data protection authority.

It would be preferable if the examination of the conditions for access could be conducted by a judicial or national supervisory authority, or at least if a review of the conditions by these authorities could take place. The sole possibility of controlling the process is ex post, through supervision by national Data Protection Authorities, which may take place months or years later. Hence, it could be argued that the current wording of the provisions does not restrict the powers of the verifying authorities in an effective manner. This could result in the strict wording of the provisions being ineffective in practice, and immigration data processed for law enforcement purposes more systematically than intended. Regrettably, it is difficult to assess whether this is so, as there is no information as to how many requests have been rejected by the verifying authorities.

Some quite good practices exist as well. For example, in Bulgaria, Estonia and the Netherlands, the task of verifying the Eurodac conditions of access is entrusted

[120] *Digital Rights Ireland* (n 43) para 62; *Tele2* (n 85) para 120. Emphasis added.

[121] Vavoula, 'The Recast Eurodac Regulation' (n 53).

[122] The operation of the verifying authority in Austria for Eurodac is entrusted to the unit dedicated to dactyloscopy (within the police, but a dedicated unit is entrusted with the task). A similar approach is taken by Belgium, where the verifying authority for Eurodac is the service of judicial identification (within the police).

to the Prosecutor's Office. In line with *OG and PI*, the intervention by a prosecutorial authority, whilst institutionally independent from the judiciary, may offer significant guarantees of impartial assessment of each individual case, as long as its legal position in the Member State in question affords them a guarantee of independence from the executive.[123] There is a downside to a prosecutor's intervention where the start of the investigation is compulsory and the prosecutor could trigger their functions by controlling access to the data. However, the legal background of a prosecutor offers stronger guarantees of independence and knowledge of the boundaries of the law than a police authority. Finally, another interesting example is provided by Malta, where the verifying authority for Eurodac is the Data Protection Office within the police. This may be a satisfactory compromise solution whereby, although access is authorised by a unit within the national police, the officers are especially trained for this task.

(iv) Data Quality as a Damocles Sword

The quality of personal data stored has been a long-standing problem of the existing databases; spelling errors, lack of documentation, insufficient language skills, technical deficiencies, incorrect transcription of names into the Latin alphabet, recording of birth dates when the precise date is unknown and lack of training are just some of the reasons why databases lack data quality.[124] For example, in the case of the VIS, it has been reported that the mechanisms securing that only data of sufficient quality were entered into the system were temporarily abolished so as to speed up the registration process.[125] Even if this was a temporary solution, given that the records are retained for 5–10 years (in cases of successful visa applications),[126] the effects of maintaining low-quality data remain long after the rectification of the procedures. If the stored information is not of sufficient quality, the possibilities of false matches multiply, particularly when using fingerprints as search keys. A possible false match would have serious repercussions for a person wrongfully identified, as they could become involved in criminal investigations or even criminal proceedings. Finally, searches in Eurodac, EES and ETIAS based on latent fingerprints – that is, incomplete fingerprints found at a crime scene – may lead to a high number of possible matches, given the wider range of correlations with partial or fragmentary prints.[127] As a result, the rates of error (false matches) could increase also for that reason.[128]

[123] Joined Cases C-509/18 *PF*, C-508/18 *OG* and C-82/19 PPU *PI* ECLI:EU:C:2019:457, paras 51–52.
[124] Vavoula, *Immigration and Privacy in the Law of the European Union* (n 2) ch 3. See Fundamental Rights Agency, Opinion 1/2018, 30.
[125] eu-LISA, 'VIS Report pursuant to Article 50(3) of Regulation (EC) No 767/2008 – VIS Report pursuant to Article 17(3) of Council Decision 2008/633/JHA' (2016) 10.
[126] VIS Regulation, Art 23.
[127] EDPS (n 54) para 61.
[128] ibid; UNHCR (n 75) 5–6.

V. The Plot Twist: Interoperability

The analysis above merely represents one part of the story. So far, the evolution of databases has followed a gradual compartmentalisation, whereby the data pots remain separate from each other, without the possibility of establishing direct communication among them. This was originally praised as a means of safeguarding the rights to privacy and personal data protection;[129] however, it is now viewed as a flaw due to fragmentation allowing 'blind spots', which must be remedied. To that end, a framework for interoperability among EU databases has been created by Regulations 2019/817[130] and 2019/818,[131] with the overarching aims of improving security in the EU, allowing for more efficient identity checks, improving detection of multiple identities and assisting in the fight against irregular migration.[132] To those ends, interoperability brings together the existing and forthcoming databases for third-country nationals, by creating four interoperability components: the European Search Portal, which will enable simultaneous queries to the underlying systems; a Biometric Matching Service, which will store templates of all biometric data recorded; a Multiple Identity Detector, to detect multiple identities; and a Common Identity Repository (CIR).

The CIR, in particular, will store an individual file for each person registered in the systems, containing both biometric and biographical data, as well as a reference indicating the system from which the data were retrieved. The CIR's main objectives are to facilitate identity checks of third-country nationals, assist in the detection of individuals with multiple identities and streamline law enforcement access to the underlying systems. Simplifying the procedure has been prompted by complaints at the national level that the current 'cascade mechanism' is a cumbersome procedure from an administrative perspective that results in delays and missed opportunities to uncover necessary information.[133] Regrettably, this claim is not substantiated by cases at the national level, whereby such access was denied in the verification process or was not provided on time. The fact that a procedure is cumbersome does not mean that it must be overturned altogether. Besides, in all cases, there is a mechanism of ex post verification of the conditions of access in urgent cases.[134] The anecdotal and fragmented data presented above further question the claim about necessity of revising the procedure, which may simply derive from overzealous law enforcement authorities that are responsible for thousands

[129] COM (2010) 385 final, 3.
[130] Regulation (EU) 2019/817 [2019] OJ L135/27 (collectively Interoperability Regulations).
[131] Regulation (EU) 2019/818 [2019] OJ L135/85 (collectively Interoperability Regulations).
[132] Interoperability Regulations, Art 2.
[133] See the Commission proposals on interoperability, COM (2017) 793 final and COM (2017) 794 final, 23 and 45.
[134] See Art 4(2) of the VIS Decision, Art 19(3) of the recast Eurodac Regulation, Art 31(2) of the EES Regulation and Art 51(4) of the ETIAS Regulation.

of searches.[135] Lack of awareness of the procedure does not dictate a revision of the existing rules. Besides, if national authorities do not make use of this functionality, it is doubtful how they could ask for their reform.[136]

Under the revised rules, a two-step process is foreseen, whereby law enforcement authorities will be able to first consult all databases to check whether records on an individual exist in any of these without obtaining prior authorisation or the need to fulfil specific conditions. In the event of a 'hit', the second step is to obtain access to each individual system that contains the matching data through the procedure prescribed for each database (hit-flag procedure).[137] Undoubtedly, interoperability will progressively lead to routine access. As noted by the European Data Protection Supervisor (EDPS), the existence of a 'hit' – that the indicated database holds a file on the individual in question – is significant, since it reveals elements of an individual's personal life, for instance, that they are visa-free travellers or asylum seekers, and, therefore, this first step of checking whether there is personal data in any of the underlying systems should also take place after fulfilling the specific conditions of access prescribed in the legal basis of each database.[138] Conversely, if there is no 'hit', the authorities may have still acquired some information as regards the individual in question, for example, that they probably belong to a specific group of third-country nationals. Importantly, it is hard to believe that, upon finding that a database holds information on a person, the verifying authority, ensuring that the conditions for access have been met, will not allow such access. This will particularly be the case when this function is to be used in cases of unknown perpetrators or victims of offences, where the existence of information on the individual in a system will pre-empt the verification of the conditions of access. In other words, not only the independence and objectivity, but also the very existence of the verification process may be biased by the two-step approach. Arguably, this new function may enable national authorities to engage in 'fishing expeditions'. Therefore, more prosecutions and/or convictions of third-country nationals may take place, merely because a pool of information exists, since no equivalent EU-wide catalogue of records on EU citizens exists. This may further sustain a divide between the EU citizens and foreigners, and raise serious non-discrimination concerns as regards the differentiated treatment between third-country nationals and EU nationals. Therefore, the establishment of the CIR may even increase the appetite to expand surveillance of movement

[135] The evaluation of the VIS speculates that the relative novelty of the system, lack of awareness among potential users and technical and administrative difficulties account for these discrepancies. See COM (2016) 655 final, 12.

[136] There is no information as to whether more Member States attempt to gain access but are denied by the verifying authority.

[137] Interoperability Regulations, Art 22.

[138] EDPS, Opinion 4/2018, 17. See also T Quintel, 'Connecting Personal Data of Third Country Nationals: Interoperability of EU Databases in the Light of the CJEU's Case Law on Data Retention' (2018) University of Luxembourg Working Paper 2/2018 https://papers.ssrn.com/sol3/papers.cfm?abstract_id=3132506.

to EU nationals, with a view to evening out the negative implications for third-country nationals.

VI. Conclusion

This chapter has examined the EU legal framework on the consultation of immigration databases by law enforcement authorities and Europol. By scrutinising the relevant rules, a clear trend towards the maximised exploitation of databases has emerged, triggered by two main drivers: the aim of combating impunity in the EU through the use of technology to detect and investigate terrorist offences and other serious crimes, and the perception that third-country nationals are risky individuals. As such, databases established primarily for immigration control have been repurposed as pools of information on suspected individuals and security risks. This understanding of third-country nationals remains even if they have undergone extensive screening processes prior to entry into the EU (as in the case of short-stay travellers), although technological means have enabled their pre-vetting and clearance in the first place. The fight against impunity has resulted in overzealous efforts to allow access to all databases for law enforcement purposes, without questioning its necessity or sufficiently respecting the principle of proportionality. This chapter has also highlighted that it is too early to assess its effectiveness, as available information remains scarce and Member States have yet to master the exploitation of these databases, or a dangerous criminal may not be found among the pool of third-country nationals. The analysis has revealed a series of privacy and data protection concerns, particularly with regard to the conditions of access, its material scope and the national authorities involved in the process. By simplifying the rules on law enforcement access, interoperability among the different systems poses further challenges for privacy and data protection; essentially, an already disproportionate procedure will be bypassed. The case of databases has clearly demonstrated that law enforcement prerogatives have trumped the protection of fundamental rights. It remains to be seen whether the effectiveness of accessing immigration databases as a policy choice will be proven (eg through convictions) or is bound to remain of limited value and will merely serve political purposes.

13

Enhancing Policing through Algorithmic Surveillance

MARIAVITTORIA CATANZARITI

I. Introduction

The fight against impunity across Europe has been exponentially accelerated by the use of algorithms-based techniques for prevention, detection and investigation, such as data analysis techniques for fraud detection, behavioural data analysis, fiscal reliability analysis, and targeting places for crimes or persons for criminal activities.[1] The increasing engagement of the public sector in technological investments has coupled with delegation mechanisms from state control techniques to private sector data mining. In 2018, most Member States signed the Declaration of Cooperation on Artificial Intelligence, committing themselves towards significant investments in deep learning technology in the field of both private and public sector data. Nonetheless, the proportion and the extent of the deployment of algorithms in the field of policing are not easily gauged, due, on the one hand, to the different meanings and dimensions of impunity and, on the other hand, to the multiple factors that shape the fight against it. On a general scale, the fight against impunity risks becoming a justification for policing that produces a shift from post-crime policing to proactive measures based on algorithmic predictions. Moreover, predictive crime solutions raise the question of their legitimacy, as they could potentially produce disparate mistreatment and undermine the presumption of innocence.

Predictive policing is based on the idea that human behaviour can be anticipated and deterred by a police action.[2] Predictive policing is more than a simple modality of the fight against impunity, as it aims at forecasting criminal events and informing actions that could prevent crime. It not only improves the capability of preventing certain crimes, but also transforms the notion of impunity and what

[1] U Pagallo and S Quattroccolo, 'The Impact of AI on Criminal Law, and Its Twofold Procedures' in W Barfield (ed), *Research Handbook on the Law of Artificial Intelligence* (London, Edward Elgar Publishing, 2018) 388.

[2] AG Ferguson, 'Policing Predictive Policing' (2017) 94 *Washington University Law Review* 1109.

is at stake. It is generally based on techniques that use algorithms to aggregate data obtained from different information chains in order to detect crime hotspots (based on behavioural and location data) and predict crimes (based on individual profiling).[3]

Technically, 'predictive policing is "not fundamentally about making crime-related predictions" but about implementing a prediction-led policing business process, which consists of a cycle of activities and decision points: data collection, analysis, police operations, criminal response, and back to data collection'.[4]

This paper looks more deeply into the dynamics of automated decision-making in the context of mass surveillance, considering three factors: the source, eg the unprecedented huge amount of data available to be collected; the delegation to a data-driven system, by which the predictive potential should enhance policing through analysis mechanisms;[5] and the role of the law and society perspective against technology neutrality, particularly in the preventive phase of algorithmic policing design.

II. A Roadmap for Preventive Justice

Over the last decades, predictive policing has been dramatically associated with the narrative of preventive justice to the detriment of civil liberties. It has determined a shift from post-crime policing to proactive statistics, in many cases undermining the presumption of innocence and other constitutional safeguards. Apparently, holistic policing through omniscient technologies – capable of learning from experience and predicting human action – is an efficient way to exert control over individuals or territories and to promise security, but studies show that the perceived success in reducing crimes is overestimated.[6] One well-known example of predictive policing software is Pred-Pol – a program developed by UCLA scientists working with the Los Angeles Police Department and now used in over 60 police departments around the USA, which identifies areas in a neighbourhood where serious crimes are most likely to occur in a particular time frame. It does not focus on individuals, but it generalises examples or clusters of facts into historically codified patterns.

[3] AG Ferguson, *The Rise of Big Data Policing: Surveillance, Race, and the Future of Law Enforcement* (New York, NYU Press, 2017).

[4] WL Perry, *Predictive Policing: The Role of Crime Forecasting in Law Enforcement Operations* (Santa Monica, RAND, 2017) 128.

[5] Algorithmwatch, 'Automating Society: Taking Stock of Automated Decision-Making in the EU' https://algorithmwatch.org/wp-content/uploads/2019/01/Automating_Society_Report_2019.pdf 9.

[6] R van Brakel and P De Hert, 'Policing, Surveillance and Law in a Pre-crime Society: Understanding the Consequences of Technology Based Strategies' (2011) 20 *Journal of Police Studies* 163.

Although predictive policing has to be kept separated from judicial support programs, the distinction is not always clear: for example, predictive mapping programs such as Correctional Offender Management Profiling for Alternative Sanctions (COMPAS) aim to minimise the risk of recidivism,[7] while individual risk assessment programs such as the Harm Assessment Risk Tool (HART) seek to identify offenders who could be eligible for deferred prosecution and inclusion in a diversionary scheme. In particular, the former can help judges to determine whether somebody should be allowed to go on probation (supervision outside prison), whereas the latter is an operational deployment of algorithmic methods within UK policing, which is an 'out of court' disposal that does not require prosecution in court.[8]

Such growing geospatial technologies and evidence-based intervention models to reduce crimes and improve public safety respond to the logic that even in democratic systems 'the goal justifies the means'. The principle behind 'judgemental atrophy', as coined by Hildebrandt,[9] is that algorithms are neutral, eg they cannot fail because they are objective,[10] even though their outcomes affect non-neutral values in a predetermined way. Nonetheless, automated decision-making cannot be considered a non-biased mechanism to ascertain the percentage of criminal behaviours because the accuracy and the irrelevance of omitted variables are highly questionable.

Moreover, predictive policing techniques are becoming convergent with mass surveillance techniques in shaping behavioural models that are not strictly connected to the purposes they pursue in theory. Surveillance is indeed broader in scope than predictive policing, as it may include programs for national security and intelligence, border control and law enforcement information sharing. However, predictive policing potentially targets huge groups of population through bulk collection. This profoundly affects the application of regulatory patterns to the social reality. Branches of public administration such as law enforcement have been transformed into single private services on demand, mostly based on customisation of demand and supply. Users of public services are likely to be treated as

[7] See *State v Loomis* 881 NW 2d 749, 761, 762 (Wis 2016), where a person was classified by COMPAS as having a high risk of reoffending and was sentenced to six years. This person appealed the ruling on the grounds that the judge, in ruling on the basis of the outcome of an algorithm whose inner functioning was not accessible and not evaluable, violated due process. The Wisconsin Supreme Court noted that COMPAS was only a means of judicial support and the sentence was not based essentially on it: as the report would not be the sole basis for a decision, sentencing that considers a COMPAS assessment would still be sufficiently individualised because courts have the discretion and information necessary to disagree with the assessment when appropriate.

[8] M Oswald, J Grace, S Urwin and GC Barnes, 'Algorithmic Risk Assessment Policing Models: Lessons from the Durham HART Model and "Experimental" Proportionality' (2018) 27 *Information & Communications Technology Law* 223, 225.

[9] M Hildebrandt, 'Law as Computation in the Era of Artificial Legal Intelligence. Speaking Law to the Power of Statistics' (2017) 68 *University of Toronto Law Journal* 2, 12.

[10] M Airoldi and D Gambetta, 'Sul mito della neutralità algoritmica' (2018) XX *The Lab's Quarterly* 4, 29.

commodities that the private sector bargains with the public authorities under the veil of algorithmic neutrality. Information sharing among public authorities and private actors has generally affected not only the shortcomings of data processing, but also the notion of individual identity and freedom.[11]

In reality, predictive policing produces linkages between the physical and virtual realms, which include not only the online/offline dimensions, but also the 'on-life' one as the result of both.[12] Algorithms shape human behaviour codifying situations and facts, stigmatising groups rather than individuals, and learning from the past: predictions may lead to static patterns that recall the idea of a caste society, in which the individual potential of change and development is far from being preserved.[13] To provide examples of such a transformation, in the field of policing, historical data from police can create a 'feedback loop' through which algorithms make predictions that strengthen social clichés as well as discrimination of minorities. Bias means that collected data may have been preferentially sampled, and therefore the data sample itself is biased.[14] The impartial statistical evidence through the intersection of neutral technology on policing practices is not necessarily reliable.[15] Such scepticism is magnified as surveillance techniques deploy technology secretly.

As noted by Neil Richards and Jonathan King, surveillance gives rise to three fundamental paradoxes: the paradox of transparency, which concerns the capability to extract data through voluntary and visible sharing and to analyse them through secret procedures; the paradox of identity, consisting in stigmatisating individual identity on the basis of past behaviours and irrespective of any possibility of human change; and the paradox of power, according to which big data appear as a tool strengthening individual knowledge, though in reality they empower the role of information intermediaries in accessing a huge amount of data.[16] As correctly pointed out by Shoshana Zuboff:[17]

> This architecture produces a distributed and largely uncontested new expression of power that I christen: 'Big Other.' It is constituted by unexpected and often illegible mechanisms of extraction, commodification, and control that effectively exile persons from their own behaviour while producing new markets of behavioural prediction and

[11] S Rodotà, 'Controllo e privacy nella vita quotidiana. Dalla tutela della vita privata alla protezione dei dati personali' (2019) 37 *Rivista Critica Del Diritto Privato* 9, 15.

[12] W Hoffmann-Riem, 'Verhaltenssteurung durch Algorithmen – Eine Herausforderung für das Recht' (2017) 142 *Archiv des öffentlichen Rechts* 1.

[13] A Mantelero, 'Personal Data for Decisional Purposes in the Age of Analytics: From an Individual to a Collective Dimension of Data Protection' (2016) 32 *Computer Law & Security Review* 238; A Mantelero 'From Group Privacy to Collective Privacy: Towards a New Dimension of Privacy and Data Protection in the Big Data Era' in B van der Sloot, L Floridi and L Taylor (eds), *Group Privacy* (Heidelberg, Springer Verlag, 2017) 139.

[14] SC Olhede and JP Wolfe, 'The Growing Ubiquity of Algorithms in Society: Implications, Impact, and Innovation' (2018) 376 *Philosophical Transactions of the Royal Society* 1.

[15] A Shapiro, 'Reform Predictive Policing' (2017) 541 *Nature* 458.

[16] N Richards and J King, 'Three Paradoxes of Big Data' (2013) 6 *Stanford Law Review* 43.

[17] S Zuboff, 'Big Other: Surveillance Capitalism and the Prospects of an Information Civilization' (2015) 30 *Journal of Information Technology* 75.

modification. Surveillance capitalism challenges democratic norms and departs in key ways from the centuries long evolution of market capitalism.

Traditionally, there is a limit to the compatibility between the use of secrecy and democratic forms of power, which consists in predicting the public use of secrecy, limited to certain cases.[18] Even though 'some democratic policies require secrecy', as observed by Thompson, 'first order secrecy requires second order publicity'.[19] The invisible use of power is, therefore, a justifiable practice insofar as it falls within a process that is itself not secret.

This is the case of algorithms that are used for speeding up processing or supporting decision-making, but are mostly based on secret systems that are not accessible to anyone, even though most of the information is meaningless albeit highly influential.[20]

The first aspect to be considered is that the data extraction is a 'one-way process, not a relationship', which produces identity fragmentation and attributes an exchange value to single fragments of the identity itself.[21]

Algorithmic surveillance indeed produces a twofold phenomenon: on the one hand, it forges the extraction process itself, which is predictive by definition, in the sense that the predetermined purpose of crimes' prevention is often only a biased presumption; on the other hand, it determines an aftermath which is not predictable, despite the fact that proxies for certain qualities as well as for relevant outcomes are known. Those qualities are defined 'target variables'.[22]

Against this background, I argue that a better setting for algorithmic predictive policing should suggest proceeding in parallel with human activities, rather than beforehand, as its aim should not be so much to predict crimes as to test and improve the ability of human actions, as well as the efficiency of a certain allocation of resources, with regard to the aim of preventing crimes. Human officers may in fact be highly influenced by the results of algorithmic predictions, whose presumed reliability drives their convictions regardless of any specific grounds, or on the basis of where they direct their attention.[23] There are, of course, similarities and differences between human policing and automated pattern recognition: pattern-based predictions may be used to trigger further human investigation (*Gefahrerforschungseingriffe*), but cannot as such justify final determinations with adverse effects on individuals (*Gefahrbeseitigungseingriffe*).[24]

[18] D Curtin, 'Second Order Secrecy and Europe's Legality Mosaics' (2018) 41 *West European Politics* 5.

[19] DF Thompson, 'Democratic Secrecy' (1999) 114 *Political Science Quarterly* 181, 182, 185.

[20] F Pasquale, *The Black Box Society. The Secret Algorithms That Control Money and Information* (Cambridge, MA, Harvard University Press, 2015) 3; M Hildebrandt, *Smart Technologies and the End(s) of Law. Novel Entanglements of Law and Technology* (Cheltenham, Edward Elgar Publishing, 2015) 133.

[21] Zuboff, 'Big Other' (n 16) 99.

[22] FZ Borgesius, *Discrimination, Artificial Intelligence, and Algorithmic Decision-Making* (Council of Europe, Strasbourg, 2018) 10.

[23] C O'Neil, *Weapons of Math Destruction* (London, Penguin Books, 2016) 91.

[24] T Rademacher, 'Predictive Policing im Deutschen Polizeirecht' (2017) 142 *Archiv des öffentliches Rechts* 366.

Moreover, pinpointing target variables is highly relevant in the field of predictive policing techniques, in order to avoid the risk of misleading outcomes. The 'black box' effect is magnified by the fact that often even police officers using the programs do not have specific knowledge of the operational logic of algorithms, as developers may refuse to reveal the algorithmic code used, as it is generally protected by copyright and trade secrets.

The second aspect to be highlighted is that the most common assumptions underlying predictive policing programs are partial and debatable.[25] First, data used to feed the program generally reflect reality without considering important variables, such as the presence of more officials or the seriousness of an event to be reported as a crime; additionally, the prediction is based on generalised historical data that do not take into account structural differences among individuals and situations; in any event, algorithms are neutral insofar as they are not associated with any historical category of discrimination, but this is not sufficient to exclude discriminatory practices; finally, they tend to give primary importance to particular pieces of information (such as location and crime date/time) over others.

The third remark regards the mismatch between algorithmic and legal code. The functioning of algorithms is generally 'self-executing' and only responds to the mere logic 'I can'; by contrast, the legal code is based on 'I can as I am allowed to' (which is clearly highlighted by the German dichotomy between *können* and *dürfen*). Whereas an algorithm can be described as a 'sequence of computational steps that transform the input into the output', machines learning algorithms are able to learn from experience and modify their processing operations autonomously.[26] The autonomy of algorithms is detached from the rules that create obstacles to their functioning as they overcome material limitations; conversely, the autonomy of the law is profoundly based on the structure of a closed and self-referential system, which generally relies on the idea that what is not forbidden is permitted.[27] Likewise, the principle 'garbage in/garbage out', according to which the quality of the output is determined by the quality of the input, so that inaccurate data cannot produce accurate results, is not entirely applicable to legal reasoning. For example, accurate data do not necessarily produce accurate results, but may produce 'false positives'. Conversely, lawful inputs into the algorithmic process are not sufficient to produce lawful outputs.

[25] TZ Zarsky, 'Transparent Predictions' (2013) 4 *University of Illinois Law Review* 1503.

[26] MH Murphy, 'Algorithmic Surveillance in the Collection Conundrum' (2017) 31 *International Review of Law, Computer & Technology* 225, 226.

[27] On this, see Consiglio di Stato, Dec 8.4.2019, n 02270/2019 REG.PROV.COLL: 'the "multidisciplinary characterization" of the algorithm (construction that certainly does not require only legal skills, but technical, IT, statistics, administrative) does not exempt from the need for the "technical formula", which in fact represents the algorithm, to be accompanied by explanations that translate it into the "legal rule" to it subtends and makes it legible and understandable, both for citizens and for the judge' (our translation).

> For example, in the area of counterterrorism, as terrorism is relatively rare compared with other phenomena, machine searches should compare and analyse data in order to be effective: due to the rarity of terrorist attacks, pattern searching is prone to mistakes. While the inherently probabilistic nature of such determinations is not a serious problem when the consequence is an online advertisement targeting an uninterested consumer, an incorrect categorisation as a terrorist can have significant human rights implications for the incorrectly targeted individual.[28]

The tension between the overwhelming capabilities of algorithms and the resilience of the legal tools can be investigated from different standpoints that tend to highlight how the character of the law as a self-reproducing system might be undermined as much as algorithms replace decision-making mechanisms.[29] The task of the legal analysis is to translate algorithmic functioning first of all into the language of the legal field of action (juridification) and then into *ex post* judicial remedies (effectiveness).[30] As law is incorporated into code-based rules that depend on information input into the system, algorithms used for legal decision-making no longer mediate between what individuals shall do and what they can or cannot do.[31]

Concepts such as proportionality, responsibility, risk management, transparency and participation all aim to make the working of algorithms compliant with legal paradigms. Beyond these standards, legal analysis should further reflect on which challenges need to be regulated as a self-reproducing social reaction.

III. Beyond Data Protection

In this section, I consider the tensions between the potential of algorithms to enhance policing and the threats to civil liberties. A data protection regime is introduced here to show how the connection between personal data processing and predictive policing techniques may trigger a set of safeguards. Neither privacy, data protection nor antitrust laws provide adequate protection, as electronic surveillance programs may affect individual liberties by producing inequality. Predictive policing systems can sometimes reproduce or amplify existing discrimination.[32]

[28] Murphy (n 25) 231.

[29] G Teubner, *Law as an Autopoietic System* (Oxford, Blackwell, 1993).

[30] CB Graber, 'Freedom and Affordances of the Net' (2018) 10 *Washington University Jurisprudence Review* 221.

[31] S Hassan and P De Filippi, 'The Expansion of Algorithmic Governance: From Code is Law to Law is Code' (2017) 17 *Facts Reports* 88 http://journals.openedition.org/factsreports/4518.

[32] Borgesius (n 21) 12: 'The COMPAS system does not use racial origin or skin colour as an input. But researches showed in 2016 that COMPAS is biased against blacks as it inserts proxies which indirectly rely on race. COMPAS … correctly predicts recidivism 61 percent of the time. But blacks are almost twice as likely as whites to be labelled a higher risk but not actually reoffend. It makes the opposite mistake among whites: they are much more likely than blacks to be labelled lower risk but go on to commit other crimes … Academic statisticians have argued that, in some cases, different standards of

One interesting aspect of the algorithmic process is, for example, the idea of 'disparate mistreatment', according to which different groups receive different error types disproportionately (for instance, individuals belonging to specific groups or minorities having major chances of getting a worse score in terms of propensity to recidivism).[33]

Predictive policing is strictly based on intrusion into the personal sphere and personal data processing. Thus, data protection may become a potential paradigm capable of encompassing several layers of safeguards even in the field of algorithmic policing, rather than being considered as a panacea.

Many authors have pointed out the limits of the Regulation EU 2016/679 (General Data Protection Regulation – GDPR) as a possible tool to better control algorithms, arguing that the right to a reasonable explanation risks resulting in the transparency fallacy determined by the fact that 'explanations are restricted both by the type of explanation sought, the multi-dimensionality of the domain and the type of user seeking an explanation'.[34]

The shift from an algorithmic transparency issue to data transparency is a slippery slope whose dynamics is recurrent: stigmatising individuals on the basis of social sorting determines a sort of customisation of social identities as well as social diseases, using the same mechanism as for the customisation of individual capabilities as end-users or consumers. Like capitalistic models that profit from induced needs to create consuming habits, social sorting elaborates on predetermined categories of social risk, which are *ex ante* input into the algorithmic process, contributing to feeding profiling techniques. One of the most significant challenges is to assess whether the model of fundamental rights protection could be of any help in addressing the issue of fragmented individual identities customised in unequal conditions. As correctly pointed out by Zuboff, 'surveillance capitalism unilaterally claims human experience as free raw material for translation into behavioural data'.[35]

For instance, customisation of behaviours enhances inequality at different layers, in terms of the possibility of getting better job opportunities and not being targeted as potential criminals.

It is not surprising that the contrast between privacy and security is fading, not only because threats to the former are under the spotlight and are commonly accepted as a failure, but also because there are worse effects than the violation of the right to privacy and data protection that undermine individual liberties and that go beyond it.[36]

fairness are incompatible mathematically, which has consequences for what discrimination prevention should or could look like.'

[33] M Hu, 'Algorithmic Jim Crow' (2017) 86 *Fordham Law Review* 633.

[34] Borgesius (n 21) 12.

[35] S Zuboff, *The Age of Surveillance Capitalism: The Fight for a Human Future at the New Frontier of Power* (New York, Public Affairs, 2019) 8.

[36] A Lodder and RP Loui, 'Data Algorithms and Privacy in Surveillance: On Stages, Numbers and the Human Factor' in Barfield (n 1) 375.

As correctly stressed by Margulies, hidden layers of computing power are used to group myriad variables.[37] Machines select materials that are relevant and indicate materials for collection and subsequent analysis.

In the following sections, this chapter aims to investigate three case studies related to individual remedies in the access to algorithmic decision-making: (i) the definition of inferences as personal data; (ii) the control of automated decision-making under GDPR and Directive EU 2016/680 (the Law Enforcement Directive, LED); and (iii) the challenge of the violation of the principle of good administration.

A. The Legal Status of Inferences

Algorithmic surveillance has reoriented privacy concerns, insofar as much emphasis has been put on data mining.[38] However, the notion of inferences has not been deeply debated by legal scholars. Inferences are very critical in term of accountability of the algorithmic process, as inferential analytics is non-verifiable and potentially compromises the reputation of and future opportunities for any individual.[39] Whereas explanations can be rendered only *ex post* after a decision has been made, inferences give a real picture of the algorithmic process during its functioning.

An interesting and not yet explored operative solution could be represented by the application of the notion of personal data to the reasonable inferences.[40] Data subjects nevertheless have the right to control data processing and collection, but not data evaluation.[41] Redefining the remit of data protection, including the justification of assessments, focusing on evaluation rather than only collection and identifiability of data subjects, by giving them the right to reverse unreasonable inferences, is the core of the right to reasonable inferences.

It has been argued that the right to an explanation of the algorithmic process – in the best case, how algorithms learn from data – as a form of transparency which promises to open the 'black box' – is unlikely to offer an exhaustive remedy to algorithmic harms.[42]

The legal status of inferences is highly controversial. Besides the debate on the nature of inferences as personal data or not, an effective remedy should be based on a definition of inferences as information relating to an identified or identifiable

[37] P Margulies, 'Surveillance by Algorithm: The NSA, Computerized Intelligence Collection and Human Rights' (2016) 68 *Florida Law Review* 1045, 1051.

[38] ibid 1091.

[39] S Watcher and B Mittelstadt, 'A Right to Reasonable Inferences: Re-thinking Data Protection Law in the Age of Big Data and AI' [2019] *Columbia Business Law Review* 494.

[40] ibid 498, 580.

[41] ibid 510, 511, 514, 568.

[42] L Edwards and M Veale, 'Slave to Algorithms? Why a Right to an Explanation Is Probably Not the Remedy You Are Looking For' (2017) 16 *Duke Law & Technology Review* 18.

natural person created through deduction or reasoning rather than mere data collection. They may include predictions and assumptions having an impact on individuals. In fact, inferences are inherent in the process of machine learning. The right to access to the proxies used in the process of algorithmic learning does not indicate much in terms of individual legitimate claims. On the contrary, the plausibility of a right to reasonable inference seems to be a balanced solution. Nevertheless, the Court of Justice, in *YS, and M and S*,[43] ruled that:

> data relating to the applicant for a residence permit contained in the minute [a document containing the reasoning of the case officer] and, where relevant, the data in the legal analysis contained in the minute are 'personal data' within the meaning of that provision, whereas, by contrast, that analysis cannot in itself be so classified.

This means that the legal analysis, which is information about the assessment and the application, should not itself be considered personal data, as 'only information relating to facts about an individual' can be defined as such.[44] This case follows the AG Opinion, according to which legal analysis is 'the legal classification of facts relating to an identified or identifiable person … and their assessment against the background of the applicable law'.[45] According to both the Opinion and the judgment, to be considered personal data, facts need to be verifiable, irrespective of whether they are expressed in a subjective or objective way. This implies that opinions as well as inferences leading to a decision, which has been the outcome of a legal analysis, will fail to be accessed and reviewed without the label of 'personal data'. Even assessments and opinions can be considered personal data. On the contrary, in *Novak*,[46] which ruled on the applicability of a data protection regime to exam scripts and to the comments of the assessor, the Court of Justice broadened the definition of personal data to include 'data in the form of opinions and assessment'[47] related to personal data. Nonetheless, in terms of effective remedies, the right of rectification does not cover the contents of the assessor's

[43] Joined Cases C-141/12 and C-372/12 *YS, M and S v Minister voor Immigratie, Integratie en Asiel* ECLI:EU:C:2014:2081, paras 54, 56, 57, 59 and 61.

[44] The definitions of personal data provided by Art 2 LED and Art 4 GDPR are similar, except for the fact that the GDPR provides for an enlargement of the notion or identifier and adds the genetic factors. 'Personal data' means any information relating to an identified or identifiable natural person ('data subject'); an identifiable natural person is one who can be identified, directly or indirectly, in particular by reference to an identifier such as a name, an identification number, location data, an online identifier or one or more factors specific to the physical, physiological, genetic, mental, economic, cultural or social identity of that natural person. As provided by recital 26 GDPR, to determine whether a person is identifiable, a controller or another person must take into account all reasonable means that are likely to be used to directly or indirectly identify the individual, such as singling out, which makes it possible to treat one person differently from another.

[45] Opinion of AG Sharpston in joined cases C-141/12 and C-372/12 *YS, M and S v Minister voor Immigratie, Integratie en Asiel* ECLI:EU:C:2013:838.

[46] Case C-434/16 *Peter Nowak v Data Protection Commissioner* ECLI:EU:C: 2017:994. The Court held that 'the written answers submitted by a candidate at a professional examination and any comments made by an examiner with respect to those answers constitute personal data'.

[47] ibid para 34.

comments, as it would exceed the scope of data protection law, which does not guarantee the lawfulness of the decision-making.[48] Both decisions did not address the definition of final inferences and subsequent decisions as personal data, taking for granted that the accuracy of the decision-making rests in the competence of administration.

Should jurisprudence define legal analysis as personal data, it may open relevant perspectives in terms of accountability of predictive policing. At the same time, it would raise opposite concerns from the point of view of effective deterrence, as it could be accessible, undermining the prevention of crimes.[49] However, whereas GDPR applies to personal data, few predictive policing programs rely on non-personal data to support police activities.

The legal definition of inferences in terms of personal data may certainly be a valuable step as it opens a set of safeguards related to a data protection regime. In this sense, data protection can be considered a trigger for attaching forms of protection to individual situations, even though it may present shortcomings, especially when inferences do not fall under the scope of personal data.

B. The Right to Control Automated Decisions

The new data protection package provides specific provisions in the field of automated individual decision-making (Article 22 GDPR and Article 11 LED).

The automated decision-making in the field of data processing for law enforcement purposes is subjected to specific and much stricter parameters compared to the general data protection. According to recital 38 LED, the data subject should have the right not to be subject to a decision evaluating personal aspects relating to him or her which is based solely on automated processing and which produces adverse legal effects concerning, or significantly affects, him or her. In any case, such processing should comply with suitable safeguards, including the provision of specific information to the data subject and the right to obtain human intervention, in particular to express his or her point of view, to obtain an explanation of the decision reached after such assessment or to challenge the decision.[50] Profiling that results in discrimination against natural persons on the basis of personal data which are by their nature particularly sensitive in relation to fundamental rights and freedoms should be prohibited under the conditions laid down in Articles 21 and 52(1) of the European Charter of Fundamental Rights.

According to Article 22 GDPR, the data subject shall have the right not to be subject to a decision based solely on automated processing, including profiling,

[48] Watcher and Mittelstadt (n 39) 503, 568, 569, 572.

[49] LB Moses and J Chan, 'Algorithmic Prediction in Policing: Assumptions, Evaluation, and Accountability' (2016) 28 *Policing and Society* 806.

[50] M Hildebrandt, 'Privacy as Protection of the Incomputable Self. From Agnostic to Agonistic Machine Learning' (2019) 20 *Theoretical Inquiries in Law* 83, 111.

which produces legal effects concerning him or her or similarly significantly affects him or her. Exceptions are foreseen in case an automated decision is necessary for entering into, or for the performance of, a contract between the data subject and a data controller; it is authorised by Union or Member State law to which the controller is subject and which also lays down suitable measures to safeguard the data subject's rights and freedoms and legitimate interests; or it is based on the data subject's explicit consent.

An aspect which can be pinpointed immediately is that Article 11 of the LED sets forth a general prohibition of decisions based solely on automated processing, unless they are authorised by EU law or the domestic law. Amongst the safeguards prompted by domestic law is the data subject's right to obtain human intervention on the part of the controller.[51]

It is by no means clear what the exact context of the 'right to obtain human intervention' is: it seems that data subjects shall have the right to reverse the decision based solely on automated processing. AG Opinion 1/15 on the EU–Canada PNR Agreement offers an interesting perspective to interpret Article 11 LED. In fact, in order to target individuals who are under reasonable suspicion of participating in terroristic offences or serious transnational crimes, the automated analyses of PNR data are deployed. Nonetheless, the AG stated that:

> since the automated analyses of PNR data necessarily involve some margin of error … any positive result obtained following the automated processing of that data must … be subject to an individual re-examination by non-automated means before an individual measure adversely affecting the air passengers concerned is adopted.[52]

In this regard, even the GDPR, as stressed by Watcher and Mittelstadt, is 'moving beyond mere data control and management (or informational self-determination,[53]

[51] According to European Commission, 'White Paper on Artificial Intelligence – A European Approach to Excellence and Trust' 21 https://ec.europa.eu/info/sites/info/files/commission-white-paper-artificial-intelligence-feb2020_en.pdf: 'The output of the AI system does not become effective unless it has been previously reviewed and validated by a human.'

[52] Grand Chamber Opinion 1/15 on the EU–Canada PNR Agreement, ECLI:EU:C:2017:592, para 173.

[53] One of the leading cases for the recognition of data protection as fundamental right was the judgment of the German Federal Court (Bundesverfassungsgericht) on the 'Population census' case in 1983, in which the right to data protection was recognised as the right to informational self-determination. In that judgment, the Court held that 'the protection of personal data is essential for free and selfdetermined development of the individual. At the same time, the self-determined development of the individual is a precondition for a free and democratic communication order. If citizens cannot oversee and control which or even what kind of information about them is openly accessible in their social environment, and if they cannot even appraise the knowledge of possible communication partners, they may be inhibited in making use of their freedom. If citizens are unsure whether dissenting behaviour is noticed and information is being permanently stored, used and passed on, they will try to avoid dissenting behaviour so as not to attract attention. They may even abstain from making use of their basic and human rights. In a potentially all-knowing state, freedom of speech and freedom of choice are virtually impossible': Bundesverfassungsgericht, decisions vol 65, 1ff.

eg Article 15) to allow data subjects to evaluate and challenge automated decisions and profiling which can be based on inferences'.[54]

Of course, the right to evaluate and challenge automated decision-making may be exercised as the result of an expansion of the notion of informational privacy, even though it is much curtailed in the field of law enforcement.

A second important aspect is that such decisions shall not be based on special categories of personal data referred to in Article 10 LED, unless suitable measures to safeguard the data subject's rights and freedoms and legitimate interests are in place. A third aspect which may open interpretative paths towards the right to reasonable inferences even in the field of law enforcement is that profiling that results in discrimination against natural persons on the basis of special categories of personal data shall be prohibited, in accordance with Union law.

This formulation underlines the idea that profiling may result in discriminatory practices, even though not originally based on special categories of data. This is very important as, according to the definition of profiling provided by Article 3(4) LED, it literally includes any form of automated processing of personal data consisting of the use of personal data to evaluate certain personal aspects relating to a natural person, in particular to analyse or predict aspects concerning that natural person's performance at work, economic situation, health, personal preferences, interests, reliability, behaviour, location or movements.

Over the last years, European Courts have focused their attention on the first phase of collection and retention, which represents the basis of potential predictive policing.[55] European case law appears to recognise that intrusion repeatedly occurs at the points of collection, retention and use – even where no human scrutiny is involved.[56] Data retention case law of the CJEU is extremely relevant for developing limitations to algorithmic surveillance, in the fields of national security, defence, prevention and the fight against serious crime. National legislation is precluded, for the purpose of fighting crime, from the general and indiscriminate retention of all traffic and location data of all subscribers and registered users relating to all means of electronic communication.[57]

[54] Watcher and Mittelstadt (n 39) 568, 588.

[55] Joined Cases C-293/12 and C-594/12 *Digital Rights Ireland and Seitlinger and Others* ECLI:EU:C:2014:238, paras 39 and 40; Joined Cases C-203/15 and C-698/15 *Tele 2 Sverige AB v Postoch telestyrelsen, and Secretary of State for the Home Department* ECLI:EU:C:2016:970; Case C-207/16 *Ministerio Fiscal* ECLI:EU:C:2018:788; Case C-623/17 *Privacy International v Secretary of State for Foreign and Commonwealth Affairs and Others* (pending).

[56] Murphy (n 25) 232.

[57] The ECtHR had the occasion to rule on surveillance programs: in particular, in the *Szabo* case (*Szabo and Vissy v Hungary* ECLI:CE:ECHR:2016:0112JUD003713814), it embraced the idea that secret surveillance measures should answer to the requirement of strict necessity, whereas in the *Zacharov* case (*Zacharov v Russia* ECLI:CE:ECHR:2015:1204JUD004714306), it pointed out that surveillance measures could be secret as far as they did not result in measures being effectively unchallengeable and outside the national judicial redress. In *Big Brothers Watch* (*Big Brothers Watch v United Kingdom* ECLI:CE:ECHR:2018:0913JUD005817013), the Court found that there has been a violation

Among national measures implementing the data protection package, the new version of the French Data Protection Act (law no 2018-493 of 20 June 2018)[58] introduces the following principles:

a) no judicial decision involving the evaluation of a person's behaviour can be based on an automated data processing designed to judge on aspects of the personality of that person;
b) no decision that produces legal effects on a person and is based on automated data processing can be taken exceeding the limitations provided by Article 22 GDPR;
c) administrative measures affecting individuals that are based on automated processing are admissible, as far as they do not involve particular categories of data;
d) such measures must contain express mention of the automated processing; in relation to them, the controller must ensure full understanding of the algorithmic processing so that the data subject has a right to explanation, in detail and in an intelligible form, regarding the conditions of the data processing.

The French Data Protection Act has furthermore established that the administration shall inform the data subjects of any measure taken on the basis of an algorithmic treatment, on the party's request, in an intelligible form and not violating any secrets protected by law, providing the following information: the degree and manner in which algorithmic treatment contributed to the decision; the data processed and their origin; the parameters of the processing and, where appropriate, their weighting, applied to the situation of the person concerned; and the transactions carried out through processing.[59]

Finally, it is interesting to compare the recent findings of the Supreme Administrative Courts in France and Italy, which, in different terms, made significant steps in assessing the extent of judicial remedies against unlawful algorithmic decision-making. It should be noted that France, differently from Italy, has adopted a specific legal framework concerning the use of algorithms by public authorities.

In 2018, the French Conseil constitutionnel was called to rule on the constitutionality of the Decree adapting French law to the GDPR.[60] Among the aspects examined, there was an alleged violation of the principle of lawful administrative decision-making, resulting in individualised decisions taken on the basis of

of Art 8 ECHR under the profiles of bulk interception and communication sharing with communication service providers. Specifically, bulk collection has been considered a valuable means for intelligence sharing, given the threat level for global terrorism and serious crime.

[58] See https://blogs.dlapiper.com/privacymatters/france-one-more-step-to-ensure-consistency-of-the-new-french-data-protection-law/.

[59] G Resta, 'Governare l'innovazione tecnologica: decisioni algoritmiche, diritti digitali e principio di uguaglianza' [2018] *Forum Disuguaglianze Diversità* 210, 234, 235.

[60] Conseil constitutionnel, décision no 2018-765.

algorithmic processing; in particular, the applicants claimed that the resort to algorithms prevents the public administration from making use of the margin of discretion depending upon each individual situation. The issue at stake was that deep learning algorithms, implying a continuous revision of algorithmic operational rules, made it impossible for the administration to understand the motivational logic underlying the automated decision. The Conseil constitutionnel rejected all the complaints, putting forward that, first of all, only deep learning algorithms should be considered precluded to the administration. The rationale behind this was that there is no delegation of regulatory power to the technological instrument, so the criteria and methods of operation of the algorithm are established *ex ante* and validated by the person in charge of the procedure. Additionally, the use of algorithmic data processing is subject to the specific conditions and guarantees provided for by law. Moreover, against individual measures taken on the basis of algorithmic treatment, in every case there is to be granted a decision that is not based solely on the automated decision making and a right of appeal against such a decision. In particular, the judge, in his role of data controller, must always be able to understand the functioning of the algorithmic data processing in order to grant the data subject a reasonable explanation – eg in detail and in an intelligible form – about how automated data processing has affected individual rights.

In April 2019, the Italian Consiglio di Stato[61] ruled on a case of public procedure for job placement lodged by applicants, who complained that the entire recruitment procedure had been managed by a computer system by means of an algorithm (whose operation would have remained unknown). In particular, it resulted in measures lacking justification, without the identification of an administrative official in charge of the assessment of the individual positions. The Court held, first, that the mechanism by which the robotic decision (ie the algorithm) is taken must be accessible, according to a reinforced declination of the principle of transparency, which also implies the full knowledge of a rule expressed in a language different from the legal language. Secondly, access to the algorithm must be guaranteed with regard to: its authors, the procedure used for its elaboration, the priorities assigned in the evaluation, the decision-making procedure of relevant selected data, the compliance of the robotic procedure to the provisions and the purposes established by law or by the administration itself, and the possibility of judicial review. Furthermore, the algorithmic rule must not only be accessible per se, but it must also be subject to the full knowledge of the administrative judge. Such a requirement is quintessential to control how the power has been concretely exercised, eg the modalities (even if automated) by which a decision has affected individual rights. Only in such a way can a full evaluation of the legitimacy of the law be carried out, even in the jurisdictional context decision.

[61] Consiglio di Stato, decision no 2019-2270. This judgment was confirmed by recent case-law, see Consiglio di Stato no 2019-8472, 8473, 8474.

This brief comparison between two recent judgments of the Supreme Administrative Courts in Italy and France shows how important algorithmic decision-making from the point of view of the rule of law assessment in democratic societies is, as any power affecting individuals shall be subject to the law and to judicial review. The defence of the rule of law has been recently put forward by the French Justice Reform Act (law no 2019-222, Article 33), which has introduced a provision according to which data revealing the identity of magistrates and members of the judiciary cannot be reused with the purpose or effect of evaluating, analysing, comparing or predicting their actual or alleged professional practices. Such a provision, controversial as it may be, reflects a trend that seeks to limit algorithmic decision-making even from the perspective of judicial independence, and also in the name of the right to a fair trial.

IV. Conclusions

In light of an unprecedented technological transformation that is radically shaping the space of civil liberties, the role of the law should not only be that of prompting judicial remedies and regulating responsibility, but also of reconfiguring the dimensions of human beings, technology and social action into an integrated regulatory model.

The idea that technology enables us to do all that is possible to do does not overlap with the prescribing function of law, which rather suggests that it is not allowed to do all that we can do.

Predictive policing shares with other public services the broader trend towards individual customisation, which aims at targeting groups, rather than individuals, on the basis of inferences from past historical data.

In this sense, the European data protection 'revolution' presents shortcomings in addressing algorithmic challenges, but may be triggered towards defining final inferences or final decisions as personal data. Nonetheless, the inclusion of inferences within the scope of personal data entails applying data subjects' rights provided by the GDPR to individuals affected by the misuse of inferences. Moreover, in the field of predictive policing, data protection safeguards are generally rarefied, as a data protection regime would be more like the one provided by the LED rather than the GDPR. In terms of individual protection in the case of automated decision-making, the instruments provided by the data protection package certainly seem a good step forward, but not an optimal solution. In any case, the reflection of the Court of Justice upon the legal status of inferences is of utmost significance in terms of awareness of the urgent issues at the core of data evaluation.

On the other hand, the adaptive interpretation of the principle of good administration has cast the algorithmic 'hole' upon a more fruitful path, which is making much progress towards the juridification of algorithmic decision-making. This turns out to be particularly relevant in the field of predictive policing, as it is primarily a public service whose technological insights need to be interpreted in light of the principle of good administration.

A paradigm shift that highlights the 'process' of decision-making rather than a mere *ex post* remedial logic is, in fact, a promising frontier, and it deserves to be taken seriously.

It should be borne in mind that the use of algorithmic predictions as a way to speed up or to increase the efficiency of public services, cannot be disentangled from the general phenomenon of algorithmic surveillance, which profoundly affects the sense of identity and individual freedom.

When an individual is subjected to automated decision-making, which determines better or worse chances of well-being, easier or poorer opportunities to find a good job or, in the case of predictive policing, a threat to the presumption of innocence, fair procedures established by law become the fundamental safeguard that cannot be waived.

The challenges faced by predictive policing and more broadly by the criminal justice system should be considered in striking a sustainable balance between the fight against impunity and human self-determination: 'Legum servi sumus, ut liberi esse possimus' (MT Cicerone).

14

Fighting Impunity with New Tools: How Big Data, Algorithms, Machine Learning and AI Shape the New Era of Criminal Justice*

MOJCA M PLESNIČAR, ALEŠ ZAVRŠNIK AND PIKA ŠARF

I. Introduction

The modern belief in technology and its ability to solve humanity's big questions is momentous. The use of technology is one of the most notable trends of the last few years in the attempt to guide and improve decision-making.[1] Technology has come to mean much more than merely the technical details behind the functioning of manufactured objects. Among others, Boyd and Crawford use the word 'mythology' to describe one aspect of the use of technology in the modern world to emphasise 'the widespread belief that large data sets offer a higher form of intelligence and knowledge that can generate insights that were previously impossible, with the aura of truth, objectivity, and accuracy'.[2]

Given the modern criminal justice system's incessant striving for objectivity, it is of little surprise that criminal justice has followed suit – and has begun utilising the emerging technologies in various contexts and various ways. Many of them have been able to improve the system by eliminating or diminishing the administrative burden of criminal justice professionals. This is true for the modern European context of fighting impunity as well. The instantaneous interconnectedness through the use of technology has allowed for more cooperation and a tighter net cast by individual criminal justice systems, thus to an extent

* The research leading to this article has received funding from the European Union's Horizon 2020 research and innovation programme under the Marie-Sklodowska-Curie grant agreement for project "Transmaking" project (no. 734855), and the Slovenian Research Agency, research project "Automated Justice: Social, Ethical and Legal Implications" (no. J5-9347).

[1] V Mayer-Schönberger and K Cukier, *Big Data: A Revolution that Will Transform How We Live, Work, and Think*, 1st edn (Boston, Eamon Dolan/Houghton Mifflin Harcourt, 2013).

[2] D Boyd and K Crawford, 'Critical Questions for Big Data' (2012) 15 *Information, Communication & Society* 662, 663.

preventing criminal cases and blameworthy individuals from escaping justice. Moreover, the globalised nature of modern crime, which is hard or impossible to grasp with traditional criminal justice approaches, may seem more approachable through the use of new and equally global technologies.

Nevertheless, criminal justice systems are fragile environments based on several fundamental principles that are under attack from many different quarters. While promising and potentially beneficial to the system, new technology is one such potential threat. Important considerations about fundamental human rights may and should arise when we discuss their use and implications in criminal justice and in fighting impunity.

In this chapter, we consider how the new tools have already permeated modern criminal justice and how criminal justice is responding, but also how it should be responding and, more importantly, planning ahead if we wish to maintain the values upon which criminal justice is based. The chapter is thus split into three parts. First, we look at the various ways that the new tools have already penetrated criminal justice and how they have so far performed in fighting impunity. Secondly, we address the legal issues surrounding the use of algorithms in criminal justice. Even though many of the areas of human interaction where such new tools are being utilised are delicate and the use of those tools may have tremendous consequences for an individual's life, criminal justice seems to be at the precipice of dangerous and potentially devastating consequences when new approaches are introduced without sufficient forethought and legal scrutiny. We thus finally discuss how the development of such aids may nevertheless be useful and, more importantly, the principles and considerations needed to shape them in order for them to be a useful weapon to fight impunity.

II. Automating Crime Control: The State of Affairs

Big data, coupled with algorithms and machine learning, has become a central theme of intelligence, security, defence, antiterrorist and crime policy efforts.[3] Especially in Anglo-American legal systems, the use of statistical tools for assessing criminality in criminal justice settings is nothing new and has been present for decades.[4] The development we are interested in, which has also been the main development in recent years, is their enhancement with artificial intelligence (AI).[5]

[3] In this chapter, we use the terms 'new tools' and 'automated decision-making systems' (ADMSs) to encapsulate 'big data', 'algorithms', 'machine learning' and 'artificial intelligence'. Each of these notions is highly contested and deserves a separate discussion, but a detailed analysis of the tools is not central to identifying the social and legal implications of automation of crime control, which is the primary topic of this chapter.

[4] Office of the Assistant Attorney General, 'The Promise and Danger of Data Analytics in Sentencing and Corrections Policy' (29 July 2014) www.justice.gov/sites/default/files/criminal/legacy/2014/08/01/2014annual-letter-final-072814.pdf.

[5] BE Harcourt, 'Risk as a Proxy for Race' (2015) 4 *Federal Sentencing Reporter* 237.

Other countries are also flirting with these systems for several competing reasons: to shrink budgets, to increase legitimacy with the veil of objectivity and to address the overload of cases, as well as to fight impunity.

Several stakeholders in the crime and security domain are currently using these new tools: (i) intelligence agencies, as revealed by Edward Snowden in 2013; (ii) law enforcement agencies, which are increasingly using crime prediction software such as PredPol (Santa Cruz, California), Precobs (Zürich, Munich) and Maprevelation (France);[6] (iii) criminal courts and probation commissions predicting recidivism;[7] and (iv) administrative agencies and inspectorates, eg tax and customs authorities, and environmental and food inspection services, which use the new tools to do their work more effectively.[8]

In order to better understand what they promise to do and how they perform, we will try to map out ADMSs in the fight against impunity by looking at (i) policing, (ii) courts and (iii) post-conviction procedures.

A. Predictive Policing

Police uses of machine learning tools are manifold and range from preventive activities to more investigative ones. The police use ADMSs for activities such as finding victims and following money trails to seek culprits. The tools work around the edges: they have the ability not only to focus on the 'penal couple' – the victim and the perpetrator – but can find clues and circumstantial evidence as well. With the new tools, police are (i) penetrating deeply into the preparatory phase of crimes yet to be committed and (ii) able to scrutinise already committed crimes.

With regard to the first, ex ante preventive measures, the automation tools are supposed to excavate plotters of crimes yet to be committed from large amounts of data. While researchers have shown how these can put fundamental liberties in peril, such as the presumption of innocence in pursuing so-called 'sleeping terrorists',[9] the tools may also be used in a human rights compliant manner to effectively reallocate resources and design crime prevention strategies without focusing

[6] D Wilson, 'Algorithmic Patrol: The Futures of Predictive Policing' in A Završnik (ed), *Big Data, Crime and Social Control* (New York, Routledge, 2018) 108–28; AG Ferguson, *The Rise of Big Data Policing: Surveillance, Race, and the Future of Law Enforcement* (New York, NYU Press, 2017); S Egbert, 'About Discursive Storylines and Techno-Fixes: The Political Framing of the Implementation of Predictive Policing in Germany' (2018) 3 *European Journal for Security Research* 95.

[7] BE Harcourt, *Exposed: Desire and Disobedience in the Digital Age* (London, Harvard University Press, 2015); DL Kehl and SA Kessler, 'Algorithms in the Criminal Justice System: Assessing the Use of Risk Assessments in Sentencing' (*DASH*, 2017) dash.harvard.edu/handle/1/33746041.

[8] K Izdebski (ed), 'alGOVrithms – State of Play' (ePaństwo Foundation, 2019) https://epf.org.pl/en/wp-content/uploads/sites/3/2019/05/alGOVrithms-State-of-Play-Report.pdf; M Spielkamp (ed), *Automating Society – Taking Stock of Automated Decision-Making in the EU* (Berlin, AW AlgorithmWatch gGmbH, 2019).

[9] A Završnik, 'Big Data: What Is It and Why It Matters for Crime and Social Control?' in Završnik (n 6) 3–28.

on specific, presumably risky, individuals. A distinction has thus been made between tools focusing on 'risky' individuals ('heat lists' – algorithm-generated lists identifying people most likely to commit a crime)[10] and tools focusing on risky places ('hot spot policing').[11]

With regard to the second, ex post facto uses of machine learning tools, there are many success stories in the fight against human trafficking. One of the challenges prosecutors face in these proceedings is connecting photos on websites (where sex workers or others place adverts for women selling sexual services) to actual escort adverts. The new tools, such as *Traffic Jam*, which detects the subtle differences in decor between chain hotel locations, may be significantly faster and more efficient than traditional investigations.[12] Similarly, Interpol's International Child Sexual Exploitation Image Database can facilitate the identification of victims and perpetrators in sexual child abuse cases through the analysis of, for instance, furniture and other mundane items in the background of abusive images.[13]

Chatbots acting as real people are another advancement in the fight against grooming and webcam sex tourism. In Europe, the Dutch children's rights organisation Terre des Hommes was the first non-governmental organisation to combat webcam child sex tourism by using a virtual character called 'Sweetie'.[14] The Sweetie avatar, posing as a ten-year-old Filipino girl, was used to identify offenders in chatrooms and online forums, and was operated by an agent of the organisation, whose goal was to gather information on individuals who contacted Sweetie and solicited webcam sex. While the chatbot triggers several legal repercussions in the field of substantive criminal law (eg whether the case of contacting the Sweetie avatar is punishable or not as an 'inappropriate attempt')[15] and criminal procedure (eg in which cases can the police use of such an avatar be considered 'entrapment'?),[16] it has an undisputable preventive role.

[10] J Gorner, 'Chicago Police Use "Heat List" to Prevent Violence' (*The Chicago Tribune*, 23 August 2013) www.policeone.com/chiefs-sheriffs/articles/6403037-Chicago-police-use-heat-list-to-prevent-violence/.

[11] For a successful use of the latter, see C Kadar, R Maculan, S Feuerriegel, 'Public Decision Support for Low Population Density Areas: An Imbalance-Aware Hyper-Ensemble for Spatio-Temporal Crime Prediction' (2019) 119 *Decision Support Systems* 107.

[12] L Brody, 'How Artificial Intelligence is Tracking Sex Traffickers' (*Medium*, 2019) onezero.medium.com/how-artificial-intelligence-is-tracking-sex-traffickers-276dcc025ecd.

[13] There are several other similar tools being used in a similar context, eg *TraffickCam* (J Huda, 'Snapping a Picture of your Hotel Room Could Help Stop Human Trafficking' (*FoxNews*, 2016) fox2now.com/news/snapping-a-picture-of-your-hotel-room-could-help-stop-human-trafficking) or *XIX* (L Brody, 'How Artificial Intelligence is Tracking Sex Traffickers').

[14] BW Schermer, I Georgieva, S van der Hof and BJ Koops, 'Legal Aspects of Sweetie 2.0' in S van der Hof, I Georgieva, BW Schermer and BJ Koops (eds), *Information Technology and Law Series, vol 31. Sweetie 2.0* (TMC Asser Press, 2016) 1–94.

[15] ibid.

[16] ibid; A Završnik, 'Pridobivanje oseb, mlajših od 15 let, za spolne namene' in D Korošec, K Filipčič and S Zdolšek (eds), *Veliki znanstveni komentar posebnega dela Kazenskega zakonika (KZ-1)* (Uradni List, 2018) 1041–59.

However, some of the proposed uses for crime-preventive purposes are outrageous and directly dangerous in terms of fundamental liberties. The controversial software promising to infer criminality from facial images,[17] for example, illuminated some of the deep-rooted misconceptions about what crime is and how it is defined, prosecuted and adjudicated. The once ridiculed phrenology from the nineteenth century hence entered the twenty-first century in new clothes as 'algorithmic phrenology', which can legitimise and normalise deep-rooted implicit biases about crime.[18] In the near future, further steps along the line of the corporal importance of one's body for crime control are reasonably to be expected: from analysis of walking patterns, posture and face recognition for identification purposes (eg Facebook's *DeepFace* program) to analysis of facial expressions for emotion recognition.

The described types of predictive policing have incited a considerable level of concern among scholars, who have addressed 'the rise of predictive policing'[19] and the 'algorithmic patrol'[20] as the new predominant method of policing that, in turn, affects other methods of policing. Country-specific studies on predictive policing exist in Germany,[21] France,[22] Switzerland[23] and the UK.[24] A common concern is the allure of objectivity, as well as the creative role police still have in producing inputs for automated calculations.

B. Automating Criminal Courts

The new technologies are increasingly being used in the courtroom, whereby mundane and routine work is being reduced. Moreover, human decision-making in courtrooms has long been criticised, and many see technology as a possible solution to the unpredictability and inadequacy of human decision-making. In general, courts use the new ADMSs when assessing the likelihood of something that is relevant to their decision: the defendant's threat of recidivism in sentencing

[17] X Wu and X Zhang, 'Automated Inference on Criminality Using Face Images' (2016) ArXiv abs/1611.04135.

[18] Agüera y Arcas et al, 'Physiognomy's New Clothes' (*Medium*, 2017) https://medium.com/@blaisea/physiognomys-new-clothes-f2d4b59fdd6a.

[19] Ferguson (n 6).

[20] Wilson (n 6).

[21] Egbert (n 6).

[22] C Polloni, 'Police prédictive: la tentation de "dire quel sera le crime de demain"' (*Rue89*, 2015) www.nouvelobs.com/rue89/rue89-police-justice/20150527.RUE9213/police-predictive-la-tentation-de-dire-quel-sera-le-crime-de-demain.html.

[23] C Aebi, 'Evaluation du Systeme de Prediction de Cambriolages Residentiels PRECOBS' (MA Thesis, Université de Lausanne, 2015).

[24] I Stanier, 'Enhancing Intelligence-Led Policing: Law Enforcement's Big Data revolution' in A Bunnik, A Cawley, M Mulqueen and A Zwitter (eds), *Big Data Challenges: Society, Security, Innovation and Ethics* (Palgrave Macmillan UK, 2016).

or parole decisions, or the likelihood of fleeing during criminal proceedings in bail procedures.

The most analysed and discussed examples stem from the USA, which is also where most such software is currently used.[25] A study of 1.36 million pretrial detention cases showed that a computer could predict whether a suspect would flee or reoffend better than a human judge.[26] However, while this data seems very persuasive, it is important to consider that automated decisions may in fact be less just. There will always be additional facts in a particular case that may be unique and go beyond the 40 or so parameters considered by the algorithm in that study, which might crucially determine the outcome of the deliberation process. There is thus the inevitable need for improvements ad infinitum. Moreover, the problem of selective labelling needs to be considered: we see results only for subgroups that are analysed, only for people who were released. Data that we see is data garnered based on our decisions. Furthermore, judges may have a broader set of preferences than the single variables that the algorithm focuses on.[27] Finally, there is the question of what we want to achieve with the ADMSs: minimisation of crime is an important, but not the only, goal in criminal justice – the fairness of the procedure is equally significant.

The second example has been discussed extensively in the literature. In a detailed assessment of the Correctional Offender Management Profiling for Alternative Sanctions (COMPAS) recidivism algorithm aimed at improving bail decisions, ProPublica looked at more than 10,000 criminal defendants in Broward County, Florida, and compared the predicted recidivism rates with the rate that actually occurred over a two-year period. ProPublica discovered that the system is biased against certain groups, as 'The formula was particularly likely to falsely flag black defendants as future criminals, wrongly labelling them this way at almost twice the rate as white defendants'. In forecasting who would reoffend, the algorithm correctly predicted recidivism for black and white defendants at roughly the same rate (59% for white defendants and 63% for black defendants), but made mistakes in very different ways. It misclassified the white and black defendants differently when examined over the two-year follow-up period. The case revealed yet another deficiency as regards the interpretation of algorithmic results and competing notions of fairness that the COMPAS producer Northpointe (now Equivant) and ProPublica were pursuing.[28]

Seemingly less controversially, a significant number of countries are using ADMSs for justice administration, especially for the allocation of cases to judges,

[25] Dewan, S, 'Judges Replacing Conjecture with Formula for Bail' (*New York Times*, 27 June 2015) www.nytimes.com/2015/06/27/us/turning-the-granting-of-bail-into-a-science.html.

[26] J Kleinberg, H Lakkaraju, J Leskovec, J Ludwig and S Mullainathan, 'Human Decisions and Machine Predictions' (2018) 133 *Quarterly Journal of Economics* 237. For more on positive uses, see CR Sunstein, 'Algorithms, Correcting Biases' (2019) 86 *Social Research: An International Quarterly* 499.

[27] Kleinberg et al, 'Human Decisions'.

[28] J Angwin, J Larson, S Mattu and L Kirchner, 'Machine Bias' (Propublica, 23 May 2016) www.propublica.org/article/machine-bias-risk-assessments-in-criminal-sentencing.

eg in Georgia, Poland, Serbia and Slovakia, and other public officials, such as enforcement officers in Serbia. However, while these cases are examples of indirect ADMSs, they may still significantly affect the right to a fair trial. The study alGOVrithms – State of Play[29] showed that none of the four countries using AMDSs for case allocations allow access to the algorithm and/or the source code. Independent monitoring and auditing of ADMSs is not possible, as the systems lack basic transparency. The main concern touches on how random these systems actually are, and whether they allow tinkering and can therefore be 'fooled'. What is even more worrying, ADMSs used for court management purposes are not transparent even for the judges themselves, and even less so for the public.[30]

There are several other ongoing developments touching upon courtroom decision-making. The most well-known successful case of an AI-driven chatbot, known as 'the world's first robot lawyer', was the UK-based *DoNotPay*. It managed to get 160,000 parking tickets in London and New York overturned a few years ago.[31] Several firms in the USA, Estonia, Slovenia, etc provide free legal aid through chatbots and generate legal documents and interactive templates for generating tailored documents (albeit only some of them are employing machine learning, such as Lex Machina or Ravellaw). More controversially, in Estonia, the Ministry of Justice is financing a team to design a 'robot judge' that could adjudicate small claims disputes of less than €7,000.[32]

C. Beyond Courtrooms

At the post-conviction stage, new tools are used in various ways. While predicting the criminal behaviour of prisoners in order to decide which prisoners should be released on parole can be traced to the pre-World War II period and probation agencies have used post-conviction assessments to determine the best supervision and treatment strategies for offenders in an effort to reduce the risk of recidivism,[33] the new tools are furnishing discriminatory effects. A detailed assessment of the COMPAS recidivism algorithm aimed at improving bail decisions revealed yet another deficiency as regards the interpretation of algorithmic results and competing notions of fairness that the COMPAS producer Northpointe and ProPublica were pursuing.[34] While Northpointe was optimising true positives and

[29] Izdebski (n 8).

[30] ibid.

[31] B Barrett, 'Security News This Week: Hero Chatbot Lawyer Overturns 160,000 Parking Tickets' (*Wired*, 7 February 2016) www.wired.com/2016/07/security-news-week-hero-chatbot-lawyer-overturns-160000-parking-tickets/?intcid=inline_amp.

[32] E Niiler, 'Can AI Be a Fair Judge in Court? Estonia Thinks So' (*Wired*, 25 March 2019) www.wired.com/story/can-ai-be-fair-judge-court-estonia-thinks-so/amp?__twitter_impression=true.

[33] Office of the Assistant Attorney General (n 4).

[34] A Chouldechova, 'Fair Prediction with Disparate Impact: A Study of Bias in Recidivism Prediction Instruments' (*arXiv*, 24 October 2016) arxiv.org/abs/1610.07524.

true negatives for black and white defendants, ProPublica was revealing the injustices occurring at the level of false negatives and false positives for the two groups of defendants.[35]

Moreover, automated systems are used in prisons to ascertain the criminogenic needs of offenders, which could be changed through treatment, and to monitor interventions in sentencing procedures.[36] AI is increasingly used in prisons for the automation of security as well as for rehabilitation purposes; for example, the government in England and Wales recently announced new funding for prisoners to be trained in computer coding[37] (similarly in Finland).[38] More controversially, AI tools have also been discussed in the light of alleviating the harms of solitary confinement in US prisons by employing smart assistants as 'confinement companions' for prisoners.

Outside of criminal justice, inspectors and administrative units across the public sector are using ADMSs. While not being crime prevention agencies *stricto sensu*, these agencies can nevertheless impose substantial fines and contribute to crime prevention. They include the use of ADMSs in cases of speed control, choosing batches for conducting controls and inspections and detecting frauds, and uses by securities market regulators and tax administrations. The US Securities and Exchange Commission, for instance, uses data mining to focus more precisely on sectors and companies at risk of engaging in illegal activities. In Hungary, the National Tax Authority uses risk assessment instrument,[39] while in Slovenia, the Financial Administration is using machine learning to detect tax-evasion schemes and tax fraud, and to find errors in tax reports, among other uses. They are also developing mathematical tools for data mining and prediction analysis to find future improvements in the tax system (optimising, modifying and collecting taxes).[40]

The above cases of ADMSs employed in criminal justice settings (and the wider crime control domain) show how the new tools are already being used and are here to stay. They can help in overcoming difficulties in the management of large datasets and extract new meaning from existing police datasets. Moreover, they are able to do so at a global level and allow for justice to be sought for crimes committed by offenders in one part of the world against victims in a completely different part of the world. In criminal proceedings at courts, the ADMSs can facilitate more informed decisions about the future behaviour of suspects, where such

[35] ibid.

[36] Kehl and Kessler (n 7).

[37] A Mari, 'DCMS Announces New Funding for Prison Coding Skills (*Computer Weekly*, 15 March 2019) https://prisonstudies.us14.list-manage.com/track/click?u=cb51806b184b825cd5f587a8a&id=da236c42f8&e=134997c2cd.

[38] A Newcomb, 'Finland is Using Inmates to Help a Start-Up Train Its Artificial Intelligence Algorithms' (*Fortune*, 28 March 2019) http://fortune.com/2019/03/28/finland-prison-inmates-train-ai-artificial-intelligence-algorithms-vainu/.

[39] Izdebski (n 8).

[40] Spielkamp (n 8).

decisions are needed according to existing criminal procedure rules (eg prediction of the risk of a suspect's future reoffending is already a part of pretrial detention decision-making analysis and the ADMS can substantiate the arguments for a decision in one or the other direction). Finally, administrative units across the public sector are increasingly using ADMSs to reallocate their resources more effectively.

In a broader sense, all these implementations allow us to better address the issues of impunity, at the level of discovering, prosecuting and punishing crimes that may otherwise remain untouched by the authorities. However, while we acknowledge some significant benefits of the ADMSs, we believe there has not been enough sober reflection on the downsides of new ADMSs. Hence, in the next section, we continue by outlining some concerns that should be taken into account when (or if) employing ADMSs in the specific stages and procedure of the fight against impunity.

III. The Legal Framework for the Use of Big Data, AI and Algorithms in Criminal Justice Systems

ADMSs entering the criminal justice systems around the globe do not function in a legal vacuum, since they are (or will be in the future) employed in a strictly regulated environment of criminal procedure in which numerous already established caveats apply. The right to a fair trial, including the right to effective participation in the proceedings, the equality of arms and the respect for the adversarial process are cornerstones of human rights protection in a criminal procedure, which have to be respected regardless of the new tools employed.

In this section, we address the encounter of new technologies and human rights guarantees that apply in criminal procedures first by looking into examples from the American context, since predictive tools are already widely used in the criminal justice settings in the USA and consequently the question of constitutionality of such use has already been addressed by their courts. The case of *Loomis v Wisconsin* will serve as an illustrative example of how US courts cope with this question, and we will use the judgment's flawed reasoning as the starting point for our further discussion about the human rights implications of opaque algorithms substituting human decision-making in courtrooms. In the second part of the section, we will turn to the European context and assess algorithmic tools against the background of the comprehensive human rights regime enshrined in the European Convention of Human Rights and the Charter of Fundamental Rights of the European Union. Since ADMSs are currently not used by the European Courts either to support or supplement judicial decision-making, our analysis builds on the examples from the USA, as it is impossible to be certain how ADMSs will be put into practice in Europe at this stage. However, if European countries follow the principles stipulated in the European Ethical Charter on the Use of Artificial Intelligence in Judicial

Systems and their Environment (see section IV below), we can expect that ADMSs employed in courtrooms across Europe will be at least more transparent and subjected to public oversight, which may lead to fairer decisions when compared to the USA.

A. US Law: *Loomis v Wisconsin* and Beyond

In 2013, Eric Loomis was arrested in the aftermath of a drive-by shooting in La Crosse, Wisconsin. Although he first denied any involvement in the shooting, he later pleaded guilty to two less severe charges, for which he was sentenced to six years of imprisonment with five years of extended supervision. In preparation for sentencing, the court relied on the presentence investigation report (PIR), which included the defendant's risk assessment based on the calculation of the COMPAS risk assessment tool. COMPAS identified Loomis as an individual who presented a high risk to society due to a high risk of reoffending.[41] Loomis appealed against the decision of the court. He argued that the use of the COMPAS risk assessment tool in sentencing violated his due process rights, since:

> (1) it violate[d] his right to be sentenced based upon accurate information, in part because the proprietary nature of COMPAS prevent[ed] him from assessing its accuracy; (2) it violate[d] his right to an individualised sentence; and (3) it improperly use[d] gendered assessments in sentencing.[42]

The Supreme Court of Wisconsin rejected Loomis's claims and upheld the decision of the Circuit Court, thereby confirming the constitutionality of risk assessment algorithms in sentencing.[43]

With regard to Loomis's first claim, the Court adjudicated that the defendant had the opportunity to verify and refute the accuracy of the COMPAS risk assessment since he could ensure the accuracy of the information on which the risk assessment was based. The Court thus rejected the defendant's claim that knowledge of the methodology behind COMPAS, which is protected as a trade secret and is therefore not known either by the defendant or by the court, is essential to guarantee his right to be sentenced upon accurate information. However, we find such reasoning of the Court problematic due to at least two reasons. First, the defendant has no insight into how the COMPAS algorithm uses and weights the input data.[44] Secondly, the argument of the court builds on the premise that

[41] *State v Loomis* 881 NW 2d 749 (Wis 2016) 754 (US).

[42] ibid.

[43] IM Beriain, 'Does the Use of Risk Assessments in Sentences Respect the Right to Due Process? A Critical Analysis of the *Wisconsin v Loomis* Ruling' (2018) 17 *Law, Probability and Risk* 45, 46; K Freeman, 'Algorithmic Injustice: How the Wisconsin Supreme Court Failed to Protect Due Process Rights in *State v Loomis*' (2016) 18 *North Carolina Journal of Law & Technology* 75, 89.

[44] See eg our discussion of COMPAS in section II. Freeman, 'Algorithmic Injustice'.

risk assessment is always correct as long as the defendant provides accurate and complete data, yet this presumption itself is inherently misleading.[45]

The Supreme Court also rejected further claims alleged by the defendant. It stated that COMPAS risk assessment is just one of the circumstances that are included in the PIR. Additionally, the Court had the possibility to depart from the proposed algorithmic risk assessment, which provided sufficient possibility to individualise the defendant's criminal sanction. Regarding Loomis's assertions that the risk assessment tool unconstitutionally considers gender as one of the relevant factors, the Court ruled that such use, in fact, serves the purpose of accuracy instead of discrimination, which benefits the entire judicial system. In any event, the defendant failed to prove that the Court actually considered gender when imposing the criminal sanction in the case at hand.[46]

The decision of the Court completely disregards the fact that the accuracy of algorithmic calculations is primarily dependent on the quality of training data, since the algorithmic output only reflects biases originating from the input data ('garbage in/garbage out').[47] In order to eliminate errors and avoid the reproduction of existing biases, first, input data has to be cleaned by either correcting or removing flawed, corrupt, incomplete and inaccurate data; and secondly, the code of the algorithm has to be repeatedly assessed and reprogrammed in the process of model training.[48] The software behind the COMPAS risk assessment algorithm as well as the input data is confidential, which makes it impossible to eliminate or even mitigate potential disparate effects and biases, therefore creating the effect of a black box.[49] The Court, however, did not completely overlook the risks of imposing criminal sanctions based on a secret algorithm since it highlighted some necessary limitations in the use of COMPAS risk assessment as well as issued a series of warnings in order to caution judges not to over-rely on algorithmically produced scores.[50]

US judges are therefore faced with a difficult task: while the use of risk assessment algorithms in sentencing is at least desirable, if not mandatory, their accuracy must nevertheless be assessed and measured in the final decision to comply with the defendant's due process rights. Judges often do not have (and even cannot have) the knowledge necessary to evaluate the accuracy of algorithmic calculations and are therefore susceptible to the effect of automation bias, ie 'the use of automation as a heuristic replacement for vigilant information seeking and

[45] Angwin et al (n 28).

[46] *State v Loomis* (n 41).

[47] S Barocas and AD Selbst, 'Big Data's Disparate Impact' (2016) 104 *California Law Review* 671, 683; D Lehr and P Ohm, 'Playing with the Data: What Legal Scholars Should Learn about Machine Learning' (2017) 51 *University of California, Davis Law Review* 653, 656.

[48] Lehr and Ohm, 'Playing with the Data.'

[49] See generally F Pasquale, *The Black Box Society: The Secret Algorithms that Control Money and Information* (Cambridge, MA, Harvard University Press, 2015); D Keats Citron and F Pasquale, 'The Scored Society: Due Process for Automated Predictions' (2014) 89 *Washington Law Review* 1.

[50] *State v Loomis* (n 41).

processing'.[51] Decision-makers, including judges, often rely too heavily on or attribute greater weight to computer-generated decisions and calculations, even if they know they could be inaccurate, incomplete or even completely wrong.[52]

Loomis is not the only case in which a US court had to address the tension between due process rights on the one hand and the secrecy surrounding the governmental use of proprietary algorithmic tools on the other. However, the decisions of two other courts adjudicating on the issue were inherently different from the decision reached by the Supreme Court of Wisconsin in *Loomis*. The first case concerned the constitutionality of a value-added statistical model (Education Value-Added Assessment System, EVAAS) used to measure teachers' effectiveness, which could form the basis for the termination of their employment.[53] Plaintiffs argued, inter alia, that the use of a proprietary algorithm violated their 'procedural due process right, due to lack of sufficient information to meaningfully challenge terminations based on low EVAAS scores'. The District Court in Houston concurred. Although the teachers were provided with some information about EVAAS, the limited information provided was not enough to replicate the teachers' scores, which would, without access to the proprietary information, remain a black box.

Similarly, a court in Idaho decided that the Idaho Department of Health and Welfare violated due process rights of individuals with developmental disabilities by decreasing individuals' budgets provided for Medicaid assistance based on a secret calculation of the Adult Budget Calculation Tool.[54] Therefore, it is far from clear whether the application of a secret algorithm in decision-making processes would in general present a violation of due process rights and the decision of the court depends on the circumstances of each individual case.

B. EU Law

Although none of the EU Member States' judicial systems are currently using algorithms as tools either to support or to entirely substitute human decision-making, it is undeniable that judicial systems in Europe are undergoing a digital transformation in order to improve their performance and efficiency.[55] The application of information and communication technology in judicial processes has

[51] KL Mosier, LJ Skitka, S Heers and M Burdick, 'Automation Bias: Decision Making and Performance in High-Tech Cockpits' (1997) 8 *International Journal of Aviation Psychology* 47, 47.

[52] Freeman (n 43).

[53] *Houston Federation of Teachers v Houston Independent School District* 251 F Supp 3d 1168 (SD Tex 2017). Only a summary judgment was reached in the case, since the parties settled their dispute before the Court had the opportunity to adjudicate on the merits.

[54] *KW v Armstrong* 180 F Supp 3d 703 (D Idaho, 28 March 2016). For more on the case and eventual settlement see ACLU Idaho, *KW v Armstrong* (2016) www.acluidaho.org/en/cases/kw-v-armstrong.

[55] European Commission for the Efficiency of Justice (CEPEJ), Guidelines on How to Drive Change Towards Cyberjustice (Strasbourg 2016) para 1 https://rm.coe.int/16807482de.

enabled more effective case management, availability of case law through online search engines, online dispute resolution mechanisms, advanced legal analytic tools, and faster and easier communication between all parties involved.[56] Above all, the digital environment is producing the data that is necessary to fuel further development of the predictive ability of algorithmic tools. Risk assessment algorithms are currently widely used by the private sector (eg insurance companies, legal departments and law firms).[57] On the other hand, EU countries are much more reluctant to introduce such tools in judicial processes, but at a time when numerous Member States are facing substantial case backlogs due to an increasing number of cases pending before their courts, this idea seems more and more appealing. Before introducing algorithms in any decision-making process, let alone in criminal procedures, it is essential to ensure compliance with fundamental human rights enshrined in the European Convention on Human Rights (ECHR)[58] and the Charter of Fundamental Rights of the European Union (the Charter),[59] as well as with the relevant data protection law.

Since no court in the EU or within the Council of Europe (CoE) has ever addressed the question of the legality of algorithmic tools in criminal justice systems, it is uncertain whether their use could be compatible with the guarantees of fair trial provided in Article 6 ECHR and Article 47 of the Charter, particularly with the right to participate effectively in the trial and respect for adversarial process, and under what circumstances and limitations.[60] Article 6 ECHR guarantees the accused a right to participate effectively in the trial. The right to effective participation may be violated in a variety of different situations, ranging from poor acoustics in the courtroom[61] to preventing the accused to be present at the trial or to examine a witness testifying against him.[62] The latter is also one of the minimal guarantees of fair trial contained in Article 6(3) ECHR and normally requires that all evidence against the accused is produced in his presence at a public hearing, which gives the defendant an effective opportunity to challenge the evidence against him.[63] The right to confrontation does not apply only to witnesses, as the term is usually understood under national law, since it has an autonomous

[56] ibid Pt 1.

[57] CEPEJ, European Ethical Charter on the Use of Artificial Intelligence in Judicial Systems and their Environment (Strasbourg 2018) 14 https://rm.coe.int/ethical-charter-en-for-publication-4-december-2018/16808f699c.

[58] Convention for the Protection of Human Rights and Fundamental Freedoms (European Convention on Human Rights, as amended) (ECHR).

[59] Charter of Fundamental Rights of the European Union [2012] OJ C326/391.

[60] Some authors argue that the use of algorithmic tools in criminal procedure could also violate some other aspects of the right to fair trial, in particular the right to a natural judge, the right to an independent and impartial tribunal, presumption of innocence and equality of arms; however, we cannot agree with this contention.

[61] *Stanford v the United Kingdom* Series App no 16757/90 (ECHR 11 April 1994).

[62] *Hermi v Italy* App no 18114/02 (ECHR 18 October 2006).

[63] *Al-Khawaja and Tahery v United Kingdom* App nos 26766/05, 2228/06 (ECHR 15 December 2011); *Asani v the former Yugoslav Republic of Macedonia* App no 27962/10 (ECHR 1 February 2018).

meaning in the Convention system that goes beyond its ordinary meaning and also includes experts, expert witnesses and victims. In any case in which the deposition serves to a material degree as the basis for a conviction of the defendant, it constitutes evidence for the prosecution to which the Convention guarantees apply.[64] The right enshrined in Article 6(3)(d) can even be applied to documentary evidence[65] and computer files[66] relevant to the criminal accusations against the defendant. Therefore, in order to ensure effective participation in a trial, the defendant must also be able to challenge the algorithmic score that is the basis of his conviction.

However, the right to confrontation is not absolute and may be restricted if certain conditions are met. The traditional approach of the European Court of Human Rights was that the right to a fair trial is violated if a conviction is based solely or to a decisive degree on an uncontested statement ('sole or decisive rule').[67] However, in *Al Khawaja and Tahery*, the European Court of Human Rights partially departed from its previous jurisprudence, stating that the admission of untested evidence will not automatically result in a breach of Article 6(1) ECHR. When assessing the overall fairness of the trial, the court has to take into account whether it was necessary to admit such evidence and whether there were sufficient counterbalancing factors, including strong procedural safeguards.[68]

The problems posed by black-box algorithms are very similar to those presented by anonymous witnesses or undisclosed documentary evidence – although the situations are not identical, they both endanger the right to a fair trial, and in a very similar way. In both cases, the ability of the defence to discredit either a testimony or an algorithmic assessment is thwarted since the defence inevitably lacks the necessary information to be able to do so. At least some degree of disclosure is necessary in order to ensure that the defendant has the opportunity to challenge the evidence against him and to counterbalance the burden of anonymity. Absent or anonymous witnesses, although not incompatible with the right to a fair trial per se, can only participate in a criminal procedure as a measure of last resort and under strict conditions ensuring that the defendant is not placed at a disadvantage. If we apply the same *ratio* and assess the potential violation of the right to participate effectively in the trial due to the use of algorithmic tools in criminal proceedings through the prism of balance between the effects resulting from the opacity of the algorithm and the reasons for limiting the defendant's right, we can conclude that judgment based on a calculation produced by a proprietary algorithm (such as the COMPAS risk assessment tool used in the *Loomis* case) would constitute a violation of the right to a fair trial.

[64] *Luca v Italy* App no 33354/96 (ECHR 27 February 2001).
[65] *Mirilashvili v Russia* App no 6293/04 (ECHR 11 December 2008).
[66] *Georgios Papageorgiou v* Greece App no 59506/00 (9 May 2003).
[67] *Doorson v the Netherlands* App no 20524/92 (ECHR 26 March 1996).
[68] *Al-Khawaja and Tahery v United Kingdom* (n 63).

IV. How should Technologies be Shaped?

Whenever a new technology is introduced into a working system, it should be obvious that important action is required much before that actually happens. This is even more essential when introducing technologies that are still under development and not very well understood by non-professionals or even professionals. Authors refer to this conundrum as the 'pacing problem', or the problem of regulatory connection, pointing towards the asynchronicity between the accelerating development of technology and the slowness of regulatory action.[69]

Artificial intelligence as a whole is emblematic of this. It appears that much of the needed considerations were not addressed before the introduction of algorithm-based decision-making in the US courts. In contrast, European countries have shown much more restraint, scepticism and prudence in these matters. However, striking the right balance between being too welcoming and too restrictive towards innovation is a hard task that the literature addresses as the 'uncertainty paradox', or the Collingridge dilemma.[70] The impasse Collingridge explained is between the potentially stifling effect that overzealous regulation might have on the development of (promising) technology on the one hand, and the ineffectiveness of regulation that comes into force too late – when the technology is already ingrained in everyday life – on the other hand.[71]

There are two basic approaches to overcome this issue. The first, the precautionary principle, advises against using any innovation that could cause significant damage until it is proven to be safe.[72] The second, principles-based regulation, proposes renouncing precise rules on technology and replacing them with broad guiding principles that would frame the acceptable development and use of any newly developed technology.[73]

It is rather obvious that banning AI in general until it is proven to be harmless is not attainable in a modern society already permeated (and often aided) by AI. However, the discussion might be different if limited to a specific field, such as the law, or, even more specifically, criminal law, and some authors have indeed

[69] M Fenwich, EPM Vermeulen and W Kaal, 'Regulation Tomorrow: Or, What Happens When Technology Is Faster Than the Law? (2017) 6 *American University Business Law Review* 561; A Butenko and P Larouche, 'Regulation for Innovativeness or Regulation of Innovation?' (2015) 7 *Law, Innovation & Technology* 52.

[70] D Collingridge, *The Social Control of Technology* (Frances Pinter, 1980); Butenko and Larouche, 'Regulation for Innovativeness or Regulation of Innovation?'

[71] Collingridge, *The Social Control of Technology.*

[72] Butenko and Larouche (n 69).

[73] GE Marchant, 'The Growing Gap between Emerging Technologies and the Law', in GE Marchant, BR Allenby and JR Herkert (eds), *The Growing Gap between Emerging Technologies and Legal-Ethical Oversight: The Pacing Problem* (Amsterdam, Springer Netherlands, 2011) 19–33; WA Kaal, 'Dynamic Regulation for Innovation' in M Fenwick, WA Kaal, T Kono and EPM Vermeulen (eds), *Perspectives in Law, Business & Innovation* (Rochester, NY, Springer, 2016).

suggested that perhaps stopping before it is too late might be the better option.[74] However, the latter option of setting overarching principles seems a more attainable one, and it is indeed one of the approaches taken by various institutions towards regulating AI in general[75] and in criminal justice more specifically.[76]

The European Commission for the Efficiency of Justice (CEPEJ), working within the CoE, has recently adopted one such pioneering document, the European Ethical Charter on the Use of Artificial Intelligence in Judicial Systems and their Environment[77] (AI Charter), following a detailed study on the matter in its appendices. The main premise of the AI Charter, with which we find it hard not to agree, could be summarised as realising that AI is likely to be unavoidable in the future, but that we need to be very selective as to what tools and where we allow it in justice systems.

The study adjoining the AI Charter rightly sees the area of criminal justice as an especially delicate one. In fact, the use of predictive tools in criminal justice is one of the areas where use should be considered with the most reservations.[78] The opportunity for misuse on the one hand and the consequences of such misuse on the other hand both seem too serious to be worth experimenting with.

Regardless, the CEPEJ has adopted five core principles to guide development and implementation in all areas of delivering justice, including criminal justice:

- The *principle of respect of fundamental rights* entails ensuring that both the design and implementation of artificial intelligence tools and services are compatible with fundamental rights.
- The *principle of non-discrimination* aims at specifically preventing the development or intensification of any discrimination between individuals or groups of individuals.
- The *principle of quality and security* demands the use of certified sources and intangible data with models conceived in a multi-disciplinary manner, in a secure technological environment.
- The *principle of transparency, impartiality and fairness* requires making data processing methods accessible and understandable, and authorising external audits.
- Finally, the *principle 'under user control'* precludes a prescriptive approach and ensures that users are informed actors and in control of their choices.

[74] F Contini, 'Rethinking Judiciaries: Dilemmas and Challenges for Practitioners and Researchers' (2019) in Linking Generations for Global Justice Congress Program, www.iisj.net/sites/default/files/190618_final_programme.pdf.

[75] See,eg the new OECD principles on AI: OECD, 'Recommendation of the Council on Artificial Intelligence' (2019) OECD/LEGAL/0449.

[76] CEPEJ, 'European Ethical Charter on the Use of Artificial Intelligence in Judicial Systems and Their Environment' (2018).

[77] ibid.

[78] ibid Appendix II.

These principles are sound and reasonable, and portray a thoughtful approach to introducing these new tools in various aspects of delivering justice. However, as principles, they perform at a very abstract level, and we will undoubtedly come across very practical dilemmas they are unable to resolve. We wish to briefly consider some of those issues in the following paragraphs.

The principle of transparency, impartiality and fairness may be at odds with the current state of development of such tools. Machine learning and algorithmic modelling are matters that are hard to understand for non-professionals, but, more importantly, their best performing variants work as black boxes, with data coming in and decisions coming out, but with no real easy insight into why and how that happens, as we have seen in the *Loomis* case discussed above. Things get even more complex with the concept of deep learning, using artificial neural networks. It is clear that further developments might improve the opacity of present-day algorithms and technologies, but for the time being, transparency is not much more than an illusion.[79]

Moreover, this principle is directly tied to the question of validity and verification. We believe that, even in cases where the new tools are already being used today, these issues have not been resolved satisfactorily. EPIC (a public interest research centre) gives a good visualisation of what the state of validation is in the USA.[80] It reports that out of the 50 states using different types of predictive algorithms, only 10 have conducted validity studies. Companies marketing such models do offer assurances about their robustness, but typically choose not to make them thoroughly transparent.[81] Even if tested by their authors, the robustness and performance they are looking for in the algorithm may not be the one most conducive to justice, as explained in the second part of this chapter. We acknowledge that the precaution of stringent validation and verification is counterproductive in a world where development is driven by profit. Moreover, development in the field of the new technologies we are discussing is often incremental, building upon previous (less than satisfactory) versions and ideas. However, the field of criminal justice seems too delicate to allow for much room for a trial-and-error approach.

Finally, the principles of transparency, impartiality and fairness may also be addressing another crucial issue at hand. So far, European criminal justice has, for the most part, escaped the privatisation trend ongoing in the USA and other parts

[79] W Samek, T Wiegand and KR Müller, 'Explainable Artificial Intelligence: Understanding, Visualizing and Interpreting Deep Learning Models' (2017) arXiv:1708.08296 [cs.AI]; R Goebel et al., 'Explainable AI: The New 42?', in Machine Learning and Knowledge Extraction (Hamburg, 2018) 295–303.

[80] EPIC, 'Algorithms in the Criminal Justice System' https://epic.org/algorithmic-transparency/crim-justice/.

[81] N Diakopoulos, 'Algorithmic Accountability Reporting: On the Investigation of Black Boxes' (Columbia Journalism School, Tow Centre for Digital Journalism, 2014) http://towcenter.org/wp-content/uploads/2014/02/78524_Tow-Center-Report-WEB-1.pdf. Such was the above-mentioned case of ProPublica reporting on COMPAS's performance.

of the world. Private prisons, for example, and other privatisation initiatives are largely not mainstream in the European context (with the exception of England and Wales). The development of the new tools might change this dynamic, as knowledge and experience will most likely be concentrated in private hands. It seems necessary, however, to consider the consequences of entering into such partnerships and the potentially clashing interests of all those involved.

Furthermore, we find that the principle 'under user control' is an absolutely necessary and worthwhile cause, but is perhaps not aligned with the reality of decision-making. It is hard to imagine any judge countering an AI-suggested decision more than once if, the first time they do so, the public determines that their decision was wrong and the AI-suggested decision was right.[82]

V. Conclusion

As we have seen, there are potentially significant benefits to the use of new tools in criminal justice. Academics have been criticising various criminal justice systems for decades, and some of the solutions seem to be within reach if only we would entrust decisions to machines instead of humans. Our society's general lack of trust in criminal justice systems[83] fits very nicely in the new rhetoric of improvement-by-algorithms.

Despite writing that tongue-in-cheek, we genuinely believe there is room for improvement that might someday be filled by new technologies. We believe that new technologies might sometime in the future help humans make not just quicker, but also better decisions in all or at least some aspects of criminal justice decision-making. With regard to our overarching topic of impunity, new technologies might indeed help future police, prosecution and courts to make better decisions, allowing them to significantly address and diminish impunity in ways that today seem unfeasible. In fact, in some instances, especially at the level of policing and focusing on prosecution in international investigations, some of those tools are already achieving that.

When looking at the fight against impunity as a process that encompasses all levels of criminal justice, it becomes clear that stopping at the level of policing is not enough. Overcoming impunity means improving not only the detection, but also the prosecution, the adjudication and the subsequent punishment of offenders.

[82] Consider the example of Massachusetts governor Michael Dukakis and his failed presidential campaign in 1988 – among others reasons, the result of outrage after one of the offenders he had released from prison on furlough committed a new crime after not returning from his weekend furlough. See eg DC Anderson, *Crime and the Politics of Hysteria: How the Willie Horton Story Changed American Justice* (New York, Crown, 1995).

[83] As seen through various emanations in different systems – eg the 'Black Lives Matter' movement in the USA, the backlash after the 'La manada' case in Spain, low scores in public trust measurements in Slovenia, etc.

If the new tools were indeed able to offer us fairer decisions in all stages of criminal justice decision-making, impunity might become a more achievable aim.

However, we firmly believe that contemporary warnings about the lack of transparency, lack of accuracy, ingrained bias, etc of these new technologies should not be overlooked as mere Luddites' outcries, but carefully studied and considered. Moreover, just understanding the limitations of new technology is no longer enough – we need to be able to convey those limitations to decision-makers in a manner that is understandable and accentuates the weight of the decision to use or not use them in criminal justice.

As ever, it is tempting to overlook today's problems because we are gazing into tomorrow's solutions. It is also, as ever, wrong. We thus believe that there is still a rather long way to go until the discussed new tools will actually be an aid in fighting impunity, and we believe we should not be rushing on this way.

PART E

The Fight against Impunity and the External Dimension of the AFSJ

15

International Fight against Impunity and EU Counter-Terrorism Law: The Case of Foreign Terrorist Fighters

ERMIONI XANTHOPOULOU AND THEODORE KONSTADINIDES

I. Introduction

The criminalisation of preparatory acts of terrorism is a relatively recent phenomenon, which has become more prominent with the rise of foreign fighters on the continent.[1] The question of how to deal with returning terrorist fighters (commonly referred to as Foreign Terrorist Fighters, or FTFs) has been pertinent since Daesh declared the creation of a 'caliphate' in Syria in 2014 and encouraged supporters to travel to the region.[2] The criminalisation of travelling, a conduct that would not otherwise be illegal if it was not accompanied with a criminal intention, forms the most current example of the international fight against impunity in relation to terrorism. This is a delicate area not the least because, inter alia, it is challenging to prove the terrorist purpose of the travel in question, but also because it is hard to decide who to prosecute, ie whether to draw a line between those travelling abroad for terrorist purposes and those who facilitate or organise such travel.

The EU framework of legal developments pertaining to FTFs is important because it has legitimised the expansion of the criminalisation scope to an otherwise innocent *actus reus*: namely, visiting a third state to join a terrorist group and/

[1] For a history of foreign fighters going back 1000 years, see D Malet, *Foreign Fighters* (Oxford, Oxford University Press, 2013). See also E Schmitt and S Sengupta, 'Thousands Enter Syria to Join ISIS Despite Global Efforts' (*New York Times*, 26 September 2015) www.nytimes.com/2015/09/27/world/middleeast/thousands-enter-syria-to-join-isis-despite-global-efforts.html.

[2] FTFs have been defined as 'individuals, driven mainly by ideology, religion and/or kinship, who leave their country of origin or their country of habitual residence to join a party engaged in an armed conflict': A de Guttry, F Capone and C Paulussen, 'Introduction' in A de Guttry, F Capone and C Paulussen (eds), *Foreign Fighters under International Law and Beyond* (The Hague, TMC Asser Press/Springer Verlag, 2016) 2.

or returning to the EU with the aim of carrying out a terrorist attack. EU criminal legislation in the field reveals the urgency of dealing with FTF conduct that for long has remained unpunished and unaddressed. In particular, Directive 2017/541 on combating terrorism confronts the FTFs issue with regard to the security threat that such mobility might pose to the Member States.[3] It does so by updating the EU legal framework and extending the list of preparatory acts and behaviours to be criminalised.[4]

This chapter does not provide an overview or a holistic analysis of the EU's revised legal framework on combating terrorism; rather, it focuses on the criminalisation of travel as a prima facie example of the expansion in the context of contemporary counter-terrorism frameworks. Its aim is twofold: first, to help the reader understand why, in light of the seriousness of the threat and the need to stem the flow of FTFs, criminalising a neutral concept such as travel is preferable to previous approaches of criminalising terrorism offences or softer national responses. Given the degree of elusiveness of the threat under study, we argue that the risk of FTF impunity challenges the limits of what constitutes a public wrong that leads to harm.[5] Accordingly, FTF impunity pushes the boundaries of criminalisation further as a preventive response to impunity. In particular, it is argued that EU harmonisation of criminalisation of FTF-related offences manifests itself as pre-crime and precautionary criminalisation (ie prosecution for preparatory acts in the absence of a link to a specific terrorist act) for the purpose of preventive justice.[6] Secondly, beyond deciphering the justification pertaining to the criminalisation of travel, we wish, through comparison, to familiarise the reader with the scope and limits of external influences to the EU's legal response. This is especially so since EU secondary legislation concerning FTFs has implemented

[3] Directive (EU) 2017/541 of the European Parliament and the Council on combating terrorism and replacing Council Framework Decision 2002/475/JHA and amending Council Decision 2005/671/JHA [2017] OJ L88/6.

[4] In order to prevent terrorist attacks and eliminate the impunity of conducts that closely relate to them, Directive 2017/541 expands criminalisation in several directions with a view to widening the scope of terrorism offences. It does not limit itself to the criminalisation of traveling: according to the revised legal framework, training or being trained as a terrorist and providing or collecting funds with the intention that terrorist offences, offences related to terrorist groups or terrorist activities will be committed, now constitute criminal acts. It also creates, in Art 5, the offence of the public provocation to commit a crime by distributing, whether online or offline, a message with the intent to incite the commission of a terrorist offence, such as by glorifying terrorist acts.

[5] J Child and D Ormerod, *Essentials of Criminal* Law (Oxford, Oxford University Press, 2017) ch 1; more generally, see J Horder, 'Harmless Wrongdoing and the Anticipatory Perspective on Criminalisation' in GR Sullivan and I Dennis (eds), *Seeking Security: Pre-empting the Commission of Criminal Harms* (Oxford, Hart Publishing, 2012); A Duff, *Answering for Crime* (Oxford, Hart Publishing, 2007).

[6] See J McCulloch and S Pickering, 'Pre-crime and Counter-terrorism: Imagining Future Crime in the War on Terror' (2009) 49 *British Journal of Criminology* 628. The authors define 'pre-crime' as follows: 'Pre-crime links coercive state actions to suspicion without the need for charge, prosecution or conviction. It also includes measures that expand the remit of the criminal law to include activities or associations that are deemed to precede the substantive offence targeted for prevention.' See also V Mitsilegas, 'From Overcriminalisation to Decriminalisation. The Many Faces of Effectiveness in European Criminal Law' (2014) 5 *New Journal of European Criminal Law* 415.

key international legal standards at the EU level.[7] What is also important in this regard is to increase awareness about the extent to which the EU's FTF agenda is in synchrony with the relevant constitutional safeguards stemming from regional and international human rights instruments with regard to traveller risk assessment, profiling and the right to a fair trial.

The methodology the chapter uses is doctrinal and comparative. First, it observes and analyses the relevant international legal responses pertaining to FTF impunity. It then compares them in order to highlight convergences and divergences in relation to the terminology used to demarcate the scope of criminalisation of FTFs. The analysis is based on principles of criminal and EU constitutional law, and is framed as 'convergences' and 'divergences' in a global approach. While the EU legal order is influenced by external initiatives that frame the choices of pre-crime and precautionary criminalisation by setting out minimum definitions of criminal offences, the chapter locates a number of shortcomings in this approach.

Overall, it is argued that the extension of criminalisation to a highly disputed and hardly verifiable conduct constitutes a quick-fix and rather repressive response to the fight against impunity in the specific area of FTFs. Pre-crime criminalisation towards FTFs does not fully take into account the specific characteristics of domestic legal systems regarding investigation, prosecution and punishment in the Member States. Instead, it renders counter-terrorism laws more susceptible to being ratcheted up to oppression by certain national governments that may relish the opportunity to impose draconian punishments against suspects (not merely their own nationals and residents). Such an approach may in turn have serious repercussions for the observance of the rule of law in the EU and may give rise to new areas of FTF impunity pertaining to international crimes.

II. International Fight against Foreign Terrorist Fighters at Different Levels of Governance

It is well known that effective cooperation in the fight against impunity regarding terrorist offences is in global demand. Indeed, rarely has the fight against impunity been so dynamic. Not only does the threat of contemporary terrorism cross borders faster than at any other time in history, but also spontaneous domestic legal responses were soon seen as insufficient to contain it.[8] The latter explains why terrorism and other related offences present impunity challenges. As such,

[7] This has been noted during discussions about amending the Framework Decision on Terrorism, taking stock of the phenomenon of FTFs and recent international developments such as the adoption of UNSC Resolution 2178 in 2014 and the Council of Europe Additional Protocol to the Convention on the prevention of terrorism from 2015.

[8] VV Ramraj, M Hor, K Roach and G Williams, *Global Anti-terrorism Law and Policy* (2nd edn, Cambridge, Cambridge University Press, 2012).

the way the threat has been addressed since the first wave of global-scale terrorist attacks such as 9/11 has been within the auspices of transnational regimes such as the EU or the UN.

While the above is true, we shall not forget that Member States have the primary responsibility for counter-terrorism, with international organisations playing a supporting role in view of the cross-border nature of the threat. In the context of FTFs, domestic sanctions include the deprivation of citizenship and other administrative measures suspending persons' freedom to leave their state. As such, beyond looking at the strength of international or regional coordinated responses and cooperation, it is important to examine the extent to which such concerted efforts have led to what has been described as 'constitutional migrations of norms'.[9] International organisations need to be able to square the competing interests of combating terrorism while respecting constitutional safeguards at different levels of governance.

A. Initiatives at the UN Security Council Level against FTF Impunity

The trend towards anticipating risks as a driving response in international counter-terrorism law was first identified by the UN Security Council. Not only did the Security Council recognise the growing threat posed by FTFs, but it also called on all UN Member States to take measures at preventing the flow of FTFs to conflict zones. UN Security Council Resolution (UNSCR) 2178 (2014) defines FTFs as

> individuals who travel to a State other than their States of residence or nationality for the purpose of the perpetration, planning, or preparation of, or participation in, terrorist acts or the providing or receiving terrorist training, including in connection with armed conflict.

It calls for the adoption of wide-ranging measures against FTFs, while at the same time its scope of application extends beyond fighters who travel to join 'terrorist groups'. The reference 'including in connection with armed conflict' somewhat blurs the demarcating line that divides terrorism from armed conflict, which is governed by a distinct body of law altogether.[10]

Despite definitional semantics, UNSCR 2178 echoes the spirit of UNSCR 1373, which was adopted after 9/11, in the sense that it forms part of the UN's concerted effort to adopt a quasi-legislative role by mandating UN Member States to bring

[9] F Fabbrini and VC Jackson (eds), *Constitutionalism across Borders in the Struggle Against Terrorism* (Cheltenham, Edward Elgar Publishing, 2016) 101–90. The authors use this term to refer to the paradigm transfers in legally addressing the harm and risk that is posed by terrorism. Constitutional migrations across the globe stem from the global character of the danger, the commonality of the values that are threatened and the comparable regulatory challenges to states that aim to secure constitutional freedoms but also the efficiency of counter-terrorism policies.

[10] Resolution 2178 (2014) of 24 September 2014.

to justice those planning or perpetrating terrorist acts.[11] It was adopted under Chapter VII of the UN Charter and is therefore binding upon UN Member States. It also enjoys primacy in relation to any other international agreement in accordance with Article 103 of the UN Charter. In this dispensation, the UNSC seems to be addressing not only the foreign fighters' conduct in the context of armed conflict, but also the terrorist risk those fighters pose when returning home – in other words, to use the Preamble's wording, 'terrorism in all forms and manifestations'. As such, with Resolution 2178, the UNSC abstains from its previous piecemeal approach in relation to terrorism, which, despite disagreements about a common definition of terrorism, achieved some success in bringing the international community together against crimes linked to terrorism.[12]

UNSCR 2178 followed up two previous Resolutions[13] in which the threat of FTFs was recognised, as well as the duty of the participating states in preventing and suppressing the flow of terrorists. Along the same lines, Resolution 2195 (2014)[14] reiterated that participating states should prevent the movement of terrorists or terrorist groups. Effective border controls should be used to achieve this goal. Following the 2015 Charlie Hebdo terrorist attacks in Paris, the global calls for securitisation were strengthened, in a spirit of emergency and renewed panic. As a response, UNSCR 2249 (2015)[15] reaffirmed previous Resolutions and urged UN Member States to intensify their efforts to stem the flow of FTFs to Iraq and Syria, to prevent and suppress the financing of terrorism, and to implement previous Resolutions. As argued, with respect to UNSC Resolution 2178, the above Resolutions encourage a broad reading of the term FTF by the respective UN Member States which goes beyond the field of international terrorism (as defined by UNSCR 1566), which falls under the purview of the UN. This approach is somewhat reminiscent of the UNSCR 1373 system, which became a legal basis for counter-terrorism beyond any foreseeable duration of the crisis following the events of 9/11.

Additional to the UN's quasi-legislative function and the broad and permanent character of the above measures, another issue that crops up relates to the potential abuse by certain UN Member States of their new legal obligations stemming from UNSCR 2178. An area which merits particular attention is the lack of restraint insofar as the wideness of definition of the categories of perpetrators who are deemed to be 'terrorists' according to a UN Member State is concerned. This is especially important for the principle of legality, in that prosecution and

[11] See also how UNSCR 1390 (2002) broadened the temporary smart sanctions system against the leaders of the Taliban into a permanent global terrorist list of Al-Qaida and Taliban terrorists.

[12] See A Gioia, 'The UN Conventions on the Prevention and Suppression of International Terrorism' in G Nesi (ed), *International Cooperation in Counter-terrorism: The United Nations and Regional Organizations in the Fight against Terrorism* (Farnham, Ashgate Publishing, 2006).

[13] Resolution 1373 (2001) of 28 September 2001; Resolution 2170 (2014) of 15 August 2014.

[14] Resolution 2195 re: cutting the illicit financial resources of the so-called Islamic State (ISIL) (2014) of 19 December 2014.

[15] Resolution 2249 (2015) of 20 November 2015, point 6.

sanction should take place in a manner which duly reflects the seriousness of the offence. In particular, the broad wording of UNSCR 2178 carries the dangerous potential of being hijacked by certain oppressive governments in order to target organised (peaceful) campaigns by political groups, religious organisations, indigenous groups and refugees, and to adopt restrictive measures against travelling, training and funding.

Last but not least, perhaps a more symbolic than substantive point pertains to the fact that the UNSCR 2178 does not refer to the UN's own compliance with human rights in its efforts to counter-terrorism.[16] Instead, it reaffirms in its Preamble that it is the Member States that 'must ensure that any measures taken to counter-terrorism comply with all their obligations under international law, in particular international human rights law', and 'that respect for human rights, fundamental freedoms and the rule of law are complementary and mutually reinforcing with effective counter-terrorism measures …' Such commitment from the part of the UN Member States, however, does not dovetail with the language of the Resolution, which, as mentioned, has the potential to give credibility to gross fundamental rights violations in the name of counter-terrorism and the phenomenon of FTFs.

Against the view that national laws are more susceptible to being ratcheted up to new levels of oppression as a result of UNSCR 2178, some commentators argue that the actual problem with the Resolution lies elsewhere. While its proneness for abuse is a legitimate concern, it has been argued that the problem is located in the failure of UN Member States to 'implement its dictates – stemming from both lack of political will and capability'. As such, it has been submitted that Member States should put their resources on more relative gains, such as preventing violent extremism – a smaller aspect of the Resolution.[17]

B. Initiatives at Council of Europe Level against FTF Impunity

The shift to pre-crime has also been manifest at the regional level. The Additional Protocol to the Council of Europe Convention on Prevention of Terrorism adopted by the Council of Europe (CoE) incorporated the key provisions of UNSCR 2178 (2014) and contributed to its implementation.[18] The Protocol was

[16] In this regard, see UNSCR 1822 (2008), which reaffirmed 'the need to combat by all means, in accordance with the Charter of the United Nations and international law, including applicable international human rights, refugee, and humanitarian law, threats to international peace and security caused by terrorist acts'.

[17] C Kopitzke, 'Security Council Resolution 2178 (2014): An Ineffective Response to the Foreign Terrorist Fighter Phenomenon' (2017) 24 *Indiana Journal of Global Legal Studies* 309.

[18] N Piacente, 'The Contribution of the Council of Europe to the Fights against Foreign Terrorist Fighters' (2015) 1 *Eucrim* 12.

concerned with the regional implementation of several acts, including the 'act of travelling abroad for the purpose of terrorism' that supplemented the provisions of the Convention. It urged states to take measures both at the national level and through international cooperation in order to set a minimum standard for criminalisation of recruitment to and receipt of training for terrorism and the act of travelling abroad for the purpose of terrorism. The Protocol further offered definitions for the behaviours 'participating in an association or group for the purpose of terrorism', 'receiving training for terrorism', 'travelling abroad for the purpose of terrorism' and 'organising or otherwise facilitating travelling abroad for the purpose of terrorism'.

In particular, 'travelling abroad for the purpose of terrorism' was defined as travelling to a state 'which is not that of the traveller's nationality or residence, for the purpose of the commission of, contribution to or participation in a terrorist offence, or the providing or receiving of training for terrorism'.[19] Signatory states were obliged to adopt measures necessary for the criminalisation of travelling 'from its territory or by its nationals, when committed unlawfully and intentionally, as a criminal offence under its domestic law. In doing so, each Party may establish conditions required by and in line with its constitutional principles.'[20] The attempt to undertake such travel should also be criminalised.[21] For the purposes of prosecution, certain conditions have to be fulfilled, and these are set out in the Explanatory Report to the Additional Protocol.[22] First, the real purpose of travelling has to be established. Secondly, it must be found that the conduct is intentional and unlawful. Thirdly, criminalisation of the act must be clearly specified and connected to the purpose of terrorism that is proven by evidence submitted to an independent court that will scrutinise each case according to national law, criminal procedure and the rule of law.

It is worth mentioning that the European Commission signed the Additional Protocol in October 2015, leaving an open question as to whether this is a matter for Member States or the 'European Commission's assertion of exclusive EU competence'.[23] Having said that, by 2018, most EU Member States' governments had submitted a bill to their parliaments proposing to both ratify the Additional Protocol to the Convention and transpose EU Directive 2017/541 (discussed in the next section) on combating terrorism. In some Member States, proposed legislative amendments included extensions of the terrorist offence and the provisions on receiving training, travel and terrorist financing. For instance, Sweden's proposal

[19] Art 4(1) of the Additional Protocol.
[20] Art 4(2) of the Additional Protocol.
[21] Art 4(3) of the Additional Protocol.
[22] Explanatory Report to the Additional Protocol to the Council of Europe Convention on the Prevention of Terrorism (Riga, 22 October 2015).
[23] See UK Parliament, written statement by Lord Bates, 22 October 2015, HLWS258 www.parliament.uk/business/publications/written-questions-answers-statements/written-statement/Lords/2015-10-22/HLWS258/.

included the extension of criminal liability on 'hijacking' to include 'hijacking by any technological means'.[24]

C. Initiatives at the EU Level against FTF Impunity

The aftermath of the Charlie Hebdo massacre in Paris on 7 January 2015 led to a new era of counter-terrorism and security law that called for the strengthening and modernisation of previous EU legislation. These calls for legislative reform were again addressed to different levels of governance within and beyond the states, and were posed in the same spirit of emergency as the previous wave of securitisation in the aftermath of 9/11 terrorist attacks.[25] At the EU level, the above-mentioned Directive 2017/541 on combating terrorism was adopted in 2017 in a spirit of urgency, setting an implementation deadline of September 2018. Directive 2017/541 agrees with the EU counter-terrorism strategy to fight terrorism globally and make Europe safer that focuses on the four pillars, namely prevent, protect, pursue and respond.[26] The 'changing security situation in the EU', especially with reference to the phenomenon of FTFs, appeared sufficient to justify the lack of an impact assessment (ex ante) despite warnings that the definitions of travel for terrorism and terrorist intent were unclear and risked a conflict between security and fundamental rights.[27] Notwithstanding such concerns, Article 9 of the Directive criminalised travelling for the purpose of committing, contributing to or participating in terrorist offences, or providing or receiving terrorist training. On a similar note, Article 10 required Member States to criminalise the organisation and facilitation of such travel for terrorism.

Reforming the EU counter-terrorism framework in 2017 was broadly influenced by the relevant responses of the UNSC.[28] At the Informal Meeting of Justice and Home Affairs Ministers in Riga in January 2015, it was agreed to reconsider the common understanding among EU Member States of terrorist offences in light of Resolution 2178 (2014).[29] In particular, emphasis was placed

[24] See permanent delegation of Sweden to OSCE, Code of Conduct on Politico-Military Aspects of Security for 2018 www.osce.org/forum-for-security-cooperation/380395?download=true.

[25] The post-9/11 legal response provides for administrative sanctions to those suspected of being associated with terrorism. The sanctions include travel bans and freezing of property, and do not require a criminal conviction.

[26] In the EU Strategy for Combating Radicalisation and Recruitment to Terrorism of 2014, it is highlighted that prevention of radicalisation and recruitment to terrorism requires a 'long-term, proactive and comprehensive approach': Preamble, recital 31.

[27] See European Parliamentary Research Service, 'The Return of Foreign Fighters on EU soil: Ex Post Evaluation', Pe 621 811 (May 2018) www.europarl.europa.eu/RegData/etudes/STUD/2018/621811/EPRS_STU(2018)621811_EN.pdf.

[28] European Commission, 'The European Agenda on Security' (Communication) COM (2015) 185 final; Council of the European Union, Document 16880/14 (18 December 2014), where the Council invited the Commission to consider a reform.

[29] Council of the European Union, Document 5855/15 (2 February 2015). The Parliament also recognised the need to harmonise relevant offences in European Parliament, Resolution of 11 February 2015 on anti-terrorism measures, P8_TA (2015)0032.

on 'the joint efforts of the internal and external dimension in fighting terrorism, and the phenomenon of the foreign terrorist fighters', which was described as 'crucial'.[30] In the same spirit, in April 2015, the Commission adopted the European Agenda on Security, including a reform on counter-terrorism legislation with the purpose of harmonising FTF-related offences.[31] The wake of recent terrorist attacks in Europe as well as the flow of FTFs to ongoing conflicts in Syria, Iraq and Libya necessitated the adoption of new measures for the strengthening of the pre-existing EU security framework. The new challenges posed a situation of emergency that was addressed in light of the ultimate goal of developing a 'Security Union' in order to plug gaps in the EU's security coordination. The Security Union's mission includes terrorism and organised crime, especially the EU's ability to track criminals and use technology to counter the dissemination of online terrorist content and prevent incidents from occurring. The Commission has emphasised in particular that

> it is important that Member States make full use of existing information systems to detect and identify foreign terrorist fighters when crossing the external borders. Work is also on-going on the use of battlefield information to prosecute foreign terrorist fighters.[32]

The coordination of investigations and prosecutions in particular became key to countering the threat posed by FTFs. Beyond the establishment of a European Counter-Terrorism Centre at Europol to provide support to Member States, the EU signed the Additional Protocol to the CoE Convention on Prevention of Terrorism and the Commission simultaneously tabled a proposal for a Directive to transpose the rules criminalising FTFs.[33] This proposal resulted in the adoption of the above-mentioned Directive 2017/541 on combating terrorism. The Directive was based on Article 83(1) TFEU. It amended the previous legislative framework based exclusively on Framework Decisions, which were the main legislative acts used within EU's competences in police and judicial cooperation in criminal justice matters prior to the Lisbon Treaty.[34]

The purpose of Directive 2017/541 is to broaden the scope of terrorism offences in EU law, an objective which was initiated by its predecessor Framework Decision 2002/475/JHA. To this end, the Directive criminalised certain forms of conduct that did not previously fall within the scope of

[30] ibid 7.

[31] In the words of the Commission, 'build a common understanding of the offences of foreign terrorist fighters': COM (2015) 185 final (n 28) 14.

[32] Communication from the Commission to the European Parliament, the European Council and the Council, '20th Progress Report Towards an Effective and Genuine Security Union', COM (2019) 552 final, 2.

[33] European Commission, 'Proposal for a Directive of the European Parliament and of the Council on combating terrorism and replacing Council Framework Decision 2002/475/JHA on combating terrorism' COM (2015) 625 final.

[34] Council Framework Decision 2002/475/JHA on combating terrorism [2002] OJ L164/3; Council Framework Decision 2008/919/JHA amending Framework Decision 2002/475/JHA on combating terrorism [2008] OJ L330/21. The deadline for implementation was on 8 September 2018.

criminal law.[35] Travelling or being trained for the purpose of terrorism were not explicitly criminalised before, and they were first explicitly mentioned by Resolution 2178 (2014), before being explicitly incorporated into the Additional Protocol to the CoE Convention on the Prevention of Terrorism. The revised rules require Member States to take necessary measures:

> to ensure that travelling to a country other than that Member State for the purpose of committing, or contributing to the commission of, a terrorist offence as referred to in Article 3, for the purpose of the participation in the activities of a terrorist group with knowledge of the fact that such participation will contribute to the criminal activities of such a group as referred to in Article 4, or for the purpose of the providing or receiving of training for terrorism as referred to in Articles 7 and 8 is punishable as a criminal offence when committed intentionally.[36]

Member States must also take necessary measures regarding the criminalisation of organising or otherwise facilitating travelling for the purpose of terrorism, including through logistical and material support.[37] The EU legislature has thus also expanded criminalisation by redefining the scope of the offence in relation to terrorist financing covering more activities. Accordingly, it criminalised the provision and receipt of training for terrorism and collecting funds to that effect.[38] A range of additional measures include, inter alia, the criminalisation of travelling for the purpose of terrorism.[39] The latter should be considered in light of the broader revised framework, with heightened border security and immigration control that increased border security checks for all persons, including EU citizens, strengthening information exchange among Member States.[40]

[35] Directive (EU) 2017/541 on combating terrorism and replacing Council Framework Decision 2002/475/JHA and amending Council Decision 2005/671/JHA [2017] OJ L88/6–21, Art 1 provides that 'This Directive establishes minimum rules concerning the definition of criminal offences and sanctions in the area of terrorist offences, offences related to a terrorist group and offences related to terrorist activities, as well as measures of protection of, and support and assistance to, victims of terrorism'.

[36] ibid Art 9.

[37] ibid Art 10.

[38] ibid Art. 7, 8 and 11.

[39] The Council adopted a regulation amending the Schengen borders code to reinforce checks against relevant databases which applies to all external borders, both at entry and exit, on all persons, including those who enjoy the right to free movement: Regulation (EU) 2016/399 of the European Parliament and of the Council of 9 March 2016 on a Union Code on the rules governing the movement of persons across borders (Schengen Borders Code) [2016] OJ L77/1; Council of the European Union, Document 13416/14 (26 September 2014). The EU's action is also concerned with the strengthening of information exchange via SIS II by increasing the functions of the system: Commission Implementing Decision (EU) 2015/219 of 29 January 2015 replacing the Annex to Implementing Decision 2013/115/EU on the Sirene Manual and other implementing measures for the second generation Schengen Information System (SIS II) [2015] OJ L44/75; European Commission, 'Stronger and Smarter Information Systems for Borders and Security' (Communication) COM (2016) 205 final.

[40] It is worth mentioning that the EU Passenger Name Record Directive (Directive 2016/681, [2016] OJ L119/132) implementation deadline was May 2018. See also Commission's legislative proposal for an EU Travel and Information Authorisation System (ETIAS) to provide prior checks for visa-exempt third-country nationals travelling to the Schengen area; EU Entry-Exit System (EES) re: enhancing security at the external EU borders.

III. Convergence between EU and International Standards in Relation to FTFs

A. Governance Convergence

It is now apparent that the criminalisation of terrorism travel by EU law follows a global criminalisation trend[41] initiated by the UNSC which is perceived as the bellwether of legislative change of existing norms in global administrative law regarding FTFs.[42] As mentioned, the UNSC has assumed a quasi-legislative role, with UNSCR 2178 (2014) being received as a legal mandate for Member States. The intervention of the CoE in this context of FTF global standard setting has been a legitimising factor for the UNSC at the regional level. It has also augmented the Resolution's implementation at the national level, enabling it to serve as a benchmark for the EU legislator. EU leaders, in their turn, have recognised the need for a comprehensive, global approach ever since the early stages of discussing the issue of FTFs, calling for specific counter-terrorism measures that will promote cooperation with UN and regional initiatives.[43]

The convergence of different approaches and their connection is not surprising, considering the nature of the threat and the response that has so far been required to fight terrorism, which has followed a top-down approach. As Directive 2017/541 acknowledges in its Preamble, 'the cross-border nature of terrorism requires a strong coordinated response and coordination within and between the Member States' and 'the global character of terrorism necessitates an international answer'.[44] Hence, the EU has adopted a holistic counter-terrorism response, taking part in building an overall universal framework. This approach complies with the orthodox view that EU acts must always be interpreted and their scope delimited, to the extent possible, consistent with the relevant rules of international law, and in particular Article 3(5) TEU, which provides that 'the EU shall uphold and promote … the strict observance and the development of international law'.

The above dependence of EU law upon international law is also manifest in the CJEU's case law, which recently held that an application for asylum can be rejected

[41] Vavoula highlights that 'The insertion of terrorism travel as a criminal offence at the EU level is anything but an isolated phenomenon; therefore, it must be viewed within a broader global security context': N Vavoula, 'Alternative, Informal, and Transitional Types of Criminal Justice and the Legitimacy of New Sanction Models in the Global Risk Society' in U Sieber et al (eds), *Alternative, Informal, and Transitional Types of Criminal Justice and the Legitimacy of New Sanction Models in the Global Risk Society* (Berlin, Duncker & Humblot, 2018) 309.

[42] B Kingsbury, N Krisch and Richard Stewart, 'The Emergence of Global Administrative Law, Law and Contemporary Problems' (2005) 68 *Law and Contemporary Problems* 15; V Mitsilegas, 'The European Union and the Global Governance of Crime' in V Mitsilegas et al (eds), *Globalisation, Criminal Law and Criminal Justice: Theoretical, Comparative and Transnational Perspectives* (Oxford, Hart Publishing, 2015) 153.

[43] Statement by the heads of state or government following an informal meeting on 12 February 2015.

[44] Preamble, recital 7.

if the asylum seeker has partaken in the activities of a terrorist network.[45] In a preliminary reference to the CJEU, the French Conseil d'État asked the CJEU to throw light on the circumstances in which an applicant for asylum can be excluded from refugee status for 'acts contrary to the purposes and principles of the United Nations' where he has had a criminal conviction for participation in the activities of a terrorist group but has not himself committed a terrorist act. The CJEU decided that it is not necessary for the asylum seeker to have committed, instigated or participated in the commission of terrorist acts. It did so by referring to UNSCR 2178, emphasising that the UNSC has expressed 'grave concern over the acute and growing threat posed by foreign terrorist fighters'. It then turned to Directive 2017/541 and highlighted that the exclusion of refugee status laid down in the Directive cannot be confined merely to the actual perpetrators of terrorist acts. Rather, it extends to all persons who engage in activities of recruitment, organisation, transportation or equipment of individuals who travel to a state other than their state of residence or nationality for terrorist purposes.

While, therefore, Member States may adopt measures which restrict the freedom of movement and residence of EU citizens and their family members, irrespective of nationality, on grounds of public policy or public security, it has to be noted that a case-by-case assessment is necessary before a measure can be based on such grounds. The CJEU recently confirmed this approach in two joint cases involving EU citizens who had either been banned from entering a Member State themselves or had relatives who were banned from residing in a Member State, on account of having participated in war crimes (Bosnia and Afghanistan).[46] In particular, the CJEU held that one cannot automatically infer from a decision to refuse asylum on war crime grounds that the individual in question poses a genuine, present and sufficiently serious threat. This is important in making a future assessment of FTF conduct, taking into consideration the passage of time and subsequent involvement, as well as their connection to a family resident in a Member State, to decide whether they remain a threat and if their exclusion is proportionate.

B. Constitutional Safeguards Convergence

All international pre-crime responses pertaining to FTFs in this chapter refer to those constitutional safeguards that need to be respected when states eventually adopt implementation legislation. At the same time, these responses that precede the substantive offence targeted for prevention contradict some of the principles that are listed therein. On the one hand, we notice a convergence of a willingness

[45] Case C-573/14 *Commissaire Général aux Réfugiés et aux Apatrides v Mostafa Lounani* [2017] ECLI:EU:C:2017:71.

[46] Joined Cases C-331/16 and C-366/16 *K and HF* ECLI:EU:C:2018:296.

to respect constitutional safeguards, while, on the other hand, there is a convergence in overlooking these promises by stretching principles of criminal justice that must be taken into consideration during the criminalisation process.[47] These trends have created a tension between, on the one hand, the ideal of 'impartial criminal justice' and, on the other hand, the 'politically charged concept of national security'.[48]

With reference to constitutional safeguards, Resolution 2178 (2014) states that any action that is necessary for states to take should be consistent with international human rights law, international refugee law and international humanitarian law.[49] In the same spirit, Resolution 2249 (2015) reaffirms that 'Member States must ensure that any measures taken to combat terrorism comply with all their obligations under international law, in particular international human rights, refugee and humanitarian law'. Equally, the Additional Protocol to the Council of Europe specifies that when a state criminalises travelling abroad it 'may establish conditions required by and in line with its constitutional principles'.[50] Indeed, Article 8 of the Protocol is dedicated to constitutional safeguards. States should respect, in particular, the right to freedom of movement, freedom of expression, freedom of association and freedom of religion, and criminalisation should be subject to the principle of proportionality. Criminal law and criminal justice in this respect should be applied with due regard to the legitimate aims pursued and to their necessity in a democratic society. Any form of arbitrariness or discriminatory or racist treatment should be avoided according to Article 8 of the Additional Protocol to the CoE Convention. In the Explanatory Notes,[51] it is expressly specified that Article 8, which contains 'conditions and safeguards', is a legally binding provision. Specific reference is made to the rule of law, and it is underlined that any measures taken by Member States must comply with this principle.[52]

As far as EU law is concerned, such proclamations to respect constitutional safeguards are included in the Preamble of the Directive, where Member States' human rights obligations are recognised.[53] Yet, at the same time, as remarked by a commentator,

> the legal net is being cast wider in many European Union Member States to increase the chance of successfully prosecuting returnees, individuals who have attempted to travel to Syria and a group of sympathizers who might pose a threat in their home countries.[54]

[47] A Ashworth, *Principles of Criminal Law* (Oxford, Oxford University Press, 2013) 24.
[48] McCulloch and Pickering (n 6).
[49] Resolution 2178 (2014), para 5.
[50] Resolution 2249 (2015), Art 4(2).
[51] Explanatory Report to the Additional Protocol to the Council of Europe Convention on the Prevention of Terrorism, note 18.
[52] ibid note 17.
[53] Preamble, recital 35.
[54] See L van der Heide, 'Preventing Terrorism in the Courtroom – the Criminalisation of Preparatory Acts of Terrorism in the Netherlands' (2015) 26 *Security and Human Rights* 162.

Despite any convergence in recognising the common framework of constitutional safeguards at different levels of governance, pre-crime and pre-emption appears to be the dominant pattern of convergence, which is next explained.

C. Shift to Pre-crime and Pre-emption Convergence

We have observed that the counterterrorist reform of EU law derives from the expansion of criminalisation in the principal international instruments against terrorism. It is contended that all different levels have criminalised travelling, a non-harmful conduct per se, when accompanied by any of three intentions: (i) to commit or contribute to the commission of a terrorist offence; (ii) to participate in the activities of a terrorist group, knowing that such participation will contribute to the criminal activities of that group; or (iii) to provide or receive training for terrorism.

The expansion of pre-crime measures in relation to FTFs is due primarily to the introduction of a new criminal conduct – that of travelling abroad when accompanied with a relevant guilty mind. The offence as defined in EU law does not require the actual commission of harm, which in this regard is identical to UNSCR 2178/2014 and the CoE Additional Protocol to the Convention for the Prevention of Terrorism. In other words, the convergence of the underpinning patterns of the international approach to terrorism is characterised by moving the criminalisation target away from the actual harm. This new focus on pre-crime and precautionary criminalisation as a means to strengthen the legal framework and tackle the causes of terrorism has resulted in a preventative logic that has permeated the legal sphere.[55]

Pre-crime and precautionary criminalisation in the global fight against impunity should be understood in light of the overlying urgency narrative which has affected the speed of adopting new security measures as the immediate reaction to recent terrorist attacks on the continent. This approach raises similarities to that concerning the previous wave of criminalisation in EU counter-terrorism law, which also legitimised legislative changes by relying on a pre-emptive narrative.[56] Urgency has therefore again bred new legislation that aims to prevent the infliction of harm and the future commission of criminal acts.[57] The criminalisation of the act of travelling with an ulterior intent that does not correspond to an element

[55] Scheinin sees the Resolution as a new wave of panic similar to the post-9/11 spirit: M Scheinin, 'Back to Post-9/11 Panic? Security Council Resolution on Foreign Terrorist Fighters' (*Just Security*, 2014) www.justsecurity.org/15407/post-911-panic-security-council-resolution-foreign-terrorist-fighters-scheinin/; Vavoula (n 41) 314.

[56] C Murphy, *EU Counter-Terrorism Law: Pre-Emption and the Rule of Law* (Oxford, Hart Publishing, 2015) 22–27.

[57] D Cole, 'The Difference Prevention Makes: Regulating Preventive Justice, Criminal Law & Philosophy' (2015) 9 *Criminal Law and Philosophy* 510.

of *actus reus* of the offence (ie the commission of terrorist acts) is a prima facie example of preventive justice. The focus is placed on travel that is criminalised in addition to other preparatory acts, such as terrorist recruitment and funding, which were already regarded as illegal behaviours for the purpose of EU law. The rationale is that by criminalising the mobility of potential future terrorists their future acts that constitute security threats will be prevented.

Mobility forms the *actus reus* of an individual – a new offence accompanied by a *mens rea* in relation to a suspected future act that is presumably the ultimate goal of the person who will be charged with this offence. Therefore, intention is the only guilty element of the offence, as the *actus reus* leads to no harm itself. That might be very difficult to prove beyond 'any reasonable doubt' as the standard that must be met by the prosecution's evidence in a criminal prosecution. In this respect, the European Parliament suggested that prosecuting authorities should use 'objective, factual circumstances'.[58] However, the final text of Directive 2017/541 does not refer to factual circumstances.[59] This is not surprising, considering that prosecuting authorities are assumed to be doing this anyway. Such a provision, namely directing prosecuting authorities to use 'objective, factual circumstances' when determining intention, would be out of place in a legal text.

Additional to mobility forming the required *actus reus* for the FTF crime, Directive 2017/541 also includes a provision in relation to attempts to commit a terrorist offence which is even more controversial through the lens of criminalisation principles, such as *ultima ratio* and harm theory, as the proportionality of criminalisation has not been substantiated. As a result, the scope of Article 9 of Directive 2017/541 is very broad, as it may include travelling to countries which do not constitute conflict zones as well as other Member States. The scope of Directive 2017/541 does not include the travelling of returnees from other states. Yet, Directive 2017/541 allows Member States to 'criminalise preparatory acts undertaken by a person entering a state with the intention to commit or contribute to the commission of a terrorist offence' which is a paradox.[60]

What is more, the Directive refers to vague terms whose interpretation is unclear vis-à-vis the 'facilitation' of travelling abroad. This vagueness may indirectly further expand the scope of the offence, as criminal law should be clear, precise and certain.[61] Amongst the critics, Mitsilegas argues that all citizens exercising their rights to move freely are now treated as suspected foreign fighters, which jeopardises the relationship of trust between them and the state.[62] Directive 2017/541 is also problematic as it is not in compliance with a number of

[58] 'Draft Report on the proposal for a Directive of the European Parliament and of the Council on combating terrorism and replacing Council Framework Decision 2002/475/JHA on combating terrorism' (COM (2015) 0625 – C8-0386/2015–2015/0281(COD)), 9 March 2016, 10.

[59] Directive 2017/541, Preamble, recital 8.

[60] ibid recital 12.

[61] Charter of Fundamental Rights of the European Union [2012] OJ C326/02, Art 49.

[62] V Mitsilegas, *EU Criminal Law after Lisbon* (Oxford, Hart Publishing, 2016) 259.

fundamental rights. In light of human rights law, the measure breaches the right to leave a country, including one's own. The right is guaranteed in Article 2 of Protocol No 4 to the European Convention on Human Rights (the Convention) and is a prerequisite to the enjoyment of a number of other human rights. Moreover, in light of EU constitutional law, Article 9 of the Directive 2017/541 does not comply with the fundamental right to free movement.

IV. Divergence: Scope and Limits of External Influences

While the fight against the impunity of terrorism at the level of EU law is largely based on international law, it has been noted that 'the EU's participation in these external norms is also relevant for the study of the EU's role in the world'.[63] As seen in this chapter, the global approach to counter-terrorism is based on a fairly homogeneous approach, at the heart of which lies the prevention of impunity for terrorist crimes. Still, it is worth observing some differences across the various legal approaches considered so far in order to more closely examine the trends with regard to a common legal terminology in justifying FTF pre-crime and precautionary criminalisation.

From a comparative perspective, the Additional Protocol to the CoE Convention does not follow exactly the same terminology as UNSC Resolution 2178 (2014). For example, the terms 'perpetration' and 'planning and preparation' are substituted with the terms 'commission' and 'contribution', respectively.[64] It appears that the CoE accepted the Security Council Resolutions at the regional level by following their approach to a large extent. This divergence is positive as it comes from a human-rights-oriented organisation that frames the fight against terrorism impunity as, inter alia, a threat to the enjoyment of human rights, as one could argue that living in a secure area is a prerequisite to the enjoyment of fundamental rights. In fact, security is recognised by some as a right, and this reading is not a new one.[65] However, the security-right analogy may be dangerous in that it could lead to pre-emptive securitisation.[66]

[63] E Fahey, 'Joining the Dots: External Norms, AFSJ Directives and the EU's Role in Global Legal Order' (2016) 41 *EL Rev* 105.

[64] Explanatory Report to the Additional Protocol to the Council of Europe Convention on the Prevention of Terrorism, note 52.

[65] R Powell, 'The Right to Security of Person in European Court of Human Rights Jurisprudence' (2007) 6 *European Human Rights Law Review* 649; I Loader and N Walker, *Civilising Security* (Cambridge, Cambridge University Press, 2007).

[66] S Fredman, 'The Positive Right to Security' in BJ Goold and L Lazarus (eds), *Security and Human Rights* (Oxford, Hart Publishing, 2007); M Valverde, 'Governing Security, Governing Through Security' in R Daniels, P Macklem and K Roach (eds), *The Security of Freedom: Essays on Canada's Anti-terrorism Bill* (Toronto, Toronto University Press, 2001) 83; L Lazarus, 'The Right to Security – Securing Rights or Securitising Rights' in R Dickinson et al (eds), *Examining Critical Perspectives on Human Rights* (Cambridge, Cambridge University Press, 2012).

As far as EU law is concerned, the drafters of Directive 2017/541 chose the language of the Convention instead of the Resolution. For example, they chose the word 'commission' instead of 'perpetration', and 'contribution' instead of 'planning' and 'preparation'.[67] Contribution is arguably a broader term, and could refer to behaviours other than planning and preparation. Considering that Member States will legislate at domestic level to transpose the Directive, the drafters might have chosen a broader term to allow for a greater national leeway in an area that is sensitive and crucial. However, this might allow Member States to criminalise behaviours that are loosely connected to a harm that is already a potential one and which is prevented.

The above begs the question: how does the departure from the core principles of criminalisation affect constitutional safeguards? Such departure might affect constitutional safeguards in ways that relate to the constitutional character of criminalisation principles. Criminalisation principles are closely linked to constitutional safeguards in the sense that they determine the reach of criminal law vis-à-vis an individual's liberty and draw the limits of the state's lawful coercion as performed by both criminalisation and penology.[68] Criminalisation principles are the specific manifestations of constitutional safeguards in the field of criminal law and delimitate the relationship of citizen and state in an area where the state is allowed to exercise coercion and social control. Therefore, criminalisation principles have traditionally been seen as the sword and the shield of the citizen, and any departure from those principles might have significant effects on the relationship of trust between the state and the citizen.[69]

Although UNSC Resolution 2178, the Additional Protocol to the CoE Convention on Prevention of Terrorism and Directive 2017/541 refer to limitations to 'securitisation' that stem from constitutional safeguards, these are neither specified in the same way nor given the same emphasis. In particular, the Directive makes many more references to constitutional safeguards in the Preamble's recitals than the other two documents. This might be explained in light of the fact that the UNSC Resolution 2178 was criticised by commentators in respect of the preparatory offences, such as terrorist recruitment and funding, as they arguably raise challenges to freedom of expression, non-discrimination and the respect of political rights.[70] So, the EU legislator, by recognising all potential freedoms that the Directive might encroach upon, seems conscious of these early concerns that were voiced regarding UNSC Resolution 2178. These are, however, non-binding recitals of the Preamble of Directive 2017/541, whereas the drafters of the Additional Protocol to the CoE Convention included Article 8, a legally binding provision, to demarcate the criminalisation process by reference to specific constitutional

[67] Preamble, recital 52.

[68] N Peršak, *Criminalising Harmful Conduct* (Berlin, Springer, 2007) 9–33.

[69] Mitsilegas (n 62) 259 rightly notes that treating mobile citizens as suspects of being terrorist fighters risks the relationship of trust between the citizen and the state.

[70] Scheinin (n 55).

safeguards. Nevertheless, their reference in the Preamble is not without significance, considering the increasingly important interpretative role a Preamble plays. In addition, a very thorough analysis in relation to the restriction of the right to free movement is conducted in the Explanatory Report to the Additional Protocol to the CoE Convention,[71] but a similar analysis is missing from the Directive. This is surprising considering the fundamental status that the right to free movement has in EU law.

It is also worth underlying that Directive 2017/541 includes minimum standards and that its implementation at domestic level might lead to further divergences and reveal further shortcomings resulting from its interpretation. Member States might interpret FTF conduct broadly, which could be dangerous especially in relation to evidencing intention when citizens move to other states which might be conflict zones or other countries, as the Directive does not specify. Evidencing intention will be specified by national laws, will be exercised by prosecuting authorities and lawyers and will be heard by judicial authorities, who will rule on the verdict. For some of these, simply travelling to a conflict or 'suspect' zone might be seen as sufficient to indicate a terrorist purpose for the evidentiary standard of proof necessary for prosecution or even to prove the intention for the purpose of conviction.[72] A potential divergence in prosecution is therefore expected, and it will be interesting to see how domestic prosecutors make decisions on who is suspected, stopped while travelling and charged with the offence, what evidentiary standards authorities require and how they understand several terms which are vague, such as that of 'contribution'.

Having said that, it should be noted that the legal basis of the Directive 2017/541, Article 83 TFEU, allows Member States to 'establish minimum rules concerning the definition of criminal offences and sanctions'. Member States will thus maintain a broad scope of discretion which might lead to different approaches to achieve the binding result of the Directive. Therefore, the EU's competence per se allows for such divergences and provides for ways to address any dysfunctions stemming from that, ie by means of the preliminary reference procedure through which the CJEU may provide for a consistent harmonised interpretation of contested terms. Still, these concerns should not be underestimated and deserve further attention. Differentiating approaches to implementing Directive 2017/541 might lead to different degrees of criminalisation across the EU Member States. As the Directive only provides for minimum rules concerning the definition of criminal offences, it only obliges Member States to follow the 'floor' and not the 'ceiling' of criminalisation, as expected. As a result, a preparatory conduct might

[71] Explanatory Report to the Additional Protocol to the Council of Europe Convention on the Prevention of Terrorism (Riga, 22 October 2015).

[72] The Meijers Committee shares this concern and indicate the difficulties that humanitarian organisations might face: Meijers Committee, 'Note on the Proposal for the Directive on Combatting Terrorism' CM1603 (Standing Committee of Experts on International Immigration, Refugee and Criminal Law, 2016) 7.

be a crime in one Member State but not in another. Considering that the targeting conduct involves mobility within and outside the EU, several degrees of harmonisation could allow the phenomenon of 'forum shopping' for potential criminal offenders when designing their activities, as they could choose paths of 'minimal' criminalisation. Therefore, certain acts that will be considered as criminal in the jurisdiction of some Member States might remain unpunished if the 'offender' chooses a path where their actions do not fall within the scope of domestic criminal law.

Despite the relatively homogenised legal approach in pre-crime and precautionary criminalisation, local divergence might arise. The UK, Ireland and Denmark do not participate in this Directive. They are, however, bound by the Additional Protocol to the CoE Convention and the Security Council Resolutions. It comes as a surprise that the UK opted out, since prior to Brexit it took part in related security-oriented measures of EU criminal law.[73] Notwithstanding the UK's withdrawal from the EU, the recent UK Counter-Terrorism and Border Security Act 2019 has caught up with international and European legislation through the extension of sentences for terrorism offences, including the so-called 'designated area offence'. This is the offence of entering, or remaining in, an area outside the UK that has been designated in regulations made by the Home Secretary. The offence carries the maximum penalty of 10 years' imprisonment, but will not apply retrospectively for UK FTFs who travelled to Iraq or Syria unless they assist in future conflict. As with the application of EU law on FTFs, there are bound to be difficulties with the exceptions contained in the Counter-Terrorism and Border Security Act 2019 in prosecuting and punishing crimes against humanity committed by Daesh regarding travellers providing humanitarian aid or working as journalists, or simply travelling for the purpose of providing care for an ill relative.[74]

V. Conclusion

As discussed, the international fight against impunity of serious cross-border crimes has transcended different levels of legal governance and is a driving force for the criminalisation of harmful or dangerous conduct at the EU level. This is evident in the recent reform of the EU counter-terrorism legislation, which aims to address threats such as the so-called FTFs. In the EU context, criminalisation appears to be the main legal response to tackle unprecedented criminality with

[73] Ministry of Justice and Home Office, *Fifth Annual Report to Parliament on the Application of Protocols 19 and 21 to the TEU and the TFEU in Relation to EU Justice and Home Affairs (JHA) Matters* (Cm 90061, February 2015) www.gov.uk/government/uploads/system/uploads/attachment_data/file/401463/46831_Cm_9006_accessible.pdf.

[74] See Council of Europe, Committee on Legal Affairs and Human Rights, 'Prosecuting and Punishing the Crimes against Humanity or Even Possible Genocide Committed by Daesh' Doc 14402 (22 September 2017).

a cross-border character. The recent Directive 2017/541 on combating terrorism and reforming previous EU legislation expanded criminalisation to the act of travelling when conducted with specific criminal intent.

Since EU legislative choices in the field have been shaped to a great extent by international initiatives, this chapter has attempted to define the scope and limits of external influences on the EU choices of criminalisation vis-à-vis FTFs. It did so by identifying common global patterns at the EU and the international sphere that demonstrate a convergence towards a global approach in fighting impunity of certain crimes. The chapter has also exhibited the limits of external influences to EU law by highlighting the divergence in the EU's approach from that of international law. In this respect, we considered the extent to which EU constitutional law principles have played a role as red lines, demarcating the EU's approach.

Despite its flaws, including the standard of evidence, questions over jurisdiction as well as the general shroud of ambiguity surrounding the status of returnees from other states, Directive 2017/541 provides a blueprint for the EU to build a more coherent future response to combat the impunity that FTFs often enjoy. Yet, while legal means can reduce the ability of FTFs to carry out attacks by linking them with extremist networks, what we have witnessed so far are quick fixes based on a rather repressive approach which may endanger international constitutional safeguards protecting constitutional rights (both recognition and enforcement of individual legal rights) and limiting abuses of power.

More is needed, therefore, to address radicalisation, discourage European citizens from committing crimes abroad and reintegrate FTFs in the EU as a polity of states and people. This is particularly crucial since the international fight against FTFs relates not only to those involved in active combat, but also to non-combatants who may have provided other kinds of trivial support to proscribed terrorist networks. As the territory controlled by Daesh has shrunk considerably as a result of the international coalition of forces, the return of FTF combatants and non-combatants is imminent in Europe and will test the EU's various mechanisms, and its ability and authority to address impunity within the scope of application of EU law.

16

Impunity and EU or Member States' Extradition Agreements with Third Countries

STEFANO SALUZZO

I. Introduction

In a series of recent judgments, the Court of Justice of the European Union (CJEU) has intervened on certain questions regarding the extradition of European citizens to third countries. Such cases have raised a number of sensitive issues both at the international and at the European level. The traditional system of extradition to third countries is still largely based on bilateral agreements concluded by Member States and this calls into question the limits of Member States' foreign powers with regard to EU law obligations. Moreover, the execution of extradition requests from third countries has highlighted the need to strike a (difficult) balance between the exigencies of preventing spaces of impunity while avoiding possible discriminations based on nationality within the EU legal order.

This chapter addresses the issue from the perspective of both international and EU law, which are strictly intertwined in such situations. On the one hand, Member States are required to comply with extradition requests coming from third countries by virtue of an international agreement and in order to prevent situations of impunity; on the other hand, their discretion in this context is limited by certain fundamental principles of EU law, especially the freedom of movement and the prohibition of discriminations based on nationality. The analysis thus attempts to clarify the legal obligations of states, by looking at the recent case law of the CJEU and reading it in the light of international rules governing extradition matters. This will also require a more general analysis of the relationship between Member States' international agreements concluded with third countries and EU law obligations.

II. Extradition Requests for the Purpose of Prosecution

The first case in which the CJEU had the opportunity to deal with the question of prevention of impunity and non-discrimination of European citizens emerged in the context of a 1993 bilateral extradition agreement between Russia and Latvia.[1]

The case originated from the extradition of Mr Petruhhin, an Estonian national, requested by Russia to the Latvian government. Mr Petruhhin was arrested in Latvia and a request from Russia was later received on the basis of a bilateral extradition treaty existing between Russia and Latvia. Mr Petruhhin filed an appeal against the Latvian public prosecutor's decision to grant the extradition, claiming that, under a treaty concluded in 1992 among Estonia, Latvia and Lithuania on judicial assistance and judicial relations, he enjoyed the same protection as Latvian nationals against unjust extradition.[2]

The Supreme Court of Latvia, to which the proceedings had been transmitted, on its own initiative recognised that the matter was raising not just the issue of the effects of the 1992 agreement, but also a more general problem of the scope of application of the nationality exception provided by the Russia–Latvia extradition treaty in relation to the prohibition of discrimination, deriving from EU citizenship. Indeed, since the nationality exception only refers to the nationals of the contracting states and does only apply on the territory of those countries, the non-recognition of the same protection to other EU citizens could amount to an unjust discrimination on grounds of nationality, forbidden by Article 18(1) TFEU and by Article 2(2) of the Charter of Fundamental Rights. The Latvian court referred various questions to the Court of Justice, asking, first, whether, in case of an extradition request from a third country, a Member State is obliged to guarantee the same level of protection to all EU citizens and, secondly, whether the national judge should apply to the extradition proceedings the conditions for extradition of the Member State of which the person concerned is a national or that in which he has his habitual residence. Moreover, the referring court also raised the issue of obligations of Member States deriving from Article 19(2) of the Charter, which provides for protection in the event of removal, expulsion or extradition.[3]

A. The Scope of Application of EU Law

Both Advocate General (AG) Bot and the Court of Justice held that EU law was applicable to the case, including the principle of non-discrimination.

[1] Case 182/15 *Aleksei Petruhhin* ECLI:EU:C:2016:630.

[2] The claim was based on the fact that the extradition agreement concluded in 1993 between Latvia and Russia only provided for the nationality of one of the contracting states as a ground to refuse the extradition request. However, according to Art 1 of the earlier 1992 agreement, the rights of the nationals of one of the contracting parties shall enjoy the same protection on the territory of all other contracting parties. By relying on this provision, Mr Petruhhin was seeking an extension of the nationality exception enshrined in the extradition agreement between Russia and Latvia.

[3] ibid para 17.

Some intervening governments had claimed that, since the Union had no competence regarding extradition matters, the extradition of Mr Petruhhin fell outside the scope of EU law.[4] Indeed, Member States are currently still free to conclude bilateral extradition treaties with third countries, since the related competence has not been attributed exclusively to the EU and an exclusive competence of the Union cannot be derived from the pre-emption doctrine. Even if the EU has concluded a number of extradition agreements with third countries, these only supplement Member States' international agreements on extradition matters, by providing additional and uniform rules.[5] This could not exclude, however, that the situation of Mr Petruhhin fell outside the scope of EU law.

According to a settled case law of the CJEU, a main feature of the status of EU citizen is the right not to suffer any discrimination on grounds of nationality within the scope of application *ratione personae* of the Treaty.[6] In order for EU law to cover a specific situation, both the personal and the material scope of application should be assessed. Even if the difference between the two has sometimes been unclear,[7] it is usually accepted that the personal criterion is satisfied by possessing the nationality of a Member State, while the material scope – which encompasses the right to equal treatment – includes those situations involving the exercise of a fundamental freedom guaranteed by the Treaties, in particular the freedom to move and to reside in another Member State.[8] Thus, the sole fact that a situation falls within a retained competence of the Member States does not *per se* exclude that certain factual elements of that situation are governed by EU law, specifically by the right of free movement.[9] Moreover, when Member States act in a field covered by their own competence, as is the case for the execution of a bilateral extradition treaty, they must do so in a manner consistent with EU law, thus paying due regard to individual rights derived from primary and secondary EU provisions.[10]

It is on this premise that the AG affirmed that Articles 18 and 21 TFEU were applicable to Mr Petruhhin's situation: by moving from his country of origin to Latvia, he had exercised his right to free movement under EU law.

[4] See *Petruhhin* (n 1) Opinion of AG Bot, para 33.

[5] S Peers, *EU Justice and Home Affairs Law* (Oxford, Oxford University Press, 2012) 750. On the relationship between EU law and extradition agreements of Member States, see F Casolari, 'EU Member States' International Engagements in AFSJ Domain: Between Subordination, Complementariity and Incorporation' in C Flaesh-Mougin and LS Rossi (eds), *La dimension extérieure de l'espace de liberté, de sécurité et de justice de l'Union européenne après le Traité de Lisbonne* (Brussels, Bruylant, 2013) 23.

[6] Case 85/96 *Martìnez Sala* ECLI:EU:C:1998:217, para 62.

[7] See E Spaventa, 'Seeing the Wood Despite the Trees: On the Scope of Union Citizenship and Its Constitutional Effects' (2008) 45 *CML Rev* 13, 14.

[8] Case 224/98 *Marie Natalie D'Hoop v Office national de l'emploi* ECLI:EU:C:2002:432, para 29.

[9] At the same time, there can be situations not covered by EU law even if the matter falls partly under an EU legislative measure. See Joined Cases 446/12 and 449/12 *WP Willems and Others v Burgemeester van Nuth and Others* ECLI:EU:C:2015:238, para 47ff.

[10] This is a traditional construction of the Court's case law, which has been confirmed also in relation to the exercise of Member States' foreign powers. See, eg Case 533/08 *TNT Express Nederland BV v AXA Versicherung AG* [2010], para 52.

Consequently, he was entitled to the same treatment of nationals of the host state.[11] Contrary to what the intervening Member States had observed, the exercise by Mr Petruhhin of his freedom of movement throughout the Union territory is, according to the AG, perfectly sufficient to trigger the protection deriving from both the citizenship status and the principle of non-discrimination, since the factual situation involved the necessary link with EU law, notwithstanding the fact that extradition matters are still a retained competence of Member States.[12]

The Court of Justice confirmed the position of the AG, by recognising that the exercise by Mr Petruhhin of his freedom of movement constituted a sufficient basis to consider the extradition proceedings covered by the protection of EU law against discrimination.[13] This passage reveals how relevant the judgment could be for future extradition requests coming from third countries and addressed to Member States. The assessment made by the CJEU, even if referred only to the specific situation, has broad implications for extradition matters.[14] In fact, if one considers that EU law applies whenever a citizen of the EU has exercised his freedom of movement, this will entail that all extradition requests related to a citizen who is not a national of the requested Member State will essentially be covered by EU law.[15] Moreover, this is likely to happen not just when the movement from one Member State to another is voluntary, but also when the individual has been previously surrendered by virtue of a cooperation instrument, such as the European Arrest Warrant (EAW).[16]

Once the applicability of Articles 18 and 21(1) TFEU to the case at hand had been established, it was quite evident that the nationality exception enshrined in extradition treaties constitutes a discrimination on grounds of nationality that is forbidden by EU law. Whether this discrimination could be justified on the basis of legitimate reasons, such as the need to prevent risks of impunity, is a different issue, which needs to be addressed separately.[17]

[11] Opinion of AG Bot, *Petruhhin* (n 4) para 34.

[12] ibid para 39.

[13] *Petruhhin* (n 1) paras 30–31.

[14] A Klip, 'Europeans First!: Petruhhin, an Unexpected Revolution in Extradition Law' (2017) 25 *European Journal of Crime, Criminal Law and Criminal Justice* 195. See also R Niblock and A Oehmichen, 'Local Law Repercussions on EU Extradition Law: Perspectives from Continental Europe and England and Wales' (2017) 8 *New Journal of European Criminal Law* 116.

[15] Note also that the extension of the protection to mere EU citizens having exercised the freedom of movement would be much wider in this case than the one usually applicable to optional grounds of refusal of EAW execution in relation to non-nationals. See n 20 below and the case law cited therein.

[16] Although with the limits set forth by Art 16 of the EAW Framework Decision on multiple requests and the criteria provided therein. Moreover, under Art 28(4) of the EAW Framework Decision, 'a person who has been surrendered pursuant to a European arrest warrant shall not be extradited to a third State without the consent of the competent authority of the Member State which surrendered the person. Such consent shall be given in accordance with the Conventions by which that Member State is bound, as well as with its domestic law'.

[17] See the next section.

B. Preventing Impunity: The Clash between the Nationality Exception and the Principle of Non-discrimination

The main point of interest in *Petruhhin* is the Court of Justice's assessment of the compatibility with EU law of nationality exceptions enshrined in extradition agreements. The question raised by the Latvian Supreme Court concerned the possibility of extending the protection of nationals against extradition to habitual or permanent residents. International law provides examples of treaties allowing for the non-extradition of residents beside nationals, but they are usually restricted to certain countries (in particular, Scandinavian states)[18] and, in any case, the protection is expressly granted by the extradition treaty itself.[19] Evidently, the referring court was also trying to draw an analogy with the EAW system, in which the requested Member State has the possibility to refuse the surrender of nationals of another Member State having resided on its territory for a number of years should it apply this exception to its own nationals.[20]

Both the AG and the Court of Justice went beyond this question and addressed the issue from a wider perspective. First, they analysed whether the nationality exception in extradition treaties[21] could be considered as a discrimination on grounds of nationality; secondly, they considered the extent to which this derogation from the principle of non-discrimination could be justified in the pursuit of a legitimate aim, such as to avoid the risk of impunity of the requested person.

The rule on the non extradition of nationals has its origins in national legislations of civil law countries. It has lately been codified in the majority of extradition agreements, although it has not reached the status of customary international law.[22] The rationale behind the rule is traditionally identified in a general distrust in the legal system of third countries and in the need for the state to protect its own

[18] See Z Deen-Racsmány, 'Modernizing the Nationality Exception: Is the Non-extradition of Residents a Better Rule?' 2006) 75 *Nordic Journal of International Law* 36. See, eg Art 6, para 1, let b) of the 1957 European Convention on Extradition; see also Art 15, para 3, let a) of the 2002 London Scheme for Extradition within the Commonwealth.

[19] Mr Petruhhin had claimed before the Latvian authorities that he enjoyed the same protection as Latvian nationals by virtue of the agreement between Latvia, Estonia and Lithuania. However, it would have been difficult to recognise that the mentioned agreement was applicable in relation to a third country, given the principle of relativity of treaties.

[20] On the notion of residence and the requirements deriving from the principle of non-discrimination in relation to an EAW execution, see Case 66/08 *Kozłowski* ECLI:EU:C:2008:437, paras 36–54; Case 123/08 *Dominic Wolzenburg* ECLI:EU:C:2009:616, paras 43–46; Case 42/11, *Lopes da Silva Jorge* ECLI:EU:C:2012:517, paras 40–45. See generally L Marin, '"A Spectre Is Haunting Europe": European Citizenship in the Area of Freedom, Security and Justice' (2011) 17 *European Public Law* 705; S Peers, 'The European Arrest Warrant: The Dilemma of Mutual Recognition, Human Rights and EU Citizenship' in A Rosas, E Levits and Y Bot (eds), *The Court of Justice and the Construction of Europe: Analyses and Perspectives on Sixty Years of Case-law* (The Hague, TMC Asser Press, 2013) 533.

[21] Even if the CJEU made reference to 'national rules on extradition', the nationality exception was also provided by Art 62 of the 1992 extradition agreement between Latvia and Russia.

[22] JM Thouvenin, 'Le principe de non extradition des nationaux' in *Droit international et nationalité. Colloque de Poitiers* (Paris, Pedone, 2012) 127, 131–32.

nationals from prosecution in other jurisdictions. At the same time, the nationality exception is usually deemed not applicable to individuals who have acquired the nationality of the requested state after the extradition request.

In the first part of the reasoning, the Court of Justice followed the Opinion of the AG, by considering that the nationality exception, insofar as it produces a different treatment of EU citizens, amounts to a discrimination on grounds of nationality under EU law. The protection of nationals against extradition also negatively affects the freedom of movement within the Union.[23]

Many intervening states, together with the European Commission, have observed before the Court of Justice that the difference in treatment of EU citizens is justified under the need to combat the impunity of persons suspected of having committed an offence abroad. In fact, where extradition is requested by a third state, avoiding any room for impunity should be considered as a legitimate objective under EU law. Indeed, the Court had already recognised that the prevention of impunity amounts to an interest of the Union.[24] Following this argument, AG Bot observed that a proper discrimination could only occur when the two categories of EU citizens are in a comparable situation. In the context of an extradition request, a comparable situation means that both EU citizens can be prosecuted in the requested EU Member State for an offence committed in the requesting third state. This is where the principle *aut dedere aut judicare* becomes relevant.

The *aut dedere aut judicare* principle is a long-established feature of international extradition law, according to which the state, when deciding to refuse the extradition of the requested person, has the duty to prosecute him according to its national rules.[25] The principle has assumed various forms in international practice. In the so-called 'Hague Formula' (from the 1970 Hague Convention for the Suppression of Unlawful Seizure of Aircraft),[26] the state is under an obligation to prosecute the person responsible for the behaviours described in the Convention, but it can avoid the execution of the obligation if it extradites the perpetrator to another requesting state party.[27] Conversely, there are cases in which the principle is applicable just in relation to a refusal to extradite on the grounds of nationality

[23] *Petruhhin* (n 1) paras 31–32. The reasoning is close to the one followed by the Court in Case 34/09 *Ruiz Zambrano* ECLI:EU:C:2011:124, paras 44–45. See also M Böse, 'Mutual Recognition, Extradition to Third Countries and Union Citizenship: *Petruhhin*' (2017) 54 *CML Rev* 1781, 1787.

[24] Case 129/14 *Spasic* ECLI:EU:C:2014:586, paras 63–64, 72.

[25] For an overview of instruments providing for the obligation to prosecute or to extradite, see C Mitchell, Aut Dedere, aut Judicare: *The Extradite or Prosecute Clause in International Law* (Geneva, Graduate Institute Publications, 2009).

[26] See ILC, 'Final Report – Working Group on the Obligation to Extradite or Prosecute (*aut dedere aut iudicare*)', UN Doc A/CN.4/L.844 (5 May–6 June and 7 July–8 August 2014) para 15ff. The Hague Formula has been codified in a number of international conventions dealing with extradition, including the 1984 United Nations Convention against Torture and Other Cruel, Inhuman or Degrading Treatment or Punishment.

[27] This kind of mechanism is accompanied by the duty to criminalise a certain conduct and to establish jurisdiction over it. In this regard, see ICJ *Questions relating to the obligation to prosecute or extradite (Belgium v Senegal)* (Merits) [2012] ICJ Rep 2012, 422, para 74.

exception. For instance, the UN Convention against Organised Crime provides that a state refusing the extradition solely on the grounds of nationality 'shall, at the request of the State Party seeking extradition, be obliged to submit the case without undue delay to its competent authorities for the purpose of prosecution'.[28] In order to abide by the principle and avoid incurring international responsibility, the refusing state must have the capacity to exercise jurisdiction over the offences concerned. Thus, the question of the jurisdictional basis for prosecution – whether provided by international or national law – is a logical priority when dealing with the *aut dedere aut judicare* principle.[29]

AG Bot had observed that, when the requested state has the jurisdiction to try and prosecute the offender, the nationality exception cannot be justified under EU law. In fact, the state can extend the protection against extradition to all EU citizens, provided that it can respect the principle of *aut dedere aut judicare*. In the latter case, indeed, the risk of impunity, which would justify the derogation from the prohibition of discrimination, would be overcome by the possibility for the requested state to directly prosecute the offender. The risk, however, persists when the Member State 'has not made provision in its domestic law for jurisdiction allowing it to try a national of another Member State suspected of having committed an offence on the territory of a third State'.[30] Since Latvia, according to its national criminal code, had no jurisdiction to try Mr Petruhhin for the behaviours realised in the Russian territory, the AG concluded that the difference in treatment deriving from the nationality exception should be considered legitimate.

The Court of Justice started from the same premise, but it reached a quite different conclusion. Considering that the nationality exception certainly constitutes a difference in treatment prohibited under Article 18 TFEU, it confirmed that contrasting the risk of impunity is a legitimate objective in EU law, which has to be attained by Member States according to the principles of necessity and proportionality, and thus by 'less restrictive measures'.[31] According to the Court, the principle *aut dedere aut judicare* provides a guidance to identify less restrictive measures, insofar as it allows the protection against extradition to be extended to other EU citizens provided that at least one Member State has the jurisdiction to prosecute the offender. Here, the Court deviates from AG Bot's Opinion, by affirming that, within the EU legal order, even where the requested Member State has no jurisdiction over the offender's conduct, it can always resort to the EAW mechanism in order to surrender the offender to the Member State possessing the jurisdiction to prosecute him. This would generally be the state of nationality, and in fact the Court noted that Latvia could have surrendered Mr Petruhhin

[28] See Art 16, para 10 of the United Nations Convention against Transnational Organized Crime.

[29] See M Böse, 'EU Substantive Criminal Law and Jurisdiction Clauses: Claiming Jurisdiction to Fight Impunity?' ch 5 in this book.

[30] Opinion of AG Bot, *Petruhhin* (n 4), paras 64–65.

[31] *Petruhhin* (n 1), para 38.

to the competent Estonian authorities for the purpose of prosecution. Moreover, Member States that are requested by a third country to extradite a person can also resort to the EU's exchange information system in order to identify which Member State can exercise jurisdiction over acts committed abroad.[32] The application of all the cooperation and mutual assistance instruments provided by EU law will thus be sufficient to strike the balance between the necessity to avoid the risk of impunity and the guarantee of fundamental freedoms and principles of EU law.

C. EU International Agreements on Extradition

The issue of discriminations based on nationality arising out of extradition requests is not limited to Member States' bilateral extradition agreements. Extradition for the purpose of prosecution might also be requested by third countries on the basis of international agreements concluded solely by the EU.

Today, the only treaty providing for an EU-only extradition regime is the one established by the 2003 EU–US extradition agreement. The agreement is binding upon all the Member States by virtue of Article 216 TFEU, although the EU is the sole subject bound by it at the international level. The agreement sets forth some principles regarding extradition from and to the US, while certain specific issues are left to existing bilateral agreements concluded by Member States with the US.

On April 2018, the CJEU rendered a judgment on an extradition request filed to Germany by the US in relation to an Italian national, Mr Pisciotti, allegedly responsible for having established a cartel in the US. Once again, the essence of the case lies in the interpretation of Articles 18 and 21 TFEU in the context of extradition for the purpose of prosecution. The applicability of EU law here was established quite easily, the request being based on a treaty concluded directly by the EU.[33]

In this case, the protection of nationals against extradition did not stem from the EU–US agreement, but from a bilateral Germany–US extradition treaty concluded in 1978.[34] Again, the CJEU was asked to rule on the possibility of extending the protection to citizens of other Member States (having exercised their freedom of movement) and on the availability of less restrictive means that would grant due consideration to the objective of preventing impunity. According

[32] ibid para 48.

[33] Case C-191/16 *Romano Pisciotti v Bundesrepublik Deutschland* ECLI:EU:C:2018:222, para 31.

[34] Bilateral treaties are still relevant in the context of extradition from and to the US, by virtue of a reference contained in Art 17 of the EU–US extradition treaty: '1. This Agreement is without prejudice to the invocation by the requested State of grounds for refusal relating to a matter not governed by this Agreement that is available pursuant to a bilateral extradition treaty in force between a Member State and the United States of America. 2. Where the constitutional principles of, or final judicial decisions binding upon, the requested State may pose an impediment to fulfilment of its obligation to extradite, and resolution of the matter is not provided for in this Agreement or the applicable bilateral treaty, consultations shall take place between the requested and requesting States.'

to Mr Pisciotti, this requirement would have been satisfied by a prosecution for the same offences conducted by the German authorities.

The Court, however, disagreed, confirming the *Petruhhin* findings on the priority of the EAW mechanism and, consequently, of the Member State possessing jurisdiction over the specific offence. Only in a case where the Member State possessing jurisdiction has not issued an EAW may the individual be extradited.[35] In the case at issue, the Italian authorities had been informed of the situation and decided not to start any proceedings against him. Given the Italian authorities' decision not to issue an EAW, the CJEU held that Germany had not breached EU law by surrendering Mr Pisciotti to the US.

In general terms, the *Pisciotti* judgment clarifies the extent of the Member States' obligation to refuse extradition in order to respect EU law. The priority to the *judicare* element can be established only when one of the Member States possesses a valid title to jurisdiction and is willing to exercise it. However, the CJEU seems to underestimate – as it already did in the previous *Petruhhin* case – the possibility of the requested Member State exercising vicarious jurisdiction in accordance with its national rules.[36]

III. Extradition Requests for the Purpose of Enforcement of Sentences

In November 2018, the CJEU returned to the issue of the compatibility of nationality exceptions in the context of an extradition requested to a Member State by a third country.[37] In the *Raugevicius* case, however, the legal framework was somewhat different from that of *Petruhhin*. The extradition request, addressed by Russia to Finland, had the purpose of obtaining the surrender of Mr Raugevicius, a Lithuanian and Russian national, to make him serve in Russia a sentence issued by a Russian judge. The request was not based on a bilateral extradition treaty, but on the 1957 European Convention on Extradition, which provides for a nationality exception framed in terms of a right for the states parties and not of an obligation. Moreover, Article 6(2) of the 1957 Convention enshrines a formula which recalls the *aut dedere aut iudicare* principle.[38] In this specific case, however, a stricter obligation not to extradite nationals was also provided by the Finnish Constitution and legislation.

[35] *Pisciotti* (n 33) paras 50–55.

[36] MJ Costa, 'The Emerging EU Extradition Law. Petruhhin and Beyond' (2017) 8 *New Journal of European Criminal Law* 192, 201. On vicarious jurisdiction see Böse, (n 29).

[37] Case 247/17 *Denis Raugevicius* ECLI:EU:C:2018:898.

[38] See 1957 European Convention on Extradition, Art 6(2): 'If the requested Party does not extradite its national, it shall at the request of the requesting Party submit the case to its competent authorities in order that proceedings may be taken if they are considered appropriate.'

Once it had been established that EU law (and the freedom of movement) applied to the case, the Court reaffirmed the principle by virtue of which Member States are required to respect EU law obligations even when they are acting in a field of retained competences. Accordingly, Member States shall not disregard EU law for the sole fact that they are executing an international agreement concluded with a third country. In this sense, it is quite clear to the Court that a protection based on nationality, such as the one applicable in case of Mr Raugevicius, would give rise to a discrimination within the meaning of Article 21 TFEU[39] and to a limitation of the freedom of movement. In order to consider this limitation as legitimate, the requested Member State would have to assess whether there are less restrictive means to achieve the objective of preventing impunity. However, in this case, no reference could be made to the *aut dedere aut iudicare* principle, as the extradition request was not made for the purpose of prosecution.[40] The Court then referred to an alternative solution:

> in order to prevent the risk of such persons remaining unpunished, there are mechanisms under national law and/or international law which make it possible for those persons to serve their sentences, in particular, in the State of which they are nationals and, in doing so, increase their chances of social reintegration after they have completed their sentences.[41]

The CJEU concluded that, where the national legislation of the Member State, or the applicable international regime, would allow the state to refuse the extradition of its own nationals and make them serve the sentence in their country of nationality,[42] this protection might be extended to other EU citizens.

This reasoning was reinforced by the fact that the same Finnish law provided for such an alternative. Under the 1987 law on international cooperation for the enforcement of certain criminal sanctions, penalties involving the loss of liberty imposed by a court of a foreign state 'may be enforced in Finland if the convicted person … is a Finnish national or a foreign national permanently residing in Finland and the convicted person has agreed to enforcement'. The CJEU, drawing an argument from the *Wolzburg* case,[43] could thus confirm that Finnish nationals and nationals of other EU Member States residing permanently in Finland are in a comparable situation when the latter demonstrate a certain degree of integration into the host state's society.[44] This led to the conclusion

[39] *Raugevicius* (n 37) para 30.

[40] The Supreme Court of Finland, ie the referring court, and a number of intervening states have also submitted that the application of the principle *aut dedere aut iudicare* in this context would have amounted to a violation of the *ne bis in idem*.

[41] *Raugevicius* (n 37) para 36. The CJEU also makes reference to the 1983 Convention on the Transfer of Sentenced Persons, to which all Member States and the Russian Federation are parties.

[42] This would anyway require the consent of both the requesting country and the requested subject. Under the relevant Finnish law, the consent of the foreign state imposing the criminal sanction is also required.

[43] *Dominic Wolzenburg* (n 20) para 67.

[44] *Raugevicius* (n 37) paras 46–47.

that Articles 18 and 21 TFEU should bar extradition of European citizens residing permanently in another Member State against extradition for the purpose of enforcing a custodial sentence.

The Court certainly established an important restriction, especially in comparison with the previous *Petruhhin* case. Member States may afford the same treatment to other Member States' nationals on the condition that they are permanent residents within the meaning of Directive 2004/38 and can demonstrate their integration into the Member State's society.[45] In this context, the previous case law of the CJEU on permanent residence and the whole debate around the notion of social integration in the EU legal order will certainly become relevant.[46]

IV. The Limits to Member States' Foreign Powers in the Context of Extradition Agreements

The outlined recent trends in Member States' extradition agreements raise some questions as regards Member States' management of their foreign relations and the limits deriving to them from EU law. The interest of impunity prevention constitutes a tool to balance competing interests and allow a margin of manoeuvre to Member States when they are requested to execute their international obligations. However, the Court has set some clear limits to Member States' action.

A. The Execution of Extradition Agreements

As a first remark, it must be observed that the judgments on extradition requested to Member States by third countries confirms the previous case law of the CJEU on the exercise of Member States' retained foreign powers. Member States are required to comply with EU law obligations both in the conclusion and the execution of international agreements concluded with third countries. In the *Raugevicius* case, the Court confirmed that

> in the absence of EU legal provisions on the extradition of nationals of Member States to Russia, Member States retain the power to adopt such provisions, those Member States are required to exercise that power in accordance with EU law, in particular, the prohibition on discrimination laid down in Article 18 TFEU and the freedom to

[45] See S Montaldo, 'Offenders' Rehabilitation and the Cross-Border Transfer of Prisoners and Persons Subject to Probation Measures and Alternative Sanctions: A Stress Test for EU Judicial Cooperation in Criminal Matters' (2019) 5 *Revista Brasileira de Direito Processual Penal* 925.

[46] In this regard, see S Montaldo, 'Us and Them: Restricting EU Citizenship Rights through the Notion of Social Integration' (2017) *Freedom, Security and Justice: European Legal Studies* 34; S Coutts, 'The Absence of Integration and the Responsibilities of Union Citizenship' (2018) 3 *European Papers* 761.

move and reside within the territory of the Member States guaranteed by Article 21(1) TFEU.[47]

Retained powers imply the possibility for Member States to conclude international agreements with third countries or, more generally, to manage their international relations. Nonetheless, they are not free from constraints.[48] Indeed, it is usually assumed that their exercise is subjected to procedural and substantial obligations imposed by the duty of loyalty and the primacy of EU law.[49] The former requires Member States to prevent conflict of rules by means of a duty of abstention from international action or of consultation with EU institutions,[50] while the latter imposes the precedence of EU law over incompatible international commitments assumed towards third states.

In the traditional construction, however, it is upon the Member States' competent authorities to decide whether and how to comply with an international obligation owed to a third country. The decision will be determined also by the margin of discretion left by international law, which will define the extent of a concrete conflict with EU law. The state will be free to decide how to act by balancing different and concurrent obligations. Otherwise, according to a settled position of the CJEU, it will be required to apply EU law and disregard its international obligations.[51]

It is thus remarkable that in the line of cases dealing with extradition requests from third countries, the CJEU has preferred to essentially maintain control over this balancing operation. Indeed, once the Court established that the objective of preventing impunity, pursued by bilateral extradition treaties, constituted a legitimate objective of EU law, it had the opportunity to determine the result of the proportionality test, by giving priority to internal mechanism of judicial cooperation.[52] At the same time, this conclusion and its consequences stem precisely from the duty of loyalty under Article 4(3) TEU.[53]

[47] *Raugevicius* (n 37) para 45.

[48] See J Klabbers, 'Restraints on the Treaty-Making Power of Member States Deriving from EU Law: Towards a Framework for Analysis' in E Cannizzaro (ed), *The European Union as an Actor in International Relations* (The Hague, Kluwer, 2002) 151, 175: 'even where the formal power still remains with the Member States, they cannot use their power in any which way they please'. See, eg CJEU, Case C-307/97 *Saint Gobain v Finanzamt Aachen-Innerstadt* ECLI:EU:C:1999:438, para 57; CJEU, Case C-55/00 *Gottardo v INPS* ECLI:EU:C:2002:16, paras 33–34.

[49] M Cremona, 'EU External Relations: Unity and Conferral of Powers' in L Azoulai (ed), *The Question of Competence* (Oxford, Oxford University Press, 2014) 65.

[50] E Neframi, 'The Duty of Loyalty: Rethinking Its Scope through Its Application in the Field of EU External Relations' (2010) 47 *CML Rev* 323; A Thies, 'Le devoir de coopération loyale dans l'exercise des compétences externes de l'Union européenne et des Etats membres' in E Neframi (ed), *Objectifs e compétences dans l'Union européenne* (Brussels, Bruylant, 2012) 326ff.

[51] Case 537/11 *Manzi v Capitaneria di Porto di Genova* ECLI:EU:C:2014:19, para 41.

[52] This with the only exception of cases in which the Member State has no jurisdiction over a certain offence or has decided not to exercise its title of jurisdiction, as the Italian authorities did in the *Pisciotti* case. In that regard, the Court has not followed the opinion of AG Bot, suggesting that Arts 18 and 21 TFEU were violated due to the refusal of the Italian authorities to prosecute Mr Pisciotti in Italy. See Case 191/16 *Romano Pisciotti* ECLI:EU:C:2018:878, Opinion of AG Bot, paras 52–55.

[53] *Petruhhin* (n 1) para 42.

The balancing exercise is particularly complex, given the broad interpretation of the scope of application of EU law with regard to Member States' international agreements[54] and the concrete risks of impunity left for prosecuted or sentenced individuals. The principles established for the first time in *Petruhhin* now seem confirmed, as the Court has recognised that discrimination based on nationality may be legitimate in order to prevent spaces of impunity, although priority must be given to the jurisdiction of the state of nationality by resorting to the EAW mechanism.

It is somehow surprising that neither the referring court nor the Court of Justice mentioned Article 351 TFEU, the so-called 'subordination clause', which gives precedence over EU law to Member States' international commitments assumed before 1 January 1958 or before their accession. Since Latvia became a Member of the Union only on 1 May 2004, it would have been reasonable to consider its treaty with Russia as a prior agreement prevailing on EU law obligations under Article 351(1) TFEU.[55] The reason for avoiding any reference to the subordination clause could have resided in the will to exclude any possible conflict between the latter and fundamental rights of EU citizens, such as the protection against discrimination. It should be recalled, in fact, that in the *Kadi* case the CJEU made clear that international obligations of Member States, even when covered by Article 351 TFEU, cannot derogate from fundamental rights guaranteed within the EU legal order.[56]

However, Article 351 TFEU does not merely provide for a derogation to the principle of primacy of EU law.[57] Instead, it also establishes certain obligations Member States have under EU law in relation to conflicting treaty obligations. In particular, according to Article 351(2) TFEU, to the extent that the agreement is incompatible with the Treaties, Member States are required 'to take all the appropriate steps to eliminate the incompatibilities established'. Moreover, Member States 'shall, where necessary, assist each other to this end and shall, where appropriate, adopt a common attitude'.[58] Among these steps, Member States are first of all expected to interpret treaty provisions in accordance with obligations deriving

[54] See also the previous decision of the CJEU in Case 473/15 *Peter Schotthöfer and Florian Steiner GbR v Eugen Adelsmayr* ECLI:EU:C:2017:633.

[55] The Court can also reformulate the questions referred to include aspects of EU law not expressly addressed by the national judge. See K Lenaerts, I Maselis and K Gutman, *EU Procedural Law* (Oxford, Oxford University Press, 2014) 235. See also Case C-513/03, *Heirs of MEA van Hilten-van der Heijden* ECLI:EU:C:2006:131, paras 23–27; Joined Cases C-307/09 to C-309/09 *Vicoplus et al v Minister van Sociale Zaken en Werkgelegenheid* ECLI:EU:C:2011:64, paras 22–25.

[56] See Joined Cases C-402/05 and C-415/05 *Kadi and Al Barakaat International Foundation* [2008] ECLI:EU:C:2008:461, para 304, where the Court stated that Art 351 TFEU 'may in no circumstances permit any challenge to the principles that form part of the very foundations of the Community legal order, one of which is the protection of fundamental rights'.

[57] R Schütze, *An Introduction to European Law* (Cambridge, Cambridge University Press, 2012) 138.

[58] These duties also derive from the principle of sincere cooperation enshrined in Art 4(3) TEU. See P Koutrakos, *EU International Relations Law* (Oxford, Hart Publishing, 2015) 324; see also Case 205/06 *Commission v Austria* [2008] ECLI:EU:C:2008:391, Opinion of AG Maduro, paras 33–34.

from EU law.[59] Beside this, the Member State concerned has to amend the incompatible treaty provision by entering into negotiation with its counterpart. The CJEU, however, has qualified the provision of Article 351(2) TFEU as an obligation of result, so that, when amendments are not suitable to solve the conflict or when an agreement with the third country concerned is not reached, Member States have to terminate the treaty.[60]

As already observed, in the *Petruhhin* judgment, the Court refrained from expressly qualifying the relationship between the principle of non-discrimination and the nationality exception of the extradition agreement as a conflicting one. In the last paragraph, however, I have tried to demonstrate that such a conflict – in a normative sense – exists and can extend to a wide range of Member States' extradition agreements concluded with third countries. This implies that, should these agreements fall within the temporal scope of application of Article 351(2) TFEU, Member States will be under the obligation to amend them in order to include a protection for all EU citizens having exercised their freedom of movement or, as a last resort, to terminate them. This could appear to be a rather drastic solution. If the Court had applied Article 351 TFEU, it could have had the opportunity to clarify the scope and the content of Member States' obligations in relation to extradition agreements conflicting with EU law.

B. The Impact of the EU Charter of Fundamental Rights

Once the applicability of EU law is established in relation to a certain situation, this also triggers the obligation for Member States to act in conformity with the Charter.[61] The Court has confirmed that 'situations cannot exist which are covered in that way by European Union law without those fundamental rights being applicable'.[62] This holds true not only when national authorities are implementing EU law, but also in cases in which Member States enjoy a wide margin of discretion or even adopt measures derogating from EU law.[63]

In the context of extradition requests, Article 19(2) of the Charter makes clear that no one can be extradited to a state where there is a serious risk that he or she would be subjected to the death penalty, torture or other inhuman or degrading

[59] Case 216/01 *Budějovický Budvar, národní podnik v Rudolf Ammersin GmbH* [2003] ECLI:EU:C:2003:618, para 169.

[60] Provided that the termination – usually made by means of a denunciation – is possible under international law. See Case 62/98 *Commission v Portugal* [2000] ECLI:EU:C:2000:358, para 34.

[61] According to Art 51 of the Charter, 'The provisions of this Charter are addressed to the institutions and bodies of the Union with due regard for the principle of subsidiarity and to the Member States only when they are implementing Union law'.

[62] Case 617/10 *Åkerberg Fransson* [2013] ECLI:EU:C:2013:105, para 21.

[63] For a comprehensive analysis, especially in relation to criminal cooperation matters, see S Montaldo, *I limiti della cooperazione in materia penale nell'Unione europea* (Naples, Editoriale Scientifica, 2015) 464–69.

treatment or punishment.[64] Accordingly, any EU citizen entitled by virtue of Articles 20 and Article 21 TFEU to remain on the territory of a Member State other than that of nationality also enjoys the protection of the Charter against extradition.[65]

In the *Petruhhin* case, Mr Petruhhin had claimed before the Latvian Supreme Court that his extradition to Russia would have been barred – regardless of the principle of non-discrimination – on grounds of Article 19(2) of the Charter. The CJEU reiterated that the decision of a Member State to extradite a national of another Member State who had availed himself of his freedom of movement falls within the scope of EU law and therefore needs to comply with the Charter.[66] This is the first time the CJEU has applied the protection under Article 19 of the Charter to extradition towards third countries.[67] The requirements identified by the Court had thus extensively drawn upon its previous case law on the EAW.

A Member State which has received an extradition request from a third country is required to verify the presence of certain elements, excluding the risks envisaged by Article 19(2) of the Charter. The evaluation must be first conducted in the light of the European Court of Human Rights case law on the interpretation of Article 3 of the Convention on Human Rights.[68] Beside this, the CJEU made reference to its previous judgment *Aranyosi and Căldăraru*, in which it established that, in order to determine the existence of a risk of inhuman or degrading treatment, the competent national authority must rely on information that is objective, reliable, specific and properly updated.[69] It is interesting to note that the Court – supported by AG Bot[70] – has deemed that the content of the protection afforded to individuals by Article 19 of the Charter is essentially the same as that provided in Article 4 of the Charter, on the prohibition of torture and inhuman or degrading treatment. By reference to the *Aranyosi and Căldăraru* judgment, the Court has thus made clear that the standards of protection applicable in the case of an EAW

[64] The provision incorporates well-settled international standards deriving from human rights law. See the Explanations relating to the Charter of Fundamental Rights of the European Union on Article 19 (2007/C 303/02), expressly recalling the case law of the European Court of Human Rights.

[65] E Guild, 'Article 19' in S Peers, T Hervey, J Kenner and A Ward (eds), *The EU Charter of Fundamental Rights – A Commentary* (Oxford, Hart Publishing, 2014) 549.

[66] *Petruhhin* (n 1) para 52, expressly recalling the *Fransson* judgment of 2013.

[67] In the subsequent *Raugevicius* case, the Court confirmed that the protection granted by the Charter also covers extradition requests for the purpose of enforcement of sentences. See *Raugevicius* (n 37) para 49.

[68] *Petruhhin*, Opinion of AG Bot (n 4) para 77ff.

[69] The national authority can consider, inter alia, judgments of international courts, such as the European Court of Human Rights, judgments of the courts of the requesting state and also decisions, reports or other documents produced by the Council of Europe or under the aegis of the United Nations. See Joined Cases C-404/15 and C-659/15 *Pál Aranyosi e Robert Căldăraru* [2016] ECLI:EU:C:2016:198, paras 88–89.

[70] See *Petruhhin*, Opinion of AG Bot (n 4) para 83, affirming that the methodology defined by the Court in relation to the European arrest warrant can be transposed to the case in which the Member State receiving an extradition request from a third country must ascertain the requirements sets forth in Art 19(2) of the Charter.

also apply in relation to extradition requests received by Member States from third countries. National competent authorities are thus required to assess not just the general situation existing in the requesting state, but more specifically the real risk of one of the situations described by Article 19(2) of the Charter in relation to the concrete circumstances of the case.[71]

In relation to extradition cases, it is now undisputed that the Charter further restricts the margin of discretion left to Member States and that it will always prevail even in situations where the request could, in principle, be executed by relying on the need to prevent spaces of impunity.

V. 'Justifying' EU Law: The *aut dedere aut iudicare* Principle

The judgments of the CJEU related to extradition agreements present certain peculiarities also as regards the approach towards international law. Although the Court is generally considered as having an 'unfriendly' relationship with the international legal order,[72] it is worth noting that in these cases it has made an effort to take into consideration the position of Member States vis-à-vis third countries' interests.

This is particularly evident where the Court makes reference to the *aut dedere aut iudicare* principle. To a certain extent, the principle becomes the international facet of the internal objective of preventing impunity. By making such reference, the Court acknowledges the existence of a principle of international law which would justify, in the eyes of the third country requesting extradition, refusal based on the principle of non-discrimination.[73] It is certainly true that the strict connection between the *aut dedere aut iudicare* principle and the objective of preventing impunity has led the Court to consider the former as one of the elements of the proportionality test, thus removing it from the discretion of the Member States. However, this paves the way for reinforcing the legitimacy of Member States' refusal of extradition requests on the international level.[74] In other words, the

[71] A Pozdnakova, 'Aleksei Petruhhin: Extradition of EU Citizens to Third Countries' (2017) 2 *European Papers* 209, 219. In the recent *Generalstaatsanwaltschaft* judgment, the CJEU made clear that the assessment must also take into consideration 'the real risk of inhuman or degrading treatment to which the person surrendered would be exposed as a result of the conditions of his detention in the prison in which he is likely to be incarcerated'. See Case 220/18 *Generalstaatsanwaltschaft* [2018] ECLI:EU:C:2018:589, para 90.

[72] J Klabbers, *The European Union in International Law* (Paris, Pedone, 2012).

[73] See Institut de droit international, 'New Problems of Extradition: Session of Cambridge 1983', Art VII: 'While every State should in principle remain free to refuse the extradition of its nationals, it should in that event try the offence under its own law.'

[74] Moreover, this would solve some of the complexities in identifying the proper forum for prosecution. In relation to the *Lockerbie* case, see A Aust, 'Lockerbie: The Other Case' (2000) 49 *International and Comparative Law Quarterly* 278.

principle is the tool Member States have at their disposal at the international level to attain the objective of preventing impunity.[75]

On the other hand, the way in which the CJEU made reference to the *aut dedere aut iudicare* principle may create some uncertainties.

It seems, in fact, that the Court considered the *aut dedere aut judicare* principle as a general principle applicable to a wide range of situations. However, this is not the case in the international legal order, within which the principle has not acquired a customary nature, given the fragmented practice in relation to its codification.[76] It is thus clear that, notwithstanding the fact that in the *Petruhhin* case the principle was applicable,[77] there could be situations in which it has no relevance. What will happen in those cases remains an unsettled question. Following the Court's reasoning, this will essentially depend on the applicability of the *aut dedere aut judicare* principle in each specific case. In cases where the principle is not enshrined in the bilateral treaty or is not provided anywhere else, it could not be invoked to justify the extension of EU citizenship rights vis-à-vis third states.[78]

VI. Conclusions

The line of cases analysed in this chapter highlights the tensions between general principles of EU law and international law tools of mutual legal assistance. Refusing extradition requests on the basis of the non-discrimination principle may prove particularly difficult for EU Member States. Preventing impunity, in fact, is not only an internal objective of the EU legal order, but also part of the legitimate interests and expectations of the requesting third country.[79] Member States may rely on an extensive interpretation of the nationality exception, which would bring EU citizens within the notion of 'citizens of the other party'. Such a unilateral approach, however, has to be accepted by the other parties to the extradition agreement and may give rise to disputes over the correct treaty execution. The extent to which the obligation to prosecute or extradite is suitable to accommodate

[75] In a particular version of the principle whereby the *judicare* element takes priority. See MJ Costa (n 36) 199.

[76] See ILC (n 26) para 49ff. An international customary norm on the *aut dedere aut judicare* principle could perhaps be established in relation to certain specific crimes, such as terrorism or torture. See A Caligiuri, *L'obbligo aut dedere aut judicare nel diritto internazionale* (Milan, Giuffrè, 2012) 225ff.

[77] Even if no mention of such a clause is to be found in the reported provisions of the Latvia–Russia extradition agreement. The applicability of the principle could, however, be derived from the UN Convention against Transnational Organised Crime, since Mr Petruhhin was suspected of having participated in a transnational large-scale drug trafficking organisation.

[78] The same holds true for situations in which no Member State of the EU has jurisdiction to prosecute the offender. However, since most European national legislation provides for active nationality as a ground for the exercise of criminal jurisdiction, this remains an unlikely scenario.

[79] Böse (n 23) 1791.

the interests at stake largely depends on the specific legal framework applicable to a certain case. It is certainly true that the CJEU has established a clear priority of internal judicial cooperation mechanisms, but it has also confirmed that this priority is subject to the condition of being equally effective as regards the prevention of impunity. In such a scenario, Member States' extradition agreements still constitute the major instruments of judicial cooperation with third countries, although their functioning is now subject to the strict limits of EU law. And this result, far from being a mere procedural obstacle for Member States, seems to reinforce the path of the Court in using EU citizenship to define the borders and the extension of a proper 'Union territory'.[80]

[80] L Azoulai, 'Transfiguring European Citizenship: From Member States Territory to Union Territory' in D Kochenov (ed), *EU Citizenship and Federalism – The Role of Rights* (Cambridge, Cambridge University Press, 2017) 178.

17

Commercial Data Transfers and Liaison Officers: What Data Protection Rules Apply in the Fight against Impunity When Third Countries Are Involved?

CHRISTINA ECKES AND DOMINIQUE BARNHOORN

I. Introduction

Data protection is one of the great challenges of the twenty-first century. More and more data is stored, transferred, sold and analysed. It is used to enforce the law and to influence public opinion, including elections and referenda.[1] Once data leaves the jurisdiction of the European Union, it is accepted that the data protection rules are different and that the level of protection is lower than within the EU legal order. Nonetheless, large quantities of personal data leave EU territory every day as part of routinised commercial interaction. In addition, the EU invites seconded civil servants from third countries, who do not fall within the jurisdiction of the EU, cannot be held accountable in the same way and do not answer to the same rules, to work in its agencies and have access to data.

This chapter addresses the question of whether and under what circumstances data protection should prevail over the fight against impunity. It focuses on data cooperation between the EU and the USA in the context of crime prevention and law enforcement. It examines the limited control mechanisms that are in place to ensure data protection after data has been transferred or otherwise shared in the highly relevant and controversial context of commercial transfers of personal data and in the academically rather neglected context of liaison officers seconded from the USA to EU agencies within the area of freedom, security and justice (AFSJ).

[1] On the latter point, see: https://www.theguardian.com/news/series/cambridge-analytica-files. On the latter point, see www.theguardian.com/news/series/cambridge-analytica-files. On the latter point, see www.theguardian.com/news/series/cambridge-analytica-files.

The objective is to identify limits imposed by data protection requirements on data sharing as a means of fighting impunity, responsibilities of EU actors for data that is collected and processed within the EU's jurisdiction, be it public or private actors, and limits of the EU's control over data flows in the twenty-first century.

The paper is structured as follows. Section II briefly sketches the EU's legal framework for data protection. Section III turns to transfers of personal data in the context of commercial transactions and national security. It engages with the Court of Justice of the European Union (CJEU)'s recent case law on data protection, including the cases of *Schrems I* and *Schrems III*, which specifically concern the rules and guarantees that apply to commercial data transfers. National security exemptions in the EU data protection framework are examined and it is explained why they cannot apply to data transfers to third countries. This makes it very difficult to determine what standard of protection must apply in the third country for the data transfer to be legal under EU law. EU secondary law also does not require the same or even an equivalent level of protection. The section concludes with the checks and balances within the EU's data protection framework, and reflects on whether a differentiated approach toward data transfers between the EU and third countries is desirable. Section IV focuses on the specific example of data transfers via liaison officers in the AFSJ. Liaison officers are introduced as intermediate actors between two administrations – in this case, Europol and the US administration. It examines whether and how EU data protection standards could apply to liaison officers deployed from the USA to Europol. Section V then argues that protection of data that leaves the jurisdiction of the EU cannot be guaranteed at the same level as data within the jurisdiction of the EU. Similarly, when seconded civil servants of third countries are given access to data within the EU institutions, agencies and bodies, they are not subject to the same data protection rules as the EU's or Member States' civil servants. Ultimately, the two cases of commercial data transfers and the deployment of liaison officers demonstrate that data cooperation always comes at some cost in terms of data protection.

II. EU Data Protection Framework

Data protection is guaranteed within the European Union as a fundamental right in Articles 7 (respect for private and family life) and 8 (protection of personal data) of the Charter of Fundamental Rights (CFR). The right's personal scope is 'everyone'. In addition, Article 16 TFEU serves as a specific legal basis for adopting legislation to give effect to this right. The main secondary pieces of legislation are the 2016 General Data Protection Regulation (GDPR) and the 2016 Directive on the processing of personal data for authorities responsible for preventing, investigating, detecting and prosecuting crimes.[2]

[2] Regulation (EU) 2016/679 of the European Parliament and of the Council of 27 April 2016 on the protection of natural persons with regard to the processing of personal data and on the free movement

In May 2018, the GDPR replaced the previously applicable Data Protection Directive of 1995 (DPD)[3] for (inter alia) the specific issue of transferring personal data to third countries. In relation to data transfer to third countries, Article 45 GDPR replaced Article 25 DPD. Both provisions require an 'adequate' level of protection.[4] The Commission adopts general 'adequacy decisions' that address the general level of protection within the third country.[5] The Data Protection Authorities (DPAs) examine specific requests from individuals. 'Adequacy' implies that the standard does not have to be the same but that in fact data transfer is legal when a different, lower standard applies after the data has left the jurisdiction of the EU.

In 2016, the EU concluded an umbrella agreement with the USA on data transfers to the USA for law enforcement purposes. The EU placed a number of demands on the USA for the agreement to be concluded, such as that the US Judicial Redress Act extends the protection of the US Privacy Act of 1974 to EU citizens.[6] In addition, the USA also adopted the US Freedom Act 2015. However, it is fairly uncontroversial that domestic legal rules in the USA and international commitments do not guarantee a level of protection equivalent to the protection in the EU. They do not exclude access to personal data on a generalised basis, which was specifically found to be illegal under EU law (*Digital Rights Ireland*),[7] and which also interferes with the core of the right to private life as it is protected under the CFR and the European Convention of Human Rights (ECHR). In terms of remedies provided, the USA does not offer the full scope required under EU law (possibility to judicially enforce access, rectification and erasure).[8]

Within the EU legal order, international agreements rank between primary and secondary law. This means, in principle, that international commitments cannot be reviewed in the light of secondary law and that secondary law is interpreted in line with international agreements (consistent interpretation). Exceptions to this general hierarchy can be argued on the basis of the CJEU's line of case law of *Mangold* and *Kücükdeveci*,[9] where secondary law gives specific expression to a

of such data, and repealing Directive 95/46/EC (General Data Protection Regulation) [2016] OJ L119/1 (GDPR); Directive (EU) 2016/680 of the European Parliament and of the Council of 27 April 2016 on the protection of natural persons with regard to the processing of personal data by competent authorities for the purposes of the prevention, investigation, detection or prosecution of criminal offences or the execution of criminal penalties, and on the free movement of such data, and repealing Council Framework Decision 2008/977/JHA [2016] OJ L119/89.

[3] Directive 95/46/EC of the European Parliament and of the Council of 24 October 1995 on the protection of individuals with regard to the processing of personal data and on the free movement of such data [1995] OJ L281/31.

[4] Art 25(1) DPD; Art 45(1) GDPR.

[5] Art 25(6) DPD; Art 45(1) GDPR; see also recitals 103–07 GDPR, emphasising the Commission's role and the EU's commitment to fundamental rights.

[6] Judicial Redress Act of 2015.

[7] Joined Cases C-29312 and C-594/12 *Digital Rights Ireland and Seitlinger and Others* ECLI:EU:C:2014:238.

[8] Art 8 CFR.

[9] Case C-144/04 *Werner Mangold v Rüdiger Helm* ECLI:EU:C:2005:709; Case C-555/07 *Seda Kücükdeveci v Swedex GmbH & Co KG* ECLI:EU:C:2010:21.

general principle of EU law or a fundamental right protected under the Charter.[10] In these exceptional cases, secondary law is in fact understood as a concretisation of the general principle or right under primary law and as such can influence the interpretation and validity of international agreements. In the present context, one could imagine that certain core principles of the GDPR could be considered an expression of the general right to protection of personal data. This would exclude that international agreements with the USA could disregard the protection provided under the GDPR.

If this were not the case, however, the general hierarchy (international agreements rank between primary and secondary law) means that, in principle, the executive could, subject to principles of coherence and sincere cooperation, conclude international agreements even if they are contrary to secondary law adopted by the European Parliament and the Council acting as co-legislators on a proposal of the Commission. To put it more crudely, if the GDPR is not the expression of the right to the protection of personal data as enshrined in Articles 7 and 8 CFR, there may be room for a doctrinal argument that the Council and the Commission could depart from the GDPR's standard when they negotiate (the Commission under a mandate from the Council) different rules with a third country.

A. Data Transfers and National Security

(i) Data Transfer to the USA: Schrems I *and the Privacy Shield*

The case of *Schrems I*[11] was in several respects a wake-up call, reminding us of the difficulties of protecting personal data once it has left the jurisdiction of the EU. Based on the DPD (because the GDPR had not yet been adopted) and on principled considerations drawn from Articles 7 and 8 CFR, the CJEU declared invalid the transfer regime between the EU and the USA.[12] It interpreted the adequate level of protection under the DPD as meaning an 'essentially equivalent' level of protection.[13]

The Commission found that data protection rules in the USA do not generally offer an adequate standard of protection but, with its 'adequacy' decision on the EU–US Safe Harbour regime (2000), endorsed the practice that companies self-certify that they meet a number of principles (safe harbour principles) and the US authorities check this within their competences.[14] The Commission had

[10] See also Case C-414/16 *Egenberger* ECLI:EU:C:2018:257 (Art. 21 and 47 CFR); Case C-569/16 *Bauer* ECLI:EU:C:2018:871 (Art 31(2) CFR).

[11] Case C-362/14 *Maximillian Schrems v Data Protection Commissioner* ECLI:EU:C:2015:650.

[12] Case C-362/14 *Schrems v Data Protection Commissioner* ECLI:EU:C:2015:650.

[13] Ibid, para 73–4.

[14] Decision 2000/520/EC, Commission Decision of 26 July 2000 pursuant to Directive 95/46/EC of the European Parliament and of the Council on the adequacy of the protection provided by the safe

also repeatedly criticised the level of protection provided by the safe harbour regime,[15] and politically worked – albeit without great success – with the US authorities to improve it.[16] Relevant also for the public perception of data transfers to the USA were Edward Snowden's revelations in 2013 that under the PRISM programme the NSA is able to access personal data stored on US servers in an essentially unrestricted manner.

Max Schrems brought a complaint to the Irish DPA intended to stop the transfer of his personal data from Facebook Ireland to Facebook Inc in the USA. The Irish DPA declined to open an investigation because of the Commission's Safe Harbour Decision, despite the fact that the Decision confirmed the DPA's powers to stop data transfer in individual cases.[17] Schrems challenged the DPA's decision not to open an investigation before the Irish High Court, which referred a preliminary question to the CJEU. The Irish High Court specifically voiced doubts that US practices satisfied Articles 7 and 8 of the EU's CFR, as interpreted by the CJEU in *Digital Rights Ireland*.[18] In response, the CJEU emphasised the crucial role of national DPAs in the data protection framework within the EU,[19] and ruled that they had the obligation to investigate the level of protection in individual cases. If the national DPA finds fault with the data transfer, it must refer the case to a national court, which should ask a question to the CJEU as the only authority that can invalidate the Commission's adequacy decisions. The CJEU also invalidated the Commission's Safe Harbour Decision,[20] essentially because of the formal reason that the Safe Harbour regime was not based on legally binding obligations under either domestic US law or international law, but instead relies on a self-certification regime.

Moreover, the Court, recalling *Digital Rights Ireland*,[21] concluded that the Safe Harbour regime allowed for too far-reaching exceptions, including for national security matters. In essence, domestic law and international commitments of the third country would have to offer sufficient safeguards limiting the storage of personal data, access to that data by public authorities and further use of the data. Domestic law and international commitments would further have to offer remedies to individuals allowing them to access their data and, if need be, having it corrected or erased.

harbour privacy principles and related frequently asked questions issued by the US Department of Commerce [2000] OJ L215/7 (Decision 2000/520/EC).

[15] Commission, 'Rebuilding Trust in EU–US Data Flows' (Communication) COM (2013) 846 final of 27 November 2013; Commission, 'The Functioning of the Safe Harbour from the Perspective of EU Citizens and Companies established in the EU' (Communication) COM (2013) 847 final of 27 November 2013.

[16] ibid.

[17] Art 3 of Decision 2000/520/EC.

[18] *Digital Rights Ireland* (n 7).

[19] See also Case C-288/12 *Commission v Hungary* [2014] ECLI:EU:C:2014:237.

[20] Art 25(6) DPD.

[21] *Digital Rights Ireland* (n 7).

After *Schrems I*, more than 4000 US companies, which had previously relied on the Safe Harbour regime, had to find new ways to continue making data transfers. Many switched to either Binding Corporate Rules or Standard Contractual Clauses (SCCs), both of which are more burdensome on the companies that use them and more limited in scope. SCCs are model clauses, approved by the Commission (SCC decision), that create contractual obligations between data controllers and data processors that govern the transfer of data. In 2016, the Safe Harbour regime was succeeded by the Privacy Shield. SCCs (and the Commission's SCC decision) remain relevant when businesses withdraw voluntarily from the Privacy Shield. The legal framework is construed to allow for derogation from an 'adequate' level of protection. It permits transfer of data to third countries which do not ensure an adequate level of protection on a more cumbersome case-by-case basis (SCC and SCC Decision).[22]

Besides the SCC, severe doubts about the adequacy of data protection under the Privacy Shield persist. Since its entry into force, several non-governmental organisations have tried and failed to challenge the Privacy Shield adequacy decision.[23] The Privacy Shield consists of 23 privacy principles,[24] together with official representations and commitments by various US authorities. It also relies on self-certification with the Department of Commerce. The Commission had confirmed the adequacy of the Privacy Shield within the framework established by the 1995 Data Protection Directive (Privacy Shield Decision 2016).[25]

Several institutional actors within the EU voiced concerns about the adequacy of the Privacy Shield. On 28 November 2017, the Article 29 Working Party, which has now been replaced by the European Data Protection Board, made recommendations to bring the Privacy Shield into compliance with the GDPR.[26] On 5 July 2018, the European Parliament's Committee on Civil Liberties, Justice and Home Affairs (LIBE Committee) adopted a non-binding resolution recommending that the Commission suspend the EU/US Privacy Shield unless the USA takes a number of specified steps to improve data protection.[27]

[22] Commission Implementing Decision (EU) 2016/2297 of 16 December 2016 amending Decisions 2001/497/EC and 2010/87/EU on standard contractual clauses for the transfer of personal data to third countries and to processors established in such countries, under Directive 95/46/EC of the European Parliament and of the Council [2016] OJ L344/100.

[23] General Court, order of 22 November 2017, Case T-670/16 *Digital Rights Ireland v Commission*; action brought on 9 December 2016, Case T-738/16 *La Quadrature du Net and Others v Commission.*

[24] eg on data integrity and purpose limitation.

[25] Commission Implementing Decision (EU) 2016/1250 of 12 July 2016 pursuant to Directive 95/46/EC of the European Parliament and of the Council on the adequacy of the protection provided by the EU–US (notified under document C(2016) 4176) (Text with EEA relevance) [2016] OJ L207/1, recital 13.

[26] Article 29 Data Protection Working Party, EU–US Privacy Shield – First Annual Joint Review, adopted 28 November 2017, WP 255/17 https://ec.europa.eu/newsroom/just/document.cfm?doc_id=48782.

[27] European Parliament resolution of 5 July 2018 on the adequacy of the protection afforded by the EU–US Privacy Shield (2018/2645(RSP)) www.europarl.europa.eu/sides/getDoc.do?type=TA&reference=P8-TA-2018–0315&format=XML&language=EN.

The discussions demonstrate that a number of political actors remain doubtful about the level of protection offered under the Privacy Shield. The CJEU would certainly give additional fuel to these criticisms if it took the position in *Schrems III* that the data transfer to Facebook Inc was contrary to EU law, even if the case, narrowly construed, concerned data transfer under the SCC.

(ii) Data Transfers and National Security: Schrems III[28]

In his 2015 complaint to the Irish DPA, Max Schrems specifically alleged that his personal data transferred to the USA was 'made available to US Government authorities under various known and unknown legal provisions and spy programs such as the PRISM program'.[29] *Schrems III* hence specifically focuses on the consequences of the fact that US authorities access and process personal data originating in the EU for national security purposes. As Facebook Ireland was not relying on the Privacy Shield for transferring data of Mr Schrems to Facebook Inc in the USA, *Schrems III* directly only concerned transfers of data pursuant to SCC.

The Irish DPA had serious concerns with regard to the remedies offered for infringement, the restrictive standing requirements and the fact that the SCC were not binding on the US Government. It brought a case to the Irish High Court (*Schrems III*),[30] which found that the DPA raised well-founded concerns and again referred a question to the CJEU.[31] The Irish High Court inquired in particular whether the CFR applied to the transfer of personal data transferred from the EU to the USA for commercial purposes under SCCs and whether the possibility that this data is further processed for national security purposes infringes Articles 7, 8 and 47 CFR.

In the context of the investigations in *Schrems III*, five US experts,[32] selected by Max Schrems,[33] Facebook[34] and the Irish Data Protection Commissioner (DPC),[35] gave testimony, including more generally about the protection offered in the USA. Facebook's first expert, Swire, confirmed that the Foreign Intelligence Surveillance Court provides independent and effective oversight

[28] Reference for a preliminary ruling from the High Court (Ireland) made on 9 May 2018 – Case C-311/18 *Data Protection Commissioner v Facebook Ireland Limited, Maximillian Schrems*.

[29] www.europe-v-facebook.org/comp_fb_ie.pdf.

[30] Case C-498/16 *Schrems II* [2018] ECLI:EU:C:2018:37 concerned jurisdictional matters and is irrelevant here.

[31] See *The Data Protection Commissioner v Facebook Ireland Ltd & anor* [2017] IEHC 545 http://courts.ie/Judgments.nsf/768d83be24938e1180256ef30048ca51/8131a5dde8baf9ff802581b70035c4ff?OpenDocument.

[32] https://iapp.org/resources/article/schrems-2-0-expert-testimony/.

[33] Ashley Gorski of the American Civil Liberties Union. https://iapp.org/media/pdf/resource_center/Schrems-testimony-Gorski.pdf.

[34] Professor Peter Swire of the Georgia Institute of Technology and Professor Stephen Vladeck of the University of Texas. Testimonies available at https://iapp.org/media/pdf/resource_center/Schrems-testimony-Swire.pdf and https://iapp.org/media/pdf/resource_center/Schrems-testimony-Vladeck.pdf.

[35] Testimonies not publicly available.

over US Government surveillance. Facebook's second expert, Vladeck, acknowledged shortcomings in the existing US legal regime with regard to redress of unlawful government data collection, but concluded that these shortcomings are not 'nearly as comprehensive – or that standing is as categorical an obstacle – as the DPC Draft Decision [and related materials] suggest'. What is certain is that the level of data protection in the USA is not at the same standard as in the EU and that EU's political institutions have no means, other than diplomatic and economic, to push for higher protection.

In *Schrems I*, the CJEU confirmed that the term 'adequate level of protection' in Article 25(6) of Directive 95/46/EC does not require a level of protection *identical* to the guarantees offered within the EU legal order. Instead, the third country must ensure a level of protection of fundamental rights that is 'essentially equivalent' to that guaranteed within the Union.[36] The means deployed may differ, but they must, in practice, prove effective. This allows for deviation, including not reaching the same level of protection in specific circumstances. This is thus the core question: does the USA offer an 'essentially equivalent' level of protection?

The Court has taken principled decisions not only in *Schrems I*, but in a much longer line of case law, even when this meant interrupting data transfer or the work of national security actors. It regularly forced political and economic actors to reconsider existing practices. Examples are the CJEU's rulings in *Digital Rights Ireland* and *Tele2*.

Digital Rights Ireland concerned the Data Retention Directive, which regulates the retention of metadata. Metadata is the information on a telecommunication, including location of the user, duration of the connection, subject-matter heading of emails and websites visited. It does not contain the personalised content of a communication. Prima facie, metadata may appear less problematic than personal data. However, in bulk, and with technically possible automated analysis tools, it can, in particular over time, amount to very sensitive information on a person.[37] Some interpreted *Digital Rights Ireland* as ruling that the general duty of retention is disproportionate.[38] Others argued that the Court accepted compensation for the general duty of retention by strict access requirements.[39]

The case of *Tele2* also concerned the retention of communications data and the necessary safeguards to protect it.[40] The issue was whether the Swedish and UK legislation imposing an obligation on public communications providers to retain traffic and location data was compatible with EU law. The Court used the standard of 'strictly necessary', and required that access to information be subject to a prior

[36] *Schrems I* (n 11) paras 73–74.

[37] I Cameron, 'Balancing Data Protection and Law Enforcement Needs: *Tele2 Sverige* and *Watson*' (2017) 54 *CML Rev* 1467, 1469 and references therein.

[38] ibid 1470ff.

[39] ibid.

[40] Joined Cases C-203/15 *Tele2 Sverige AB v Post- och telestyrelsen* and C-698/15 *Secretary of State for the Home Department v Tom Watson and Others* ECLI:EU:C:2016:970; Cameron, 'Balancing Data Protection and Law Enforcement Needs' (n 37).

check by a court or independent authority, whose task it was to ensure that access was limited to requests that met this standard.[41]

Whether current practices meet an 'essentially equivalent' level of protection is precisely the issue in *Schrems III*. If the Court holds that current practices do not meet an 'essentially equivalent' level of protection, it will again be the task of the EU's political institutions and the US Government to find new ways of making data transfer possible and compliant with European data protection rights. First of all, this raises practical issues: is it, in practice, even possible to limit the access and processing rights of national security and law enforcement authorities of third states within the jurisdiction of the third state? Increasing mass surveillance and technological development will make this ever more difficult. Ultimately, compliance depends on the willingness of the third state. To ensure a certain entrenchment that makes non-compliance more difficult, the CJEU required national and international law commitments, rather than only administrative practice, in *Schrems I*.

Secondly, the underlying questions are: how far is it normatively justifiable to accept that private businesses transfer data to other countries in which the data subject is not able to enjoy the same level of protection? How far is it normatively justifiable to impose European data protection standards on businesses in – and, by extension, government authorities of – third countries? The answers to these questions are two sides of the same coin. The extraterritorial effects of European regulation and standards,[42] sometimes also called the Brussels effect,[43] is a hotly debated issue, not only in the area of data protection.

B. National Security Exemptions: A Blind Spot in the Checks and Balances of the EU's Data Protection System?

(i) National Security Exemptions and Substantive Standards of Protection

Schrems III specifically raised the question of whether the national security exemption in Article 4(2) TEU limited the application of EU data protection laws where national security is concerned and what the meaning of Article 3(2) Data Protection Directive, now Article 2(2) GDPR, is in this context.

Generally speaking, national security is a reserved national competence. This is expressed in Article 4(2) TEU, but also in recital 16 of the GDPR. However, the EU is competent to regulate commercial data transfers. Union and Member States then have the competence to derogate from EU law for reasons of national

[41] *Digital Rights Ireland* (n 7).

[42] C Kuner, 'Extraterritoriality and Regulation of International Data Transfers in EU Data Protection Law' (2015) 5 *International Data Privacy Law* 235.

[43] A Bradford, 'The Brussels Effect' (2012) 107 *Northwestern University Law Review* 1.

security (Article 3(2) DPD and Article 23 GDPR). These derogation clauses do not establish a standard of protection that needs to be complied with even in circumstances when national security concerns are argued. They only express the general commitment to the principle of proportionality. They are specifically addressed to the Union and the Member States.[44] Also, according to formal logic, these national security exemptions under EU law – that is, clauses that allow derogation from EU law – can only apply to the exercise of public power by authorities of those bound by EU law – that is, Member States – and hence arguably only for the purpose of protecting the national security of the Member States (and possibly the EU). The derogation clauses do not apply directly to third states or their national security authorities.

Prima facie, this leaves third countries in a position where they cannot directly rely on any national security exemption under EU law. What rules should then apply to access and processing of personal data of EU citizens by national security and law enforcement authorities of third states? This is what Article 45 GDPR addresses when regulating data transfers to third countries that offer adequate protection. Adequate protection means in particular that access and processing of personal data for national security and law enforcement purposes is regulated in that third country in a way that offers essentially equivalent protection.

Even when Member States rely on national security concerns within the scope of the GDPR and derogate from the usual data protection rules, they remain bound by EU law. Within the Union's system of fundamental rights protection, the two core questions are: is the CFR applicable? Is the ECHR applicable?

The application of the CFR is limited to actions of the Member States when they implement EU law (Article 51 CFR). This has been interpreted by the CJEU as meaning 'within the scope of EU law'[45] and continues to be interpreted roughly along the same lines as in the CJEU's pre-Lisbon Treaty case law,[46] arguably clarifying that it is sufficient that EU law objectives are affected.[47] When Member States derogate from EU law – that is, within the scope of application of the GDPR – their actions must comply with the CFR. In principle, however, when Member States exercise reserved competences and pursue national security objectives (eg data processing that does not fall within the scope of the GDPR), their actions do not fall within the scope of EU law.[48] However, even then they do not act in a law-free space.

First of all, the ECHR is in principle applicable to all actions of the Member States, irrespective of the scope of EU law and irrespective of the competence division between the EU and its Member States. Article 8 ECHR protects personal data and restricts storage and use of personal data. Article 15 ECHR allows,

[44] Art 23 GDPR.

[45] See C-617/10 *Fransson* ECLI:EU:C:2013:280; C-206/13 *Siragusa* ECLI:EU:C:2014:126.

[46] Case 5/88 *Wachauf* ECLI:EU:C:1989:321; Case C-260/89 *ERT* ECLI:EU:C:1991:254.

[47] See *Fransson* (n 45); *Siragusa* (n 45).

[48] Case C-446/12 *Willems* ECLI:EU:C:2015:238 illustrates that where a Member State uses data collected under an EU regulation for purposes outside that regulation, it acts outside of the scope of EU law.

in exceptional cases, for a declaration of a state of emergency, which leads to a general restriction of Convention rights; yet, the state of emergency exception is not applicable to the current discussion. The Irish High Court inquired whether the ECHR was directly applicable through EU law.[49] Secondly, the CJEU clarified that Member States, also when exercising their reserved competences, are bound by a general duty to respect the founding provisions of EU law, including general principles.[50]

The issues of mass surveillance and data transfers to third countries have been brought not only before the CJEU, but also before the European Court of Human Rights (ECtHR). The ECtHR confirmed in the cases of *Zakharov* and *Szabo* how seriously it takes data protection.[51] In early 2019, two relevant cases were referred to the Grand Chamber of the ECtHR. The first concerns complaints by journalists, individuals and rights organisations about three different surveillance regimes: (i) the bulk interception of communications; (ii) intelligence sharing with foreign governments; and (iii) the obtaining of communications data from communications service providers.[52] The second concerns a complaint brought by a public interest law firm alleging that legislation permitting the bulk interception of electronic signals in Sweden for foreign intelligence purposes breached its privacy rights.[53] So far, no specific principles have been developed that could give useful guidance on the point of how far personal data could and should be protected beyond the jurisdiction of the contracting parties of the ECHR. Yet, the pending cases give the ECtHR further occasion to develop the right to data protection in Europe.

EU Member States hence remain bound by the right to the protection of personal data under the ECHR, including when EU law does not apply. Even when acting with the objective of protecting national security, they must continue to adhere to the ECHR. Within the EU, this general commitment to a shared interpretation of human rights protection is also the very basis of mutual trust between Member States, on which all cooperation, including data exchange, depends.

(ii) Checks and Balances within the EU

The CJEU's data protection case law also has repercussions for the balance of powers within the EU. *Schrems I* is an example of decentralisation of power to the

[49] See formulation of question 1: http://curia.europa.eu/juris/document/document.jsf?text=&docid=204046&pageIndex=0&doclang=en&mode=lst&dir=&occ=first&part=1&cid=6451273.

[50] See Case C-192/05 *Tas-Hagen and Tas* ECLI:EU:C:2006:676; Case C-135/08 *Rottmann* ECLI:EU:C:2010:104; Case C-438/05 *Viking* ECLI:EU:C:2007:772. For an ongoing discussion of the relevance of general principles beyond the scope of the Charter, see C Amalfitano, *General Principles of EU Law and the Protection of Fundamental Rights* (Cheltenham, Edward Elgar Publishing, 2018).

[51] *Zakharov v Russia* App no 47143/06 (2016) 63 EHRR 17 (ECtHR, 4 December 2015); *Szabo v Hungary* App no 37138/14 (2016) 63 EHRR 3 (ECtHR, 12 January 2016).

[52] *Big Brother Watch and Others v the United Kingdom* App nos 58170/13, 62322/14 and 24960/15 (ECtHR, 13 September 2018).

[53] *Centrum för rättvisa v Sweden* App no 35252/08 (ECtHR, 19 June 2018).

Member States. Article 25(6) DPD confers a power on the Commission to make a finding that a particular third country ensures an adequate level of protection so that, in principle, personal data may be transferred from any EU Member State to a non-EU state. It remains the task of the national DPA to ensure that the level of protection in the individual case is adequate pursuant to the criteria set out in Article 25(2) DPD.[54]

The Court confirmed the important role of national DPAs under this framework and emphasised that it needs to conduct autonomous inquiries into the level of data protection in each individual case, even if the Commission has overall found the transfer regime adequate.

Tele2, by contrast, is a case in which more decentralisation would have been possible and desirable. The AG in *Tele2* suggested more decentralisation. The Court rejected the AG's Opinion; however, the Court's decision in this regard has been criticised.[55]

Decentralisation and shared responsibilities at different levels of government introduce a mechanism of checks and balances, which seems capable of contributing significantly to the overall level of protection. At the same time, the way the control mechanism is constructed in *Schrems I*, ultimately requiring a reference to the CJEU, makes it highly likely that data protection cases end up before the Court of Justice. This allows the Court to develop and enforce a uniform level of protection. It is also inevitably a form of centralisation. Overall, the mechanism of checks and balances inherent in the EU's legal framework for data protection involves a number of different authorities with the mandate to ensure and enforce a high level of protection. It seems prone to strengthen the level of protection over time rather than to lower it.

C. Concluding Remarks

Both 2018 and 2019 have been characterised by increasing geo-economic tensions, such as sanctions, tariffs, free trade agreements and investment protection. Data flows across the globe continue to grow exponentially. Commercial data is of ever greater economic relevance, and any limitations imposed by the CJEU or any other EU institution are likely to be received as actions that form part of this growing tension. Data is not only used for law enforcement purposes, but is also highly relevant, for example, for the good functioning of democracies, including national elections in EU Member States and elections to the European Parliament. This is the context in which the debate on protection of personal data after commercial data transfers should be placed.

The CJEU has time and again upheld EU data protection standards in different situations – when data is transferred to third countries (*Schrems I*), when data

[54] Art 25(1) DPD.
[55] Cameron (n 37).

is accessed and processed by telecommunications providers (*Tele2*) and when data is retained, including for future law enforcement purposes (*Digital Rights Ireland*). It is certain that the EU data protection standards do not apply when data is transferred to third countries and that the EU has only limited means to enforce the agreements made with the third country. Requiring the same standard would be practically impossible. It would also raise normative questions if US authorities would have to act pursuant to EU standards, adopted by political representatives of the EU and national citizens. The question remains what is an essentially equivalent level of protection and how can it be ensured in practice? This is what is necessary in order to justify allowing commercial data transfers on a large scale.

III. Impunities Surrounding the Deployment of Liaison Officers

A. Legal Basis and Tasks of Liaison Officers

Cooperation and coordination between police, judicial authorities and other competent authorities within the AFSJ is one of the core objectives laid down in the TFEU to ensure security in the EU.[56] The many challenges stipulated in the Treaties reflect the EU's growing international perspective. Over the past two decades, cooperation between the EU and third countries has increased sharply.[57] Correspondingly, a significant amount of EU secondary law and EU (policy) documents on security and migration[58] stresses the importance of cooperation between competent authorities between the EU and external actors. To establish

[56] Art 67(3) TFEU on criminal matters in the area of freedom, security and justice.

[57] J Monar, 'The EU's Growing External Role in the AFSJ Domain: Factors, Framework and Forms of Action' (2014) 27 *Cambridge Review of International Affairs* 147, 149; RA Wessel, L Marin and C Matera, 'The External Dimension of the EU's Area of Freedom, Security and Justice' in C Eckes and T Konstadinides (eds), *Crime Within the Area of Freedom, Security and Justice: A European Public Order* (Cambridge, Cambridge University Press, 2011), 277.

[58] Recitals 1, 3 and 4 of Council Regulation (EC) 377/2004 of 19 February 2004 on the creation of an Immigration Liaison Officers network [2004] OJ L64/1 (ILO Regulation); Art 54 and recital 20 of Regulation (EU) 2016/1624 of the European Parliament and of the Council of 14 September 2016 on the European Border and Coast Guard [2016] OJ L251/1 (Frontex Regulation); concluded bilateral agreements between Frontex and third countries: Canada, Turkey and the USA; C Jones, 'Briefing: Frontex: Cooperation with Non-EU States' (*Statewatch*, March 2017) www.statewatch.org/analyses/no-309-frontex-third-countries-agreements.pdf, 12; Art 8(3) of Regulation (EU) 2016/794 of the European Parliament and the Council of 11 May 2016 on the European Union Agency for Law Enforcement Cooperation [2016] OJ L135/53 (Europol Regulation).

Council of the European Union report, 'Outcome of the EU – US Justice and Home Affairs Senior Officials Meeting, Valetta 1–2 March 2017'; Commission, 'Establishing a New Partnership Framework with Third Countries under the European Agenda on Migration' (Communication) COM (2016) 385 final; Commission, 'Proposal for a Regulation of the EP and the Council on the Creation of a European Network of Immigration Liaison Officers' COM (2018) 303.

and maintain links between EU and third-country authorities, one of the instruments used is the deployment of liaison officers from third countries within the EU and vice versa.[59] The objective and tasks for liaison officer secondment focuses on 'coordination and cooperation between police and judicial authorities'.[60] This is in line with the objectives stipulated in the general provisions on the AFSJ set out in the TFEU.

The deployment of liaison officers is based on a variety of legal instruments: EU Regulations,[61] bilateral cooperation agreements[62] and Memoranda of Understanding[63] concluded between an EU authority and a third-country authority, often in the areas of security or migration. The instruments are, however, ambiguous about which is the competent jurisdiction that subjects liaison officers to administrative or judicial review, as well as the applicable legal regime. As it is unclear which legal regime implicitly or explicitly applies to the liaison officer, it is also unclear what data protection standards apply to them.

The same legal instruments list generally defined tasks of liaison officers, but fail to qualify their actual reach or legal effect, which is relevant in determining what rules and consequent control mechanisms may apply to these liaison officers. A wide array of responsibilities for liaison officers are visible in annual reports of EU AFSJ agencies[64] and job vacancies for liaison officers.[65] The responsibilities vary from far-reaching (ie use of EU and Member State databases for police and migration purposes;[66] assistance and facilitation of the swift exchange of information;[67]

[59] HCH Hofmann and AH Türk, *EU Administrative Governance* (Cheltenham, Edward Elgar Publishing, 2006) 343.

[60] Art 27(3) of the Council Decision of 28 February 2002 setting up Eurojust with a view to reinforcing the fight against serious crime [2002] OJ L63/1 (hereafter Eurojust Dec); Art 8(1) Europol Regulation; ArtArt. 12(3) and 54 Frontex Regulation.

[61] Europol Regulation (ibid); ILO Regulation (n 56).

[62] Two types of cooperation agreement exist in the legal interaction between EU AFSJ agencies and non-EU states or other entities outside the EU: strategic and operational agreements. Both types of agreement are aimed at enhancing cooperation between the EU agency and the non-EU state concerned. There is, however, one major difference: strategic agreements do not allow for the exchange of personal data, whereas the operational agreements do. See, eg the Annexes to the Europol cooperation agreements (n 72 and n 96).

[63] Interpol–Europol Memorandum of Understanding; Memorandum of Understanding between Eurojust–United Nations Office on Drugs and Crime (UNODC).

[64] Europol, *Europol Review 2016–2017* (2018) 64; Frontex, *A Year in Review: First 12 Months of the European Border and Coast Guard Agency* (2017) 3–5.

[65] See, eg the job vacancy for British immigration liaison officers posted 17 May 2016 by the British High Commission Office – Foreign and Commonwealth Office under https://fco.tal.net/vx/mobile-0/appcentre-ext/brand-2/candidate/so/pm/4/pl/1/opp/368-Immigration-Liaison-Officer/en-GB (job advertisement no longer available).

[66] Art 8(3), (4) Europol Regulation; exchange of information via liaison officers, via long established channels between EU Member States and third countries: 'Europol–USA Agreement: Was It Really Needed?' (*Statewatch*, 2006) www.statewatch.org/news/2006/jul/01europol-usa.htm.

[67] Art 8(3) Europol Regulation; Art 2(1) Council Regulation 377/2004; Council of the European Union outcome report, 'Meeting with Eurojust Contact Points and Liaison Magistrates appointed by Member States: Complementarity, Synergies and Cooperation, 16–17 October 2014' (20 February 2015) 4 www.eurojust.europa.eu/doclibrary/Eurojust-framework/ejstrategicmeetings/Outcome%

providing support for the decision quality of visa decisions[68]) to less far-reaching (ie network building;[69] advisory roles[70]).

B. Liaison Officers: A Short Introduction

A specific, highly relevant, but relatively unexplored tool in crime prevention cooperation is the secondment of liaison officers in the EU's area of freedom, security and justice (AFSJ). The deployment of liaison officers raises data protection concerns that could be characterised as the flipside of those discussed in the first section on commercial data transfers. It does not primarily concern what happens to data once it has left the jurisdiction of the EU and its Member States, but it does concern whether and how EU data protection rules apply to administrative officers from third countries, when they work within the EU administration and within the EU's jurisdiction.

Liaison officers are administrative agents who connect two or more administrative authorities of different jurisdictions. It is their objective to support their home administration in the enforcement of its laws. This support manifests itself in cooperation and coordination actions mainly situated in the area of security, justice and migration.The home administration is an executive body responsible for administration or enforcement in a particular policy area that deploys a liaison officer to a receiving (host) administration.[71] Once at the host administration, liaison officers carry out multiple executive tasks entrusted to them. One of those tasks discussed more extensively in this section is the easing of a swift exchange of (non)-personal information between the home and host administration. This practice of data transfers via liaison officers highlights conflicting legal issues. When liaison officers are deployed from third countries to administrative authorities within the EU, it becomes unclear under which jurisdiction they fall and what data protection rules apply. These 'non-EU state' liaison officers are in many cases regarded as a 'formal representative' of the sending administration.[72] They fall outside the EU's data protection framework described above. Put differently: liaison officers

20report%20of%20the%20meeting%20with%20Eurojust%20Contact%20Points%20and%20Liaison%20Magistrates%20(16–17%20October%202014)/Outcome-report_EJ-contact-points-liaison-and-magistrates-meeting_2015–02–20_EN.pdf.

[68] British Immigration liaison officer job vacancy (n 65).

[69] E Aydinli and H Yön, 'Transgovernmentalism Meets Security: Police Liaison Officers, Terrorism, and Statist Transnationalism' (2011) 24 *Governance: An International Journal of Policy, Administration and Institutions* 66, 67.

[70] Council outcome report, 'Meeting with Eurojust Contact Points and Liaison Magistrates' (n 67).

[71] Liaison officers can also be seconded in other policy areas to ease cooperation between administrations, such as in the areas of migration and justice.

[72] Art 2(1), Annex 4 of the Agreement on Operational and Strategic Co-operation between the Republic of Colombia and the European Police Office; Art 2, Annex III of the Agreement on Operational and Strategic Co-operation between the Government of HSH the Sovereign Prince of Monaco and Europol; Art 2, Annex III of the Agreement between the Republic of Iceland and Europol.

seconded from third countries are exempted from EU data protection standards, including when they act within the EU.

C. Liaison Officers as Intermediate Agent in the Area of Freedom, Security and Justice: The Example of Europol

Cooperation between the EU AFSJ agencies is necessary to enable large-scale collaboration in the fight against crime. AFSJ agencies are executive, specialised bodies constituted under Title V of the TFEU and responsible for the enforcement EU laws in that specific field.[73] The scope of cooperation in the field of security has increasingly developed beyond the EU's external borders and pushes the EU to cooperate with third-country security agencies. This changing landscape towards more cooperation with third-country authorities is already subject to an extensive scholarly debate in different areas such as human rights,[74] conflict of jurisdictions[75] and the application of EU data protection standards.[76] Liaison officers are, however, sidelined in that debate. A thorough study of US liaison officers seconded to Europol is therefore specifically interesting when linked to impunity from data protection standards.[77] This is a space in EU law where the European data protection standards do not apply, including within the EU administration when and because external actors are involved.

Europol is a particularly pertinent example highlighting these spaces where external agents – that is, US liaison officers – retrieve data from the EU administration and transfer it to their home administration. Europol is designed to operate in partnership with law enforcement agencies, government departments *and* the private sector.[78] This further widens the potential access of third-country liaison officers to EU data when they are deployed to Europol. In the close cooperation between public and private parties for law enforcement purposes, liaison officers act as intermediaries with a broad formal and informal network to get access to data regarded as necessary. To give some insight into the numbers of non-EU state liaison officers based in the EU: 243 liaison officers are placed at Europol, 51 of

[73] Agencies established on the basis of the TFEU articles on the area of freedom, security and justice: Europol, Eurojust, Frontex and, in the future, the European Public Prosecutors Office (EPPO).

[74] M Fink, 'Frontex Working Arrangements: Legitimacy and Human Rights Concerns Regarding Technical Relationships' (2012) 28 *Merkourios-Utrecht Journal of International and European Law* 20; JJ Rijpma, 'External Migration and Asylum Management: Accountability for Executive Action Outside EU Territory' (2017) 2 *European Papers* 571.

[75] M Böse, 'EU Substantive Criminal Law and Jurisdiction Clauses: Claiming Jurisdiction to Fight Impunity?', ch 5 in this book.

[76] M Eliantonio, 'Information Exchange in European Administrative law: A Threat to Effective Judicial Protection?' (2016) 23 *Maastricht Journal of European and Comparative Law* 531.

[77] The Europol website mentions, among others, FBI, Secret Service, NYPD, US customs authorities: www.europol.europa.eu/partners-agreements.

[78] ibid.

whom are deployed from third countries.[79] This is not a negligible proportion of the total amount of 1294 Europol employees. When non-EU state liaison officers access databases set up and maintained in the EU's geographical jurisdiction, to what extent is that data protected under the EU data protection rules, as specified in EU secondary law and the case law of the Court of Justice? The following section shows the differences in the selection and deployment procedures of liaison officers seconded by an EU Member State and those seconded by a third country to Europol.

(i) Selection Procedure for EU Member State Liaison Officers

Liaison officers function as a 'hub for information exchange between the law enforcement authorities for the EU Member States'.[80] Every EU Member State is obliged to select and deploy at least one liaison officer to Europol.[81] Europol's Founding Regulation provides some rules on the procedure for secondment of Member State liaison officers to Europol.[82] First, each EU Member State establishes or designates a national unit to function as the liaison body between Europol and the competent authorities of that Member State. The national unit is led by an official appointed by the Member State.[83] A Member State national unit must be competent under national law to fulfil the tasks assigned in the Regulation, which mainly boil down to a very broad 'coordinating role' and 'cooperation between Member States'.[84] This means in particular facilitating access to national law enforcement databases and other relevant data necessary for cooperation with Europol.[85] The organisation and staff of a particular national unit is subject to national law.[86] As an exemption to this rule, Member States may still allow direct contacts between their competent authorities and Europol – and may directly exchange information – without involvement of the national unit.[87]

The second step of liaison officer deployment is their designation by the respective national unit to Europol.[88] It is not clear from the Regulation, however, if the national unit designates a liaison officer from the national unit itself or from one of the competent authorities of the Member State. What is clear, though, is that the national unit instructs liaison officers.[89] In any case, Member States' liaison officers are subject to the national law of the designating Member State and remain subject

[79] www.europol.europa.eu/about-europol/statistics-data.
[80] Art 7(3) and recital 3 Europol Regulation.
[81] Art 8(1) Europol Regulation.
[82] Art. 7 and 8 Europol Regulation.
[83] Art 7(2) Europol Regulation.
[84] Recital 14 Europol Regulation.
[85] Art 8(3) Europol Regulation.
[86] Art 7(4) Europol Regulation.
[87] Art 7(5) Europol Regulation.
[88] Art 8(1) Europol Regulation.
[89] Art 8(2) Europol Regulation.

to the EU data protection framework.[90] That premise is relevant for non-EU state liaison officers seconded to Europol – they remain subject to their national law, and hence to their own national data protection standards.

(ii) US Liaison Officers Seconded to Europol

The Europol Founding Regulation provides rules for the conclusion of cooperation agreements between Europol and third countries.[91] These types of arrangements allow the exchange of non-personal and personal data to 'the extent necessary to fulfil the tasks' of Europol.[92] The selection and secondment of non-EU state liaison officers to Europol is also regulated in these cooperation agreements. Often, they refer to an annex or liaison agreement that specifies the tasks, status and obligations of liaison officers. The USA concluded such an operational agreement with Europol in 2001, in which the secondment of liaison officers is laid down.[93] The cooperation agreement (labelled the '2001 Agreement') states vaguely that the liaison officers' functions, tasks and status will be subject to consultations with a view to concluding a liaison agreement. The questions arise what specific parties are involved in these 'consultations', as the liaison agreement is still closed from public view,[94] and how data protection is arranged in case of (personal) information exchange. The exchange of personal data and data protection is arranged in a supplemental agreement to the 2001 Agreement, but contains a large number of ambiguities related to data protection. The next section outlines these ambiguities and other spaces in law in which the US liaison officers transfer data to the USA.

D. Do European Data Protection Standards Apply to US Liaison Officers at Europol?

US liaison officers deployed at Europol are not subject to the same level of European data protection rules. In essence, the USA–Europol cooperation agreement allows the exchange of personal data,[95] despite the fact that the personal data is not protected by EU data protection rules during and after the transfer. The following subsection sets out the legal structure under which US liaison officers (and other non-EU state liaison officers) operate when seconded to Europol.

[90] Art 8(3) and (4) Europol Regulation.
[91] Art 25 Europol Regulation.
[92] Recital 32 Europol Regulation.
[93] Art 8 of the Agreement between the United States of America and the European Police Office.
[94] This is different from other cooperation agreements with third countries, eg the Agreement between the Kingdom of Norway and the European Police Office.
[95] www.europol.europa.eu/newsroom/news/today-brazil-and-europol-signed-agreement-to-expand-cooperation-to-combat-cross-border-criminal-activities.

(i) Gaps in European Law Regarding Information Exchange

US liaison officers seconded to Europol are not subject to the laws and regulations of the EU that lay down data protection rules within the EU. Like many other non-EU state liaison officers deployed at Europol, US liaison officers are a formal representative of the USA with respect to Europol.[96] Not being members of the Europol staff themselves and subject to their own national laws, US liaison officers do not, for example, fall under the general Regulation 2018/1725 applicable to the Union institutions, bodies, offices and agencies who process personal data.[97] The scope of the Data Protection Regulation for EU institutions reveals that it does not apply to the processing of operational personal data by Europol.[98] In addition, the Europol Regulation explicitly allows data transfers between Europol and third countries on the basis of cooperation agreements concluded between the two administrations.[99]

Furthermore, the above-introduced GDPR does not apply since competent authorities for the purposes of prevention, investigation, detection or prosecution of criminal offences are exempted.[100] This means that an adequacy decision – in the US case, the Privacy Shield framework – does not apply to the law and practices of US liaison officers either. In the above-discussed context, the Privacy Shield protects EU personal data that is transferred to the USA for commercial purposes. It is not relevant for data transferred for law enforcement purposes. Directive 2018/680 on data processing by competent authorities for the purposes of law enforcement does not apply either, as the addressees are the EU Member States and (understandably) not third countries. The Umbrella Agreement does apply to personal data transferred between US liaison officers and Europol, but does not provide the same level of data protection. Hence, a legal vacuum in data protection standards is revealed in the case of US liaison officers deployed at Europol.

(ii) Data Protection Standards in the Supplemental Agreements?

As intermediaries between two agencies, liaison officers seconded from US security agencies to Europol carry out tasks outside the scope of application of EU rules on data protection. Data protection rules that apply to the law enforcement cooperation arrangement between the USA and Europol, on the basis of

[96] This is acknowledged in other cooperation agreements: Art 2(1), Annex 4 of the Colombia–Europol cooperation agreement; Annex to the Moldova–Europol cooperation agreement; Art 2(1), Annex 4 of the cooperation agreement between the Former Yugoslav Republic of Macedonia and Europol.

[97] Regulation (EU) 2018/1725 of 23 October 2018 of the European Parliament and the Council on the protection of natural persons with regard to the processing of personal data by Union institutions, bodies, offices and agencies and on the free movement of such data [2018] OJ L295/39.

[98] Ibid Art 2(3). The exemption of Europol is of a temporary nature.

[99] Art 25(3) Europol Regulation.

[100] Art 2(2)d GDPR.

which liaison officers are seconded, are laid down in the supplemental agreement between Europol and the USA on the exchange of personal data.[101] The agreement has a broad scope under which the parties may exchange information, including personal data, in accordance with the provisions of the agreement.[102] However, the agreement lacks basic data protection standards, such as control or supervisory mechanisms of the actors responsible for data transfers between the two administrative authorities. In vague terms, the agreement states that information supplied by Europol 'shall be available to competent US federal authorities' and available for use by competent US state or local authorities, provided that they agree to observe the provisions of the agreement.[103] How this practice of data use is supervised or controlled remains, however, ambiguous. US liaison officers seconded to Europol are not covered by EU data protection rules. They are subject to their national data protection laws, though these are, as argued earlier in this chapter, not the same as the European data protection standards.

IV. Conclusions: Impunities from Data Protection?

This chapter has identified what rules apply to data cooperation with the USA in two illustrative cases of commercial data transfers and liaison officers. The two cases illustrate two sides of the same coin: data protection when data leaves the jurisdictions of the EU and its Member States to the USA, and when external officers – that is, US liaison officers – are deployed to the EU administration. The chapter demonstrates that in both cases the level of data protection is not the same as within the jurisdictions of the EU and its Member States. It also highlights the difficulties of ensuring a sufficient level of protection or even establishing what rules precisely apply and who applies them.

One conclusion is that it lies in the nature of the involvement of third countries that gaps and impunities cannot be fully ruled out. International cooperation both in the context of commercial data transfers and in the context of law enforcement cooperation has become more and more widespread, relevant and even unavoidable in the past decades. The remaining question is: how can a sufficient level of data protection be ensured? How can the EU institutions ensure that certain rules apply?

In the context of commercial data transfers, the problem of ensuring sufficient protection of personal data of EU citizens continues to persist even after the Court of Justice has interfered and after several political attempts were made in order to achieve better and more formal guarantees of data protection from the

[101] Supplemental Agreement between the Europol Police Office and the United States of America on the Exchange of Personal Data and Related Information.

[102] Art 3(1) Supplemental Agreement.

[103] Art 7(1) a and b Supplemental Agreement.

US Government. US companies have shown willingness to comply with EU rules, even if under US law they are not legally obliged to do so.[104] However, in particular the rules on access of national security agencies to data of EU citizens collected by commercial actors and judicial protection from infringements of data protection rights in the USA remain issues that are approached very differently in the EU and in the USA. Both issues further are not in the hands of commercial actors. In fact, commercial actors in the USA are often not in the position to deny access by national security agencies.

EU secondary law and the case law of the CJEU take a decentralised approach, in which both the European Commission and national DPAs both play a role in assessing the level of protection. The Commission makes a general assessment of the situation in the third country and 28 national DPAs assess the individual case. Together, this division of tasks seems to pave the way for a race to the top rather than a race to the bottom.

In the context of US liaison officers seconded to the EU, the greatest problem is the level of unclarity of the rules applying to data transfers. The cooperation agreement concluded between Europol and the USA contains a vast, multi-interpretable list of areas of crimes that allow the exchange of information. This has the consequence that data protection rights are not safeguarded with the same legal certainty and at a level comparable to the level guaranteed within the EU. A question for further examination that is equally highly relevant in this context is what control or accountability rules actually apply to non-EU state liaison officers.

[104] F Marotta-Wurgler, 'Understanding Privacy Policies: Content, Self-Regulation, and Markets' (2016) New York University Law and Economics Working Papers 4–2016 https://lsr.nellco.org/cgi/viewcontent.cgi?article=1439&context=nyu_lewp.

18

The Court of Justice of the European Union and the International Criminal Court: The Fight against Impunity between Complementarity and Mandatory Requirements

AURORA RASI

I. Introduction

In its recent case law, the Court of Justice of the European Union put much emphasis on the objective of the EU to fight against impunity. Its legal basis was identified in Article 3(2) TEU:[1] 'the objective of preventing the risk of impunity for persons who have committed an offence is to be seen in the context of the prevention and combating of crime' and it 'must be considered, in the context of Article 3(2) TEU, to be a legitimate objective of EU law'.[2]

Determining what fighting against impunity generally entails for the EU (and not only for the EU) is a challenging task, which falls outside the scope of the present chapter. More modestly, for our examination, it is sufficient to note that, among many other aspects, fighting against impunity implies, first and foremost, ensuring ascertainment of criminal responsibility. In other words, preventing impunity entails first of all that every person who has allegedly committed a criminal offence must be held accountable: the territory of the EU must not be a safe haven, so there should be no possibility for a person alleged to be responsible for a crime not to face a criminal trial.[3]

[1] Art 3(2) TEU entails that 'The Union shall offer its citizens an area … in which … is ensured … the prevention and combating of crime'.

[2] Court of Justice, judgment of 10 April 2018, Case C-191/16 *Pisciotti* [GC] ECLI:EU:C:2018:222, para 47. For some notes on this judgment, see P Mori, 'L'estradizione di un cittadino UE verso uno Stato terzo: il caso Pisciotti dinanzi alla Corte di giustizia' [2018] *Il diritto dell'Unione europea* 595.

[3] In this sense, see Eurojust, 'Strategy of the EU Genocide Network to Combat Impunity for the Crime of Genocide, Crimes against Humanity and War Crimes within the European Union and its Member States' (November 2014) 4ff.

This objective is not the exclusive task of the Court of Justice (the Court). Quite the contrary, the Court is only one among a plurality of judicial organs which pursue it. The judicial doctrine on the fight against impunity must, therefore, be contextualised against a larger background. Indeed, by taking into consideration the wider context of international law, it emerges that the goal of preventing impunity is one of the main imperatives of the international community as a whole. It has been, and still is, concretely pursued through the establishment of a number of international judges, whose activities are primarily, if not exclusively, devoted to preventing impunity.[4]

Limiting the survey only to the last three decades, the goal of defeating impunity has been served by the international community through the establishment of ad hoc tribunals, namely the International Criminal Tribunal for the former Yugoslavia (ICTY) and the International Criminal Tribunal for Rwanda (ICTR),[5] and also through the setting up of the world's first permanent international criminal jurisdiction, namely the International Criminal Court (ICC).[6]

The Preamble of the Rome Statute (the Statute) solemnly and plainly proclaims that the ultimate aim of the ICC is 'to put an end to impunity for the perpetrators' of war crimes, crimes against humanity, genocides and crimes of aggression (together,

[4] See United Nations, Security Council, 'The Rule of Law and Transitional Justice in Conflict and Post-conflict Societies – Report of the Secretary General', UN Doc S/2004/616 (23 August 2004) para 38ff. For a historical survey of the attempts, successful or not, made by the international community in the fight against impunity, see *ex multis* WA Schabas, *The Trial of the Kaiser* (Oxford, Oxford University Press, 2018); M Cherif Bassiouni, 'Combating Impunity for International Crimes' (2000) 71 *University of Colorado Law Review* 409; G Acquaviva, 'International Criminal Courts and Tribunals as Actors of General Deterrence? Perceptions and Misperceptions' [2015] 895/896 *International Review of the Red Cross* 784; P Akhavan, 'Beyond Impunity: Can International Criminal Justice Prevent Future Atrocities' [2001] 95 *American Journal of International Law* 7.

[5] As specified by the Secretary General in the report annexed to the Statute of the ICTY, it was mandatory, at that time, to take effective measures in order to bring to justice the persons who were responsible for the heinous crimes perpetrated on the territory of the former Yugoslavia since 1991. With this goal in mind, the report declared that 'the establishment of an international tribunal would enable this aim to be achieved': *cf* 'Report of the Secretary General Pursuant to Paragraph 2 of Security Council Resolution 808', UN Doc S/25704 (3 May 1993) para 10. Similarly, the United Nations decided to establish the ICTR as 'the establishment of an international tribunal for the prosecution of persons responsible for genocide and [other] violations of international humanitarian law [in the territory of Rwanda between the 1 January 1994 and 31 December 1994] will contribute to ensuring that such violations are halted and effectively redressed': *cf* Security Council Resolution 955 (1994) of 8 November 1994, UN Doc S/RES/955(1994), 2). *cf* also the general definition of impunity stated in N Roht-Arriaza, 'General Obligation of States to Take Effective Action to Combat Impunity' in F Haldemann and T Unger (eds), *The United Nations Principles to Combat Impunity: A Commentary* (Oxford, Oxford University Press, 2018) 45: 'Impunity arises from a failure by States to meet their obligations to investigate violations; to take appropriate measures in respect of the perpetrators, particularly in the area of justice, by ensuring that those suspected of criminal responsibility are prosecuted, tried and duly punished.'

[6] The Rome Statute of the International Criminal Court, adopted at the Rome Conference on 17 July 1998, entered into force on 1 July 2002, 'the first day of the month after the 60th day following the date of the deposit of the 60th instrument of ratification, acceptance, approval or accession with the Secretary-General of the United Nations' (Art 126, para 1 of the Statute). *cf* United Nations, Treaty Series, vol 2187, no 38544, Depositary: Secretary-General of the United Nations. At the time of writing, there were 122 States Parties to the Statute. The list of States Parties is available at https://asp.icc-cpi.int/en_menus/asp/states%20parties/Pages/the%20states%20parties%20to%20the%20rome%20statute.aspx.

international crimes): these acts 'must not go unpunished' and 'their effective prosecution must be ensured'.[7] Far from describing a mere distant and ideal goal, the Preamble's words have been read by the ICC as 'a compendious expression … of the serious and urgent concerns that frame the mandate that the States Parties have given the ICC': among the paragraphs of the Preamble, 'A particularly luminous beacon … is the determination of the States Parties "*to put an end to impunity* for the perpetrators of …"' international crimes.[8]

The Court of Justice case law can obviously be analysed 'in splendid isolation'. This methodology can give good results insofar as it only focuses on the European judicature. However, this approach would disregard two elements: first, that the fight against impunity is recognised as an interest pertaining not only to the EU, but rather to the entire international community; secondly, that it is effectively pursued by international criminal tribunals even more than by the Court of Justice. Therefore, there is a paramount interest, both doctrinal and practical, to analyse the case law of the Court of Justice against the wider background composed of the activities of other international criminal forums. It is precisely this overall enquiry that is attempted in the present chapter. Clearly, the obvious differences, in their structure and function, between the Court of Justice and the international criminal tribunals, oblige us to carry on the comparative analysis with the greatest care. In the light of this caveat, this chapter will proceed to a parallel analysis of the techniques respectively used by the Court of Justice and by the ICC, in search of their analogies, albeit remote, and their dissimilarities, obvious though they may be.[9]

The starting point of the enquiry (section II) will be an analysis of the first technique used by the Court of Justice to attain the goal enshrined in Article 3(2) TEU and by the ICC to attain the goal enshrined in the Preamble of the Statute. It consists of enlarging the scope of EU law and international law where application of domestic procedural rules could directly or indirectly have prevented a national trial from starting or from being carried on. The subsequent section (section III) will focus on the second technique used by the two courts which consists, in a sense logically opposed to the former, of narrowing down the scope of EU law and international law, and giving priority to national rules, where application of individual rights protected by EU law and international law could directly or indirectly have prevented a national criminal proceeding from starting or being carried on. The last section will take stock of the analogies and dissimilarities in the use of these techniques by the two courts and will offer some conclusive remarks.

[7] *cf* Preamble of the Statute, paras IV and V.

[8] ICC, *The Prosecutor v William Samoei Ruto and Joshua Arap Sang, Decision on Prosecutor's Application for Witness Summonses and resulting Request for State Party Cooperation*, Trial Chamber V (A), 17 April 2014, no ICC-01/09-01/11-1274-Corr, para 64 (emphasis in the original).

[9] The choice to focus only on the ICC, and thus to not focus on the ICTY or the ICTR, was made because the ICC is the sole international criminal court still in action. The ICTY mandate lasted from 1993 to 2017 (see ICTY, 'International Criminal Tribunal for the former Yugoslavia – 1993–2017' www.icty.org), while the ICTR functions were concluded in 2015 (see International Residual Mechanism for Criminal Tribunals, 'The ICTR in Brief' https://unictr.irmct.org/en/tribunal).

II. Fighting against Impunity by Enlarging the Scope of Supranational Law

A. The Court of Justice

As previously mentioned, in a number of cases, the Court of Justice has extensively interpreted the scope of EU law in order to prevent national procedural provisions from increasing the risk of impunity, namely the risk that an alleged criminal will not face a criminal trial,[10] for individuals suspected of having perpetrated a criminal offence.

This technique was applied by the Grand Chamber of the Court in *Kolev*, a case that probably provides one of the clearest examples of this case law.[11] Nikolay Kolev, a Bulgarian national, was suspected by the Bulgarian authorities of having committed a sophisticated tax fraud. This conduct would have entailed criminal responsibility under Articles 215, 301 and 321 of the Bulgarian Criminal Code (collectively, Article 215). Significantly, Article 215 implements Article 325 TFEU, which imposes on the Member States the obligation to 'counter fraud and any other illegal activities affecting the financial interests of the Union'.[12] In 2012, a criminal proceeding against Kolev started in Bulgaria, but it was soon halted following the invocation by Nikolay Kolev of Articles 368 and 369 of the Bulgarian Code of Criminal Procedure (collectively, Article 369). These provisions impose closing the criminal proceedings upon a request by the accused where, within a certain (and very limited) period, no indictment has been issued and submitted to the court by the prosecutor. Significantly, no margin of discretion was granted to the national judge under Article 369. The judge was bound to close the proceedings even if the accused had contributed to the lapse of time by abusing his or her procedural rights.[13] Before closing the proceeding against Kolev, the Bulgarian judge referred to the Court of Justice a question of interpretation related to the consistency of Article 369 with Article 325 TFEU.[14]

The Grand Chamber initially seemed to conceive of the obligation enshrined in Article 325 TFEU as a classical obligation of result. Once it was pointed out that

[10] For the notion of impunity adopted in the present chapter see section I above.

[11] Court of Justice, judgment of 5 June 2018, Case C-612/15 *Kolev and Others* [GC] ECLI:EU:C:2018:392. For other examples, see Court of Justice, judgment of 5 December 2017, Case C-42/17 *MAS and MB* [GC] ECLI:EU:C:2017:936; judgment of 8 September 2015, Case C-105/14 *Taricco and Others* [GC] ECLI:EU:C:2015:555.

[12] *Kolev and Others* (ibid) paras 24ff, 50, 56–57 and 68. In particular, Kolev was suspected of having demanded, together with other individuals, 'bribes from drivers of lorries and cars crossing the border between Bulgaria and Turkey in order not to carry out customs inspections and not to document any irregularities identified' (ibid para 24).

[13] ibid paras 20–21, 24–35, 60 and 62.

[14] ibid para 37.

the Member States are required 'to provide for penalties that are effective, proportionate and dissuasive' in cases of tax fraud, the Court admitted that the criminal penalties laid down by Bulgarian law met these standards.[15] If the reasoning had stopped at that point, the Court should have logically concluded in favour of the full consistency of Article 369 with Article 325 TFEU. The practical consequence of this interpretation would have been that Nikolai Kolev, as other alleged perpetrators of criminal offences directly or indirectly relevant for EU law, could evade trial. Inexorably, a situation of impunity would have been determined.

Strikingly, the Grand Chamber continued its reasoning by enlarging the scope of Article 325 TFEU so as to include national procedural measures designed to ensure the effectiveness of the substantive penalties provided for by Bulgarian law.[16] In particular, in the view of the Court of Justice, Article 325 TFEU compels states to adopt all 'the measures necessary' to prevent the risk of impunity, described by the Court as 'a systemic risk' that tax frauds 'may go unpunished'.[17] In particular, national legislators must 'ensure that the procedural rules … are not designed in such a way that there arises, for reasons inherent in those rules, a systemic risk that [tax frauds] may go unpunished'.[18]

The broad interpretation of Article 325 TFEU thus enabled the Grand Chamber to determine that national procedural provisions also come within the purview of EU (criminal) law. In particular, Article 325 TFEU would have been breached by all national procedural criminal provisions producing effects (directly or indirectly) on application of (domestic provisions implementing) EU rules. Indeed, the Court concluded that every national provision 'liable to impede the effectiveness of criminal prosecution and the punishment of acts that may be categorised as [tax frauds]', such as Article 369, would be in conflict with EU law.[19] The logical consequence of this assumption was to empower the national court to set aside all national procedural rules whose application may have prevented the full effectiveness of Article 325 TFEU.[20]

[15] ibid paras 53 and 58.

[16] ibid para 64.

[17] ibid para 65.

[18] ibid. It is interesting to note that this passage seems clearer in the Italian ('un rischio sistemico d'impunità') and in the French ('un risque systémique d'impunité') versions of the judgment than in the English one.

[19] ibid paras 63 and 68.

[20] ibid para 76. Very interestingly, in a more recent case, Case C-310/16 *Dzivev and Others* ECLI:EU:C:2019:30 (judgment of 17 January 2019), the Court of Justice set a limit to the wide ranging interpretation of Art 325 TFEU developed in *Kolev*. In *Dzivev*, the Court recalled that Member States shall 'ensure that the rules of criminal procedure, laid down by national law, permit effective investigation and prosecution of' tax frauds (para 29), and 'that it is for the national courts to give full effect to the obligations under Article 325(1) TFEU and to disapply national provisions which, in connection with proceedings concerning serious VAT infringements, prevent the application of effective and deterrent penalties' (para 32). However, the Court stated that these obligations meet a limit, namely 'the necessary

B. The International Criminal Court

Interestingly, in the frame of its policy of positive complementarity, the ICC used a similar technique to encourage states to conduct criminal proceedings, and thus to fight against impunity. To attain this goal, the ICC has significantly enlarged the scope of the Statute.

As explained by the ICC itself, the expression 'positive complementarity' 'refers to all activities [or] actions whereby national jurisdictions are strengthened and enabled to conduct genuine national investigations and trials of crimes included in the Rome Statute'.[21] Undoubtedly, among the activities in which positive complementarity materialises, a prominent place has to be given to the pressure exerted by the ICC on states to adopt national measures effectively implementing the Statute.[22] The problem arises, however, as to the scope of the notion of 'national measures effectively implementing the Statute'. Whereas one could naturally expect that substantial criminal measures come within the purview of this notion, it is more controversial whether procedural rules also fall within it.

Unhesitatingly, the ICC answered the question in the affirmative. States must adopt not only substantive criminal measures designed to put into effect the measures spelling out the criminal behaviours coming within the scope of the Statute, but also those procedural provisions designed to bestow the effectiveness of these prohibitive measures. In the view of the Court, these two normative fields – composed of substantive and procedural provisions respectively – seem to have identical relevance. Consequently, the mere presence, in the national legal order, of a procedural provision potentially hampering, directly or indirectly, the conducting of effective criminal trials implies that the legal order as a whole (and the state to which it pertains) does not abide by the Statute.[23]

observance of the principle of legality and the rule of law which is one of the primary values on which the European Union is founded, as is indicated in Article 2 TEU' (para 34).

[21] *cf* ICC, Assembly of States Parties, Resolution ICC-ASP/8/Res.9 of 25 March 2010, Appendix, 'Report of the Bureau on Stocktaking: Complementarity – Taking Stock of the Principle of Complementarity: Bridging the Impunity Gap' https://asp.icc-cpi.int/iccdocs/asp_docs/RC2010/RC-11-Annex.V.c-ENG.pdf, para 16; Office of the Prosecutor, 'Statement of the Prosecutor Luis Moreno Ocampo to Diplomatic Corps – The Hague, Netherlands, 12 February 2004' www.icc-cpi.int/NR/rdonlyres/0F999F00-A609-4516-A91A-80467BC432D3/143670/LOM_20040212_En.pdf, 1: 'A positive approach to complementarity [implies that,] [r]ather than competing with national systems for jurisdiction, we will encourage national proceedings wherever possible.' On positive complementarity, *cf*, *ex multis*, W Burke-White, 'Reframing Positive Complementarity' in C Stahn and MM El Zeidy (eds), *The International Criminal Court and Complementarity: From Theory to Practice* (Cambridge, Cambridge University Press, 2009) 341ff.

[22] ICC, Appendix (ibid) para 17. Other activities are, for instance, 'training of police, investigators and prosecutors', 'training of judges and training of defence counsel' and 'construction of physical infrastructure, such as courthouses and prison facilities' (ibid).

[23] In practical terms, this means that states must adopt not only substantive rules describing and prohibiting international crimes, but also procedural rules suitable for the conduction of effective criminal trials. Returning to the examples previously mentioned, as for the ICC, national provisions establishing how witnesses shall be heard in the courtroom now fall within the scope of the Statute. See ICC, Assembly of States Parties, Resolution ICC-ASP/16/Res.6 of 14 December 2017, paras 7–8.

Far from being merely hortatory, the ICC's concern for effective national criminal procedural rules is real and urgent. States' compliance with the described far-reaching obligation flowing from the Statute is regularly verified by the ICC, which collects periodical reports on the 'state of the art'[24] and classifies, in a freely accessible database, all the relevant national criminal provisions (that is, having a substantive and procedural nature) of the states which accepted the ICC's jurisdiction.[25]

Positive complementarity is rooted in an extensive interpretation of the scope of international criminal law in general, and of the Statute in particular. It implies that the Statute's purview is broad enough to encompass not only national criminal provisions having a substantive nature, but also those provisions having a procedural nature. In all evidence, positive complementarity is grounded on the premise that national provisions merely related to the ascertainment of criminal responsibility, even minor procedural rules, also fall within the scope of international criminal law, on the condition, of course, that their application may directly or indirectly affect the effectiveness of the substantive rules.

C. Partial Conclusive Remarks

There is, then, a common thread between the case law of the Court of Justice and the strategies adopted by the ICC to prevent impunity. Both judicial organs have argued that, when the possibility for a national criminal trial to be started or to be carried on is hampered because of the effects of a national procedural provision, the goal of fighting against impunity requires the procedural provision to be set aside. Moreover, this assumption seems to be grounded, both in the Court of Justice and in the ICC's reasoning, on the same premise: the scope of EU and international provisions establishing the objective to fight against impunity must be interpreted as implying for states the overall obligation to make their criminal system, considered as a unitary corpus composed of both substantial and procedural provisions, fully functional to conduct criminal trials. As is evident, the EU and international provisions establishing the objective of preventing impunity are considered, both by the Court of Justice and by the ICC, as pre-eminent over national criminal provisions.

In the same sense, see, *ex multis*, ICC, Assembly of States Parties, Resolution ICC-ASP/7/Res.3 of 21 November 2008, para 37.

[24] *cf*, eg ICC, Assembly of States Parties, 'Report of the Bureau on Complementarity' (22 November 2017, no ICC-ASP/16/33); 'Report of the Bureau on Complementarity' (17 November 2010, no ICC-ASP/9/26); 'Report of the Bureau on the Plan of Action for Achieving Universality and Full Implementation of the Rome Statute of the International Criminal Court' (24 October 2008, no ICC-ASP/7/19).

[25] The database, named 'Legal Tools', is freely accessible through the ICC's website (www.icc-cpi.int) or directly at www.legal-tools.org. In the database, there is collected general information about every state's legal system, about its criminal law and procedures, and about legal provisions that are particularly relevant for ascertainment of the responsibility of the alleged perpetrators of international crimes.

III. Fighting against Impunity by Narrowing Down the Scope of Supranational Law

A. The Court of Justice

The Court of Justice has contributed to pursuing the objective of combating impunity through the use of an alternative interpretative technique, consisting of narrowing down (ie interpreting restrictively) the scope of EU law when the application of an EU provision conferring individual rights precludes national jurisdictions from holding criminal proceedings against individuals who, by taking advantage of EU law, could avert a trial.

This technique has been used, for instance, by the Grand Chamber of the Court in *Petruhhin*.[26] In 2014, Russia requested Latvia to extradite Aleksei Petruhhin, an Estonian national who lived in Latvia and was indicted of drug trafficking under Russian law, in order to start a criminal proceeding against him. Latvia authorised the extradition, and Petruhhin, invoking both EU law and Latvian law, filed an appeal against the decision. He invoked Article 18 TFEU and Article 62 of the Agreement of 3 February 1993 between the Republic of Latvia and the Russian Federation on Judicial Assistance and Judicial Relations in Civil, Family and Criminal Matters (the Agreement): Article 18 TFEU prohibits 'any discrimination on grounds of nationality' among the EU citizens; Article 62 of the Agreement states that 'Extradition shall not be granted if … the person whose extradition is requested is a national of the Contracting Party'. Since Petruhhin was an EU citizen, who had exercised the right of free movement according to Article 21 TFEU and had decided to live in Latvia, he argued that Article 18 TFEU should be applied in the case and, consequently, he should enjoy the same level of protection granted by Latvian law to Latvian citizens against extradition to Russia.[27]

Charged with the matter, the Court of Justice acknowledged that Latvian law provided, per se, for a discrimination based on nationality among EU citizens in enjoyment of freedom of movement.[28] On the basis of this premise, one could reasonably expect the Court to hold that Latvia, by applying Articles 18 and 21 TFEU in the case, should have granted to Petruhhin the same standard of protection against extradition to Russia granted to its nationals. However, as pointed out by AG Bot in his Opinion in the case, this holding would not have been entirely free of drawbacks: since Latvian law prohibits starting criminal proceedings

[26] Court of Justice, judgment of 6 September 2016, Case C-182/15 *Petruhhin* [GC] ECLI:EU:C:2016:630. For another example, see Court of Justice, judgment of 27 May 2014, Case C-129/14 PPU *Spasic* [GC] ECLI:EU:C:2014:586. On *Petruhhin*, see S Saluzzo, 'Impunity and EU or Member States' Extradition Agreements with Third Countries', ch 16 in this book.

[27] *Petruhhin* (ibid) paras 13–17.

[28] ibid paras 32–33: 'the unequal treatment which allows the extradition of a Union citizen who is a national of another Member State, such as Mr Petruhhin, gives rise to a restriction of freedom of movement, within the meaning of Article 21 TFEU'. *cf* also *Pisciotti* (n 2) para 44.

against a foreign national for acts allegedly committed outside the Latvian territory, Petruhhin would have remained in Latvia and would never have been held accountable for the alleged misdeeds.[29]

The Court of Justice then highlighted other arguments pointing to a different conclusion. First, the Court noted that one of the objectives pursued by the EU under Article 3(2) TEU is to prevent impunity.[30] Secondly, it stressed that 'extradition is a procedure whose *aim is to combat the impunity* of a person who is present in a territory other than that in which he has allegedly committed an offence'.[31] Moreover, the Court noted that when a national judge, such as the Latvian one, 'has no jurisdiction to try cases concerning … acts when neither the perpetrator nor the victim of the alleged offence is a national of that Member State', extradition proves to be the only means for a criminal trial to be held.[32]

In other words, the objective of securing compliance with Article 3(2) TEU, and therefore of preventing Mr Petruhhin from fleeing justice, led the Court to interpret restrictively the scope of the EU provisions conferring rights related to free movement of persons across the EU territory. The Court concluded this reasoning by specifying that 'national rules, such as those at issue in the main proceedings, … appear appropriate to achieve the objective pursued' by the EU, that is to fight against impunity.[33]

In practical terms, this holding can be explained by the necessity to allow the Russian judge to conduct a criminal trial against Petruhhin. In legal terms, it entails that a national rule producing a discrimination among EU citizens on the ground of their nationality should not be set aside, in spite of its at least apparent conflict with Articles 18 and 21 TFEU, because it contributes to pursuing the EU's goal of preventing impunity. In turn, this entails that the scope of the principle of non-discrimination, in the field of the fundamental freedoms of the EU, could be narrowed down in order to pursue the objective enshrined in Article 3(2) TEU.

It should be noted that the reasoning of the Court continued by looking for

> an alternative measure less prejudicial to the exercise of the rights conferred by Article 21 TFEU which would be equally effective in achieving the objective of preventing the risk of impunity for a person alleged to have committed a criminal offence.

This was actually found.[34] However, the availability of an alternative measure does not undermine the first statement of the Court, namely that the protection

[29] *cf* Opinion of AG Bot delivered on 10 May 2016, Case C-182/15 *Petruhhin* ECLI:EU:C:2016:330. AG Bot underlined that 'a national of a Member State other than the Republic of Latvia, such as Mr Petruhhin, … cannot be prosecuted in Latvia for an offence which he is suspected of having committed in Russia' (para 68). Thus, Petruhhin, if not transferred to Russia because of the rights conferred on him by EU law, would not have faced a trial at all.

[30] ibid para 36.

[31] ibid para 39 (emphasis added).

[32] ibid.

[33] ibid para 40.

[34] ibid paras 41 and 50. As is well known, the alternative measure was represented by quite a complex procedure: 'when a Member State to which a Union citizen, a national of another Member State, has

granted by Articles 18 and 21 TFEU to EU citizens can be confined when the goal of fighting against impunity is at stake. Indeed, the Court initially admitted this possibility, and only subsequently investigated how to 'reduce the reduction' of the protection of Petruhhin's rights.

B. The International Criminal Court

Like the Court of Justice, the ICC has also used (albeit rarely) interpretative techniques consisting of narrowing down the scope of rights conferred on individuals by international law when a broad interpretation of the relevant provisions would have entailed the closing of a national criminal trial.

This technique has been used in the decision on the admissibility of the *Al-Senussi* case.[35] In 2013, Libya was investigating Abdullah Al-Senussi, the former chief of the Libyan intelligence service and one of the closest aides of Muammar Gaddafi, for the crimes against humanity he had allegedly committed. Being about to start a proceeding on the same case, the ICC was called upon to assess whether the Libyan proceedings compelled the ICC to declare its own case inadmissible under Article 17 of the Statute. This provision entails that the ICC can only open proceedings if no national jurisdiction is carrying on a criminal proceedings on the same case or if the national jurisdiction, even if it has opened a proceedings on the same case, is actually unwilling or unable to prosecute: in other words, the ICC can only open a proceeding if there is no other ongoing 'genuine' exercise of jurisdiction.[36] Thus, the ICC jurisdiction could only be lawfully exercised in the *Al-Senussi* case if the Libyan proceedings failed to meet the standards required by the Statute and so proved not to be a genuine exercise of jurisdiction.

moved receives an extradition request from a third State with which the first Member State has concluded an extradition agreement, it must inform the Member State of which the citizen in question is a national and, should that Member State so request, surrender that citizen to it, in accordance with the provisions of Framework Decision 2002/584, provided that that Member State has jurisdiction, pursuant to its national law, to prosecute that person for offences committed outside its national territory' (ibid para 50).

[35] *cf* ICC, *Situation in Libya, Case of the Prosecutor v Saif Al-Islam Gaddafi and Abdullah Al-Senussi, Decision on the admissibility of the case against Abdullah Al-Senussi*, Pre-Trial Chamber I, 11 October 2013, no ICC-01/11-01/11-466-Red (Al-Senussi admissibility decision). For a survey of the ICC proceeding against Abdullah Al-Senussi, *cf* ICC, *Gaddafi Case, The Prosecutor v Saif Al-Islam Gaddafi – Formerly The Prosecutor v Muammar Mohammed Abuminyar Gaddafi, Saif Al-Islam Gaddafi and Abdullah Al-Senussi* www.icc-cpi.int/libya/gaddafi.

[36] *cf* Art 17 of the Statute; WA Schabas, 'The International Criminal Court: A Commentary on the Rome Statute' (Oxford, Oxford University Press, 2016) 446ff; WA Schabas and MM El Zeidy, 'Article 17: Issues of Admissibility' in O Triffterer and K Ambos (eds), *The Rome Statute of the International Criminal Court: A Commentary* (Munich, CH Beck/Oxford, Hart Publishing/Baden-Baden, Nomos, 2016) 781ff; Stahn and El Zeidy (n 21); JT Holmes, 'Complementarity: National Courts versus the ICC' in A Cassese, P Gaeta and J Jones (eds), *The Rome Statute of the International Criminal Court: A Commentary* (Oxford, Oxford University Press, 2002) 667ff.

The issue was particularly thorny. Whereas Libya's willingness and ability to prosecute Al Senussi was uncontroversial, the national proceedings was being conducted in violation of the fundamental rights of the accused. As plainly admitted by Libya, since his extradition and imprisonment in September 2012, Al Senussi's right to meet a lawyer had been denied; nor had he been granted the right even to appoint a lawyer, despite having been deprived of his liberty, interrogated and confronted with evidence materials, and despite requesting to talk with a lawyer on numerous occasions, even though the Libyan criminal procedural code had established the right of the accused to be represented by a lawyer.[37]

One could reasonably expect the ICC to hold that, because of the violation of Al Senussi's fundamental rights, the national proceedings did not meet the standards of 'judicial proceedings', and therefore could not bar the exercise of the ICC jurisdiction.[38] Several arguments pleaded in this direction. First, Article 21 of the Statute directs the ICC to interpret all provisions it is competent to apply 'consistent[ly] with internationally recognized human rights', and the ICC had actually more than once interpreted Article 21 as imposing the duty to interpret all provisions of the Statute in accordance with human rights law.[39] Secondly, the

[37] *Decision on the admissibility of the case against Abdullah Al-Senussi* (n 35) paras 7 and 230–33. See also the Report of Human Right Watch, referred to by the Pre-Trial Chamber at para 231 of the mentioned decision: Human Right Watch, *Libya: Ensure Abdallah Sanussi Access to Lawyer* (17 April 2013) www.hrw.org/news/2013/04/17/libya-ensure-abdallah-sanussi-access-lawyer.

[38] This argument would not be a novelty in the case law of the ICC. While dealing with the situation in Uganda, in 2008 the Pre-Trial Chamber was called to evaluate the possibility for traditional justice mechanisms to take precedence over the ICC jurisdiction under Art 17 of the Statute. In that case, mechanisms such as, for instance, *Mato Oput*, were even mentioned in Art 1 of the Agreement on Accountability and Reconciliation Between the Government of the Republic of Uganda and the Lord's Resistance Army (*cf* Security Council, 'Annex to the Letter dated 16 July 2007 from the Permanent Representative of Uganda to the United Nations Addressed to the President of the Security Council', no S/2007/435). *Mato Oput* was described as 'the traditional rituals performed by the Acholi [population] to reconcile parties formerly in conflict, after full accountability', and consists in 'a ritual [during which] the offender must admit responsibility, ask for forgiveness, drink sheep's blood mixed with the mato oput root, and pay compensation' to the victims: *cf* AK Krikscinn, 'Uganda's Response to International Criminal Court Arrest Warrants: A Misguided Approach?' (2008) 16 *Tulane Journal of International and Comparative Law* 213, 234. However, the ICC disregarded all mechanisms such as *Mato Oput* and implicitly (re)affirmed its jurisdiction on the cases (*cf* ICC, *Situation in Uganda, The Prosecutor v Joseph Kony, Vincent Otti, Okot Odhiambo, Dominic Ongwen, Request for Further Information from the Republic of Uganda on the Status of Execution of the Warrants of Arrest*, 18 June 2008, no ICC-02/04-01/05-299). Interestingly, Human Rights Watch argued that a prominent place among the reasons which led the ICC to do so ought to be identified in the lack of fair-trial guarantees for the accused in this sort of procedures: 'Internationally recognized fair trials standards would need to be rigorously observed in any national alternative to ICC prosecutions. The Ugandan government would need to demonstrate that any national alternative respects such standards both in principle and in practice … They include [the right to benefit from] adequate time and facilities to prepare a defense': Human Right Watch, 'Benchmarks for Assessing Possible National Alternatives to International Criminal Court Cases against LRA Leaders' (May 2007) 7.

[39] Actually the ICC, in its case law, has often used the parameter established by Art 21 to interpret other statutory provisions. For instance, the ICC did so in interpreting Art 82 of the Statute, when stressed that: 'Like every other article of the Statute, article 82 must be interpreted and applied in

accused's right to be assisted by legal counsel during the criminal trial is certainly part of human rights law and, in particular, is one of the 'minimum guarantees' of the criminal trial under Article 14(3) of the International Covenant on Civil and Political Rights, which is, moreover, echoed by Article 67 of the Statute.[40]

Following this line of argument, one could reasonably expect the ICC to interpret the admissibility criteria stated in Article 17 of the Statute in the light of the internationally recognised standards of human rights protection, such as the right of the accused to benefit from legal assistance. Consequently, one would have expected the ICC to rule that the Libyan proceedings had failed to abide by the notion of genuine judicial proceedings, or even the notion of judicial proceedings at all, enshrined in the Statute, which would have been enough to hamper the ICC's exercise of jurisdiction under Article 17.[41] Thus, the ultimate consequence would have been that the national proceeding should have been closed in order to give precedence to the international one.

However, the ICC's reasoning unhesitatingly pointed in the opposite direction. It did not consider Article 21, its previous case law related to this provision or human rights law, not even Article 67 of the Statute. On the contrary, the Court decided to let the national proceedings continue by applying only Article 17 of the Statute. In particular, the ICC specified that the violation of Al Senussi's right to benefit from legal assistance 'does not justify a finding of unwillingness' and that the Court could not state 'that Libya will be unable to … ensure the provision of adequate legal representation for Mr Al-Senussi': under Article 17, 'The case against Mr Al-Senussi is *therefore* inadmissible before the Court'.[42]

accordance with internationally recognized human rights, as declared in article 21 (3) of the Statute' (ICC, *Situation in the Democratic Republic of Congo, Judgment on the Prosecutor's Application for Extraordinary Review of Pre-Trial Chamber I's 31 March 2006 Decision Denying Leave to Appeal*, 13 July 2006, no ICC-01/04-168, para 38).

[40] Art 14, para 3, lett b) and d) of the 1966 International Covenant on Civil and Political Rights: 'In the determination of any criminal charge against him, everyone shall be entitled to the following minimum guarantees, in full equality: [t]o have adequate time and facilities for the preparation of his defence and to communicate with counsel of his own choosing; … to defend himself in person or through legal assistance of his own choosing; … to have legal assistance assigned to him, in any case where the interests of justice so require, and without payment by him in any such case if he does not have sufficient means to pay for it.' It is noteworthy that Art 67 of the Statute also lists, among the 'minimum guarantees' to be granted to the accused in the proceedings conducted by the ICC, precisely the right 'To have adequate time and facilities for the preparation of the defence and to communicate freely with counsel of the accused's choosing in confidence'. This is not a matter of surprise. As has already been pointed out, Art 67 of the Statute was inspired by Art 14, para 3 of the International Covenant on Civil and Political Rights. *cf*, *ex multis*, WA Schabas and Y McDermott, 'Article 67 – Rights of the Accused' in Triffterer and Ambos (n 36) 1650ff.

[41] In this sense, *cf* Human Right Watch, 'Benchmarks for Assessing Possible National Alternatives' (n 38) 7: 'Internationally recognized fair trials standards would need to be rigorously observed in any national alternative to ICC prosecutions … International fair trial standards are largely contained in the International Covenant on Civil and Political Rights (ICCPR) and are crucial to a trial's legitimacy. They include the following rights: … adequate time and facilities to prepare a defense; … have a lawyer of the accused's own choosing.'

[42] *Decision on the admissibility of the case against Abdullah Al-Senussi* (n 35) paras 292, 308 and 311 (emphasis added). The inadmissibility of the case was confirmed by the Appeals Chamber,

These conclusions cannot but flow from a narrow interpretation of the scope of the relevant provisions of the Statute and, in particular, of those referring to human rights law. By failing to consider these rules in its reasoning, the ICC seems to have asserted that they do not provide for standards that are useful for evaluating the genuineness of national proceedings. National jurisdictions can thus conduct national trials aimed at ascertaining the commission of international crimes even in breach of one of the most fundamental rights conferred on individuals by international law.

C. Partial Conclusive Remarks

There is, then, a second common thread between the case law of the Court of Justice and that of the ICC. Both judicial organs have accepted the possibility for an EU or international provision conferring individual rights to be set aside when the effects of this provision could hamper a national criminal trial from starting or from being continued. This argument seems to be grounded, in the case law of both the Court of Justice and the ICC, on the very same premise: that the scope of EU and international provisions conferring individual rights can be limited, by means of interpretation, when their effects (may) collide, directly or indirectly, with the objective of fighting against impunity. Necessarily, this premise is rooted in another assumption: that the duty to protect individual rights, even fundamental rights, can be balanced with the requirement of preventing impunity and can, in certain cases, be recessive.

IV. Conclusions

A tentative conclusion emerging from the brief parallel analysis of the judicial strategies followed by the Court of Justice and by the ICC is that both courts have greatly increased the chances for national criminal trials to be conducted.

With regard to the ICC, the juridical basis of this phenomenon can be easily explained. The Court was established, as a last resort tool, in order to replace those states which fall short of their duty to prosecute individuals for acts allegedly constituting international crimes. The exercise of the ICC jurisdiction thus constitutes just a part of the two-tier strategy adopted by the Statute to combat impunity. This task must be primarily performed through the exercise of national jurisdiction. In its Preamble, the Statute specifies that 'the most serious crimes of

which strenuously defended the decision issued by the Pre-Trial Chamber. See ICC, *Situation in Libya, Case of the Prosecutor v Saif Al-Islam Gaddafi and Abdullah Al-Senussi, Judgment on the appeal of Mr Abdullah Al-Senussi against the decision of Pre-Trial Chamber I of 11 October 2013 entitled 'Decision on the admissibility of the case against Abdullah Al-Senussi'*, Appeals Chamber, 24 July 2014, no ICC-OI/II-OI/IIOA6, para 189ff.

concern to the international community as a whole must not go unpunished[,] and that their *effective prosecution must be ensured by taking measures at the national level*': 'it is the duty of every State to exercise its criminal jurisdiction over those responsible for international crimes'.[43] In other words, the main concern of the Statute is to push states to conduct criminal proceedings; in this perspective, the exercise of jurisdiction by an international court constitutes a (mere) residuary means of action to be activated only when states fail to abide by their primary duty to prosecute.[44]

Giving priority to the exercise of national jurisdiction is thus a statutory imperative that takes pre-eminence vis-à-vis other concerns and cannot but pervade the interpretative activity of the ICC. This does not necessarily entail that the Court shall give priority to the national jurisdiction in every possible case. However, this 'ideal aspiration' to use states as a tool to achieve the international objective of preventing impunity can, at least partially, explain the multifaceted interpretation of the scope of the Statute developed by the ICC.

On the contrary, the legal turf on which the Court of Justice grounded its case law seems less evident. In other words, it seems less simple to understand on what legal basis the Court has, in a certain sense, sacrificed individual rights, even those of paramount importance in the EU legal order, on the altar of the fight against impunity.

In order to (try to) identify the legal basis of the reasoning developed by the Court of Justice, we must reconsider the logic underlying *Kolev* and *Petruhhin*. These two judgments may turn out to be less diverse than they seem at first sight: in both decisions, the reasoning of the Court hinges on an analogous chain of arguments. First, the Court identified an individual right, granted by national law in *Kolev* and by EU law in *Petruhhin*: Kolev was entitled to ask for the closing of the criminal trial against himself and Petruhhin was entitled not to be treated in a discriminatory manner vis-à-vis Latvian nationals. Secondly, the Court of Justice ascertained that the exercise of this individual right might collide with the pursuit of the objective of preventing impunity, established in Article 3(2) TEU: by exercising their rights, Kolev and Petruhhin would indeed have averted any criminal trial. Thirdly, in both cases, the Court settled the 'normative conflict' between the conferring-right provision and the objective described in Article 3(2) TEU by declaring the pre-eminence of the interest to prevent impunity and the subservience of the interest underlying the individual right.

[43] Preamble of the Statute, paras IV and VI (emphasis added). *cf* para X: the ICC 'shall be [only] complementary to national criminal jurisdictions'; section III.B above.

[44] This spirit seems well epitomised by the Prosecutor of the ICC when, called on to illustrate the implications of the complementary nature of the Court, he stated that the opening of numerous international proceedings would be absolutely not a success for the ICC: 'On the contrary, the absence of trials by the ICC, as a consequence of the effective functioning of national systems, would be a major success': ICC, Office of the Prosecutor, 'Paper on Some Policy Issues before the Office of the Prosecutor' (September 2003) 4.

Significantly, in both *Kolev* and *Petruhhin*, the Court of Justice attained the same practical result: Nikolay Kolev was no longer able to invoke his right to claim interruption of the national criminal proceedings; and Aleksei Petruhhin was no longer able to invoke his right not to be discriminated (and then, practically speaking, not to be extradited to Russia). In both cases, this inability ultimately permitted the national proceedings against Kolev and Petruhhin to be carried on. In other words, in both cases, the Court of Justice accepted that an individual could be divested of a right protected by EU law where the exercise of this right could have hampered the pursuit of a paramount goal, namely the fight against impunity.

This line of reasoning is not a novelty in the Court of Justice case law. Not unsurprisingly, one may be tempted to detect some elements of analogy with the chain of arguments that feature in the case law on mandatory requirements. In *Rewe*, and its progeny, the Court of Justice held that national provisions whose application can interfere with the exercise by individuals of fundamental freedoms of the EU may be consistent with EU law 'in so far as [they] may be recognized as being necessary in order to satisfy mandatory requirements'.[45] In turn, the notion of mandatory requirements encompasses an open set of interests which a state can lawfully pursue in spite of the interferences produced by one of the fundamental freedoms of the EU.[46] This is certainly not the right place to dwell in full on a sophisticated and controversial doctrine, such as that of the EU mandatory requirements. This doctrine is evoked, rather than explored, here, with the sole purpose of pinpointing some methodological analogies between the line of reasoning which led to the development of this doctrine and the line of reasoning which led the Court of Justice to the findings in the case law mentioned in the previous sections.

When applying the doctrine of mandatory requirements, the Court of Justice usually develops a threefold argument. First, it ascertains the existence of an individual right granted by EU primary law. Secondly, it admits that the application of a certain national provision may hamper, or even prevent, the exercise of this right. Thirdly, the Court determines that the national provision at stake aims to pursue 'overriding requirements of public interest',[47] and therefore it can be applied in national proceedings even if interferes with implementation of

[45] Court of Justice, judgment of 20 February 1979, Case C-120/78 *Rewe v Bundesmonopolverwaltung für Branntwein* ECLI:EU:C:1979:42, para 8.

[46] *cf*, *ex multis*, C Barnard, *The Substantive Law of the EU: The Four Freedoms* (Oxford, Oxford University Press, 2016); S Enchelmaier, 'Article 36 TFEU: General' in P Oliver (ed), *Oliver on Free Movement of Goods in the European Union* (Oxford, Hart Publishing, 2010) ch 7; M Józon, 'The Enlarged EU and Mandatory Requirements Law' (2005) 11 *European Law Journal* 549; E Spaventa, 'On Discrimination and the Theory of Mandatory Requirements' (2000) 3 *Cambridge Yearbook of European Legal Studies* 457; V Hatzopoulos, 'Exigences essentielles, impératives ou impérieuses: une théorie, des théories ou pas de théorie du tout?' (1998) 34 *Revue trimestrielle de droit européen* 191.

[47] *cf*, *ex multis*, Court of Justice, judgment of 16 December 2008, Case C-205/07 *Gysbrechts and Santurel Inter* [GC] ECLI:EU:C:2008:730, para 45ff.

EU law.[48] The practical consequence of this doctrine is clear: individuals are deprived of the possibility to invoke, in front of the national judge, a provision of EU law conferring a right on them because, by so doing, they would hamper the pursuit of a national paramount goal which is, moreover, protected by EU law as well.

In spite of the many differences, one can reasonably assume that the legal reasoning developed by the Grand Chamber of the Court in *Kolev* and in *Petruhhin* has signs of close resemblance to the doctrine of mandatory requirements and, in particular, its methodological gist. As mentioned, this doctrine hinges on the premise that individuals are not entitled to exercise a right bestowed on them by EU law, if this conduct may result in hindering or affecting the attainment of a major legal interest.[49]

It does not seem unreasonable to infer that the Court of Justice, where ruling on normative conflicts between individual rights and the need to prevent impunity, has considered the fight against impunity as a mandatory requirement – that is, as an overriding requirement of public interest for the European Union – which can set aside or limit the enjoyment of fundamental rights under EU law.

[48] For other judgments related to the issue of mandatory requirements *cf*, *ex multis*, Court of Justice, judgment of 16 January 2003, Case C-14/00 *Commission v Italy* ECLI:EU:C:2003:22; judgment of 20 September 1988, Case 302/86 *Commission v Denmark* ECLI:EU:C:1988:421; judgment of 14 July 1981, Case 155/80 *Oebel* ECLI:EU:C:1981:177.

[49] Among all the differences, it can be noted that mandatory requirements are national legal interests and not (necessarily) EU ones, and that the provisions that are not applicable because of their conflict with the mandatory requirement at stake pertain to EU law and not to national law.

INDEX

Algorithmic surveillance
assumptions, partial and debatable nature, 244
automated decisions, right to control—
accessibility of mechanism, need for etc, 253
adverse legal effects, protection from, 249–50
data retention case law—
France and Italy, in, 252–4
importance, 251
discrimination, profiling leading to, 249, 251
evaluation and challenge, 250–1
French legislation, 252, 254
generally, 249–54
human intervention, right to, 250
informational privacy, expansion, 251
job placement procedure, 253
judge as data controller, 253
legal provisions, 249
prohibition, 249, 250, 251
public administration, effect on, 252–3
rule of law, defence, 254
safeguards, need for, 249, 251
biased data sample, effect, 242
civil liberties, effect on—
automated decisions, right to control *see* automated decisions, right to control *above*
data protection, redefining remit, 247
exam scripts etc, data protection regime, 248
explanation of process, right to, 247
General Data Protection Regulation, limitations, 246
generally, 240, 245–7
inferences, legal status, 247–9
legal analysis, whether comprising personal data, 248, 249
privacy, right to, 246, 247
proxies used, right to, 248
reasonable inference, right to, 248
rectification, right, 248–9
COMPAS, 241
concepts to aid compliance with legal paradigms, 245
data protection, beyond *see* civil liberties, effect on *above*
discrimination, causing, 245
disparate mistreatment, 246
extraction process forged by, 243
fair procedures developed by law, need for, 255
feedback loop, creation, 242
generally, 8–9, 239–40, 254–5
goal justifying means, 241
HART, 241
human activities, in parallel with, 243
human behaviour shaped by algorithms, 242
human self-determination, fight against impunity and, 255
individual customisation, 254
inequality, surveillance programs producing, 245, 246
judgemental atrophy, principle behind, 241
juridification, progress towards, 254
legal code, mismatch with, 244–5
non-predictable aftermath, 243
paradoxes, 242
physical and virtual realms, linkages between, 242
Pred-Pol, 240
proactive approach, 240
roadmap for preventive justice, 240–5
secrecy and democracy, limit to compatibility between, 243
target variables, 243, 244
transparency, shift from algorithmic to data, 246
types of algorithms-based techniques, 239
Area of freedom, security and justice
alternative cooperation mechanisms in, 180–2
approximation of criminal law—
functions, 179
importance, 180
better lawmaking to help bring about, 75

construction of EU as, 21, 22, 41, 44
digital evidence *see* **Digital evidence**
integration, effect of fight against impunity on, 3–4, 18, 20, 41
key role of fight against impunity, 22
liaison officer as intermediate agent in *see under* **Data protection**
mutual recognition principle *see* **Mutual recognition**
ne bis in idem principle, and, 110
reimagining impunity in, 41–5
time, extension and shortening, 43
transnational *ne bis in idem see* **Transnational *ne bis in idem***

Artificial Intelligence
approach to use, 271, 272
banning, difficulties, 271–2
confinement companions, as, 264
core principles to guide development and implementation, 272–4
Declaration of Cooperation on, 239
European Charter on, 9, 265–6, 272
generally, 8, 9, 271
introduction—
failure to address potential problems, 271
precautionary principle, use, 271
principles-based regulation, 271
predictive policing *see* **Algorithmic surveillance; Automated decision-making system**
prisons, use in, 264, 274

Automated decision-making system
Adult Budget Calculation Tool, 268
automating criminal courts—
assessment of recidivism or flight, 261–2
COMPAS recidivism algorithm, 262
errors in interpretation of results etc, 262, 263–4
fairness of procedure, importance, 262
generally, 261–3
justice administration, for, 262–3
robot judge, attempt to design, 263
robot lawyer, 263
studies—
alGOVrithms – State of Play, 263
pretrial detention cases, 262
ProPublica, by, 262
US, in, 262
UK-based *DoNotPay*, 263
bail decisions, 263
case backlogs, to deal with, 269
COMPAS risk assessment tool, use, 266–7, 270
confrontation, and right to, 269–70
core principles to guide development and implementation, 272–4
criminal sanctions, risk of imposing, 267
criminogenic needs of offenders, ascertaining, 264
due process, tension with, 268
environment for, regulated nature, 265
EU, in, 268–70
EVAAS, 268
fair trial, and, 269, 270
future approach, 274–5
generally, 258–9, 265–6, 274–5
global use, 264
human rights implications—
EU law, 268–70
generally, 265–6
US case law, 266–8
input data, importance, 267
post-conviction stage—
discriminatory effects, furnishing, 263
future behaviour, predicting, 264–5
generally, 263–5
parole, 263
prisons, use in, 264
precautionary principle, use, 271
predictive policing—
chatbots, 260
child sex tourism, 260
common concerns, 261
country-specific studies, 261
emotion recognition from facial expressions, 261
facial images, inferring criminality from, 261
generally, 259–61
heat lists, 260
hot spot policing, 260
human trafficking, 260
presentence investigation report, reliance on, 266
pretrial detention—
future behaviour, predicting, 265
study, 262
principles-based regulation, 271
prisons, use in, 264, 274
problems presented by, 270
public sector use, 264
resources, allocation, 265

risk assessment tool, use—
EU, in, 269
US, in, 266–8
shaping technology, 271–4
stakeholders, 259
training data, importance, 267
untested evidence, 270
witnesses, absent or anonymous, 270

Biometric Matching Service
purpose, 235

Common Identity Repository
purpose, 235
Conflict of jurisdiction
assessment of rules construed to deal with—
challenges as to practical implementation, 131–3
choice of prosecuting State after act, 130
effectiveness of criminal procedures, effect of choice based on, 131
fighting impunity and punishing crime, problems as to, 129
infringement of *ne bis in idem* principle, prevention, 130
lack of foreseeability, problems flowing from, 130–1
legal framework—
challenges arising from, 128–31
future reform, 133–4
parallel criminal proceedings, 129, 130
shortcomings, 128–31
transfer of proceedings, 132
criminal prosecutions, possible future prohibition, 135
Eurojust
factors, taking into account, 126–7
Framework Decision 2009/948/JHA, and, 122, 125
goals of EU rules, 130
Guidelines, 122, 125, 126–8
jurisdiction, choosing, 128
parallel proceedings, stance towards, 132, 133
penalty levels, relevance, 127
role, 126–8
rules introduced by—
challenges as to practical implementation, 131–3
generally, 119
written opinions from, 126
European Arrest Warrants, non-execution, 128
evidence, relevance of where located, 131
factors determining jurisdiction, 131–22
fighting impunity—
link with, 134–5
significant challenges presented by, 135
forum shopping, risk, 121, 131
Framework Decision 2009/948/JHA—
application, effect, 123
Charter of Fundamental Rights, and, 123
contents, 123
EU rules in parallel to, 125
Eurojust Guidelines, and, 122, 125, 126–8
generally, 122–4
infringement of *ne bis in idem* principle, prevention, 130
procedure in, 122
purpose, 122
special legislative provisions, and, 124–5
fundamental rights, EU's duty to protect, 134
generally, 117–19
Greek Criminal Code, application, 120–1
lack of legislation as to, 119
legal framework, future reform, 133–4
location of suspect and other parties etc, relevance, 131
mutual recognition instruments, effect, 127–8
ne bis in idem principle—
coincidence as critical factor, 121
Directives, 124, 125
evoking, 119
forum shopping, risk, 121, 131
Framework Decision *see* Framework Decision 2009/948/JHA *above*
future infringement, possibility, 129
Greece, approach in, 120–1
lex specialis, 124
national law, and, 119–22
partial impunity, risk, 121
self-standing concept, as, 121
Spain, in, 121
special legislative provisions, 124–5
suitability, 119
nullum crimen nulla poena sine lege processu, effect on, 119
parallel criminal proceedings, 129, 130, 132, 133, 135
positive conflicts—
EU law favouring, 118
problematic nature, 118
preliminary presumption, making, 127
problems for consideration, 117–19

prosecution based on territoriality, 127
rules to deal with *see* assessment of rules construed to deal with *above*
territoriality principle, 132
Confiscation order
Regulation on Mutual Recognition of Freezing Orders and Confiscation Orders, 201
Court of Justice
approach to fight against impunity, 339
case law—
general study, 341
individual rights, sacrificing, 352–4
mandatory requirements, application of doctrine, 353–4
setting aside of fundamental rights, 351
extradition case, in, 346–8
fundamental rights, setting aside—
generally, 352–4
mandatory requirements, application of doctrine, 353–4
generally, 339–41, 345, 351–4
legal order, role in shaping and creating, 3, 4
mandatory requirements, application of doctrine, 353–4
national procedural provisions, approach to—
enlarging scope of supranational law, 342–3
extradition case, in, 346–8
generally, 342–3, 345
narrowing scope of supranational law, 346–8
role, 10
supranational law—
enlargement of scope, 342–3, 345
narrowing scope, 346–8
tax fraud, 342–3
TFEU, enlargement of scope, 343
Criminal jurisdiction *see* **Jurisdiction**

Data protection
cooperation between EU and external actors, need for, 329–30
data transfers—
communication data, retention, 324–5
essentially equivalent level of protection, whether current practices meeting, 325
geo-economic tensions, effect, 328
legislation, compatibility with EU law, 324–5
liaison officer, and *see* liaison officer *below*
metadata: meaning, 324
national security, and—
CJEU rulings, 324, 328–9
Data Retention Directive, and, 324
exemptions *see* national security exemptions *below*
level of protection required outside EU, 324
USA, data transfer from Ireland to, 323–4
national security exemptions—
checks and balances within EU, 327–8
decentralisation and shared responsibilities, effect, 328
substantive standards of protection, and, 325–7
third countries, to—
generally, 329
see also USA, to *below*
USA, to—
adequacy of data protection, fears as to, 322
contrary to EU law, whether, 323
Facebook personal data, transfer, 321, 323
generally, 320–3, 328–9
lower level of protection in USA, 324
Privacy Shield, 322–3
Safe Harbour regime, 320–2
Snowden revelations, 321
EU framework—
assessing level of protection, 337
Data Protection Authorities, 319
data transfers *see* data transfers *above*
decentralised approach, 337
international commitments—
executive's power to conclude, 320
generally, 319–20
nature, 319–20
review, restriction on, 319
secondary law, interpretation, 319
legislation, 318–20
USA, agreement with, 319
fundamental right, as, 318
generally, 317–18, 336–7
information exchange, crimes allowing for, 337
liaison officer—
administrative agents, as, 331
deployment—
data protection concerns, 331

legal instruments as to, 330
third countries, from, 331–2
exemption from EU standards, where, 332
generally, 331–2
home administration, support for, 331
intermediate agent in AFSJ—
Europol, to—
generally, 332–3
numbers of officers, 332–3
selection procedure for EU Member State officer, 333–4
US officer seconded to *see* US liaison officers at Europol *below*
generally, 332–3
legal basis, 330
non-EU, control and accountability, 337
objective, 331
responsibilities, 330–1
tasks, 331
limited control mechanisms, 10
prevalence, 10
US liaison officers at Europol—
cooperation agreement, 337
EU standards, whether applicable, 334–6
gaps in EU information exchange law, 335
generally, 334, 337
supplemental agreements, standards in, 335–6
US rules, subject to, 336

Database
access to—
overzealous efforts to, 237
proportionality, importance, 237
consulting, under revised rules, 236
evolution, nature, 235
generally, 8, 9, 235–7
immigration *see* **Immigration database**
interoperability components, 235
non-discrimination concerns, under revised rules, 236
Regulations, 235
risk technology tool, as, 224
surveillance of EU nationals, possible increase under revised rules, 236–7
use of data other than for original purpose of collection, 224–5

Digital evidence
agreements with USA, 39–40
draft EU Regulation on use etc—
CLOUD Act, comparison with, 39
generally, 36–8
EU's role in global developments etc, 40
European Commission's approach, 43
fundamental rights—
concerns as to protection, 37–9, 41
limited scrutiny, risks, 40
private providers, protection by, 38
safeguarding, 45
generally, 36–40, 45
human rights' perspective, EU strategy and, 40
judicial cooperation, attempt to change internal paradigm, 39
mutual trust, effective privatisation, 38
private sector—
co-option by state, 36
EU's approach, problems with, 40
public authority, cooperation with, 37, 38
rule-of-law perspective, EU strategy and, 40, 45
standards, EU's negotiation, 40

E-evidence *see* **Digital evidence**

EU Budget
Corpus Juris, and, 14
importance, 14
protection *see* **European interest** (protection)
VAT fraud, 16

EU policy preparation and evaluation
better lawmaking—
criteria, implementation in area of EU criminal law *see* implementation of better lawmaking *below*
economic integration, as response to, 68
failure to fully embrace, 69
guidelines and toolboxes, 75
guiding nature, 74
high-quality legislation, need for, 68
institutional agreements, 65, 67
integration, as response to objections to, 75
Joint Practical Guide, 68
meaning, 64
mutual recognition, role, 75
open and transparent approach, need for, 65
origins and application of concept, 64–8
procedure for, 66–7
relevance, 75
trust in EU, to enhance, 75
COVID-19, need to coordinate response to, 65
distrust among electorate, 65

European Public Prosecutor's Office *see* **European Public Prosecutor's Office**
generally, 63, 74–6
impact assessments of initiatives, 66, 67, 75
implementation of better lawmaking—
challenges, 71
Commission, assessment by, 69
Framework Decision on Organised Crime, 69
fundamental rights, gaps in EU legislation, 69
generally, 68–72
last resort, use of criminal law as, 70
safe havens, prevention, 71
security of citizens, move to enhance 70
strategy on criminal justice, 71
trust etc in EU, enhancement, 75
Juncker Commission, 65
methods of strengthening the fight against impunity, 76
migration-related crimes, 75
minimum rules to protect suspects, 64
monitoring and measurement of measures, difficulties, 71
proportionality principle, and, 66
recommendations for embedding fight against impunity in, 74–6
refugee crisis, effect, 75
reinforcement through, 63
serious criminality, attempts to reduce prevalence, 76
subsidiarity, respect for, 66
trust in EU institutions, need for, 64

European Arrest Warrant
detention not including periods of curfew, 23
enforcement of custodial sentence, 24
extradition, and *see* **Extradition**
fair trial, risk of not receiving, 202
fine, restriction on imposition, 23
freedom of movement, and, 302
fundamental rights, where state in violation of, 204–5
generally, 7
inhumane or degrading treatment, risk, 202, 203
issue—
sincere cooperation principle, 32
test prior to, 73–4
mandatory refusal ground, 201
minor's criminal responsibility, no power to substitute assessment, 23
nationality exception, 303
non-execution, 128
periods of deduction of sentence, whether applicable, 23
procedural safeguards in execution, 23
refusal—
grounds for, 202–3
restriction on power of, 202
violations justifying, 203–4
sincere cooperation, and, 32
surrender of person by competent authority, 161–2
systemic deficiencies in detention conditions, where, 202
USA, extradition to, 33

European interest
communications, unlawful interception, 19–20
crimes affecting, challenges posed by, 137–8
protection—
accused persons' rights, 19
assimilation principle, 15–16
communications, unlawful interception, 19–20
Court of Justice, 15–21
EU laws, 15, 16, 18
European Public Prosecutor's Office's role, 91, 141
generally, 14, 15
harmonisation, through, 16, 18, 20, 45
Italian Constitutional Court's approach, 17, 18
limitation periods, approach to, 17–18, 44, 45
national laws—
amendment where necessary, 19
disapplication, 16, 17
EU law obligations, interaction with, 20
fundamental rights, respect for, 18, 19, 20
legality and rule of law, respect for, 20
priority for national enforcement, 45
use, 15
TFEU Article 325, 15–20
purpose, 141
value of offences against, 72
VAT fraud, 16, 19

European Investigation Order
generally, 7, 201

European Public Prosecutor's Office
applicable law, 145–7
benefits, 72

Central Office, 143
College's role, 143
competence—
allocation, offence linked to criminal conduct, 149
conflict *see* conflict of competence with national authorities *below*
national authority's decision, as to, 150
Regulation, under, 148
shared with national authorities, 148
conflict of competence with national authorities—
de facto impunity arising, risk, 150
EU's financial interests, offences as to, 148
evocation, exercise of right, 149
generally, 147–50
national authority taking over case, 150
non-participating Member State, 151–2
offence inextricably linked to criminal conduct, 149
reference of case to national authorities, 149–50
Regulation, and, 148
resolution mechanisms, 148
transnational dimension, where, 149
consultation and notification procedures, 146
contradictory opinions of different members, effect, 145
creation, 20, 41, 72
decision to prosecute, interactions behind, 144
deterrent effect, weaknesses in, 153
EU financial interest, protecting, 91
European Delegated Prosecutor—
cross-border crimes, 146, 147
decisions on whether to prosecute 144
disagreements with other parties, effect, 144
dismissal of case by, objections to, 145
reallocation of case, 144–5
role, 143
fight against impunity, whether legitimate objective, 153
fragmented nature of body, 146
generally, 6, 21, 72–4, 76, 137–8, 152–3
impunity—
de facto, prevention, 140
fight against: meaning, 138–9
meaning, 138–40
Regulation, in, 141–2
see also **Impunity**
investigative measures, procedures to follow, 145
judicial independence, inability to ensure, 76
justification for, 72
meaning, 143
Member State judicial systems, need to strengthen, 73
missed opportunity, as, 21
mutual recognition instruments, recourse to, 147
national implementing laws, coherence dependent on, 148
national level, work at, 143
national prosecutors, strengthening hand of, 72
Permanent Chambers' work, 143–4
Poland and Hungary not part of, 74
rationale behind establishment, 21
recommendations for improvement, 152–3
Regulation as to—
adoption, 21, 137
applicable law, 145–7
fight against impunity, and, 142–52, 153
generally, 137–8, 152–3
loopholes, 142
purpose, 137
role, 41, 76, 141
special scheme for investigations, 147
structure and design—
Central Office, 143
centralised level, 143
decentralised level, 143
generally, 21, 142–5
weaknesses, 142–5
Swiss system, as model for change, 153
European Supervision Order
applied measures, supervision, 160
breach of measure, 162
consultation with foreign courts, 167–8
crucial nature, in applying national regulations etc, 169
decision on supervision measures—
adaptation of measures, 161
alternative measures, refusal to recognise, 161
cooperation duties, 161–2
enforceable nature of, 159–60
meaning, 159
procedure, 161–2
withdrawal from duty to supervise, 161

decision-making process, need to alter, 166
European Arrest Warrant, and *see* **European Arrest Warrant**
European Judicial Network, role to be played by, 167
family and social ties, preservation, 164
Framework Decision 2009/829/JHA—
application, limited, 162
definitions, 159
implementation by, 157
limitations, 162
mutual recognition, application, 158, 159, 162
non-residents, previous treatment, 158–9, 165
package of other measures, as part of, 159
purpose, 158, 159
structure and functioning *see* structure and functioning *below*
supervision measures, list, 165
fundamental rights, respect for, 169
generally, 7, 157–8, 169
innocence, enhancing presumption of, 163–4
insignificant number of cases, 162–3
Ireland not within, 162
mutual recognition instrument, as, 163
non-residents—
non-custodial measure, right to, 165
pretrial detention, 158–9, 164–6
positive aspects, 159
potentiality, 169
pretrial detention—
challenging, 166
consultation between competent authorities, 168
consultation with foreign court prior to, 167–8
explanation for, 166
home arrest as form of, 168
judicial evaluation, scope, 166
overuse, 164–6
reduction in use of, need for, 167
strict interpretations, good reasons to overcome, 168
purpose, 159
reasons not to concede failure of, 169
right to ask for, 166
specificities—
cultural change in practitioners, need for, 166–7, 169
education etc, need for, 168
foreign courts, consultation with, 167–8
generally, 162–3, 169
innocence, enhancing presumption of, 163–4
limited application, 163
pretrial detention *see* pretrial detention *above*
strict interpretations, good reasons to overcome, 168
structure and functioning—
alternative measures, application, 160
competent authorities, list and identification etc, 160
costs of procedure, 162
definitions, 159
generally, 158–9
national competent authorities, powers etc, 160
procedure, 161–2
supervision measures, 159–60
studies on—
lack, 163
need for, 166
unsatisfactory application, 7
Europol
liaison officer in AFSJ—
generally, 332–3
selection procedure for EU Member State officer, 333–4
US officer seconded to Europol, 334
Extradition
Aranyosi test, 31
aut dedere aut judicare principle—
EU law, justification, 314–15
non-discrimination on nationality grounds, 304–6
death penalty, torture etc in requesting state, effect, 312–13
enforcement of sentence, request for purpose—
EU law, supremacy, 308
Finnish nationals, 308
foreign national resident in Finland, 308
generally, 307–9
legal alternatives, existence, 308
prohibition, 309
protection for Member State nationals, 309
right to refuse, 308
EU citizen—
citizenship, protection afforded by, 31, 32, 33
Court's reluctance to use citizenship as protection, 42–3

Finland, residence in, 33
in transit via another EU State, 33
permanent resident, 33–4
USA request for extradition, 33
EU international agreements, 306–7
EU law—
justifying, 314–15
need to respect, 308
non-discrimination principle *see* non-discrimination on nationality grounds *below*
European Arrest Warrant—
freedom of movement, and, 302
priority of mechanism, Member State's jurisdiction, 307
see also **European Arrest Warrant**
freedom of movement, effect of right to, 301–2
generally, 9–10, 31, 315–16
limits to Member States' foreign powers—
CJEU's approach, 310–12
competent authorities' role, 310
discrimination, legitimacy, 311
EU Charter of Fundamental Rights, impact, 312–14
EU obligations, compliance with, 309–10, 311 12
execution of extradition agreements, 309–12
inhuman or degrading treatment etc, risk, 312, 313
matters to be ascertained by Member State, 313
protection for EU citizens, 312
retained powers, 310
TFEU subordination clause, relevance, 311–12
national approach, risks to citizen, 35
non-discrimination on nationality grounds—
aut dedere aut judicare principle, relevance, 304–6
EU citizen's right, 301, 302
European Arrest Warrant, issue, 303
generally, 303–6
judicial analysis, 303–6
legitimacy of discrimination, 311
requested state having jurisdiction to prosecute, where, 305
scope, 303
prosecution, request for purpose—
generally, 300
Russia, from Latvia *see* Russia-Latvia treaty *below*
unjust discrimination, whether, 300
protection from, 31, 32, 35
reasons for, 31
Russia-Latvia treaty—
Charter protection, and, 300
Estonian citizen, 300
generally, 300–2
nationality exception, effect, 300
see also third countries from EU *below*
third countries from EU—
bilateral agreements, power to make, 301
Charter protection, and, 300
exchange information system, use, 306
freedom of movement, protection afforded by, 301–2
fundamental freedoms etc, importance, 306
generally, 32, 33, 34, 299
non-discrimination principle—
generally, 300
see also non-discrimination on nationality grounds *above*
Russia, from Latvia *see* Russia-Latvia treaty *above*
scope of application of EU law, 300–2
see also limits to Member States' foreign powers *above*
third countries to EU—
bilateral agreements, power to make, 301
generally, 31, 42
unjust, whether, 300
US, agreement with, 306–7

Foreign Terrorist Fighters
convergence between EU and international standards—
asylum seeker associated with terrorism, 289–90
CJEU's case law, 289–90
constitutional safeguards convergence, 290–2
Directive 2017/541, 289, 290
governance convergence, 289–90
pre-crime and pre-emption convergence, shift to *see* pre-crime and pre-emption convergence *below*
TEU, 289
UNSC as bellwether for change, 289
Council of Europe's initiatives—
Additional Protocol, 284–5
generally, 284–6

Member States' response, 285–6
travelling abroad for the purpose of terrorism: meaning, 285
see also EU initiatives *below*
criticism of EU approach, 281
Directive 2017/541—
elements of offence, 293
exclusion of refugee status in, 290
fundamental rights, non-compliance with, 293–4
generally, 280, 286, 287–8, 298
Preamble, 289, 291
divergence, scope and limits of external influences—
Additional Protocol and UNSC Resolution, 294
constitutional safeguards, effect on, 295–6
Directive 2017/541—
CoE Convention, and, 295
countries not participating in, 297
minimum rules, 296
EU competence allowing for divergence, 296
generally, 294–7
local divergence, 297
Member States' discretion, effect, 296–7
pre-emptive securitisation, risk, 294
UK legislation, 297
domestic sanctions, 282
EU initiatives—
Additional Protocol, 287
border security, 288
Charlie Hebdo massacre, in response to, 286
Directive 2017/541, 280, 286, 287–8
European Agenda on Security, adoption, 287
European Counter-Terrorism Centre, 287
four pillars, 286
generally, 286–8
immigration control, 288
information exchange, 288
Security Union, development, 287
travelling for terrorist purposes, 286, 288
UNSC approach, response to, 286–7
see also Council of Europe's initiatives *above*
future challenges, 298
generally, 279–81, 297–8
hijacking by any technological means, 286
international fight against—
Council of Europe's initiatives *see* Council of Europe's initiatives *above*
generally, 281–2
UN Security Council's initiatives *see* UN Security Council's initiatives *below*
meaning—
risk of abuse by oppressive governments, 284
UN definition, 282
pre-crime and pre-emption convergence—
actus reus, mobility as, 293
destination, broad scope of Directive, 293
facilitation of travelling abroad, 293
generally, 292–4
harm theory, 292
intention as guilty element, 293
legislation, 292
mens rea, as to suspected future act, 293
pre-crime criminalisation, 281, 293
required intentions, 292, 293
ultima ratio, 293
urgency leading to, 292
see also Directive 2017/541 *above*
returning, dealing with, 279
travelling, criminalisation—
generally, 279–80
global trend, 289
pre-crime and pre-emption convergence *see* pre-crime and pre-emption convergence *above*
required intentions for, 292
UN Security Council's initiatives—
abusive nature of, risk, 284
Charlie Hebdo attacks, following, 283
effective border controls, need for, 283
fundamental freedoms etc, compliance with, 284
generally, 282–4
human rights etc, compliance with, 284
potential abuse of legal obligations, 283
prevention of violent extremism, 284
rule of law etc, compliance with, 284
Framework Decision 2008/584/JHA
generally, 7
Framework Decision 2008/909/JHA
background, 194
double criminality, abolition, 195
duties under, 195
European Enforcement Order, introduction, 194
executing Member State: meaning, 194
flaws in, 197

fundamental rights issues, and—
generally, 203–5
lack of test, 205
prisoner's rights, 205
generally, 191–4, 206
judicial cooperation tool, as, 206
mutual recognition principle, application, 195
partial recognition, 195
prisoner transfer *see* **Prisoner transfer**
provisions, 194–7
purpose, 191, 197
report on status of implementation, 196–7
social rehabilitation, and *see* **Social rehabilitation**
Framework Decision 2009/829/JHA
European Supervision Order *see* **European Supervision Order**
generally, 7–8
Framework Decision 2009/948/JHA *see under* **Conflict of jurisdiction**
Freedom of movement
impunity risk, and, 198
restrictions, justification, 32
Freezing order
Regulation on Mutual Recognition of Freezing Orders and Confiscation Orders, 201
Fundamental rights
child sexual abuse, 52, 53
Court of Justice's approach, 51–2
criminal law as threat and protection, 49, 60
criminalisation approach, whether governed by, 53–6
detention—
power to detain in, 202
systemic deficiencies in detention conditions, where, 202
see also **European Arrest Warrant**
digital evidence *see under* **Digital evidence**
emergence in EU legal order, 50–3
EU as fundamental rights actor, 49
EU law, prohibition on national law compromising primacy etc, 201
function of, in EU criminal law, 49
generally, 47–50, 60–1
human rights *see* **Human rights**
human trafficking, 60
impunity rationales based on—
areas of crime and definitions of offences, 58–60
generally, 56
institutional perspective, 57–8
precise subject of rationale, 58–60
incrimination, justification for, 60, 61
individual rights, problems determining, 54
information sharing *see under* **Information sharing**
invoking, 52
judicial cooperation, shift in relationship with, 203
law enforcement concerns trumping, 237
minimum norms, adoption, 51
mutual recognition, underpinning, 24, 25, 26, 42
national interest, weighed against, 112
ne bis in idem principle—
authorities hindering each other, where, 111
civic order, as rational principle of, 99
Court of Justice's approach, 102–4, 108–12
criminal and administrative law, parallel application of—
case law developments, 105–12
criminal prosecution followed by administrative one, 108
financial offences, 105–12
generally, 105–12, 116
reopening criminal case, 109
VAT, failure to pay, 109–12
violation of principle, whether, 105
criticism, 104
double punishment, protection against, 110–11
dual proceedings' compliance with, 106–7
effect, 99
enforcement requirement from CISA Article 54, 112–14, 116
exception to rule, to avoid impunity, 114–15, 116
false positives and false negatives, 99–101
financial offences—
fines, imposition to deter, 112
generally, 105–12
need to safeguard interests, 111
framing question of impunity and, 104–5
generally, 99–100, 116
higher level of protection, where, 111
human rights against national interests, 112
idem, judicial interpretation, 103
justification of approach taken, 102–4
limitations' system, 111
lowering of protection, 107

multiple charges, acceptability of bringing, 107
multiple procedures, acceptability of initiating, 107
nature of, 115
novum rule, need for, 114–15, 116
objectivity in assessing facts, need for, 103
overly protective, whether, 104
purpose, 107
reopening of case, 114
rule of law, and, 99–100
sufficiently strong, whether, 102
transnational *see* **Transnational *ne bis in idem***
whether working to advantage of criminals, 101
positive obligations *see* **Positive obligations**
protection—
European Arrest Warrant, and *see* **European Arrest Warrant**
false positives and false negatives, 99–101
fight against impunity, and, 200–3
generally, 31, 49, 206
issue with regard to judicial cooperation, as, 200
limitation to fight against impunity, as, 192
limits, 52
ne bis in idem principle *see ne bis in idem* principle *above*
reductionist nature of fundamental rights-oriented approach, 53–6, 61
setting aside, to prevent impunity, 351
sexual exploitation, 60
substantive criminal law—
impunity rationales *see* impunity rationales based on *above*
reach, relevant factors, 55–6
terrorism—
Directives, 52, 58–9
violation of rights, as, 52, 58
Treaty of Lisbon, effect, 50–1
violation—
examples, 52, 58
procedural, 54, 55

Globalisation
digital evidence, use *see* **Digital evidence**
generally, 36–40

Human rights *see also* **Fundamental rights**
foundational value of EU, as, 50
positive obligations concept, 47
private life, respect for, 48
protection for, 47
purpose, 47
rape—
legal interpretation, as violation of rights, 48
mentally ill person, 47–8

Immigration database
access to—
ancillary objective, 214–19
asylum seekers' data, 212, 221, 222
bona fide persons, possible exclusion, 225
conditions of, court review, 232, 233
designation process *see* designation process *below*
Europol, by, 210, 214–19, 227, 228, 231
ex post control of process, 233
exceptional or disproportionate, whether, 226–8
fundamental rights, trumping, 237
generally, 209–10, 237
harmonised rules, Table, 215–18, 225–6
immigration data, 223
law enforcement authorities, by, 210, 214–19, 233
limited value, 237
modalities—
clarity and limits *see* progressive refinement of modalities of access *below*
Table showing, 215–18
necessity, threshold for—
EES, 226–7
ETIAS, 226–7, 228
Eurodac, 226
VIS, 226, 227, 228
normalisation *see* normalisation of law enforcement access *below*
overzealous efforts, 237
personal data, interference with protection, 219
political purposes, serving, 237
preventive justice through risk assessment, as, 224
private life, interference with, 219, 237
proportionality, importance, 237
Prüm Decision, under, 222
refinement of modalities *see* progressive refinement of modalities of access *below*
restrictions, 214, 219

revised rules, under, 236–7
stigmatising effect, 224
unlawful, 233
verifying authority, 230
Charter, need to fulfil requirements, 219–20
contents, 210
data quality, lack, 234
designation process—
designated authority—
flexibility in allocation, 231
intelligence service, as, 231–2
role, 230
EU intervention in, 230
Europol, access by, 231
independent authority, need for, 231, 233
national level authorities, 230–4
operating units, list, 230
prosecutorial authority, intervention by, 234
verification process, 232–4
verifying authority, 230, 233, 234
Dublin system, administration, 212
false matches due to lack of data quality, 234
fingerprinting, 212, 213, 234
generally, 209–10, 237
multipurpose nature, 214, 225
normalisation of law enforcement access—
administrative purposes, databases for, 223
asylum seekers' data, 212, 221, 222
biometric data, inclusion, 222
duration of retention period, 222
EES data, access to, 222–3
erosion of purpose limitation principle, 223–4
ETIAS data, 223
Eurodac, 221
generally, 220–4
Hague Programme, justification in, 220
immigration data, 223
preventive justice through risk assessment, access as, 224
Prüm Decision, under, 222
statistics as to searches, 220–1
stigmatising effect, 224
third-country nationals deemed de facto risky, 224
VIS Decision, Preamble, 220
passenger name record data, use, 224–5
personal data, interference with protection, 219
previous convictions of third-country nationals, 213–14
private life, interference with, 219
progressive refinement of modalities of access—
clarity and limits, 225–34
data quality, lack, 234
designation process *see* designation process *above*
exceptional or disproportionate access to data, whether, 226–8
generally, 225–6
harmonised rules, 215–18, 225–6
national authorities, 230–4
nature of changes, 225–34
necessity, threshold for *see under* access to *above*
problematic features, 226
Table, 215–18
terrorism and serious crimes, defining, 228–30
purpose, 210
repurposing, 237
risk technology tool, as, 224
Schengen area, security within, 210–11, 214
security risk, whether traveller posing, 213
serious crimes, and, 228–30, 237
short-stay visas, as to, 211
'Smart Borders Package', 212
surveillance of EU nationals, possible increase under revised rules, 236–7
terrorism, and, 228–30, 237
third-country nationals, disadvantageous position, 224, 225, 237
types—
ECRIS-TCN, 213–14
EES, 212–13, 214, 219, 222–3
ETIAS, 213, 214, 219, 223
Eurodac, 212, 214, 219, 221, 226
generally, 209
SIS II, 210–11, 214
VIS, 211, 214, 226
use of stored data for law enforcement purposes, 224–5
visa-free travellers, monitoring, 213
Impunity
acceptable and necessary, where, 100
concepts relevant to fight against, 3, 13
concerns inherent in fight against, 4, 5
counterterrorism law, and fight against, 9
cross-border dimension, in, 1, 2
de Vabre's view, 1
elusive nature of meaning, 1
EU developments, and, 3

European Public Prosecutor's Office *see* **European Public Prosecutor's Office**
fight against—
Court of Justice's role *see* **Court of Justice**
EPPO Regulation, whether legitimate objective, 153
generally, 339–41
International Criminal Court's role *see* **International Criminal Court**
legal basis, 339
meaning, 138–9
purpose, 141
generally, 1–10, 13–14
grounds for concern, 2–3
integration process, and, 3–4, 18, 20, 41
interests of EU, need to protect, 13
meaning, 100, 138–40, 192
objective, 1
preventing risk, as EU objective 141
public interest, and, 4
questions raised by concept, 1
rationale, whether justifying criminalisation, 5
reimagining in Europe's Area of Justice, 41

Information sharing
access, types—
hybrid, 173
mediated, 172–3
unmediated, 173
companies' role *see* private actors *below*
cross-border access to information—
alternative cooperation dynamics, 180–2
approximation and mutual recognition, importance, 179–80
e-evidence proposal *see* e-evidence proposal *below*
integration dynamics, 179–2
law enforcement authorities, by, 174–82
data cooperation—
European Investigation Order, 173–4
generally, 10, 171
judicial cooperation, and, 179–80
privatisation, 186
data selectors, use, 185
databases *see* **Database**
due process guarantees of requests, concerns, 186–8
e-evidence proposal—
concerns and calls for safeguards, 176–7
CLOUD Act, relevance, 178
data protection requirements, in line with, 177
Directive—
legal representatives, appointment, 176
Regulation as alternative to, 181
European Preservation Order Certificate, 176, 183, 187, 188
European Production Order Certificate, 176, 183, 187, 188
generally, 7, 175–9
immunities and privileges in criminal proceedings, 178
internet access services, inclusion, 176
law enforcement authority's role see law enforcement authority *below*
legal basis, suitability, 181–2
ongoing investigations, relevance to, 182
policy consequences, 184
privatisation of mutual trust, 186
production order, 175, 183, 187, 188
production request, 175
Regulation, proposed *see* Regulation on e-evidence *below*
remedies to protect rights, 178
traditional MLA agreements, shift away from, 181
US developments, effect, 178–9
enforcement jurisdiction, legal uncertainty as to, 184
fundamental rights—
challenge to, 172
concerns as to, taking into account, 187
MLA requests, whether encroaching on, 186
protection, 174, 189
General Data Protection Regulation, risk of clash with, 185
generally, 7, 171–2, 188–9
harmonisation etc of law, as cornerstone of judicial cooperation, 179–80
issuing judicial authority, 183
judicial decision, recognition throughout EU, 182
law enforcement authority—
access to data, 185
data providers outside EU, powers as to, 184
General Data Protection Regulation, risk of clash with, 185
issuing state, in, 184–5
jurisdiction, legal uncertainty as to, 184
legality of requested data, verification, 184
sovereignty of other states, interaction with, 184

legal basis for, difficulties in choosing, 181–2
legal foreseeability, concerns, 186–8
multiple jurisdictions, access governed by, 184
mutual legal assistance instruments—
challenges to, 175, 189
fundamental rights protection *see* fundamental rights *above*
generally, 189
lowest degree of informational integration, 171
purpose, 171
shift away from, 181
mutual recognition, as cornerstone of judicial cooperation, 179–80
national legislation as point of reference, 180
need for, to combat crime etc, 189
politics of information control, changes, 185
private actors—
beyond public-private divide, 185–8
criteria for role played by, lack, 187–8
decision-making and policy implementation, effect on, 186
defence difficulties, 188
delegation of states' responsibilities to, 187
examples, 185
fundamental rights assessments, 1888
government access to data held by, 185
individual rights protection, difficulties in providing, 187
public judicial authorities, acting as, 187
security professionals, as, 185
small service providers, 188
subcategories, 188
transfer of data by, to public authorities, 186
privatisation of security, 175, 185, 187
public prosecutor—
independence from, determining, 183
law enforcement authority, as, 183
Regulation on e-evidence—
EU data protection package, references to, 177
ongoing investigation application to, 182
scope, 176, 177, 184
suitability, 180–1
service providers outside EU, jurisdiction over, 184
sovereignty of states, effect on, 184, 189
systems for, 8
territorial sovereignty, safeguards, 182
time of essence, where, 175
transactional and content data, production, 183
voluntary disclosure, 175
Integration
fight against impunity as driver for advancing, 3–4, 18, 20, 41
fundamental rights, protection, 41
Internal borders
lack of *see* **Area of freedom, security and justice**
Internal market
criminal opportunities provided by, 2
free movement of crimes and offenders, 2
internal driver, 3
International cooperation
EU's standards and values, maintenance, 31, 34–5
extradition *see* **Extradition**
fundamental rights, need to protect, 31
generally, 30–5
legitimate objective of EU law, 34
national approach, risks to citizen, 35
objective, Court's acceptance as, 42
restrictions, 34
International Criminal Court
aim, 340–1
case law, setting aside of fundamental rights, 351
generally, 340–1, 345, 351–4
national rule, concern for effective, 345
parallel national proceedings, where—
accused fundamental rights, violation, 349, 351
generally, 348–51
judicial proceedings, need to meet standards, 349, 350
legal representation, whether accused denied, 349, 350
priority, 352
positive complementarity, 344–5
role, 10, 351
Rome Statute—
enlargement of scope, 344–5
human rights, importance, 349–50, 351
interpretation of Article 21, 349, 350
minimum guarantees under, 350
positive complementarity, and, 344–5
Preamble, aim in, 340–1, 351–2
supranational law—
enlargement of scope, 344–5
narrowing scope, 348–51
setting aside of fundamental rights, 351

Judicial cooperation
enhancement, 73
European Arrest Warrant *see* **European Arrest Warrant**
Framework Decision 2008/584/JHA on *see* **Framework Decision 2008/584/JHA**
human rights, and, 8
mutual recognition, and, 7
Judicial systems
effectiveness, need to enhance, 73
Member States, scrutinisation, 73
Poland and Hungary, accusations against, 73
Jurisdiction
active personality principle, 85–7, 89
autonomous clauses in EU criminal law, 87–8
common interest in fighting crime, countries having, 83
concepts, 80–1
conflict *see* **Conflict of jurisdiction**
Convention on Human Rights, 85
cooperation instruments, use, 80
crimes committed outside the EU—
active personality and domicile principle, 93–4, 95, 97
domestic law, subject to, 97
erosion of trust, through criminal's easy escape, 94
EU financial interests, 92–3
EU law and interest, reliance on, 95
generally, 92–6
genuine link, need for, 92
human trafficking and sexual abuse, 94
passive personality principle, 94, 95
protective principle, reliance on, 92
terrorism, 93
transfer of proceedings, Convention on, 96
trial in home country, as legitimate interest, 95
vicarious jurisdiction as alternative to extradition, 95
crimes committed within the EU—
active personality principle, recourse to, 89
Court of Justice intervention against Member State, 91
decision not to prosecute, overriding, 91
discretion open to Member States, 90
Europa-Delikt, 90
European Arrest Warrant, failure to execute, 89
European Public Prosecutor's Office's role, 91
extraterritorial jurisdiction, need for, 90
financial interest, protection, 90, 91, 96–7
generally, 89–92, 96
Market Abuse Directive, 92
no duty to prosecute, where, 89
no safe havens, 89
over- or under-punishment, risks, 91
punitive approach, factors favouring, 91
systemic deficiencies in national systems, where, 91
territorial jurisdiction, duty to exercise, 89
vicarious jurisdiction, recourse to, 89
defendant's rights, need to balance, 96
Directives—
Attacks against Information Systems, on, 83
autonomous jurisdictional clauses in, 87–8
Combating Terrorism, on, 84, 86
Counterfeiting Currencies, on, 84
extraterritorial jurisdiction, and, 86
human trafficking and sexual abuse etc, 94
extraterritorial—
active personality, need for, 85–7
crimes committed outside the EU *see* crimes committed outside the EU *above*
crimes committed within the EU *see* crimes committed within the EU *above*
measures to harmonise, 80
protective principle, reliance on, 92, 96
symbolic only, where, 97
see also **Conflict of jurisdiction**
factors determining, 132–3
Framework Decisions, 83–4
generally, 6, 79–80, 88–9, 96–7
international treaties, clauses originating from—
aut dedere aut iudicare principle—
recent treaties, in, 86
universal jurisdiction, 84–5, 96
vicarious jurisdiction, 82–4, 89
autonomous clauses in EU Criminal law, 87–8
Directives *see* Directives *above*
European Convention, 86
extraterritorial jurisdiction based on genuine link, 85–7
Framework Decisions, 86
generally, 81–2, 88–9, 96–7
Geneva Conventions, 84
UN Conventions, 84, 86
ne bis in idem, 6

networking jurisdiction, use, 79
normative framework to avoid and resolve conflicts, 80
nullum crimen, nulla poena sine lege principle, 85
primary and derivative, 81
types of jurisdiction—
adjudicate, to, 80, 97
enforce, to, 81, 97
prescribe, to, 80, 97
primary and derivative, 81
universal, 79, 84–5
vicarious, 82–4, 89

Legal order
conceptual appraisal of concept of impunity in, 5
Court of Justice's role in shaping, 3, 4
morphology in context of, determining, 5
Legal space
EU as, importance, 4

Mandatory requirements
doctrine, application, 353–4
Multiple Identity Detector
purpose, 235
Mutual recognition
application of principle, 22
automaticity in interstate cooperation, 22
balancing act with development of criminal law, 76
better regulation flowing from, 75
concerns fostering EU legislation on, 7
Directives, rights covered by, 25–6
dual criminality, no need to verify, 23
earned trust, based on, 24
enforcement objectives of issuing state, prioritising, 24
European Arrest Warrant *see* **European Arrest Warrant**
European integration, effect on, 26
fundamental rights underpinning, 24, 25, 26, 42
generally, 41, 45
importance in fight against impunity, 180
instruments, adoption, 22
judicial cooperation, 7, 180
judicial authority and independence underpinning, 25
law enforcement cooperation, and, 180
legislative harmonisation, effect, 25
limited success of European concept, 22–3
Member State's enforcement objectives, emphasis on achievement, 22
mutual trust and comity among national judiciaries, 179
programme of measures to implement principle, 194
purpose, 22
rule of law underpinning, 24, 25
safeguards underpinning, 24, 25
speed as key feature, 22
successful, implication, 179
Mutual trust
privatisation, 38
public and private sector, between, 38
suspension by Council of the EU, 74

Ne bis in idem
conflict of jurisdiction, and *see* **Conflict of jurisdiction**
criminals, whether working to advantage of, 101
fundamental right, as *see under* **Fundamental rights**
transnational *see* **Transnational *ne bis in idem***

Policing
algorithmic surveillance, enhanced through *see* **Algorithmic surveillance**
predictive *see* **Algorithmic surveillance; Automated decision-making system**
Positive obligations
criminalisation of conduct, 48–9
fundamental rights *see* **Fundamental rights**
inferred obligations, 47
rape cases, 47–8
Predictive policing *see* **Algorithmic surveillance**
Prisoner
cross-border transfer *see* **Prisoner transfer**
protection of rights, 8
Prisoner transfer
consent requirement, 195
enforcement of sentence—
cross-border transfer, 7
responsibility for, 196
European Arrest Warrant, and *see* **European Arrest Warrant**
executing Member State: meaning, 194
Framework Decision 2008/909/JHA, and *see* **Framework Decision 2008/909/JHA**

fundamental rights, objection where risk of violation, 205
partial recognition and execution, 195
procedure for authorising—
generally, 195
speed, mechanism enhancing, 196
recognition of decision, time for, 195
start of transfer procedure, failure to inform prisoner, 196
violation of rights—
objection where risk, 205
right to bring action, 206

Rule of law
importance, 192
impunity for those undermining, 76
mutual recognition underpinning, 24, 25
promotion etc, through fight against impunity, 192
respect for, in national laws, 20

Sanction
duty, imposition, 2
Social rehabilitation
cross-border transfer, effect, 199
executing Member State—
enforcement and execution rights, 198
meaning, 194
family, social or professional ties, existence 199
fight against impunity, and clash with, 198
Framework Decision 2008/909/JHA, under, 191, 206
generally, 8
issuing Member State's right to determine sentence, 199
judgment, request for recognition, 199
legal fragmentation, effect, 199
limitation to fight against impunity, as, 192–3
reduction in sentence, whether prisoner entitled to, 198–9
work in prison contributing to, 199
Surveillance
algorithmic surveillance *see* **Algorithmic surveillance**
artificial Intelligence *see* **Artificial Intelligence**
databases *see* **Database**
role, 8

Technology
algorithmic surveillance *see* **Algorithmic surveillance**
artificial Intelligence *see* **Artificial Intelligence**
automated decision-making system *see* **Automated decision-making system**
databases *see* **Database**
generally, 257–8
objectivity, search for, 257
shaping, 271–4
threat, as, 258
Terrorism
dealing with—
challenges presented by, 281–2
domestic sanctions, 282
draconian treatment, risk, 281
Foreign Terrorist Fighters *see* **Foreign Terrorist Fighters**
future challenges, 298
generally, 297–8
Member States' primary responsibility, 282
oppressive treatment, risk, 281
preparatory acts, criminalisation, 279
returning fighters, dealing with, 279
travelling, criminalisation, 279
Transnational *ne bis in idem*
application, decisive factor, 28
bis, Court's interpretation, 27, 28
Court's approach, 27–30, 52
domestic *ne bis in idem* cases, and, 30
enforcement views of 'second' Member State, relevance, 28–9, 30
extraterritorial protection, 26
free movement, potential effect on, 30
fundamental rights protection, and *see* **Fundamental rights** (*ne bis in idem* principle)
generally, 26–30, 42
harmonisation, and, 44
idem, Court's interpretation, 28
limitation of principle, 29
mutual trust in Member State systems, 27
not arising, where, 30
Schengen—
Convention, use, 27
heritage, 26–7
idem, and, 28

security rationale within fundamental right, 30
time, extension and shortening, 43
two-fold aim, 52
unilateral perceptions of enforcement, and, 30

Travelling
criminalisation, 279–80
Foreign Terrorist Fighters *see* **Foreign Terrorist Fighters**

www.ingramcontent.com/pod-product-compliance
Ingram Content Group UK Ltd.
Pitfield, Milton Keynes, MK11 3LW, UK
UKHW020232290926
15470UKWH00002B/505

9 781509 926879